Perspectives on Employee Staffing and Selection

Readings and Commentary

The Irwin Series in Management and The Behavioral Sciences

L. L. Cummings and E. Kirby Warren, Consulting Editors
John F. Mee, Advisory Editor

Perspectives on Employee Staffing and Selection

Readings and Commentary

GEORGE F. DREHER
School of Business
University of Kansas

PAUL R. SACKETT
Department of Psychology
University of Illinois
at Chicago

1983

RICHARD D. IRWIN, INC.
Homewood, Illinois   60430

ISBN 0-256-02948-2

Library of Congress Catalog Card No. 82–84267

Printed in the United States of America

1 2 3 4 5 6 7 8 9 0 ML 0 9 8 7 6 5 4 3

To Sheila and Pat

Preface

This book is about meeting organizational staffing needs through either external hiring or internal promotion or transfer. The focus is on how people differ from each other and how organizations can use information about these differences to make sound personnel selection decisions. Eleven chapters are organized within three major sections with each chapter's reading(s) preceded by an introduction and followed by a commentary or discussion designed to provide both within- and between-chapter integration. A careful reading of each chapter's introduction should prove particularly valuable for readers approaching this material for the first time. We hope the commentaries will provide provocative reading irrespective of the degree of past exposure to the selection literature.

Part 1 addresses a variety of conceptual issues that set the stage for much of the remainder of the book. Chapter 1 is devoted to the validation processes or the methods used to provide evidence that a selection procedure is related to subsequent work behavior or job performance. Models of selection system fairness are introduced in Chapter 2, and the developing area of validity generalization is the focus of Chapter 3. The usefulness or economic utility of a selection device is the final topic for this section. Throughout there is ample evidence that selection research is undergoing change and that it represents a dynamic research area for the 1980s. Numerous conceptual controversies remain; concepts once thought to be well understood are now often painfully unclear. An appreciation of these issues is essential background for the last two sections of the book.

The impact of the external environment on employment practices is perhaps the dominant issue in personnel management today and is the topic for Part 2. The major sources of regulations governing selection practices are reviewed in Chapter 5 while Chapter 6 focuses on labor market issues. The goal of Chapter 5 is to trace the development of the abstract concept known as *equal employment opportunity*. Regulations and court interpretations are reviewed, and the current practice of defining equal opportunity in terms of the results achieved (statistical parity) is discussed. The difficult issue of defining a firm's labor market is the focus for Chapter 6. This is a critical issue for at least two reasons. First, there is the potential for base rate and selection ratio change as recruiting efforts are directed toward different labor market segments. This is central to the broader question of

ix

decision making in the personnel selection area. Second, one procedure for determining *adverse impact* is to make a comparison of the employer's internal work force with the race, sex, and ethnic percentages associated with the defined prospective employee pool. The relationship between staffing decisions and labor markets, as influenced by base rates and selection ratios, is the primary area of discussion in this chapter's commentary.

The chapters of Part 3 address specific selection practices from theoretical, legal, and utility perspectives. Work sample tests, assessment center procedures, biographical data, the employment interview, and psychological tests are the methods reviewed. While not a complete list of employee selection procedures, they were drawn from a continuum ranging from direct samples of job behavior (work sample tests) to highly inferential measurement strategies (psychological tests). Due to space limitations, we chose to be representative not comprehensive.

The book is intended for use by graduate or advanced undergraduate students in Personnel/Human Resource Management and Industrial/Organizational Psychology. The goal has been to provide students with an exposure to high-quality original writing in the personnel selection area. Hopefully this has been achieved with a level of integration not commonly found in a book of readings. Also, an attempt was made to focus on the current controversies of the field. We believe this collection of readings can be used alone as the sole book in a selection course if supplemented by lectures and other outside readings chosen by the instructor as necessary. We purposely omitted important foundation material. It is critical that students be exposed to a variety of applied measurement concepts before focusing on this book. A survey personnel management course would serve this purpose. At a minimum, students need a basic exposure to the job analysis and performance measurement literatures as well as a working knowledge of the concepts of correlation and linear regression if they are to take full advantage of the readings and commentary to follow.

ACKNOWLEDGMENTS

Many colleagues and students have contributed to this project. The selection of readings resulted from our experiences in teaching graduate-level selection courses at the University of Kansas and the University of Illinois at Chicago. We thank these students for their reactions and guidance. Special thanks need to go to the Irwin reviewers, particularly Richard Arvey, for numerous helpful suggestions. Finally, the most important contributors were the authors who allowed us to use their original articles. We particularly want to thank Paul Sparks for writing an article specifically for this book. We believe it made a very unique and important contribution.

George F. Dreher
Paul R. Sackett

Contents

Part 1

Personnel Decisions:
Principles and Concepts

Chapter 1

Models for
Selection Research

INTRODUCTION

This book is about obtaining new employees either from outside the organization or through promotion or transfer within. Recruiting activities generate applicants for jobs, and selection decisions must then be made that attempt to choose the subset of applicants, or the applicant, most likely to succeed. This chapter focuses on how organizations determine the degree to which their selection procedures are job related.

A central issue in the area of personnel selection continues to be the development of various ways of showing that a selection procedure is related to successful performance on the job. Validation studies try to do this. Validation refers to the process of providing evidence that a selection procedure (e.g., a test, interview, or scored application blank) is related to or predictive of subsequent job performance. Historically, validation strategies have emphasized either an empirical approach (criterion-related validity) or an approach based upon the logic of how the selection procedure is developed (content validity). Demonstrating the job relatedness of a selection procedure is critical from at least two vantage points. First, even a slight increase in the job relatedness for a selection device can translate into substantial cost savings. For example, as you will note in a subsequent chapter, Schmidt, Hunter, Mckenzie, and Muldrow (1979) were able to demonstrate that very large productivity gains could be achieved in the federal government by using a more valid test to select new computer programmers. The introduction of job-related selection techniques often represents a very cost-effective way of increasing productivity; thus, sound management practice will often dictate the introduction of valid selection procedures.

The second reason for stressing the use of job-related selection procedures is that such procedures help meet state and federal equal employment opportunity requirements. For example, if there is adverse impact (e.g., a smaller proportion of minority applicants meet hiring standards than non-minority applicants) associated with a hiring device, an employer may need to demonstrate that the procedure is job related. Guidelines for demonstrating job relatedness have been provided by the federal government (Equal Employment Opportunity Commission, Civil Service Commission, Department of Labor, & Department of Justice, 1978). These guidelines offer detailed treatments of both empirical and content-oriented procedures. A violation of equal employment law can have serious financial consequences for the firm.

This chapter will introduce you to the validation process. In practice, validation has tended to become a technology based on a set of accepted beliefs and assumptions. However, a second goal of this chapter is to demonstrate that selection research represents, in actuality, a dynamic and complex process with many controversies and questions left unanswered.

Before introducing the readings for this chapter, it is necessary to review some fundamental terms and processes associated with traditional approaches to selection research. It will become apparent that this review is simplistic, suggesting a degree of clarity where there is actually considerable complexity and controversy. It should, however, make the readings more meaningful. The commentary will then explore the current controversies in some detail.

Types of Validity

Selection specialists have historically described the validation process in terms of three broad classes of validity evidence. Each will be summarized, and then examples of the steps followed will be presented for three of the more commonly used strategies.

Criterion-related validity. This type of validation evidence relies on actually comparing performance on some type of selection procedure with performance on the job. That is, the observed relationship between scores on the selection procedure and one or more independent criteria serves as evidence of job relatedness. There are two general forms of the criterion-related approach, predictive and concurrent. When using the concurrent approach, present employees make up the study's sample. To illustrate, assume that a paper and pencil personnel test is to serve as the selection device. The first step is to have a sample of current employees complete the employment test (a test that was not in use when these employees were selected). Then, at approximately the same time, performance measures (e.g., supervisory ratings, production records, etc.) are collected for all sample members. Concurrent validity evidence usually is then provided in the form of a correlation coefficient or what is termed a *validity coefficient*. A sufficiently large correlation between the test and the current measure of job performance serves as evidence of validity.

One form of the predictive approach begins by administering the test to applicants. In this type of predictive design, the test should not be used for making selection decisions. After an appropriate time period, the persons hired serve as a follow-up group. Their job performance is measured, and as in the concurrent design, the correlation between the test score and the measure of job performance is computed.

Since the fundamental reason for using tests or other selection procedures is to make predictions regarding subsequent success on the job, there is considerable controversy surrounding the use of the concurrent design. It has been assumed that present job holders and applicants differ on a set of key factors. These differences are assumed to invalidate the concurrent approach since in theory one always wants to make predictive statements. The concurrent approach serves only to estimate predictive validity since job holders and applicants are likely to differ on characteristics ranging from motivation to perform well on the selection device to job-related knowledge and skills (Jennings, 1953, Rothe, 1947; Thorndike, 1949). For example, with additional job experience, employees may develop skills that are then reflected in test scores. If experience affects test scores, it also may affect the correlation between test scores and some measure of job performance.

Content validity. This strategy involves a systematic study of the job to determine important job behaviors and required knowledge and skills. The job analysis is used to define a relevant job-content domain, and then a selection procedure is developed or constructed by sampling from the job-content domain. Appropriate sampling often results in a selection procedure that is a miniature replica of certain job components or even the job as a whole. Content validity may more appropriately be defined as "content-oriented test construction" since, unlike the criterion-related approach, it focuses on the selection device itself. Criterion-related approaches focus on the relationship between the selection device and some criterion variable. The content-based strategy can be characterized as a rational, judgmental process that is applicable in a limited number of employment settings. Selection procedures developed on the basis of a content-oriented strategy serve to measure current knowledge, skill, or ability levels. Thus, it is not appropriate to use procedures of this type to measure knowledge or skills learned after an individual is hired. This means that the approach is not applicable for many entry-level jobs.

Construct validity. The construct validation process is much more complex than either so-called content validity or the various forms of criterion-related validity. It involves a program of research that includes traditional content and criterion-related studies. The approach attempts to identify constructs believed to underlie successful job performance such as achievement motivation, numerical ability, or verbal ability. The problem is to establish that the selection procedure serves to measure the construct and that the construct is indeed required for successful job performance. Given the complexity associated with the approach, a general lack of professional guidance on how to apply the approach to employment problems, and the need to conduct what amounts to multiple content and criterion-related studies, the approach is rarely used by selection specialists.

Some Illustrations

The use of a concurrent model is not new. For example, in 1916 Hugo Munsterberg, a Harvard professor, administered a series of what he termed *mental tests* to a group of 23 employees of a New England wholesaling firm

(Burtt, 1917). Twelve tests were administered and the employees also were rated by their managers with reference to their ability as salesmen. The test results for the five top-rated salesmen were compared with the test results for the five worst-rated salesmen. Five of the tests provided sufficient test-score differences between the two groups to lead the researcher to a variety of interpretive statements. For example, it was hypothesized that a test of letter rearrangement may prove useful in differentiating salesmanship ability. Also note that mean test-score differences were compared between the top- and bottom-rated employees. This illustrates that criterion-related validation does not have to rely on correlational statistical techniques.

In a more recent article, Latham, Saari, Pursell, and Campion (1980) followed a predictive model in one of three reported validation studies. A systematic job analysis was used to develop a performance-appraisal instrument and a standardized employment interview. The interview (a particular type of standardized procedure called a situational interview) was administered to 56 applicants for entry-level work in a paper pulp mill. Thirty were female and all were black. All 56 applicants who had been interviewed were subsequently hired. The employees' job performance was then measured, using the performance-appraisal procedure developed in the early stages of the research. Performance was evaluated 12 months after the employees were hired. Separate analyses were performed, resulting in correlations between rated performance in the interview and performance on the job of .39 for females and .33 for blacks. This study illustrates the common steps followed in most criterion-related studies. The procedure begins with a job analysis that then is used to develop predictors (selection procedures) and criterion measures (measures of success on the job). Scores on both sets of variables are then collected (using either a concurrent or predictive design) and analyzed.

Finally, an example of content-oriented test construction or content validation is provided by Schoenfeldt, Schoenfeldt, Acker, and Perlson (1976). They describe the procedures associated with the development of a content-oriented industrial reading test. In discussions with management concerning what new employees in entry-level operating jobs must know when hired, "it was determined that reading was the one skill that could not be learned on-the-job" (p. 582). Related to this was the finding that many industrial accidents in the company's plants were the result of failure to read and comprehend job-related instructions and procedures.

The first step was to define the job-content domain. The domain included all nonproprietary material read by entry-level employees at selected plants. The researchers further defined the comprehension skills associated with successfully reading the stimulus materials. This survey of job-related reading was essentially a job analysis focusing on the one skill required of entry-level employees.

The next step was to sample from the content domain and construct the employment test. The authors describe a comprehensive strategy of sampling that, among other things, weighted the selected materials by frequency and importance and included reading passages specific to the various participating plants. For example, 54 percent of the test content covered safety-related material, 31 percent focused on operating procedures, 13 percent covered such day-to-day operations as logbook entries and schedules, and 2 percent were devoted to various other topics.

Finally, the test was administered to applicants and current employees to study item characteristics and determine a relevant passing score. Note that what is being described as content validation is basically a systematic procedure for constructing a test.

The three readings that follow are conceptual. Dunnette (1963) develops a more complex model for guiding criterion-related validation research. He argues that the traditional model has ignored issues related to the subgrouping of tests, people, jobs, and situations. Essentially, Dunnette advocates moving beyond simply asking whether a selection technique works to asking under what circumstances different techniques are likely to be useful. Some components of Dunnette's model have been tested and have not received support. For example, validation studies subgrouping on the basis of race have not supported the hypothesis that cognitive ability tests are predictive of job performance for certain racial groups but not others. This issue will be developed in further detail in subsequent chapters. Other components of Dunnette's model have not been studied and still represent promising directions for future research. While the article is somewhat dated, it is of considerable historical importance since much of the regulatory environment in the personnel selection area still reflects the underlying principles developed in the Dunnette article.

In the second reading, Guion (1974) struggles with the meaning of the terms *criterion-related validity, content validity, construct validity,* and *job relatedness.* His article is particularly useful in describing appropriate sampling techniques when constructing content-oriented tests.

Finally, in one of the few clear statements on the topic, Tenopyr (1977) reflects on the differences between content and construct validity. The commentary addresses additional findings and controversies that have recently emerged. This should move the reader from the belief that prevailed until recently that selection research was a well-developed technology with few, if any, issues left unanswered to an understanding of the dynamic nature of selection research.

REFERENCES

Burtt, H. E. Professor Munsterberg's vocational tests. *Journal of Applied Psychology,* 1917, *1,* 201–213.

Dunnette, M. D. A modified model for test validation and selection research. *Journal of Applied Psychology,* 1963, *47,* 317–323.

Equal Employment Opportunity Commission, Civil Service Commission, Department of Labor, & Department of Justice. Adoption by four agencies of uniform guidelines on employee selection procedures. *Federal Register,* 1978, *43,* 38290–38315.

Guion, R. G. Open a new window: Validation and values in psychological measurement. *American Psychologist,* 1974, *29,* 287–296.

Jennings, E. E. The motivation factor in testing supervisors. *Journal of Applied Psychology,* 1953, *37,* 168–169.

Latham, G. P., Saari, L. M., Pursell, E. D., & Campion, M. A. The situational interview. *Journal of Applied Psychology,* 1980, *65,* 422–427.

Rothe, F. H. Distributions of test scores of industrial employees and applicants. *Journal of Applied Psychology,* 1947, *31,* 480–483.

Schmidt, F. L., Hunter, J. E., Mckenzie, R. C., & Muldrow, T. W. Impact of valid selection procedures on work-force productivity. *Journal of Applied Psychology,* 1979, *64,* 609–626.

Schoenfeldt, L. F., Schoenfeldt, B. B., Acker, S. R., & Perlson, M. R. Content validity revisited: The development of a content-oriented test of industrial reading. *Journal of Applied Psychology,* 1976, *61,* 581–588.

Tenopyr, M. L. Content-construct confusion. *Personnel Psychology,* 1977, *30,* 47–54.

Thorndike, R. L. *Personnel selection: Test and measurement techniques.* New York: John Wiley & Sons, 1949.

A Modified Model for Test Validation and Selection Research*

MARVIN D. DUNNETTE

Nearly 35 years ago, Clark Hull (1928) discussed the level of forecasting efficiency shown by the so-called modern tests of the time. He noted that the upper limit for tests was represented by validity coefficients of about .50 corresponding to a forecasting efficiency of only 13 percent. He regarded the region of forecasting efficiency lying above this point as being inaccessible to the test batteries of the day, and he viewed with pessimism the use of test batteries for predicting occupational criteria. Hull, of course, failed to emphasize that the accuracy of practical decisions might better be assessed against zones of behavior (e.g., passing versus failing in a training program) rather than against the metrical continuum assumed in the calculation of his index of forecasting efficiency. Further, he gave no attention to the varying effects of different selection ratios on the accuracies obtainable with even rather low correlation coefficients. Even so, we should be somewhat dismayed by the fact that today our tests have still not penetrated the

region of inaccessibility defined so long ago by Hull. Ghiselli's (1955) comprehensive review of both published and unpublished studies showed average validities ranging in the .30s and low .40s; an average validity of .50 or above was a distinct rarity. These low validities have apparently led many psychologists to become disenchanted with test and selection research. Some have disappeared into other endeavors such as the study of group influences, interaction patterns, and the like. Others have sought refuge in the hypothesis testing models of statistical inference and have implied validity for tests showing *statistically* (but often not *practically*) significant differences between contrasting groups (see Dunnette & Kirchner, 1962). Nunnally (1960) comments:

> We should not feel proud when we see the psychologist smile and say "the correlation is significant beyond the .01 level." Perhaps that is the most he can say, but he has no reason to smile [p. 649].

Even less defensible, perhaps, has been the tendency for many to persist in doing selection *without* conducting selection research or test validation. The ordinary defenses for such practice run the gamut— from claiming near miracles of clinical insight in personnel assessment to the recounting of anecdotes about instances of

* M. D. Dunnette, "A Modified Model for Test Validation and Selection Research," *Journal of Applied Psychology* 47 (1963), pp. 317–23. Copyright 1963 by the American Psychological Association. Reprinted/Adapted by permission of the publisher and author. This paper was read at the 70th annual convention of the American Psychological Association held in St. Louis in the fall of 1962.

selective accuracy (counting the "hits" and forgetting the "misses") and finally to the old cliché that "management is well-satisfied with the methods being employed." We cannot and should not try to avoid the fact that the statistics of selection (i.e., validity coefficients) are far from gratifying and offer little support to anyone claiming to do *much* better than chance in the selection process.

It seems wise, therefore, to discuss the possibility of improving our batting average in test validation and selection research. Selection programs will go on—with or without psychologists—but I believe we now have the capability for penetrating the region of inaccessibility outlined by Hull.

First, let us examine the classic validation or prediction model. This model has sought simply to link predictors, on the one hand, with criteria, on the other, through a simple index of relationship, the correlation coefficient. Such a simple linkage of predictors and criteria is grossly oversimplified in comparison with the complexities actually involved in predicting human behavior. Most competent investigators readily recognize this fact and design their validation studies to take account of the possible complexities—job differences, criterion differences, etc.—present in the prediction situation. Even so, the appealing simplicity, false though it is, of the classic model has led many researchers to be satisfied with a correspondingly simplified design for conducting selection research. Thus, the usual validation effort has ignored the events—on the job behavior, situational differences, dynamic factors influencing definitions of success, etc.—intervening between predictor and criterion behavior. I believe that the lure of this seemingly simple model is, to a great extent, responsible for the low order of validities reported in the Ghiselli (1955) review. It is noteworthy that the studies reviewed by Ghiselli show no typical level of predic-

tion for any given test or type of job. In fact, there seems to be little consistency among various studies using similar tests and purporting to predict similar criteria. The review also suggests that the magnitude of validity coefficients is inversely proportional to the sample size employed in the studies. This can perhaps be explained, in part, by sampling error, but it may also be due to the relatively greater homogeneity possible within smaller groups of subjects. It appears, in other words, that the varying levels of prediction shown by the various studies are related somehow to the appropriateness (or lack thereof) of the classic prediction model for the particular set of conditions in the study being reported. It seems wise, therefore, to consider a prediction model which more fully presents the complexities which are only implied by the classic model.

Guetzkow and Forehand (1961) have suggested a modification of the classic validation model which provides a richer schematization for prediction research and which offers important implications for the direction of future research. Their model along with certain additional modifications is shown in Figure 1. Note that the modified prediction model takes account of the complex interactions which may occur between predictors and various predictor combinations, different groups (or types) of individuals, different behaviors on the job, and the consequences of these behaviors relative to the goals of the organization. The model permits the possibility of predictors being differentially useful for predicting the behaviors of different subsets of individuals. Further, it shows that similar job behaviors may be predictable by quite different patterns of interaction between groupings of predictors and individuals'or even that the same level of performance on predictors can lead to substantially different patterns of job behavior for different individuals. Finally, the model recognizes the annoying reality that

Figure 1
A Modified Model for Test Validation and Selection Research

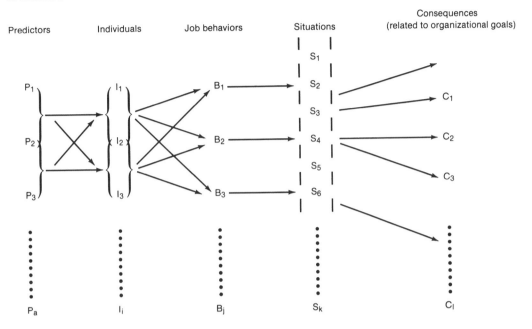

the same or similar job behaviors can, after passing through the situational filter, lead to quite different organizational consequences.

This modified and more complex prediction model leads to a number of important considerations involving the emphases to be followed by future validation research:

First, we must be willing to back off a step or two from global measures of occupational effectiveness—ratings, volume of output, and other so-called criteria of organizational worth, and do a more careful job of studying actual job behavior—with particular focus on behavioral or stylistic variations among different individuals with the same jobs. Most previous validation research has been overly concerned with predicting organizational consequences without first determining the nature of possible linkages between such consequences and differences in actual job behavior. It is true that industrial psychologists should continue to be concerned about predicting organizational consequences. Certainly, the

modified model implies no lessening of such an interest. What is hoped, however, is that the more careful analysis of the behavioral correlates of differences in organizational consequences will lead to broader understanding of them and, eventually, to their more accurate prediction.

Secondly, as implied by the point just made, the modified model demands that we give up our worship of *the* criterion (Dunnette, 1963). I believe that our concept of *the* criterion has suggested the existence of some single, all encompassing measure of occupational success against which predictors must be compared. Our modified model demands that we work with multiple measures of individual behavior and organizational consequences. I suggest therefore that we cease talking about *the* criterion problem and that we discard the notion of a so-called ultimate criterion. Such action should result in a research emphasis which will be less restrictive and less simple-minded and more aware of the necessity of analyzing and predicting the many facets of occupational success.

Thirdly, the modified model implies nothing concerning the form of the relationships to be expected. One of the unfortunate consequences of utilizing the classic validation model was its overemphasis on the correlation coefficient as almost the sole statistic of validation research. The notion of a simple linkage between predictor and criterion led easily to the equally simple assumption of the applicability of the linear, homoscedastic model for expressing the magnitude of relationships. Kahneman and Ghiselli (1962), in investigating relationships between 60 aptitude variables and various criteria, showed that 40 percent of the scatter diagrams departed significantly from the linear, homoscedastic model, and 90 percent of these departures held up on cross-validation. This is an important finding for it points up the necessity in future validation research of adopting a methodology taking account of the very great likelihood of nonlinear, heteroscedastic models. Our more complex prediction model, focusing as it does on the complex linkages between predictors and consequences, implies also the necessity of adopting more complex and sophisticated tools of analysis in studying these linkages.

Fourth, and most obviously, our modified model demands that we develop a sort of typology for classifying people, tests, job situations, and behaviors according to their relative predictability. Future validation research must define the unique conditions under which certain predictors may be used for certain jobs and for certain purposes. Research studies should, therefore, be devoted to the definition of homogeneous subsets within which appropriate prediction equations may be developed and cross-validated. This idea is not particularly startling nor even new. But it has *not* been applied widely in the conduct of selection research. The modified model rather explicitly directs us to carry out such

subgrouping studies in order to learn more about the complex linkages between predictors and consequences. Fortunately several studies already are available which confirm the advantages of studying differential patterns of validity for various subgroups. A brief review of some of these research approaches should illustrate the utility of applying our more complicated model to validation research.

With respect to job groupings, Dunnette and Kirchner (Dunnette, 1958; Dunnette & Kirchner, 1958, 1960) have studied the different patterns of validities obtained when careful techniques of job analysis are used to discover groupings of jobs which are relatively homogeneous in terms of actual responsibilities. Substantially different validities were obtained for engineers grouped according to functional similarities (research, development, production, and sales), salesmen (industrial and retail), and clerical employees (stenographers and clerk typists). These studies highlight the necessity of studying job differences and the differential predictability of effectiveness in various job groupings. More generally, an emphasis on the varying predictability of different job activities is inherent in the methods of synthetic validity (Balma, Ghiselli, McCormick, Primoff, & Griffin, 1959) and in the use of the *J* coefficient developed by Primoff (1955).

Everyone recognizes the possibility of situational effects on the validity of psychological predictions, but there is a paucity of research designed to estimate systematically the magnitude of such effects. Perhaps the best example of such research is provided by Vroom (1960). He showed that various aptitude tests (verbal and nonverbal reasoning, arithmetic reasoning) predicted ratings of job success most effectively for persons who were highly motivated. Job effectiveness in nonmotivating situations showed either no relationship or negative relationships with tested abilities. In a second study with Mann (Vroom &

Mann, 1960), it was shown that the size of work groups strongly influenced employee attitudes toward their supervisors. Employees in small groups preferred democratic or equalitarian supervisors; employees in large work groups preferred authoritarian supervisors. In a significant series of studies, Porter (1962) is also investigating situational factors such as hierarchical level, firm size, and job function as they affect managerial perceptions of their jobs. More emphasis needs to be given to these and other situational factors in validation studies, particularly as they serve to operate as moderating variables (Saunders, 1956) in behavioral predictions.

Many studies have shown different validities for different subgroups of individuals. For example, Seashore (1961) summarized a vast number of scholastic success studies which show almost uniformly that the grades of women (in both high school and college) are significantly more predictable than those of men. It is also well established that differing patterns of validity are typically obtained for subgroups differing in amounts of education and/or years of job experience. It may seem obvious that such factors as sex, education, and experience provide useful moderating variables in validation research. However, researchers also have identified variables which are much less *obvious* but which *do* make substantial differences in the patterns and magnitudes of validities obtained. For example, Grooms and Endler (1960) showed that the grades of anxious college students were much more predictable ($r = .63$) with aptitude and achievement measures than were the grades of nonanxious students ($r = .19$); and Frederiksen, Melville, and Gilbert (Frederiksen & Gilbert, 1960; Frederiksen & Melville, 1954) have shown that interest in engineering (as measured by the Strong test) has a higher validity for predicting grades for noncompulsive engineers than for compulsive ones. Berdie (1961) showed that the grades of engineer-

ing students with relatively consistent scores on an algebra test were more predictable from the total test score than were the grades of students with less consistent scores.[1] Ghiselli (1956, 1962) has developed a method for dividing persons, on the basis of a screening test, into more and less predictable subgroups. The advantage of his method is that no a priori basis is necessary for the identification of subgroups; the method depends simply on the development of one or more predictor tests to facilitate the subgrouping process.

The identification of more and less predictable subgroups of persons, whether based on logical factors (such as sex, education, or experience) or on methods such as those employed by Berdie and Ghiselli, places a special burden on the investigator to demonstrate the stability of his results. Although the studies cited above were cross-validated (i.e., checked on hold-out groups), the validity generalization and/or extension of such results has not often been measured. This needs to be done. The results so far reported with these methods are promising indeed, but they will take on greatly added significance when it is demonstrated that they hold up over time.

Less research has been directed at identifying subsets of predictors showing differential patterns of validity. However, Ghiselli (1960, 1962) has also contributed methodology in this area and has succeeded in significantly enhancing prediction by identifying, again through the development and use of screening tests, the particular predictor which will do the most valid job for each individual.

General approaches to the development of "types" have been made by a number of investigators. Gaier and Lee (1953) and

---

[1] The algebra test of 100 items was divided into 10 subtests of equal difficulty. The measure of consistency for each student was simply the sum of squares of the deviations of his 10 scores from his mean score on all 10 subtests.

Cronbach and Gleser (1953) summarize a variety of methods of assessing profile similarity and conclude that available indexes are simply variants of the general Pythagorean formula for the linear distance between two points in *n*-dimensional space. Lykken (1956) has questioned the psychological meaning of such "geometric similarity" and he proposes a method of actuarial pattern analysis which requires no assumptions concerning the form of the distribution and which defines similarity in psychological rather than geometric terms. His method consists simply of investigating criterial outcomes for subjects classified together into cells on the basis of similar test scores. In a recent study, he and Rose (Lykken & Rose, 1963) demonstrate that the method is more accurate in discriminating between neurotics and psychotics on the basis of MMPI scores than either clinicians' judgments or a statistical technique based on equations derived from a discriminant function analysis. Lykken's method of actuarial pattern analysis is the same as Toops' (1959) method of developing subgroups or "ulstriths" based on biographical and test similarities and then writing different prediction equations for each of the subgroups so identified. It is interesting to note that computers have now given us the capability for carrying out many of Toops' suggestions—which at one time were regarded as wild-eyed, idealistic, and unrealistic. McQuitty (1957, 1960, 1961) also has developed methods for discovering the diagnostic and predictive significance of various response patterns. His techniques, in addition to the methods proposed by Lykken and Toops, constitute the most extensive attack made to date on the problem of developing differentially predictable subsets or types.

These studies and methods mark the bare beginnings of efforts to take account of complexities which have been ignored by the oversimplified prediction model of the past. It appears that subgrouping of tests, people, jobs, situations, and consequences is necessary to a thorough understanding of what is going on in a prediction situation. The widespread acceptance of the modified model which we have been discussing should lead to a new and refreshing series of questions about problems of selection and placement. Instead of asking whether or not a particular selection technique (test, interview, or what have you) is any good, we will ask under *what circumstances* different techniques may be useful. What sorts of persons should be screened with each of the methods available, and how may the various subgroups of persons be identified and assigned to optimal screening devices? Finally, what job behaviors may be expected of various people and how may these behaviors be expected to aid or to detract from accomplishing different organizational objectives which may, in turn, vary according to different value systems and preferred outcomes?

What are the implications of these trends for the selection function in industry? Primarily, I believe they suggest the possibility of a new kind of selection process in the firm of the future. The selection expert of tomorrow will no longer be attempting to utilize the same procedure for all his selection problems. Instead, he will be armed with an array of prediction equations. He will have developed, through research, a wealth of evidence showing the patterns of validities for different linkages in the modified prediction model—for different predictors, candidates, jobs, and criteria. He will be a flexible operator, attentive always to the accumulating information on any given candidate, and ready to apply, at each stage, the tests and procedures shown to be optimal.

REFERENCES

Balma, M. J., Ghiselli, E. E., McCormick, E. J., Primoff, E. S., & Griffin, C. H. The development of processes for indirect or synthetic validity: A symposium. *Personnel Psychol.*, 1959, *12*, 395–400.

Berdie, R. F. Intra-individual variability and predictability. *Educ. psychol. Measmt.*, 1961, *21*, 663–676.

Cronbach, L. J., & Gleser, Goldine. Assessing similarity between profiles. *Psychol. Bull.*, 1953, *50*, 456–473.

Dunnette, M. D. Validity of interviewer's ratings and psychological tests for predicting the job effectiveness of engineers. St. Paul: Minnesota Mining and Manufacturing Company, 1958. (Mimeo)

Dunnette, M. D. A note on *the* criterion. *J. appl. Psychol.*, 1963, *47*, 251–254.

Dunnette, M. D., & Kirchner, W. K. Validation of psychological tests in industry. *Personnel Admin.*, 1958, *21*, 20–27.

Dunnette, M. D., & Kirchner, W. K. Psychological test differences between industrial salesmen and retail salesmen. *J. appl. Psychol.*, 1960, *44*, 121–125.

Dunnette, M. D., & Kirchner, W. K. Validities, vectors, and verities. *J. appl. Psychol.*, 1962, *46*, 296–299.

Frederiksen, N., & Gilbert, A. C. Replication of a study of differential predictability. *Educ. psychol. Measmt.*, 1960, *20*, 759–767.

Frederiksen, N., & Melville, S. D. Differential predictability in the use of test scores. *Educ. psychol. Measmt.*, 1954, *14*, 647–656.

Gaier, E. L., & Lee, Marilyn. Pattern analysis: The configural approach to predictive measurement. *Psychol. Bull.*, 1953, *50*, 140–148.

Ghiselli, E. E. *The measurement of occupational aptitude.* Berkeley: Univer. California Press, 1955.

Ghiselli, E. E. Differentiation of individuals in terms of their predictability. *J. appl. Psychol.*, 1956, *40*, 374–377.

Ghiselli, E. E. Differentiation of tests in terms of the accuracy with which they predict for a given individual. *Educ. psychol. Measmt.*, 1960, *20*, 675–684.

Ghiselli, E. E. The prediction of predictability and the predictability of prediction. Paper read at American Psychological Association, St. Louis, September 1962.

Grooms, R. R., & Endler, N. S. The effect of anxiety on academic achievement. *J. educ. Psychol.*, 1960, *51*, 299–304.

Guetzkow, H., & Forehand, G. A. A research strategy for partial knowledge useful in the selection of executives. In R. Taguiri (Ed.), *Research needs in executive selection.* Boston: Harvard Graduate School of Business Administration, 1961.

Hull, C. L. *Aptitude testing.* Yonkers, N.Y.: World Book, 1928.

Kahneman, D., & Ghiselli, E. E. Validity and nonlinear heteroscedastic models. *Personnel Psychol.*, 1962, *15*, 1–11.

Lykken, D. T. A method of actuarial pattern analysis. *Psychol. Bull.*, 1956, *53*, 102–107.

Lykken, D. T., & Rose, R. J. Psychological prediction from actuarial tables. *J. clin. Psychol.*, 1963, *19*, 139–151.

McQuitty, L. L. Isolating predictor patterns associated with major criterion patterns. *Educ. psychol. Measmt.*, 1957, *17*, 3–42.

McQuitty, L. L. Hierarchical linkage analysis for the isolation of types. *Educ. psychol. Measmt.*, 1960, *20*, 55–67.

McQuitty, L. L. A method for selecting patterns to differentiate categories of people. *Educ. psychol. Measmt.*, 1961, *21*, 85–94.

Nunnally, J. The place of statistics in psychology. *Educ. psychol. Measmt.*, 1960, *20*, 641–650.

Porter, L. W. Some recent explorations in the study of management attitudes. Paper read at American Psychological Association, St. Louis, September 1962.

Primoff, E. S. *Test selection by job analysis.* Washington, D.C.: United States Civil Service Commission, Test Development Section, 1955.

Saunders, D. R. Moderator variables in prediction. *Educ. psychol. Measmt.*, 1956, *16*, 209–222.

Seashore, H. G. Women are more predictable than men. Presidential address, Division 17, American Psychological Association, New York, September 1961.

Toops, H. A. A research utopia in industrial psychology. *Personnel Psychol.*, 1959, *12*, 189–227.

Vroom, V. H. *Some personality determinants of the effects of participation.* Englewood Cliffs, N.J.: Prentice-Hall, 1960.

Vroom, V. H., & Mann, F. C. Leader authoritarianism and employee attitudes. *Personnel Psychol.,* 1960, *13,* 125–139.

Reading 2

Open a New Window
*Validities and Values in Psychological Measurement**

ROBERT M. GUION

DEFINITIONS OF VALIDITY

Validity, in the history of testing, has been a confused concept, although the basic ideas have been present from the beginning. Criterion-related, content, and construct validities were all implicit when Galton said,

> One of the most important objects of measurement . . . is to obtain a general knowledge of the capacities of man by sinking shafts, as it were, at a few critical points. In order to ascertain the best points for the purpose, the sets of measurements should be compared with an independent estimate of the man's powers. We may thus learn which of the measures are most instructive [DuBois, 1970, p. 22].

The criterion problem was acknowledged by Hull (1928): "the most formidable problem encountered by the aptitude psychologist is the location of a trial group of subjects from whom a *valid* and reliable

* R. G. Guion, "Open a New Window: Validities and Values in Psychological Measurement," *American Psychologist* 29 (1974), pp. 287–96. Presented under the title, "Open a New Window," as the presidential address to the Division of Industrial and Organization Psychology at the meeting of the American Psychological Association, Montreal, August 29, 1973. Copyright 1974 by the American Psychological Association. Reprinted/adapted by permission of the publisher and author.

quantitative criterion of *aptitude* may be obtained [p. 374, italics added]."

The construct problem was in Brigham's (1930) complaint:

> Most psychologists working in the test field have been guilty of a *naming fallacy* which easily enables them to slide mysteriously from the score in the test to the hypothetical faculty suggested by the name given to the test. Thus, they speak of . . . perception, memory, intelligence, and the like while the reference is to a certain objective test situation [pp. 159–160].

Brigham was particularly critical of combining independent tests and giving the composite a unitary name. If tests are independent, he argued, they are measuring different things and therefore should not be given a common name. If he were addressing you, his title might come from a different song: "When will they ever learn?"

Constructs, content sampling, and relations with criteria were all intertwined in discussions of validity as the extent to which tests measure what they "purport" to measure (Boynton, 1933; Hunt, 1937; South, 1938). The 1954 *Technical Recommendations* clarified things somewhat, but the "clarification" sparked controversy, such as the opposing positions of Bechtoldt (1959) and Loevinger (1957). Content validity was largely ignored outside of educational circles; industrial psychologists certainly paid little attention to it until the term was thrust upon them in federal regulations. Nearly 20 years after the "clarification," debate still rages over the meanings of these terms. What's more, because of legal issues we have a different term, *job-relatedness,* which must somehow fit into the scheme.

I offer here my understanding of what these terms mean, and I shall illustrate that understanding with examples from a study of packers.[1]

Workers on this job packed their products—golf balls—a dozen to a carton. Two types of assessment were considered as possible predictors. There was a series of anthropometric measures, of which I shall concentrate only on the simplest, arm length. The other was a home grown dexterity test. The criterion was a brief work sample: the time required to pack a set of eight cartons.

Criterion-Related Validity

Criterion-related validity is the extent to which scores on one variable, usually a predictor, may be used to infer performance on a different and operationally independent variable called a criterion. For convenience we often speak of criterion-related validities in terms of correlation coefficients, but the statistic has nothing to do with the definition.

We can describe two of the measures in the packing study in conventional criterion-related terms. Arm length correlates with speed in packing with a coefficient of $-.46$; the validity coefficient for the dexterity test is $-.41$. These seem quite satisfactory.

The names of the predictors are not im-

portant. The information about validity is in the correlation coefficients and the regression equations on which they are based. The information I have given would have been as complete had I simply said that variables A and B have validities of $-.46$ and $-.41$, respectively. The nature of the measurement is not what is important to this statement. The important fact being reported is that these variables can be used to predict job performance within the limits of accuracy defined by the correlation coefficient.

The criterion in this conventional validation study is quite different from the sort of criterion desired by early testers. In contemporary practice, a criterion usually grows out of a given problem. The problem here is straightforward: How can we select people who will package golf balls more quickly? Pioneers in mental measurement phrased a different question: How can we find a measure in real life that will reflect the attribute our test is measuring? They would have accepted job performance as a criterion for dexterity, but looking for a criterion for a measure of arm length would have seemed awfully silly to them.

The point is that criterion-related validities serve two distinctly different purposes. In some cases, as in the early history of testing, the emphasis is on the test. In other cases, as in selection research, the focus is on the criterion. In the first type, one refers to the validity of the test scores. In the latter case, however, the reference is to the validity of the relationship. In the packing study the validity coefficient tells us nothing at all about one measurement other than that it tends to be related to another measurement. It gives as much information about the validity of the criterion as of the validity of the test. This is an uncommon way to look at these correlations, but it is useful; it may point to some understanding of the performance measure. Understanding criteria is every bit as important as understanding tests.

---

[1] David P. Jones of Bowling Green State University and I plan to report the study elsewhere; here I refer only to those parts of the study that illustrate certain ideas.

Construct Validity

When we speak of understanding, we are talking about construct validity, the degree to which scores may be used to infer how well a stated hypothetical construct describes individual differences among the people tested. Construct validity is not expressible in such simple terms as validity coefficients; it is a judgment based on many kinds of information: procedures followed in developing the test, results of experiments testing specific implications of the construct, and patterns of correlations with other measures. The data used to judge the construct validity of a measure may also help to validate the construct; as data accumulate, ideas about the construct may be modified. Describing a construct is more than merely naming it.

Can any of the measures in the packing study be evaluated in terms of construct validity? What construct is being measured by the criterion? If I suggest that the construct we wanted to measure is productivity, as different from production, then I must define what productivity implies. Productivity may imply, for example, endurance at a high rate of performance over an extended period of time in varying conditions of work. Does the timing of a job sample for a few minutes imply endurance? I think not. We cannot defend the criterion in terms of construct validity unless we define the construct simply as short-term speed in packing golf balls—and in such a tautology we are more interested in reliability.

Can we praise the construct validity of the dexterity test? It so happens that we can. The construct of manual dexterity has been established in experimental and factor-analytic literature. This test has been found in factor analysis to have a substantial dexterity loading (Bourassa & Guion, 1959). This is not enough evidence, but it is some; it places this particular test in a well-established network of relationships.

What about the construct validity of the cloth tape measure used to indicate arm length? Here again is a tautology. What sort of a construct, other than physical distance from one end of an arm to the other, could we possibly have in mind? Of course we could say distance is a construct, simply declare the measurement valid, and forget the whole thing. Actually, construct validity is not a very useful idea for physical measurement. There are well-established, well-defined units by which length is measured. A tape measure is not evaluated by experimental or correlational studies placing their results in some nomological net. It is evaluated in terms of its reliability and of the accuracy of its units. These are quite different questions (Guion, 1965).

Let us examine the same three measures from the point of view of content validity. Content validity refers to the fidelity with which a measure samples a domain of tasks or ideas; it is the degree to which scores on the sample may be used to infer performance on the whole.

Consider a test of addition of two single-digit integers. Figure 1 defines the content domain; there are 10 possible digits for the top number and 10 for the lower. The resulting matrix allows 100 possible combinations. If the content domain is defined with every combination weighted equally, then an arithmetic test of less than 100 problems will be a valid sample of the domain if equal numbers of cells are selected for each row and each column of the matrix. With three cells in each column and each row, randomly chosen within this constraint, Figure 1 specifies a 30-item test that will be judged adequate in terms of content validity.

It is up to those concerned about content validity to define a domain appropriately for their situation. If someone defines a domain using the same matrix, but differing in the weights to be given, the 30-item test indicated here would have inadequate content validity. Figure 2 shows the changed definition: Problems using the smaller numbers have only half the weight

Figure 1
Sampling of Arithmetic Problems with Equally Weighted
Domain

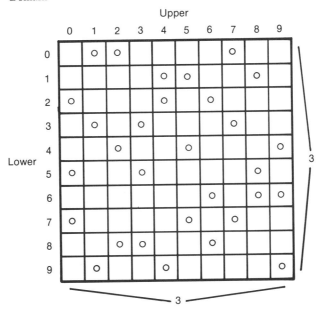

Figure 2
Sampling of Arithmetic Problems with Larger Integers More
Heavily Weighted

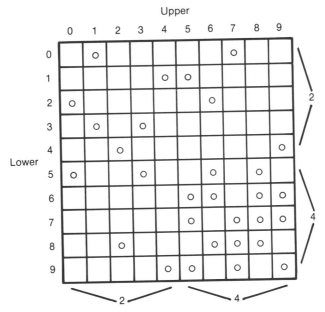

of those using the larger ones. Relatively more items must be selected from the lower right quadrant to yield adequate content validity according to this definition of the domain.

In real industrial problems, content domains are harder to diagram, but the principles are the same. To speak of content validity, there must be a content domain from which to draw a sample. It must be analyzed in terms of elements; elements must be weighted in some way (perhaps in terms of such characteristics as frequency of occurrence, importance, or complexity); and content validity must be judged in terms of how well the domain as defined has been sampled.

The content validity of our packing criterion depends on the definition of the domain of packing tasks. If I define the domain as packing fragile items, this measure lacks content validity, for golf balls are not fragile. If the job of packing golf balls includes crating the cartons, sealing the crates, and stacking them on pallets, and *if I define the content domain as including all of these activities,* then *this* work sample lacks content validity. If, however, I define the content domain simply as the repetitive packing of cartons of golf balls as quickly as possible, then this work sample has substantial content validity.

Can we talk about the content validity of the measure of arm length? Some people will. I will not. Merely recording the number of inches encompassed in the outstretched arm does not, as far as I can tell, sample any defined domain of content. The measure is therefore not reasonably described in terms of content validity.

What about the content validity of the dexterity test? The *construct* of dexterity has been operationally defined with several kinds of related tasks; these tasks could define a content domain. The present test calls on only one of these tasks, so it is not a very good sample. Yet if I am satisfied that I am measuring the construct adequately, I am not likely to worry about content validity. Personally, I tend to think of content validity as a special case of construct validity. Where the task chosen adequately measures the construct, the need for representative sampling of tasks is not apparent to me.

Let us take stock. What has or can be said about validity? First, for any measure there are many validities, not just one. It is and has long been recognized as silly to speak of *the* validity of a test. Second, it is an erroneous shorthand to speak of the validities of the measures themselves; what we really refer to are the validities of *inferences* from the measures (Cronbach, 1971). When we speak of *criterion-related* validity we refer to the use of test scores to infer criterion levels. When we speak of *construct* validity, we refer to the use of test scores to infer degrees to which a particular construct describes the persons, organizations, or objects measured. When we speak of *content* validity, we refer to the use of test scores to infer levels of achievement the persons, organizations, or objects would exhibit in the total domain. These are different facets or "aspects" of validity, and all three kinds of inferences should be valid for most tests. However, the kind of validity statement we seek in any given measurement situation depends on the kinds of inferences we wish to make. This is fundamentally a value judgment. Third, in industrial psychology, the most frequently valued inference is the inference about future performance on a valued criterion. The valued criterion is usually (although not necessarily) either a sample of a performance domain or a performance construct that is identifiably different from the constructs measured by predictors. That is, in employment testing, the validity of major interest is the validity of the *hypothesis* of a predictive relationship between test scores and job performance. Fourth, the validities of criteria need to be investigated. Finally, I suggest that an employment test may pro-

vide a basis for inferences that have criterion-related validity, or construct validity,
or content validity, or all of these, and still
not be job related.

Job-Relatedness

I am not willing to equate "validity" and
"job-relatedness." Criterion-related validity is evidence of job-relatedness only if the
criterion measure is a valid measure of
overall job performance, an element or
sample of performance, or a construct related to job behavior.

Construct validity is evidence of job-relatedness only if the construct is related to
the job. To defend an employment test on
the basis of construct validity, one must
first argue from job or need analysis that a
particular construct is related to job behavior. Then he must show that the test has
acceptable validity for measuring that construct. What he has at this point is the hypothesis that the construct, as operationally
defined by the predictor, can be used to
infer levels of valued job behavior. This is a
hypothesis of criterion-related validity, and
it fairly begs to be tested, "where technically feasible."

If it is clearly feasible to do the criterion-
related study, it should be done. Where it
is clearly *not* feasible to do the study, the
defense of the predictor can rest on a combination of its construct validity and the rational justification for the inclusion of the
construct in the predictive hypothesis.
Where the issue is not clear, we will argue.
My position is that I would rather trust the
use of valid measures of predictor constructs in a well-developed hypothesis than
a typical, done-for-convenience criterion-
related study. I think my preference offers
better evidence of job-relatedness.

*   *   *   *   *

So far, these comments implied an assumption that inexperienced people will be
hired who will have to learn the job. The

employment test is therefore a *predictor* of
performance, not a *measure* of it.[2]

No such assumption is made when content validity is invoked. Either experienced
workers will be hired, or applicants will be
expected to have already mastered certain
prerequisite components of the job
through prior training.

The job-relatedness of content sampling
depends on the definition of the content
domain. In the most extreme case, one
might define job content by listing every
nontrivial task performed. A representative sample from this complete catalog of
tasks clearly has both content validity and
job-relatedness. Despite its virtue, however, it can only be used to select people
who already know how to handle the job. If
the domain is defined more narrowly as a
skill or area of knowledge that can reasonably be expected in applicants and is prerequisite to learning necessary additional skills
or information, and if a test is a valid sample of this content, then the test is job related to whatever extent the domain it samples is job related.

How much abstraction is permissible before one questions whether a test is sampling *job* content? Figure 3 may clarify this
problem. The large block on the left represents the defined content domain. The
smaller blocks represent different ways to
sample from that domain. The most direct
sample, and therefore the closest, is a probationary period; what could have higher
content validity than a well-planned probationary period? Next is the completion of a

---

[2] In the *Griggs* decision, the Supreme Court has
said, "What Congress has forbidden is giving these
devices and mechanisms controlling force unless they
are demonstrably a reasonable measure of job performance." At first glance, in the context of this discussion, the quoted phrase might be interpreted as requiring content validity. This is an unreasonable
interpretation. One cannot "measure" job performance among applicants who have not yet performed
on the job. One can *predict* job performance, or one
can measure performance on tasks that are samples of
the job. Either of these is a job-related use of tests and
probably satisfies the intent of the phrase.

Figure 3

A Progression of Methods for Sampling Job-Relevant Content for the Assessment of Candidates

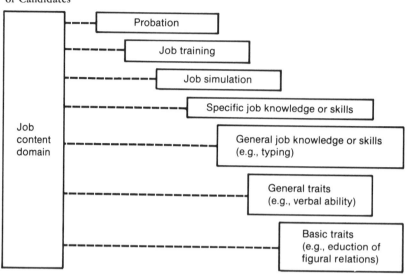

training program designed to teach a representative sample of job tasks. The third, a simulation exercise, can be a good sample of job content.

As we move to the right, to the use of conventional tests, the sampling is progressively less direct. The farther one goes in assessment from a direct sampling, the greater the inferential leap necessary to relate test content to job content. Where shall we draw the line? How far can we go and still claim to be sampling the content of the job? For the present, I will say only that the greater the inferential leap required, the less relevant content validity is in assessing the job-relatedness of a test; that is, the domain being sampled validly is a less satisfactory definition of the *job* domain.

I have argued that a measure can be described as valid and still not be job related. I will also argue that a requirement may be job related even where the measurement concepts of validity are not applicable. The usual example of a bona fide occupational qualification, the requirement that the men's room attendant be male, may soon be archaic, but I think it illustrates the point.

Certain educational requirements may also be job related even where the validity of inferences as described in the *Standards* is not especially relevant. Consider only one example: the requirement of a degree in mechanical engineering for one who is to design heavy equipment. Possession of the degree does not reflect any homogeneous construct. Its content validity for a job-content domain is probably low; it includes performance in nonengineering subjects, many of the engineering subjects studied may be irrelevant to the particular job, and many aspects of the job may not have been reflected in the work toward the degree. In short, the knowledge and skill required to obtain the degree is a sample of a different domain from that of the job. Yet, personally, I would consider a degree in engineering related to the job of designing heavy equipment.[3]

When I say this, I am implying a hypothesis that people with the degree are more likely to be able to perform the required tasks than are people without the degree.

---

[3] This is not a general endorsement of educational requirements, many of which are highly questionable.

This is a testable hypothesis, but the interests of society are not well served by hiring a lot of nonengineers to design heavy equipment just to do a criterion-related validation study. Moreover, the logic of the hypothesis seems so clear to me that I would accept the requirement as job related without any further evidence of the validity of the hypothesis.

In short, I view job-relatedness as the extent to which the hypothesis of a relationship between the hiring requirement and job behavior can be accepted as logical. If there are gaps in the logical arguments, or if it is based on weak assumptions, then evidence of validity may be useful to support claims of job-relatedness. But validity and job-relatedness are not the same.

*   *   *   *   *

REFERENCES

American Psychological Association, American Educational Research Association, & National Council on Measurements Used in Education (Joint Committee) Technical recommendations for psychological tests and diagnostic techniques. *Psychological Bulletin,* 1954, *51,* 201–238.

American Psychological Association, American Educational Research Association, & National Council on Measurement in Education (Joint Committee). *Standards for educational and psychological tests and manuals.* Washington, D.C.: American Psychological Association, 1966.

Attneave, F. *Applications of information theory to psychology.* New York: Holt, 1959.

Bechtoldt, H. P. Construct validity: A critique. *American Psychologist,* 1959, *14,* 619–629.

Bourassa, G. L., & Guion, R. M. A factorial study of dexterity tests. *Journal of Applied Psychology,* 1959, *43,* 199–204.

Boynton, P. L. *Intelligence: Its manifestations and measurement.* New York: Appleton, 1933.

Brigham, C. C. Intelligence tests of immigrant groups. *Psychological Review,* 1930, *37,* 158–165.

Cronbach, L. J. Test validation. In R. L. Thorndike (Ed.), *Educational measurement.* (2nd. ed.) Washington, D.C.: American Council on Education, 1971.

DuBois, P. H. *A history of psychological testing.* Boston: Allyn & Bacon, 1970.

Fitts, P. M. The information capacity of the human motor system in controlling the amplitude of movement. *Journal of Experimental Psychology,* 1954, *47,* 381–391.

Guion, R. M. *Personnel testing.* New York: McGraw-Hill, 1965.

Guion, R. M. A note on organizational climate. *Organizational Behavior and Human Performance,* 1973, *9,* 120–125.

Hull, C. L. *Aptitude testing.* Yonkers, N.Y.: World Book, 1928.

Hunt, T. *Measurement in psychology.* New York: Prentice-Hall, 1937.

Loevinger, J. Objective tests as instruments of psychological theory. *Psychological Reports,* 1957, *3,* 635–694.

Schneider, B. *The perceived environment: Organizational climate.* (Tech. Rep. 2) College Park: University of Maryland, Department of Psychology, June 1973.

South, E. B. *A dictionary of terms used in measurements and guidance.* New York: Psychological Corporation, 1938.

Standing, T. E. An application of information theory to individual worker differences in satisfaction with work itself. Unpublished doctoral dissertation, Bowling Green State University, 1971.

Standing, T. E. Satisfaction with the work itself as a function of cognitive complexity. Paper presented at the meeting of the American Psychological Association, Montreal, Canada, August 31, 1973.

Content–Construct Confusion*

MARY L. TENOPYR

The confusion between content validity and construct validity runs rampant in psychology today. Possibly nothing has highlighted this confusion so much as the various efforts to develop guidelines on test validation. For example, in the various drafts of the pending Equal Employment Opportunity Coordinating Council Uniform Guidelines on Employee Selection Procedures there appears a statement to the effect that content validity alone is not sufficient justification for tests intended to measure psychological processes. Yet are all tests not intended to measure processes or constructs? Is not, for example, the ability to type a construct?

Standards for Educational and Psychological Tests (American Psychological Association, 1974) gives general definitions of various aspects of validity, but unfortunately, emphasizes the interrelatedness of the various aspects of validity—criterion-related, content, and construct and does not appear to draw the warranted distinctions among these aspects. Thus, there is inadequate professional guidance to which to refer when one wishes to compare the various aspects of validity.

The distinction between criterion-related validity and the other aspects of validity is not so clear as one might wish. However, it appears to be the distinction between the content and the construct aspects of validity which has resulted in the most confusion among both practitioners and theoreticians. Cronbach (1970) defines the two aspects of validity as follows: "Content validity is evaluated by showing how well the content of the test samples the class of situations about which conclusions are to be drawn. Construct validity is evaluated by investigating what psychological qualities a test measures; i.e., by determining the degree to which certain explanatory concepts or constructs account for performance on the test." (p. 444)

These definitions obviously are not mutually exclusive; in the ensuing discussion, I will make several relevant points which may help to clarify the content-construct problem.

First, validity refers to the accuracy of inferences about test *scores* (Cronbach, 1970).

Second, all inferences which should be made about employment selection procedures are concerned with prediction (broadly defined) and decision-making.

* M. L. Tenopyr, "Content–Construct Confusion," *Personnel Psychology* 30 (1977), pp. 47–54. Copyright 1977 by Personnel Psychology, Inc. Reprinted/Adapted by permission of the publisher and author. These comments were given at a conference on content validity, July 18, 1975, Bowling Green State University.

Third, any inference relative to prediction and, furthermore, all inferences relative to test scores, are based upon underlying constructs. In other words, we assume that common constructs underlie both test scores and specified job behaviors.

Fourth, that which is commonly known as "content validity" deals with inferences about test construction, not inferences about test scores. Therefore, "content validity" cannot be equated with other aspects of validity (Messick, 1975). That which is commonly called content validation is usually merely propaedeutic to and not synonymous with construct validation.

Fifth, content-oriented test development, to be useful in an employment situation, must always take constructs into account. Also test interpretation should imply constructs. The notion of criterion-referenced test interpretation, in particular, has no applicability in employment selection.

Sixth, there should be no real conflict about whether content or construct validation is appropriate in a given situation. The question instead is one of for which *class* of constructs is evidence of traditional content validity alone enough to justify the contention that these constructs are being measured and if the predictive inferences made from the measurements are sufficiently accurate.

Some of the preceding points may represent a departure from conventional thinking, so each in order will be developed further. First, validity refers to the accuracy of inferences about test *scores*. I need not say that one should never speak about *the* validity of a test. Furthermore, it should be readily apparent that it is not the test which is valid, it is the inferences made from test scores. As Cronbach (1970) has pointed out, there can be as many validities related to a test as there are inferences about the scores. It is, again, almost patronizing to discuss the notion of multiple versus single validities and the fact that validity

is based on inferences, not tests. However, these two points should probably be accentuated in the interest of making material which will follow more comprehensible.

The second point is that all inferences which should be made about employment selection procedures are concerned with prediction. Various distinctions have been made about inferences possible from tests. Some of these distinctions have had limited usefulness in particular situations, but insofar as employment testing is concerned, such distinctions have probably only added to the confusion. In particular, the distinction between descriptive and predictive inferences (Tukey, 1960) has been a source of problems. Cronbach (1970) distinguishes between inferences relevant to specific decisions, the nature of which is known in advance of testing, and descriptive inferences, which may at some time be used for various decisions. The primary distinction between the two is the immediacy and degree of knowledge of the nature of decisions involved. A parallel may be drawn between this distinction and the one which psychologists sometimes make relative to content validity. It has been suggested that a test validated by criterion-related methods is used for prediction or decision-making, whereas a content valid test describes the level of skill a person brings to a job. Both of these statements are true, of course, but I contend that we should be concerned mainly with the predictive aspects of tests used for employment decisions. We should not be primarily concerned with the descriptive aspects of inferences from a content developed test. Surely scores from a well-developed typing test can be used to describe a person's skill at manipulating a typewriter, but description is not our primary purpose when we use a typing test to make hiring decisions. We would not care about a mere description of an individual's typing ability unless we were deciding whether to employ him or her. We essentially use the typing score to *predict* how successfully someone will perform a job involving typing.

Nor is it useful to make the aptitude-achievement distinction in employment testing. Often it has been said that tests like the typing tests are measures of achievement, whereas most other tests are aptitude tests. Whether a test is an aptitude or an achievement test depends on how it is used. It does not depend upon how specific the ability is which is being measured. When a job knowledge test and a spatial reasoning test are being used to assess progress in training, they are both achievement tests. When they are both used to predict employment success, they are both aptitude tests.

A particular problem extant in employment psychology today is that of the licensing or certification test. Those who construct such tests appear to treat them as pure achievement tests and argue that a licensing test only assures prospective employers or the public that a person has the necessary knowledge and skills to practice in a given profession or trade. However, the assurance of minimum skills is merely an aspect of prediction. It is predicted that those not possessing the minimum skills will do a poorer job of professional practice than those who do possess those skills.

In fact, any test which is used for decision-making relative to prediction is essentially an aptitude test. Anytime we make an employ/not employ decision on the basis of a test we are using an explicit or implicit prediction. Thus, there is no conceptual difference between a typing or licensing test used for employment, and a traditional aptitude test, e.g., one of abstract reasoning.

These who argue for either a descriptive or an achievement-oriented interpretation of tests like the typing test can often marshal impressive logical arguments for such interpretation, but their logic fails when they reach the point of exact score interpretation. It is difficult, if not impossible, to establish a meaningful critical score on

an employment test unless one uses a predictive framework. A critical score on a content-oriented test has no meaning unless it can be related to some level of job behavior. For example, what does the proverbial 70 percent mean in terms of job behavior? What does typing straight copy at 40 words per minute mean in terms of typing on the job?

Writers of government guidelines have not eliminated the confusion. They have spoken of "content validity" without any reference to the predictive nature of tests purported to have this type of validity, but when they have written of interpretation of content valid tests, they acknowledge that scores on such tests must have some relationship to job behavior.

The third major point to be discussed is that not only are inferences from content-based tests used for employment decisions predictive in nature, they are also based upon constructs. For such a test to be useful in employment decision-making, there must be common constructs underlying both test performance and job behavior. We may look at a factor, as derived from factor analysis, as an elementary definition of a construct. Also, we know from elementary factor theory that the correlation between any two variables equals the sum of the cross-products of their common factor loadings. Putting it more simply, to have high predictive value, a test must essentially involve the same constructs to the same degree as a measure of the job behavior. It would seem, then, that any interpretation of a content-based employment test strictly in terms of tasks is inadequate. A content-based test or any other test used for prediction, must share common constructs with job behavior.

The obvious relationship between content and construct validity cannot be ignored; however, content and construct validity cannot be equated. My fourth point exemplified this. Content validity deals with inferences about test construction; construct validity involves inferences about test *scores*. Since by definition, all validity is the accuracy of inferences about test scores, that which has been called "content validity" is not validity at all. Typical content validity is an indication of how well test content samples a larger universe of content. Although, as some authors (Cronbach, 1970) have stated, there are hints of constructs involved in content validation; Melton (1966) implied, strictly speaking, judgments about content validity should be reserved for the operational, observable aspects of test construction. In other words, the question in content validation may be reduced to, "How good a sample is the behavior required by the test of the behavior in the universe?" Reduced to its simplest terms, traditional content validity involves the results of a comparison of test tasks and universe tasks and says nothing about the processes involved in accomplishing the tasks. At the minimum, content validation may be considered propaedeutic to construct validation. At the maximum, content validity may be assumed to be one type of evidence of construct validity. The latter interpretation in employment testing appears to be reasonable only in the case in which test tasks and job tasks match so well that there can be little question that common constructs underlie performance on both.

The method of test interpretation has some bearing here. The notion of criterion-referenced test interpretation, in particular, has no application in an employment setting. Such interpretation, based on standards rather than peer group performance tends to negate individual differences which are at the heart of construct interpretations. Also they tend to obscure the predictive nature of all employee selection methods. A predictive model again implies individual differences. To get from criterion-referenced scores into a predictive mode implicitly involves a change from comparison with standards to a comparison with peers.

In most employment testing situations, the relationship between test constructs and job constructs is not readily apparent. This leads us to my fifth point which is that much content-oriented test development must take constructs into account. There are various ways of accomplishing this, and the notion is not particularly new. In fact, educators long ago developed the task-by-process method of outlining tests. The procedure is not completely without merit.

However, typically the processes are chosen arbitrarily from one or another taxonomy of processes and have no relationship to constructs which have been defined by the more sophisticated methods. For example, one so-called process sometimes used in outlining is "analyzing." However, nowhere in the literature of construct definition can one find evidence of a single construct "ability to analyze." When test writers deal in terms of such vaguely defined concepts, the end result is likely to be a test with highly correlated parts which really cannot be assumed to represent different constructs.

Another procedure which might be applied in relating constructs to the content-oriented test development is to combine content and criterion-related methods. This procedure admittedly is not feasible in many instances, and it is usually particularly inappropriate in criterion development. The method I propose is to do a thorough job of content-oriented test construction and follow it with a token criterion-related study. The study would lend support to construct interpretations and also solve the problem of setting a meaningful critical score. It is important to note that I am not suggesting a criterion-related study on a grand scale, including differential prediction studies and similarly complicated embellishments, but merely a small study which is essentially confirmatory in nature and yields some reasonable means for establishing a critical score or other method of score interpretation.

A third possibility is to include construct information in the job analysis which is the basis for the content-oriented test. I am convinced that analysis based on tasks or duties alone is usually not a sound basis for content-oriented test construction. At its worst it leads to a fantastic amount of redundancy in measurement. It is well known through employing multiple regression techniques in a prediction problem that four or five short aptitude tests can usually account for most of the predictable variance in the criterion. Some of the test batteries developed on the basis of job analysis and content-oriented test development methods require many hours to administer and yet involve no more common factors than the typical short battery of aptitude tests. Their users should not be surprised if such long test batteries, when subjected to a criterion-related study, yield a large number of negative regression weights for variables which serve as suppressor variables. It is to be noted that the only function suppressor variables serve is to remove redundancy in measurement. A simple example might be in order at this point. A factor analysis based upon importance ratings of secretarial duties resulted in a number of factors relating to typing. A different test was developed for each factor. However, when the tests were administered, they were found to be so highly correlated that a single test would suffice to cover all task-based factors. True, as a result of the study the test construction and correlation data provided evidence to support not using a strict work sample approach and yielded evidence of construct validity for a simple speed typing test. However, the research time and effort required hardly justified the results.

A possibly better approach which I have planned, but not as yet applied, involves factor analysis of task information and construct information together. This approach implies the existence of an appropriate taxonomy of constructs and a means of evaluating each with respect to its applicability to the job.

One possible procedure would be as follows:

1. Obtain task ratings, e.g., importance or frequency.
2. Obtain construct ratings, e.g., degree required or importance.
3. Factor task ratings to obtain task factors.
4. Project construct ratings on task factors (Mosier, 1938).

The method should yield a reasonably sound basis for regrouping tasks and for eliminating tasks which are redundant insofar as the involvement of underlying constructs is concerned.

The procedure has a big disadvantage because of the nature of factors which are derived from task ratings. Often task factors represent only duties which occur together. For example, if taking shorthand and making coffee are both part of the job, they may form a factor. If setting up a lathe and sweeping up chips are part of a job, they may define a factor. Obviously, superimposing constructs on factors such as these will yield equivocal results. Another problem, not to be ignored, is that of getting sufficient subjects to do such sophisticated analyses. One can easily find oneself in the position where he or she has more variables than subjects.

Another procedure might be to start with a task-by-ability matrix with all entries representing importance of the ability for the task. Mean ratings could be factored, resulting in ability factors. The factor scores of the tasks on those factors could then be examined. Again, there is a serious problem of getting enough subjects and meeting other conditions for the analysis.

The interbattery and simultaneous factor analysis methods probably have some application here, and I believe that a refined method of getting construct task factors can be developed.

A note of caution must be interjected here. The mathematical refinements I have been discussing may be in the category of using a micrometer to measure an elephant. Job analysis of necessity involves considerable subjectivity; any mathematical formulations of the type I have discussed must be viewed not as substitutes for, but as aids to, sound professional judgment.

My final point is that the decision on whether to use construct, content, or criterion-related validity should not rest on "whether mental processes are measured." It is clear that processes and underlying constructs are involved in all measurement. I have indicated that, at its best, that known as content validity is one form of evidence for construct validity. I have, in addition, suggested some methods which may serve to make it better evidence.

However, I have not addressed the question of when so-called traditional content validity should be allowed as the sole evidence of construct validity. The answer to that question appears to require some means of classifying constructs and placing them on various continua. For example, I can envision a continuum from simple to complex or from having observable manifestations to not having such manifestations. In lieu of such a classificatory system, I can only make tentative suggestions as to the constructs for which so-called content validity is an appropriate sole source of evidence. I suggest these constructs be limited to acquired skills, well defined physical characteristics, specific knowledge, well de-

fined preferences (e.g., for shift work), and the like. To go far beyond those constructs which are simple and easily measured is to stretch to inferences of dubious scientific quality. Certainly there are gray areas in which decisions on appropriate validity evidence are not easy. However, my general advice is, "If you want to use inferences about test construction to justify inferences about test scores, stay with simple, well defined constructs with easily observable manifestations."

REFERENCES

American Psychological Association, American Educational Research Association, and National Council on Measurement in Education. *Standards for educational & psychological tests.* Washington, D.C.: American Psychological Association, 1974.

Cronbach, L. J. Test validation. In R. L. Thorndike (Ed.), *Educational measurement* (2nd ed.). Washington, D.C.: American Council on Education, 1971, 443–507.

Melton, A. W. Individual differences and theoretical process variables. In R. M. Gagne (Ed.), *Learning and individual differences.* Columbus, Ohio: Charles E. Merrill, 1966, 238–252.

Messick, S. The standard problem: Meaning and values in measurement and evaluation. *American Psychologist.* 1975, 30, 955–966.

Mosier, C. I. A note on Dwyer: The determination of the factor loadings of a given test. *Psychometrika,* 1938, 3, 297–299.

Tukey, J. W. Conclusions vs. decisions. *Technometrics.* 1960, 2, 423–433.

COMMENTARY

The discussion that follows focuses on current controversies surrounding the various criterion-related validation strategies. This is not to suggest that content-oriented procedures are less controversial or that they are less important. It simply reflec·· the content of this and subsequent chapters. A conceptual review of the conten. validation process will be found in the chapter that reviews the assessment center technique (see Dreher & Sackett, 1981) while content-oriented applications are characterized in the work-sample chapter (see Robinson, 1981). In addition, the second and third readings from the current chapter (Guion, 1974; Tenopyr, 1977) are devoted to discussing the distinctions and similarities associated with the different forms of validity evidence, with a particular focus on content-oriented approaches. For example, few have discussed with greater clarity than Tenopyr (1977) the issue of when content-oriented test construction should serve as the sole justification for using a selection device.

What follows is in four sections. The first three concern specific issues related to the generation of criterion-related validity evidence. The fourth introduces a modified approach to selection research proposed by Roberts, Hulin, and Rousseau (1978). Each represents a departure from the traditional view of the validation process that prevailed for many years.

Concurrent versus Predictive Designs

Concurrent validity has long been viewed as an inadequate substitute for predictive validity. In his widely read book, Dunnette argued that the "predictive strategy is definitely necessary because it yields a kind of information about test responses impossible to obtain from strictly concurrent comparisons" (1966, p. 117). A more recent statement regarding concurrent designs comes from Cascio:

> *Unfortunately, concurrent validity is often used as a substitute for predictive validity. That is, both predictor and criterion data are gathered from present employees, and it is assumed that if workers who score high (low) on the predictor also are rated as excellent (poor) performers on the job, the relationships should also hold for job applicants. . . . These arguments are baseless. . . . The criterion-related validities are not equivalent or substitute procedures, and it is simply illusory to think so. (1978, pp. 91–92)*

The official position as stated in the *Principles for Validation and Use of Personnel Selection Procedures* (APA, 1975; APA, 1980) seems to have shifted in the latest edition of the document. In 1975 the predictive model was "to be preferred in most employee selection research" (p. 5). The 1980 version is as follows:

> *The other design is the* concurrent *model in which both predictor and criterion information are obtained for present employees at approximately the same time. The research literature clearly indicates that well conducted concurrent studies can provide useful estimates of predictive validity (Bemis, 1968; Pearlman, Schmidt, & Hunter, 1980). Both types of criterion-related studies are susceptible to the effects of range restriction. However, the test scores obtained in concurrent studies may also be influenced by additional job knowledge, different motivation, or added maturity of incumbents vs. applicants. A concurrent study with appropriate controls should yield results very comparable to those of a predictive study. (p. 7)*

Thus, there is perhaps growing awareness of the usefulness of the concurrent approach. While there are clear conceptual differences between concurrent and predictive designs, Barrett, Phillips, and Alexander (1981) argue that "frequently the conceptual distinction between predictive and concurrent validity has been exaggerated. More importantly, the differences that may exist have never been shown to render concurrent validity inaccurate as an estimate of predictive validity" (p. 1). They argue that some degree of range restriction operates in most designs (concurrent and predictive), that is, the sample used in the validation research may not include persons with extreme scores on the experimental selection device or the criterion variable. This serves to limit the maximum possible correlation that can be obtained. Also, while there may be other differences between applicants and current employees on such factors as the motivation to do well on the selection device, maturity, and job-related knowledge, there have been few empirical demonstrations that these differences lead to highly inaccurate validity estimates when using the concurrent approach.

Perhaps the best argument stressing the superiority of predictive designs comes from Guion and Cranny (1982). They correctly state that there is a wide variety of predictive and concurrent designs, not two simple strategies. Five common predictive models identified by Guion and Cranny follow:

Follow-up random.   This is the basic approach that serves as the standard with the greatest conceptual merit. Here, applicants are tested on the experimental selection procedure but the results of testing are not used to make hiring decisions. In fact, decision makers are not allowed to review test scores either before or after a hiring decision is made. The applicants are then selected randomly and placed on the job. Test scores are then correlated with subsequent measures of job performance. The criterion data are collected after the employees have been working for an appropriate period of time. As in all designs, the goal is to generalize study results to subsequent applicant groups.

Follow-up present.   Applicants are tested using the experimental procedure but selection is based on the system the organization currently uses. Test scores are then correlated with measures of job performance, again gathered after an appropriate time interval. Note that when using this model there is the possibility of range restriction on both the predictor and criterion variable. If the experimental test is correlated with the procedure in use, this will clearly restrict the range of predictor scores, since low-scoring individuals will not be hired. Likewise, if the experimental procedure is predictive of performance, some degree of restriction on the criterion also will occur.

Select by test.   Applicants are tested using the experimental procedure and then selected on the basis of these test scores. The highest-scoring individuals on the experimental procedure are selected. After an appropriate time interval, criterion data are collected and compared (usually using correlational techniques) with the test scores. Here there is likely to be considerable range restriction, depending on the selection ratio. If all the applicants are hired (selection ratio equals 1.00) the design is equivalent to the "follow-up random" approach. But as the proportion of applicants hired decreases, additional range restriction is introduced.

Hire, then test.   Soon after being hired, employees are tested, using the experimental procedure. Later, criterion data are collected and correlated with predictor scores. The degree of range restriction associated with this design will depend on whether or not the initial selection was based on a variable correlated with the trial predictor.

Shelf research.   The files of current employees are reviewed for reference to scores on selection procedures that may or may not have been used to make hiring decisions. Filed test scores, often collected at different time intervals from the date of hire, are then correlated with measures of job performance as they become available.

While these are all predictive designs, Guion and Cranny (1982) evaluate each on the basis of potential for making statistical corrections for range restriction. They argue that most predictive designs allow for range restriction corrections while most concurrent designs do not. Thus, concurrent designs will almost always result in poorer estimates of the true predictive validities of selection procedures.

The question raised by Barrett et al. (1981) is still appropriate however. While concurrent designs differ from predictive designs in terms of the likely degree of range restriction produced, the degree to which statistical corrections can be made, the motivation levels of test takers, and the impact of job experience and maturity on test scores, it still is an empirical question as to how comparable predictive and concurrent validities are in actual employment settings. If, for certain predictor types in certain selection situations, reasonably accurate validity estimates result from a concurrent strategy, the design can be of considerable value given the associated cost and time savings. An illustration of a high degree of correspondence comes from the Pearlman, Schmidt, and Hunter study of clerical occupations. They located a large number of validity coefficients associated with general ability tests. "The unweighted average of the mean validities across test types rounded to an identical .21 for both predictive and concurrent studies" (Pearlman et al., 1980, p. 381).

Sample Size Requirements

When planning a validation study one must consider the minimum number of cases needed to provide a reasonable chance of detecting validity when in fact it exists. Until recently, many researchers assumed that sample sizes from 30 to 50 were adequate for criterion-related validation studies. Guion (1965) estimated that typical validation studies were based upon samples of 40 to 50, under the best of circumstances. This reliance on small sample sizes was often the result of organizational constraints (e.g., a small number of applicants) but also reflected a belief that small random samples in the 40 to 50 range are sufficient to allow the researcher to uncover true validity when it exists.

The use of small samples in validation research has been convincingly challenged by Schmidt, Hunter, and Urry (1976). They consider two other factors, in addition to sample size, that reduce the likelihood that the typical validity study will result in a statistically significant correlation when there is an actual relationship in the population. First, an unreliable criterion variable will attenuate the estimated validity. For example, if the true validity of a selection procedure is .40 and the measure of job performance used in the study has a reliability of .70, then the expected value of the computed correlation between scores on the selection procedure and job performance is $\sqrt{.70}\,(.40)$ or .33. The sample size needed to provide a good chance of detecting a coefficient of .33 is greater than that required to detect a coefficient of .40. The second factor identified by Schmidt et al. (1976) was range restriction. Recall that the best way to generalize results to subsequent applicant samples is to conduct a study that uses unrestricted predictor scores from a group of applicants. If the study is conducted on a sample that has been selected on the basis of scores on the experimental test, the computed correlation coefficient will underestimate the operational validity of the test. What sample size is then required to provide a good chance, say 90 percent, of detecting that a test with a true validity of .35 is valid? To answer this question one must also consider the degree of range restriction that operates in the study and the reliability of the criterion variable. Schmidt et al. (1976) provide tables taking these and other factors into account. Consider a situation where the true validity of the test is .35 and there is no restriction of range on the test for the sample used in the study. This would be similar to using the follow-up random design described earlier. Either all or a random sample of applicants would be used in the validation study. Also, assume the reliability of the criterion variable to be .70. To provide a 90 percent chance of detecting that the test is in fact valid, a sample size of 98 would be required (using an alpha level of .05 and a one-tailed statistical test). This is well above the sample requirements previously viewed as appropriate. It also represents an idealized validation strategy. To be more realistic, assume that a "select by test" predictive design is used. Here, top-scoring applicants are selected and become the validation sample. If 50 percent of the applicants are selected this results in considerable range restriction on the selection device. Again, assume that the true validity of the test is .35 and the criterion reliability equals .70. Using this type of predictive design a sample of 256 would be required to provide a 90 percent chance of detecting that the test is valid. The point is, only under certain conditions (low range restrictions, high criterion reliability, and high true validity) will required sample sizes approach the range once thought appropriate. It is interesting to note that sample size requirements are determined largely by the type of validation design used. Relatively large sample sizes are required when using Guion and Cranny's (1982) select by test strategy, while smaller sample sizes will normally be required when using the follow-up random approach. Thus, choosing an appropriate research design and determining an appropriate sample size for the study are interrelated problems.

Subgroup Validity

Dunnette (1963) argued that by subgrouping tests, people, jobs, situations, and consequences, a higher degree of predictive accuracy could be achieved. Recall that he noted the pessimism Clark Hull displayed in 1928 concerning the use of test batteries for predicting occupational criteria. For Hull, validity coefficients in the range of .50 represented the upper limit for occupational tests. As will become apparent in subsequent chapters, even today a validity coefficient approaching .50 is extremely rare. For Dunnette, one explanation for low validity coefficients and variation among coefficients generated in different studies takes the form of what some term *moderator variables*. "As classically defined, a moderator variable is one at different levels of which the relationship between a second and third variable may be expected to differ" (Owens, 1978, p. 243). Or, as defined by Saunders (1956), the term refers to conditions under "which the predictive validity of some psychological measure varies systematically in accord with some other independent psychological variable" (p. 209). These definitions are deceptively clear, while in reality defining the meaning associated with the term *moderator variable* has resulted in considerable confusion. The notion of a moderator in the classic sense is not implied in the discussion to follow. Given the limited scope of this text, the interested reader should review a more detailed treatment of this topic, such as provided by Zedeck (1971). Here, the concept of subgroup validity perhaps best applies. By creating homogeneous subgroups, researchers have attempted to increase the predictability of performance (or other meaningful criteria). For example, Locke, Mento, and Katcher (1978) "found that ability predicted performance better in groups which were homogeneous with respect to motivation than in those which were motivationally heterogenous" (p. 269). Note that the degree to which performance was predicted was enhanced in homogeneous groups. Ability predicted performance best when motivation was either high *or* low. Computing a correlation on the basis of a combined group (motivationally hetergeneous) resulted in decreased predictive accuracy. Essentially, this is a process of controlling a main effect variable (i.e., a variable causally linked to performance). In this case, ability (also a main effect variable) will serve as a better predictor of performance when motivation (a second main effect variable) is controlled. Another example comes from Abelson (1952). In this study the academic performance of females was more predictable than that of males. Following the logic of using homogeneous subgroups, one might explain this finding by arguing that females are more homogeneous with respect to motivation to perform in academic settings than males (Locke et al., 1978). Note that this is a very different statement from saying that ability will be predictive of performance only when motivation is high. This last statement implies that ability is causally linked to performance only under certain circumstances (i.e., when individuals possess a certain degree of motivation). Or, at the very least, it implies that ability acts on or affects performance differently, depending upon the level of motivation.

In the area of personnel selection, subgroup analyses have taken multiple forms. The area receiving the greatest attention has focused on subgrouping on the basis of race and sex. This, of course, has occurred as a result of the civil rights legislation passed in the 1960s, since minorities and women are members of protected classes.

It was hypothesized that employment tests generate lower validity coefficients when applied to minorities and women. The research evidence, as applied to black-white differences, indicates that cognitive-ability tests are equally valid (or at least the magnitude of the difference is very small) for both groups (Linn, 1978). Thus, in this restricted sense, subgrouping on the basis of race has not confirmed this early suspicion. However, limited research suggests that the hypothesis may still be viable for male-female subgroups (Arvey, 1979, p. 93). The topic of male-female and minority-nonminority subgroup validity will be discussed in greater detail in the following chapter, which focuses on the broader question of selection system fairness. Therefore, we will now turn our attention to a related question. Is validity situation or job specific? This issue also will be treated in a more detailed fashion in subsequent chapters, but it needs to be briefly developed here to make a point regarding subgroup validity.

When one examines validity coefficients obtained using the same predictor for what seem to be similar jobs (but in different organizations or different subunits of the same organization) the validities differ, producing a distribution of coefficients. Historically, the variance associated with this distribution has been interpreted as evidence that validities are situation specific. Likewise, when using the same predictor for different jobs (even within similar job families) different validity values are usually obtained. In a series of studies, based upon a model formulated by Schmidt and Hunter (1977), it has been shown that much of the observed variation in validities associated with cognitive employment tests can be accounted for by considering a variety of statistical artifacts. For example, study differences in sample size, criterion reliability, and range restriction seem to account for most of the observed variability. This, however, is a different problem from that Dunnette (1963) considered. He was concerned with procedures that would provide the capability of "penetrating the region of inaccessibility outlined by Hull" (p. 318). That is, he hoped to generate validity coefficients above .50. While the work of Schmidt and his colleagues helps explain why validity coefficients vary across studies, the mean estimates of true validity in most of their reports are still in the .20 to .40 range. Thus, there still may be a variety of variables that, if used to form subgroups, would result in higher mean validity coefficients.

A Dynamic Selection Model

In an attempt to integrate individuals, environments, and responses within the context of a dynamic model of job performance and selection, Roberts, Hulin, and Rousseau (1978) stress, among other things, two issues related to the current discussion. First, following Dunnette (1963), they argue that:

> *Without adequate conceptualization and assessments of response-relevant environmental characteristics in selection studies, influences of these characteristics must be assigned to the category of errors of prediction. Such assignment has the inevitable result of reducing the apparent predictability of performance (p. 123).*

The key here is the use of the term *response-relevant*. Subgrouping based on this type of variable should result in greater predictive accuracy. Consider the following as illustrations of the usefulness of incorporating response-relevant situational variables within the context of more traditional validation research. Of particular interest is a study by Brown (1981) which examined the validity of a biodata instrument used to select salesmen in the life insurance industry. (This instrument is the subject of the reading by Thayer included in Chapter 9.) Validity evidence for the instrument was available from 12 different companies, with sample sizes ranging from 406 to 3,590. Observed validities in the 12 companies ranged from .128 to .264. Brown divided the 12 companies into 2 groups, representing more effective and less effective management of recruiting and selection practices. The more effective companies had high average production levels, had greater success in hiring applicants with high test scores, and made more use of personal recruiting sources. After correcting for range restrictions and criterion reliability, the mean validity for the effectively managed companies was .32, compared with a mean validity of .22 for the less-effectively managed companies. This study provides an excellent example of a situational variable affecting the level of validity found across organizations.

Brown (1979), in another life insurance industry study, found some initially disturbing findings: applicants hired despite lower scores appeared to be more likely to succeed than applicants with higher scores. Managers making hiring decisions were not given actual test scores, but merely told that the applicant had passed or failed the test. Some applicants were hired despite a failing test score. Dividing his sample into "hired and passed" and "hired despite failing" groups, Brown found that the test was valid within each group, e.g., the closer a failing applicant came to the test cutoff the greater the likelihood of success, and the higher a passing applicant scored, the greater likelihood of success. However, applicants with a "high fail" score were more likely to succeed than applicants with a "low pass" score. These findings were interpreted as resulting from increased managerial commitment to applicants hired despite failing scores. The manager is going out on a limb to hire such an applicant, and thus has a greater stake in the applicant's success, leading to more care in training and supervision. This research suggests that the supervisor's personal stake in and commitment to the success of a new hire is a situational variable worthy of attention. The two studies by Brown provide examples of using environmental variables to explain validity differences across organizations (e.g., finding higher validities in companies with effective management strategies) and to explain differences across individuals in likelihood of job success (e.g., managerial commitment to applicants hired despite failing scores increasing the applicants' likelihood of success).

In his 1975 essay on organizational climate, Schneider offers the proposition that performance is a function of ability and a climate which stresses the display of individual differences. Also working in the life insurance industry, Schneider found a correlation of .07 between the Aptitude Index Battery and performance. He used organizational climate data to form clusters of agencies and found that validities for these clusters ranged from −.01 to .26. The highest validity was found in agencies which were highest on supervisory support, concern for new employees, agent autonomy and agent morale, lowest on intraagency conflict, and average in supervisory structure.

Following this research, Schneider (1978) reviewed other studies of ability-situation interaction research. One situational variable leading to conflicting findings is the type of incentive system used. In a laboratory study, Weinstein and Holzbach (1973) found an ability-performance correlation of .46 when all subjects received the same pay and an ability-performance correlation of .08 in a pay-for-performance condition. Pritchard, Dunnette, and Jorgenson (1972) created an organization in which subjects performed clerical work for six days. Ability-performance correlations were higher under incentive pay ($r = .75$) than under hourly pay ($r = .65$) conditions. While the impact of incentive systems is yet to be fully determined, incentive systems represent a potentially important situational variable.

Finally, Bray, Campbell, and Grant (1974) investigated the effects of early career job challenge on the accuracy of predictions made as part of the Management Progress Study, AT&T's large-scale assessment center study (see Chapter 8 for additional discussion of this research). Overall, 64 percent of the candidates predicted to reach middle management did so, while 32 percent of those predicted to fail reached middle management. However, among those predicted to reach middle management, 76 percent of those with highly challenging first assignments did so, as opposed to 33 percent of those with unchallenging assignments. Among those predicted to fail, 61 percent of those with highly challenging first assignments proved the prediction wrong by reaching middle management, as opposed to 5 percent of those with unchallenging assignments. Early career challenge appears to be a situational variable with a powerful effect on job performance.

A wide variety of intraorganizational situational variables have been examined, including early job challenge, managerial effectiveness, supervisory commitment to the new employee, organizational climate, incentive systems, and job characteristics. While by no means an exhaustive literature review, the above discussion illustrates both the variety of situational variables which have been studied and the variety of research strategies available for examining these variables.

The above discussion has focused on intraorganizational situational variables. Near, Rice, and Hunt (1980) offer a conceptual framework interrelating work and nonwork variables. They identify a variety of extraorganizational variables, including demographic characteristics (e.g., marital status), community variables (e.g., raised in an urban versus rural environment, health, nonwork leisure activities), and family life variables (e.g., family size, home emotional climate). Their review focuses on the impact of these variables on reactions to work (e.g., job satisfaction) rather than on performance. The variables they identify are commonly included as part of biographical data questionnaires used for selection purposes (Chapter 9 focuses in detail on the use of biographical data). It is interesting to note that the research strategies used in examining intra- and extraorganizational situational variables are quite different. As we saw earlier, research dealing with intraorganizational variables typically uses the situational variable to enhance the accuracy of predictions made using other predictors. Either the situational variable is used to form subgroups of individuals, or organizations for which validity of other predictors are examined separately, or else an interaction between the situational variable and other predictors is examined. On the other hand, extraorganizational variables measured by a biodata questionnaire are typically used directly as predictors of job success.

One final way in which situational variables play a role in selection research is the restriction of range in performance due to situational constraints. If, for example, strong informal workgroup norms dictate that daily output should stay within a narrow range, the correlation between any predictor and performance will be low. Any factor which restricts the range of performance also restricts the degree to which performance can be predicted. Peters and O'Connor (1980) have identified a number of situational constraints on performance, including (1) the lack of information needed to do the job; (2) the lack of tools, equipment, materials, or supplies needed to do the job; (3) the help needed from others to do the job; (4) the training and experience needed to do the job; (5) the time needed to do the job; and (6) physical work environment which restricts job performance due to such factors as heat, cold, or noise. It is important to note that a situational constraint which lowers the performance of all employees by, say, 10 units per day, will not affect validity. In such a case, the range of performance is unaffected. Only when the range is restricted is validity affected. Peters and O'Connor offer some limited support that situational constraints restrict the performance of higher performers more than that of lower performers, thus restricting the range of performance. A simple example: using a typewriter on which the keys jam when one reaches a rate of 80 words per minute puts an artificial upper boundary on performance.

The second issue developed by Roberts et al. (1978) addresses a more radical departure from the traditional validation model. They propose that environmental characteristics can directly influence the characteristics of people, not just their responses in employment settings. Traditional validation research, particularly as it relates to cognitive abilities, assumes that person-centered traits are stable. As employees mature and experience the work environment they may change in predictable ways. Thus, "individual characteristics assessed before organizational entry may be only indirectly related to the same characteristics assessed in the same individuals after experience in an organization" (Roberts et al., 1978, p. 124). This relates directly to the design of validation studies and may form the basis for integrating the traditional predictive and concurrent designs discussed earlier in this chapter. Individual characteristics may influence early work experiences which in turn may influence individual characteristics that are the precursors of subsequent behavior.

REFERENCES

Abelson, R. P. Sex differences in predictability of college grades. *Educational and Psychological Measurement,* 1952, *12,* 638–644.

American Psychological Association, Division of Industrial-Organizational Psychology. *Principles for the validation and use of personnel selection procedures.* Dayton, Ohio: The Industrial-Organizational Psychologist, 1975.

American Psychological Association, Division of Industrial-Organizational Psychology. *Principles for the validation and use of personnel selection procedures.* (2d ed.). Berkeley, Calif.: The Industrial-Organizational Psychologist, 1980.

Arvey, R. D. Fairness in selecting employees. Reading, Mass.: Addison-Wesley, 1979.

Barrett, G. V., Phillips, J. S., & Alexander, R. A. Concurrent and predictive validity designs: A critical reanalysis. *Journal of Applied Psychology,* 1981, *66,* 1–6.

Bartlett, C. J., Bobko, P., Mosier, S. B., & Hannan, R. Testing for fairness with a moderated multiple regression strategy: An alternative to differential analysis. *Personnel Psychology,* 1978, *31,* 233–241.

Bemis, S. E. Occupational validity and the general aptitudes test battery. *Journal of Applied Psychology,* 1968, *52,* 240–244.

Berlew, D. E., & Hall, D. T. The socialization of managers: Effects of expectation on performance. *Administrative Science Quarterly,* 1966, *11,* 207–224.

Bray, D. W., Campbell, R. J., & Grant, D. L. *Formative years in business: A long-term AT&T study of managerial lives.* New York: John Wiley & Sons, 1974.

Brown, S. H. Validity distortions associated with a test in use. *Journal of Applied Psychology,* 1979, *64,* 460–462.

Brown, S. H. Validity generalization and situational moderation in the life insurance industry. *Journal of Applied Psychology,* 1981, *66,* 664–670.

Cascio, W. F. *Applied psychology in personnel management.* Reston, Virginia: Reston Publishing, 1978.

Dreher, G. F., & Sackett, P. R. Some problems with applying content validity evidence to assessment center procedures. *Academy of Management Review,* 1981, *6,* 551–560.

Dunnette, M. D. A modified model for test validation and selection research. *Journal of Applied Psychology,* 1963, *47,* 317–323.

Dunnette, M. D. *Personnel selection and placement.* Belmont, Calif.: Brooks/Cole, 1966.

Ghiselli, E. E. The validity of aptitude tests in personnel selection. *Personnel Psychology,* 1973, *26,* 461–478.

Guion, R. M. *Personnel Testing.* New York: McGraw-Hill, 1965.

Guion, R. M. Open a new window: Validities and values in psychological measurement. *American Psychologist,* 1974, *29,* 298–296.

Guion, R. M., & Cranny, C. J. A note on concurrent and predictive validity designs: A critical reanalysis. *Journal of Applied Psychology,* 1982, *67,* 239–244.

Linn, R. L. Single-group validity, differential validity, and differential prediction. *Journal of Applied Psychology,* 1978, *63,* 507–512.

Locke, E. A., Mento, A. J., & Katcher, B. L. The interaction of ability and motivation in performance: An exploration of the meaning of moderators. *Personnel Psychology,* 1978, *31,* 269–280.

Near, J. P., Rice, R. W., & Hunt, R. G. The relationship between work and nonwork domains: A review of empirical research. *Academy of Management Review,* 1980, *5,* 415–429.

Owens, W. A. Moderators and subgroups. *Personnel Psychology,* 1978, *31,* 243–247.

Pearlman, K., Schmidt, F. L., & Hunter, J. E. Validity generalization results for tests used to predict job proficiency and training success in clerical occupations. *Journal of Applied Psychology,* 1980, *65,* 373–406.

Peters, L. H., & O'Connor, E. J. Situational constraints and work outcomes: The influence of a frequently overlooked construct. *Academy of Management Review,* 1980, *5,* 391–397.

Pritchard, R. D., Dunnette, M. D., & Jorgenson, D. O. Effects of perceptions of equity and inequity on worker performance and satisfaction. *Journal of Applied Psychology,* 1972, *56,* 75–94.

Roberts, K. H., Hulin, C. L., & Rousseau, D. M. *Developing an interdisciplinary science of organizations.* San Francisco: Jossey-Bass, 1978.

Robinson, D. D. Content-oriented personnel selection in a small business setting. *Personnel Psychology,* 1981, *34,* 77–87.

Saunders, D. R. Moderator variables in prediction. *Educational and Psychological Measurement,* 1956, *16,* 209–222.

Schmidt, F. L., & Hunter, J. E. Development of a general solution to the problem of validity generalization. *Journal of Applied Psychology,* 1977, *62,* 529–540.

Schmidt, F. L., Hunter, J. E., & Urry, V. W. Statistical power in criterion-related validation studies. *Journal of Applied Psychology,* 1976, *61,* 473–485.

Schneider, B. Organizational climates: An essay. *Personnel Psychology,* 1975, *28,* 447–479.

Schneider, B. Person-situation selection: A review of some ability-situation interaction research. *Personnel Psychology,* 1978, *31,* 281–297.

Tenopyr, M. L. Content-construct confusion. *Personnel Psychology,* 1977, *30,* 47–54.

Weinstein, A. G., & Holzback, R. L. Impact of individual differences, reward distribution, and task structure on productivity in a simulated work environment. *Journal of Applied Psychology,* 1973, *58,* 296–301.

Zedeck, S. Problems with the use of moderator variables. *Psychological Bulletin,* 1971, *76,* 295–310.

Chapter 2

Differential Validity and Selection Fairness

INTRODUCTION

The previous chapter was primarily concerned with issues related to providing validity evidence. The focus for this chapter is also related to that, addressing the issue of *fairness* or *equality* in employment opportunity. A variety of social and legal influences have led researchers to propose models of test fairness that provide statistical definitions of unfair employment practices. Details regarding the legal environment and what constitutes discrimination on the basis of membership in a protected class will be provided in a subsequent chapter. Here, the goal is to familiarize the reader with the basic concepts associated with conducting a fairness analysis. Thus, it is an extension of the previous chapter in the sense that it will concentrate on using data, usually generated using a criterion-related methodology, to make statements about selection-system fairness. A secondary goal will be to briefly review (when appropriate) research results based on different definitions of fairness.

The concept of selection-system fairness is extremely complex. Before studying the reading for this chapter (Hunter & Schmidt, 1976) it is necessary to review some basic statistical or what are called psychometric models of fairness. Unfortunately, as stressed by Hunter and Schmidt, definitions based on purely statistical grounds do not make explicit the ethical positions taken by the models' advocates. The question of fairness is an ethical question for which resolution ultimately depends on values and beliefs. While the question of selection-system validity is important, fairness in employment opportunity rests on how the selection system is used or how specific hiring decisions are made. The reading by Hunter and Schmidt serves to move us away from attempting to resolve ethical disputes using purely statistical concepts. Decisions regarding the fairness of a selection plan, or the strategy used in making actual hiring decisions (e.g., setting a minimum passing score on a selection test, using different standards for different groups), are ultimately judged by different interest groups. Individual, corporate, and national interests will often not coincide. "Finding the worker best for a vacancy is to some degree at cross-purposes with identifying the job best for the individual. And both of these may run counter to the public interest. That interest clearly is served when high standards are used to select technicians for nuclear power plants. Critics doubt the public is served when excellent technical talent is bought up by the makers of video games or soft drinks" (Cronbach, 1980, p. 39).

Accommodation among individual, corporate, and national interests is most likely to result from the use of complex utility analyses. The values or utilities associated with different outcomes of selection must be made explicit by the user of the selection system. Then different strategies can be evaluated against this type of value-laden standard. However, full accommodation is unlikely since individuals and institutions will usually differ in their perceived utilities.

Five statistical definitions of fairness are described in what follows. Each provides guidance in determining whether or not a selection system is being used in a fair and equitable manner. These definitions are not consistent nor are they complete. Other statistical models of fairness have been proposed (e.g., see Cole, 1973; Darlington, 1971; Guion, 1966). After reviewing some general themes encountered in the fairness literature, two formal models of fairness will be summarized. The models of Cleary (1968) and Thorndike (1971) will be described here and then critically evaluated by Hunter and Schmidt (1976) who make explicit the ethical positions associated with each statistical approach.

As will become clear, there is no certain answer as to what constitutes an unfair employment practice. As stated earlier, the advance specification of utilities is central to providing some degree of resolution to questions of this type. While it is beyond the scope of this text, considerable work has been devoted to decision-theoretic models that focus on utility specification as a first step in the analysis. The interested reader is advised to review the work of Gross and Su (1975), Cronbach (1976), Petersen and Novick (1976), and Hunter, Schmidt, and Rauschenberger (1977) for an introduction to this evaluative strategy.

Five Definitions of Fairness

Pure quota model.   Here, the selection system is regarded as fair when the proportion of selected applicants belonging to each focal group (e.g., males, females, blacks, whites, and persons 40 to 70 years of age) is equal to the group's fair-share quota. The problem is to determine the appropriate quota. Groups that have significant numbers of members in a firm's relevant labor market may claim that fair selection will result when the proportion of those hired equals the population ratio. Thus, if the relevant labor market is defined as a standard metropolitan statistical area (SMSA) whose population is 30 percent black and 70 percent white, a fair selection procedure will admit three blacks to every seven whites. However, as you will note in a subsequent article by Gastwirth and Haber (1976), defining a "relevant" labor market is no simple task.

Fair-share quotas can be defined in any number of ways. In a firm that has few minority employees, the introduction of a new selection strategy that selects minorities in proportion to the relevant external labor market may not alleviate the internal imbalance for many years. Thus, minority-conscious affirmative action plans may require hiring quotas that greatly exceed the proportions encountered in a particular SMSA. These plans can remain in effect until the percentage of minority employees approximates the percentage of minorities in the local labor market.

Culture-free model.   Here, selection is fair when the selection ratios are equal across groups. If 40 percent of the majority applicants are hired, this definition asks that approximately 40 percent of the minority applicants also be hired. As with the pure quota model, rules regarding how to select applicants from the various subgroups can be made using performance-relevant factors or can be based on factors totally irrelevant to expected performance levels. The system is judged fair if selection ratios are equal across groups. Interestingly, this is essentially the definition federal enforcement agencies use when making a determination of adverse impact. "A selection rate for any race, sex, or ethnic group which is less than four fifths (4/5) (or eighty percent) of the rate for the group with the highest rate will generally be regarded by the Federal enforcement agencies as evidence of adverse impact. . . ." (Equal Employment Opportunity Commission, Civil Service Commission, Department of Labor, & Department of Justice, 1978, p. 38297). Since organizations can defend the use of selection procedures that result in adverse impact against minority groups by showing that the selection procedure is job related, this is not the definition of fairness advanced by government agencies. The concept of adverse impact will be discussed at length in a subsequent chapter devoted to the legal environment, while the fairness model advocated by federal enforcement agencies is yet to be discussed in this section of the text. However, note that "the greater the severity of adverse impact on a group, the greater the need to investigate the possible existence of unfairness" (EEOC et al., 1978, p. 38301).

Differences in validity.   Few issues have received greater attention and at the same time been as irrelevant to the issue at hand, than the debate over the hypotheses regarding *single-group* validity and *differential* validity. In the 1960s, with little theoretical underpinning, employment tests were hypothesized to be less valid for minority group members than for members of the majority group. This hypothesis took two forms, with Boehm (1972) providing explicit definitions of each. She defined a situation where *differential* validity exists as one where: "*(a)* there is a significant difference between the correlation obtained for one ethnic group and the correlation of the same device with the same criterion obtained for the other group, and *(b)* the validity coefficients are significantly different from zero for one or both groups" (p. 33). She defined *single-group* validity as a situation "where a given predictor exhibits validity significantly different from zero for one group only, and there is no significant difference between the two validity coefficients" (p. 33).

While there are a variety of controversies related to interpreting research in this area, two key issues will be reviewed here. First, each definition is based on the use of inferential statistical techniques. When addressing the differential-validity question, one attempts to determine if the observed difference in sample validity coefficients reflects a true population difference. The likelihood of making an incorrect no-difference conclusion will increase as sample sizes decrease. Conversely, with large samples, one is almost certain to find a statistically significant difference between validity coefficients. In addition, validity coefficient comparisons suffer from other artifactual problems, such as differential range restriction and criterion reliability differences. A more important question is "whether differences in validity are generally so small that they are of no practical consequence or whether they are big enough to routinely require separate validation where feasible" (Linn, 1978, p. 510). The research evidence in this area strongly suggests that the magnitude of validity differences is very small.

Even a finding of equivalent correlation coefficients says little regarding possible unfairness. Linn (1978) correctly supports the view that differential validity is a pseudo problem. So do Bobko and Bartlett (1978), who argue that:

> a focus on subgroup validity differences distracts attention from the more global problems of test fairness and differential prediction. The argument about the existence of differential validity may be replaced by arguments about the existence of differential prediction. (p. 13)

This point can be illustrated by referring to Figure 2–1. This represents a situation where there is no subgroup validity difference but where there is a

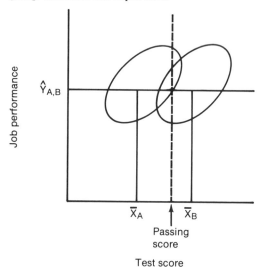

Figure 2–1
Likely Bias Against Group A Even Though Subgroup Validities Are Equivalent

significant mean score difference on the predictor variable. Note that there is no difference in average job performance. Assume that both coefficients are statistically different from zero and that they are not statistically different from each other. While there is no single-group or differential validity, the use of a single passing score on the test would, by most definitions, be biased against the group with the lowest mean test score. This needed focus on differential prediction leads to our next definition.

Cleary's regression model. Since the presence or absence of single-group or differential validity cannot serve alone as an indication of unfair discrimination, models that take into account both the slopes and intercepts of subgroup regression lines have been advocated. Cleary (1968) used this regression line framework and defined unfairness as follows:

> [A] test is biased for members of a subgroup of the population if, in the prediction of a criterion for which the test was designed, consistent nonzero errors of prediction are made for members of the subgroup. In other words, the test is biased if the criterion score predicted from the common regression line is consistently too high or too low for members of the subgroup. With this definition of bias, there may be a connotation of "unfair," particularly if the use of the test produces a prediction that is too low. (p. 115)

This definition is based on a comparison of the common regression line (the equation derived from the total sample) with the separate subgroup regression lines. If the criterion score predicted from the common regression line consistently over or underpredicts for members of a subgroup, the selection test is considered biased. Since the article by Hunter and Schmidt (1976) will provide a full definition and critique of the Cleary model, only one illustration of the Cleary approach will be presented here.

Suppose a criterion-related validity study had been conducted to evaluate the fairness of a personnel test which was to be used to hire entry-level clerical employees. Separate studies were performed for males and females with the corresponding regression lines computed as follows:

$$\text{Common line} \quad \hat{Y}_T = .123X + 9.46$$
$$\text{Male line} \quad \hat{Y}_m = .063X + 12.86$$
$$\text{Female line} \quad \hat{Y}_F = .102X + 9.94$$

Assume that the validity coefficients associated with each group are statistically different from zero but not different from each other. The coefficient for the male group equals .21 while the female coefficient equals .28. The subgroup mean scores on the test are 38.48 for males and 35.24 for females. Using five representative test scores the three regression lines give different results:

Test score	Predicted criterion score		
	Common regression line	Male regression line	Female regression line
28	12.90	14.62	12.80
32	13.40	14.88	13.20
36	13.89	15.13	13.61
40	14.38	15.38	14.02
44	14.87	15.63	14.43

If the common regression line had been used to hire persons on the basis of the predicted criterion score the test would be viewed as biased, using a Cleary definition of fairness. The common line consistently underpredicts the performance of males. Further elaboration of the Cleary model is saved for Hunter and Schmidt (1976).

Thorndike's constant ratio model. The Thorndike (1971) model represents a form of quota setting. He proposed that "the qualifying scores on a test should be set at levels that will qualify applicants in the two groups in proportion to the fraction of the two groups reaching a specified level of performance" (p. 63). This is equivalent to saying that selection is fair when the selection ratio is proportional to the success ratio across groups. Imagine that an organization has completed a follow-up random predictive validity study. Recall that this research design requires either hiring all applicants, irrespective of how well they performed on the experimental selection device, or selecting randomly from the applicant pool. After an appropriate time interval performance measures are gathered for all members of the research sample. Suppose the organization was able to develop a criterion-referenced performance-appraisal system. That is, each individual is compared to a specified level of performance, not to each other as in a norm-referenced system. Based on this information, the proportions of minority and majority group members exceeding the specified performance level are determined. If 35 percent of the minority group and 50 percent of the majority group exceed this standard, subsequent selection would be fair if 35 percent of the minority applicants and 50 percent of the majority applicants are hired. Or, following the notion of proportional selection ratios, if the number of job openings requires that only 20 percent of the majority applicant group be hired, selection would be fair if 14 percent of the minority applicants are hired.

As is the case for the Cleary model, Hunter and Schmidt (1976) will provide a more detailed definition and critique of the Thorndike approach. At this point let us say only that the Cleary and Thorndike models will almost always conflict and that Thorndike's approach usually gives preference to persons coming from groups having lower average test scores.

REFERENCES

Bobko, P., & Bartlett, C. J. Subgroup validities: Differential definitions and differential prediction. *Journal of Applied Psychology,* 1978, *63,* 12–14.

Boehm, V. R. Negro-white differences in validity of employment and training selection procedures. *Journal of Applied Psychology,* 1972, *56,* 33–39.

Cleary, T. A. Test bias: Prediction of grades of Negro and white students in integrated colleges. *Journal of Educational Measurement,* 1968, *5,* 115–124.

Cole, N. S. Bias in selection. *Journal of Educational Measurement,* 1973, *10,* 237–255.

Cronbach, L. J. Equity in selection—where psychometrics and political philosophy meet. *Journal of Educational Measurement,* 1976, *13,* 31–41.

Cronbach, L. J. Selection theory for a political world. *Public Personnel Management,* 1980, *9,* 37–50.

Darlington, R. B. Another look at culture fairness. *Journal of Educational Measurement,* 1971, *8,* 71–82.

Equal Employment Opportunity Commission, Civil Service Commission, Department of Labor, & Department of Justice. Adoption by four agencies of Uniform guidelines on employee selection procedures. *Federal Register,* 1978, *43,* 38290–38315.

Gastwirth, J. L., & Haber, S. Defining the labor market for equal employment standards. *Monthly Labor Reiew,* 1976, *99,* 3, 32–36.

Gross, A. L., & Su, W. Defining a "fair" or "unbiased" selection model: A question of utility. *Journal of Applied Psychology,* 1975, *60,* 345–351.

Guion, R. M. Employment tests and discriminatory hiring. *Industrial Relations,* 1966, *5,* 20–37.

Hunter, J. E., & Schmidt, F. L. Critical analysis of the statistical and ethical implications of various definitions of test bias. *Psychological Bulletin,* 1976, *83,* 1053–1071.

Hunter, J. E., Schmidt, F. L., & Rauschenberger, J. M. Fairness of psychological tests: Implications of four definitions of selection utility and minority hiring. *Journal of Applied Psychology,* 1977, *62,* 245–260.

Linn, R. L. Single-group validity, differential validity, and differential prediction. *Journal of Applied Psychology,* 1978, *63,* 507–512.

Peterson, N. S., & Novick, M. R. An evaluation of some models for culture-fair selection. *Journal of Educational Measurement,* 1976, *13,* 3–39.

Thorndike, R. L. Concepts of culture-fairness. *Journal of Educational Measurement,* 1971, *8,* 63–70.

Critical Analysis of the Statistical and Ethical Implications of Various Definitions of Test Bias*

JOHN E. HUNTER and FRANK L. SCHMIDT

In the last several years there has been a series of articles devoted to the question of the fairness of employment and educational tests to minority groups (Cleary, 1968; Darlington, 1971; Thorndike, 1971). Although each of these articles came to an ethical conclusion, the basis for that ethical judgment was left unclear. If there were only one ethically defensible position, then this would pose no problem. But such is not the case. The articles that we review have a second common feature. Each writer attempts to establish a definition on purely statistical grounds, that is, on a basis that is independent of the content of test and criterion and that makes no explicit assumption about the causal explanation of the statistical relations found. We argue that this merely makes the substantive considerations implicit rather than explicit.

* * * * *

* J. E. Hunter and F. L. Schmidt, "Critical Analysis of the Statistical and Ethical Implications of Various Definitions of Test Bias," *Psychological Bulletin* 83 (1976), pp. 1053–59. Copyright 1976 by the American Psychological Association. Reprinted/Adapted by permission of the publisher and author.

THREE ETHICAL POSITIONS

Unqualified Individualism

The classic American definition of an objective advancement policy is giving the job to the person "best qualified to serve." Couched in the language of institutional selection procedures, this means that an organization should use whatever information it possesses to make a scientifically valid prediction of each individual's performance and always select those with the highest predicted performance. From this point of view, there are two ways in which an institution can act unethically. First, an institution may knowingly fail to use an available, more valid predictor; for example, it may select on the basis of appearance rather than scores on a valid ability test. Second, it may knowingly fail to use a more valid prediction equation based on its available information; for example, it may administer a more difficult literacy test to blacks than to whites and then use a cut-off score for both groups that assumes they both took the same test. In particular, if in fact race, sex, or ethnic group membership were a valid predictor of performance in a given situation over and above the effects of other measured variables, then the unqualified individualist would be ethically bound to use such a predictor.

Quotas

Most corporations and educational institutions are creatures of the state or city in which they function. Thus, it has been argued that they are ethically bound to act in a way that is "politically appropriate" to their location. In particular, in a city whose population is 45 percent black and 55 percent white, any selection procedure that admits any other ratio of blacks and whites is "politically biased" against one group or the other. That is, any politically well defined group has the "right" to ask and receive its "fair share" of any desirable product or position that is under state control. These fair share quotas may be based on population percentages or on other factors irrelevant to the predicted future performance of the selectees (Darlington, 1971; Thorndike, 1971).

Qualified Individualism

There is one variant of individualism that deserves separate discussion. This position notes that America is constitutionally opposed to discrimination on the basis of race, religion, national origin, or sex. A qualified individualist interprets this as an ethical imperative to refuse to use race, sex, and so on, as a predictor even if it were in fact scientifically valid to do so. Suppose, for example, that race were a valid predictor of some criterion, that is, assume that the mean difference between the races on the criterion is greater than that that would be predicted on the basis of the best ability test available. This would mean that the use of race in conjunction with the ability test would increase the multiple correlation with the criterion. That is, prediction would be better if separate regression lines were used for blacks and whites. To the

unqualified individualist, on the other hand, failure to use race as a predictor would be unethical and discriminatory, since it would result in a less accurate prediction of the future performance of applicants and would "penalize" or underpredict performance of individuals from one of the applicant groups. The qualified individualist recognizes this fact but is ethically bound to use one overall regression line for ability and to ignore race. Thus, the qualified individualist relies *solely* on measures of ability and motivation to perform the job (e.g., scores on valid aptitude and achievement tests, assessment of past work experiences, etc.).

Definition of *Discrimination*

There is one very important point to be made before leaving this issue: The word *discriminate* is *not* ambiguous. The qualified individualist interprets the word *discriminate* to mean *treat differentially*. Thus, he will not treat blacks and whites differently even if it is statistically warranted. However, the unqualified individualist also refuses to discriminate, but he uses a different definition of that word. The unqualified individualist interprets *discriminate* to mean *treat unfairly*. Thus, the unqualified individualist would say that if there is in fact a valid difference between the races that is not accounted for by available ability tests, then to refuse to recognize this difference is to penalize the higher performing of the two groups. Finally, the person who adheres to quotas will also refuse to discriminate, but he will use yet a third definition of that word. The person who endorses quotas interprets *discriminate* to mean *select a higher proportion of persons from one group than from the other group*. Thus, the adherents of all three ethical positions accept a constitutional ban against discrimination, but they differ in their views of how that ban is to be put into effect.

*   *   *   *   *

The Cleary Definition

Cleary (1968) defined a test to be *unbiased* only if the regression lines for blacks and whites are identical. The reason for this is brought out in Figure 1, which shows a hypothetical case in which the regression line for blacks lies above the line for whites and is parallel to it. Consider a white and a black subject, each of whom have a score of A on the test. If the white regression line were used to predict both criterion scores, then the black applicant would be underpredicted by an amount Δy, the difference between his expected score making use of the fact he is black and the expected score assigned by the white regression line. Actually, in this situation in order for a white subject to have the same expected performance as a black whose score is A, the white subject must have a score of B.

That is, if the white regression line under-predicts black performance, then a white and black are only truly equal in their expected performance if the white's test

score is higher than the black's by an amount related to the amount of underprediction. Similarly, if the white regression line always overpredicts black performance, then a black subject has equal expected performance only if his test score is higher than the corresponding white subject's score by an amount related to the amount of overprediction. Thus, if the regression lines for blacks and whites are not equal, then each person will receive a statistically valid predicted criterion score only if separate regression lines are used for the two races. If the two regression lines have exactly the same slope, then this can be accomplished by predicting performance from two separate regression equations or from a multiple regression equation with test score and race as the predictors. If the slopes are not equal, then either separate equations must be used or the multiple regression equation must be expanded by the usual product term for moderator variables. Thus, we can view Cleary's definition of an unbiased test as an attempt

Figure 1
A Case in Which the White Regression Line Underpredicts Black Performance

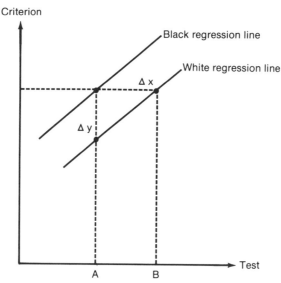

to rule out disputes between qualified and unqualified individualism.

If the predictors available to an institution are unbiased in Cleary's sense, then the question of whether to use race as a predictor does not arise. But if the predictors are *biased,* the recommended use of separate regression lines is clearly equivalent to using race as a predictor of performance. Thus, although Cleary may show a preference for tests that meet the requirements of both unqualified and qualified individualism, in the final analysis, her position is one of unqualified individualism.

A Cleary-defined unbiased test is ethically acceptable to those who advocate quotas only under very special circumstances. In addition to identical regression lines, blacks and whites must have equal means and equal standard deviations on the test, and this in turn implies equal means and standard deviations on the performance measure. Furthermore, the proportion of black and white applicants must be the same as their proportion in the relevant population. These are conditions that rarely occur.

Linn and Werts (1971) have pointed out an additional problem for Cleary's definition—the problem of defining the fairness when using less than perfectly reliable tests. Suppose that a perfectly reliable measure of intelligence were in fact an unbiased predictor in Cleary's sense. But because perfect reliability is unattainable in practice, the test used in practice will contain a certain amount of error variance. Will the imperfect test be unbiased in terms of the regression equations for blacks and whites? If black applicants have lower mean IQs than white applicants, then the regression lines for the imperfect test will *not* be equal. This situation is illustrated in Figure 2. In this figure we see that if an unreliable test is used, then that test produces the double regression line of a biased test in which the white regression

line overpredicts black performance. That is, by Cleary's definition, the unreliable test is biased against whites in favor of blacks.[1,2]

Cleary's critics question whether the failure to attain perfect reliability (impossible under any circumstances) should be adequate grounds for labeling a test as biased. But suppose we first consider this question from a different viewpoint. Suppose there were only one ethnic group, whites, for example. Assume that Bill has a

---

[1] This phenomenon would account for perhaps half of the overprediction of black grade-point average in the literature. In standard score units, the difference in intercepts due to unreliability is $\Delta Y = (1 - r_{XX}) \times (\mu_w - \mu_B)$, where r_{XX} is the test reliability and $\mu_W - \mu_B$ is the white–black mean difference on the criterion (about 1 SD). For $r_{XX} = .80$, this would be only .2 SD, whereas in the data reported in Linn (1973), the overprediction is about .37 SD.

[2] The reader may wonder why we show so much concern with the reliability of the test and no concern with the reliability of the criterion. Actually, despite its large effect on the validity coefficient, no amount of unreliability in the criterion has any effect on the regression line of criterion on predictor. Let the true score equations for X and Y be $X = T + e_1$ and $Y = U + e_2$, and let the regression true score equation be $U = \alpha T + \beta$. Then the observed regression line will not have the same coefficients. Let the observed regression line be $Y = aX + b$. The slope of the observed regression line will be

$$a = r_{XY}\frac{\sigma_Y}{\sigma_X} = (r_{TU}r_{TX}r_{UY})\frac{\sigma_Y}{\sigma_X} = r_{TU}\frac{\sigma_T}{\sigma_X}\frac{\sigma_U}{\sigma_Y}\frac{\sigma_Y}{\sigma_X}$$

$$= r_{TU}\frac{\sigma_U}{\sigma_T}\frac{\sigma_T}{\sigma_X}\frac{\sigma_T}{\sigma_X} = \left(r_{TU}\frac{\sigma_U}{\sigma_T}\right)\left(\frac{\sigma_T{}^2}{\sigma_X{}^2}\right)$$

$$= \alpha r_{XX}.$$

That is, the slope of the observed regression line is the slope of the true score regression line multiplied by the reliability of X. However, note that the slope of the observed regression line is completely independent of the reliability of Y. The intercept of the observed regression line is given by:

$$b = \mu_Y - a\mu_X = \mu_U - a\mu_T = \mu_U - r_{XX}\alpha\mu_T.$$

Thus, the intercept is also affected by the reliability of X, but is completely independent of the reliability of Y. Since the slopes of the true score regression equations are equal (assuming equal standard deviations, as we have in this article) any differences in the regression lines will be equal to the difference between the intercepts and hence independent of r_{YY}. In the case in which the true score regression lines are the same, the difference between the observed regression lines is $b_W - b_B = (1 - r_{XX})(\mu_{UW} - \mu_{UB})$.

Figure 2
Regression Artifacts Produced by Unreliability in a Cleary-Defined
Unbiased Test

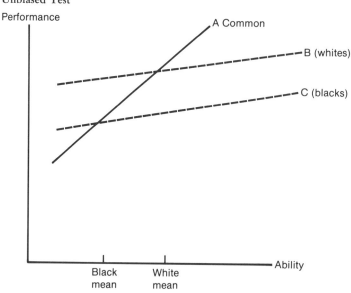

A is the common regression line for a perfectly reliable ability test. B and C are the
regression lines for whites and blacks, respectively, for a test of reliability .50.

true ability level of 115 and Jack has an ability of 110. If ability is a valid predictor of performance in this situation, then Bill has the higher expected performance; and if a perfectly reliable test is used, Bill will invariably be admitted ahead of Jack. But suppose that the reliability of the ability test is only .50. Then the two obtained scores will each vary randomly from their true values, and there is some probability that Bill's will be randomly low while Jack's is randomly high—that is, some probability that Jack will be admitted ahead of Bill. If the standard deviation of the observed ability scores is 15, then the difference between their observed scores has a mean of 5 and a standard deviation of 21. The probability of a negative difference is then .41. Thus, the probability that Bill is admitted ahead of Jack drops from 1.00 to .59.

The unreliable test is in fact sharply biased against better qualified applicants. This bias, however, is not directly racial or cultural in nature. It takes on the appearance of a racial bias only because the pro-portion of better qualified applicants is higher in the white group. Thus, the bias created by random error works against more applicants in the white group, and thus, on balance, the test is biased against that group as a whole. But at the individual level, such a test is no more biased against a well-qualified white than a well-qualified black. The question then is whether Cleary's (1968) definition is defective in some sense in labeling this situation as biased. If so, it may perhaps be desirable to modify the definition to apply only to bias beyond that expected on the basis of test reliability alone.

While on the topic of reliability, we should note that as the reliability approaches .00, the test becomes a random selection device and is hence utterly reprehensible to an individualist of either stripe. On the other hand, a totally unreliable test would select blacks in proportion to the number of black applicants and hence might well select in proportion to population quotas. Ironically, the argument that tests are biased against blacks because they are unreliable is not only false, it is exactly opposite to the truth.

Let us consider in detail the comparison of whites and blacks on the unreliable test. We first remark that it is a fact that on the average, whites with a given score have a higher mean performance than do blacks who have that same score. Thus, the use of a single regression line will in fact mean that whites near the cutoff will be denied admission in favor of blacks who will, on the average, not perform as well. Cleary's (1968) definition would clearly label such a situation biased. Furthermore, in this situation the partial correlation between race and performance with observed ability held constant is not zero. Thus, race makes a contribution to the multiple regression because with an unreliable ability test, race is in fact a valid predictor of performance after ability is partialed out. That is, from the point of view of unqualified individualism, the failure to use race as a second predictor is unethical. If the test is used with only one regression line, then the predictors are in fact biased against whites. If two regression lines are used, then each person is being considered solely on the basis of expected performance.

Thus, in summary, we feel that Cleary's critics have raised a false issue. To use an unreliable predictor is to blur valid differences between applicants, and an unreliable test is thus, to the extent of the unreliability, biased against people or groups of people who have high true scores on the predictor. Thus, from the point of view of an unqualified individualist, an unreliable test is indeed biased. On the other hand, a qualified individualist would object to this conclusion. Use of separate regression lines is statistically optimal because the unreliable test does not account for all the real differences on the true scores. But the qualified individualist is ethically prohibited from using race as a predictor and therefore can employ only a single regres-

sion equation. He can, however, console himself with the fact that the bias in the test is not specifically racial in nature. And, of course, he can attempt to raise the reliability of the test.

Thorndike's Definition

Thorndike (1971) began his discussion with the simplifying assumption that the slope of the two regression lines is equal. There are then three cases. If the regression lines are identical, then the test satisfies Cleary's (1968) definition. If the regression line for blacks is higher than that for whites (as in Figure 1), then Thorndike labels the test "obviously unfair to the minor group." On the other hand, if the regression line for whites is higher than that for blacks, then he does *not* label the test as obviously unfair to whites. Instead, he has an extended argument that the use of two regression lines would be unfair to blacks. Clearly there must be an inconsistency in his argument and indeed we ultimately show this.

Thorndike noticed that whereas using two regression lines is the only ethical solution from the point of view of unqualified individualism, it need not be required by an ethics of quotas. In particular, if the black regression line is lower, then blacks will normally show a lower mean on both predictor and criterion. Suppose that blacks are one standard deviation lower on both and that validity is .50 for both groups. If we knew the actual criterion scores and set the cutoff at the white mean on the criterion, then 50 percent of the whites and 16 percent of the blacks would be selected. If the white regression line were used for both groups, then 50 percent of the whites and 16 percent of the blacks would be selected. However, if blacks are selected using the black regression line, then because the black regression line lies .5 standard deviations below the white regression line, blacks will have to have a larger score to be selected (i.e., a cutoff two sigmas above the black mean instead of one), and hence fewer blacks will be selected. Thus, if the predictor score is used with two regression lines, then 50 percent of the whites but only 2 percent of the blacks will be admitted. Thorndike argued that this is unfair to blacks as a group. He then recommended that we throw out individualism as an ethical imperative and replace it with a specific kind of quota. The quota that he defined as the fair share for each group is the percentage of that group that would have been selected had the criterion itself been used or had the test had perfect validity. In the above situation, for example, Thorndike's definition would consider the selection procedure fair only if 16 percent of the black applicants were selected.

What Thorndike has rediscovered has long been known to biologists: Bayes's law is cruel. If one of two equally reproductive species has a probability of .49 for survival to reproduce and the other species has a probability of .50, then ultimately the first species will be extinct. Maximization in probabilistic situations is usually much more extreme than most individuals expect (Edwards & Phillips, 1964).

What then was Thorndike's contradiction? He labeled the case in which the black regression line was higher than the white line as "obviously unfair to the minor group." But his basis for this was presumably unqualified individualism. In effect, he said that if blacks perform higher than whites over and above the effects of measured ability, then this fact should be recognized and blacks should have a correspondingly higher probability of being selected. That is, if the black regression line is higher, then separate regression lines should be used. But if separate regression lines are used, then the number of whites selected would ordinarily be drastically reduced. In fact, the number of whites selected would be far below the Thorn-

dike-defined fair share of slots. The mathematics of unequal regression lines (i.e., of Bayes's Law) is the same for a high black curve as for a high white curve: The use of a single regression line lowers the validity of the prediction but tends to yield selection quotas that are much closer to the quotas that would have resulted from clairvoyance (i.e., much closer to the selection quotas that would have resulted had a perfectly valid test been available). Thus, Thorndike's inconsistency lies in his failure to apply his definition to the case in which the white regression line underpredicts black performance. The fact that because of a technicality (i.e., racial equality on the performance measure), this effect would not manifest itself in Thorndike's (1971) Case 1 should not be allowed to obscure this general principle.

If only one regression line is to be used, then a test will meet the Thorndike quotas only if the mean difference between the groups in standard score units is the same for both predictor and criterion. For this to hold for a Cleary-defined unbiased test, the validity of the test must be 1.00—a heretofore unattainable outcome.

Once Thorndike's position is shown to be a form of quota setting, then the obvious question is, Why his quotas? After all, the statement that 16 percent of the blacks can perform at the required level would not apply to the blacks actually selected and is in that sense irrelevant. In any event, it seems highly unlikely that this method of setting quotas would find support among those adherents of quotas who focus on population proportions as the proper basis of quota determination. Thorndikean quotas will generally be smaller than population-based quotas. On the other hand, Thorndike-determined quotas may have considerable appeal to large numbers of Americans as a compromise between the requirements of individualism and the social need to upgrade the employment levels of minority group members.

There is another question that must be raised concerning Thorndike's position: Is it ethically compatible with the use of imperfect selection devices? We will show that Thorndike's selection rule is contradictory to present test usage, that is, that according to Thorndike we must fill N vacancies not by taking the top N applicants but by making a much more complicated selection. Consider the following example: Assume that one is using a test score of 50 ($\bar{X}$ = 50, SD = 10, r_{xy} = .50) as a cutoff and that the data show that 50 percent of those with a test score of 50 will be successful. Applicants with a score of 49 would all be rejected, though for r_{xy} = .50 about 48 percent of them would have succeeded had they been selected (a score of 49 is $-.1$ sigmas on X and implies an average score of $-.05$ on the criterion with a sigma of .87). Thus, applicants with a test score of 49 can then correctly state, If we were all admitted, then 48 percent of us would succeed. Therefore, according to Thorndike, 48 percent of us should be admitted. Yet we were all denied. Thus, you have been unfair to our group, those people with scores of 49 on the test. That is, strictly speaking Thorndike's ethical position precludes the use of any predictor cutoff in selection, no matter how reasonably determined. Instead, from each predictor category one must select that percentage that would fall above the criterion cutoff if the test were perfectly valid. For example, if one wanted to select 50 percent of the applicants and the validity were .60, then one would have to take 77 percent of those who lie 1 SD above the mean, 50 percent of those within 1 SD of the mean, and 23 percent of those who fall 1 SD below the mean. And Thorndike's definition could be interpreted, of course, as requiring the use of even smaller intervals of test scores.

There are several problems with this procedure. First, one must attempt to explain to applicants with objectively higher qualifications why they were not admitted—a rather difficult task and from the point of view of individualism, an unethical one. Second, the general level of performance will be considerably lower than it would have been had the usual cutoff been used. In the previous example, the mean performance of the top 50 percent on the predictor would be .48 standard score units, whereas the mean performance of those selected by the Thorndike ethic would be .29. That is, in this example, using Thorndike's quotas has the effect of cutting the usefulness of the predictor by about 60 percent. (These calculations are shown in the appendix.)

One possible reply to this criticism would be that Thorndike's definition need not be interpreted as requiring application to all definable groups. The definition is to be applied only to "legitimate minority groups," and this would exclude groups defined solely by obtained score on the predictor. If agreement could be reached that, for example, blacks, Chicanos, and Indians are the only recognized minority groups, the definition might be workable. But such an agreement is highly unlikely. On what grounds could we fairly exclude Polish, Italian, and Greek Americans, for example?

Perhaps an even more telling criticism can be made. In a college or university, performance below a certain level means a bitter tragedy for a student. In an employment situation, job failure can often be equally damaging to self-esteem. In the selection situation described above, the percentage of failure would be 25 percent if the top half were admitted, but one third if a Thorndikean admission rule were used. Furthermore, most of the increase in failures comes precisely from the poor-risk admissions. Their failure rate is two thirds. Thus, in the end, a Thorndikean rule may be even more unfair to those at the bottom than to those at the top.

* * * * *

ETHICAL POSITIONS, STATISTICAL DEFINITIONS, AND PROBLEMS

In this section, we briefly relate each ethical position to its appropriate statistical operation and point out some of the advantages and disadvantages of each approach.

Unqualified Individualism

The ethical imperative of individualism is to apply to each person that prediction procedure which is most valid for that person. Thus, white performance should be predicted by that test which has maximum validity for whites. Black performance should be predicted using that test which has maximum validity for blacks. The person with the highest predicted criterion score is then selected.

There is no reason why the test used to select blacks need be the same as that used to select whites. Indeed, if there is a more valid test for blacks, then it is ethically wrong *not* to use it. Furthermore, in situations in which the mean black criterion performance is lower than that for whites, the number of blacks admitted is maximized by using that test which has maximum validity for blacks.

Consider the alternative. Suppose there is a group for which the test used has low validity. For simplicity assume no validity at all. Then, the predicted criterion score for everyone in that group is the same— the mean criterion score for that group. Thus, either everyone in that group is accepted or everyone in that group is rejected. If that group is in fact highly homogeneous on the criterion, then this is perfectly reasonable. But if the zero validity group has the same degree of spread on the criterion as other groups, then this lack of discrimination poses ethical problems: either a great many poor prospects are being admitted, or a great many excellent prospects are being overlooked. Because

selection ratios are typically low (say 50 percent or less), this means that the use of a low validity test for some groups is likely to mean that that group is virtually eliminated. Thus, indeed, it is important to seek the maximum validity test for any group. But there is little evidence to suggest that different demographic groups will in fact require different tests. In an age of mass culture, this seems a very implausible hypothesis for most such groups. For example, the research evidence strongly indicates that differential validity by race is no more than a chance phenomenon (Schmidt, Berner, & Hunter, 1973). The same may later be shown with respect to other population subgroups, thus greatly reducing the scope of this problem. The problem would not thus be eliminated, however; although the same tests may be valid across population subgroups and regression slopes may be equal, there is much research evidence (Reilly, 1973; Schmidt & Hunter, 1974; Ruch, Note 1) that intercepts often differ significantly. That is, the same test may be a maximum validity test for many groups, but it need not therefore be unbiased by Cleary's definition. Thus, some adjustment for differences in group intercepts would still have to be made.

Qualified Individualism

For the most part, the qualified individualist is also concerned with maximum validity. However, should there be a subgroup for whom there was low validity, it would pose greater problems for the qualified individualist because he cannot give different tests to different groups. Thus, should such a case ever be found, the qualified individualist would presumably respond by searching for a less valid test (for the population as a whole) that had less variability in subgroup validity.

There is another, more subtle but perhaps more real, problem that advocates of qualified individualism must face. The ethical imperative here requires that the prediction equation that has maximum validity for the entire population—without regard to group membership—be identified and employed. But there is a problem with this solution. Suppose, for example, that for a certain city college the black regression line falls below the white regression line, that is, race is a valid predictor for that college. Use of race as a predictor is, of course, forbidden to the qualified individualist, but there may be alternative ways of increasing the overall validity of the prediction equation that are equally objectionable. For example, if race is a valid predictor, then a properly coded version of the student's address may also be a valid predictor and increase overall validity. This "indirect indicator of race" would probably be detected and rejected, but a more subtle cue might not be properly identified. In particular, the most subtle problem is the one facing the test constructor: If the black regression line falls below the white regression line, then the introduction of items whose content is biased against blacks would increase the overall validity of the test. If the separate regression lines of the unqualified individualist are used, then racially biased test material would have no effect on the selection of applicants. But if that is forbidden, then material biased against blacks would lower the black scores on the predictor and hence make their scores using the white regression line more accurate. That is, the introduction of material biased against blacks would reduce the overprediction of black performance and hence raise the validity of a one-regression-line use of the test.

The problem, in its general form, is that any measured variable which correlates with race, sex, religion and so on (i.e., shows group differences), can be considered to be an indirect (and imperfect) indicator of group membership. Because he is forbidden to use group membership itself as a predictor even if valid, the qualified

individualist may be tempted to substitute indirect indicators of group membership that may be unfair. How can he decide whether a given race-correlated predictor is fair or unfair? We discuss two such criteria: (a) Is the relation between predictor and criterion an "intrinsic" one? (b) Is the within-groups validity high enough?

The first criterion is the apparent intrinsicness of the relationship between the predictor and performance. If the predictor is a job sample test (e.g., a typing test) assessing the skills actually required on the job, there is little doubt that the relation is intrinsic. Scores on a written achievement test could also easily pass this test, as would a face-valid aptitude test. Scores on a weighted biographical information inventory, on the other hand, would be allowed only if they were able to meet the second, less subjective standard: high validity coefficients for both groups separately. Thus, the qualified individualist's answer to the question posed in the example above is that if the material to be added to the test appears to have an intrinsic relation to performance, it is ethically admissible. It is not biased against blacks as blacks but merely against applicants (of whatever race) who are less capable of performing well on the criterion. The fact that there happen to be more blacks with low ability (percentage-wise) than whites is an ethically irrelevant fact.

While the preceding distinctions are regarded as crucial among qualified individualists, they receive short shrift from those committed to other ethical positions. Those who are *un*qualified individualists will argue that parental income is an indicator of motivation to do well in school or on the job and that such motivation is surely intrinsic to high performance. That is, the unqualified individualist says that the question of whether a variable is intrinsically related to performance is subject to empirical test: If it is correlated with performance, then it is intrinsically related, whereas if it is not correlated, then it is not. Those who promote quotas will also reject validity of the intrinsic–extrinsic distinction. They argue that *ability* just means whether or not you went to a good school and is thus highly contaminated with extrinsic elements. The qualified individualist may offer scientific theories in arguing his case, but his opponents will simply argue that the theories are wrong. And the data we have in 1975 will *not* decide the argument.

Is there a less subjective way to test for an intrinsic relation between the predictor and the criterion? Certainly one test is within-groups validity. If the relation is intrinsic, then there should be a correlation for each group separately. But how high should that correlation be? Certainly statistical significance is no answer. If a college were gathering data on a new test on an entering class of 4,000, then it would only take a within-groups validity of .01 to be significant. On the other hand, if we set some standard, such as .10, we run into another problem. If the within-groups validity of some piece of biographical information were .10, while the correlation with race were .70, it would be clear that most of the validity of the test would lie in its serving as an indirect indicator of race. Indeed, one might well consider requiring that the correlation with race be less than the within-groups validity.

*   *   *   *   *

Quotas

The main technical question for an adherent of quotas is, Whose? Once the quotas have been set, the only remaining ethical question is how to select from within each group. Although some would use random selection within groups, most would evoke individualism at this point. With this assumption, the optimal strategy for filling quotas can be stated. For each group, ob-

tain predicted criterion performance using that test which has maximum validity for the given group. If the test with maximum validity for blacks is not the test with maximum validity for whites, then it is unethical to use the same test for both.

The major problem for a quota-based system is that the criterion performance of selectees as a whole can be expected to be considerably lower than under unqualified or even qualified individualism. In college selection, for example, the poor-risk blacks who are admitted by a quota are more likely to fail than are the higher scoring whites who are rejected because of the quota. Thus, in situations in which low-criterion performance carries a considerable penalty, being selected on the basis of quotas is a mixed blessing. Second, there is the effect on the institution. The greater the divergence between the quotas and the selection percentages based on actual expected performance, the greater the difference in mean performance in those selected. If lowered performance is met by increased rates of expulsion or firing, then the institution is relatively unaffected, but (*a*) the quotas are undone and (*b*) there is considerable anguish for those selected who don't make it.[5] On the other hand, if the institution tries to adjust to the candidates selected by quotas, there may be great cost and inefficiency. Finally, there is the one other problem that academic institutions must face. Quotas will inevitably lower the average performance of graduating seniors, and hence lower the prestige rating of the school. Similar considerations apply in the case of the employment setting. In both cases, the effect of these

---

[5] Furthermore, the public image of the institution may suffer as much from the higher rate of expulsion as from the charge of discrimination in hiring. For example, if we read the trial records correctly, there is a company that deliberately reduced its entrance standards to hire more blacks. However, these people could not then pass the internal promotion tests and hence accumulated in the lowest level jobs in the organization. The government then took them to court for discriminatory promotion policies!

changes on the broader society must also be considered. These effects are difficult to assess, but they may be quite significant.

CONCLUDING REMARKS

We have presented three ethical positions with respect to the use of tests and other psychological devices in selecting people for entry into various kinds of institutions, and we have shown these ethical positions to be irreconcilable. We have also reviewed a number of attempts to define the fair or unbiased use of tests or other devices and have shown them to be related to different ethical positions. Moreover, we have shown that the scientific principles used to justify the statistical procedures vary considerably in their plausibility from one concrete selection situation to another. Indeed we feel that we have shown that any purely statistical approach to the problem of test bias is doomed to rather immediate failure.

The dispute reviewed in this article is typical of ethical arguments—the resolution depends in part on irreconcilable values. Furthermore, even among those who agree on values there will be disagreements about the validity of certain relevant scientific theories that are not yet adequately tested. Thus, we feel that there is no way that this dispute can be objectively resolved. Each person must choose as he sees fit (and in fact we are divided). We do hope that we have clarified the issues to make the choice more explicitly related to the person's own values and beliefs.

REFERENCE NOTE

1. Ruch, W. W. A re-analysis of published differential validity studies. In R. E. Biddle (Chair), *Differential validation under Equal Employment Opportunity Commission and Office of Federal Contract Compliance testing and selection regulations.* Symposium presented at the meeting of the American Psychological Association, Honolulu, September 1972.

REFERENCES

Cleary, T. A. Test bias: Prediction of grades of Negro and white students in integrated colleges. *Journal of Educational Measurement,* 1968, *5,* 115–124.

Darlington, R. B. Another look at "cultural fairness." *Journal of Educational Measurement,* 1971, *8,* 71–82.

Edwards, W., & Phillips, L. D. Man as transducer for probabilities in Bayesian command and control systems. In M. W. Shelley II & G. L. Bryan (Eds.), *Human judgements and optimality.* New York: Wiley, 1964.

Reilly, R. R. A note on minority group test bias studies. *Psychological Bulletin,* 1973, *80,* 130–132.

Schmidt, F. L., Berner, J. G., & Hunter, J. E. Racial differences in validity of employment tests: Reality or illusion? *Journal of Applied Psychology,* 1973, *58,* 5–9.

Schmidt, F. L., & Hunter, J. E. Racial and ethnic bias in psychological tests: Divergent implications of two definitions of test bias. *American Psychologist,* 1974, *29,* 1–8.

Thorndike, R. L. Concepts of culture-fairness. *Journal of Educational Measurement,* 1971, *8,* 63–70.

COMMENTARY

This commentary is purposely brief, given the clear message provided in the Hunter and Schmidt (1976) article. Their position serves as an appropriate summary and is similar to the stance taken by other writers (e.g., see Novick & Ellis, 1977). Essentially, they argue that the utility of a particular outcome depends on the perspective taken and that a particular outcome may not simultaneously serve the interests of the individual, the institution, and society at large. However, there are a few remaining issues worthy of additional attention and these will be addressed in the brief commentary that follows.

Fairness and Professional Practice

The Uniform Guidelines on Employee Selection Procedures (Equal Employment Opportunity Commission, Civil Service Commission, Department of Labor, and Department of Justice, 1978) acknowledge that the "concept of fairness or unfairness of selection procedures is a developing concept" (p. 38301). Irrespective of this stated position, the guidelines provide a definition of unfairness that is consistent with the Cleary definition:

> *When members of one race, sex, or ethnic group characteristically obtain lower scores on a selection procedure than members of another group, and the differences in scores are not reflected in differences in a measure of job performance, use of the selection procedure may unfairly deny opportunities to members of the group that obtains the lower scores.* (p. 38301)

The guidelines also advocate empirical investigation of fairness, when feasible. Thus, there is the expectation that regression equations will differ and that even small disparities can have practical consequences for members of protected groups. They seem to reject the notion that empirical research can establish, as a generalizable principle, the null hypothesis. Examining regression line differences on a case-by-case basis is therefore viewed as appropriate. Finally, if an unfair selection situation is discovered, the guidelines provide two courses of corrective action. First, the user may revise or replace the selection instrument so that regression line differences are no longer meaningful. Or, the user "may continue to use the selection instrument operationally with appropriate revisions in its use to assure compatibility between the probability of successful job performance and the probability of being selected" (EEOC et al., 1978, pp. 38301, 38302).

The position taken in the current *Principles for Validation and Use of Personnel Selection Procedures* (APA, 1980) is less definitive, but emphasizes the maximization of opportunities for each individual. This document advocates the use of the most valid selection procedures by stating that the "interests of employers, applicants, and the public at large are best served when selection is made by the most valid means available" (p. 3). However, in the final analysis, the *Principles* do not advocate any one model of fairness and stress the need to make advance specification of utilities. Thus, as suggested by Hunter and Schmidt (1976), the resolution of fairness questions can depend in part on potentially irreconcilable values.

To be somewhat more optimistic, Novick and Ellis (1977) suggest that a socially desirable and constitutionally acceptable solution is possible. They argue that consideration should not be given to a person's race, sex, or ethnic group, "but to the relative advantage or disadvantage experienced by a person and to the utility of the contribution to society that can be expected from that person as a result of any particular allocation of resources or comparative advantage" (p. 306). Also the concept of protecting the individual has been strengthened in a recent Supreme Court decision. The court argued that the principal focus of Title VII of the Civil Right Act "is the protection of the individual employee, rather than the protection of the minority group as a whole" (*Connecticut et al.* v. *Teal et al.*, 1982, p. 13). Again, we save a detailed discussion of the legal environment for a subsequent chapter.

In summary, it is clear that professional standards are not yet fully established in this area. There does, however, seem to be an evolving concensus regarding the necessity of using decision-theoretic methods when examining selection system fairness.

Research Evidence

Earlier, we took the position that testing hypothesis regarding single-group and differential validity is irrelevant to the issue of fairness. This rather strong statement is not totally accurate, but we made it deliberately to emphasize an important point. While large differences between minority and nonminority validity coefficients can represent a sufficient condition for arguing that the selection system is unfair, the existence of meaningful validity differences does not represent a necessary condition for unfair selection system use. That is, as illustrated in the introduction, the absence of differential validity does not preclude a finding of unfairness. Nevertheless, a large research literature has been generated that focuses on the question of validity differences. The empirical studies have primarily examined black-white validity differences when using aptitude tests as predictor variables. Reviews of this literature generally conclude that differential and single-group validity are found only at chance levels and that minority-nonminority validity differences are very small. The interested reader is directed to reviews of this literature by Boehm (1972, 1977), Linn (1978), and Schmidt, Berner, and Hunter (1973). Note, however, that few conclusions can be drawn regarding the use of other selection procedures or other subgroup comparisons (e.g., male-female validity differences).

The more important question of regression line differences also has received considerable research attention. Here, comparisons of regression line slopes and intercepts are made for various subgroups. Arvey (1979, pp. 98–101) provides a useful summary of these studies and concludes that "regression lines generally do not differ with regard to their slopes" but a difference in "intercept values appears to be a relatively common phenomenon" (p. 101). Interestingly, minority group members tend to be overpredicted rather than underpredicted.

REFERENCES

American Psychological Association, Division of Industrial-Organizational Psychology. *Principles for validation and use of personnel selection procedures.* (2d ed.). Berkeley, Calif.: The Industrial-Organizational Psychologist, 1980.

Arvey, R. D. *Fairness in Selecting Employees.* Reading, Mass.: Addison-Wesley, 1979.

Boehm, V. R. Negro-white differences in validity of employment and training selection procedures: Summary of research evidence. *Journal of Applied Psychology,* 1972, *56,* 33–39.

Boehm, V. R. Differential prediction: A methodological artifact? *Journal of Applied Psychology,* 1977, *62,* 146–154.

Connecticut v. *Teal,* 29 EPD 32, 820.

Equal Employment Opportunity Commission, Civil Service Commission, Department of Labor, and Department of Justice. Adoption by four agencies of uniform guidelines on employee selection procedures. *Federal Register,* 1978, *43,* 38290–38315.

Hunter, J. E., & Schmidt, E. L. Critical analysis of the statistical and ethical implications of various definitions of test bias. *Psychological Bulletin,* 1976, *83,* 1053–1059.

Linn, R. L. Single-group validity, differential validity, and differential prediction. *Journal of Applied Psychology,* 1978, *63,* 507–512.

Novick, M. R., & Ellis, D. D. Equal opportunity in educational and employment selection. *American Psychologist,* 1977, *32,* 306–320.

Schmidt, F. L., Berner, J. G., & Hunter, J. E. Racial differences in validity of employment tests: Reality or illusion? *Journal of Applied Psychology,* 1973, *58,* 5–9.

Chapter 3

Validity Generalization

INTRODUCTION

In an often-quoted epilogue to his chapter on recruiting, selection, and job replacement in the *Handbook of Industrial and Organizational Psychology*, Guion (1976) states that the inability to generalize validity findings from one setting to another is the major hurdle separating selection as technology from selection as science. A set of generalizable laws, specifying the types of predictors which would be valid for a given job, would move selection from technology to science, but by the conventional interpretation of existing validity evidence, validity is situation specific. When one examines validity coefficients obtained from using the same predictor for what seem to be identical jobs in different organizations, or different subunits in the same organization, one finds substantial differences, leading to the conclusion that separate validation is required in each setting.

The reading by Schmidt and Hunter offers an alternative explanation for observed differences in validities across situations, namely that true validity *does* generalize across situations and that observed differences are statistical artifacts due to defects in the validity studies (e.g., small sample sizes, range restriction, and criterion unreliability). Schmidt and Hunter propose the pooling of results from validity studies for a given test type and a given job grouping, and the determination of how much of the variability in validity coefficients can be accounted for by these statistical sources of error. If most of the variation in validities can be accounted for by these errors, the situational specificity argument is discredited, and validity generalization becomes possible.

The Schmidt-Hunter procedure is one approach to transporting validity evidence from one setting to another. The commentary discusses a variety of other approaches for use in the many situations where the Schmidt-Hunter procedure is not feasible (e.g., a substantial number of validity coefficients for a given predictor for a given job are not available).

REFERENCE

Guion, R. M. Recruiting, selection, and job replacement. In M. D. Dunnette (Ed.), *Handbook of industrial and organizational psychology.* Chicago: Rand McNally, 1976, 777–828.

The Future of Criterion-Related Validity*

FRANK L. SCHMIDT

JOHN E. HUNTER

For the last 50 years or so, personnel psychology, as a profession and a science, has been stunted and made sterile by the near-universal belief in the erroneous law of small numbers (Tversky and Kahneman, 1971). The law of small numbers holds that the law of large numbers applies to small numbers as well. The law of large numbers correctly states that large random samples will be highly representative of the population from which they are drawn. Those who erroneously assume that small samples will be similarly representative are endorsing the law of small numbers. The result is a gross overestimation of the amount of information contained in small-sample studies.

We are now on the threshold of a new era. We are beginning to recognize and reject our belief in the law of small numbers. We are beginning to appreciate the grossly distorting effects it has had on progress and development in our field.

In general terms, the effect of belief in the law of small numbers has been to create the impression of complexity and even chaos where in fact there was order and simplicity. That is, the effect was to obscure the essential lawfulness of the phenomena of our field and cause us to conclude falsely that the objects of our study were situational, capricious, and perhaps unknowable.

* * * * *

SAMPLE SIZE AND THE TECHNICAL FEASIBILITY OF CRITERION-RELATED VALIDITY STUDIES

For years the dominant belief had been that sample sizes in the 30 to 50 range were adequate to make criterion-related validity studies technically feasible. The authors, along with Vern Urry, recently published a study demonstrating that this traditional belief is erroneous (Schmidt, et al., 1976). Our study showed that such sample sizes are almost invariably too small to produce acceptable levels of statistical power. When sample sizes are in the 30–50 range, statistical power is typically in the .25 to .50 range. That is, if the test is in fact valid, such studies will correctly detect the validity only 25 to 50 percent of the time. Sample sizes required to produce statistical power of .90 are much larger, often ranging above 200 or 300. Sample sizes required

---

* Excerpted from F. L. Schmidt and J. E. Hunter, "The Future of Criterion-Related Validity," *Personnel Psychology* 33 (1980), pp. 41–60. Copyright 1980 by Personnel Psychology, Inc. Reprinted/Adapted by permission of the publisher and author.

for specific levels of range restriction, criterion reliability, and true validity are presented in the tables included in our study. This study demonstrated more clearly than any other that personnel psychologists have traditionally been believers in the law of small numbers. They have grossly overestimated the amount of information contained in small samples.

SITUATIONAL SPECIFICITY OF TEST VALIDITIES AND THE PROBLEM OF VALIDITY GENERALIZATION

Our statistical power study demonstrated that criterion-related validity studies are technically feasible much less frequently than personnel psychologists have generally believed. Taken together with the belief that test validities are situationally specific, this fact would seem to indicate that criterion-related validity cannot be employed in many settings. If validity is situationally specific, then it must be determined separately for each situation; if a criterion-related validity study is not feasible in a given situation, then it follows that this validity strategy cannot be employed in that situation. But suppose it can be shown that the doctrine of situational validity rests on the erroneous belief in the law of small numbers.

The empirical basis for the principle of situational specificity has been the fact that considerable variability in observed validity coefficients is typically apparent from study to study even when jobs and tests appear to be similar or essentially identical (Ghiselli, 1966). The orthodox explanation for this phenomenon is that the factor structure of job performance is different from job to job and that the human observer or job analyst is simply too poor an information receiver and processor to detect these subtle but important differences. That is, there are mysterious, unknown and maybe unknowable moderator variables operating,

causing a test to be valid in one setting but not in another. Therefore, it is concluded, empirical validation is required in each situation, and validity generalization is impossible (Ghiselli, 1966, p. 28; Guion, 1965, p. 126; Albright, Glennon, and Smith, 1963, p. 18). This harsh "fact" is widely lamented, and it is said that our inability to solve the problem of validity generalization is perhaps the most serious shortcoming in selection psychology today (Guion, 1976; APA, Division of Industrial-Organization Psychology, Note 1). The inability to generalize validities precludes development of general principles of selection that could take our field beyond a mere technology to the status of a science (Guion, 1976).

But there is evidence suggesting that much of the variance in the outcomes of validity studies within job-test combinations may be due to statistical artifacts. Schmidt, Hunter, and Urry (1976) have shown that under typical and realistic validation conditions, a valid test will show a statistically significant validity in only about 50 percent of studies. As one specific example, they showed that if true validity for a given test is constant at .45 in a series of jobs, if criterion reliability is .70, if the prior selection ratio on the test is .60, and if sample size is 68 [the median over 406 published validity studies (Lent, Aurbach, and Levin, 1971a)] then the test will be reported to be valid 54 percent of the time and invalid 46 percent of the time (two-tailed test, $p = .05$). These are the kinds of results that are in fact observed in the literature (Ghiselli, 1966; Lent et al., 1971b).

When sample size is adequate to provide appropriate levels of statistical power, the observed results are quite different. In a well executed large sample series of studies, it was found that when Army occupations were classified rationally into job families, tests showed very similar validities and regression weights for all jobs within a given family (Brogden, Note 2). Further, new jobs assigned rationally to job families also fit this pattern. Brogden has concluded that when methodological artifacts are controlled and large samples are used, obtained validities are in fact stable and similar across time and situations for similar jobs.

If the variance in validity coefficients across situations for job-test combinations is due to statistical artifacts, then obviously the doctrine of situational specificity is false and validities are generalizable. We have developed a method for testing this hypothesis (Schmidt and Hunter, 1977; Schmidt and Hunter, Pearlman and Shane, 1979; Pearlman, Schmidt, and Hunter, 1980; Schmidt, Gast-Rosenberg, and Hunter, Note 3). This method can be explained conceptually as follows. One starts with a fairly large number of validity coefficients for a given test-job combination, and computes the variance of this distribution. From this variance, one then subtracts variance due to various sources of error. There are at least seven sources of error variance:

1. Differences between studies in criterion reliability.
2. Differences between studies in test reliability.
3. Differences between studies in range restriction.
4. Sampling error (i.e., variance due to $N < \infty$).
5. Differences between studies in amount and kind of criterion contamination and deficiency (Brogden and Taylor, 1950).
6. Computational and typographical errors (Wolins, 1962).
7. Slight differences in factor structure between tests of a given type (e.g., arithmetic reasoning tests).

In a purely analytical substudy, Schmidt et al. (1979) showed that the first four sources alone are capable, under specified and realistic circumstances, of producing as much variation in validities as is typically observed from study to study. They then turned to analyses of empirical data. Using 14 distributions of validity coefficients from the published and unpublished literature for various tests in the occupations of clerical worker and first-line supervisor, they found that artifactual variance sources (1) through (4) accounted for an average of 63 percent of the variance in validity coefficients, with a range from 43 percent to 87 percent. In an earlier study (Schmidt and Hunter, 1977), it was found that sources (1), (3) and (4) alone accounted for an average of about 50 percent of the observed variance in distributions of validity coefficients presented by Ghiselli (1966, p. 29). Pearlman et al. (1980) focused on various clerical occupations. This study contained 24 distributions of validity coefficients against measures of overall training success. For these distributions, artifactual sources (1) through (4) accounted for an average of 70 percent of the observed variance, with a range from 19 percent to 100 percent. This study also examined 32 distributions of validity coefficients against measures of overall job proficiency. In these data, the same artifacts accounted for an average of 75 percent of observed variance, with a similar range (23–100 percent). Schmidt et al. (Note 3) studied the occupation of computer programer. For the four distributions in this study, artifacts (1) through (4) accounted for an average of 61 percent of observed variance in validity coefficients, with a range from 41 percent to 71 percent. In each of these four studies, controlling only three or four statistical artifacts left little remaining variance in which moderators could operate. If one could correct for all seven sources of error variance, one would, in all likelihood, consistently find that the residual variance was zero or near zero. That is, it is likely that the small amounts of remaining variance in the studies cited here are due to the sources of artifactual variance not corrected for. Thus there is now strong evidence that the observed variation in validities from study to study for similar test-job combinations is artifactual in nature. These findings cast considerable doubt on the situational specificity hypothesis.

Rejection of the situational specificity doctrine obviously opens the way to validity generalization. Furthermore, validity generalization is possible in many cases even if the situational specificity hypothesis is not rejected. After correcting the *mean* of the validity distribution for attenuation due to criterion unreliability and for range restriction (based on average values of both), and after properly correcting the residual *SD*, one may find that a large percentage, say 90 percent, of all values in the distribution lie above the minimum useful level of validity. In such a case, one can conclude with 90 percent confidence that the estimate of true validity would be at or above this minimum level in a new situation involving the same test-type and job without carrying out a validation study of any kind. Only a job analysis is necessary, in order to ensure that the job at hand is a member of the class of jobs on which the validity distribution was derived. Furthermore, there is now strong evidence that the job analysis need not be a detailed analysis of job tasks or behaviors. Despite longstanding belief to the contrary, general job analyses sufficient to classify jobs into broad occupational groups (e.g., clerical work) are all that is required for validity generalization purposes (Schmidt, Hunter and Pearlman, Note 4).

In Schmidt and Hunter (1977), this procedure allowed validity generalization for two of the four validity distributions, even though only three sources of artifactual variance could be corrected for. In the later study (Schmidt, et al., 1979) in which it was possible to correct for four sources of error variance, 12 of the 14 corrected distributions had 90 percent or more of validities above levels that would typically be indicative of significant practical utility (cf. Hunter and Schmidt, in press). In

Pearlman et al. (1980), 48 of the 58 distributions fell into this category, and in Schmidt et al. (Note 3), the count was four out of five.

But it should be noted that focusing on the value at the bottom of the distribution can be deceptive. The best estimate of test validity is the mean of the corrected validity distribution, not the value at the foot of the 90 percent confidence interval. The estimated 90 percent confidence value would be a very biased estimate of test validity. Furthermore, it is conservative (that is, biased downward) even as an estimate of the 90 percent confidence value, because artifacts not corrected for inflate the standard deviation used to estimate the 90 percent confidence value. Suppose all of the corrections described above could be made, including corrections for variance due to clerical and typographical errors and differences between studies in amount and kind of criterion contamination. How much variance would then remain within which the hypothesized situational moderators (*or moderator variables of any kind*) could operate? The evidence indicates that very little would remain. This question is examined more fully in another paper (Schmidt and Hunter, 1978). These results, in our interpretation, refute the situational specificity hypothesis in the case of cognitive aptitude tests.

In addition to validities for individual tests and test types, validities for test combinations or batteries can also be estimated. This can be done in one of two ways. In some cases (e.g., Schmidt et al., Note 3; Schmidt et al., 1979), distributions of validity coefficients will be available for test combinations or sums. These coefficients can be used with the validity generalization model in the usual manner. For example, in a study focusing on the prediction of proficiency in clerical work. Schmidt et al. (1979) report 53 validity coefficients for tests for which total scores were a composite of verbal, quantitative, and perceptual speed subscores. The mean of this corrected distribution was .60 and the value at the 10th percentile was .20. Validities for composite scores will rarely be available from the literature in sufficient numbers, however, and therefore researchers will typically have to rely on the second approach. This procedure requires that one be able to obtain estimates of predictor intercorrelations in the applicant pool. Data on predictor intercorrelations are typically more readily available than validity data. In addition, N's are usually larger. In most cases, published correlations (e.g., from test manuals) computed on similar groups will be sufficiently accurate. Validities are, of course, estimated for each predictor from the validity generalization model. One then has all the information necessary to estimate multivariate validities, based on either rational (including equal) or least squares regression weights. If regression is used, little or no shrinkage would be expected, assuming the predictor intercorrelations were based on a large sample; validities will almost invariably have been based on large samples. On the other hand, equal weighting of predictors is apt to produce validities almost as high as those produced by regression weights (Schmidt, 1971, 1972).

In summary, this research demonstrates that the widespread belief that validity generalization is never possible is fallacious and based ultimately on belief in the law of small numbers. Indeed, this research strongly suggests that, for cognitive aptitude tests, the situational specificity hypothesis is false and that validity generalization is always possible.

*   *   *   *   *

REFERENCE NOTES

1. American Psychological Association, Division of Industrial-Organizational Psychol-
ogy. *Principles for the validation and use of personnel selection procedures.* Dayton, Ohio. The Industrial-Organization Psychologist, 1975.

2. Brogden, H.E. Personal communication, 1970.

3. Schmidt, F. L., Gast-Rosenberg, I., & Hunter, J. E. Test of a new model of validity generalization: Results for computer programers. *Journal of Applied Psychology,* 1980, *65,* 643–661.

4. Schmidt, F. L., Hunter, J. E., & Pearlman, K. Task differences as moderators of aptitude test validity in selection: A red herring. *Journal of Applied Psychology,* 1981, *66,* 166–185.

REFERENCES

Albright, L. E., Glennon, J. R., & Smith, W. J. *The uses of psychological tests in industry.* Cleveland: Howard Allen, 1963.

Brogden, H. E., & Taylor, E. K. A theory and classification of criterion bias. *Educational and psychological measurement,* 1950, *10,* 159–186.

Ghiselli, E. E. *The validity of occupational aptitude tests.* New York: Wiley, 1966.

Grant, D. L., & Bray, D. W. Validation of employment tests for telephone company installation and repair occupations. *Journal of Applied Psychology,* 1970, 54, 7–14.

Guion, R. M. *Personnel testing.* New York: McGraw-Hill, 1965.

Guion, R. M. Recruiting, selection, and job placement. In Dunnette, M. D. (Ed.), *Handbook of Industrial-Organizational Psychology.* Chicago: Rand McNally, 1976.

Lent, R. H., Aurbach, H. A., & Levin, I. S. Research and design and validity assessment. *Personnel Psychology,* 1971, *24,* 247, 274. (a)

Lent, R. H., Aurbach, H. A., & Levin, I. S. Predictors, criteria, and significant results. *Personnel Psychology.* 1971, *24,* 519–533. (b)

Pearlman, K., Schmidt, F. I., & Hunter, J. E. Test of a new model of validity generalization: Results for job proficiency and training criteria in clerical occupations. *Journal of Applied Psychology,* 1980, *65,* 373–406.

Schmidt, F. L. The relative efficiency of regression and simple unit predictor weights in applied differential psychology. *Educational and Psychological Measurement,* 1971, *31,* 699–714.

Schmidt, F. L. The reliability of differences between linear regression weights in applied differential psychology. *Educational and Psychological Measurement,* 1972, *32,* 879–886.

Schmidt, F. L., & Hunter, J. E. Development of a general solution to the problem of validity generalization. *Journal of Applied Psychology,* 1977, *62,* 529–540.

Schmidt, F. L., & Hunter, J. E. Moderator research and the law of small numbers. *Personnel Psychology,* 1978, *31,* 215–231.

Schmidt, F. L., Hunter, J. E., Pearlman, K., & Shane, G. S. Further tests of the Schmidt-Hunter Bayesian validity generalization procedure. *Personnel Psychology,* 1979, *32,* 257–281.

Schmidt, F. L., Hunter, J. E., & Urry, V. W. Statistical power in criterion-related validity studies. *Journal of Applied Psychology,* 1976, *61,* 473–485.

Tversky, A., & Kahneman, D. Belief in the law of small numbers. *Psychological Bulletin,* 1971, *76,* 105–110.

Wolins, L. Responsibility for raw data. *American Psychologist,* 1962, *17,* 657–658.

COMMENTARY

Schmidt and Hunter have proposed and tested an elegant approach to testing the hypothesis that validity is situation specific. To summarize briefly, they noted that the personnel-selection field has not properly taken into account the statistical power (e.g., likelihood of detecting validity if true validity exists) of validity studies. Due to small sample size, the power of the typical validity study is low, and thus variability in validity coefficients should be expected. They proposed obtaining a group of validity coefficients for a given job and test type and determining empirically how much of the variation in validity coefficients could be accounted for by differences in sample size and also by a variety of other sources of error, such as differences in criterion reliability and range restriction. Correcting for these sources of error reduces the standard deviation of the distribution of validity coefficients. If these errors are found to account for a large amount, such as 75 percent, of the variance in validity coefficients, one could reject the situational specificity hypothesis and conclude that validity findings for that test and job type will be generalizable to other organizations. The technical details of the procedure can be found elsewhere (see Schmidt & Hunter (1977) for the original formulation of the model; see Callender & Osburn (1980) for a critique and a modified model). As the reading showed, the model has been applied in a variety of settings, with the consistent finding that much of the variability in validity coefficients can be explained as statistical artifact, thus allowing Schmidt and Hunter to tentatively conclude that validity generalization is always possible for cognitive-ability tests.

It is important to note that Schmidt and Hunter's work has focused on cognitive-ability tests, and they are careful to limit their conclusions to those. Whether similar findings will be obtained for other predictors is an empirical question. The model has been applied to predictors other than ability tests. Schmidt, Hunter, and Caplan (1981) investigated the use of a biographical background survey for maintenance jobs in the petroleum industry and found that 75 percent of the variance in validity coefficients could be accounted for by statistical artifacts. However, the mean of the corrected distribution was −.05, indicating the generalizable conclusion that this predictor will *not* be valid for maintenance jobs. A second investigation of the generalizability of biographical data was provided by Brown (1981), who examined the validity of a biographical inventory used to select life insurance agents in 12 large insurance firms. He found that 62 percent of the variance in validity was due to artifacts, and that the mean of the corrected distribution was .256. After correcting for the sources of error, the standard deviation of the distribution of validity coefficients was .0249. Using this figure to construct a confidence interval, one finds that the lower boundary of a 95 percent confidence interval is .188, leading to the conclusion that the biodata instrument will be valid if used by other insurance companies. Thus, mixed findings emerge from the limited examination of the generalizability of biodata as a predictor of job success. Schmidt and Hunter (1977) investigated the use of a finger dexterity test for bench workers, and found that though the mean corrected validity coefficient was .39, the confidence interval included the value zero. Thus, validity is not generalizable in this case. There are as yet no published findings dealing with other predictors.

One cautionary note regarding the application of the validity generalization model is in order, namely, the need to attend to the quality of criterion measures used in the studies being pooled. For example, elsewhere (Chapter 8) we point out that most assessment center validation studies suffer from possible criterion contamination, i.e., knowledge of a subordinate's assessment center performance may influence performance evaluations, or promotion decisions, thus producing an inflated validity coefficient. Thus, while one could gather a large number of validity coefficients from assessment-center users and apply the generalization model, we would not find the results meaningful.

The availability of the Schmidt-Hunter model offers a strong incentive for cooperation among firms in a given industry. Petroleum and electric utilities are but two examples of industries which are pooling research evidence in order to apply the model. But what of industries which do not have a history of conducting selection research, and thus do not have large numbers of validity coefficients available? We will devote the remainder of this commentary to a discussion of alternate approaches to the general problem of the need to make selection decisions in a setting where empirical validation is not feasible, a number of which involve transporting validity evidence across situations. The problem of transporting validity evidence becomes one of interest to far more employers in light of Schmidt, Hunter, and Urry's (1976) conclusion that the statistical power of typical small-sample validity studies is relatively low. In many cases, sample sizes of 100 or more are needed to achieve statistical power of .90, thus permitting a reasonable degree of confidence that validity will be detected if it exists. Validity studies are technically feasible for far fewer employers when an N of 100 is required than when an N of 30 is seen as sufficient. We will discuss six strategies one might consider if conducting one's own criterion-related validity study is unfeasible, or which one might consider as alternatives to conducting one's own study.

Strategy 1

The first strategy involves organizing an industrywide clearinghouse for validity studies in which studies are grouped according to job and test type, and applying the Schmidt-Hunter model for those job/test combinations where a substantial number of studies can be found. We believe that this would be feasible for a relatively small number of industries and that opportunities to apply the Schmidt-Hunter model will be exhausted relatively quickly. Industries without a history of selection research certainly should not attempt to quickly generate large numbers of small-sample studies in order to apply the model. The model is an elegant device for making sense out of previously gathered but flawed information. Firms considering industrywide efforts where previous studies are not available are advised to consider strategy 2.

Strategy 2

The second strategy involves the pooling of resources by a number of firms to conduct a high-quality validity study. We will briefly discuss several aspects of this approach. The first is the role of job analysis. This procedure will insure that similarly titled jobs in various participating organizations are sufficiently similar to justify grouping the jobs for a cooperative validation study. The appropriate methodology for this step is unclear at present. Schmidt, Hunter, and Pearlman (1981) concluded that substantial differences in job tasks do not have a marked effect on the validities of cognitive-ability tests, leading them to conclude that detailed task-oriented job analysis is not necessary. Whether this finding will be generalizable to other predictors is as yet unknown. In addition, we find their conclusion suspect. Their data shows that regardless of task differences, validity of cognitive-ability tests is greater than zero; however, their data shows that true between-job validities for a given test type will frequently differ by .2 or greater, which we view as a meaningful difference. In the interim, we recommend a detailed task inventory, since this can serve as a data base for investigating the effects of task differences on validity and for identifying required abilities.

The second aspect of this approach is predictor selection and/or development. The experiences of various firms in the industry may lead to the identification of potentially useful predictors; alternatively, new predictors can be developed based on the job analysis.

The third aspect of this approach is criterion development. We cannot overemphasize the importance of developing (and assessing the reliability of) good performance measures. A thorough treatment of criterion measurement is beyond the scope of this book; however, we suggest careful identification of performance dimensions, the use of multiple raters, rater training, and making clear that ratings are for experimental purposes only and will not be used operationally. (See Latham & Wexley (1981) and Carroll & Schneier (1982) for detailed treatments of performance appraisal.)

The fourth aspect of this approach concerns the design of the study. By pooling the resources of multiple organizations, a very large sample size may be obtained. The sample size should be carefully constructed to insure adequate representation of firms with characteristics hypothesized as possible moderator variables. For example, in a cooperative study dealing with selecting store managers in the supermarket industry, organizational structure (centralized versus decentralized) and organizational size (sales under $2 million versus $2 to $3 million versus over $3 million) were identified as potentially critical differences between participating firms, and thus attempts were made to include an equal number of stores in each category (Baehr & Burns, undated). Note that if one plans to compute separate validity coefficients for centralized versus decentralized organizations, care must be taken that each subgroup has sufficient sample size to insure adequate statistical power.

Thus, this second strategy involves pooling resources—time, effort, money, and job applicants—across organizations in order to conduct a validity study that would be beyond feasibility in terms of cost and/or sample size for any one firm.

Strategy 3

The third strategy involves locating a firm which has conducted a technically sound validity study, using job analysis to determine the extent of job similarity between the two firms and carefully searching for situational differences which would be likely to limit the generalizability of validity findings from one setting to the other. For example, a realtor with a 10-person sales force might find that another realtor with a 200-person sales force had conducted a validity study. Job analysis indicates virtually identical tasks are performed in the two firms; both firms draw from the same applicant pool. No situational differences are found (e.g., both firms operate on a commission basis, both focus on residential real estate in the same price range, both have a 10 to 1 salesperson-to-manager ratio). Transportability of validity results appears possible. However, if the large firm offered a base salary while the small firm operated solely on a commission basis, the generalizability of findings becomes questionable. As was seen in Chapter 1, empirical evidence regarding situational moderators of validity is not common but sorely needed.

The first three strategies for dealing with situations in which conducting one's own validity study is not feasible involve generalizing evidence obtained at least in part from other organizations. The remaining three strategies do not involve transporting validity.

Strategy 4

The fourth strategy is to rely on content validity to show the job relatedness of the predictors being used. This is not a viable alternative; we mention it solely because content validity has historically been offered as a fallback position when empirical validation is not feasible. As discussed elsewhere (see Chapters 1 and 8), what is referred to as "content validity" is better viewed as "content-oriented test construction," and constitutes one form of evidence for the construct validity of the predictor. Content validity should not be viewed as substitute for criterion-related validity, since the two are addressing separate questions. Criterion-related validity refers to making inferences about predictor scores, (i.e., it tests the hypothesis that scores can be used to predict job performance). Content validity refers to the adequacy with which predictor content adequately samples a content domain. However, a system for scoring the content sample must be devised, and inferences about scores are outside the realm of content validity (Guion, 1978).

Strategy 5

The fifth strategy involves obtaining rational estimates of validity from experienced personnel psychologists. Schmidt and Hunter (1980) note that they found no significant difference between empirical findings and rational estimates in reanalyzing data from the only study to date which makes the comparison (Parry, 1968). Procedurally, experienced psychologists would be given complete information about the predictor and the criterion and asked to estimate the validity coefficient that would result if a technically sound study were carried out, and the estimates of a number of psychologists would be averaged. At present, this strategy is little more than speculation. Much work will be needed before the merits of obtaining rational estimates of validity can be assessed. It is possible that rational estimates match empirical estimates simply because psychologists are aware of previous empirical findings. This might limit the value of the approach in novel settings where no previous validity evidence is available.

Strategy 6

The sixth strategy involves the use of synthetic validity, originally defined by Balma (1959) as the "inferring of validity in a specific situation from a logical analysis of jobs into their elements, a determination of test validities for these elements, and a combination of elemental validities into a whole" (p. 395). In essence, while sample size for any one job may be too small for validation to be feasible, one could combine jobs having common job elements and possibly obtain a large enough sample across jobs to validate predictors against performance on them. For example, Guion (1965) found that jobs in one small firm consisted of various combinations of seven types of responsibilities: salesmanship, creative judgment, customer relations, routine judgment, leadership, ability to handle detail work, and ability to organize work. By obtaining independent performance measures for each of these elements, and pooling the jobs requiring each element, Guion determined which of a battery of tests predicted performance on each element. For any given job, one then determines which elements are involved, and the appropriate predictors for each element are used for selection. The complexity of the procedure is probably the major reason for the relative infrequency of the use of synthetic validity.

Thus, six different strategies which may be considered when empirical validation is technically unfeasible have been described: applying the Schmidt-Hunter model to the results of existing validity studies, pooling resources across firms for a cooperative validation study, transporting validity results from another firm based on job and situational similarity, relying on content validity, using rational estimates of validity, and using synthetic validity. We have noted the conceptual problems with content validity and the lack of evidence regarding the merits of rational estimates of validity. However, a firm that is serious about valid selection but lacks the resources for empirical validation does have of number of available alternatives.

It should be noted that the Uniform Guidelines on Employee Selection Procedures encourage cooperative studies (Sec. 8) and allow the use of validity studies conducted by other firms (Sec. 7) if the validity study in question meets the technical requirements for validation set forth in the guidelines (see Chapter 5), unless there are variables in the users' situation which are likely to affect validity significantly (see Chapter 1 for a discussion of the effects of situational variables on validity). The potential for generalizing validity across situations has been recognized in a district court opinion in *Pegues* v. *Mississippi State Employment Service*. In this case, black plaintiffs challenged the use of the General Aptitude Test Battery. The court upheld the use of the GATB:

> *Empirical research has demonstrated that validity is not perceptually changed by differences in location, differences in specific job duties or applicant populations. Valid tests do not become invalid when these circumstances change. Plaintiffs' allegation that validity is specific to a particular location, a particular set of tasks and to a specific applicant population, or in other words, that a valid test in one set of circumstances is not valid in circumstances not perfectly identical is not true.*

Thus, progress is being made in the area of validity generalization. Application of generalization procedures to a wide range of predictors is needed before the doctrine of the situational specificity of validity is abandoned. The work of Schmidt and Hunter has challenged the situational specificity doctrine and serves to take personnel selection another step toward moving beyond its status as a technology and closer to the development of a science of selection.

REFERENCES

Baehr, M. E., & Burns, F. M. The improvement of selection and utilization procedures for personnel in the supermarket industry. Undated report, Industrial Relations Center, University of Chicago.

Balma, M. J. The concept of synthetic validity. *Personnel Psychology,* 1959, *12,* 395–396.

Brown S. H. Validity generalization and situational moderation in the life insurance industry. *Journal of Applied Psychology,* 1981, *66,* 664–670.

Callender, J. C., & Osburn, H. G. Development and test of a new model of validity generalization. *Journal of Applied Psychology,* 1980, *65,* 543–558.

Carroll, S. J., & Schneier, C. E. *Performance appraisal and review systems.* Glenview, Ill.: Scott, Foresman, 1982.

Guion, R. M. An illustrative study of synthetic validity. *Personnel Psychology,* 1965, *18,* 49–63.

Guion, R. M. "Content validity" in moderation. *Personnel Psychology,* 1978, *31,* 205–213.

Latham, G. P., & Wexley, K. N. *Increasing productivity through performance appraisal.* Reading, Mass.: Addison-Wesley, 1981.

Parry, M. E. Ability of psychologists to estimate validities of personnel tests. *Personnel Psychology,* 1968, *21,* 139–147.

Pegues v. *Mississippi State Employment Service* (22 FEP Cases 392).

Schmidt, F. L., & Hunter, J. E. Development of a general solution to the problem of validity generalization. *Journal of Applied Psychology,* 1977, *62,* 529–540.

Schmidt, F. L., & Hunter, J. E. The future of criterion-related validity. *Personnel Psychology,* 1980, *33,* 41–60.

Schmidt, F. L., Hunter, J. E., & Caplan, J. R. Validity generalization results for two jobs in the petroleum industry. *Journal of Applied Psychology,* 1981, *66,* 261–273.

Schmidt, F. L., Hunter, J. E., & Pearlman, K. Task differences and validity of aptitude tests in selection: A red herring. *Journal of Applied Psychology,* 1981, *66,* 166–185.

Schmidt, F. L., Hunter, J. E., & Urry, V. M. Statistical power in criterion-related validity studies. *Journal of Applied Psychology,* 1976, *61,* 473–485.

Chapter 4

Decision Making and Utility Measurement

INTRODUCTION

One of the basic questions which must be answered in the theory and practice of personnel selection is, "What is the practical value of a predictor of a given validity?" Approaches to assessing the utility of a selection procedure have changed dramatically in the last 60 years; we will briefly review these changes.

I. Utility as a Function of Validity

The Pearson product-moment correlation coefficient is generally used to describe the degree of relationship between a predictor and a criterion. Early solutions to the problem of the usefulness of a predictor were based simply upon algebraic manipulations of this coefficient. Kelley (1923) developed a measure of the utility of a predictor based on the degree to which the obtained correlation coefficient reduced the standard error of estimate (i.e., the standard deviation of the errors of prediction occurring when a less than perfectly valid predictor—x—is used to predict a criterion $-y$). The formula for the standard error of estimate is $S_{est} = S_y \sqrt{1 - r_{xy}^2}$. Thus, the error in predicting a criterion score from a predictor value is reduced as the correlation coefficient becomes larger. The reduction of errors of prediction is a function of $\sqrt{1 - r_{xy}^2}$, which Kelley terms the coefficient of alienation.

Using this as an index of utility, a validity coefficient of .43 is needed to reduce the standard error by 10 percent; a coefficient of .86 is needed to reduce the standard error by 50 percent. Thus, the coefficient of alienation suggests that high validities are needed to predict even slightly better than a random guess.

In his 1928 work, *Aptitude Testing,* Clark Hull discussed utility in terms of a statistic he referred to as the Index of Forecasting Efficiency (E). This is defined as: $E = 1 - \sqrt{1 - r_{xy}^2}$. E represents the percent of perfect forecasting efficiency of a predictor in predicting a criterion score. Note that this statistic is simply one minus Kelly's coefficient of alienation. Using this as a measure of utility, the efficiency of a correlation of .50 is only 13 percent. Hull's answer to the question of the usefulness of a predictor of given validity is as follows:

> Below .45 or .50, practically useless for differential prognosis.
>
> From .50 to .60, of some value.
>
> From .60 to .70, of considerable value.
>
> From .70 to .80, of decided value but rarely found.
>
> From .80 to .90, not obtained by present methods. (p. 276)

Hull noted that the zone of low forecasting efficiency is exactly the zone where practically all obtained correlations fall. Although this may be somewhat disappointing, he stated that "the sooner these facts are fully realized the better for all" (p. 275).

Hull also pointed out the error of interpreting the correlation coefficient directly as the percent of criterion variance accounted for by the predictor. It is the squared correlation coefficient—which Hull called the coefficient of determination—which gives the percentage of a variance accounted for. Looking at utility in terms of the coefficient of determination does not provide much improvement over the rather dismal conclusions arrived at through the use of the index of forecasting efficiency. Regardless of the way in which the correlation coefficient is manipulated, evaluating the utility of a predictor based on validity coefficients suggests that the use of tests in personnel selection be abandoned. Ghiselli (1973) states that the mean validity coefficient for on-the-job criteria for all tests is .22, and for training criteria, .39. If a correlation under .50 is useless, personnel testing is indeed in trouble.

Looking at Hull's work with the benefit of hindsight, it is interesting to note that he touched upon two concepts which would later become important in evaluating the utility of a predictor. First, in a footnote he anticipated the important distinction between the use of predictors for individual and for institutional decisions. While the predictor may not do a good job of accurately predicting *individual* performance, the *average* performance of individuals selected using a moderately valid test would be higher than the average performance of individuals selected without the test. He noted that in an employment setting with a large number of applicants relative to the number of openings, the cutoff could be set high enough that a predictor with a validity coefficient of less than .50 could be useful. This comment predates by more than 10 years the formal presentation of the same concept by Taylor and Russell. Second, Hull hinted at the necessity of considering the cost of selection in evaluating the utility of a predictor. Psychometrically, he believed that a predictor should be evaluated on the basis of forecasting efficiency. Practically, he recognized the need to consider the cost of selection.

II. Taylor-Russell: New Hope for Personnel Selection

Acknowledging the hint from Hull, Taylor and Russell (1939) set out to demonstrate that, under the usual paradigm used for the selection of employees, fairly small correlations—i.e., .20—can be much more useful than would be suggested by applying the index of forecasting efficiency to such a correlation. At the heart of the Taylor-Russell approach is a move away from individual prediction to institutional decision making. Consider the following example.

A given test bears a moderate linear relationship with a criterion. Two individuals obtain scores of 60 to 70 on the test; both perform identically on the job. According to an individual prediction model, an error has been made: the person with the higher score would be predicted to outperform the individual with the lower score. Assume, however, that the organization uses the test with a cutoff of 50: anyone scoring above 50 is hired. The organization ignores test score differences among those scoring above or below 50; applicants are assigned to one of two conditions: select or reject. The organization then evaluates the performance of those selected, relative to the performance of a group selected without the test. Taylor and Russell operationalized this by dichotomizing the criterion, separating individuals into "satisfactory" and "unsatisfactory" groups, and then comparing the proportion of satisfactory employees selected with and without the test. Thus, under the model no prediction that the person scoring 70 will outperform the person scoring 60 is made. Rather, with a test cutoff of 50, both are simply predicted to fall into the satisfactory group. If they do fall there, the test has achieved its purpose. Thus, a situation that would be viewed as an error in prediction using an individual prediction model would be seen as accurate prediction using an institutional decision-making model.

As the above discussion indicates, the Taylor-Russell model dichotomizes both the predictor and the criterion, thus categorizing individuals into one of four categories: (1) Selected and satisfactory, known as "true positives"; (2) selected but unsatisfactory, known as "false positives"; (3) rejected but would have been satisfactory, known as "false negatives"; and (4) rejected and unsatisfactory, known as "true negatives." Note that the model applies to a situation where predictor data is collected on a group of current employees, and thus performance data is available for all. The model asks the hypothetical question, "What would be the outcomes of using a given predictor with a given cutoff score?"

The reproduction of a diagram from the Taylor-Russell article will facilitate a description of their treatment of utility. In Figure 4–1, line TT' represents the test cutoff score while line SS' represents the criterion score separating satisfactory and unsatisfactory employees. In many cases, the location of line SS' is somewhat arbitrary as an objective means of identifying a performance level above which employees will be considered satisfactory may not be available.

From Figure 4–1, several important ratios are derived. The base rate—the proportion of employees considered satisfactory if the test is not used—is defined as $(A + D)/(A + B + C + D)$. The selection ratio—the proportion of individuals selected using a given predictor cutoff—is defined as $(A + B)/(A + B + D)$. The accuracy of the predictor, viewing true positives and true negatives as correct decisions, is $(A + C)/(A + B + C + D)$. At this point an important value judgment is made, namely that the organization

Figure 4–1

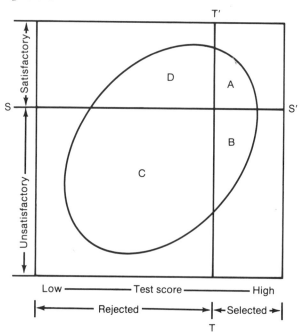

will consider only the performance of those selected in determining the utility of the test. The consequences of properly or improperly rejecting an applicant are ignored. This point will be taken up further in the commentary. If those rejected are ignored, decision accuracy can be redefined as $A/(A + B)$, commonly known as the success ratio.

It is clear that this ratio varies as either the selection ratio or base rate vary. As the selection ratio decreases and approaches zero, the ratio of $A/(A + B)$ increases and approaches unity. As the base rate increases and approaches unity, the ratio of $A/(A + B)$ also approaches unity. Thus, simply knowing the validity of a predictor-criterion relationship provides little information as to the usefulness of the predictor. If the selection ratio is very high, no predictor, however valid, will increase the proportion satisfactory among those selected to any great extent. If the base rate is high, the vast majority of employees selected at random perform satisfactorily, therefore no predictor, however valid, will provide much improvement.

In cases where neither base rate nor selection ratio are extreme values, predictors with validities previously considered useless can be beneficial. Consider a predictor with a validity of .35. Using r^2, the coefficient of determination, this predictor accounts for only about 12 percent of the criterion variance. However, given the information that only 10 percent of employees selected without the test are satisfactory and that there are 50 applicants for 10 positions—a selection ratio of .20—the predictor is quite useful. Given this information, a predictor with a validity of .20 will improve the proportion of satisfactory employees from .10 to .20: twice as many satisfactory employees as without the predictor. Taylor and Russell provide a series of tables showing values of $A/(A + B)$—the proportion of satisfactory employees—as a function of the base rate, the selection ratio, and the validity coefficient.

The key to the Taylor-Russell conception of utility is that errors of prediction are redefined. A salesman selling $100,000 worth of merchandise despite predicted sales of $80,000 would be treated as an error in a validity-based utility model. In the Taylor-Russell scheme this would be a successful prediction if $75,000 is the baseline for success. Error is defined solely as failure where success was predicted (area B in Figure 4–1). This conception gave new life to personnel selection: rather than evaluating predictors in terms of how far removed they were from perfect individual prediction, the Taylor-Russell conception considered predictors in terms of improvement over a base rate of success.

Although of tremendous value to the personnel selection field, the Taylor-Russell approach is not without flaws. The problems with the approach center on the effects of dichotomizing the criterion measure to create satisfactory and unsatisfactory groups of employees. As pointed out earlier, the decision as to where to draw the line between satisfactory and unsatisfactory performance is often somewhat arbitrary. Two managers with differing standards as to what constitutes acceptable performance may evaluate the same group of employees quite differently: according to one manager's standards, 90 percent of the employees may be satisfactory; according to the other's stricter standards, only 50 percent may be satisfactory. With different base rates of success, the Taylor-Russell model leads to different conclusions about the potential value of a given predictor.

A second difficulty is that by forming this performance dichotomy, real differences in performance are ignored. An employee whose production is twice the minimum standard is considered of equal value to the employee who just makes the minimum. Both of these problems can be eliminated by developing utility models which do not require a dichotomous criterion. Naylor and Shine (1965) have developed a model which expressed utility as the mean criterion performance of those selected using a predictor compared to the mean criterion performance of those selected without the predictor. Using mean criterion performance of those selected rather than the proportion of satisfactory employees among those selected avoids both the artificial dichotomy issue and the problems of acknowledging differences in performance.

III. When Selection "Pays Off"

In the Taylor-Russell utility model, as the selection ratio decreases the gain from the use of any predictor with positive validity increases. From this, one might logically conclude that the utility of a predictor is maximized as the selection ratio becomes extremely small. Brogden (1949) points out the fallacy of this conclusion: the more individuals tested for any position, the greater the cost of selection. The cost of selection must be evaluated against the relative value to the organization of an exceptional employee as opposed to an average employee. Unless the value of one employee over another exceeds the cost of selection, the predictor, regardless of its validity, is of no benefit to the organization.

Thus, Brogden adds two variables not considered in the Taylor-Russell utility model. First, one must consider the variance of the value of employees to the organization. If the variance is small, i.e., the difference in production, turnover, absences, accidents, etc. between an exceptional employee and a poor employee is minimal, the use of valid predictors may not have a significant effect on productivity. If the variance is large, a selection program may be of great value. Put simply, characteristics of the criterion also affect the utility of a predictor. Second, the cost of selection per individual hired affects utility. If the cost of testing and processing one applicant is $20, the cost per individual hired is $40 if the selection ratio of .50; if the selection ratio is .01, the cost per individual hired is $2,000. Since these two factors—the criterion variance and the cost of testing—must be considered together in assessing the utility of a test, the two must be measured in the same units. Brogden suggests that both be measured in dollars, since cost of testing is already in dollars.

Using this information, Brogden developed a model for assessing the utility of a selection strategy. He demonstrated that the validity coefficient, r_{xy}, is the percentage of the possible savings which would be obtained by using a perfect predictor. He showed that r_{xy} could be expressed as the ratio of the mean performance of those selected using the predictor to the mean performance of those selected if selection were done on the basis of the criterion, (i.e., perfect prediction) with both measures expressed in standard *(z)* score form. In other words, a correlation of, say, .30 means that at any given selection ratio, the mean performance score of those selected using that predictor is 30 percent of the difference between the mean performance score that would be obtained using a perfectly valid predictor and the mean performance score that would be obtained without the predictor. Thus, the usefulness of a predictor is a direct linear function of validity.

According to Brogden, the mean gain in productivity in dollars per selectee (ΔU/selectee) is $r_{xy} SD_y \bar{z}_{xs} - C/p$ where SD_y is the standard deviation of performance in dollars, $\bar{z}_{xs}$ is the mean predictor score of those selected, expressed in standard score form, C is the cost of selection per applicant, and p is the proportion of applicants hired: the selection ratio. Let us examine how each component of the formula affects utility. The role of r_{xy} was discussed above—utility increases linearly as validity increases. SD_y incorporates the notion that a predictor of given validity will be more useful if the value of differences in performance is large. $\bar{z}_{xs}$, the mean predictor score of those selected, is the mechanism by which the selection ratio is incorporated into the utility formula. $\bar{z}_{xs}$ will increase as the selection ratio decreases. Thus, utility increases as r_{xy} increases, as SD_y increases, and as $\bar{z}_{xs}$ increases. However, the cost of selection increases as the selection ratio decreases; these costs are subtracted from the productivity gain due to selection to arrive at the overall utility figure. This equation requires only that the predictor-criterion relationship be linear; alternative formulas can be used if more restrictive assumptions are made, e.g., that test scores are normally distributed (Schmidt, Hunter, McKenzie, & Muldrow, 1979). Specifically, $\bar{z}_{xs}$ can be replaced by ϕ/p, where ϕ is the ordinate of the normal distribution at the cutoff score and p is the selection ratio. If one has a table of areas of the normal curve which gives ordinate values (many current statistics books no longer include this value in the table), ϕ/p may be easier to obtain than computing $\bar{z}_{xs}$.

The above equation provides the means for giving a bottom-line answer to the question of determining the productivity gain, in dollars, which would result from using a given predictor. Also worthy of mention is the work of Cronbach and Gleser (1965), who pointed out that this formulation applies only to single-stage selection decisions. They have expanded the approach to utility discussed above to deal with placement as well as selection decisions, with sequential as well as single stage decisions, and with multivariate as well as univariate information.

To summarize, the response to the question, "How useful is a predictor of given validity?" has changed dramatically over the years. Three major conceptual frameworks have been identified:

1. A predictor is evaluated in terms of how well it predicts a given job-related criterion for each individual tested.
2. A predictor is evaluated not in terms of individual prediction but rather as the extent to which it improves the proportion of applicants selected who will be successful on the job.
3. A predictor evaluated in terms of the value to the organization of the selection strategy used, as opposed to the value of using other strategies with the same or with other predictors.

The shift from the first to the second represented a change in viewpoint from individual to institutional decisions; the shift from the second to the third was a shift from an emphasis on the number of successes and failures resulting from a selection procedure to emphasis on the "payoff" resulting from the adoption of the selection procedure.

IV. Applications of Utility Models

As we have seen, the basic equation giving the average increase in criterion performance, expressed in dollar terms, resulting from the implementation of a valid selection procedure has been available for more than 30 years. One would presume that this model would routinely be applied by psychologists as a means of justifying their validation efforts and of gaining financial support for further selection research. Yet, until the past few years, the model was rarely used. Consider for a moment the components of the Brogden utility model: the validity coefficient, the standard deviation of the criterion in dollar terms, and the mean predictor score of those selected in standard-score terms. While the first and third are routinely obtained as part of a validity study, the second—the standard deviation of performance—has proved to be the stumbling block limiting the applicability of the model. As initially proposed, one would need to measure the contribution, in dollars, of each individual to the overall efficiency of the organization and then compute the mean and standard deviation of these values. Included in the measure of the value of each employee would be such factors as quantity and quality of objects or services produced, errors, accidents, damage to equipment, social effectiveness in dealing with the public, and supervisory costs (Brogden and Taylor, 1950). Cost-accounting procedures would be used to assess each of these variables.

Application of this procedure has come to be regarded as extremely difficult, if not totally unfeasible. Even for a position like drill operator, where both costs—raw materials, labor costs, machine usage—and benefits—the market value of a finished piece—are tangible, the accounting procedure proved to be extremely time consuming and to require considerable subjective judgment (Roche, 1965). Applying accounting procedures to jobs involving analytical or interpersonal skills, rather than psychomotor skills, to jobs with less tangible raw materials and end products, and to jobs involving a wide variety of tasks and responsibilities, appeared to be such a monumental task that the utility formulas remained virtually unused until the past few years.

New interest in utility was generated by the publication of an article by Schmidt, Hunter, McKenzie, and Muldrow (1979) outlining a radically different approach to estimating the standard deviation of performance. They suggested obtaining global estimates of the value of employees performing at the 15th, 50th, and 85th percentile from groups of job experts, such as supervisors. Averaging the estimates of the supervisors, the difference between the average value of an employee at the 15th percentile and an employee at the 50th percentile represents an estimate of the standard deviation of performance, since the 15th percentile represents a value approximately one standard deviation below the mean if a distribution is normal. Similarly, the difference between the 50th and 85th percentiles represents another estimate of the standard deviation. If these global estimates prove to be meaningful, a straightforward method of assessing the utility of selection procedures would result. Schmidt et al.'s article, applying this procedure to the position of computer programmer and then using the standard deviation estimates to determine the utility of a programming aptitude test, is included below.

The commentary discusses the implications of the Schmidt et al. approach and then considers an alternative approach to estimating the standard deviation of performance. The commentary then moves to an issue sidestepped by the utility models discussed here, namely, the individual, organizational, and societal consequences of rejecting job applicants.

REFERENCES

Brogden, H. D. When testing "pays off." *Personnel Psychology,* 1949, *2,* 171–185.

Brogden, H. E., & Taylor, E. K. The dollar criterion—applying the cost accounting concept to criterion construction. *Personnel Psychology,* 1950, *3,* 133–154.

Cronbach, L. J., & Gleser, G. C. *Psychological tests and personnel decisions.* Urbana: University of Illinois Press, 1965.

Ghiselli, E. E. The validity of aptitude tests in personnel selection. *Personal Psychology,* 1973, *26,* 461–477.

Hull, C. L. *Aptitude testing.* New York: World Book, 1928.

Kelley, T. L. *Statistical methods.* New York: MacMillan, 1923.

Naylor, J. C., & Shine, L. C. A table for determining the increase in mean criterion score obtained by using a selection device. *Journal of Industrial Psychology,* 1965, *3,* 33–42.

Roche, W. J., Jr. A dollar criterion in fixed treatment employee selection. In L. J. Cronbach and G. C. Gleser (Eds.), *Psychological tests and personnel decisions.* Urbana: University of Illinois Press, 1965.

Schmidt, F. L., Hunter, J. E., McKenzie, R. C., & Muldrow, T. W. Impact of valid selection procedures on work-force productivity. *Journal of Applied Psychology,* 1979, *64,* 609–626.

Taylor, H. C., & Russell, J. T. The relationship of validity coefficients to the practical effectiveness of tests in selection. *Journal of Applied Psychology,* 1939, *23,* 565–578.

Impact of Valid Selection Procedures on Work-Force Productivity*

F. L. SCHMIDT
J. E. HUNTER
R. C. McKENZIE
T. W. MULDROW

Questions concerning the economic and productivity implications of valid selection procedures increasingly have come to the fore in industrial-organizational psychology. Dunnette and Borman's chapter in the *Annual Review of Psychology* (1979) includes, for the first time, a separate section on the utility and productivity implications of selection methods. This development is due at least in part to the emphasis placed on the practical utility of selection procedures in some of the litigation in recent years involving selection tests. Hunter and Schmidt (in press) have contended, on the basis of a review of the empirical literature on the economic utility of selection procedures, that personnel psychologists have typically failed to appreciate the magnitude of productivity gains that result from use of valid selection procedures. The major purpose of this study is to illustrate the productivity (economic utility) implications of a valid selection procedure in the occupation of computer programmer in the federal government and in the economy as a whole.

* * * * *

* F. L. Schmidt, J. E. Hunter, R. C. McKenzie, and T. W. Muldrow, "Impact of Valid Selection Procedures on Work-Force Productivity, *Journal of Applied Psychology* 64 (1979), pp. 609–26. Copyright 1979 by the American Psychological Association. Reprinted/Adapted by permission of the publisher and author.

[One] major reason for neglect of the powerful Brogden-Cronbach-Gleser utility model was the difficulty of estimating SD_y.

. . . The generally recommended procedure for estimating SD_y uses cost-accounting procedures. Such procedures are supposed to be used to estimate the dollar value of performance of a number of individuals (cf. Brogden & Taylor, 1950a), and the SD of these values is then computed. Roche's (1961) dissertation illustrates well the tremendous time and effort such an endeavor entails. This study (summarized in Cronbach and Gleser, 1965, pp. 256–266) was carried out on radial drill operators in a large midwestern plant of a heavy equipment manufacturer. A cost-accounting procedure called *standard costing* was used to determine the contribution of each employee to the profits of the company. The procedure was extremely detailed and complex, involving such considerations as cost estimates for each piece of material machined, direct and indirect labor costs, overhead, and perishable tool usage. There was also a "burden adjustment" for below-standard performance. But despite the complexity and apparent objectivity, Roche was compelled to admit that "many estimates and arbitrary allocations entered into the cost accounting" (Cronbach & Gleser, 1965, p. 263). Cronbach, in commenting on the study after having discussed it with Roche, stated that some of the cost-accounting procedures used were unclear or questionable (Cronbach & Gleser, 1965, pp. 266–267) and that the accountants perhaps did not fully understand the utility estimation problem. Thus even given great effort and expense, cost-accounting procedures may nevertheless lead to a questionable final product.

Recently, we have developed a procedure for obtaining rational estimates of SD_y. This method was used in a pilot study by 62 experienced supervisors of budget analysts to estimate SD_y for that occupation. Supervisors were used as judges because they have the best opportunities to observe actual performance and output differences between employees on a day-to-day basis. The method is based on the following reasoning: If job performance in dollar terms is normally distributed, then the difference between the value to the organization of the products and services produced by the average employee and those produced by an employee at the 85th percentile in performance is equal to SD_y. Budget analyst supervisors were asked to estimate both these values; the final estimate was the average difference across the 62 supervisors. The estimation task presented to the supervisors may appear difficult at first glance, but only 1 out of 62 supervisors objected and stated that he did not think he could make meaningful estimates. Use of a carefully developed questionnaire to obtain the estimates apparently aided significantly; a similar questionnaire was used in the present study and is described in the Method section. The final estimate of SD_y for the budget analyst occupation was $11,327 per year ($SE_M$ = $1,120). This estimate is based on incumbents rather than applicants and must therefore be considered to be an underestimate.

As noted earlier, it is generally not critical that estimates of utility be accurate down to the last dollar. Utility estimates are typically used to make decisions about selection procedures, and for this purpose only errors large enough to lead to incorrect decisions are of any consequence. Such errors may be very infrequent. Further, they may be as frequent or more frequent when cost-accounting procedures are used. As we noted above, Roche (1961) found that even in the case of the simple and structured job he studied, the cost accountants were frequently forced to rely on subjective estimates and arbitrary allocations. This is generally true in cost accounting and may become a more severe problem as one moves up in the occupational hierarchy. What objective cost-accounting techniques, for example, can be used to assess the dollar value of an executive's impact on the morale of his or her subordinates? It is the jobs with the largest SD_y values, that is, the jobs for which $\Delta \bar{U}$/selectee is potentially greatest, that are handled least well by cost-accounting methods. Rational estimates—to one degree or another—are virtually unavoidable at the higher job levels.

Our procedure has at least two advantages in this respect. First, the mental standard to be used by the supervisor-judges is the estimated cost to the organization of having an outside consulting firm provide the same products and/or services. In many occupations, this is a relatively concrete standard. Second, the idiosyncratic tendencies, biases, and random errors of individual experts can be controlled by averaging across a large number of judges. In our initial study, the final estimate of SD_y was the average across 62 supervisors. Unless this is an upward or downward bias in the group as a whole, such an average should be fairly accurate. In our example, the standard error of the mean was $1,120. This means that the interval $9,480–$13,175 should contain 90 percent of such estimates. (One truly bent on being conservative could employ the lower bound of this interval in his or her calculations.)

Methods similar to the one described here have been used successfully by the Decision Analysis Group of the Stanford Research Institute (Howard, Note 2) to scale otherwise unmeasurable but critical variables. Resulting measures have been used in the application of decision-theoretic principles to high-level policy decision making in such areas as nuclear power plant construction, corporate risk policies, investment and expansion programs, and hurricane seeding (Howard, 1966; Howard, Matheson, & North, 1972; Matheson, 1969; Raiffa, 1968). All indications are that the response to the work of this group has been positive; these methods have been judged by high-level decision makers to contribute valuably to improvement of socially and economically important decisions.

In most cases, the alternatives to using a procedure like ours to estimate SD_y are unpalatable. The first alternative is to abandon the idea of a utility analysis. This course of action will typically lead to a gross (implicit) underestimate of the economic value of valid selection procedures. This follows if one accepts our contention (Hunter & Schmidt, in press) that the empirical studies that are available indicate much higher dollar values than psychologists have expected. The second alternative in most situations is use of a less systematized, and probably less accurate, procedure for estimating SD_y. Both of these alternatives can be expected to lead to more erroneous decisions about selection procedures.

The Present Study

The procedure for estimating SD_y described here assumes that dollar outcomes are normally distributed. One purpose of the present study is the evaluation of that assumption.

The present study has three purposes: (a) to illustrate the magnitude of the productivity implications of a valid selection procedure, (b) to demonstrate the application of decision-theoretic utility equations, and (c) to test the assumption that the dollar value of employee productivity is normally distributed.

The major reason for our choice of the job of computer programmer was the remarkably accurate validity estimates for this job that a previous study (Schmidt, Rosenberg, & Hunter, Note 3) had provided. Applying the Schmidt–Hunter (Schmidt et al., 1979) validity generalization model to all available validity data for the Programmer Aptitude Test (PAT; Hughes & McNamara, 1959; McNamara & Hughes, 1961), this study found that the percentage of variance in validity coefficients accounted for in the case of job proficiency criteria for the PAT total score was 94 percent. This finding effectively refutes the situational specificity hypothesis. The estimated true validity was .76. Thus the evidence is strong that the (multivariate) total PAT score validity is high for predicting performance of computer programmers and that this validity is essentially constant across situations (e.g., different organizations; Schmidt et al., Note 3). Since it is total score that is typically used in selecting programmers, this study concerns itself only with total score validity. Because the PAT is no longer available commercially, testing costs had to be estimated. In this study, we assumed a testing cost of $10 per examinee.

METHOD

Definition of Relevant Job Group

This study focused on selection of computer programmers at the GS-5 through GS-9 levels. GS-5 is the lowest level in this occupational series. Beyond GS-9, it is unlikely that an aptitude test like the PAT would be used in selection.

Applicants for higher level programmer positions are expected (and required) to have considerable developed expertise in programming and are selected on the basis of achievement and experience, rather than directly on aptitude. The vast majority of programmers hired at the GS-9 level are promoted to GS-11 after 1 year. Similarly, all but a minority hired at the GS-5 level advance to GS-7 in 1 year and to GS-9 the following year. Therefore, the SD_y estimates were obtained for the GS-9 through GS-11 levels. Statistical information obtained from the Bureau of Personnel Management Information Systems of the U.S. Office of Personnel Management indicated that the number of programmer incumbents in the federal government at the relevant levels (GS-5 through GS-9) was 4,404 (as of October 31, 1976, the latest date for which figures were available). The total number of computer programmers at all grade levels was 18,498. For 1975–1976, 61.3 percent of all new hires were at the GS-5 through GS-9 levels. The number of new hires governmentwide in this occupation at these levels was 655 and 565 for calendar years 1975 and 1976, respectively, for an average yearly selection rate of 618. The average tenure of computer programmers hired at GS-5 through GS-9 levels was determined to be 9.69 years.

Data from the 1970 U.S. Census (U.S. Bureau of the Census, 1970) showed that there were 166,556 computer programmers in the U.S. in that year. Because the growth rate has been rapid in this occupation recently, this figure undoubtedly underestimates the current number of programmers. However, it is the most recent estimate available. In any event, the effect of underestimation on the utility results is a conservative one. It was not possible to determine the number of computer programmers that are hired yearly in the U.S. economy. For purposes of this study, it was assumed that the turnover rate was 10 percent in this occupation and that therefore .10 × 166,556, or 16,655, were hired to replace those who had quit, retired, or died. Extrapolating from the fed-

eral to the private sector work force, it was assumed that 61.3 percent of these new hires were at occupational levels for which the PAT would be appropriate. Thus it was assumed that .613 × 16,655, or 10,210 computer programmers could be hired each year in the U.S. economy using the PAT. In view of the current rapid expansion of this occupation, it is likely that this number is a substantial underestimate.

It was not possible to determine prevailing SRs for computer programmers in the general economy. Because the total yearly number of applicants for this job in the government could not be determined, it was also impossible to estimate the government SR. This information lack is of no real consequence, however, since it is more instructive to examine utilities for a variety of SRs. Utilities were calculated for SRs of .05, .10, .20 . . . .80. The gains in utility or productivity as computed from Equation 4 are those that result when a valid procedure is introduced where previously no procedure or a totally invalid procedure has been used. The assumption that the true validity of the previous procedure is essentially zero may be valid in some cases, but in other situations the PAT would, if introduced, replace a procedure with lower but nonzero true validity. Hence, utilities were calculated assuming previous procedure true validities of .20, .30, .40, and .50, as well as .00.

Estimating SD_y

Estimates of SD_y were provided by experienced supervisors of computer programmers in 10 federal agencies. These supervisors were selected by their own supervisors after consultation with the first author. Participation was voluntary. Of 147 questionnaires distributed, 105 were returned (all in usable form), for a return rate of 71.4 percent. To test the hypothesis that dollar outcomes are normally distributed, the supervisors were asked to estimate values for the 15th percentile ("low-performing programmers"), the 50th percentile ("average programmers"), and the 85th percentile ("superior programmers"). The resulting data thus provide two estimates of SD_y. If the distribution is approximately normal, these two estimates will not differ substantially in value.

The instructions to the supervisors were as follows:

> The dollar utility estimates we are asking you to make are critical in estimating the relative dollar value to the government of different selection methods. In answering these questions, you will have to make some very *difficult judgments*. We realize they are difficult and that they are judgments or estimates. You will have to ponder for some time before giving each estimate, and there is probably no way you can be absolutely certain your estimate is accurate when you do reach a decision. But keep in mind three things:
>
> (1) The alternative to estimates of this kind is application of cost accounting procedures to the evaluation of job performance. Such applications are usually prohibitively expensive. And in the end, they produce only imperfect estimates, like this estimation procedure.
> (2) Your estimates will be averaged in with those of other supervisors of computer programmers. Thus errors produced by too high and too low estimates will tend to be averaged out, providing more accurate final estimates.
> (3) The decisions that must be made about selection methods do not require that all estimates be accurate down to the last dollar. Substantially accurate estimates will lead to the same decisions as perfectly accurate estimates.

Based on your experience with agency programmers, we would like for you to estimate the yearly value to your agency of the products and services

produced by the average GS 9-11 computer programmer. Consider the quality and quantity of output typical of the *average programmer* and the value of this output. In placing an overall dollar value on this output, it may help to consider what the cost would be of having an outside firm provide these products and services.

> Based on my experience, I estimate the value to my agency of the average GS 9-11 computer programmer at _____ dollars per year.

We would now like for you to consider the *"superior" programmer*. Let us define a superior performer as a programmer who is at the 85th percentile. That is, his or her performance is better than that of 85 percent of his or her fellow GS 9-11 programmers, and only 15 percent turn in better performances. Consider the quality and quantity of the output typical of the superior programmer. Then estimate the value of these products and services. In placing an overall dollar value on this output, it may again help to consider what the cost would be of having an outside firm provide these products and services.

> Based on my experience, I estimate the value to my agency of a superior GS 9-11 computer programmer to be _____ dollars per year.

Finally, we would like you to consider the *"low performing" computer programmer*. Let us define a low performing programmer as one who is at the 15th percentile. That is, 85 percent of all GS 9-11 computer programmers turn in performances better than the low performing programmer, and only 15 percent turn in worse performances. Consider the quality and quantity of the output typical of the low-performing programmer. Then estimate the value of these products and services. In placing an overall dollar value on this output, it may again help to consider what the cost would be of having an outside firm provide these products and services.

> Based on my experience, I estimate the value to my agency of the low performing GS 9-11 computer programmer at _____ dollars per year.

The wording of this questionnaire was carefully developed and pretested on a small sample of programmer supervisors and personnel psychologists. None of the programmer supervisors who returned questionnaires in the study reported any difficulty in understanding the questionnaire or in making the estimates.

Computation of Impact on Productivity

Using a modification of Equation 4, utilities that would result from 1 year's use of the PAT for selection of *new hires* in the federal government and the economy as a whole were computed for each of the combinations of SR and previous procedure validity given above. When the previous procedure was assumed to have zero validity, its associated testing cost was also assumed to be zero; that is, it was assumed that no procedure was used and that otherwise prescreened applicants were hired randomly. When the previous procedure was assumed to have a nonzero validity, its associated cost was assumed to be the same as that of the PAT, that is, $10 per applicant. As mentioned above, average tenure for government programmers was found to be 9.69 years; in the absence of other information, this tenure figure was also assumed for the private sector. $\Delta \bar{U}$/selectee per year was multiplied by 9.69 to give final $\Delta \bar{U}$/selectee. Cost of testing was charged only to the first year.

Building all of these factors into Equation 4, we obtain the equation actually used in computing the utilities:

$$\Delta U = t N_s (r_1 - r_2) SD_y \phi / p \\ - N_s (C_1 - C_2) / p \quad (6)$$

where ΔU = the gain in productivity in dollars from using the new selection procedure for 1 year; t = tenure in years of the average selectee, here 9.69; N_s = number selected in a given year (this figure was 618 for the federal government and 10,210 for the U.S. economy); r_1 = validity of the new procedure, here the PAT (r_1 = .76); r_2 = validity of the previous procedure (r_2 ranges from 0 to .50); C_1 = per-applicant cost of the new procedure, here $10; and C_2 = per-applicant cost of previous procedure, here 0 or $10. The terms SD_y, ϕ, and p are as defined previously. The figure for SD_y was the average of the two estimates obtained in this study. Note that although this equation gives the productivity gain that results from substituting *for 1 year* the new (more valid) selection procedure for the previous procedure, these gains are not all realized the first year. They are spread out over the tenure of the new employees.

RESULTS AND DISCUSSION

Estimation of Yearly SD_y

The two estimates of SD_y were similar. The mean estimated difference in dollar value of yearly job performance between programmers at the 85th and 50th percentiles in job performance was $10,871 ($SE$ = $1,673). The figure for the difference between the 50th and 15th percentiles was $9,955 ($SE$ = $1,035). The difference of $916 is roughly 8 percent of each of the estimates and is not statistically significant. Thus the hypothesis that computer programmer productivity in dollars is normally distributed cannot be rejected. The distribution appears to be at least approximately normal. The average of these two estimates, $10,413, was the SD_y figure used in the utility calculations below. This figure must be considered an underestimate, since it applies to incumbents rather than to the applicant pool. As can be seen from the two standard errors, supervisors showed better agreement on the productivity difference between "low-performing" and "average programmers" than on the difference between "average" and "superior" programmers.

Impact on Productivity

Table 1 shows the gains in productivity in millions of dollars that would result from

Table 1
Estimated Productivity Increase from 1 Year's Use of the Programmer Aptitude Test to Select Computer Programmers in the Federal Government (in Millions of Dollars)

Selection ratio	True validity of previous procedure				
	.00	.20	.30	.40	.50
.05	97.2	71.7	58.9	46.1	33.3
.10	82.8	60.1	50.1	39.2	28.3
.20	66.0	48.6	40.0	31.3	22.6
.30	54.7	40.3	33.1	25.9	18.7
.40	45.6	34.6	27.6	21.6	15.6
.50	37.6	27.7	22.8	17.8	12.9
.60	30.4	22.4	18.4	14.4	10.4
.70	23.4	17.2	14.1	11.1	8.0
.80	16.5	12.2	10.0	7.8	5.6

1 year's use of the PAT to select computer programmers in the federal government for different combinations of SR and previous procedure validity. As expected, these gains increase as SR decreases and as the validity of the previous procedure decreases. When SR is .05 and the previous procedure has no validity, use of the PAT for 1 year produces a productivity gain of $97.2 million. At the other extreme, if SR is .80 and the procedure the PAT replaces has a validity of .50, the gain is only $5.6 million. The figures in all cells of Table 1 are large—larger than most industrial-organizational psychologists would, in our judgment, have expected. These figures, of course, are for total utility. Gain per selectee for any cell in Table 1 can be computed by dividing the cell entry by 618, the assumed yearly number of selectees. For

example, when SR = .20 and the previous procedure has a validity of .30, the gain per selectee is $64,725. As indicated earlier, the gains shown in Table 1 are produced by 1 year's use of the PAT but are not all realized during the first year; they are spread out over the tenure of the new employees. Per-year gains for any cell in Table 1 can be obtained by dividing the cell entry by 9.69, the average tenure of computer programmers.

Table 2 shows productivity gains for the economy as a whole resulting from use of the PAT or substitution of the PAT for less valid procedures. Table 2 figures are based

Table 2
Estimated Productivity Increase from 1 Year's Use of Programmer Aptitude Test to Select Computer Programmers in U.S. Economy (in Millions of Dollars)

Selection ratio	True validity of previous procedure				
	.00	.20	.30	.40	.50
.05	1,605	1,184	973	761	550
.10	1,367	1,008	828	648	468
.20	1,091	804	661	517	373
.30	903	666	547	428	309
.40	753	555	455	356	257
.50	622	459	376	295	213
.60	501	370	304	238	172
.70	387	285	234	183	132
.80	273	201	165	129	93

on the assumed yearly selection of 10,210 computer programmers nationwide. Again, the figures are for the total productivity gain, but gain per selectee can be computed by dividing the cell entry by the number selected. Once mean gain per selectee is obtained, the reader can easily compute total gain for any desired number of selectees. As expected, these figures are considerably larger, exceeding $1 billion in several cells. Although we have no direct evidence on this point, we again judge that the productivity gains are much higher than most industrial-organizational psychologists would have suspected.

In addition to the assumptions of linearity and normality discussed earlier, the productivity gain figures in Tables 1 and 2 are based on two additional assumptions. The first is the assumption that selection proceeds from top-scoring applicants downward until the SR has been reached. That is, these analyses assume that selection procedures are used optimally. Because of the linearity of the relation between test score and job performance, any other usage of a valid test would result in lower mean productivity levels among selectees. For example, if a cutting score were set at a point lower than that corresponding to the SR and if applicants scoring above this minimum score were then selected randomly (or selected using other nonvalid procedures or considerations), productivity gains would be considerably lower than those shown in Tables 1 and 2. (They would, however, typically still be substantial.)

The second additional assumption is that all applicants who are offered jobs accept and are hired. This is often not the case, and the effect of rejection of job offers by applicants is to increase the SR and thus lower the productivity gains from selection. For example, if a SR of .10 would yield the needed number of new employees given no rejections by applicants, then if half of all job offers are rejected, the SR must be increased to .20 to yield the desired number of selectees. If the validity of the previous procedure were zero, Table 1 shows that rejection by applicants would reduce productivity gains from $82.8 to $66.0 million, a reduction of $16.8 million. If the validity of the previous procedure were nonzero, job rejection by applicants would reduce both its utility and the utility of the new test. However, the function is multiplicative and hence the utility of the more valid procedure would be reduced by a greater amount. Therefore, the utility advantage of the more valid procedure over the less valid procedure would be reduced. For example, Table 1 shows that if the va-

lidity of the previous procedure were .30, the productivity advantage of the more valid test would be $50.1 million if the needed workers could be hired using a selection ratio of .10. But if half of the applicants rejected job offers, we would have to use a SR of .20, and the advantage of the more valid test would drop by one fifth to $40 million.

Hogarth and Einhorn (1976) have pointed out that utility losses caused by job offer rejection can often be offset in part by additional recruiting efforts that increase the size of the applicant pool and, therefore, restore use of smaller SRs. They present equations that allow one to compute the optimal number of additional applicants to recruit and test and the optimal SR under various combinations of circumstances.

The PAT is no longer available commercially. Originally marketed by Psychological Corporation, it was later distributed by IBM as part of package deals to computer systems purchasers. However, this practice was dropped around 1974, and since then the PAT has not been available to most users (Dyer, Note 4). This fact, however, need create no problems in terms of validity generalization. The validity estimates from Schmidt et al. (Note 3) generalize directly to other tests and subtests with the same factor structure. The three subscales of the PAT are composed of conventional number series, figure analogies, and arithmetic reasoning items. New tests can easily be constructed that correlate 1.00, corrected for attenuation, with the PAT subtests.

The productivity gains shown in Tables 1 and 2 are based on an estimated true validity of .76 for the PAT total score (Schmidt et al., Note 3). For many jobs, alternative selection procedures with known validities of this magnitude may not be available. However, the methods used here would be equally applicable. For example, if the alternate selection procedure has an estimated true validity of .50, Equation 6 can be used in the same way to estimate values comparable to those in Tables 1 and 2. Obviously, in this case, all productivity gain would be smaller and there would be no productivity gain at all from substituting the new procedure for an existing procedure with validity of .50. But work-force productivity will often be optimized by combining the existing procedure and the new procedure to obtain validity higher than either procedure can provide individually. This fact is well known in personnel psychology, and we therefore do not develop it further here.

It should be noted that productivity gains comparable to those shown in Tables 1 and 2 can probably be realized in other occupations, such as clerical work, in which lower SD_y values will be offset by the larger numbers of selectees. Pearlman, Schmidt, and Hunter (1980) present extensive data on the generalizability of validity for a number of different kinds of cognitive measures (constructs) for several job families of clerical work.

There is another way to approach the question of productivity gains resulting from use of valid selection procedures. One can ask what the productivity gain would have been had the entire incumbent population been selected using the more valid procedure. As indicated earlier, the incumbent population of interest in the federal government numbers 18,498. As an example, suppose this population had been selected using a procedure with true validity of .30 using a SR of .20. Then had the PAT been used instead, the productivity gain would have been approximately $1.2 billion [$9.69 \times 18,498 \times (.76 - .30) \times 10,413 \times .28/.20$]. Expanding this example to the economy as a whole, the productivity gain that would have resulted is $10.78 billion.

Obviously, there are many other such examples that can be worked out, and we encourage readers to ask their own questions and derive their own answers. However, virtually regardless of the question, the answer always seems to include the conclusion that it does make a difference—an important, practical difference—how people are selected. We conclude that the implications of valid selection procedures for work-force productivity are much greater than most of us have realized in the past.

Finally, we note by way of a necessary caution that productivity gains in individual jobs from improved selection cannot be extrapolated in a simple way to productivity gains in the composite of all jobs making up the national economy. To illustrate, if the potential gain economywide in the computer programmer occupation is $10.78 billion and if there are N jobs in the economy, the gain to be expected from use of improved selection procedures in all N jobs will not in general be as great as N times $10.78 billion. Since the total talent pool is not unlimited, gains due to selection in one job are partially offset by losses in other jobs. The size of the net gain for the economy depends on such factors as the number of jobs, the correlation between jobs of predicted success composites ($\hat{y}$s), and differences between jobs in SD_y. Nevertheless, potential net gains for the economy as a whole are large. The impact of selection procedures on the economy as a whole is explored in detail in Hunter and Schmidt (in press).

REFERENCE NOTES

3. Schmidt, F. L., Rosenberg, I. G., & Hunter, J. E. *Application of the Schmidt–Hunter validity generalization model to computer programmers.* Personnel Research and Development Center, U.S. Civil Service Commission, Washington, D.C., 1978.

4. Dyer, P. Personal communication, April 20, 1978.

REFERENCES

Cronbach, L. J., & Gleser, G. C. *Psychological tests and personnel decisions*. Urbana: University of Illinois Press, 1965.

Dunnette, M. D., & Borman, W. C. Personnel selection and classification systems. *Annual Review of Psychology*, 1979, *30*, 1477–1525.

Hogarth, R. M., & Einhorn, H. J. Optimal strategies for personnel selection when candidates can reject offers. *Journal of Business*, 1976, *49*, 478–495.

Howard, R. A. (Ed.). *Proceedings of the Fourth International Conference on Operational Research*. New York: Wiley, 1966.

Howard, R. A., Matheson, J. E., & North, D. W. The decision to seed hurricanes. *Science*, 1972, *176*, 1191–1202.

Hughes, J. L., & McNamara, W. J. *Manual for the revised Programmer Aptitude Test*. New York: Psychological Corporation, 1959.

Hunter, J. E., & Schmidt, F. L. Fitting people to jobs: The impact of personnel selection on national productivity. In E. A. Fleishman (Ed.), *Human performance and productivity*, in press.

Matheson, J. E. Decision analysis practice: Examples and insights. In, *Proceedings of the Fifth International Conference on Operational Research (OR 69)*. London: Tavistock, 1969.

McNamara, W. J., & Hughes, J. L. A review of research on the selection of computer programmers. *Personnel Psychology*, 1961, *14*, 39–51.

Pearlman, K., Schmidt, F. L., & Hunter, J. E. Test of a new model of validity generalization: Results for job proficiency and training criteria in clerical occupations. *Journal of Applied Psychology*, 1980, *65*, 373–406.

Raiffa, H. Decision analysis. In, *Introductory lectures on choices under uncertainty*. Reading, Mass.: Addison-Wesley, 1968.

Roche, U. J. The Cronbach-Gleser utility function in fixed treatment employee selection (Doctoral dissertation, Southern Illinois University, 1961). *Dissertation Abstracts International*, 1961–62, *22*, 4413. (University Microfilms No. 62-1570). (Portions reproduced in L. J. Cronbach & G. C. Gleser (Eds.), *Psychological tests and personnel decisions*. Urbana: University of Illinois Press, 1965.)

Schmidt, F. L., Hunter, J. E., Pearlman, K., & Shane, G. S. Further tests of the Schmidt–Hunter validity generalization model. *Personnel Psychology*, 1979, *32*, 257–281.

U.S. Bureau of the Census. *Census of population: 1970. Subject reports* (Final Rep. PC (2)-7A). Washington, D.C.: Author, 1970.

COMMENTARY

Schmidt, Hunter, McKenzie, and Muldrow's (1979) conclusions about the value of the productivity increase attributable to the use of a valid test are eye-opening. In the introduction, we discussed the basic utility formula giving the average dollar value of the increase in productivity per new hire per year resulting from the use of a valid test. By considering the average tenure of programmers and the number of programmers hired annually, Schmidt et al. are able to estimate the total value to one employer—the federal government—and to the national economy as a whole of using the test. It must be noted that their conclusions cannot be accepted unless one first accepts the method of measuring each component of the utility model. Of most concern is their rational-estimate approach to assessing the standard deviation of performance. A skeptic looking at their work might react as follows:

1. Evidence that the rational-estimate approach to assessing SD_y produces a measure approximating the true value of SD_y is lacking.
2. While agreement among supervisors is no guarantee that the estimates are valid, agreement would at least suggest that their estimates are potentially meaningful. Yet there was tremendous variability in the estimates. Schmidt et

al. report a standard error of $1,673 for the difference between the 50th and 85th percentiles. We know that the standard error equals the standard deviation divided by $\sqrt{N-1}$; with $N = 105$, $\sqrt{N-1}$ equals about 10.2. Thus the standard deviation of the estimate of SDy is $17,064—far greater than the mean estimate of SD_y of $10,871. Thus, these estimates vary so greatly among supervisors to make interpretation of the findings questionable.

3. The instructions to "consider what the cost would be of having an outside firm provide these products and services" may result in a potentially large overestimate of the actual value of the products and services. One typically pays a premium for the services of a consultant or a temporary help agency: one is paying for convenience and administrative ease as well as for services rendered.

4. As noted by Cascio (1982), the procedure lacks face validity in that the basis of each supervisor's judgment is unknown.

Recently, Schmidt, Hunter, and Pearlman (1982) have provided some evidence to support their rational-estimate approach. They report that in 29 studies where actual worker output was measured, the standard deviation of output averaged 21 percent of mean output. They also report that their rational estimate approach typically yields an SD_y of about 40 percent of salary. Thus, if one accepts an assumption that the yearly dollar value of output of the typical worker is about twice his/her salary, the rational estimates appear reasonable.

We will briefly describe one alternative to the Schmidt et al. procedure. Cascio (1982) describes the development of a procedure called the Cascio-Ramos Estimate of Performance in Dollars (CREPID). Rather than relying on a global estimate, CREPID is a measure of the value of the performance of each individual; the standard deviation of these measures is computed to obtain SD_y. The technique is based on the assumption that the mean salary for a given job represents the economic value of an average performer. A series of frequency, importance, consequences of error, and difficulty ratings is used to determine the relative weight, in percentage terms, of each major job activity. Thus, for the position of accounting supervisor, the activity of receiving questions on billing problems from suppliers, and investigating and furnishing answers might be found to have a weight of 15.7 percent. These percentage figures are then used to determine the dollar value of each activity. If the mean salary of accounting supervisors is $35,000, the value of average performance on the above activity is 15.7 percent of the total, or $5,495. Next, the performance of each employee is rated on each activity on a scale from 0.00 to 2.00, where a rating of 1.00 represents performance at the 50th percentile. Multiplying these ratings by the dollar value of each activity and summing across activities gives an employee's dollar value to the firm. Thus, an accounting supervisor rated 1.5 on the above activity would have a dollar value of $8,242.50 on that activity ($5,495 × 1.5); summing across activities gives his/her total value. Once the value of each employee is determined, SD_y is found by computing the standard deviation of the values. Note that the performance-rating scale used constrains the possible value of performance: an employee rated 2 on all work activities would have a total value twice as high as an average employee rated 1 on each activity. Different scales should be used if studying the job indicates that much wider variation between the value of the best employees and average employee is expected. Gilbert (1978) claims that ratios of best to average performance vary widely across jobs, with ratios typically more than 5 to 1 for sales jobs, around 3 to 1 for management jobs, and lower for routine jobs.

No data is yet available comparing the results of utility analysis using CREPID with results using Schmidt et al.'s global-estimate approach. As we saw above,

Schmidt et al. (1982) state that the economic value of products and services is typically twice the average worker's salary, while CREPID assumes an equivalence between economic value and salary. Thus, it seems likely that the two approaches may result in substantially different estimates of SD_y. Research using multiple techniques for the same job is needed. Clearly, utility assessment is still in its early stages; given the importance of the problem we can expect substantial progress in the next few years.

As Schmidt et al. (1979) point out, their utility analysis is based on the assumption that all applicants who are offered the jobs accept them. In addition, it is implicitly assumed that the organization's applicant pool is a representative sample of the potential applicant pool. If these assumptions are not met, the utility of a valid selection device decreases. If some combination of factors, such as low pay and benefits, poor working conditions, and routine work, result in applicants turning down job offers, the productivity gain due to selection will decrease. If these same factors deter well-qualified job seekers from applying, the productivity gain due to selection will decrease. In sum, an organization must be able to recruit and be successful in hiring well-qualified applicants in order to reap the full benefit of using a valid selection device.

These issues become important as one moves beyond looking at one organization and considers an entire occupation. What would happen if, upon reading the Schmidt et al. article, all employers of computer programmers began using the Programmer Aptitude Test? What if each one looked at Schmidt's Table 2 and decided to use the test with a selection ratio of .10, i.e., select the top 10 percent of the applicant pool? If, nationwide, the number of people seeking programming jobs equals the number of jobs available, a zero-sum situation exists. A fixed number of people will be allocated among various employers; for each employer hiring an above average applicant another hires a below average applicant. The total utility gain would be zero. Fortunately, this is typically not the case: the number of job seekers commonly exceeds the number of jobs. However, in some situations the ratio of applicants to jobs may approach 1.0, or even drop below 1.0, resulting in a zero-sum situation. As pointed out in Chapter 6, the demand for computer programmers may exceed the supply in the 1980s.

When one moves from examining the utility of valid selection procedures in a single firm to examining the effects of selection on the national economy, the utility models discussed thus far become suspect. As we pointed out in the introduction, the Taylor-Russell approach, the Brogden utility formula, and the Schmidt et al. modification of the Brogden formula all disregard the rejected applicant. The formulas consider only the value to the firm of the performance of selected applicants. Consider the following quadrant diagram:

	Predictor score	
Criterion	*Reject*	*Accept*
Satisfactory	False Negative	True Positive
Unsatisfactory	True Negative	False Positive

Figure 4–2

A Heuristic Model of the Consequences of a Negative Employment Decision

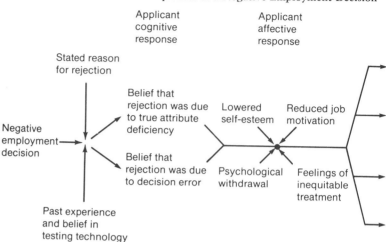

Conceptually, there is a gain or a loss associated with each of the four outcomes above. The value of each outcome may be different, depending on whether one takes the perspective of the individual job seeker, the organization, or society as a whole. For example, while the individual job seeker clearly regards a false negative outcome as having a strong negative utility value, organizations typically are concerned with maximizing performance among those selected and view a false negative outcome as neutral, e.g., as having neither positive nor negative implications for organizational success. We believe that in order to obtain a balanced viewpoint regarding the utility of selection systems, models examining the consequences of all outcomes should be used. In an attempt to draw attention to the often neglected area of the consequences of rejection in utility models, we present Figure 4–2, a model of possible consequences of negative employment decisions. The model identifies possible cognitive responses to rejection, namely, a belief that rejection was due to the applicant truly not possessing the skills or attributes needed for the job or belief that rejection was not due to a deficiency on the part of the applicant but rather to a decision error. The model next identifies possible affective responses, such as reduced self-esteem and job motivation, and identifies possible behavioral responses, such as seeking additional training or education, seeking jobs not requiring the same skills, or withdrawal from the work force. The model then notes that the outcomes of the behavioral responses differ, depending on whether the rejected applicant is classified as a false negative or a true negative. For example, seeking a job requiring lesser skills leads to manpower underutilization—a negative societal outcome—if the applicant is a false negative, but leads to an increased likelihood of a person-job fit—a positive societal outcome—if the applicant is a true negative. Finally, the model notes that whether an applicant believes that rejection was due to a true attribute deficiency or to a decision error is likely to depend in part on the applicants' past experience with and belief in selection technology (e.g., a belief that tests are infallible versus a belief that tests are nonsense) and on the means by which rejection is communicated to the applicant (e.g., "you're not qualified" versus "your qualifications are impressive but we found someone even better" versus no response at all versus explanation of testing procedures and individual counseling).

Figure 4-2 *(concluded)*

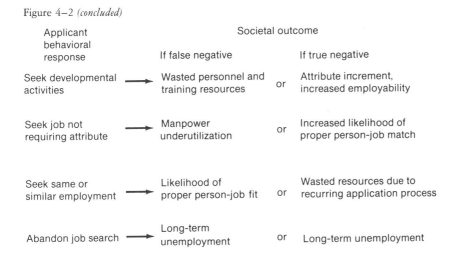

Applicant behavioral response	Societal outcome	
	If false negative	If true negative
Seek developmental activities	Wasted personnel and training resources or	Attribute increment, increased employability
Seek job not requiring attribute	Manpower underutilization or	Increased likelihood of proper person-job match
Seek same or similar employment	Likelihood of proper person-job fit or	Wasted resources due to recurring application process
Abandon job search	Long-term unemployment or	Long-term unemployment

The model is simply heuristic at present: very little is known about the hypothesized linkages. We view this as an area where research is needed, eventually leading to some prescriptive statements about what can be done to increase the likelihood that rejection can lead to positive outcomes: a redirected job search in the case of a true attribute deficiency and continued search without loss of self-esteem in the case of a decision error.

Recall that this chapter began with the seemingly simple question, "How useful is a selection procedure of a given validity?" From straightforward answers based on correlation coefficients, we have seen the development of complex models incorporating base rates, selection ratios, testing costs, and the value of differences in job performance. Measuring the value of differences in job performance has proved to be the major methodological obstacle to utility estimation; our discussion has indicated that the problem is not yet resolved. Finally, we have seen that organizations do not operate in a vacuum while selecting employees and that labor market characteristics, such as applicant supply, must be considered in utility measurement, particularly when projections about the value of scientific selection to the economy as a whole are made.

REFERENCES

Cascio, W. F. *Costing human resources: The financial impact of behavior in organizations.* Boston: Kent Publishing, 1982.

Gilbert, T. F. *Human competence.* New York: McGraw-Hill, 1978.

Schmidt, F. L., Hunter, J. E., McKenzie, R. C., & Muldrow, T. W. Impact of valid selection procedures on work-force productivity. *Journal of Applied Psychology,* 1979, *64,* 609–626.

Schmidt, F. L., Hunter, J. E., & Pearlman, K. Assessing the economic impact of personnel programs on workforce productivity. *Personnel Psychology,* 1982, *35,* 333–347.

Part 2

The Impact of the External
Environment on Personnel Selection

Chapter 5

The Legal Environment

DISCRIMINATION IN EMPLOYEE SELECTION:
THE LEGAL FRAMEWORK

INTRODUCTION

The term *discrimination* has multiple meanings, leading to considerable confusion about how it applies to employee selection. In its initial meaning, discriminate means simply to differentiate or distinguish. In this context, discrimination is occurring every time one applicant is selected for a job and another rejected, regardless of the basis for the selection decision. The second dictionary definition of discriminate is "to act on the basis of prejudice." This appears to be the layman's understanding of the term: discrimination connotes the intentional use of what appears to be irrelevant information as the basis for an employment decision. Using an example we have actually encountered, a job applicant who is told, "Sorry, you're a Libra and we only hire Tauruses," is likely to feel that he or she has been discriminated against.

Neither of these definitions matches the current legal use of the term. Legal recourse against what is felt to be a discriminatory act is available only to members of protected classes, e.g., groups specifically protected by the various antidiscrimination laws. Thus, Title VII of the Civil Rights Act of 1964 forbids discrimination on the basis of race, color, religion, sex, and national origin; the Age Discrimination in Employment Act of 1967 protects individuals between 40 and 70 years of age; the Vocational Rehabilitation Act of 1973 prohibits discrimination on the basis of handicap; and some state fair employment practice laws, which generally mirror Title VII, go beyond Title VII and add additional protected classes, such as homosexuals and obese individuals. Referring back to our earlier example, note that astrological sign is not included among the protected classes. While many may believe that it is unfair to deny someone employment on the basis of astrological sign, nonetheless, the practice apparently does not violate any of the existing antidiscrimination laws. (Government employees, however, could file a constitutional claim.) This highlights an important point: an employer is *not* required to be rational in making selection decisions, so long as the procedures used do not discriminate on the basis of membership in a protected class.

Exactly what constitutes discrimination on the basis of membership in a protected class is not made explicit in the text of antidiscrimination laws. Consider Title VII of the Civil Rights Act of 1964, which defines unlawful employment practices as follows:

> It shall be an unlawful employment practice for an employer:
>
> 1. to fail, refuse to hire, discharge any individual, or otherwise to discriminate against any individual with respect to his compensation, terms, conditions or privileges of employment because of the individual's race, color, religion, sex, or national origin; or
> 2. to limit, segregate, or classify employees or applicants for employment in any way which would deprive, or tend to deprive, any individual of employment opportunities or otherwise adversely affect his stature as an employee because of such individual's race, color, religion, sex, or national origin.

The only other explicit reference to employee selection found in Title VII is the Tower amendment (initially proposed by Senator John Tower of Texas) which states: "Nor shall it be an unlawful employment practice to give and to act upon the results of any professionally developed ability test, provided that such test, its administration or action upon the results is not designed, intended or used to discriminate because of race, color, religion, sex or national origin" (Sec. 703h).

Attempts to clarify which selection practices will and will not be acceptable under Title VII have come from two sources. First, Title VII created the Equal Employment Opportunity Commission and empowered this agency to issue interpretive guidelines to aid employers in complying with the law. Several iterations of guidelines on employee selection procedures have been issued, the most recent in 1978. These guidelines will be considered in detail later in this chapter. Second, a number of court decisions have been handed down which clarify the statutory language of Title VII. For example, the 1971 Supreme Court decision in *Griggs* v. *Duke Power Company* dealt with the issue of whether discriminatory intent had to be shown, and concluded that the effects, rather than the intent, of a selection procedure determined whether or not the procedure was discriminatory.

Under our current understanding of Title VII, three basic types of discrimination can occur:

1. *Evil intent.* This refers to the most basic, blatant type of discrimination, in which an employer explicitly refuses to consider members of a protected class (e.g., "We don't hire women for laborer positions").
2. *Differential treatment.* This refers to the use of different selection procedures or the application of different standards to members of protected classes. Some examples follow:
   - Married women applying for real estate sales positions are told that an interview with their husbands is required in order to determine

whether the husband objects to the wife working irregular hours; no such spouse interview is required for male applicants.

- References of black applicants are carefully checked; those of white applicants are not.
- Women are asked about their plans for marriage and having children during an interview; men are not. (Asking men the same questions but disregarding the answers given by men is still differential treatment: a different standard is being applied to women than is applied to men.)

3. *Adverse impact.* This refers to the use of an apparently neutral selection procedure which has the effect of excluding members of a protected class at a higher rate. Some examples follow:
    - Requiring a high school diploma in an area where a much smaller percentage of blacks than whites have completed high school.
    - Imposing a 5'8" height requirement will exclude more women and hispanics than white males.
    - A preference for homeowners may exclude blacks at a higher rate than whites.

There are two critical factors to note about adverse impact. First, if adverse impact is shown, the employer bears the burden of proof of demonstrating that the requirement is job related. For example, if a job analysis indicates that lifting 75-pound sacks of sand constitutes a significant part of the job in question, a lifting test may be used despite the fact that the test has adverse impact against women. (Procedures for demonstrating the job relatedness of selection procedures are discussed in detail in Chapters 1, 2, and 3.) Thus, a finding of adverse impact does not necessarily indicate that the selection procedure is discriminatory; rather, adverse impact establishes what is known as a prima facie case ("at first view") which shifts the burden of proof to the employer. The second important point to note about adverse impact is that there is no implication of intent to discriminate on the part of the employer. An employer may be acting in good faith in implementing a selection procedure which is later found to have adverse impact. Thus adverse impact is quite far removed from the dictionary definition of discrimination as "acting on the basis of prejudice."

The three types of discrimination outlined here constitute a useful framework for determining whether a selection practice is susceptible to legal challenge. For instance, if approached by the job applicant discussed earlier who was denied a job because of astrological sign and asked for your opinion, you would analyze the situation as follows:

1. While month of birth is being used explicitly as the basis for an employment decision, this is not included among the protected classes.
2. Is the astrological sign test used for all applicants? If applied to women, and not men, for example, it may be a case of differential treatment.
3. Is there evidence of adverse impact? The authors are unaware of any such evidence, but if it were shown that, say, substantially more males

than females were born in May, adverse impact against members of a protected class could result. While clearly an improbable example, it does serve to illustrate an important point, namely, that a showing of adverse impact requires empirical evidence and that whether or not a selection procedure has adverse impact may not be intuitively obvious, and may not be revealed until data are collected and analyzed.

Chapter Outline

The first reading in this section is a description by Cascio and Awad of the legal framework affecting employee selection. Executive orders, laws (e.g., the Civil Rights Act of 1964, the Age Discrimination Act of 1967), and constitutional issues are reviewed.

Significant Supreme Court decisions are then reviewed by a compilation of case summaries published during the last 10 years in the *Monthly Labor Review*. First *Griggs* v. *Duke Power, Albemarle* v. *Moody, Washington* v. *Davis,* and *Connecticut* v. *Teal* are presented to highlight a sequence of cases which contributed to increased clarity regarding the legal restrictions associated with employee selection. They also serve to highlight the standards used by courts when reviewing an employer's defense. The last two cases focus on a different but related issue. The *Manhart* and *Weber* cases are used to illustrate the complex interrelationships between the provisions of Title VII and the establishment of Affirmative Action programs. The commentary is devoted to disentangling this controversy. The third reading, by Glazer, examines the shift over time from an emphasis on providing opportunities for individuals regardless of membership in a protected class to a statistical parity approach focusing on determining each affected group's "fair share" of jobs. Finally, the 1978 Uniform Guidelines on Employee Selection Procedures are included for reference and detailed review by the serious student.

Personnel Decisions in the Context of Civil Rights Legislation*

WAYNE F. CASCIO
ELIAS M. AWAD

Employers in the public and private sectors, employment agencies, unions, and joint labor-management committees controlling apprentice programs are subject to the various nondiscrimination laws. Government contractors and subcontractors are subject to *executive orders*. Many business organizations are employers as well as government contractors and, therefore, are directly subject both to nondiscrimination laws and to executive orders.

In this section we consider only the major civil rights laws. . . . Let us consider the legal principles expressed in the following:

1. The United States Constitution.
2. The Civil Rights Acts of 1866 and 1871.
3. The Equal Pay Act of 1963.
4. The Civil Rights Act of 1964 (as amended by the Equal Employment Opportunity Act of 1972).
5. The Age Discrimination in Employment Act of 1967 (as amended in 1978).

6. The Rehabilitation Act of 1973.
7. Executive Orders 11246, 11375, and 11478.

* * * * *

THE UNITED STATES CONSTITUTION

Due Process

The Fifth Amendment states, "No person shall . . . be deprived of life, liberty, or property, without due process of law. . . ." This is a prohibition upon the federal government, just as the Fourteenth Amendment (discussed later) is a prohibition against certain actions by state governments. Due to its wide applicability and necessarily abstract nature, the "due process" clause of the Fifth Amendment does not speak directly to specific subjects, such as employment discrimination. Therefore, when a suit is filed alleging violation of due process of law, judicial interpretation on an ad hoc or case-by-case basis is usually required. For this reason, the courts prefer to defer to existing statutory law (i.e., law enacted by Congress) when possible, because it is more specific.

* * * * *

* Excerpted from: W. F. Cascio and E. M. Awad, *Human Resources Management: An Information Systems Approach* (Reston, Va.: Reston Publishing, 1981), pp. 100–109, 549–52. Reprinted with permission of Reston Publishing Company, A Prentice-Hall Company, 11480 Sunset Hills Road, Reston, Virginia 22090.

Equal Protection

The Fourteenth Amendment, a prohibition on certain actions by state governments, was enacted to provide equal protection for all under the law. It states:

All persons born or naturalized in the United States and subject to the jurisdiction thereof, are citizens of the United States and of the State wherein they reside. No state shall make or enforce any law which shall abridge the privileges and immunities of citizens of the United States; nor shall any state deprive any person of life, liberty, or property, without due process of law; nor deny to any person within its protection the equal protection of the laws.

This constitutional guarantee requires that all persons similarly situated be treated alike, both in the privileges conferred and in the liabilities imposed upon them.

* * * * *

CIVIL RIGHTS ACTS OF 1866 AND 1871

The Right to Make and Enforce Contracts for Employment

The Thirteenth and Fourteenth Amendments both grant Congress the power to enforce their provisions by enacting appropriate legislation. Section 1981 of the Civil Rights Act of 1866 grants all citizens

the same right in every state and territory to make and enforce contracts, to sue, be parties, give evidence, and to the full and equal benefit for all laws and proceedings for the security of persons and property as is enjoyed by white citizens.

In *Johnson* v. *Railway Express Agency* (1975), the Supreme Court held that while Section 1981 on its face relates primarily to racial discrimination in the making and enforcement of contracts, it also provides a federal remedy against discrimination in private employment on the basis of race. It is a powerful remedy. Under Section 1981, individuals are entitled to both equitable and legal relief, including compensatory and, under certain circumstances, punitive damages. And unlike Title VII (discussed later), back-pay awards are not limited to 2 years.

Deprivation of Constitutional Rights

Section 1981 of the Civil Rights Act of 1866 is often used in conjunction with Section 1983 of the Civil Rights Act of 1871, which grants all citizens the right to sue if they feel they have been deprived of any rights or privileges guaranteed by the Constitution and laws.

EQUAL PAY ACT OF 1963: EQUAL PAY FOR EQUAL WORK REGARDLESS OF SEX

This act was passed as an amendment to the Fair Labor Standards Act (FLSA) of 1938. For those employers already subject to the FLSA (i.e., those engaged in commerce or in the production of goods for commerce), the Equal Pay Act specifically prohibits sex discrimination in the payment of wages, except

where such payment is made pursuant to (i) a seniority system; (ii) a merit system; (iii) a system which measures earnings by quantity of production, or (iv) a differential based on any other factor other than sex: *Provided,* that an employer who is paying a wage rate differential in violation of this subsection shall not, in order to comply with the provisions of this subsection, reduce the wage rate of any employee.

Note the last five lines of the law. In correcting any inequity under the Equal Pay Act, companies ordinarily must raise the lower rate. Thus, following the 1972 extension of the act to include outside salespersons, managers, and executives,

AT&T signed a consent agreement to bring the initial pay of women promoted to managerial positions up to the initial pay of men who were so promoted. Since initial pay had previously been related to past earnings (which were lower for the women), the cost to the company was estimated at $30 million.

The Equal Pay Act, the first in the series of federal nondiscrimination laws passed during the 1960s, is administered, as of July 1979, by the EEOC. Wages withheld in violation of its provisions are viewed as unpaid minimum wages or unpaid overtime compensation under the FLSA.

THE CIVIL RIGHTS ACT OF 1964: EQUAL EMPLOYMENT OPPORTUNITY

The Civil Rights Act of 1964 is divided into several sections or titles, each dealing with a particular facet of discrimination (e.g., voting rights, public accommodations, public education). For our purposes, Title VII is particularly relevant.

Title VII has been the principal body of federal legislation in the area of fair employment. Through it the Equal Employment Opportunity Commission (EEOC) was instituted to ensure compliance by employers, employment agencies, and labor organizations. We will consider the organization and operation of the EEOC in greater detail in a following section.

Nondiscrimination on the Basis of Race, Sex, Religion, or National Origin

Employers are bound by the provision of Section 703(a) of Title VII, as amended, which states:

> It shall be an unlawful employment practice for an employer
> 1. to fail or to refuse to hire or to discharge any individual with respect to his compensation, terms, conditions, or privileges of employment, because of such individual's race, color, religion, sex, or national origin; or
> 2. to limit, segregate, or classify his employees or applicants for employment in any way which would deprive or tend to deprive any individual of employment opportunities or otherwise adversely affect his status as an employee, because of such individual's race, color, religion, sex, or national origin.

Nondiscrimination in Apprenticeship Programs

Section 703(b) of Title VII forbids

> discrimination against any individual because of his race, color, religion, sex, or national origin in admission to, or employment in, any program established to provide apprenticeship or other training.

A further provision of the act, Section 704(a), prohibits discrimination against an employee or applicant because he or she has opposed an unlawful employment practice or made a charge, testified, assisted, or participated in a Title VII investigation, proceeding, or hearing. Finally, Section 704(b) prohibits notices or advertisements relating to employment from indicating any preference, limitation, specification, or discrimination on any of the prohibited factors unless it is in relation to a bona fide occupational qualification (discussed later).

Prior to 1972, Title VII was primarily aimed at (1) private employers with 25 or more employees, (2) labor organizations with 25 or more members, and (3) private employment agencies. In 1972 the Equal Employment Opportunity Act expanded this coverage to (1) both public and private employers (including state and local governments and public and private educational institutions) with 15 or more employees, (2) labor organizations with 15 or more members, and (3) both public and private employment agencies. Elected officials and their appointees are excluded from Title VII but are still subject to the Fourteenth Amendment and to the Civil Rights Acts of 1866 and 1871.

Suspension of Government Contracts and Back-Pay Awards

Two other provisions of the 1972 law are noteworthy. First, denial, termination, or suspension of government contracts is not permitted (without a special hearing) if an employer has and is following an affirmative action plan accepted by the federal government for the same facility within the past 12 months. Second, back-pay awards are limited to 2 years in Title VII cases.

Several *exemptions* to the provisions of Title VII were written into the law. Among these were the following:

Bona Fide Occupational Qualifications

Classification or discrimination in employment according to race, religion, sex, or national origin is permissible when such qualification is a bona fide occupational qualification "reasonably necessary to the operation of that particular business or enterprise" (e.g., actors, actresses, models). The burden of proof rests with the employer to demonstrate this. We hasten to add, however, that the EEOC interprets bona fide occupational qualifications quite narrowly. Preferences of the employer, coworkers, or clients are irrelevant.

Seniority Systems

Bona fide seniority or merit systems and incentive pay systems are lawful "provided that such differences are not the result of an intention to discriminate." However, since *job* or *departmental* seniority systems (in which employees continue to accrue seniority as long as they do not change jobs or departments) tend to perpetuate past discriminatory patterns, such systems are not "bona fide." *Plantwide* or *companywide* systems (in which employees retain their seniority regardless of where they move within the plant or company are preferred.

Pre-employment Inquiries

Such inquiries, for example, regarding sex and race, are permissible as long as they are not used as bases for discrimination. Besides, such inquiries are necessary to meet the reporting requirements of the federal regulatory agencies and to ensure compliance with the law.

Testing

An employer may give or act upon any professionally developed ability test provided the test is not used as a vehicle to discriminate on the basis of race, color, religion, sex, or national origin.

Preferential Treatment

It is unlawful to interpret Title VII as requiring the granting of preferential treatment to individuals or groups because of their race, color, religion, sex, or national origin on account of existing imbalances.

Veterans' Preference Rights

These are not repealed or modified in any way by Title VII.

National Security

When it is deemed necessary to protect the national security, discrimination (e.g., against members of the Communist Party) is permitted under Title VII.

Initially, it appeared that these exemptions would significantly blunt the overall impact of the law. However, it soon became clear that they would be interpreted very narrowly by both the EEOC and the courts.

AGE DISCRIMINATION IN EMPLOYMENT ACT OF 1967

Just as Title VII prohibits discrimination in employment on the basis of race, sex, religion, or national origin, employers are also mandated to provide equal employment opportunity on the basis of age. As amended in 1978, the act specifically proscribes discrimination on the basis of age for employees 40 to 70 years old unless the employer can demonstrate that age is a bona fide occupational qualification for the job in question. This law is administered, as of July 1979, by the EEOC.

THE DISABLED: PROSPECTS AND PROBLEMS

Congress enacted the Rehabilitation Act of 1973, requiring federal contractors (those receiving more than $2,500 in federal contracts annually) and subcontractors to take affirmative action to seek out qualified handicapped people and fully utilize them.

* * * * *

Legally, a person is considered handicapped if he or she satisfies one of three broad conditions:

He or she has a physical or mental impairment that substantially limits one or more of life's major activities (e.g., seeing, hearing, walking, breathing).

He or she has a record of such impairment (e.g., a former patient in a mental hospital who now is mentally sound).

He or she is regarded as having such impairment (e.g., a person who seems mentally retarded but is not).

Even alcoholics and drug addicts are considered "handicapped" under the law. However, any alcoholic or drug addict may be held to the same standards of work performance and behavior as other employees, even if the unsatisfactory work or behavior is related to the person's addiction. The law is designed to prohibit discrimination *solely* by reason of the handicap.

The omission of goals, timetables, and utilization analyses make these regulations significantly different from previous rules governing affirmative action. The original idea was and still is that, if federal contractors and recipients of federal funds are successful in making voluntary efforts to root out discrimination against the disabled, government will place fewer burdensome restrictions on them in the future.

The shift away from the "numbers game" has been replaced by an emphasis on systemic discrimination—any business practice that *results* in a denial of equal employment opportunity. Since systemic discrimination need not involve any specific action against an applicant or employee, it is harder to detect. Typically, it results from policies (or the way policies are implemented), practices, procedures, selection criteria, or decision-making criteria. For example, suppose company policy requires that all employment interviews be conducted in the offices of the personnel department. Simple enough. However, suppose personnel is located on the fourth floor of a building that has no elevators? A person in a wheelchair might never be hired simply because he or she could not apply.

Enforcement of regulations for the disabled also differs from previous affirmative action regulations. Individual complaint activity, rather than periodic onsite audit, is the primary method used. The emphasis is on "screening in" applicants, not screening them out.

* * * * *

EXECUTIVE ORDERS 11246, 11375, AND 11478:
NONDISCRIMINATION BY FEDERAL AGENCIES, CONTRACTORS, OR SUBCONTRACTORS

The executive branch of the federal government has also been involved in the area of employment discrimination, principally through the issuance of executive orders. Presidential executive orders are aimed specifically at government contractors and subcontractors. They are not new. In 1941 President Franklin D. Roosevelt issued an order outlawing discrimination in defense-related industries on the basis of race, creed, color, or national origin. Every president since Roosevelt has issued one or more orders, making enforcement more rigorous and extending coverage.

In 1965 President Johnson signed Executive Order 11246. Initially, the order prohibited discrimination on the basis of race, color, religion, or national origin by federal agencies, contractors, and subcontractors. In 1967, Executive Order 11375 prohibited sex-based discrimination as well.

Executive Order 11478, issued by President Nixon in 1969, supersedes Part I of Executive Order 11246, prescribing that employment policies in the federal government be based on merit and fitness and prohibiting discrimination on the basis of race, color, religion, sex, or national origin. The head of each federal agency is required to establish and maintain a program of equal employment opportunity, which includes, but is not limited to, "employment, upgrading, demotion, or transfer; recruitment or recruitment advertising; layoff or termination; rates of pay or other forms of compensation; and selection for training, including apprenticeship. . . ."

These requirements are almost identical to those of Title VII, except that as affirmative acts, they require companies to post special notices and also to indicate in "help wanted" ads that they are equal opportunity employers. Part II of Executive Order 11246 regulates all federal contractors or subcontractors with contracts or subcontracts of $10,000 or more (as of July 1968). Part III makes each contracting agency in the government responsible for the compliance of their contractors and subcontractors. Two groups are exempt. State and local governments need not file annual compliance reports or maintain written affirmative action compliance programs if they do not actually participate in the work covered by the contracts or subcontracts. Second, unions are wholly exempt from Executive Order 11246, but remain subject to Title VII of the Civil Rights Act of 1964.

Enforcement of Executive Orders

Considerable enforcement power accompanied Executive Order 11246, administered by the Department of Labor through its Office of Federal Contract Compliance Programs (OFCCP). Upon noncompliance with OFCCP rules and regulations (described later), the EEOC may be notified if it appears that Title VII may also have been violated, the Department of Justice may be advised to institute criminal proceedings, and the secretary of labor may cancel or suspend current contracts as well as the right to bid on future contracts. Noncompliance can become a very expensive proposition.

ENFORCEMENT OF THE LAWS: REGULATORY AGENCIES

State Fair Employment Practices Commissions

Most states have nondiscrimination laws that include provisions which express the public policy of the state, the persons to whom the law applies, and the prescribed activities of various administrative bodies. Moreover, the provisions specify unfair employment practices, procedures, and enforcement powers. Many states vest statutory enforcement powers in a state fair employment practices commission. Some of the larger municipal governments (e.g., New York City) have, in turn, passed local nondiscrimination laws and have their own enforcement bodies.

However, whenever there are inconsistencies between federal requirements and state or local requirements, the federal requirements take precedence. For example, in many states pre-employment inquiries (e.g., to identify the race or sex of applicants) are illegal, as is postemployment identification of employees by race, sex, and so on, on individual personnel records. However, in the absence of such information, federal agencies would have an extremely difficult time investigating alleged noncompliance. Thus, the federal government may request that such information be retained as long as the records will not be used to discriminate unlawfully.

Among federal agencies, equal employment authorities have been consolidated so that by July 1979 just three agencies (instead of 16 previously) had such authority. . . .

Equal Employment Opportunity Commission (EEOC)

EEOC is an independent regulatory agency whose five commissioners (one of whom is chairperson) are appointed by the president and confirmed by the Senate for terms of 5 years. No more than three of the commissioners may be from the same political party. Like the OFCCP, the EEOC sets policy and in individual cases determines whether there is "reasonable cause" to believe that unlawful discrimination has occurred. It should be noted, however, that the courts give no legal standing to EEOC rulings on whether or not "reasonable

cause" exists; each Title VII case constitutes a new proceeding.

EEOC's 59 regional and district offices throughout the country process approximately 70,000 complaints annually. Such complaints may be filed by an individual, a group, or an EEOC commissioner within 180 days of the date of an alleged violation. The latter authority is worthy of note. Originally, EEOC was given no enforcement power whatsoever. It was merely entitled to investigate complaints and to foster voluntary conciliation between the aggrieved parties. With the passage of the Equal Employment Opportunity Act in 1972, however, EEOC was granted the power to sue, either on its own behalf, when it believes unlawful discrimination to have taken place, or on behalf of a claimant.

Complaint process. Complaints filed with the EEOC are first deferred to a state or local fair employment practices commission, if there is one with statutory enforcement power. After 60 days, EEOC can begin its own investigation of the charges, whether or not the state agency takes action.

Of course, the state or local agency may immediately redefer to the EEOC. At the outset, voluntary compliance (acceptable to the government, to the respondent organization, and to the aggrieved party) is sought. If all else fails, however, court action can be taken. . . . If the defendant is a private employer, the case is taken to the appropriate federal district court; if the defendant is a public employer, the case is referred to the Department of Justice.

EEOC has also issued several sets of guidelines for Title VII compliance. Among these are guidelines on discrimination because of pregnancy, sex, religion, and national origin, guidelines on employee selection procedures, guidelines on affirmative action programs, and a policy statement on pre-employment inquiries. These guidelines are not laws, although the

Supreme Court (1975) has indicated that they are entitled to "great deference." While the purpose of the guidelines is more legal than scientific, violators will incur EEOC sanctions and possible court action.

EEOC has one other major function: information gathering. Each organization with 100 or more employees must file annually with the EEOC a form (EEO-1) detailing the number of women and members of four different minority groups employed in nine different job categories from laborers to managers and officials. Specific minority groups and blacks, Americans of Cuban, Spanish, Puerto Rican, or Mexican origin, Orientals, and American Indians (which in Alaska includes Eskimos and Aleuts). Over 260,000 forms are filed annually. Although each report cannot be examined critically at present, in the future EEOC hopes to develop computerized scanning procedures for detecting patterns of discrimination.

Office of Federal Contract Compliance Programs (OFCCP)

Until October 1978, OFCCP (a part of the Department of Labor's Employment Standards Administration) had only administrative responsibility for Executive Order 11246. Day-to-day enforcement activities were actually carried out by other federal agencies, with OFCCP monitoring their work and setting program policies.

Through an executive order issued by President Carter, OFCCP now has all enforcement as well as administrative and policy-making authority for the entire contract compliance program. "Contract compliance" means that in addition to quality, timeliness, and other requirements of federal contract work, contractors and subcontractors also must meet EEO and affirmative action requirements covering all aspects of employment, including recruitment, hiring, training, pay, seniority, pro-

motion, and even benefits. These requirements affect many people, for over 30,000 prime contractors and thousands more subcontractors provide the U.S. government with supplies, services, use of property, and construction work totaling about $11 billion each year.

Large contractors and subcontractors, those with $50,000 or more in government business and with 50 or more employees, must prepare and implement written affirmative action programs. The programs are kept on file by the employers and always reviewed during compliance investigations. In job areas where minorities or women are underrepresented, employers must establish goals and timetables for hirings and promotions. Goals and timetables are not required under the handicapped workers and veterans' laws, but all other affirmative action measures are implicit in the contractual obligation.

When a compliance review turns up problems that cannot be resolved easily, OFCCP attempts to reach a conciliation agreement with the employer. A conciliation agreement might include back pay, seniority credit, promotions, or other forms of relief for the victims of discrimination; it might also involve new training programs, special recruitment efforts, or other affirmative action measures.

The conciliation agreement is OFCCP's preferred route. It means that the contractor may continue doing government business, and the employees are guaranteed protection of their rights. But when conciliation efforts are unsuccessful, OFCCP must turn to its enforcement process. Contractors or subcontractors cited for violating their EEO and affirmative action requirements may have a formal hearing before an administrative law judge. If conciliation is not reached before or after the hearing, employers may lose their government contracts or subcontracts, they may be debarred, that is, declared ineligible for any federal contract work. Debarment is

OFCCP's ultimate weapon, for it indicates in the most direct way possible that the U.S. government is serious about EEO programs. Between 1965 and 1980, 24 companies were debarred from government work.

Reading 8

Major Supreme Court Decisions*

I. *GRIGGS* v. *DUKE POWER COMPANY*[1]

In its Dan River steam station at Draper, N.C., the Duke Power Co. maintained a hiring and promotion requirement of high school diploma for all its employees except those in the lowest paying "labor department," which was virtually reserved for blacks. When the Civil Rights Act went into effect in 1965, the company added another requirement to its criteria—a satisfactory score on two professionally designed tests, one measuring general intelligence, the other mechanical aptitude. The management claimed that these criteria were not intended for discrimination against Negroes, that they were applied to whites as well as to blacks, and that their purpose was, generally, to "improve the overall quality of the work force." (Court's language.) All of this might have been true, but the unavoidable fact was that these standards also discriminated against Negroes. . . .

A Federal district court ruled that the company's policy had ceased to be discriminatory when the 1964 law went into effect, and that the impact of past inequities could not be remedied under title VII because the law was intended for a "prospective"

application only. An appeals court agreed that there had been no intentional discrimination, but disagreed as to the law's prospective application; residual discrimination resulting from past practices was not beyond the law's remedy, it held.

In the Supreme Court, Chief Justice Burger, who delivered the Court's opinion, phrased the question brought before the bar as being "whether an employer is prohibited by the Civil Rights Act of 1964, Title VII, from requiring high school education or passing of a standardized general intelligence test as a condition of employment in or transfer to jobs when (*a*) neither standard is shown to be significantly related to successful job performance, (*b*) both requirements operate to disqualify Negroes at a substantially higher rate than white applicants, and (*c*) the job in question formerly had been filled only by white employees as part of a longstanding practice of giving preference to whites." The Court's answer was a definite "yes."

Does title VII prohibit testing of job applicants? No, it does not; educational requirements as well as test scores may be essential to determine whether a man gets the right kind of job and vice versa. And indeed, the Supreme Court said here, "Nothing in the act precludes the use of testing or measuring procedures; obviously, they are useful. . . ." But such tests and other criteria part company with propriety and legality when their avowed purpose is but a sham.

---

* Excerpted from the *Monthly Labor Review*'s monthly column, "Significant Decisions in Labor Cases."

[1] Written by Eugene Skotzo, June 1971, pp. 79–81.

Section 703(h) of the act provides that, "Notwithstanding any other provision of [title VII], it shall not be an unlawful employment practice for an employer . . . to give and to act upon the results of any professionally developed ability test provided that such test, its administration or action upon the results is not designed, intended, or used to discriminate because of race, color, religion, sex or national origin. . . ." There is no absolute prohibition of ability tests here, there is only the condition that they not be used for purposes of discrimination. Yet this somewhat involuted and negative phraseology of a conditional approval does not deprive the statutory provision of its potential for a positive function in preventing discrimination, as has been demonstrated in this case.

"What Congress has prohibited," said the High Court, "is giving these [testing] devices and mechanisms controlling force unless they are demonstrably a reasonable measure of job performance. Congress has not commanded that the less qualified be preferred over the better qualified simply because of minority origins. Far from disparaging job qualifications as such, Congress has made such qualifications the controlling factor, so that race, religion, nationality, and sex become irrelevant. . . ." Obviously, then, "The touchstone is business necessity. If an employment practice which operates to exclude Negroes cannot be shown to be related to job performance, the practice is prohibited."

There may, however, be a situation where—as the employer claimed to be true in this case—a test or other criterion is not exactly job-related, nor is the employer's motive improper. What then? Is the standard proscribed?

The Court concerned itself with this type of situation, and its answer was somewhat in line with the old saying that good intentions may, and often do, pave the road to hell. It said, "good intent or absence of discriminatory intent does not redeem employment procedures or testing mechanics that operate as 'built-in headwinds' for minority groups and are unrelated to measuring job capability." And, "Under the act, practices, procedures, or tests neutral on their face, and even neutral in terms of intent, cannot be maintained if they operate to 'freeze' the status quo of prior discriminatory employment practices."

As already mentioned, the employer sought refuge in the fact that its hiring and promotion criteria applied equally to whites and blacks. Chief Justice Burger, who delivered the opinion of the Court, referred to the petitioners' "inferior education [received] in the segregated schools" and cited Aesop's fable about the fox, the stork, and a shallow dish of milk before them: ". . . Congress has . . . provided that tests or criteria for employment or promotion may not provide equality of opportunity only in the sense of the fabled offer of milk to the stork and the fox. On the contrary, Congress has . . . required that the posture and condition of the job-seeker be taken into account. It has—to resort again to the fable—provided that the vessel in which the milk is proffered be one all seekers can use. The act proscribes not only overt discrimination but also practices that are fair in form, but discriminatory in operation. . . ."

The Court stressed more than once that "Congress did not intend by title VII . . . to guarantee a job to every person regardless of qualifications. . . . Discriminatory preference for any group, minority or majority, is precisely and only what Congress has proscribed. What is required by Congress is the removal of artificial, arbitrary, and unnecessary barriers of employment when the barriers operate invidiously to discriminate on the basis of racial or other impermissible classifications." The appellate court's holding that the practices complained of had no purpose or intent of racial discrimination was overruled.

II. *ALBEMARLE PAPER COMPANY* v. *MOODY* [2]

. . . the High Court clarified the standards by which employment tests may be validated. In 1971, the court ruled unanimously that Title VII of the Civil Rights Act of 1964 forbids the use of employment tests that have "disproportionate racial impacts" (that is, tests which yield significantly lower scores for members of one race than of another), unless the employer can show that the tests have a "manifest relation" to the jobs involved. *(Duke Power Co.)* Since that time, lower courts have struggled to develop standards to determine whether such a relationship has been shown. In this case, the Supreme Court applied the test validation guidelines developed by the Equal Employment Opportunity Commission, noting, as it had before, that such guidelines are "entitled to great deference" as an administrative interpretation of the 1964 Civil Rights Act by the agency charged with enforcing it.

The trial court also upheld Albemarle's job testing program. The company required applicants for jobs in skilled lines of progression to have a high school diploma and to pass two standardized tests (one to measure verbal and the other nonverbal ability). Shortly before the trial, Albemarle hired an industrial psychologist to study the program. He compared the test scores of current employees in 10 job groupings with ratings of those employees by their supervisors. The study showed statistically significant correlations between test scores and these ratings in some, but not all, of the job groupings. The court concluded that the tests had been sufficiently validated, but ordered the high school diploma requirement dropped as not sufficiently job related.

* * * * *

[On appeal] the Supreme Court noted that Albemarle's validation study fell short of the EEOC's guidelines in four ways:

• The study found significant correlations between test scores and ratings in only some of the job categories covered, and not all categories were included in the study. The EEOC guidelines permit validation in one area to justify use of the test in another only if "no significant differences" exist between the areas. (Albemarle's study did not analyze the jobs to determine whether any such differences exist.)

• The study compared test scores with subjective ratings. The guidelines authorize subjective ratings only under more precise standards than those employed by Albemarle.

• In most areas, the study focused on job groups near the top of the lines of progression. Under the EEOC guidelines, analyses at higher levels can validate tests for use at entry only if the "new employees will probably, within a reasonable period of time and in a great majority of cases, progress to [the] higher level."

• The study dealt almost exclusively with experienced white workers, while those actually taking the tests to gain employment were younger, generally inexperienced, and less predominantly white.

The Supreme Court therefore held that the employment tests had not been sufficiently validated. It instructed the district court to reconsider the issue in line with the EEOC guidelines. That court will also consider whether the plaintiffs should be denied backpay because of their delay in requesting it.

In a separate opinion (concurring in part and dissenting in part), Chief Justice Warren E. Burger . . . noted that the EEOC guidelines were not supported by the words of the act or by its legislative history, and that they had not been submitted to public comment as administrative regula-

---

[2] Written by Craig E. Polhemus, October 1975, pp. 57–58.

tions. "Thus, slavish adherence to the EEOC guidelines regarding test validation should not be required," the Chief Justice said.

III. *WASHINGTON v. DAVIS*[3]

Before the 1972 amendments extending Title VII of the Civil Rights Act of 1964 to the Federal Government, the primary ban on racial discrimination in Federal employment resided in the Fifth Amendment's guarantee of due process of law. Many Federal appeals courts, faced with suits alleging discrimination in violation of the Fifth Amendment (or of the parallel equal protection and due process guarantees applying to the States through the Fourteenth Amendment), turned to Title VII standards for guidance. Although most current cases alleging government employment discrimination are brought under Title VII as well as the Constitution, some pre-1972 cases are still pending on appeal. In deciding one such case, the U.S. Supreme Court recently held that the constitutional standard for determining whether employment practices improperly discriminate on the basis of race is less strict than the standard used in Title VII cases. *(Washington v. Davis.)*

The *Davis* case challenged a verbal-communications test administered to applicants for the District of Columbia police force. The plaintiffs, blacks who had been rejected because of their low test scores, claimed that the examination was not related to job performance and disqualified a disproportionately high number of blacks. A Federal district court dismissed the case, citing the efforts of the District of Columbia police department to recruit blacks and the relative equality of the proportions of blacks on the police force and in the entire metropolitan recruiting area.

On appeal, a higher court adopted, by analogy, the standards developed in Title VII cases and determined that the test was improper because it tended to exclude black applicants and because it had not been shown to be job-related. The appellate court held that the lack of discriminatory intent was irrelevant to the constitutional claim.

The Supreme Court, in turn, reversed the court of appeals. The High Court concentrated on the difference between constitutional claims and those brought under Title VII:

> As the court of appeals understood Title VII, employees or applicants under it need not concern themselves with the employer's possibly discriminatory purpose but instead may focus solely on the racially differential impact of the challenged hiring or promotion practices. This is not the constitutional rule. We have never held that the constitutional standard for adjudicating claims of invidious racial discrimination is identical to the standards applicable under Title VII, and we decline to do so today.
>
> Necessarily, an invidious discriminatory purpose may often be inferred from the totality of the relevant facts, including the fact, if it is true, that the law bears more heavily on one race than another. It is also not infrequently true that the discriminatory impact . . . may for all practical purposes demonstrate unconstitutionality because in various circumstances the discrimination is very difficult to explain on nonracial grounds. Nevertheless, we have not held that a law, neutral on its face and serving ends otherwise within the power of government to pursue, is invalid under the equal protection clause simply because it may affect a greater proportion of one race than of another. Disproportionate impact is not irrelevant, but it is not the sole touchstone of an invidious racial discrimination forbidden by the Constitution. Standing alone, it does not trigger the rule . . . that racial classifi-

---

[3] Written by Craig E. Polhemus, August 1976, pp. 41–42.

cations are to be subjected to the strictest scrutiny and are justifiable only by the weightiest of considerations.

The Court specifically criticized the rulings of "various courts of appeals . . . in several contexts, including public employment, that the substantially disproportionate impact of a statute or official practice standing alone and without regard to discriminatory purpose, suffices to prove racial discrimination violating the equal protection clause absent some justification going substantially beyond what would be necessary to validate most other legislative classifications."

Because the court saw the efforts of the police department "modestly to upgrade the communicative abilities of its employees" as a reasonable government purpose under the Constitution, it rejected the Fifth Amendment claim of discrimination.

If the test had been challenged under Title VII, the Government would have been required to establish a relationship between test scores and an accepted measure of job performance or ability. After dismissing the constitutional claim in *Davis,* the Supreme Court discussed validation techniques for determining whether the trial judge had been correct in dismissing claims brought under pre-1972 statutes implementing the constitutional ban on racial discrimination. Because the Government had introduced evidence relating test scores with subsequent performance in a police recruit training course, the High Court upheld the dismissal, noting that the plaintiffs did not challenge the advisability of the training course and that adequate communicative skills were essential to the completion of the program.

In a dissent joined by Justice Thurgood Marshall, Justice William Brennan noted that the Court's ruling did not alter the test validation standards in Title VII cases, standards that he thought should also have been applied in this case.

IV. *STATE OF CONNECTICUT v. TEAL*[4]

The 1978 Uniform Guidelines on Employee Selection Procedures adopted a "bottom-line" approach to identifying adverse impact. In general, if the total selection process did not have adverse impact against any protected groups, then the individual components of the selection process did not have to be individually evaluated. Thus, a component of the selection process (e.g., a test) which had adverse impact against blacks could be compensated for by another component (e.g., an interview) in which blacks passed at a higher rate than whites, resulting in the selection of approximately equal selection rates for blacks and whites. The bottom-line concept was not presented as a legal interpretation of Title VII, but rather as a mechanism to be used by the regulatory agencies in making prosecutorial decisions. In *Connecticut* v. *Teal* the question was whether showing that an overall selection process favored blacks constituted a defense against a charge of discrimination based on one component of the selection process which disqualified blacks at a higher rate than whites.

Four black employees of the state of Connecticut had been provisionally appointed to the position of welfare eligibility supervisor. To receive a permanent appointment to the position, they had to go through a formal selection procedure. The first step was a written test, which was passed by 54 percent of the black applicants and nearly 80 percent of the white applicants. Those passing the test were placed on an eligibility list, and past performance, supervisory recommendations, and seniority were used in making final selection decisions. Overall, 22.9 percent of the black applicants and 13.5 percent of the white applicants were promoted. The four

---

[4] This summary was prepared by the authors, as a *Monthly Labor Review* summary was not available.

blacks failed the test and filed suit, claiming that the test had adverse impact; the state responded that the fact that the overall procedure was more favorable to blacks than whites was a sufficient defense against the claim. The district court held that the bottom line figures favoring blacks were a sufficient defense; the court of appeals reversed this, noting that since the test served as a barrier to minority employment it must be shown to be job related.

The Supreme Court ruled in favor of the four black employees. According to the court, the principal focus of Title VII is the protection of the individual employee rather than the minority groups as a whole. The court stated that an employer may not discriminate against some employees on the basis of race simply because other members of the same group are treated favorably. The fact that other blacks received promotions is no consolation to the individual black rejected due to a failing score on a test which had not been shown to be job related. The test is being "used to discriminate," under the meaning of Title VII, despite the employer's effort to compensate for its effect.

Four justices dissented, arguing that while it is clearly appropriate to focus on discrimination against individuals in differential treatment cases (i.e., situations in which different standards are applied to members of one group than to members of another), the nature of disparate or adverse impact cases requires a focus on groups rather than individuals. Since group statistics (e.g., passing rates) are used as the basis for the complaint, group statistics should also be available as a defense. The dissenting opinion speculates that the majority decision may force employers either to eliminate tests and adopt quota hiring, or attempt to validate all testing procedures.

The implications of this June 1982 decision are not yet clear. The alternatives presented in the dissent—abandon testing or validate all tests—certainly do not represent the full range of options. One common response to the decision is the recommendation that employers move away from sequential multistage selection in which some applicants are rejected at each stage of the process, and instead simply combine information from all components of the selection process and make one final selection decision rather than a series of intermediate decisions, each of which is open to scrutiny.

V. McDONALD v. SANTA FE TRAIL TRANSPORTATION COMPANY[5]

[This decision] resolved the long-debated issue of whether the Civil Rights Acts of 1866 and 1964 protect whites as well as blacks and others from racial discrimination. Although the Equal Employment Opportunity Commission and courts interpreting Title VII of the 1964 act have sometimes stated that it applies to all races, a few cases have suggested otherwise. And the issue with respect to the 1866 act has been even more confused, for a key provision of that act provides that "all persons . . . shall have the same right . . . to make and enforce contracts . . . . as is enjoyed by white citizens." Some courts have concluded that this provision does not grant anything to whites. The Supreme Court disagreed. . . .

The issue arose in connection with Santa Fe Trail Transportation Co.'s discipline of three employees, two white and one black, for allegedly misappropriating 60 gallons of antifreeze. Santa Fe fired the white workers but not the black, and the discharged employees charged that their treatment violated both Title VII and the 1866 act.

In accordance with the 1973 case of *McDonnell Douglas Corp. v. Green*, the Supreme Court stated that although the em-

---

[5] Written by Craig E. Polhemus, November 1976, p. 53.

ployer was not required to employ workers who had participated in illegal activity, neither did that illegality shield the employer from the civil rights acts.

In determining what the civil rights acts require, the High Court unanimously held that the language and legislative history of Title VII unambiguously indicated that it was intended to protect whites as well as others from employment discrimination based on race. Although the legislative history of the 1866 act was (like its language) less clear, the Court also ruled that the rights of whites were guaranteed by that act.

VI. *STEELWORKERS* v. *WEBER*[6]

Voluntary affirmative action programs that utilize quotas to eliminate racial imbalances in "traditionally segregated job categories" are permissible under Title VII of the 1964 Civil Rights Act. . . . A 5-to-2 majority rejected arguments that the law prohibited such programs because, by using quotas, they discriminate on the basis of race. Instead, the Court reasoned that the legislative history of Title VII and the historical context in which the act arose "make clear that an interpretation . . . that forbade all race-conscious affirmative action would 'bring about an end completely at variance with the purpose of the statute' and must be rejected. . . ."

The voluntary plan in question, designed in 1974 by the United Steelworkers and Kaiser Aluminum, provided that half of all entrants in a craft training program be black. The plan was to remain in effect until the percentage of black craftworkers (1.83 percent in 1974) approximated the percentage of blacks in the local labor market (39 percent in 1974). During 1974, seven blacks and six whites were selected as craft trainees. The most junior black se-

---

[6] Written by Gregory J. Mounts, August 1979, pp. 56–57.

lected had less seniority than several white production workers not selected; one of these workers, Brian Weber, filed suit claiming a violation of Title VII.

Writing for the Court, Justice William Brennan emphasized the narrowness of the case: "The only question before us is the narrow statutory issue of whether Title VII *forbids* private employers and unions from voluntarily agreeing upon bona fide affirmative action plans that accord racial preferences in the manner and for the purpose provided in the Kaiser–USWA plan."

Subsections 703(a) and (d) of Title VII make it unlawful to "discriminate . . . because of . . . race" in hiring and in the selection of apprentices for training programs. Weber claimed that this language, read in the context of a 1976 Supreme Court ruling that "Title VII protects whites as well as blacks from certain forms of racial discrimination," prohibited the Kaiser–USWA plan.

Brennan acknowledged that Weber's argument "is not without force. But," he continued, "it overlooks the significance of the fact that the Kaiser–USWA plan is an affirmative action plan voluntarily adopted by private parties to eliminate traditional patterns of racial segregation. In this context, respondent's reliance upon a literal construction of §§703(a) and (d) and upon [our earlier ruling] is misplaced. It is a 'familiar rule that a thing may be within the letter of the statute and yet not within the statute, because not within its spirit, nor within the intention of its makers.' "

Brennan turned to the legislative history and found that "Congress' primary concern" in enacting the prohibition against racial discrimination in Title VII was with "the plight of the Negro in our economy." He cited the House Report which suggested that the law ". . . will create an atmosphere conducive to voluntary or local resolution of other forms of discrimination." He concluded that Congress "did not intend wholly to prohibit private and voluntary affirmative action efforts. . . ."

Brennan also found support for his view in the language and history of Section 703 (j) of Title VII. Congress wrote that nothing contained in Title VII "shall be interpreted to *require* any employer . . . to grant preferential treatment . . . to any group because of the race . . . of such . . . group." Brennan reasoned that the lawmakers could have substituted *permit* for *require* if they had intended to outlaw all voluntary race-conscious affirmative action.

Although the Court's decision removed much of the uncertainty surrounding the use of racial goals and quotas in voluntary affirmative action plans, the majority declined to expand its ruling:

> We need not today define in detail the line of demarcation between permissible and impermissible affirmative action plans. It suffices to hold that the challenged Kaiser–USWA affirmative action plan falls on the permissible side of the line. The purposes of the plan mirror those of the statute. Both were designed to break down old patterns of racial segregation and hierarchy. Both were structured to "open employment opportunities for Negroes in occupations which have traditionally been closed to them."

In dissent, Chief Justice Warren Burger complained that the majority ruling, through "intellectually dishonest means," does "precisely what both . . . sponsors and opponents agreed the statute was *not* intended to do." It illustrates, Burger noted, the old adage that "hard cases make bad law."

Justice William Rehnquist, also in dissent, scored the "Orwellian" tone of the ruling:

> Whether described as "benign discrimination" or "affirmative action," the racial quota is nonetheless a creator of castes, a two-edged sword that must demean one in order to prefer another. In passing Title VII, Congress outlawed *all* discrimina-

tion, recognizing that no discrimination based on race is benign, that no action disadvantaging a person because of his color is affirmative. With today's holding, the Court introduces into Title VII a tolerance for the very evil that the law was intended to eradicate, without offering a clue as to what the limits on that tolerance may be. We are simply told that Kaiser's racially discriminatory admission quota "falls on the permissible side of the line." By going not merely *beyond,* but directly *against* Title VII's language and legislative history, the Court has sown the wind. Later courts will face the impossible task of reaping the whirlwind.

VII. *CITY OF LOS ANGELES* v. *MANHART*[7]

It is well established that women, on average, live longer than men. As a result, individual women have been required to make greater contributions than men to employer-managed pension plans. Since the 1840's, employers have justified this arrangement by citing the greater expense of providing a pension for the average woman.

The Supreme Court recently ended this practice, ruling 6 to 2 that, when an employer's monthly pension benefits for men and women are equal, it is unlawful sex discrimination under Title VII of the 1964 Civil Rights Act to charge women higher premiums.

Writing for the Court, Justice John Paul Stevens emphasized that Title VII is concerned with the rights of individuals:

> Even if the statutory language were less clear, the basic policy of the statute requires that we focus on fairness to individuals rather than fairness to classes. Practices which classify employees in terms of religion, race, or sex tend to preserve traditional assumptions about groups rather than thoughtful scrutiny of individuals. The generalization involved

---

[7] Written by Gregory J. Mounts, July 1978, p. 39.

in this case illustrates the point. Separate mortality tables are easily interpreted as reflecting innate differences between the sexes; but a significant part of the longevity differential may be explained by the social fact that men are heavier smokers than women.

. . . An employment practice which requires 2,000 individuals to contribute more money into a fund than 10,000 other employees simply because each of them is a woman, rather than a man, is in direct conflict with both the language and the policy of the Act.

The case involved the 12,000 employees of the Los Angeles Department of Water and Power. Like many other public employers, the Department managed its own pension fund and required all employees to participate. Women were required to make monthly contributions that were 14.84 percent higher than comparable men employees.

While the women employees' suit was pending, the California Legislature enacted a law prohibiting certain municipal agencies from requiring higher pension fund contributions from women than from men. The Department amended its plan in 1975, but the litigation continued because the women sought monetary recovery for the higher premium they had paid. The district court ordered a refund of all excess contributions made between the applicability of Title VII (in 1972) and the date the plan was amended; the Ninth Circuit affirmed.

The Supreme Court struck down the lower court's award of retroactive relief, indicating that, although there is still a strong presumption in favor of such relief in Title VII cases, the nature of *Manhart* required a different conclusion. The Court noted that a change in rules affecting insurance and pension plans can have an enormous impact on the entire economy because of the large sums of money involved. Consequently, the rules "should not be applied retroactively unless the legislature has plainly commanded that result," the majority declared. The Court was also concerned that a monetary award "could be devastating for a pension fund."

Reading 9

Affirmative Action in Employment: From Equal Opportunity to Statistical Parity*

NATHAN GLAZER

. . . One place to begin is with the Civil Rights Act of 1964. In the wake of the assassination of President Kennedy and the harrowing and violent resistance in

* Excerpted from Nathan Glazer, *Affirmative Discrimination: Ethnic Inequality and Public Policy* (New York: Basic Books, 1975), pp. 43–59. Copyright © 1975 by Nathan Glazer. Reprinted by permission of Basic Books, Inc., Publishers, New York.

the South to the exercise of simple political rights by blacks, the nation decided, in an act of sweeping power, to finally fulfill the 100-year-old promise of the Emancipation Proclamation. The Act dealt with the right to vote (Title I), to use places of public accommodation (Title II), with the desegregation of public facilities (Title III), with the desegregation of public education (Title IV), with the expansion of the powers of the Commission on Civil Rights (Title V), with nondiscrimination in Federally assisted programs (Title VI), and, most significantly for employment discrimination, with equal employment opportunity (Title VII). The Act could only be read as instituting into law Judge Harlan's famous dissent in *Plessy* v. *Ferguson:* "Our Constitution is color-blind." Again and again, one could read the sonorous phrases: no discrimination or segregation "on the ground of race, color, religion, or national origin" (Titles II and VI), "on account of his race, color, religion, or national origin" (Title III), "by reason of race, color, religion, or national origin" (Title IV), "because of such individual's color, religion, sex, or national origin" (Title VII). Following the pattern of treatment of ethnic differences that had emerged from American experience, as described in Chapter I, the Act was understood as granting not *group* rights but *individual* rights. Two provisions, among others, were inserted in Title VII to protect individual rights:

> 703(h) . . . it shall not be an unlawful employment practice . . . for an employer to give and act upon the results of any professionally developed ability test provided that such test, its administration or action upon the results is not designed, intended or used to discriminate because of race, color, religion, sex or national origin. . . .
>
> 703(j) Nothing contained in this title shall be interpreted to require any employer . . . to grant preferential treatment to any individual or to any group because of the race, color, religion, sex, or national origin of such individual or group on account of an imbalance which may exist with respect to the total number or percentage of persons of any race, color, religion, sex, or national origin employed by any employer. . . .

And the statements made at the time of the debate on the bill to establish the legislative history and Congressional intent seemed clear and unambiguous:

The Civil Rights Act's floor managers in the Senate, Senator Joseph Clark of Pennsylvania and Senator Clifford Case of New Jersey, stated that ". . . It must be emphasized that discrimination is prohibited as to any individual. . . . The question in each case is whether that individual was discriminated against." [110 Cong. Rec. 7213.] Senator Clark responded to the objection that "the bill would require employers to establish quotas for non-whites" with the flat statement "Quotas are themselves discriminatory." [110 Cong. Rec. 7218.] Senator Humphrey, the majority whip, noted that "The proponents of the bill have carefully stated on numerous occasions that Title VII does not require an employer to achieve any sort of racial balance in his work force by giving preferential treatment to any individual or group." [110 Cong. Rec. 12723.] Senator Williams, explaining Sec. 703(j), stated that it would "specifically prohibit the Attorney General, or any agency of the government, from requiring employment to be on the basis of racial or religious quotas. Under [this provision] an employer with only white employees could continue to have only the best qualified persons even if they were all white." [110 Cong. Rec. 14331.]

The will of Congress and its laws must be interpreted both by administrative agencies issuing guidelines and by courts interpreting legislation and guidelines since litigation inevitably accompanies all new legislation. Thus, one may think of the law as not only the specific law as passed by Congress but as part of a troika, with the agency interpretations on the one hand and the legal interpretations on the other. The law, apparently, generally comes off a bad third in this troika, because, after all, the congressmen do not enforce the law—the agencies do—and the congressmen do not interpret the law, unless they are willing to undergo the elaborate ordeal of legislation again—the courts do.

In the case of minority employment, there was another and independent source of law: Executive orders, which go as far back as No. 8802, in 1941, issued by President Roosevelt, and ordering an end of discrimination in defense industries. Under Presidents Truman and Eisenhower, further executive orders were issued, extending the ban on discrimination by government contractors and setting up various bodies to oversee and enforce it. Executive Order No. 10925, issued by President Kennedy, for the first time used the term "affirmative action." Contractors were now to act affirmatively to recruit workers on a nondiscriminatory basis. But the capstone of the structure is Executive Order No. 11246, issued by President Johnson in 1965. "Affirmative action" was not further defined. Presumably, it meant such things as advertising the fact, seeking out qualified applicants from sources where they might be found, and the like. Executive orders, just as laws, breed their attendant throng of regulations and guidelines, which the contractor in search of government business must attend to as carefully as (indeed, more carefully than) the executive order itself. By the time we reach guidelines, the "Executive," in the form of the President and his advisors, is far away: The permanent or semipermanent officials engaged in the program of contract compliance are the chief formulators of guidelines.

In May 1968, the Department of Labor, in which the Office of Federal Contract Compliance is housed, issued further regulations expanding upon this modest phrase, "affirmative action." A "written affirmative action compliance program" is required from every major contractor and subcontractor (more than 50 employees and a contract of $50,000 or more).

A necessary prerequisite to the development of a satisfactory affirmative action program is the identification and analysis of problem areas inherent in minority employment and an evaluation of opportunities for utilization of minority group personnel. The contractor's program shall provide in detail for specific steps to guarantee equal employment opportunity keyed to the problems and needs of members of minority groups, including, when there are deficiencies, the development of specific goals and time-tables for the prompt achievement of full and equal employment opportunity. Each contractor shall include in his affirmative action compliance program a table of job classifications. . . . The evaluation of utilization of minority group personnel shall include . . . an analysis of minority group representation in all categories. [Title 41, C.F.R., 60–1.40]

It was not at all clear at this point that a "deficiency" might be an insufficient number of workers at some level of employment of some specific group compared with the number of that group in the population. "Utilization" was used but not "underutilization," and "specific goals and timetables" were required but only for the "prompt achievement of full and equal employment *opportunity*" (my italics). The shift from "opportunity" to "representation" had not yet occurred, nor was it clearly stated that only some groups were the specific object of government concern. But there was a requirement that the contractor was to file "complete and accurate reports on Standard Form 100 (EEO–1)" (60–1.7[a]), and that form, required by the Equal Opportunity Commission from employers covered by Title VII of the Civil Rights Act and government contractors and subcontractors covered by Executive Order No. 11246, did require a report on employees who were "Negroes," "Orientals," "American Indians," and "Spanish Americans." "Spanish Americans" were defined as those of "Latin American, Mexican, Puerto Rican, or Spanish origin." "Oriental" was not defined. (The EEO–1 form later changed from the usage "Spanish American" to "Spanish surnamed American.") On the basis of such a report, a "deficiency" in numbers employed in given categories might be found, but the May 1968 guidelines nowhere suggest that this is a breach of affirmative action requirements.

The next set of guidelines, dated February 5, 1970, requires more from government contractors in the way of affirmative action:

> An affirmative action program is a set of specific and result-oriented procedures to which a contractor commits himself to apply every good faith. The objective of these procedures plus such efforts is equal employment opportunity. Procedures without effort to make them work are meaningless; and effort, undirected by specific and meaningful procedures, is inadequate. [41, C.F.R., 60–2.10.]

The meaning of this new language is not completely clear, though ominous. "Opportunity," it seems, is being redefined as "result." But the specific definition of a "utilization analysis" in the guidelines, while expanded, is still oriented to "opportunity."

It is in the next set of guidelines, of December 4, 1971, that we have the creation, for purposes of Federal contract compliance, of a special category of "affected class," and a special requirement for determining whether the members of this class are "underutilized," and requirements for measures that will correct this "underutilization." The specific language involved in this order, the basis of affirmative action as required by the government from just about every substantial employer in the country, reflects the government's understanding of the causes of the differential distribution of ethnic groups in employment, and its expectations of what the pattern of employment in a nondiscriminatory society would look like.

Repeating the language of the earlier 1970 guidelines, that ". . . procedures without effort to make them work are meaningless; and effort, undirected by adequate and specific procedures, is inadequate, . . ." it now continues:

> An acceptable affirmative action program must include an analysis of areas within which the contractor is deficient in the utilization of minority groups and women, and further, goals and timetables to which the contractor's good faith efforts must be directed to correct the deficiencies and, thus to increase materially the utilization of minorities and women, at all levels and in all segments of his work force where deficiencies exist.

The point of this pronouncement is that equal employment opportunity must now be redefined, against its plain meaning, not as opportunity, but result. "Procedure" and "effort" alike are inadequate without "result." The employer is required to undertake

> . . . an analysis of all major classifications at the facility, with explanations if minorities or women are currently being underutilized in any one or more job classifications. . . . "Underutilization" is defined as having fewer minorities or women in a particular job classification than would reasonably be expected by their availability. . . . [41, C.F.R., 60–2.11.]

Some guidance is given on how to determine "underutilization" (60–2.11): In effect, the census is now to determine what is discrimination and what is affirmative action. That all this is still called "equal employment opportunity" is simply another example of the misnaming of reality in an age in which words are easily distorted into their opposites. This is the last in the series of guidelines under which the Office of Federal Contract Compliance and its multifarious branches in every agency of the executive establishment operate, and the law of the land.

Legally, the Equal Employment Opportunity Commission operates under greater restrictions than the Office of Federal Contract Compliance: After all, there is still the specific ban in the law which created it against the use of any statistics of "imbalance" to require preferential treatment.

However, with the assistance of the courts, simple imbalance—under which the EEOC can require nothing—can be redefined as itself a showing of discrimination, which permits the EEOC or the Department of Justice to require everything: back pay for classes of individuals who themselves have suffered no discrimination, the setting of quotas for employment of individuals of specific groups for given jobs, and the like. The question one may ask is: When does imbalance, under which one can do nothing, become discrimination, on the basis of which one can do everything?

The development of the law here, as interpreted by the courts, has been deeply affected by the dogged resistance by Southern states and localities to the granting of political rights to blacks and to the dismantling of the dual school system. The South was endlessly ingenious in devising regulations for registration that were on their face fair but that were used in many jurisdictions to deny the blacks the right to vote. In the Voting Rights Act of 1965, all subterfuges were finally thrust aside under a simple statistical rule: If 50 percent of the persons of voting age, according to the census, had not voted, radical and drastic Federal intervention and correction could now be undertaken. It was under this drastic statistical rule that the barriers to Negro voting in the South finally fell, and the political situation of the Negro was transformed. Similarly, in 1968, the Supreme Court, tired of endless delay in desegregating dual school systems, accepted a statistical rule for desegregation of schools, under which "freedom of choice" was outlawed. If too few blacks and whites took advantage of freedom of choice to shift their schools, that demonstrated unconstitutional discrimination had not been overcome, period.

Thus it was relatively easy for a statistical rule to develop in discrimination cases brought under the Civil Rights Act of 1964, for here, too, endless subterfuge was possible. Indeed, it was owing to the resistance of crafts unions to the entry of blacks that the first affirmative action programs requiring fixed statistical quotas for employment were instituted by the Federal government through its power as a Federal contractor, in the Philadelphia Plan in 1969, and many similar plans which followed. The argument could be made in the courts, and was, that either the statistical disproportion in employment was such that it served as a prima facie case of discrimination—under which the judge could impose whatever remedy seemed suitable to him, including fixed quotas for employment— or that the executive order's affirmative action provisions were not bound by the specific provision against preferential treatment on account of imbalance in the Civil Rights Act of 1964. Thus the statistical approach to proving discrimination spread from voting and the schools to jobs, even though one can, on the face of it, discern a very important distinction: Everyone, with minor exceptions, is expected to have the right to vote and is required to go to school, but jobs are based on qualifications and it is well-known that qualifications (such as education) will vary with race and ethnicity.

*   *   *   *   *

The Equal Employment Opportunity Commission, supported by the Department of Justice and the Federal courts, has carefully constrained the use of tests to the point where, in fact, hardly any test may be used without legal challenge. When the testing authorities of the Equal Employment Opportunity Commission are asked for an example of a test that will pass muster as legitimate, if blacks pass at a lower rate, the only example they seem to come up with is a typing test. Even that, we should point out, may not be used indiscriminately. One cannot, for example, require a higher level of typing than is current in a group of typists already employed.

Indeed, one would not be allowed to require a higher level of typing than that possessed by the poorest typist one has hired, if the higher level served to select one ethnic group or race more or less than another. Under this rule, one could guarantee that the level of typing would steadily decline.

The development of the law in these areas has become truly arcane as one Federal agency plunges ahead of another, and the other races to catch up, or the courts go beyond either. The effect is to steadily constrain any effort to set a higher standard of employment or, indeed, any standard, if it serves to have disproportionate impact, even a minor disproportionate impact, on the employment of some specific group. Any disproportion may trigger investigation and the application of stringent rules.

In effect, the EEOC is engaged in breaking the law under which it operates. "In 1970, a member of the EEOC staff told the *Harvard Law Review* that 'The anti-preferential provisions [of Title VII] are a big zero, a nothing, a nullity. They don't mean anything at all to us.'" Anyone studying their record hardly needs this direct confirmation.

*   *   *   *   *

The purpose of this determined and dogged resistance to any form of employment selection which leads to any but proportionate representation in a work force is simply that—to ensure proportionate representation of minority groups in a work force. "Affirmative action" originally meant that one should not only not discriminate, but inform people one did not discriminate; not only treat those who applied for jobs without discrimination, but seek out those who might not apply. This is what it apparently meant when first used in executive orders. In the Civil Rights Act of 1964, it was used to mean something else—the remedies a court could impose when some

employer was found guilty of discrimination, and they could be severe. The new concept of "affirmative action" that has since emerged and has been enforced with ever greater vigor combines both elements: It assumes that everyone is guilty of discrimination; it then imposes on every employer the remedies which in the Civil Rights Act of 1964 could only be imposed on those guilty of discrimination.

Affirmative action has developed a wonderful Catch-22 type of existence. The employer is required by the OFCC to state numerical goals and dates when he will reach them. There is no presumption of discrimination. However, if he does not reach these goals, the question will come up as to whether he has made a "good faith" effort to reach them. The test of a good faith effort has not been spelled out. From the employer's point of view, the simplest way of behaving to avoid the severe penalties of loss of contracts or heavy costs in back pay (to persons selected at random who have not been discriminated against, to boot), such as have already been imposed on AT&T and other employers, is simply to meet the goals.

How the EEOC is likely to look upon a failure to meet the "goals" that have been set (and that the employer must set) is grimly set forth in the *7th Annual Report:*

> As the Commission stated in Decision No. 72–0265, Title VII imposes an affirmative duty on employers and unions to end the chilling effects of past discrimination and that a continuing lack of Negro applicants for once all-white jobs only indicated that, "The effectiveness, thoroughness, and frequency of whatever efforts the respondent was making to inform Negroes that it no longer discriminates against them fall short of what is necessary."

There is a simple solution to Catch-22: proportional hiring, quotas; and every em-

ployer worth his salt knows that is the solution that the EEOC and the OFCC and the
rest of the agencies are urging upon him,

while they simultaneously explain they
have nothing of the sort in mind.

*   *   *   *   *

GUIDELINES ON EMPLOYEE SELECTION PROCEDURES

The previously cited Tower amendment to Title VII, which permits the
use of professionally developed ability tests which are not designed, intended, or used to discriminate, is the only guidance provided by Title VII
itself as to what selection practices are or are not permissable under the law.
Consequently, both the EEOC and other agencies have issued interpretive
guidelines on selection procedures. These guidelines have a long and interesting history: prior to the adoption of the Uniform Guidelines on Employee Selection Procedures by the EEOC, the Department of Justice and
Labor, the U.S. Civil Service Commission, and the Civil Rights Commission
in 1978, employers could find themselves subject to two or more contradictory sets of guidelines. A review of the various early guidelines will not be
undertaken here, as they are now primarily of historical interest. Gorham
(1977) provides an insightful review of the process leading up to the adoption of the Uniform Guidelines.

A brief summary of the major provisions of the Uniform Guidelines
follows. This is no substitute for an in-depth examination of the guidelines,
but rather is intended as an introduction prior to thorough study:

1. The guidelines apply to any employer subject to Title VII or Executive
   Order 11246.
2. The term *test* in the Tower amendment is broadly interpreted as including any selection procedure, formal or informal.
3. Any procedure having adverse impact is discriminatory unless justified.
   Adverse impact is defined as a selection rate for any protected group
   which is less than four fifths of the rate for the group with the highest
   rate.
4. In general, adverse impact computations are made for the total selection process, rather than for each component of the process. If bottom-
   line adverse impact is found, each component of the selection process
   should be examined.
5. Applicant flow records must be kept for each job in order that adverse
   impact computations can be made for males, females, blacks, whites,
   American Indians, Asians, and Hispanics. Failure to keep these records
   will result in a presumption of adverse impact.
6. Validation of selection procedures is required only if adverse impact is
   found. Changing the selection procedure to eliminate adverse impact is
   encouraged; this eliminates the need for validation.
7. Criterion-related, content, and construct validity are acceptable methods, provided that detailed technical requirements for studies of each
   type are met. These technical standards make up the bulk of the guidelines.

8. Validation alone is not adequate justification for using a selection procedure with adverse impact; the employer is also responsible for demonstrating that alternative procedures with equal validity and less adverse impact are not available.

9. Voluntary affirmative action programs are encouraged. Sharf (1979) argues forcefully that the Uniform Guidelines do not represent standards by which employers can establish the job relatedness of their selection procedures but rather constitute a mechanism to force employers to adopt a race and sex-conscious proportional hiring system. Among his arguments are the following:

   a. The validation standards are so stringent that even the largest employers would be unable to comply if the guidelines are literally applied.

   b. Although Title VII empowered the EEOC to furnish technical assistance to employers attempting to comply with the law, the EEOC and OFCCP employ a grand total of two selection professionals between them. Thus technical assistance is not provided.

   c. Even if the guidelines differ from accepted professional principles of validation, the guidelines take precedence.

   d. Despite the Supreme Court ruling in *Albemarle* v. *Moody* that it is the responsibility of the complaining party to show that other viable selection methods are available which do not have adverse impact, the guidelines place the responsibility of considering alternatives on the employer.

The enforcement agency's disdain for (and misunderstanding of) validation was made clear by former EEOC Chair Eleanor Holmes Norton (cited in Sharf, 1979):

> There is not any way in which black people tomorrow as a group are going to, no matter what kind of test you give them, score the same way that white people score. . . . I can't live with that. I think employers can. And I think test validation gives them an A–1 out. Because if you validate your tests you don't have to worry about exclusion of minorities and women any longer, you have done what it seems to me is increasingly a fairly minimal thing to do . . . [u]nless somebody pushes employers to find other ways other than tests to find qualified people. . . . But I sincerely believe that tests do not tell us very much about who is qualified to do the job. . . . If I wanted really to find out whether or not you could do the job for me, I wouldn't give you the test. I'd call around and find out about you . . . the employer community has now caught on to a nice new thing, and . . . if they continue to rely as heavily on validation they could actually undercut the purposes of Title VII. . . . Thus, I think that by giving alternatives, we relieve especially minorities of the frustration they find inevitably in taking validated tests.

In light of this overview, let us consider the complete 1978 Uniform Guidelines. It should be pointed out that a set of questions and answers intended to clarify the guidelines are available ("Questions and Answers on Uniform Guidelines . . . ," 1979).

REFERENCES

Gorham, W. A. Political, ethical, and emotional aspects of federal guidelines on employee selection procedures. In W. C. Hamner and F. L. Schmidt (Eds.), *Contemporary Problems in Personnel*. Chicago: St. Clair Press, 1977.

Questions and answers on uniform guidelines on employee selection procedures. *Federal Register*, 1979, 44, 11996–12009.

Sharf, J. L. Uniform guidelines: Competence or numbers? Unpublished manuscript, 1979.

Reading 10

Uniform Guidelines on Employee Selection Procedures*

GENERAL PRINCIPLES

SECTION 1. *Statement of purpose.*—A. *Need for uniformity—Issuing agencies.* The Federal government's need for a uniform set of principles on the question of the use of tests and other selection procedures has long been recognized. The Equal Employment Opportunity Commission, the Civil Service Commission, the Department of Labor, and the Department of Justice jointly have adopted these uniform guidelines to meet that need, and to apply the same principles to the Federal Government as are applied to other employers.

B. *Purpose of guidelines.* These guidelines incorporate a single set of principles which are designed to assist employers, labor organizations, employment agencies, and licensing and certification boards to comply with requirements of Federal law prohibiting employment practices which discriminate on grounds of race, color, religion, sex, and national origin. They are designed to provide a framework for determining the proper use of tests and other selection procedures. These guidelines do not require a user to conduct validity studies of

selection procedures where no adverse impact results. However, all users are encouraged to use selection procedures which are valid, especially users operating under merit principles.

C. *Relation to prior guidelines.* These guidelines are based upon and supersede previously issued guidelines on employee selection procedures. These guidelines have been built upon court decisions, the previously issued guidelines of the agencies, and the practical experience of the agencies, as well as the standards of the psychological profession. These guidelines are intended to be consistent with existing law.

SEC. 2. *Scope.*—A. *Application of guidelines.* These guidelines will be applied by the Equal Employment Opportunity Commission in the enforcement of title VII of the Civil Rights Act of 1964, as amended by the Equal Employment Opportunity Act of 1972 (hereinafter "Title VII"); by the Department of Labor, and the contract compliance agencies until the transfer of authority contemplated by the President's Reorganization Plan No. 1 of 1978, in the administration and enforcement of Executive Order 11246, as amended by Executive Order 11375 (hereinafter "Executive

* *Federal Register* 43, no. 166 (August 25, 1978), pp. 38295–38309.

Order 11246"); by the Civil Service Commission and other Federal agencies subject to section 717 of Title VII; by the Civil Service Commission in exercising its responsibilities toward State and local governments under section 208(b)(1) of the Intergovernmental-Personnel Act; by the Department of Justice in exercising its responsibilities under Federal law; by the Office of Revenue Sharing of the Department of the Treasury under the State and Local Fiscal Assistance Act of 1972, as amended; and by any other Federal agency which adopts them.

B. *Employment decisions.* These guidelines apply to tests and other selection procedures which are used as a basis for any employment decision. Employment decisions include but are not limited to hiring, promotion, demotion, membership (for example, in a labor organization), referral, retention, and licensing and certification, to the extent that licensing and certification may be covered by Federal equal employment opportunity law. Other selection decisions, such as selection for training or transfer, may also be considered employment decisions if they lead to any of the decisions listed above.

C. *Selection procedures.* These guidelines apply only to selection procedures which are used as a basis for making employment decisions. For example, the use of recruiting procedures designed to attract members of a particular race, sex, or ethnic group, which were previously denied employment opportunities or which are currently underutilized, may be necessary to bring an employer into compliance with Federal law, and is frequently an essential element of any effective affirmative action program; but recruitment practices are not considered by these guidelines to be selection procedures. Similarly, these guidelines do not pertain to the question of the lawfulness of a seniority system within the meaning of section 703(h), Executive Order 11246 or other provisions of Federal

law or regulation, except to the extent that such systems utilize selection procedures to determine qualifications or abilities to perform the job. Nothing in these guidelines is intended or should be interpreted as discouraging the use of a selection procedure for the purpose of determining qualifications or for the purpose of selection on the basis of relative qualifications, if the selection procedure had been validated in accord with these guidelines for each such purpose for which it is to be used.

D. *Limitations.* These guidelines apply only to persons subject to Title VII, Executive Order 11246, or other equal employment opportunity requirements of Federal law. These guidelines do not apply to responsibilities under the Age Discrimination in Employment Act of 1967, as amended, not to discriminate on the basis of age, or under sections 501, 503, and 504 of the Rehabilitation Act of 1973, not to discriminate on the basis of handicap.

E. *Indian preference not affected.* These guidelines do not restrict any obligation imposed or right granted by Federal law to users to extend a preference in employment to Indians living on or near an Indian reservation in connection with employment opportunities on or near an Indian reservation.

SEC. 3. *Discrimination defined: Relationship between use of selection procedures and discrimination.*—A. *Procedure having adverse impact constitutes discrimination unless justified.* The use of any selection procedure which has an adverse impact on the hiring, promotion, or other employment or membership opportunities of members of any race, sex, or ethnic group will be considered to be discriminatory and inconsistent with these guidelines, unless the procedure has been validated in accordance with these guidelines, or the provisions of section 6 below are satisfied.

B. *Consideration of suitable alternative selection procedures.* Where two or more selection procedures are available which serve the user's legitimate interest in efficient and trustworthy workmanship, and which are substantially equally valid for a given purpose, the user should use the procedure which has been demonstrated to have the lesser adverse impact. Accordingly, whenever a validity study is called for by these guidelines, the user should include, as a part of the validity study, an investigation of suitable alternative selection procedures and suitable alternative methods of using the selection procedure which have as little adverse impact as possible, to determine the appropriateness of using or validating them in accord with these guidelines. If a user has made a reasonable effort to become aware of such alternative procedures and validity has been demonstrated in accord with these guidelines, the use of the test or other selection procedure may continue until such time as it should reasonably be reviewed for currency. Whenever the user is shown an alternative selection procedure with evidence of less adverse impact and substantial evidence of validity for the same job in similar circumstances, the user should investigate it to determine the appropriateness of using or validating it in accord with these guidelines. This subsection is not intended to preclude the combination of procedures into a significantly more valid procedure, if the use of such a combination has been shown to be in compliance with the guidelines.

SEC. 4. *Information on impact.*—A. *Records concerning impact.* Each user should maintain and have available for inspection records or other information which will disclose the impact which its tests and other selection procedures have upon employment opportunities of persons by identifiable race, sex, or ethnic group as set forth in subparagraph B below in order to determine compliance with these guidelines. Where there are large numbers of applicants and procedures are administered frequently, such information may be retained on a sample basis, provided that the sample is appropriate in terms of the applicant population and adequate in size.

B. *Applicable race, sex, and ethnic groups for recordkeeping.* The records called for by this section are to be maintained by sex, and the following races and ethnic groups: Blacks (Negroes), American Indians (including Alaskan Natives), Asians (including Pacific Islanders), Hispanic (including persons of Mexican, Puerto Rican, Cuban, Central or South American, or other Spanish origin or culture regardless of race), whites (Caucasians) other than Hispanic, and totals. The race, sex, and ethnic classifications called for by this section are consistent with the Equal Employment Opportunity Standard Form 100, Employer Information Report EEO-1 series of reports. The user should adopt safeguards to insure that the records required by this paragraph are used for appropriate purposes such as determining adverse impact, or (where required) for developing and monitoring affirmative action programs, and that such records are not used improperly. See section 4E and 17(4), below.

C. *Evaluation of selection rates. The "bottom line."* If the information called for by sections 4A and B above shows that the total selection process for a job has an adverse impact, the individual components of the selection process should be evaluated for adverse impact. If this information shows that the total selection process does not have an adverse impact, the Federal enforcement agencies, in the exercise of their administrative and prosecutorial discretion, in usual circumstances, will not expect a user to evaluate the individual components for adverse impact, or to validate such individual components, and will not take enforcement action based upon adverse impact of any component of that process, including the separate parts of a multipart selection procedure or any separate procedure that is used as an alternative method of selection. However, in the following circumstances the Federal enforcement agencies will expect a user to evaluate the individual components for adverse impact and may, where appropriate, take enforcement action with respect to the individual components: (1) where the selection procedure is a significant factor in the continuation of patterns of assignments of incumbent employees caused by prior discriminatory employment practices, (2) where the weight of court decisions or administrative interpretations hold that a specific procedure (such as height or weight requirements or no-arrest records) is not job related in the same or similar circumstances. In unusual circumstances, other than those listed in (1) and (2) above, the Federal enforcement agencies may request a user to evaluate the individual components for adverse impact and may, where appropriate, take enforcement action with respect to the individual component.

D. *Adverse impact and the "four-fifths rule."* A selection rate for any race, sex, or ethnic group which is less than four-fifths (⁴⁄₅) (or eighty percent) of the rate for the group with the highest rate will generally be regarded by the Federal enforcement agencies as evidence of adverse impact, while a greater than four-fifths rate will generally not be regarded by Federal enforcement agencies as evidence of adverse impact. Smaller differences in selection rate may nevertheless constitute adverse impact, where they are significant in both statistical and practical terms or where a user's actions have discouraged applicants disproportionately on grounds of race, sex, or ethnic group. Greater differences in selection rate may not constitute adverse impact where the differences are based on small numbers and are not statistically significant, or where special recruiting or other programs cause the pool of minority or female candidates to be atypical of the normal pool of applicants from that group. Where the user's evidence concerning the impact of a selection procedure indicates adverse impact but is based upon numbers which are too small to be reliable, evidence concerning the impact of the procedure over a longer period of time and/or evidence concerning the impact which the selection procedure had when used in the same manner in similar circumstances elsewhere may be considered in determining adverse impact. Where the user has not maintained data on adverse impact as required by the documentation section of applicable guidelines, the Federal enforcement agencies may draw an inference of adverse impact of the selection process from the failure of the user to maintain such data, if the user has an underutilization of a group in the job category, as compared to the group's representation in the relevant labor market or, in the case of jobs filled from within, the applicable work force.

E. *Consideration of user's equal employment opportunity posture.* In carrying out their obligations, the Federal enforcement agencies will consider the general posture of the user with respect to equal employment opportunity for the job or group of jobs in question. Where a user has adopted an affirmative action program, the Federal enforcement agencies will consider the provisions of that program, including the goals and timetables which the user has adopted and the progress which the user has made in carrying out that program and in meeting the goals and timetables. While such affirmative action programs may in design and execution be race, color, sex, or ethnic conscious, selection procedures under such programs should be based upon the ability or relative ability to do the work.

SEC. 5. *General standards for validity studies.*—A. *Acceptable types of validity studies.* For the purposes of satisfying these guidelines, users may rely upon criterion-related validity studies, content validity studies or construct validity studies, in accordance with the standards set forth in the technical standards of these guidelines, section 14 below. New strategies for showing the validity of selection procedures will be evaluated as they become accepted by the psychological profession.

B. *Criterion-related, content, and construct validity.* Evidence of the validity of a test or other selection procedure by a criterion-related validity study should consist of empirical data demonstrating that the selection procedure is predictive of or significantly correlated with important elements of job performance. See section 14B below. Evidence of the validity of a test or other selection procedure by a content validity study should consist of data showing that the content of the selection procedure is representative of important aspects of performance on the job for which the candidates are to be evaluated. See section 14C below. Evidence of the validity of a test or other selection procedure through a construct validity study should consist of data showing that the procedure measures the degree to which candidates have identifiable characteristics which have been determined to be important in successful performance in the job for which the candidates are to be evaluated. See section 14D below.

C. *Guidelines are consistent with professional standards.* The provisions of these guidelines relating to validation of selection procedures are intended to be consistent with generally accepted professional standards for evaluating standardized tests and other selection procedures, such as those described in the Standards for Educational and Psychological Tests prepared by a joint committee of the American Psychological Association, the American Educational Research Association, and the National Council on Measurement in Education (American Psychological Association, Washington, D.C., 1974) (hereinafter "A.P.A. Standards") and standard textbooks and journals in the field of personnel selection.

D. *Need for documentation of validity.* For any selection procedure which is part of a selection process which has an adverse impact and which selection procedure has an adverse impact, each user should maintain and have available such documentation as is described in section 15 below.

E. *Accuracy and standardization.* Validity studies should be carried out under conditions which assure insofar as possible the adequacy and accuracy of the research and the report. Selection procedures should be administered and scored under standardized conditions.

F. *Caution against selection on basis of knowledges, skills, or ability learned in brief orientation period.* In general, users should avoid making employment decisions on the basis of measures of knowledges, skills, or abilities which are normally learned in a brief orientation period, which have an adverse impact.

G. *Method of use of selection procedures.* The evidence of both the validity and utility of a selection procedure should support the method the user chooses for operational use of the procedure, if that method of use has a greater adverse impact than another method of use. Evidence which may be sufficient to support the use of a selection procedure on a pass/fail (screening) basis may be insufficient to support the use of the same procedure on a ranking basis under these guidelines. Thus, if a user decides to use a selection procedure on a ranking basis, and that method of use has a greater adverse impact than use on an appropriate pass/fail basis (see section 5H below), the user should have sufficient evidence of validity and utility to support the use on a ranking basis. See sections 3B, 14B (5) and (6), and 14C (8) and (9).

H. *Cutoff scores.* Where cutoff scores are used, they should normally be set so as to be reasonable and consistent with normal expectations of acceptable proficiency within the work force. Where applicants are ranked on the basis of properly validated selection procedures and those applicants scoring below a higher cutoff score than appropriate in light of such expectations have little or no chance of being selected for employment, the higher cutoff score may be appropriate, but the degree of adverse impact should be considered.

I. *Use of selection procedures for higher level jobs.* If job progression structures are so established that employees will probably, within a reasonable period of time and in a majority of cases, progress to a higher level, it may be considered that the applicants are being evaluated for a job or jobs at the higher level. However, where job progression is not so nearly automatic, or the time span is such that higher level jobs or employees' potential may be expected to change in significant ways, it should be considered that applicants are being evaluated for a job at or near the entry level. A "reasonable period of time" will vary for different jobs and employment situations but will seldom be more than 5 years. Use of selection procedures to evaluate applicants for a higher level job would not be appropriate:

(1) If the majority of these remaining employed do not progress to the higher level job;

(2) If there is a reason to doubt that the higher level job will continue to require essentially similar skills during the progression period; or

(3) If the selection procedures measure knowledges, skills, or abilities required for advancement which would be expected to develop principally from the training or experience on the job.

J. *Interim use of selection procedures.* Users may continue the use of a selection procedure which is not at the moment fully supported by the required evidence of validity, provided: (1) The user has available substantial evidence of validity, and (2) the user has in progress, when technically feasible, a study which is designed to produce the additional evidence required by these guidelines within a reasonable time. If such a study is not technically feasible, see section 6B. If the study does not demonstrate validity, this provision of these guidelines for interim use shall not constitute a defense in any action, nor shall it relieve the user of any obligations arising under Federal law.

K. *Review of validity studies for currency.* Whenever validity has been shown in accord with these guidelines for the use of a particular selection procedure for a job or group of jobs, additional studies need not be performed until such time as the validity study is subject to review as provided in section 3B above. There are no absolutes in the area of determining the currency of a validity study. All circumstances concerning the study, including the validation strategy used, and changes in the relevant labor market and the job should be considered in the determination of when a validity study is outdated.

SEC. 6. *Use of selection procedures which have not been validated.*—A. *Use of alternate selection procedures to eliminate adverse impact.* A user may choose to utilize alternative selection procedures in order to eliminate adverse impact or as part of an affirmative action program. See section 13 below. Such alternative procedures should eliminate the adverse impact in the total selection process, should be lawful and should be as job related as possible.

B. *Where validity studies cannot or need not be performed.* There are circumstances in which a user cannot or need not utilize the validation techniques contemplated by these guidelines. In such circumstances, the user should utilize selection procedures which are as job related as possible and which will minimize or eliminate adverse impact, as set forth below.

(1) *Where informal or unscored procedures are used.* When an informal or unscored selection procedure which has an adverse impact is utilized, the user should eliminate the adverse impact, or modify the proce-

dure to one which is a formal, scored or quantified measure or combination of measures and then validate the procedure in accord with these guidelines, or otherwise justify continued use of the procedure in accord with Federal law.

(2) *Where formal and scored procedures are used.* When a formal and scored selection procedure is used which has an adverse impact, the validation techniques contemplated by these guidelines usually should be followed if technically feasible. Where the user cannot or need not follow the validation techniques anticipated by these guidelines, the user should either modify the procedure to eliminate adverse impact or otherwise justify continued use of the procedure in accord with Federal law.

SEC. 7. *Use of other validity studies.*—A. *Validity studies not conducted by the user.* Users may, under certain circumstances, support the use of selection procedures by validity studies conducted by other users or conducted by test publishers or distributors and described in test manuals. While publishers of selection procedures have a professional obligation to provide evidence of validity which meets generally accepted professional standards (see section 5C above), users are cautioned that they are responsible for compliance with these guidelines. Accordingly, users seeking to obtain selection procedures from publishers and distributors should be careful to determine that, in the event the user becomes subject to the validity requirements of these guidelines, the necessary information to support validity has been determined and will be made available to the user.

B. *Use of criterion-related validity evidence from other sources.* Criterion-related validity studies conducted by one test user, or described in test manuals and the professional literature, will be considered acceptable for use by another user when the following requirements are met:

(1) *Validity evidence.* Evidence from the available studies meeting the standards of section 14B below clearly demonstrates that the selection procedure is valid;

(2) *Job similarity.* The incumbents in the user's job and the incumbents in the job or group of jobs on which the validity study was conducted perform substantially the same major work behaviors, as shown by appropriate job analyses both on the job or group of jobs on which the validity study was performed and on the job for which the selection procedure is to be used; and

(3) *Fairness evidence.* The studies include a study of test fairness for each race, sex, and ethnic group which constitutes a significant factor in the borrowing user's relevant labor market for the job or jobs in question. If the studies under consideration satisfy (1) and (2) above but do not contain an investigation of test fairness, and it is not technically feasible for the borrowing user to conduct an internal study of test fairness, the borrowing user may utilize the study until studies conducted elsewhere meeting the requirements of these guidelines show test unfairness, or until such time as it becomes technically feasible to conduct an internal study of test fairness and the results of that study can be acted upon. Users obtaining selection procedures from publishers should consider, as one factor in the decision to purchase a particular selection procedure, the availability of evidence concerning test fairness.

C. *Validity evidence from multiunit study.* If validity evidence from a study covering more than one unit within an organization satisfies the requirements of section 14B below, evidence of validity specific to each unit will not be required unless there are variables which are likely to affect validity significantly.

D. *Other significant variables.* If there are variables in the other studies which are likely to affect validity significantly, the user may not rely upon such studies, but will be expected either to conduct an internal validity study or to comply with section 6 above.

SEC. 8. *Cooperative studies*—A. *Encouragement of cooperative studies*. The agencies issuing these guidelines encourage employers, labor organizations, and employment agencies to cooperate in research, development, search for lawful alternatives, and validity studies in order to achieve procedures which are consistent with these guidelines.

B. *Standards for use of cooperative studies*. If validity evidence from a cooperative study satisfies the requirements of section 14 below, evidence of validity specific to each user will not be required unless there are variables in the user's situation which are likely to affect validity significantly.

SEC. 9. *No assumption of validity.*—A. *Unacceptable substitutes for evidence of validity*. Under no circumstances will the general reputation of a test or other selection procedures, its author or its publisher, or casual reports of its validity be accepted in lieu of evidence of validity. Specifically ruled out are: assumptions of validity based on a procedure's name or descriptive labels; all forms of promotional literature; data bearing on the frequency of a procedure's usage; testimonial statements and credentials of sellers, users, or consultants; and other nonempirical or anecdotal accounts of selection practices or selection outcomes.

B. *Encouragement of professional supervision*. Professional supervision of selection activities is encouraged but is not a substitute for documented evidence of validity. The enforcement agencies will take into account the fact that a thorough job analysis was conducted and that careful development and use of a selection procedure in accordance with professional standards enhance the probability that the selection procedure is valid for the job.

SEC. 10. *Employment agencies and employment services.*—A. *Where selection procedures are devised by agency*. An employment agency, including private employment agencies and State employment agencies, which agrees to a request by an employer or labor organization to devise and utilize a selection procedure should follow the standards in these guidelines for determining adverse impact. If adverse impact exists the agency should comply with these guidelines. An employment agency is not relieved of its obligation herein because the user did not request such validation or has requested the use of some lesser standard of validation than is provided in these guidelines. The use of an employment agency does not relieve an employer or labor organization or other user of its responsibilities under Federal law to provide equal employment opportunity or its obligations as a user under these guidelines.

B. *Where selection procedures are devised elsewhere*. Where an employment agency or service is requested to administer a selection procedure which has been devised elsewhere and to make referrals pursuant to the results, the employment agency or service should maintain and have available evidence of the impact of the selection and referral procedures which it administers. If adverse impact results the agency or service should comply with these guidelines. If the agency or service seeks to comply with these guidelines by reliance upon validity studies or other data in the possession of the employer, it should obtain and have available such information.

SEC. 11. *Disparate treatment*. The principles of disparate or unequal treatment must be distinguished from the concepts of validation. A selection procedure—even though validated against job performance in accordance with these guidelines—cannot be imposed upon members of a race, sex, or ethnic group where other employees, applicants, or members have not been subjected to that standard. Disparate treatment occurs where members of a race, sex, or ethnic group have been denied the same employment, promotion, membership, or other employment opportunities as have been available to other employees or applicants. Those employees or applicants who have been denied equal treatment, because of prior discriminatory practices or policies, must at least be afforded the same opportunities as had existed for other employees or applicants during the period of discrimination. Thus, the persons who were in the class of persons discriminated against during the period the user followed the discriminatory practices should be allowed the opportunity to qualify under less stringent selection procedures previously followed, unless the user demonstrates that the increased standards are required by business necessity. This section does not prohibit a user who has not previously followed merit standards from adopting merit standards which are in compliance with these guidelines; nor does it preclude a user who has previously used invalid or unvalidated selection procedures from developing and using procedures which are in accord with these guidelines.

SEC. 12. *Retesting of applicants.* Users should provide a reasonable opportunity for retesting and reconsideration. Where examinations are administered periodically with public notice, such reasonable opportunity exists, unless persons who have previously been tested are precluded from retesting. The user may however take reasonable steps to preserve the security of its procedures.

SEC. 13. *Affirmative action.*—A. *Affirmative action obligations.* The use of selection procedures which have been validated pursuant to these guidelines does not relieve users of any obligations they may have to undertake affirmative action to assure equal employment opportunity. Nothing in these guidelines is intended to preclude the use of lawful selection procedures which assist in remedying the effects of prior discriminatory practices, or the achievement of affirmative action objectives.

B. *Encouragement of voluntary affirmative action programs.* These guidelines are also intended to encourage the adoption and implementation of voluntary affirmative action programs by users who have no obligation under Federal law to adopt them; but are not intended to impose any new obligations in that regard. The agencies issuing and endorsing these guidelines endorse for all private employers and reaffirm for all governmental employers the Equal Employment Opportunity Coordinating Council's "Policy Statement on Affirmative Action Programs for State and Local Government Agencies" (41 FR 38814, September 13, 1976). That policy statement is attached hereto as appendix, section 17.

TECHNICAL STANDARDS

SEC. 14. *Technical standards for validity studies.* The following minimum standards, as applicable, should be met in conducting a validity study. Nothing in these guidelines is intended to preclude the development and use of other professionally acceptable techniques with respect to validation of selection procedures. Where it is not technically feasible for a user to conduct a validity study, the user has the obligation otherwise to comply with these guidelines. See sections 6 and 7 above.

A. *Validity studies should be based on review of information about the job.* Any validity study should be based upon a review of information about the job for which the selection procedure is to be used. The review should include a job analysis except as provided in section 14B(3) below with respect to criterion-related validity. Any method of job analysis may be used if it provides the information required for the specific validation strategy used.

B. *Technical standards for criterion-related validity studies.*—(1) *Technical feasibility.* Users choosing to validate a selection procedure by a criterion-related validity strategy should determine whether it is technically feasible (as defined in section 16) to conduct such a study in the particular employment context. The determination of the number of persons necessary to permit the conduct of a meaningful criterion-related study should be made by the user on the basis of all relevant information concerning the selection procedure, the potential sample and the employment situation. Where appropriate, jobs with substantially the same major work behaviors may be grouped together for validity studies, in order to obtain an adequate sample. These guidelines do not require a user to hire or promote persons for the purpose of making it possible to conduct a criterion-related study.

(2) *Analysis of the job.* There should be a review of job information to determine measures of work behavior(s) or performance that are relevant to the job or group of jobs in question. These measures or criteria are relevant to the extent that they represent critical or important job duties, work behaviors or work outcomes as developed from the review of job information. The possibility of bias should be considered both in selection of the criterion measures and their application. In view of the possibility of bias in subjective evaluations, supervisory rating techniques and instructions to raters should be carefully developed. All criterion measures and the methods for gathering data need to be examined for freedom from factors which would unfairly alter scores of members of any group. The relevance of criteria and their freedom from bias are of particular concern when there are significant differences in measures of job performance for different groups.

(3) *Criterion measures.* Proper safeguards should be taken to insure that scores on selection procedures do not enter into any judgments of employee adequacy that are to be used as criterion measures. Whatever criteria are used should represent important or critical work behavior(s) or work

outcomes. Certain criteria may be used without a full job analysis if the user can show the importance of the criteria to the particular employment context. These criteria include but are not limited to production rate, error rate, tardiness, absenteeism, and length of service. A standardized rating of overall work performance may be used where a study of the job shows that it is an appropriate criterion. Where performance in training is used as a criterion, success in training should be properly measured and the relevance of the training should be shown either through a comparison of the content of the training program with the critical or important work behavior(s) of the job(s), or through a demonstration of the relationship between measures of performance in training and measures of job performance. Measures of relative success in training include but are not limited to instructor evaluations, performance samples, or tests. Criterion measures consisting of paper and pencil tests will be closely reviewed for job relevance.

(4) *Representativeness of the sample.* Whether the study is predictive or concurrent, the sample subjects should insofar as feasible be representative of the candidates normally available in the relevant labor market for the job or group of jobs in question, and should insofar as feasible include the races, sexes, and ethnic groups normally available in the relevant job market. In determining the representativeness of the sample in a concurrent validity study, the user should take into account the extent to which the specific knowledges or skills which are the primary focus of the test are those which employees learn on the job.

Where samples are combined or compared, attention should be given to see that such samples are comparable in terms of the actual job they perform, the length of time on the job where time on the job is likely to affect performance, and other relevant factors likely to affect validity differences; or that these factors are included in the design of the study and their effects identified.

(5) *Statistical relationships.* The degree of relationship between selection procedure scores and criterion measures should be examined and computed, using professionally acceptable statistical procedures. Generally, a selection procedure is considered related to the criterion, for the purposes of these guidelines, when the relationship between performance on the procedure and performance on the criterion measure is statistically significant at the 0.05 level of significance, which means that it is sufficiently high as to have a probability of no more than one (1) in twenty (20) to have occurred by chance. Absence of a statistically significant relationship between a selection procedure and job performance should not necessarily discourage other investigations of the validity of that selection procedure.

(6) *Operational use of selection procedures.* Users should evaluate each selection procedure to assure that it is appropriate for operational use, including establishment of cutoff scores or rank ordering. Generally, if other factors remain the same, the greater the magnitude of the relationship (e.g., correlation coefficient) between performance on a selection procedure and one or more criteria of performance on the job, and the greater the importance and number of aspects of job performance covered by the criteria, the more likely it is that the procedure will be appropriate for use. Reliance upon a selection procedure which is significantly related to a criterion measure, but which is based upon a study involving a large number of subjects and has a low correlation coefficient will be subject to close review if it has a large adverse impact. Sole reliance upon a single selection instrument which is related to only one of many job duties or aspects of job performance will also be subject to close review. The appropriateness of a selection procedure is best evaluated in each particular situation and there are no minimum correlation coefficients applicable to all employment situations. In determining whether a selection procedure is appropriate for operational use the following considerations should also be taken into account: The degree of adverse impact of the procedure, the availability of other selection procedures of greater or substantially equal validity.

(7) *Overstatement of validity findings.* Users should avoid reliance upon techniques which tend to overestimate validity findings as a result of capitalization on chance unless an appropriate safeguard is taken. Reliance upon a few selection procedures or criteria of successful job performance when many selection procedures or criteria of performance have been studied, or the use of optimal statistical weights for selection procedures computed in one sample, are techniques which tend to inflate validity estimates as a result of chance. Use of a large sample is one safeguard: cross-validation is another.

(8) *Fairness.* This section generally calls for studies of unfairness where technically feasible. The concept of fairness or unfairness of selection procedures is a developing concept. In addition, fairness studies generally require substantial numbers of employees in the job or group of jobs being studied. For these reasons, the Federal enforcement agencies recognize that the obligation to conduct studies of fairness imposed by the guidelines generally will be upon users or groups of users with a large number of persons in a job class, or test developers; and that small users utilizing their own selection procedures will generally not be obligated to conduct such studies because it will be technically infeasible for them to do so.

(a) *Unfairness defined.* When members of one race, sex, or ethnic group characteristically obtain lower scores on a selection procedure than members of another group, and the differences in scores are not reflected in differences in a measure of job performance, use of the selection procedure may unfairly deny opportunities to members of the group that obtains the lower scores.

(b) *Investigation of fairness.* Where a selection procedure results in an adverse impact on a race, sex, or ethnic group identified in accordance with the classifications set forth in section 4 above and that group is a significant factor in the relevant labor market, the user generally should investigate the possible existence of unfairness for that group if it is technically feasible to do so. The greater the severity of the adverse impact on a group, the greater the need to investigate the possible existence of unfairness. Where the weight of evidence from other studies shows that the selection procedure predicts fairly for the group in question and for the same or similar jobs, such evidence may be relied on in connection with the selection procedure at issue.

(c) *General considerations in fairness investigations.* Users conducting a study of fairness should review the A.P.A. Standards regarding investigation of possible bias in testing. An investigation of fairness of a selection procedure depends on both evidence of validity and the manner in which the selection procedure is to be used in a particular employment context. Fairness of a selection procedure cannot necessarily be specified in advance without investigating these factors. Investigation of fairness of a selection procedure in samples where the range of scores on selection procedures or criterion measures is severely restricted for any subgroup sample (as compared to other subgroup samples) may produce misleading evidence of unfairness. That factor should accordingly be taken into account in conducting such studies and before reliance is placed on the results.

(d) *When unfairness is shown.* If unfairness is demonstrated through a showing that members of a particular group perform better or poorer on the job than their

scores on the selection procedure would indicate through comparison with how members of other groups perform, the user may either revise or replace the selection instrument in accordance with these guidelines, or may continue to use the selection instrument operationally with appropriate revisions in its use to assure compatibility between the probability of successful job performance and the probability of being selected.

(c) *Technical feasibility of fairness studies.* In addition to the general conditions needed for technical feasibility for the conduct of a criterion-related study (see section 16, below) an investigation of fairness requires the following:

(i) An adequate sample of persons in each group available for the study to achieve findings of statistical significance. Guidelines do not require a user to hire or promote persons on the basis of group classifications for the purpose of making it possible to conduct a study of fairness; but the user has the obligation otherwise to comply with these guidelines.

(ii) The samples for each group should be comparable in terms of the actual job they perform, length of time on the job where time on the job is likely to affect performance, and other relevant factors likely to affect validity differences; or such factors should be included in the design of the study and their effects identified.

(f) *Continued use of selection procedures when fairness studies not feasible.* If a study of fairness should otherwise be performed, but is not technically feasible, a selection procedure may be used which has otherwise met the validity standards of these guidelines, unless the technical infeasibility resulted from discriminatory employment practices which are demonstrated by facts other than past failure to conform with requirements for validation of selection procedures. However, when it becomes technically feasible for the user to perform a study of fairness and such a study is otherwise called for, the user should conduct the study of fairness.

C. *Technical standards for content validity studies.*—(1) *Appropriateness of content validity studies.* Users choosing to validate a selection procedure by a content validity strategy should determine whether it is appropriate to conduct such a study in the particular employment context. A selection procedure can be supported by a content validity strategy to the extent that it is a representative sample of the content of the job. Selection procedures which purport to measure knowledges, skills or abilities may in certain circumstances be justified by content validity, although they may not be representative samples, if the knowledge, skill, or ability measured by the selection procedure can be operationally defined as provided in section 14C(4) below, and if that knowledge, skill, or ability is a necessary prerequisite to successful job performance.

A selection procedure based upon inferences about mental processes cannot be supported solely or primarily on the basis of content validity. Thus, a content strategy is not appropriate for demonstrating the validity of selection procedures which purport to measure traits or constructs, such as intelligence, aptitude, personality, commonsense, judgment, leadership, and spatial ability. Content validity is also not an appropriate strategy when the selection procedure involves knowledges, skills, or abilities which an employee will be expected to learn on the job.

(2) *Job analysis for content validity.* There should be a job analysis which includes an analysis of the important work behavior(s) required for successful performance and their relative importance and, if the behavior results in work product(s), an analysis of the work product(s). Any job analysis should focus on the work behavior(s) and the tasks associated with them. If work behavior(s) are not observable, the job analysts should identify and analyze those as-

pects of the behavior(s) that can be observed and the observed work products. The work behavior(s) selected for measurement should be critical work behavior(s) and/or important work behavior(s) constituting most of the job.

(3) *Development of selection procedures.* A selection procedure designed to measure the work behavior may be developed specifically from the job and job analysis in question, or may have been previously developed by the user, or by other users or by a test publisher.

(4) *Standards for demonstrating content validity.* To demonstrate the content validity of a selection procedure, a user should show that the behavior(s) demonstrated in the selection procedure are a representative sample of the behavior(s) of the job in question or that the selection procedure provides a representative sample of the work product of the job. In the case of a selection procedure measuring a knowledge, skill, or ability, the knowledge, skill, or ability being measured should be operationally defined. In the case of a selection procedure measuring a knowledge, the knowledge being measured should be operationally defined as that body of learned information which is used in and is a necessary prerequisite for observable aspects of work behavior of the job. In the case of skills or abilities, the skill or ability being measured should be operationally defined in terms of observable aspects of work behavior of the job. For any selection procedure measuring a knowledge, skill, or ability the user should show that (a) the selection procedure measures and is a representative sample of that knowledge, skill, or ability; and (b) that knowledge, skill, or ability is used in and is a necessary prerequisite to performance of critical or important work behavior(s). In addition, to be content valid, a selection procedure measuring a skill or ability should either closely approximate an observable work behavior, or its product should closely approximate

an observable work product. If a test purports to sample a work behavior or to provide a sample of a work product, the manner and setting of the selection procedure and its level and complexity should closely approximate the work situation. The closer the content and the context of the selection procedure are to work samples or work behaviors, the stronger is the basis for showing content validity. As the content of the selection procedure less resembles a work behavior, or the setting and manner of the administration of the selection procedure less resembles the work situation, or the result less resembles a work product, the less likely the selection procedure is to be content valid, and the greater the need for other evidence of validity.

(5) *Reliability.* The reliability of selection procedures justified on the basis of content validity should be a matter of concern to the user. Whenever it is feasible, appropriate statistical estimates should be made of the reliability of the selection procedure.

(6) *Prior training or experience.* A requirement for or evaluation of specific prior training or experience based on content validity, including a specification of level or amount of training or experience, should be justified on the basis of the relationship between the content of the training or experience and the content of the job for which the training or experience is to be required or evaluated. The critical consideration is the resemblance between the specific behaviors, products, knowledges, skills, or abilities in the experience or training and the specific behaviors, products, knowledges, skills, or abilities required on the job, whether or not there is close resemblance between the experience or training as a whole and the job as a whole.

(7) *Content validity of training success.* Where a measure of success in a training program is used as a selection procedure and the content of a training program is justified on the basis of content validity, the use should be justified on the relationship between the content of the training program and the content of the job.

(8) *Operational use.* A selection procedure which is supported on the basis of content validity may be used for a job if it represents a critical work behavior (i.e., a behavior which is necessary for performance of the job) or work behaviors which constitute most of the important parts of the job.

(9) *Ranking based on content validity studies.* If a user can show, by a job analysis or otherwise, that a higher score on a content valid selection procedure is likely to result in better job performance, the results may be used to rank persons who score above minimum levels. Where a selection procedure supported solely or primarily by content validity is used to rank job candidates, the selection procedure should measure those aspects of performance which differentiate among levels of job performance.

D. *Technical standards for construct validity studies.*—(1) *Appropriateness of construct validity studies.* Construct validity is a more complex strategy than either criterion-related or content validity. Construct validation is a relatively new and developing procedure in the employment field, and there is at present a lack of substantial literature extending the concept to employment practices. The user should be aware that the effort to obtain sufficient empirical support for construct validity is both an extensive and arduous effort involving a series of research studies, which include criterion related validity studies and which may include content validity studies. Users choosing to justify use of a selection procedure by this strategy should therefore take particular care to assure that the validity study meets the standards set forth below.

(2) *Job analysis for construct validity studies.* There should be a job analysis. This job analysis should show the work behavior(s) required for successful performance of the job, or the groups of jobs being studied,

the critical or important work behavior(s) in the job or group of jobs being studied, and an identification of the construct(s) believed to underlie successful performance of these critical or important work behaviors in the job or jobs in question. Each construct should be named and defined, so as to distinguish it from other constructs. If a group of jobs is being studied the jobs should have in common one or more critical or important work behaviors at a comparable level of complexity.

(3) *Relationship to the job.* A selection procedure should then be identified or developed which measures the construct identified in accord with subparagraph (2) above. The user should show by empirical evidence that the selection procedure is validly related to the construct and that the construct is validly related to the performance of critical or important work behavior(s). The relationship between the construct as measured by the selection procedure and the related work behavior(s) should be supported by empirical evidence from one or more criterion-related studies involving the job or jobs in question which satisfy the provisions of section 14B above.

(4) *Use of construct validity study without new criterion-related evidence.*—(a) *Standards for use.* Until such time as professional literature provides more guidance on the use of construct validity in employment situations, the Federal agencies will accept a claim of construct validity without a criterion-related study which satisfies section 14B above only when the selection procedure has been used elsewhere in a situation in which a criterion-related study has been conducted and the use of a criterion-related validity study in this context meets the standards for transportability of criterion-related validity studies as set forth above in section 7. However, if a study pertains to a number of jobs having common critical or important work behaviors at a comparable level of complexity, and the evidence satisfies subparagraphs 14B (2)

and (3) above for those jobs with criterion-related validity evidence for those jobs, the selection procedure may be used for all the jobs to which the study pertains. If construct validity is to be generalized to other jobs or groups of jobs not in the group studied, the Federal enforcement agencies will expect at a minimum additional empirical research evidence meeting the standards of subparagraphs section 14B (2) and (3) above for the additional jobs or groups of jobs.

(b) *Determination of common work behaviors.* In determining whether two or more jobs have one or more work behavior(s) in common, the user should compare the observed work behavior(s) in each of the jobs and should compare the observed work product(s) in each of the jobs. If neither the observed work behavior(s) in each of the jobs nor the observed work product(s) in each of the jobs are the same, the Federal enforcement agencies will presume that the work behavior(s) in each job are different. If the work behaviors are not observable, then evidence of similarity of work products and any other relevant research evidence will be considered in determining whether the work behavior(s) in the two jobs are the same.

DOCUMENTATION OF IMPACT AND VALIDITY EVIDENCE

SEC. 15. *Documentation of impact and validity evidence.*—A. *Required information.* Users of selection procedures other than those users complying with section 15A(1) below should maintain and have available for each job information on adverse impact of the selection process for that job and, where it is determined a selection process has an adverse impact, evidence of validity as set forth below.

(1) *Simplified recordkeeping for users with less than 100 employees.* In order to minimize recordkeeping burdens on employers

who employ one hundred (100) or fewer employees, and other users not required to file EEO-1, et seq., reports, such users may satisfy the requirements of this section 15 if they maintain and have available records showing, for each year:

(a) The number of persons hired, promoted, and terminated for each job, by sex, and where appropriate by race and national origin;

(b) The number of applicants for hire and promotion by sex and where appropriate by race and national origin; and

(c) The selection procedures utilized (either standardized or not standardized).

These records should be maintained for each race or national origin group (see section 4 above) constituting more than two percent (2%) of the labor force in the relevant labor area. However, it is not necessary to maintain records by race and/or national origin (see §4 above) if one race or national origin group in the relevant labor area constitutes more than ninety-eight percent (98%) of the labor force in the area. If the user has reason to believe that a selection procedure has an adverse impact, the user should maintain any available evidence of validity for that procedure (see sections 7A and 8).

(2) *Information on impact.*—(a) *Collection of information on impact.* Users of selection procedures other than those complying with section 15A(1) above should maintain and have available for each job records or other information showing whether the total selection process for that job has an adverse impact on any of the groups for which records are called for by sections 4B above. Adverse impact determinations should be made at least annually for each such group which constitutes at least 2 percent of the labor force in the relevant labor area or 2 percent of the applicable workforce. Where a total selection process for a job has an adverse impact, the user should maintain and have available records

or other information showing which components have an adverse impact. Where the total selection process for a job does not have an adverse impact, information need not be maintained for individual components except in circumstances set forth in subsection 15A(2)(b) below. If the determination of adverse impact is made using a procedure other than the "four-fifths rule," as defined in the first sentence of section 4D above, a justification, consistent with section 4D above, for the procedure used to determine adverse impact should be available.

(b) *When adverse impact has been eliminated in the total selection process.* Whenever the total selection process for a particular job has had an adverse impact, as defined in section 4 above, in any year, but no longer has an adverse impact, the user should maintain and have available the information on individual components of the selection process required in the preceding paragraph for the period in which there was adverse impact. In addition, the user should continue to collect such information for at least two (2) years after the adverse impact has been eliminated.

(c) *When data insufficient to determine impact.* Where there has been an insufficient number of selections to determine whether there is an adverse impact of the total selection process for a particular job, the user should continue to collect, maintain and have available the information on individual components of the selection process required in section 15(A)(2)(a) above until the information is sufficient to determine that the overall selection process does not have an adverse impact as defined in section 4 above, or until the job has changed substantially.

(3) *Documentation of validity evidence.*—(a) *Types of evidence.* Where a total selection process has an adverse impact (see section 4 above) the user should maintain and have available for each component of that pro-

cess which has an adverse impact, one or more of the following types of documentation evidence:

(i) Documentation evidence showing criterion-related validity of the selection procedure (see section 15B, below).

(ii) Documentation evidence showing content validity of the selection procedure (see section 15C, below).

(iii) Documentation evidence showing construct validity of the selection procedure (see section 15D, below).

(iv) Documentation evidence from other studies showing validity of the selection procedure in the user's facility (see section 15E, below).

(v) Documentation evidence showing why a validity study cannot or need not be performed and why continued use of the procedure is consistent with Federal law.

(b) *Form of report.* This evidence should be compiled in a reasonably complete and organized manner to permit direct evaluation of the validity of the selection procedure. Previously written employer or consultant reports of validity, or reports describing validity studies completed before the issuance of these guidelines are acceptable if they are complete in regard to the documentation requirements contained in this section, or if they satisfied requirements of guidelines which were in effect when the validity study was completed. If they are not complete, the required additional documentation should be appended. If necessary information is not available the report of the validity study may still be used as documentation, but its adequacy will be evaluated in terms of compliance with the requirements of these guidelines.

(c) *Completeness.* In the event that evidence of validity is reviewed by an enforcement agency, the validation reports completed after the effective date of these guidelines are expected to contain the information set forth below. Evidence denoted by use of the word "(essential)" is

considered critical. If information denoted essential is not included, the report will be considered incomplete unless the user affirmatively demonstrates either its unavailability due to circumstances beyond the user's control or special circumstances of the user's study which make the information irrelevant. Evidence not so denoted is desirable but its absence will not be a basis for considering a report incomplete. The user should maintain and have available the information called for under the heading "Source Data" in sections 15B(11) and 15D(11). While it is a necessary part of the study, it need not be submitted with the report. All statistical results should be organized and presented in tabular or graphic form to the extent feasible.

B. *Criterion-related validity studies.* Reports of criterion-related validity for a selection procedure should include the following information:

(1) *User(s), location(s), and date(s) of study.* Dates and location(s) of the job analysis or review of job information, the date(s) and location(s) of the administration of the selection procedures and collection of criterion data, and the time between collection of data on selection procedures and criterion measures should be provided (essential). If the study was conducted at several locations, the address of each location, including city and State, should be shown.

(2) *Problem and setting.* An explicit definition of the purpose(s) of the study and the circumstances in which the study was conducted should be provided. A description of existing selection procedures and cutoff scores, if any, should be provided.

(3) *Job analysis or review of job information.* A description of the procedure used to analyze the job or group of jobs, or to review the job information should be provided (essential). Where a review of job information results in criteria which may be used without a full job analysis (see section 14B(3)), the basis for the selection of these

criteria should be reported (essential). Where a job analysis is required a complete description of the work behavior(s) or work outcome(s), and measures of their criticality or importance should be provided (essential). The report should describe the basis on which the behavior(s) or outcome(s) were determined to be critical or important, such as the proportion of time spent on the respective behaviors, their level of difficulty, their frequency of performance, the consequences of error, or other appropriate factors (essential). Where two or more jobs are grouped for a validity study, the information called for in this subsection should be provided for each of the jobs, and the justification for the grouping (see section 14B(1)) should be provided (essential).

(4) *Job titles and codes.* It is desirable to provide the user's job title(s) for the job(s) in question and the corresponding job title(s) and code(s) from U.S. Employment Service's Dictionary of Occupational Titles.

(5) *Criterion measures.* The bases for the selection of the criterion measures should be provided, together with references to the evidence considered in making the selection of criterion measures (essential). A full description of all criteria on which data were collected and means by which they were observed, recorded, evaluated, and quantified, should be provided (essential). If rating techniques are used as criterion measures, the appraisal form(s) and instructions to the rater(s) should be included as part of the validation evidence, or should be explicitly described and available (essential). All steps taken to insure that criterion measures are free from factors which would unfairly alter the scores of members of any group should be described (essential).

(6) *Sample description.* A description of how the research sample was identified and selected should be included (essential). The race, sex, and ethnic composition of the sample, including those groups set forth in section 4A above, should be described (essential). This description should include the size of each subgroup (essential). A description of how the research sample compares with the relevant labor market or work force, the method by which the relevant labor market or work force was defined, and a discussion of the likely effects on validity of differences between the sample and the relevant labor market or work force, are also desirable. Descriptions of educational levels, length of service, and age are also desirable.

(7) *Description of selection procedures.* Any measure, combination of measures, or procedures studied should be completely and explicitly described or attached (essential). If commercially available selection procedures are studied, they should be described by title, form, and publisher (essential). Reports of reliability estimates and how they were established are desirable.

(3) *Techniques and results.* Methods used in analyzing data should be described (essential). Measures of central tendency (e.g., means) and measures of dispersion (e.g., standard deviations and ranges) for all selection procedures and all criteria should be reported for each race, sex, and ethnic group which constitutes a significant factor in the relevant labor market (essential). The magnitude and direction of all relationships between selection procedures and criterion measures investigated should be reported for each relevant race, sex, and ethnic group and for the total group (essential). Where groups are too small to obtain reliable evidence of the magnitude of the relationship, need not be reported separately. Statements regarding the statistical significance of results should be made (essential). Any statistical adjustments, such as for less then perfect reliability or for restriction of score range in the selection procedure or criterion should be described and explained; and uncorrected correlation coefficients should also be shown (essen-

tial). Where the statistical technique categorizes continuous data, such as biserial correlation and the phi coefficient, the categories and the bases on which they were determined should be described and explained (essential). Studies of test fairness should be included where called for by the requirements of section 14B(8) (essential). These studies should include the rationale by which a selection procedure was determined to be fair to the group(s) in question. Where test fairness or unfairness has been demonstrated on the basis of other studies, a bibliography of the relevant studies should be included (essential). If the bibliography includes unpublished studies, copies of these studies, or adequate abstracts or summaries, should be attached (essential). Where revisions have been made in a selection procedure to assure compatability between successful job performance and the probability of being selected, the studies underlying such revisions should be included (essential). All statistical results should be organized and presented by relevant race, sex, and ethnic group (essential).

(9) *Alternative procedures investigated.* The selection procedures investigated and available evidence of their impact should be identified (essential). The scope, method, and findings of the investigation, and the conclusions reached in light of the findings, should be fully described (essential).

(10) *Uses and applications.* The methods considered for use of the selection procedure (e.g., as a screening device with a cut-off score, for grouping or ranking, or combined with other procedures in a battery) and available evidence of their impact should be described (essential). This description should include the rationale for choosing the method for operational use, and the evidence of the validity and utility of the procedure as it is to be used (essential). The purpose for which the procedure is to be used (e.g., hiring transfer, promo-

tion) should be described (essential). If weights are assigned to different parts of the selection procedure, these weights and the validity of the weighted composite should be reported (essential). If the selection procedure is used with a cutoff score, the user should describe the way in which normal expectations of proficiency within the work force were determined and the way in which the cutoff score was determined (essential).

(11) *Source data.* Each user should maintain records showing all pertinent information about individual sample members and raters where they are used in studies involving the validation of selection procedures. These records should be made available upon request of a compliance agency. In the case of individual sample members these data should include scores on the selection procedure(s), scores on criterion measures, age, sex, race, or ethnic group status, and experience on the specific job on which the validation study was conducted, and may also include such things as education, training, and prior job experience, but should not include names and social security numbers. Records should be maintained which show the ratings given to each sample member by each rater.

(12) *Contact person.* The name, mailing address, and telephone number of the person who may be contacted for further information about the validity study should be provided (essential).

(13) *Accuracy and completeness.* The report should describe the steps taken to assure the accuracy and completeness of the collection, analysis, and report of data and results.

C. *Content validity studies.* Reports of content validity for a selection procedure should include the following information:

(1) *User(s), location(s) and date(s) of study.* Dates and location(s) of the job analysis should be shown (essential).

(2) *Problem and setting.* An explicit definition of the purpose(s) of the study and

the circumstances in which the study was conducted should be provided. A description of existing selection procedures and cutoff scores, if any, should be provided.

(3) *Job analysis—Content of the job.* A description of the method used to analyze the job should be provided (essential). The work behavior(s), the associated tasks, and, if the behavior results in a work product, the work products should be completely described (essential). Measures of criticality and/or importance of the work behavior(s) and the method of determining these measures should be provided (essential). Where the job analysis also identified the knowledges, skills, and abilities used in work behavior(s), an operational definition for each knowledge in terms of a body of learned information and for each skill and ability in terms of observable behaviors and outcomes, and the relationship between each knowledge, skill, or ability and each work behavior, as well as the method used to determine this relationship, should be provided (essential). The work situation should be described, including the setting in which work behavior(s) are performed, and where appropriate, the manner in which knowledges, skills, or abilities are used, and the complexity and difficulty of the knowledge, skill, or ability as used in the work behavior(s).

(4) *Selection procedure and its content.* Selection procedures, including those constructed by or for the user, specific training requirements, composites of selection procedures, and any other procedure supported by content validity, should be completely and explicitly described or attached (essential). If commercially available selection procedures are used, they should be described by title, form, and publisher (essential). The behaviors measured or sampled by the selection procedure should be explicitly described (essential). Where the selection procedure purports to measure a knowledge, skill, or ability, evidence that the selection procedure measures and

is a representative sample of the knowledge, skill, or ability should be provided (essential).

(5) *Relationship between the selection procedure and the job.* The evidence demonstrating that the selection procedure is a representative work sample, a representative sample of the work behavior(s), or a representative sample of a knowledge, skill, or ability as used as a part of a work behavior and necessary for that behavior should be provided (essential). The user should identify the work behavior(s) which each item or part of the selection procedure is intended to sample or measure (essential). Where the selection procedure purports to sample a work behavior or to provide a sample of a work product, a comparison should be provided of the manner, setting, and the level of complexity of the selection procedure with those of the work situation (essential). If any steps were taken to reduce adverse impact on a race, sex, or ethnic group in the content of the procedure or in its administration, these steps should be described. Establishment of time limits, if any, and how these limits are related to the speed with which duties must be performed on the job, should be explained. Measures of central tendency (e.g., means) and measures of dispersion (e.g., standard deviations) and estimates of reliability should be reported for all selection procedures if available. Such reports should be made for relevant race, sex, and ethnic subgroups, at least on a statistically reliable sample basis.

(6) *Alternative procedures investigated.* The alternative selection procedures investigated and available evidence of their impact should be identified (essential). The scope, method, and findings of the investigation, and the conclusions reached in light of the findings, should be fully described (essential).

(7) *Uses and applications.* The methods considered for use of the selection procedure (e.g., as a screening device with a cut-

off score, for grouping or ranking, or combined with other procedures in a battery) and available evidence of their impact should be described (essential). This description should include the rationale for choosing the method for operational use, and the evidence of the validity and utility of the procedure as it is to be used (essential). The purpose for which the procedure is to be used (e.g., hiring, transfer, promotion) should be described (essential). If the selection procedure is used with a cutoff score, the user should describe the way in which normal expectations of proficiency within the work force were determined and the way in which the cutoff score was determined (essential). In addition, if the selection procedure is to be used for ranking, the user should specify the evidence showing that a higher score on the selection procedure is likely to result in better job performance.

(8) *Contact person.* The name, mailing address, and telephone number of the person who may be contacted for further information about the validity study should be provided (essential).

(9) *Accuracy and completeness.* The report should describe the steps taken to assure the accuracy and completeness of the collection, analysis, and report of data and results.

D. *Construct validity studies.* Reports of construct validity for a selection procedure should include the following information:

(1) *User(s), location(s), and date(s) of study.* Date(s) and location(s) of the job analysis and the gathering of other evidence called for by these guidelines should be provided (essential).

(2) *Problem and setting.* An explicit definition of the purpose(s) of the study and the circumstances in which the study was conducted should be provided. A description of existing selection procedures and cutoff scores, if any, should be provided.

(3) *Construct definition.* A clear definition of the construct(s) which are believed to underlie successful performance of the critical or important work behavior(s) should be provided (essential). This definition should include the levels of construct performance relevant to the job(s) for which the selection procedure is to be used (essential). There should be a summary of the position of the construct in the psychological literature, or in the absence of such a position, a description of the way in which the definition and measurement of the construct was developed and the psychological theory underlying it (essential). Any quantitative data which identify or define the job constructs, such as factor analyses, should be provided (essential).

(4) *Job analysis.* A description of the method used to analyze the job should be provided (essential). A complete description of the work behavior(s) and, to the extent appropriate, work outcomes and measures of their criticality and/or importance should be provided (essential). The report should also describe the basis on which the behavior(s) or outcomes were determined to be important, such as their level of difficulty, their frequency of performance, the consequences of error or other appropriate factors (essential). Where jobs are grouped or compared for the purposes of generalizing validity evidence, the work behavior(s) and work product(s) for each of the jobs should be described, and conclusions concerning the similarity of the jobs in terms of observable work behaviors or work products should be made (essential).

(5) *Job titles and codes.* It is desirable to provide the selection procedure user's job title(s) for the job(s) in question and the corresponding job title(s) and code(s) from the United States Employment Service's dictionary of occupational titles.

(6) *Selection procedure.* The selection procedure used as a measure of the construct should be completely and explicitly described or attached (essential). If commercially available selection procedures are

used, they should be identified by title, form and publisher (essential). The research evidence of the relationship between the selection procedure and the construct, such as factor structure, should be included (essential). Measures of central tendency, variability and reliability of the selection procedure should be provided (essential). Whenever feasible, these measures should be provided separately for each relevant race, sex and ethnic group.

(7) *Relationship to job performance.* The criterion-related study(ies) and other empirical evidence of the relationship between the construct measured by the selection procedure and the related work behavior(s) for the job or jobs in question should be provided (essential). Documentation of the criterion-related study(ies) should satisfy the provisions of section 15B above or section 15E(1) below, except for studies conducted prior to the effective date of these guidelines (essential). Where a study pertains to a group of jobs, and, on the basis of the study, validity is asserted for a job in the group, the observed work behaviors and the observed work products for each of the jobs should be described (essential). Any other evidence used in determining whether the work behavior(s) in each of the jobs is the same should be fully described (essential).

(8) *Alternative procedures investigated.* The alternative selection procedures investigated and available evidence of their impact should be identified (essential). The scope, method, and findings of the investigation, and the conclusions reached in light of the findings should be fully described (essential).

(9) *Uses and applications.* The methods considered for use of the selection procedure (e.g., as a screening device with a cutoff score, for grouping or ranking, or combined with other procedures in a battery) and available evidence of their impact should be described (essential). This description should include the rationale for choosing the method for operational use, and the evidence of the validity and utility of the procedure as it is to be used (essential). The purpose for which the procedure is to be used (e.g., hiring, transfer, promotion) should be described (essential). If weights are assigned to different parts of the selection procedure, these weights and the validity of the weighted composite should be reported (essential). If the selection procedure is used with a cutoff score, the user should describe the way in which normal expectations of proficiency within the work force were determined and the way in which the cutoff score was determined (essential).

(10) *Accuracy and completeness.* The report should describe the steps taken to assure the accuracy and completeness of the collection, analysis, and report of data and results.

(11) *Source data.* Each user should maintain records showing all pertinent information relating to its study of construct validity.

(12) *Contact person.* The name, mailing address, and telephone number of the individual who may be contacted for further information about the validity study should be provided (essential).

E. *Evidence of validity from other studies.* When validity of a selection procedure is supported by studies not done by the user, the evidence from the original study or studies should be compiled in a manner similar to that required in the appropriate section of this section 15 above. In addition, the following evidence should be supplied.

(1) *Evidence from criterion-related validity studies.*—a. *Job information.* A description of the important job behavior(s) of the user's job and the basis on which the behaviors were determined to be important should be provided (essential). A full description of the basis for determining that these important work behaviors are the same as those of the job in the original

study (or studies) should be provided (essential).

b. *Relevance of criteria.* A full description of the basis on which the criteria used in the original studies are determined to be relevant for the user should be provided (essential).

c. *Other variables.* The similarity of important applicant pool or sample characteristics reported in the original studies to those of the user should be described (essential). A description of the comparison between the race, sex and ethnic composition of the user's relevant labor market and the sample in the original validity studies should be provided (essential).

d. *Use of the selection procedure.* A full description should be provided showing that the use to be made of the selection procedure is consistent with the findings of the original validity studies (essential).

e. *Bibliography.* A bibliography of reports of validity of the selection procedure for the job or jobs in question should be provided (essential). Where any of the studies included an investigation of test fairness, the results of this investigation should be provided (essential). Copies of reports published in journals that are not commonly available should be described in detail or attached (essential). Where a user is relying upon unpublished studies, a reasonable effort should be made to obtain these studies. If these unpublished studies are the sole source of validity evidence they should be described in detail or attached (essential). If these studies are not available, the name and address of the source, an adequate abstract or summary of the validity study and data, and a contact person in the source organization should be provided (essential).

(2) *Evidence from content validity studies.* See section 14C(3) and section 15C above.

(3) *Evidence from construct validity studies.* See sections 14D(2) and 15D above.

F. *Evidence of validity from cooperative studies.* Where a selection procedure has been validated through a cooperative study, evidence that the study satisfies the requirements of sections 7, 8 and 15E should be provided (essential).

G. *Selection for higher level job.* If a selection procedure is used to evaluate candidates for jobs at a higher level than those for which they will initially be employed, the validity evidence should satisfy the documentation provisions of this section 15 for the higher level job or jobs, and in addition, the user should provide: (1) a description of the job progression structure, formal or informal; (2) the data showing how many employees progress to the higher level job and the length of time needed to make this progression; and (3) an identification of any anticipated changes in the higher level job. In addition, if the test measures a knowledge, skill or ability, the user should provide evidence that the knowledge, skill or ability is required for the higher level job and the basis for the conclusion that the knowledge, skill or ability is not expected to develop from the training or experience on the job.

H. *Interim use of selection procedures.* If a selection procedure is being used on an interim basis because the procedure is not fully supported by the required evidence of validity, the user should maintain and have available (1) substantial evidence of validity for the procedure, and (2) a report showing the date on which the study to gather the additional evidence commenced, the estimated completion date of the study, and a description of the data to be collected (essential).

DEFINITIONS

SEC. 16. *Definitions.* The following definitions shall apply throughout these guidelines:

A. *Ability.* A present competence to perform an observable behavior or a behavior which results in an observable product.

B. *Adverse impact.* A substantially different rate of selection in hiring, promotion, or other employment decision which works to the disadvantage of members of a race, sex, or ethnic group. See section 4 of these guidelines.

C. *Compliance with these guidelines.* Use of a selection procedure is in compliance with these guidelines if such use has been validated in accord with these guidelines (as defined below), or if such use does not result in adverse impact on any race, sex, or ethnic group (see section 4, above), or, in unusual circumstances, if use of the procedure is otherwise justified in accord with Federal law. See section 6B, above.

D. *Content validity.* Demonstrated by data showing that the content of a selection procedure is representative of important aspects of performance on the job. See section 5B and section 14C.

E. *Construct validity.* Demonstrated by data showing that the selection procedure measures the degree to which candidates have identifiable characteristics which have been determined to be important for successful job performance. See section 5B and section 14D.

F. *Criterion-related validity.* Demonstrated by empirical data showing that the selection procedure is predictive of or significantly correlated with important elements of work behavior. See sections 5B and 14B.

G. *Employer.* Any employer subject to the provisions of the Civil Rights Act of 1964, as amended, including State or local governments and any Federal agency subject to the provisions of section 717 of the Civil Rights Act of 1964, as amended, and any Federal contractor or subcontractor or federally assisted construction contractor or subcontractor covered by Executive Order 11246, as amended.

H. *Employment agency.* Any employment agency subject to the provisions of the Civil Rights Act of 1964, as amended.

I. *Enforcement action.* For the purposes of section 4 a proceeding by a Federal enforcement agency such as a lawsuit or an administrative proceeding leading to debarment from or withholding, suspension, or termination of Federal Government contracts or the suspension or withholding of Federal Government funds; but not a finding of reasonable cause or a conciliation process or the issuance of right to sue letters under title VII or under Executive Order 11246 where such finding, conciliation, or issuance of notice of right to sue is based upon an individual complaint.

J. *Enforcement agency.* Any agency of the executive branch of the Federal Government which adopts these guidelines for purposes of the enforcement of the equal employment opportunity laws or which has responsibility for securing compliance with them.

K. *Job analysis.* A detailed statement of work behaviors and other information relevant to the job.

L. *Job description.* A general statement of job duties and responsibilities.

M. *Knowledge.* A body of information applied directly to the performance of a function.

N. *Labor organization.* Any labor organization subject to the provisions of the Civil Rights Act of 1964, as amended, and any committee subject thereto controlling apprenticeship or other training.

O. *Observable.* Able to be seen, heard, or otherwise perceived by a person other than the person performing the action.

P. *Race, sex, or ethnic group.* Any group of persons identifiable on the grounds of race, color, religion, sex, or national origin.

Q. *Selection procedure.* Any measure, combination of measures, or procedure used as a basis for any employment decision. Selection procedures include the full range of assessment techniques from traditional paper and pencil tests, performance tests, training programs, or probationary periods and physical, educational, and work experience requirements through informal or casual interviews and unscored application forms.

R. *Selection rate.* The proportion of applicants or candidates who are hired, promoted, or otherwise selected.

S. *Should.* The term "should" as used in these guidelines is intended to connote action which is necessary to achieve compliance with the guidelines, while recognizing that there are circumstances where alternative courses of action are open to users.

T. *Skill.* A present, observable competence to perform a learned psychomotor act.

U. *Technical feasibility.* The existence of conditions permitting the conduct of meaningful criterion-related validity studies. These conditions include: (1) An adequate sample of persons available for the study to achieve findings of statistical significance; (2) having or being able to obtain a sufficient range of scores on the selection procedure and job performance measures to produce validity results which can be expected to be representative of the results if the ranges normally expected were utilized, and (3) having or being able to devise unbiased, reliable and relevant measures of job performance or other criteria of employee adequacy. See section 14B(2). With respect to investigation of possible unfairness, the same considerations are applicable to each group for which the study is made. See section 14B(8).

V. *Unfairness of selection procedure.* A condition in which members of one race, sex, or ethnic group characteristically obtain lower scores on a selection procedure than members of another group, and the differences are not reflected in differences in measures of job performance. See section 14B(7).

W. *User.* Any employer, labor organization, employment agency, or licensing or certification board, to the extent it may be covered by Federal equal employment opportunity law, which uses a selection procedure as a basis for any employment decision. Whenever an employer, labor organization, or employment agency is required by law to restrict recruitment for any occupation to those applicants who have met licensing or certification requirements, the licensing or certifying authority to the extent it may be covered by Federal equal employment opportunity law will be considered the user with respect to those licensing or certification requirements. Whenever a State employment agency or service does no more than administer or monitor a procedure as permitted by Department of Labor regulations, and does so without making referrals or taking any other action on the basis of the results, the State employment agency will not be deemed to be a user.

X. *Validated in accord with these guidelines or properly validated.* A demonstration that one or more validity study or studies meeting the standards of these guidelines has been conducted, including investigation and, where appropriate, use of suitable alternative selection procedures as contemplated by section 3B, and has produced evidence of validity sufficient to warrant use of the procedure for the intended purpose under the standards of these guidelines.

Y. *Work behavior.* An activity performed to achieve the objectives of the job. Work behaviors involve observable (physical) components and unobservable (mental) components. A work behavior consists of the performance of one or more tasks. Knowledges, skills, and abilities are not behaviors, although they may be applied in work behaviors.

APPENDIX

17. *Policy statement on affirmative action* (see section 13B). The Equal Employment

Opportunity Coordinating Council was established by act of Congress in 1972, and charged with responsibility for developing and implementing agreements and policies designed, among other things, to eliminate conflict and inconsistency among the agencies of the Federal Government responsible for administering Federal law prohibiting discrimination on grounds of race, color, sex, religion, and national origin. This statement is issued as an initial response to the requests of a number of State and local officials for clarification of the Government's policies concerning the role of affirmative action in the overall equal employment opportunity program. While the Coordinating Council's adoption of this statement expresses only the views of the signatory agencies concerning this important subject, the principles set forth below should serve as policy guidance for other Federal agencies as well.

(1) Equal employment opportunity is the law of the land. In the public sector of our society this means that all persons, regardless of race, color, religion, sex, or national origin shall have equal access to positions in the public service limited only by their ability to do the job. There is ample evidence in all sectors of our society that such equal access frequently has been denied to members of certain groups because of their sex, racial, or ethnic characteristics. The remedy for such past and present discrimination is twofold.

On the one hand, vigorous enforcement of the laws against discrimination is essential. But equally, and perhaps even more important are affirmative, voluntary efforts on the part of public employers to assure that positions in the public service are genuinely and equally accessible to qualified persons, without regard to their sex, racial, or ethnic characteristics. Without such efforts equal employment opportunity is no more than a wish. The importance of voluntary affirmative action on the part of

employers is underscored by title VII of the Civil Rights Act of 1964, Executive Order 11246, and related laws and regulations—all of which emphasize voluntary action to achieve equal employment opportunity.

As with most management objectives, a systematic plan based on sound organization is crucial to the accomplishment of affirmative action objectives. For this reason, the Council urges all State and local governments to develop and implement results oriented affirmative action plans which deal with the problems so identified.

The following paragraphs are intended to assist State and local governments by illustrating the kinds of analyses and activities which may be appropriate for a public employer's voluntary affirmative action plan. This statement does not address remedies imposed after a finding of unlawful discrimination.

(2) Voluntary affirmative action to assure equal employment opportunity is appropriate at any stage of the employment process. The first step in the construction of any affirmative action plan should be an analysis of the employer's work force to determine whether percentages of sex, race, or ethnic groups in individual job classifications are substantially similar to the precentages or those groups available in the relevant job market who possess the basic job-related qualifications.

When substantial disparities are found through such analyses, each element of the overall selection process should be examined to determine which elements operate to exclude persons on the basis of sex, race, or ethnic group. Such elements include, but are not limited to, recruitment, testing, ranking certification, interview, recommendations for selection, hiring, promotion, etc. The examination of each element of the selection process should at a minimum include a determination of its validity in predicting job performance.

(3) When an employer has reason to believe that its selection procedures have the exclusionary effect described in paragraph 2 above, it should initiate affirmative steps to remedy the situation. Such steps, which in design and execution may be race, color, sex, or ethnic "conscious," include, but are not limited to, the following.

(a) The establishment of a long-term goal, and short-range, interim goals and timetables for the specific job classifications, all of which should take into account the availability of basically qualified persons in the relevant job market;

(b) A recruitment program designed to attract qualified members of the group in question;

(c) A systematic effort to organize work and redesign jobs in ways that provide opportunities for persons lacking "journeyman" level knowledge or skills to enter and, with appropriate training, to progress in a career field;

(d) Revamping selection instruments or procedures which have not yet been validated in order to reduce or eliminate exclusionary effects on particular groups in particular job classifications;

(e) The initiation of measures designed to assure that members of the affected group who are qualified to perform the job are included within the pool of persons from which the selecting official makes the selection;

(f) A systematic effort to provide career advancement training, both classroom and on-the-job, to employees locked into dead end jobs; and

(g) The establishment of a system for regularly monitoring the effectiveness of the particular affirmative action program, and procedures for making timely adjustments in this program where effectiveness is not demonstrated.

(4) The goal of any affirmative action plan should be achievement of genuine equal employment opportunity for all qualified persons. Selection under such plans should be based upon the ability of the applicant(s) to do the work. Such plans should not require the selection of the unqualified, or the unneeded, nor should they require the selection of persons on the basis of race, color, sex, religion, or national origin. Moreover, while the Council believes that this statement should serve to assist State and local employers, as well as Federal agencies, it recognizes that affirmative action cannot be viewed as a standardized program which must be accomplished in the same way at all times in all places.

Accordingly, the Council has not attempted to set forth here either the minimum or maximum voluntary steps that employers may take to deal with their respective situations. Rather, the Council recognizes that under applicable authorities, State and local employers have flexibility to formulate affirmative action plans that are best suited to their particular situations. In this manner, the Council believes that affirmative action programs will best serve the goal of equal employment opportunity.

Respectfully submitted,

HAROLD R. TYLER, Jr.
Deputy Attorney General and Chairman of the Equal Employment Coordinating Council.

MICHAEL H. MOSKOW,
Under Secretary of Labor.

ETHEL BENT WALSH,
Acting Chairman, Equal Employment Opportunity Commission.

ROBERT E. HAMPTON,
Chairman, Civil Service Commission.

ARTHUR E. FLEMMING,
Chairman, Commission on Civil Rights.

Because of its equal employment opportunity responsibilities under the State and Local Government Fiscal Assistance Act of

1972 (the revenue sharing act), the Department of Treasury was invited to participate in the formulation of this policy statement; and it concurs and joins in the adoption of this policy statement.

Done this 26th day of August 1976.

RICHARD ALBRECHT,
General Counsel,
Department of the Treasury.

Section 18. *Citations.* The official title of these guidelines is "Uniform Guidelines on Employee Selection Procedures (1978)". The Uniform Guidelines on Employee Selection Procedures (1978) are intended to establish a uniform Federal position in the area of prohibiting discrimination in employment practices on grounds of race, color, religion, sex, or national origin. These guidelines have been adopted by the Equal Employment Opportunity Commission, the Department of Labor, the Department of Justice, and the Civil Service Commission.

The official citation is:

"Section _____, Uniform Guidelines on Employee Selection Procedure (1978); 43 FR _____ (August 25, 1978)."

The short form citation is:

"Section _____, U.G.E.S.P. (1978); 43 FR _____ (August 25, 1978)."

When the guidelines are cited in connection with the activities of one of the issuing agencies, a specific citation to the regulations of that agency can be added at the end of the above citation. The specific additional citations are as follows:

Equal Employment Opportunity Commission

29 CFR Part 1607

Department of Labor

Office of Federal Contract Compliance Programs

41 CFR Part 60-3

Department of Justice

28 CFR 50.14

Civil Service Commission

5 CFR 300.103(c)

Normally when citing these guidelines, the section number immediately preceding the title of the guidelines will be from these guidelines series 1-18. If a section number from the codification for an individual agency is needed it can also be added at the end of the agency citation. For example, section 6A of these guidelines could be cited for EEOC as follows: "Section 6A, Uniform Guidelines on Employee Selection Procedures (1978); 43 FR _____, (August 25, 1978); 29 CFR Part 1607, section 6A."

ELEANOR HOLMES NORTON,
Chair, Equal Employment
Opportunity Commission.
ALAN K. CAMPBELL,
Chairman,
Civil Service Commission.
RAY MARSHALL,
Secretary of Labor.
GRIFFIN B. BELL,
Attorney General.

COMMENTARY

At this point, it should be clear that the concepts of equal employment opportunity, as defined by Title VII, and affirmative action, as defined by the regulatory agencies appear to be at odds. Much of the confusion stems from how one interprets the overall intent of Title VII with regard to employee election. Here are two differing interpretations:

1. The intent of Title VII was to eliminate barriers to minority employment resulting from discriminatory hiring practices. Irrelevant information (e.g., race, sex) should not be considered in making hiring decisions: each applicant

should be considered solely on the basis of his or her qualifications. This approach focuses on the term "opportunity" in the phrase "equal employment opportunity."

2. The intent of Title VII was to increase the representation of minority groups in all job categories in the American work force. This approach focuses on "equal (read "proportional") employment."

These interpretations are dramatically different in their implications. The first encourages employers to upgrade their selection procedures by using valid, job-related techniques. It treats individual differences as important, and encourages employers to determine what characteristics are needed for job success and to select according to these characteristics. By eliminating discriminatory practices and considering women and racial minority group members who had been excluded in the past, employers gain access to untapped resources. One can make a case that this form of equal opportunity does not constitute a burden to employers, but rather is sound business practice.

The movement from the first interpretation, which appears to be that intended by Congress in passing Title VII, to the second, which represents the philosophy and enforcement strategy of the enforcement agencies, has been described in the reading by Glazer. A critical variable in differentiating between the two approaches is *time:* how quickly will patterns of minority employment change? Seligman (1973) has outlined four approaches to increasing minority employment, which fall on a continuum from slowest to fastest:

1. *Passive nondiscrimination.* This represents our first interpretation of Title VII. By eliminating discriminatory selection procedures and irrelevant barriers to minority employment, an increase in minority representation in the work force will result. However, discrimination has been and often still is prevalent in aspects of society other than employment, e.g., education. Minorities will be less likely to possess the knowledge, skills, and abilities needed for jobs. Thus, even if the opportunity for employment is made equally available to all, increases in minority employment may come slowly until differences in, say, quality of education decrease.

2. *Active recruiting.* This represents the initial interpretation of affirmative action: taking positive steps to actively seek qualified minority applicants. At this point, equal employment opportunity (passive nondiscrimination) and affirmative action (active recruiting) are totally compatible concepts. All applicants will be considered solely on the basis of qualifications; attempts will be made to increase the pool of minority applicants. With a larger pool of minority applicants, a larger number of qualified applicants can be expected, resulting in a faster increase in minority employment than under a passive nondiscrimination policy. However, the operational result of this approach may be extreme competition between employers for the services of the cream of the minority applicant pool, with many employers documenting extensive minority recruiting campaigns resulting in the hire of relatively few minority group members.

3. *Minority preference.* This is analogous to veterans' preference for government employment: a recognition of societal debt to a particular group, resulting in members of that group being given special consideration (e.g., "bonus points") for employment. This represents a major philosophical shift from the earlier approaches. Group membership is explicitly recognized as a factor in hiring decisions. For the first time, employers are told that they may not be allowed to hire the most qualified applicant; they are to share an obligation to make right previous societal wrongs. Outcries from employers that they are being told to

engage in ineffective business practices by hiring less-qualified, or even unqualified, minority applicants have been met by a reconceptualization of "qualifications." The most extreme position is that, based on a job analysis, one can determine the minimum level of knowledge, skill, and ability needed for the job; applicants below this level are unqualified and applicants above the level are qualified. The importance of differences in qualifications and differences in subsequent job performance are downplayed. Qualifications become a dichotomy rather than a continuum. Under this logic, an employer's objectives are equally well served by any qualified applicant, and thus no hardship is imposed on employers by a minority preference form of affirmative action. (Recent research by Schmidt and his colleagues, included in Chapter 4, documents the fallacy of this argument and highlights the value of differences in performance.)

Minority preference is likely to increase minority representation at a faster rate than active recruiting. The extent of the gain depends on both the magnitude of differences between majority and minority group members on the selection device, and the manner in which minority preference is operationalized. For example, a white applicant with a test score of 70 would be preferred over a black applicant scoring 55 if 10 points are added to the score of black applicants; the black applicant would be preferred if 20 points were added. Note that while an active recruiting approach to affirmative action is compatible with a passive nondiscrimination approach to equal opportunity, a minority preference form of affirmative action clearly is not.

4. *Proportional hiring.* This represents a quota approach to increasing minority representation. One simple expansion of the philosophy behind minority preference is made: barring discrimination by employers, all groups would be represented in all jobs in proportion to their representation in the work force as a whole. Thus, an explicit numerical hiring objective can be set for minority representation in each job; the fastest way to reach this objective (barring the firing of job incumbents) is to require that a fixed proportion of openings be reserved for minority group members until the objective is met.

As has been noted earlier, nothing in either Title VII or Executive Order 11246 authorizes this form of affirmative action: it is a creation of the regulatory agencies. As pointed out by Glazer, the development of a proportional hiring approach to affirmative action is more understandable if one takes a broader view of discrimination than do most personnel professionals. When one looks at discrimination in, say, voting, a statistical approach to identifying discrimination makes sense: barring discrimination, equal proportions of various groups would be expected to be registered. The policy makers at the regulatory agencies are not employment specialists; as civil rights activists, the tendency to borrow approaches used to identify and combat discrimination in other aspects of society is understandable. While the fact that people differ in their qualifications for jobs seems to complicate the analogy between discrimination in voting and in employment, we have seen that the regulatory agencies deal with this problem by downplaying the importance of differences in qualifications.

In attempting to reconcile the conflict between equal opportunity for all individuals, regardless of group membership, and the more extreme forms of affirmative action, an examination of court decisions will be instructive. A relatively small number of fair employment practices cases have reached the Supreme Court: let us compare their interpretation of the intent of Title VII with that of the regulatory agencies. Consider *Griggs* v. *Duke Power Company:*

. . . the Act does not command that any person be hired simply because he was formerly the subject of discrimination, or because he is a member of a minority group.. Discriminatory preference for any group, minority or majority, is precisely and only what Congress has proscribed. What is required by Congress is the removal of artificial, arbitrary, and unnecessary barriers to employment when the barriers operate invidiously to discriminate on the basis of racial or other impermissible classification.

. . . Nothing in the Act precludes the use of testing or measuring procedures; obviously they are useful. What Congress has forbidden is giving these devices and mechanisms controlling force unless they are demonstrably a reasonable measure of job performance. Congress has not commanded that the less qualified be preferred over the better qualified simply because of minority origins. Far from disparaging job qualifications as such, Congress has made such qualifications the controlling factor, so that race, religion, nationality and sex become irrelevant. What Congress has commanded is that any tests used must measure the person for the job and not the person in the abstract.

Consider *Los Angeles Department of Water and Power* v. *Manhart:*

Congress has decided that classifications based on sex, like those based on national origin or race, are unlawful . . . the basic policy of the statute requires that we focus on fairness to individuals rather than fairness to classes. Practices which classify employees in terms of religion, race or sex tend to preserve traditional assumptions about groups rather than thoughtful scrutiny of individuals.

Consider *Furnco Construction Corp.* v. *Waters:*

It is clear beyond cavil that the obligation imposed by Title VII is to provide an equal opportunity for each applicant regardless of race, without regard to whether members of the applicant's race are already proportionately represented in the work force.

In light of these statements, the Court appears to clearly endorse selection processes which are blind to group membership. Preferential affirmative action programs would seem to be contrary to Title VII. Yet in *United Steelworkers of America* v. *Weber,* when asked for the first time to rule on the legality of preferential affirmative action programs, the Court ruled that Title VII did not create an absolute bar to race-conscious affirmative action plans. The court relied heavily on the language of Section 703(j), which states that preferential treatment is not required. According to the Court, Congress could have replaced "required" with "permitted" if an absolute ban on preferential treatment was intended. Thus, the voluntary nature of this plan appears to be the major factor making it permissible. Note that the term *voluntary* is being used euphemistically in this context: as Johnson (1981) notes, Kaiser's affirmative-action plan was devised after the OFCCP had determined that Kaiser was underutilizing minorities. Voluntary action refers to action undertaken without coercion or threat; clearly in this context the threat of loss of federal contracts led to the development of the plan. As noted in Justice Rehnquist's dissent, the Court's decision disregards the extensive evidence from congressional debate prior to the passage of Title VII indicating that preferential treatment would not be permitted.

What accounts for this abrupt about-face by the court? No basis for definitively answering this question is available; what follows is our interpretation of the available evidence.

According to the Court, Title VII "was primarily addressed to the problem of opening opportunities for Negroes in occupations which have been traditionally closed to them." We have previously noted that approaches to affirmative action vary on a continuum of the speed with which increased minority representation will result. The Court in *Steelworkers* appears to be concerned with speed:

> *Congress' primary concern in enacting the prohibition against racial discrimination in Title VII was with the plight of the Negro in our economy, and the prohibition against racial discrimination in employment was primarily addressed to the problem of opening opportunities for Negroes in occupations which have been traditionally closed to them. In view of the legislative history, the very statutory words intended as a spur or catalyst to cause employers and unions to self-examine and to self-evaluate their employment practices and to endeavor to eliminate, so far as possible, the last vestiges of an unfortunate and ignominious page in this country's history cannot be interpreted as an absolute prohibition against all private, voluntary, race-conscious affirmative action efforts to hasten the elimination of such vestiges. (p. III)*

Consider the facts in *Steelworkers:* selection was not on the basis of knowledge, skill, ability, or previous job performance, but rather on the basis of seniority. Also, the issue was selection to a training program where skills necessary for job performance would be acquired. Given the situation, the Court may have seen an opportunity to speed up the process of occupational integration without doing violence to an organization's interest in developing a highly qualified work force. Hence the very limited ruling: a statement that not all preferential affirmative action plans are prohibited, and that the plan in question is acceptable. We are speculating here that the Court would have ruled differently if the case had involved a situation in which job applicants were expected to already possess a set of skills clearly related to successful job performance.

By appealing to the spirit of the law and either downplaying or ignoring legislative history and previous court decisions, the decision in *Steelworkers* exemplifies ongoing debate about what constitutes the appropriate role of the Court. Is it appropriate to reason as follows? "If Congress knew in 1964 the extent to which occupational segregation would still exist in 1978, it would have treated the preferential treatment issue differently. With the advantage of hindsight we now see some forms of preferential treatment as necessary to achieve the goals of Title VII." Or is the following more appropriate? "In 1964, Congress clearly felt that preferential treatment was not needed to achieve occupational integration. If Congress feels differently today, Title VII can be amended. Our role is to interpret existing law; thus preferential treatment is forbidden." The majority in *Weber* reflects the first position; the dissent, the second.

Until clarification is received from the courts, employers face a situation in which proportional hiring strategies are endorsed by the regulatory agencies. Using valid selection strategies to rank applicants separately by race and sex and to hire proportionately from each group appears to be the safest strategy for employers to follow at present. While it does deviate from race and sex-blind qualifications-based hiring, which we consider optimal, it avoids the fallacy of equating applicants exceeding some minimal standard. Proportional hiring need not imply abandoning the development and use of the most valid selection procedures available, but rather the use of such procedures to hire the most qualified applicant within each group. How long the uneasy compromise will continue will be determined by the courts.

REFERENCE

Seligman, D. How equal opportunity turned into employment quotas. *Fortune,* March, 1973, 160–168.

Chapter 6

Labor Markets

INTRODUCTION

In the earlier chapter on decision making, we stressed the concept of maximizing the expected utility of a selection system. Recall that the base rate and selection ratio associated with a particular selection problem must be considered along with the validity and cost of the selection procedure and the costs/benefits associated with various outcomes when making decisions about whether to use a particular selection device. Essentially, alternative procedures are compared and the approach resulting in the greatest net advantage to the firm becomes the procedure of choice. The base rate reflects the proportion of applicants who, if hired, could perform at or above some minimum standard. The selection ratio is the ratio of applicants who can be accepted to the total number of available applicants. Given the centrality of these concepts to the decision-making process, it will be useful to consider each within the broader context of a labor market. Base rates and selection ratios are sensitive to the supply of and demand for labor. The first two readings focus on these issues from an aggregate perspective. Young (1982) documents the recent increase in the educational level of workers. While reports on the educational attainment of workers regularly appear in the *Monthly Labor Review* (*MLR*), Young's *MLR* article is particularly interesting because it documents change across the decade of the 1970s. The educational attainments and skills (in addition to labor force size) of persons who compose the labor force and the extent to which they match the skill requirements of jobs are key issues for this chapter. Rumberger (1981) makes the important distinction between skills individuals possess and skills jobs require. His article examines the general skill requirements of jobs in the U.S. economy. Both articles suggest that in certain occupational areas there will be an oversupply of qualified job seekers. Note, however, that as outlined by Young (1981), the situation can change rapidly as the baby-boom generation works its way through the educational system and subsequent entry-level jobs.

Finally, the different issue of defining a firm's labor market is the focus of the final reading by Gastwirth and Haber (1977). This is a critical issue for two reasons. First, one accepted procedure for determining adverse impact is to make a comparison of the employer's internal work force with the race, sex, and ethnic percentages associated with the defined prospective employee pool. The other reason relates to the potential for base rate and selection ratio change as recruiting efforts focus on different labor market segments.

REFERENCES

Gastwirth, J. L. & Haber, S. Defining the labor market for equal employment standards. *Monthly Labor Review,* 1976, *99, 3,* 32–36.

Rumberger, R. W. The changing skill requirements of jobs in the U.S. economy. *Industrial and Labor Relations Review,* 1981, *34,* 578–589.

Young, A. M. Educational attainment of workers, March 1981. *Monthly Labor Review,* April 1982, pp. 52–55.

Educational Attainment of Workers, March 1981*

ANNE MCDOUGALL YOUNG
Division of Labor Force Studies, Bureau of Labor Statistics

Employers continue to use education as one of the basic qualifications for hiring and promotion, and in recent years the educational level of workers has increased dramatically. In March 1981, there were almost as many workers age 25 to 64 who had completed a year or more of college as had ended their formal education with a high school diploma. (See Table 1.) Each of these two groups accounted for about 40 percent of the work force. As recently as 1970, only 26 percent of the workers had completed any college after high school.[1] (See Table 2.) This change reflects primarily the coming of age of the more highly educated baby boom generation,[2] and, to a lesser extent, early retirement among older and generally less educated workers.

To cope with the very large number of students who reached college age between the mid-1960's and early 1970's, the education industry expanded both in physical plant and staff. The number of institutions of higher education increased by 47 percent from 1963 to 1978, from 2,132 to 3,134, and the number of full-time equivalent teaching staff rose from 242,000 to 597,000.[3] Over half (55 percent) of the new institutions were 2-year public colleges. The relatively easy accessibility of these colleges enabled many students to attend without leaving home and often while working at a full-time job. Indeed, among persons under age 35, part-time students accounted for half of the growth in total college enrollment during the 1970–80 decade.[4]

The relationship between men and women in terms of educational attainment did not change over the decade, except among the youngest group. The proportion of men with a year or more of college continued to be almost 6 percentage points above that of women, while women remained less likely to be high school dropouts. However, among workers 25 to 34— the age group comprising the largest part of the baby boom generation—the male-female difference in the proportion with some college narrowed substantially. Close to half of all workers in that age group had completed some college.

PARTICIPATION RATES

More education has historically been associated with higher rates of labor force participation, a pattern that persisted in March 1981. College graduates had the highest labor force participation rates, and

* Anne McDougall Young, "Educational Attainment of Workers, March 1981," *Monthly Labor Review*, April 1982, pp. 52–55.

Table 1
Labor Force Status of Persons Age 25–64, by Sex and Years of School Completed, March 1980 and
March 1981 (numbers in thousands)

| | Men | | | Women | | |
| | 1980 | | | 1980 | | |
Years of school completed	Original	Revised	1981	Original	Revised	1981
Total population	49,848	50,782	51,840	53,664	54,777	55,813
Total labor force	44,755	45,417	46,363	32,010	32,593	33,910
High school:						
Less than 4 years	10,022	10,103	9,963	5,885	5,999	5,889
4 years only	16,017	16,232	16,917	14,586	14,801	15,635
College:						
1 to 3 years	7,880	8,042	8,083	5,566	5,686	6,086
4 years or more	10,837	11,040	11,402	5,974	6,106	6,300
Labor force participation rate (in percent)	89.8	89.4	89.4	59.6	59.5	60.8
High school:						
Less than 4 years	79.4	78.8	79.3	43.9	43.7	44.2
4 years only	92.2	91.9	91.2	61.4	61.2	62.4
College:						
1 to 3 years	92.7	92.4	92.0	66.5	66.4	68.0
4 years or more	95.5	95.3	95.4	73.6	73.4	74.3

NOTE: See text footnote 1 regarding revised numbers. Due to rounding, sums of individual items may not equal totals.

high school dropouts, the lowest. (See Table 2.)

Participation rates for men have continued their historical drift downward among all age and educational attainment groups except college graduates under age 55. This general trend among men has been observed over the past 25 years.[5] Accounting in part for this trend are more widely available disability and pension benefits, which have made early retirement possible. Persons in poor health or who have been out of work for a number of months, have been the most likely to retire before age 65,[6] and workers with less education are in these circumstances more often than are persons with extensive education.

While men have reduced their labor force participation, rates for women have increased at all levels of educational attainment and at all ages except among those 55–64 years of age. Among women age 25 to 34, the sharp rise in participation rates between 1970 and 1981 reflected the trend toward delayed marriage and childbearing. Increases in participation were also sub-

stantial among women 35 to 54, although to a lesser degree than among younger women. Most of the women over age 35 were married (72 percent), and such factors as expanded job opportunities in the white-collar and service sectors, as well as inflationary pressure on family budgets, boosted their labor force activity.

OCCUPATIONS

The increase in the proportion of more highly educated workers was supported by growth in the demand for a trained labor force. Computerized design and manufacturing operations, word processing and other new business machines, engineering development, biological research, and changing medical care procedures all needed personnel with sufficient education to use the new technology which became available during the 1970's.[7] Consequently, the proportion of workers in professional-technical and managerial occupations increased from 26 percent in 1970 to 29 percent in 1981. (See Table 3.)

Table 2
Years of School Completed by Persons in the Labor Force, and Labor Force Participation Rates, by Age and Sex, March 1970 and March 1981

Years of school completed	25 to 64 years		25 to 34 years		35 to 44 years		45 to 54 years		55 to 64 years	
	1970	1981	1970	1981	1970	1981	1970	1981	1970	1981
Labor force										
Men										
Total: Number (thousands)	39,302	46,363	11,211	17,312	10,518	11,982	10,429	9,847	7,142	7,222
Percent	100.0	100.0	100.0	100.0	100.0	100.0	100.0	100.0	100.0	100.0
High school: Less than 4 years	37.5	21.5	25.1	13.4	35.7	19.9	41.2	29.2	54.5	33.3
4 years only	34.5	36.5	40.4	37.8	34.6	36.7	34.0	35.2	25.9	34.6
College: 1 year or more	27.9	42.0	34.5	48.8	29.7	43.4	24.8	35.6	19.6	32.1
1 to 3 years	12.2	17.4	15.3	22.3	12.1	16.4	11.4	13.4	8.8	12.9
4 years or more	15.7	24.6	19.2	26.5	17.6	27.0	13.4	22.2	10.8	19.2
Women										
Total: Number (thousands)	22,458	33,910	5,735	12,945	6,014	8,904	6,516	7,189	4,198	4,872
Percent	100.0	100.0	100.0	100.0	100.0	100.0	100.0	100.0	100.0	100.0
High school: Less than 4 years	33.5	17.4	23.6	10.5	32.5	16.7	35.5	23.0	45.6	28.6
4 years only	44.3	46.1	48.2	43.6	47.2	47.0	45.6	49.2	33.0	46.7
College: 1 year or more	22.1	36.5	28.3	46.0	20.3	36.2	18.9	27.8	21.5	24.7
1 to 3 years	10.9	17.9	13.1	22.2	10.5	17.3	9.8	13.8	10.3	13.9
4 years or more	11.2	18.6	15.2	23.8	9.8	18.9	9.1	14.0	11.2	10.8
Labor force participation rates										
Men										
Total	93.5	89.4	96.5	94.7	97.1	95.0	94.6	91.0	83.4	71.3
High school: Less than 4 years	89.3	79.3	95.1	89.3	94.7	89.0	91.5	83.7	79.4	62.1
4 years only	96.3	91.2	98.2	96.1	98.2	95.8	96.3	92.7	88.8	73.6
College: 1 to 3 years	95.6	92.0	95.7	94.2	98.7	96.0	97.5	92.8	87.5	76.8
4 years or more	96.3	95.4	95.4	96.1	98.8	98.3	97.4	98.2	90.0	84.3
Women										
Total	48.9	60.8	45.6	67.4	51.3	66.5	54.4	61.7	43.7	42.1
High school: Less than 4 years	42.9	44.2	40.3	47.4	47.6	52.9	47.9	48.5	36.7	32.7
4 years only	51.3	62.4	45.5	66.9	52.7	67.9	57.8	65.0	49.4	45.3
College: 1 to 3 years	50.8	68.0	45.5	71.6	52.7	72.8	57.0	66.9	50.6	50.7
4 years or more	60.9	74.3	57.6	78.7	57.7	74.0	67.5	76.3	64.1	54.7

NOTE: The labor force participation rate is the percent of the civilian population in the labor force. Due to rounding, sums of individual items may not equal totals.

Table 3

Occupation of Employed Persons Age 18 and Over, by Years of School Completed and by Sex, March 1970 and March 1981 (in percent)

Years of school completed	Total		Professional-technical	Managers	Sales	Clerical	Craft	Operatives	Nonfarm laborers	Service	Farm
	Number (in thousands)	Percent									
Both sexes:											
1970	75,658	100.0	14.8	10.9	5.9	17.7	13.1	18.1	4.1	11.8	3.6
1981	96,644	100.0	16.9	12.1	6.2	18.7	12.9	13.8	3.9	13.1	2.6
Men:											
1970	47,062	100.0	14.4	14.8	5.5	7.5	20.4	19.9	6.3	6.1	5.0
1981	55,005	100.0	16.4	15.4	6.1	6.3	21.2	16.5	6.0	8.6	3.5
Women:											
1970	28,596	100.0	15.5	4.5	6.5	34.6	1.1	15.1	.4	21.0	1.4
1981	41,639	100.0	17.6	7.7	6.4	35.2	1.8	10.3	1.1	19.2	.9
High school:											
Less than 4 years:											
Men:											
1970	17,326	100.0	1.4	8.4	2.8	4.5	25.7	29.4	10.7	8.3	8.8
1981	11,741	100.0	1.5	7.0	2.2	3.8	26.4	28.7	11.0	12.2	7.2
Women:											
1970	8,585	100.0	1.8	3.3	6.5	14.7	1.7	30.4	.8	37.9	2.8
1981	6,779	100.0	2.4	3.9	5.5	15.2	2.8	27.3	2.1	39.0	1.9
4 years only:											
Men:											
1970	16,563	100.0	6.9	15.5	5.9	9.9	25.0	21.5	5.4	6.2	3.7
1981	20,966	100.0	5.7	12.7	5.3	6.9	29.1	21.0	6.9	9.0	3.5
Women:											
1970	13,053	100.0	6.7	4.7	7.3	50.0	1.1	12.0	.3	17.0	.9
1981	19,556	100.0	6.0	7.1	6.9	45.5	2.0	10.9	1.2	19.6	.8
College:											
1 to 3 years:											
Men:											
1970	6,334	100.0	19.7	22.3	10.8	12.8	13.1	9.7	3.3	5.7	2.4
1981	10,096	100.0	15.6	19.1	9.0	9.9	18.9	10.6	4.8	10.4	1.8
Women:											
1970	3,799	100.0	22.1	6.8	7.2	46.6	.6	2.9	.2	13.0	.7
1981	8,226	100.0	19.7	9.8	7.5	42.9	1.3	2.7	.8	14.9	.5
4 years or more:											
Men:											
1970	6,837	100.0	60.6	22.4	6.8	4.3	2.5	1.4	.3	.9	.8
1981	12,200	100.0	50.0	25.4	8.7	4.5	4.7	1.8	.8	2.9	1.2
Women:											
1970	3,159	100.0	80.9	4.1	1.9	10.6	.3	.5	—	1.6	.2
1981	7,080	100.0	61.9	10.3	4.4	16.6	.8	1.3	.3	3.9	.5

The number of college graduates in the professions increased substantially over the decade. But because there were so many more graduates competing for available positions, those finding professional-technical jobs represented a smaller percentage of all graduates—54 percent in 1981 compared with 67 percent in 1970. The situation was intensified by the relative lack of growth in the demand for teachers, as the baby boom generation passed through the schools. This trend was especially important for the greatly increased number of women with college degrees. Whereas 50 percent of the employed female graduates were teachers in 1970, that proportion had declined to 29 percent in 1981.

A greater proportion of the college graduates were managers in 1981. This was, in part, a response to the growth of large scale enterprises, such as banking and investment services, in which the increased quantity and variety of transactions have created more complex management situations.[8] College graduates were also more likely to be salesworkers, often as specialists in technical services and equipment, and small but growing proportions were in blue-collar and service occupations.

Many workers who had completed their formal education with 1 to 3 years of college had earned certificates and other awards of achievement. During 1970–71 to 1977–78, the number of associate degrees conferred increased by 63 percent.[9] Among the recipients in 1977–78, 59 percent had been in occupational curricula such as science or engineering, data processing, or health sciences. Nevertheless, between 1970 and 1981, the proportion of workers with only 1 to 3 years of college who held white-collar jobs decreased 12 percentage points among men and almost 3 percentage points among women. Increased employment in craft and service work accounted for most of the change among men. The relatively smaller change among women reflected their continuing concentration in clerical occupations and their modest gain in the management field.

Workers with no formal education beyond high school were at an increasing disadvantage, compared to those with 1 to 3 years of college, in finding employment in professional-technical and managerial occupations. The proportion of male high school graduates with no college who were blue-collar workers rose from 52 to 57 percent over the decade. The proportion of women with no education beyond high school who were in clerical jobs dropped from 50 to 46 percent—with some shifting to managerial jobs and some to service jobs.

In March 1981, most high school dropouts were employed as operatives, nonfarm laborers, and service workers. These occupations frequently do not require a high school diploma as a condition of employment. However, the average educational attainment has risen substantially in these jobs, and is now well over 12 years. Thus, even for these relatively unskilled occupations, dropouts faced increased competition from workers with more education.

The educational composition of the labor force may undergo several changes in the near future. First, the baby boom generation will have worked its way through the educational system by the mid-1980's, putting an end to the bulge in the number of workers in entry level jobs. Second, the next wave of labor force entrants will be smaller, and the relative shortage of new high school and college graduates may lead to more readily available entry level jobs. On the other hand, these workers will face continuing competition for advancement from the huge group which preceded them. And third, modifications of national priorities and possible changes in spending patterns in both the private and public sectors may shift the demand for more highly educated workers from one occupational group to another.

NOTES

[1] Data in this report are based on tabulations from the March 1981 Current Population Survey (CPS), conducted for the Bureau of Labor Statistics by the Bureau of the Census. The data relate to the labor force 25 to 64 years of age, unless otherwise specified. The data have been inflated using population weights based on results from the 1980 census. The March 1980 data in Table 1 have also been revised to bring them in line with the new population weights and to make them comparable with the March 1981 data. Previously published data for the years 1971 through 1980 reflected population weights projected forward from the 1970 census.

As Table 1 shows, the number of persons age 25 to 64 years old was revised upward by 2 million, and the number in the labor force was estimated to be 1.2 million greater than originally reported. Despite these significant changes in the data for 1980, the various relationships and percentages based on the new estimates are similar to those based on the previously published estimates. For example, the labor force participation rate for persons with 4 years of high school was estimated at 74.4 percent using the 1970 weights and 74.2 percent using the 1980 weights.

For a more complete description of changes in labor force data stemming from the use of 1980 census population weights in the CPS, see "Revisions in the Current Population Survey Beginning in January 1982," *Employment and Earnings*, February 1982.

Because the March estimates are based on a sample, they may differ from the figures that would have been obtained from a complete census. Sampling variability may be relatively large in cases where the numbers are small. Small es-timates, or small differences between estimates, should be interpreted with caution. This report is the latest in a series on this subject. The most recent was published in the *Monthly Labor Review*, "Trends in educational attainment among workers in the 1970's," July 1980, pp. 44–47. Data on the educational attainment of the population are published by the Bureau of the Census in *Current Population Reports*, Series P–20.

[2] The expression "baby boom generation" usually refers to persons born between 1946 and 1964. The rate of births to women 15 to 44 years of age rose to over 24 per 1,000 in 1946, over 25 per 1,000 in 1957, and remained over 21 per 1,000 through 1964. See *Historical Statistics of the United States, Colonial Times to 1970*, Part 1 (Bureau of the Census, 1975), Table B 5–10.

[3] *The Condition of Education*, 1975 Edition (U.S. Department of Education, National Center for Education Statistics), table 67; *The Condition of Education*, 1980 Edition, Tables 3.7 and 3.10; and unpublished data from the National Center for Education Statistics.

[4] Unpublished data from the October 1970 and 1980 supplements to the Current Population Survey (CPS), Bureau of Labor Statistics.

[5] *Employment and Training Report of the President, 1980*, table A–4.

[6] Karen Schwab, "Early Labor Force Withdrawal of Men: Participants and Nonparticipants Aged 58–63," *Social Security Bulletin*, August 1974, pp. 24–38.

[7] *Occupational Outlook for College Graduates, 1978–79* edition (Bureau of Labor Statistics).

[8] Ibid.

[9] *The Condition of Education*, 1980 edition, table 1–11.

The Changing Skill Requirements of Jobs in the U.S. Economy*

RUSSELL W. RUMBERGER

Most labor market research treats skills as characteristics of individuals, not of jobs. Yet there may be an important distinction between the skills possessed by individuals and the skills required by the jobs they hold. This study examines the general skill requirements of jobs in the U.S. economy and documents changes in the aggregate distribution of these requirements between 1960 and 1976.

Focus on the skills of individuals arises from the neoclassical view of the labor market, which forms the basis of a large quantity of research. According to this view, skills are embodied in individuals in the form of "human capital"[1] and earnings reflect the marginal products of individuals, on the basis of the assumption that individual skills are effectively utilized by firms because of substitution among workers and between labor and capital.[2]

The idea of skill requirements being associated with jobs also has a conceptual basis, however. Thurow posits a "job competition" model of the labor market in which marginal products are associated with jobs and not individuals.[3] In this view workers are first allocated to available jobs and then trained to perform the tasks associated with them. Because this allocation process is based on the available supplies of both individuals and jobs, workers may actually possess more skills than are necessary to perform the tasks of their jobs adequately. Other views of the labor market also endorse the notion of job skills. In screening theory, education serves as a credential, in part, implying that some individuals may be allocated to jobs in which some of their skills remain unused.[4] And in a Marxist framework, Braverman argues, the development of capitalism causes jobs to be frag-

* R. W. Rumberger, "The Changing Skill Requirements of Jobs in the U.S. Economy," *Industrial and Labor Relations Review*, 34 (1981), pp. 578–89. Reprinted with permission from the *Industrial and Labor Relations Review*, Vol. 34, 1981, 578–589. © 1981 by Cornell University. All rights reserved.

The author is a research associate at Stanford University. Support for this project was provided by the Employment and Training Administration, U.S. Department of Labor. The author wishes to acknowledge advice and assistance from Henry Levin, Martin Carnoy, Lewis Mayhew, Laura Best, and Thomas Daymont.

[1] Gary S. Becker, *Human Capital* (New York: National Bureau of Economic Research, 1964).

[2] Some observers question whether earnings are proportional to marginal products. See Peter T. Gottschalk, "A Comparison of Marginal Productivity and Earnings by Occupation," *Industrial and Labor Relations Review*, 31, no. 3 (April 1978), pp. 368–78.

[3] Lester C. Thurow, *Generating Inequality* (New York: Basic Books, 1975), pp. 75–97.

[4] Paul Taubman and Terence Wales, *Higher Education: An Investment and a Screening Device* (New York: McGraw-Hill, 1974).

mented and routinized over time, irrespective of the skills workers possess.[5]

In addition to its theoretical importance, the study of job skill requirements is useful in addressing policy issues. Measuring the skill requirements of jobs serves as one means of assessing the demand for skilled labor. By contrasting the skill content of jobs in the economy with the skills possessed by the labor force, policy makers get some indication of how well the supply of skilled labor is keeping abreast of available jobs. The recent debate on the economic decline of college graduates illustrates the usefulness of this approach.

Jobs skills, especially of a general nature, are often acquired in school. Except for occasional shortages, most observers view the educational system as a highly effective vehicle for producing the skills required to maintain the growth of the economy. In the 1960s, for example, it appeared that the increasing supply of college-educated workers entering the labor market was simply meeting the rising demand for skilled labor. In recent years, however, the supply of skilled labor may have outstripped demand. Some observers contend that many college graduates must now accept positions formerly held by high school graduates.[6] Others claim, however, that such upgrading is necessary because of technological advances that require a more skilled labor force.[7] Yet little evidence exists to support either claim.

The present study examines changes in job skill requirements. Specifically, it asks the following questions: (1) Has the overall skill content of jobs increased, remained steady, or decreased in recent years? (2)

What factors have contributed to any observed change? In particular, what has been the effect of: (*a*) changes in the distribution of employment among different occupations, and (*b*) changes in the skill requirements of particular occupations?[8]

Some previous researchers have assessed changes in the overall skill level of jobs in the economy by using information on job skill requirements from various editions of the *Dictionary of Occupational Titles* (DOT), a sourcebook that is issued periodically by the U.S. Employment Service[9] A few of these have based their estimates on skill requirements of individual jobs at one particular time, taken from a single edition of the DOT, and the distribution of employment among jobs at two or more

---

[5] Harry Braverman, *Labor and Monopoly Capital* (New York: Monthly Review Press, 1974), pp. 251–56.

[6] Ivar Berg, *Education and Jobs: The Great Training Robbery* (New York: Praeger Publishers, 1970).

[7] Carnegie Commission on Higher Education, *College Graduates and Jobs* (New York: McGraw-Hill, 1973).

[8] The research reported in this paper was conducted as part of a larger project that compared changes in the general skill requirements of jobs with changes in the skills of the American workforce reflected in educational attainments. The results of the larger project are reported in Russell W. Rumberger, *Overeducation in the U.S. Labor Market* (New York: Praeger Publishers, 1981). The entire project only examined general skill requirements, not specific skill requirements. The latter represents an important topic for future research.

[9] Previous studies include R. S. Eckaus, "The Economic Criteria For Education and Training," *Review of Economics and Statistics* 46. no. 2 (May 1964), pp. 181–90; James G. Scoville, "Education and Training Requirements for Occupations," *Review of Economics and Statistics* 48. no. 4 (November 1966), pp. 387–94; Morris A. Horowitz and Irwin L. Herrnstadt, "Changes in the Skill Requirements of Occupations in Selected Industries," in the National Commission on Technology, Automation, and Economic Progress, *The Employment Impact of Technological Change* (Washington, D.C.: (Government Printing Office, 1966), pp. II-223–87; Ivar Berg, *Education and Jobs* (New York: Praeger Publishers, 1970); V. Lane Rawlins and Lloyd Ulman, "The Utilization of College-Trained Manpower in the United States," in *Higher Education and the Labor Market*, ed. Margaret S. Gordon, (New York: McGraw-Hill, 1974), pp. 195–235; Lloyd V. Temme, *Occupation: Meanings and Measures* (Washington, D.C.: Bureau of Social Science Research, 1975); Ivar Berg, Marcia Freedman, and Michael Freeman, *Managers and Work Reform* (New York: Free Press, 1978); and Kenneth I. Spenner, "Temporal Changes in Work Content," *American Sociological Review*, 44, no. 6 (December 1979); pp. 968–75.

times.[10] As a result, these researchers have attributed changes in the aggregate distribution of skill requirements to shifts in employment among occupations but have ignored changes in the skill requirements of individual jobs. Other investigators have examined changes in the skill requirements of individual jobs, using two successive editions of the DOT, but have ignored shifts in the distribution of employment, which would also produce changes in the aggregate distribution of job skill requirements.[11] The present study attempts to overcome these limitations by using estimates of individual job skill requirements from two editions of the DOT together with information on the distribution of employment in two years—1960 and 1976.[12] In addition, the study makes use of the most recent edition of the DOT (1977), thereby providing an indication of recent changes in skill requirements.

METHODOLOGY

The conceptual framework of this research is based on the assumption that the skill requirements of jobs are in some way specifiable and measurable, or, stated differently, that there is an average skill requirement associated with each job in the economy. A worker holding a particular job must attain the average skill level for that job in order to perform the tasks of the job adequately. Functional requirements are not to be confused with the hiring requirements established by employers, however, which are dictated in part by market conditions. Although the skill requirements of some jobs could vary over the long run with changes in the skills of workers in those jobs, employers may be unable or unwilling to alter the tasks of a job in the short run to take advantage of a particular worker's skills. This notion of relatively fixed skill requirements forms the basis of the present study.

This research is divided into two empirical tasks. The first is to estimate the distribution of skill requirements *within* major census occupation groups (professional, managerial, and service, for example) at two points in time using two separate estimates of skill requirements for individual jobs. Net changes in aggregate skill levels between 1960 and 1976 can then be disaggregated into two factors: changes in the distribution of employment among jobs and changes in the skill requirements of individual jobs.

The second task is to estimate the distribution of skill requirements across the economy as a whole, using the estimates produced in the first task. In this case it is possible to disaggregate net changes in aggregate skill levels into three factors: changes in the distribution of employment among major occupation groups (*inter-occupational group shifts*), changes in the distribution of employment among jobs within major occupation groups (*intra-occupational group shifts*), and changes in the skill requirements of individual jobs.

Two types of information are required to derive these empirical estimates. The first, information on the skill requirements of individual jobs, is taken from the two most recent editions of the *Dictionary of*

[10] See, for example, Eckaus, "The Economic Criteria," and Scoville, "Education and Training Requirements."

[11] Examples include Horowitz and Herrnstadt, "Changes in the Skill Requirements," Spenner, "Temporal Changes," and Rawlins and Ulman, "The Utilization of College-Trained Manpower."

[12] These two years were chosen for several reasons. At the time of this study, 1976 was the most recent year for which employment data were available. The year also corresponded quite closely with the release of the most recent edition of the DOT in 1977. The other year, 1960, marked the beginning of a decade characterized by rapid technological change that some people believe greatly increased the demand for skilled labor. Employment data were also readily available for that year. This base year did not correspond as well, however, to the 1965 release date of the other edition of the DOT used in the study. This matter is discussed in the next section.

Occupational Titles—the third edition, issued in 1965, and the fourth, issued in 1977.[13] The DOT contains comprehensive descriptions of all jobs in the U.S. economy, which include estimates of the general and specific skill requirements (General Educational Development—GED and Specific Vocational Preparation—SVP) for each job. The estimates represent the skills required for a worker to achieve "average performance in a particular job."[14] The distributions of general skill requirements based on the GED estimates from the DOT are used in this study.

The second type of information required, that on the distribution of employment, comes from census data: the 1960 1/1000 Public Use Sample and the March 1976 Current Population Survey (CPS). Data on the current occupation of the employed population, 14 years and older, pro-

vided the distribution of employment for each year.[15]

The major methodological task in this research involved producing estimates of skill requirements for individual census occupation codes on the basis of DOT information. This task was necessary because the DOT and census data employ different occupational coding schemes. In addition, the coding schemes changed between the third and fourth editions of the DOT and between the 1960 and 1970 censuses. Going from one scheme to the other requires a sample of occupations coded under both systems.

Fortunately such a sample was prepared for two previous Current Population Surveys, 1966 and 1971. The 1966 CPS was used to construct a matrix that cross-references 1960 census occupation codes and third edition DOT occupation codes.[16]

---

[13] U.S. Employment Service, *Dictionary of Occupational Titles*, 2 vols., 3rd ed. (Washington, D.C.: Government Printing Office, 1965); U.S. Employment Service, *Dictionary of Occupational Titles*, 4th ed. (Washington, D.C.: Government Printing Office, 1977). Information in the third edition of the DOT was collected mostly in the early 1960s, while information in the fourth edition was collected between 1965 and the mid-1970s. See U.S. Employment Service, *Dictionary*, 4th ed., p. xiv. There may be some bias introduced because the years for which employment distributions are assessed—1960 and 1976—may not correspond exactly with the years in which the skill requirements of jobs were measured.

[14] U.S. Employment Service, *Dictionary*, 3d ed., Vol. 2, Appendix B, p. 651. These estimates were derived primarily by government experts observing workers performing their jobs. They represent the functional or performance requirements of jobs, not the hiring requirements dictated by employers. Consequently, differences in estimated skill levels should measure changes in skill requirements of particular jobs and not changes in employers' tastes for certain worker traits. However, because job analysts also employ other techniques to obtain information on jobs, there is no guarantee that skill requirements are completely independent of employers' preferences or hiring requirements. We can only assume this to be the case. For a full description of the procedures used to obtain DOT information, see U.S. Department of Labor, *Handbook for Analyzing Jobs* (Washington, D.C.: Government Printing Office, 1972).

[15] Initially both the employed and unemployed were included in the two files. But only the employed were actually used in the final estimates since it was felt that they would give a more accurate picture of the jobs that actually exist in the economy. Of course there are more jobs than those held by the employed population because there are always a number of vacant or unfilled jobs. But since the analysis focuses on the distribution of skill requirements, the actual numbers are relatively unimportant. There may be some bias introduced by excluding the unemployed, however. In both years persons who did not report an occupation were also excluded. There were no such cases in 1976 (since occupations were allocated); in 1960 4.7 percent of the cases were dropped. The final sample sizes were 64,945 in 1960 and 54,194 in 1976.

[16] The matrix was constructed originally by Anne R. Miller, "Occupations of the Labor Force According to the Dictionary of Occupational Titles," (Philadelphia: Population Studies Center, Pennsylvania University, 1971). The advantage of using the CPS data is that it weights the distribution of DOT occupations *within* each census occupation code based on the number of people employed in each job. In some previous studies, DOT characteristics were assigned to census codes using unweighted averages of the DOT job characteristics associated with each particular census code. Examples include Eckaus, "The Economic Criteria," Scoville, "Education and Training Requirements," Berg, *Education and Jobs,* and Rawlins and Ulman, "The Utilization of College-Trained Manpower."

With this matrix and data on the character-istics of jobs in the DOT, every census oc-cupation code was assigned the probability of having a particular DOT job characteris-tic, including a specific GED level.[17] This information was then merged with the 1960 sample of occupations.

A similar set of procedures was used to assign GED levels to the 1976 sample of occupations. In this case 1970 census occu-pation codes and third edition DOT codes were cross-referenced in the 1971 CPS.[18] Another cross-reference was used to trans-late third edition DOT information into fourth edition DOT information.[19] Using these two cross-references, every 1970 census occupation code was assigned the probability of having a particular GED level based on both the third and fourth editions of the DOT.[20] This information was then merged with the 1976 sample of occupations.[21]

EMPIRICAL RESULTS

Changes in the aggregate distribution of skill levels can result from both changes in the distribution of employment among jobs and changes in the skill levels of indi-vidual jobs. The distribution of employ-ment that existed among major occupation groups in 1960 and 1976 is exhibited in Table 1. The occupation groups are defined according to the census classification scheme, since it is the most widely used and well-known system for examining em-ployment patterns. The figures in Table 1 show that between 1960 and 1976 the per-centage of workers employed in all white-collar occupations (except sales workers) and in service occupations (except private houshold workers) increased while the per-centage of workers employed in blue-collar

---

[17] These estimates were made by Robert E. B. Lu-cas, "Working Conditions, Wage Rates, and Human Capital" (Ph.D. dissertation, Massachusetts Institute of Technology, 1972). Lucas produced estimates for 295 out of 297 1960 census occupation codes, leaving some codes without information on job characteris-tics. He also subdivided two census categories into ten industry subgroups. Instead of using these subdivided categories, I assigned individuals the mean values of GED from the subgroups within each code. Finally, neither Lucas nor I produced separate estimates for whites and blacks or men and women. To the degree that blacks hold lower skilled jobs than whites, even within the same census category, estimates may over-state the aggregate skill requirements of jobs. This bias is probably less acute for women since the major-ity are employed in female-dominated jobs. Yet some critics claim that the requisite skills for some female-dominated occupations may be understated. See Patri-cia C. Sexton, "Women and Work," U.S. Department of Labor R&D Monograph No. 46 (Washington D.C.: Government Printing Office, 1977), pp. 39–40.

[18] Census coders were sometimes unable to assign a DOT code based on respondent's job information in the 1971 CPS. These cases, comprising 14 percent of the original sample, were excluded from the cross-reference. It is difficult to assess the degree to which the excluded cases may have biased the estimates, al-though there is no evidence to indicate that the errors should not be random. Moreover, this problem un-doubtedly affected the 1966 CPS as well. Any result-ing bias should be similar, therefore, and comparisons between 1960 and 1976 should accurately reflect ac-tual changes.

[19] The cross-reference translated third edition codes into equivalent fourth edition codes. Of course, between the third and fourth editions of the DOT, some occupation codes were added and some were deleted. The added codes mean that some occupations in the 1971 CPS sample may have been coded with a particular third edition DOT code, when another, fourth edition code would have represented that occu-pation more accurately. But unless the new codes cre-ated in the fourth edition of the DOT are, on average, associated with higher skill levels than third edition codes (and recent evidence suggests they are not—see Spenner, "Temporal Changes," p. 971), estimated skill levels for census occupations should be reasona-bly accurate. The problem with deleted codes was mi-nor. In the 1971 CPS sample, fewer than .1 percent of the cases with third edition codes could not be matched to fourth edition codes. In these instances third edition information was used.

[20] The GED scale is composed of three compo-nents. Only the highest of the three were selected from the fourth edition of the DOT in order to corre-spond to the single estimate available from the third edition of the DOT.

[21] A small number of cases (.1 percent) in the 1976 sample of occupations were not assigned DOT infor-mation because some occupations were not present in the 1971 CPS. These cases were excluded from the analysis.

Table 1
Occupation Group of Employed Population,
1960 and 1976 (percent distribution)[a]

Occupation Group	1960	1976
White-collar workers	43.1	50.1
Professional and technical workers	11.9	15.2
Managers and administrators	8.6	10.6
Sales workers	7.6	6.5
Clerical workers	15.0	17.8
Blue-collar workers	38.5	32.4
Craft and kindred workers	14.1	12.6
Operatives	19.3	15.2
Nonfarm laborers	5.1	4.6
Service workers	11.6	14.4
Private household workers	2.8	1.8
Other service workers	8.8	12.6
Farm workers	6.7	3.2
Farmers	4.2	1.7
Farm laborers	2.5	1.5
Total	100.0	100.0

[a] Distributions may not add to 100.0 because of rounding.
Source: Calculated from the 1960 1/1000 Public Use Sample and the March 1976 Current Population Survey, U.S. Bureau of the Census.

and farming occupations decreased. The growth in white-collar employment itself is often heralded as an indication of the increasing employment opportunities in the more rewarding and demanding portion of the job hierarchy. But the terms "white-collar" and "blue-collar" actually reveal little about job content or requisite job skills:

> "White-collar" is a label that presupposes an essential difference between the structure of labor in the factory and in the office. It is a category of social ideology rather than of social science and has evoked the image of a system of social stratification that regards office work as a higher-status occupation than factory work, administration as more prestigious than manual labor, or, indeed, any occupation related directly to the production of goods. The bare fact is that "white-collar" is less a description of an actual group of workers than a conceptual tool for a specific perspective on social class.[22]

---

[22] Stanley Aronowitz, *False Promises* (New York: McGraw-Hill, 1973), p. 292.

In reality some blue-collar jobs may require far more skills than many white-collar jobs. Thus, changes in the distribution of employment favoring white-collar occupations will not necessarily increase the overall distribution of skill requirements in the economy.

This point is further illustrated by examining the distribution of skill requirements (GED levels) *within* major census occupation groups.[23] Three separate estimates of aggregate skill requirements for each occupation group are shown in Table 2. The first row (1960:3) shows the distribution of skill requirements in 1960 based on the third edition of the DOT; the second row (1976:3) shows the distribution of skill requirements in 1976 based on the third edition of the DOT; and the third row (1976:4) shows the distribution of skill requirements in 1976 based on the fourth edition of the DOT. Differences between rows one and two reflect changes in the distribution of employment among jobs within each occupation group, assuming the same skill requirements for individual jobs. Since a number of individual occupations comprise each occupation group, changes in the distribution of employment among these occupations can produce changes in the distribution of skills within each group. Differences between rows two and three reflect changes in the skill requirements of individual jobs (based on the third and fourth editions of the DOT). That is, given

---

[23] There are 6 GED levels, with 6 representing the highest skill level and 1 the lowest. Although the scale does not correspond directly to educational requirements of jobs, a correspondence can be used to illustrate differences. Roughly, GED levels 5 and 6 correspond to a college education, 3 and 4 to a high school education, and 1 and 2 to an elementary school education. See Eckaus, "The Economic Criteria." As Eckaus points out, this equivalency is based on personal judgment, not empirical validation. For a discussion of the problem of translating GED levels into educational equivalents, see Sidney A. Fine, "The Use of the Dictionary of Occupational Titles as a Source of Estimates of Educational and Training Requirements," *Journal of Human Resources*, 3, no. 3 (Summer 1968), pp. 363–75.

Table 2
Job Skill Requirements of Employed Population, by Occupation Group, 1960 and 1976 (percent distribution)[a]

Occupation Group	Year: DOT[b]	Job Skill Requirement[c]					
		1	2	3	4	5	6
Professional workers	1960:3	0.1	0.4	2.9	16.4	55.9	24.3
	1976:3	0.0	0.4	3.1	16.5	56.2	23.6
	1976:4	0.0	0.4	2.8	10.1	66.9	19.5
Managers	1960:3	0.0	0.9	8.2	47.9	29.5	13.5
	1976:3	0.1	0.5	6.2	45.2	32.8	14.9
	1976:4	0.0	0.6	6.0	51.1	36.7	5.3
Sales workers	1960:3	0.2	0.7	53.5	41.8	3.5	0.5
	1976:3	0.0	0.8	50.4	42.9	4.6	1.1
	1976:4	0.0	6.4	25.4	63.4	4.3	0.2
Clerical workers	1960:3	0.5	2.7	45.3	46.5	4.8	0.2
	1976:3	0.2	2.7	41.1	50.0	5.8	0.4
	1976:4	0.1	2.3	21.7	71.9	3.4	0.3
Craft workers	1960:3	0.4	3.0	24.2	68.7	3.0	0.8
	1976:3	0.2	3.0	24.2	68.0	4.0	0.4
	1976:4	0.1	2.3	21.7	71.9	3.4	0.3
Operatives	1960:3	3.0	30.1	54.9	9.2	0.7	0.2
	1976:3	3.2	35.7	53.3	7.0	0.4	0.1
	1976:4	2.2	36.1	50.3	10.7	0.4	0.1
Laborers	1960:3	12.5	63.7	14.3	4.7	0.5	0.0
	1976:3	12.9	56.4	25.7	4.5	0.2	0.1
	1976:4	5.5	62.7	27.1	4.3	0.2	0.0
Private household workers	1960:3	0.4	12.0	84.8	2.6	2.3	0.0
	1976:3	0.1	11.1	86.3	2.4	0.0	0.0
	1976:4	0.6	10.6	86.4	2.3	0.0	0.0
Service workers	1960:3	5.3	26.0	49.4	18.1	1.1	0.1
	1976:3	5.6	24.7	46.2	21.0	2.0	0.3
	1976:4	7.5	20.2	44.9	25.0	2.1	0.1
Farmers	1960:3	0.7	2.5	5.3	90.9	0.5	0.0
	1976:3	0.3	4.0	7.1	87.6	0.6	0.0
	1976:4	0.2	4.9	6.5	87.3	0.8	0.0
Farm laborers	1960:3	11.7	28.9	53.4	5.5	0.5	0.1
	1976:3	6.3	37.3	47.7	8.1	0.4	0.0
	1976:4	5.5	40.9	44.8	8.4	0.2	0.0

[a] Distributions may not add to 100.0 because of rounding.
[b] Year and edition of the DOT on which distributions are based.
[c] Job skill requirements are indexed by GED levels, which represent the general skills required for a worker to achieve average performance in a particular job.
Sources: Calculated from the 1960 1/1000 Public Use Sample and the March 1976 Current Population Survey, U.S. Bureau of the Census; and the Dictionary of Occupational Titles, 3d and 4th eds., U.S. Employment Service.

the same distribution of employment among jobs, the aggregate distribution of skills within each occupation group can change as the skill requirements of individual occupations are altered.

Ignoring these changes for the moment, the table reveals the variation of job skills both *within* and *between* major occupation groups. *Within* each group there is a distribution of requisite job skills that reflects the varying composition of each group's jobs. For example, in 1960 about 80 percent of professional occupations were in the high-skilled categories (GED levels 5 and 6), while about 20 percent required middle-level skills (GED levels 3 and 4). Thus, simply referring to professional occupations as highly skilled jobs ignores the fact that there is a fairly wide range of jobs within this category, requiring a wide range of job skills.

There are also major differences in the distributions of job skills *between* major groups. The professional group is well represented in the high-skilled categories. So is the managerial group. But over half of all managerial jobs require only middle-level skills. Farm and craft jobs have the next highest distributions of job skills. The majority of clerical sales occupations, included in the white-collar group, occupy the middle range of job skills. Finally, operatives, service workers, and laborers hold jobs that occupy the middle and lower ranges of the spectrum. These distributions illustrate the variation in job skills among occupation groups and point out how many blue-collar jobs do, in fact, require more skills than some white-collar jobs, especially clerical and sales jobs.

The distribution of skill requirements within each occupation group changed between 1960 and 1976 both because of changes in the distribution of employment among jobs and because of changes in the skill requirements of individual jobs. Changes in employment patterns (1960:3 and 1976:3), however, produced only slight changes. Substantial changes, on the other hand, were due to revisions in the DOT estimates of skill requirements (1976:3 and 1976:4). Most important, there was a decline in the percentage of the highest skilled jobs (GED level 6). In both the professional and managerial categories there were substantial decreases at this level (from 23.6 percent to 19.5 percent in the former and from 14.9 percent to 5.3 percent in the latter). This result is quite surprising. It may reflect an increasing proletarianization of managerial and profes-

sional occupations that some critics say results in a division of the most complicated and skilled jobs in the economy into lower skilled components. Although there was a reduction of skill requirements at the highest level, there were increases in skills at the next highest level (GED level 5) within professional and managerial occupations. Sales and clerical occupations showed some increase in requisite skills in the middle level (GED level 4) and decreases in the lower levels (GED levels 2 and 3). All other groups exhibited little change due to revisions in the DOT estimates of skill requirements.

The distributions appearing in Tables 1 and 2 were then used to estimate the distribution of job skills for the economy as a whole. These results appear in Table 3. Column 1 shows the aggregate distribution of skill requirements in 1960 based on the third edition of the DOT. Column 2 estimates the distribution of GED levels assuming the same distribution of GED levels *within* each major occupation group in 1976 as in 1960 and accounting only for changes in employment *among* major groups. Differences between columns 1 and 2, shown in column 6, provide an estimate of changes in aggregate skill requirements between 1960 and 1976 due solely to *inter*-group shifts in employment between the two years. Column 3 shows the actual distribution of skill requirements in 1976 based on the third edition of the DOT. Differences between columns 2 and 3, shown in column 7, provide an estimate of changes in skill requirements between 1960 and 1976 due simply to *intra*-group shifts in employment. Column 4 shows the distribution of job skills in 1976 based on the fourth edition of the DOT. Differences between columns 3 and 4, shown in column 8, reflect changes in skill requirements between 1960 and 1976 due solely to revisions in the estimates of skill requirements between the third and fourth

Table 3
Changes in Job Skill Requirements of Employed Population, 1960 and 1976

Job skill requirement[b]	Percent distribution[a]			
	1960:3 actual[k] 1	1976:3 predicted[d] 2	1976:3 actual[k] 3	1976:4 actual[f] 4
1	2.2	2.1	1.9	1.6
2	13.5	12.6	13.0	13.2
3	35.1	33.6	32.2	29.8
4	33.6	32.5	33.0	35.4
5	11.0	13.5	14.2	16.1
6	4.3	5.4	5.4	3.6

	Total net change[g]	Components of change		
		Inter-group shifts[h]	Inter-group shifts[i]	Skill changes[j]
	5	6	7	8
1	− .6	− .1	− .2	− .3
2	− .3	− .9	+ .4	+ .2
3	−5.3	−1.5	−1.4	−2.4
4	+1.8	−1.1	+ .5	+2.4
5	+5.1	+2.5	+ .7	+1.9
6	− .7	+1.1	0	−1.8

[a] Distributions may not add to 100.0 because of rounding.
[b] Job skill requirements are indexed by GED levels, which represent the general skills required for a worker to achieve average performance in a particular job.
[c] Distribution of GED levels in 1960 based on the 3rd edition of the DOT.
[d] Predicted distribution of GED levels in 1976 based on the 3rd edition of the DOT, assuming the same distribution of GED levels within major, census occupational groups in 1976 as in 1960 and accounting only for changes in employment among groups.
[e] Distribution of GED levels in 1976 based on the 3rd edition of the DOT.
[f] Distribution of GED levels in 1976 based on the 4th edition of the DOT.
[g] Difference between columns 1 and 4.
[h] Difference between columns 1 and 2.
[i] Difference between columns 2 and 3.
[j] Difference between columns 3 and 4.
Sources: Calculated from the 1960 1/1000 Public Use Sample and the March 1976 Current Population Survey, U.S. Bureau of the Census; and the Dictionary of Occupational Titles, 3d and 4th eds., U.S. Employment Service.

editions of the DOT. The overall net differences between the distribution of skill levels in 1960 based on the third edition of the DOT and distribution of skill levels in 1976 based on the fourth edition of the DOT appear in column 5.

With this table it is possible to examine the three components of change that took place between 1960 and 1976:

(1) *Inter-occupational group shifts in employment (column 6).* This factor confirms the popular notion that shifts in employ-

ment have raised the overall skill requirements of jobs in the economy. The two highest GED levels (5 and 6), which roughly correspond to skills normally acquired in college, increased while the percentage of workers having jobs requiring the lowest four levels (high school or less) decreased.

(2) *Intra-occupational group shifts in employment (column 7).* This factor did little to change the overall distribution of job skills although there was an increase in the per-

Table 4
Job Skill Requirements of Employed Population, 1940–1976 (percent distribution)[a]

Job skill requirement[b]	Equivalent years of schooling[c]	1940[d]	1950[d]	1960[e]	1976[f]
1	4	9.0	5.9	2.2	1.6
2	7	19.6	16.5	13.5	13.2
3	10	42.9	44.7	35.2	29.8
4	12	21.4	25.5	33.6	35.4
5	16	5.8	5.0	11.0	18.1
6	18	1.9	2.4	4.3	3.6
Mean equivalent year of schooling		9.7	10.1	11.1	11.4

[a] Distributions may not add to 100.0 because of rounding.

[b] Job skill requirements are indexed by GED levels, which represent the general skills required for a worker to achieve average performance in a particular job.

[c] The maximum years in schooling equivalent to a particular GED level. From Eckaus, "Economic Criteria."

[d] Estimates are for the civilian labor force and are based on the 2nd edition of the DOT.

[e] Estimates are for the employed population and are based on the 3rd edition of the DOT.

[f] Estimates are for the employed population and are based on the 4th edition of the DOT.

Sources: 1940 and 1950—R. S. Eckaus, "The Economic Criteria for Education and Training," *Review of Economics and Statistics* 46, no. 2 (May 1964), p. 188; 1960—Calculated from the 1960 1/1000 Public Use Sample, U.S. Bureau of the Census and the Dictionary of Occupational Titles, 3d ed., U.S. Employment Service; 1976—Calculated from the March 1976 Current Population Survey, U.S. Bureau of the Census and the Dictionary of Occupational Titles, 4th ed., U.S. Employment Service.

centage of skilled jobs (GED levels 4 and 5) and a decrease in the percentage of middle-level jobs (GED level 3).

(3) *Changes in the skill requirements of individual jobs (column 8).* This factor showed unexpected results. Revisions in the estimated skill requirements of jobs from the DOT reduced the percentage of highly skilled jobs (GED level 6). There were, however, increases in the percentage of jobs requiring middle-skill levels (GED levels 4 and 5).

The net result of these changes (column 5) was to increase the percentage of jobs in the upper-middle range of skills (GED levels 4 and 5). Because of revisions in the DOT estimates of skill requirements, however, the percentage of jobs at the highest skill level (GED level 6) actually declined in spite of shifts in employment favoring more skilled jobs. In addition, there were

decreases in the percentage of low-skilled jobs (GED level 1 to 3).

It is instructive to compare the present estimates with estimates from earlier periods. Eckaus calculated the distribution of general skill requirements (GED levels) for 1940 and 1950 based on the second edition of the DOT.[24] His estimates are presented in Table 4, together with the present esti-

_____

[24] Eckaus, "The Economic Criteria." Eckaus based his estimates on the characteristics of a sample of 4,000 jobs from the DOT. See U.S. Employment Service, "Estimates of Worker Trait Requirements for 4,000 Jobs as Defined in the Dictionary of Occupational Titles," (Washington, D.C.: G.P.O., 1957). Eckaus estimated skill levels by matching DOT titles to census occupation codes and then taking unweighted averages of GED levels within each census code. Since his estimates are based on a single edition of the DOT, changes in aggregate skill levels between 1940 and 1950 reflect shifts in employment among jobs, but not changes in the skill levels of individual jobs.

mates for 1960 and 1976. An average skill level is also shown for each year, based on an educational equivalent for GED levels proposed by Eckaus. The figures reveal that since 1940 there has been a steady increase in the skill levels of jobs in the U.S. economy. This has largely resulted from a decrease in low-skilled jobs and an increase in high-skilled jobs: the percentage of jobs in the lower two GED categories (jobs requiring less than a high school education) decreased from 29 percent in 1940 to 15 percent in 1976, while the percentage of jobs in the two highest GED categories (jobs requiring a college education) increased from 8 percent in 1940 to 22 percent in 1976. The percentage of jobs in the middle two categories (those requiring a high school education) changed little in this period (from 64 percent in 1940 to 65 percent in 1976). Overall, average GED levels (in educational equivalents) increased 18 percent in the 36-year period, with the greatest increase taking place between 1950 and 1960.

SUMMARY AND CONCLUSIONS

This research examined changes in the aggregate distribution of job skill requirements between 1960 and 1976. Two factors contributed to these changes: shifts in the distribution of employment among jobs in the economy and changes in the skill requirements of individual jobs. Their combined effect was to narrow the distribution of skill requirements in this period. In other words, there was a decrease in both low-skilled and high-skilled jobs and an increase in jobs requiring middle-level skills. The most surprising result was the observed decrease in the percentage of jobs requiring the highest level of skills, a decrease due solely to revisions in the estimates of individual skill requirements in the fourth edition of the DOT. Comparisons with earlier periods reveal that job

skill requirements have continued to rise since 1940, although the greatest increases occurred prior to 1960.

These results should be interpreted with some caution. While the methodology used to produce the estimates was straightforward, its application was problematic. The major difficulty in all studies of this kind is combining occupational information from the *Dictionary of Occupational Titles* with census data. Future efforts should be directed toward improving ways of utilizing information from these two rich data sources.

Another limitation of this study is that it focused on general skill requirements, or those most closely associated with educational training. There may be other skill requirements that are equally important to successful job performance. Some of those skills may be specific to particular jobs, skills often acquired from on-the-job or occupational training programs. Others may be interpersonal skills—affective traits needed for workers to interact effectively with other workers.[25] Additional effort should be directed toward a more complete analysis of job requirements, including affective and cognitive traits.

Even with these limitations, the present findings are illuminating. They also raise a number of questions. For example, what explains the observed trends in the distribution of jobs skills? The most important factor appears to be employment shifts that favor higher skilled jobs. But why does there appear to be a reduction in jobs requiring the highest level skills? Two explanations come to mind. One is that general skills, at least in some jobs, are being replaced by more specific skills. Another is that technology is reducing the skill levels of jobs in the economy. Although it is of-

[25] See, for example, Herbert Gintis, "Education, Technology, and the Characteristics of Worker Productivity," *American Economic Review* 61, no. 2 (May 1971), pp. 266–79.

ten assumed that technology tends to raise requisite job skills, some observers argue that technology may actually reduce job skills by simplifying job tasks.[26] Either of these explanations could account for the observed decrease in high-skilled jobs.

In addition to its intrinsic merit, the study of skill requirements is a practical tool for examining employment opportunities for skilled workers. The present estimates show that opportunities for high-skilled employment increased but modestly in recent years, during a period when the supply of skilled labor, especially college-educated workers, grew substantially.[27] As a result, a growing number of workers, particularly college graduates, may hold jobs for which they are overqualified. This situation could have grave social consequences. It could promote job dissatisfaction, for example, and adversely affect productivity in the workplace.[28] It also suggests that the social return to schooling is declining—that society's large investment in the skills of the American workforce is being wasted as more workers accept jobs incommensurate with their level of training. Moreover, the situation is likely to worsen as the educational skills of the workforce continue to increase with younger, more educated workers replacing older, less educated workers.[29]

One reaction to this situation is for employers to make better use of their workers' skills and training. Changes of this type are evidently occurring through such innovations as job rotation and participatory management;[30] but whether these changes continue to be adopted and whether they will significantly increase the aggregate skill requirements of jobs in the economy remain to be seen.

APPENDIX

The following equations describe the procedures of estimating the distributions of skill requirements in mathematical form:

Let S_{ij} represent the probability that job j requires a skill level i. The sum of these probabilities across all skill levels equals unity:

$$(1) \qquad \sum_{i=1}^{A} S_{ij} = S_{\cdot j} = 1$$

where A represents the number of discrete skill levels. The subscript i is dropped in subsequent equations.

The first task is to estimate the distribution of skill requirements *within* major occupation groups at two points in time (t_1 and t_2) using two separate estimates of skill requirements for individual jobs (S^1 and S^2). The distribution of skill requirements for occupation group k at t_1, based on the first estimate of skill requirements is simply:

$$(2) \qquad S_k^{11} = \frac{\sum\limits_{j=1}^{B_k} N_j^1 S_j^1}{\sum\limits_{j=1}^{B_k} N_j^1}$$

where N_j^1 represents the number of people holding job j at t_1, S_j^1 represents the skill requirement for job j at t_1, and B_k represents the number of jobs in occupation group k. The distribution of skill requirements for occupation

---

[26] Braverman, *Labor and Monopoly Capital,* and James R. Bright, "The Relationship of Increasing Automation and Skill Requirements," in the National Commission on Technology, Automation, and Economic Progress, *The Employment Impact of Technological Change* (Washington, D.C.: Government Printing Office, 1966, pp. II-203–21.

[27] Members of the civilian labor force with one or more years of college increased from 19 percent in 1959 to 31 percent in 1976. U.S. Department of Labor, *Employment and Training Report of the President* (Washington, D.C.: Government Printing Office, 1979), p. 304.

[28] See Rumberger, *Overeducation,* chap. 5.

[29] U.S. Bureau of Labor Statistics, *Occupational Outlook for College Graduates,* 1978–79 ed., Bulletin 1956 (Washington, D.C.: Government Printing Office, 1978).

[30] See, for example, Martin Carnoy and Derek Shearer, *Economic Democracy* (White Plains, N.Y.: Sharp Publishers, 1980), chap. 4; and Richard D. Rosenberg and Eliezer Rosenstein, "Participation and Productivity: An Empirical Study," *Industrial and Labor Relations Review* 33, no. 3 (April 1980), pp. 355–67.

group k at t_2 can be calculated two ways: first, based on S_j^1, the original estimate of skill requirements for individual jobs:

(3) $$S_k^{21} = \frac{\sum_{j=1}^{B_k} N_j^2 S_j^1}{\sum_{j=1}^{B_k} N_j^2}$$

and then based on S_j^2, the revised estimate of individual skill requirements:

(4) $$S_k^{22} = \frac{\sum_{j=1}^{B_k} N_j^2 S_j^2}{\sum_{j=1}^{B_k} N_j^2}$$

Differences between Equations 2 and 3 reflect changes in the distribution of employment among jobs within occupation group k. Differences between Equations 3 and 4 reflect changes in the skill requirements of individual jobs within occupation group k.

Based on the above estimates the aggregate skill requirements across all occupations in the economy can be estimated. The overall distribution of skill requirements t_1 is:

(5) $$S^1 = \frac{\sum_{k=1}^{C} N_k^1 S_k^{11}}{\sum_{k=1}^{C} N_k^1}$$

where $N_k^1 = \sum_{j=1}^{B_k} N_j^1$ represents the number of people holding jobs in occupation group k at

t_1 and C represents the number of occupation groups. The distribution of skill requirements at t_2 can be calculated three ways: first, based on S_k^{11}, which assumes the same skill levels within occupation groups as at t_1:

(6) $$S^{2'} = \frac{\sum_{k=1}^{C} N_k^2 S_k^{11}}{\sum_{k=1}^{C} N_k^2}$$

then based on S_k^{21}, which accounts for shifts in employment among jobs within each occupation group:

(7) $$S^{2''} = \frac{\sum_{k=1}^{C} N_k^2 S_k^{21}}{\sum_{k=1}^{C} N_k^2}$$

and finally based on S_k^{22}, which accounts for revised estimates of the skill requirements for individual jobs:

(8) $$S^2 = \frac{\sum_{k=1}^{C} N_k^2 S_k^{22}}{\sum_{k=1}^{C} N_k^2}$$

Differences between Equations 6 and 5 reflect *inter*-occupational group shifts in employment. Differences between Equations 7 and 6 reflect *intra*-occupational group shifts in employment. And differences between Equations 8 and 7 reflect changes in the estimated skill requirements of individual jobs.

Defining the Labor Market for Equal Employment Standards*

Commuting Patterns and Labor Force Characteristics in an Area Can Be Used to Estimate a Firm's Labor Supply

JOSEPH L. GASTWIRTH and SHELDON E. HABER

The Civil Rights Act of 1964 banned race, sex, ethnic background, and religious discrimination in hiring and pay practices. Differences about implementation of the law have led to complaints to the Equal Employment Opportunity Commission and much adjudication in the courts. Some of the issues subject to litigation have been wage discrimination, hiring discrimination, and discrimination in initial job placement and promotions. Explicit criteria for measuring nonwage discrimination remain to be developed. Criteria for measuring discrimination in hiring are particularly important because individuals excluded from desirable jobs for which they are qualified are often forced to accept less desirable ones where employment is unstable and opportunities for promotion are few. Moreover, discrimination from desirable jobs induces an excess supply of labor in the less desirable jobs, which in turn lowers the wage rate for such jobs.[1]

This article presents a model for defining and estimating the fraction of a firm's labor pool that is black (or another minority). An essential part of the problem is delineating the labor market of relevance. The objective of this article is to develop a practical procedure for utilizing empirical data to define the proper labor pool. The procedure does not define a specific geographic area as the labor market; rather it weights areas according to their proximity to the place of employment. For illustrative purposes only, the model of long-term equal employment guidelines developed in this article is applied to a recent court case involving racial discrimination; refinements and extensions of the model are briefly discussed at the end.

DELINEATING THE LABOR MARKET AREA

In a variety of cases the courts have used the percent of blacks in the total populations of a city, Standard Metropolitan Statistical Area (SMSA), State, or region as a basis for determining if particular firms have engaged in hiring discrimination.[2] This is one approach to use as a basis for estimating fair employment standards. Another way of looking at the problem is to use the pool of individuals who are potential candidates for employment, that is, to employ the labor force concept which restricts the group to be considered to those

* J. L. Gastwirth and S. Haber. "Defining the Labor Market for Equal Employment Standards," *Monthly Labor Review* 99, no. 3, (1976), pp. 32–36.

16 years or older who are looking for work.[3] Thus, people under 16 years of age and those who are not working or seeking work would not be considered potential employees. Besides the need to define the geographic area of a labor market, it is necessary to determine the pool of potential employees available to a specific firm.

The concept of a labor market stems from neo-classical economic theory. Under conditions of pure competition and perfect knowledge, a uniform wage rate should prevail within a labor market for a given type of labor. (It is also necessary to assume that transportation costs, search costs, and the opportunity costs of commuting time are essentially constant for all participants in the labor market.) The area over which such wage uniformity is observed defines the labor market in question. However, the cost of transit varies between individuals so that a theoretical labor market can never be actually realized. Hence, labor markets are officially defined in terms of criteria which are observable and subject to measurement. For example, Standard Metropolitan Statistical Areas are defined in terms of population and interarea commuting patterns of workers.[4] While defining a labor market in this manner has advantages for purposes of statistical description and for many analytical studies, it is inadequate for determining the labor pool of a particular firm, since a worker given two equal job opportunities would tend to choose the one with the smaller transit cost.

Although it is difficult to obtain precise information concerning the influence of distance (and time) between job and home on individuals' choice of jobs, a recent Bureau of Labor Statistics job finding survey found that "jobseekers generally restricted their job search to a relatively short distance from their homes. About 4 out of 10 look no farther than 10 miles and another 3 out of 10 went up to 25 miles."[5] In an earlier investigation, Albert Rees and George P. Shultz found that 65 to 80 percent of workers, in 11 out of the 12 occupations they studied, traveled less than 10 miles to work.[6] Both studies show that distance traveled to work depends on income (earnings), occupation, and sex. Generally, blue-collar and female workers look for work nearer home.[7]

Since people prefer to work nearer home, in describing a firm's labor market greater importance or weight should be given to nearby areas than to distant ones.[8] This can be contrasted with the statistical definition of a labor area which has fixed boundaries and for which it is implicitly assumed that the probability of a worker seeking employment in each subarea is the same, rather than being dependent on the location of the worker's residence relative to potential places of work.

MODEL FOR ESTIMATING FAIR EMPLOYMENT STANDARDS

The preceding section indicates the need to develop a procedure which utilizes empirical data, both government and private, in a way that provides consistent, reliable information for setting standards concerning the proportion of a firm's work force which reasonably should be composed of minority members. As noted, the kind of data that is needed pertains to the location of prospective workers vis-a-vis the location of a given firm. A probability model considering proximity of residence to job location is presented below.

Consider a plant whose workers come from K distinct residential areas, $A_1, \ldots A_K$, ordered by increasing distance to the plant.[9] For each residential area, let L_i be the area's total labor force and b_i be the fraction of minority members (say blacks) in the area's labor force. Then the fraction of blacks in the entire labor market is $\Sigma b_i L_i / \Sigma L_i$. Let p_i be the probability that a resident of the ith area applies to the firm. The probability that an applicant is black, $P(B)$, is given by

$$P(B) = \frac{\sum_{i=1}^{k} L_i p_i b_i}{\sum_{i=1}^{k} L_i p_i} = \sum_{i=1}^{k} \frac{(L_i p_i)}{\Sigma L_i p_i} \cdot b_i$$

$$= \Sigma q_i b_i \quad (1)$$

where the denominator of the first term above is the expected number of applicants to the plant from all areas and the numerator is the expected number of black applicants. Notice that

$$q_i = \frac{L_i p_i}{\Sigma L_i p_i}$$

is the fraction of a firm's labor pool residing in the ith area and that its values form a probability distribution.

Although one knows that the p_i's decrease as distance to work increases, it is difficult to estimate these values directly. Fortunately, one can estimate $P(B)$ by obtaining the labor forces, L_i, from census data and the values of q_i from applicant records at a firm or labor force data.[10] For our purposes, applicant data are preferable since they reflect the preference of the local labor force in the area to work near home and, implicitly, the availability of transportation within the entire area. When applicant data are unavailable, the data on commuting patterns reported in the census can be used; however, these data are published only for Standard Metropolitan Statistical Areas and their largest subareas.

Two problems should be mentioned which could require separate analysis. First, estimating the q_i's from residence patterns of current employees may be misleading if an employer locates in a predominantly white area in order to discriminate against minorities. In this case, an underestimate of $P(B)$ would be obtained. Second, the use of applicant data itself can lead to an underestimate of $P(B)$ where an employer has a past reputation of discrimination (the "chilling effect" often cited in court decisions) or an overestimate if an activist

group floods a firm with minority applicants. By examining the applicant flow for a period of years, one can see if sharp changes took place and the reasons for them can be explored.

In 1973, a U.S. district court found the Detroit Edison Co. guilty of racial discrimination[11] *in part* on the basis that while blacks form 41.3 percent of the resident labor force in the city of Detroit and 17 percent of the metropolitan labor force, only 8 percent of the utility's employees were black. In view of these statistics and the fact that 55 percent of the company's work force is employed in the city of Detroit, the court ordered that hiring for some specified departments and jobs be on the basis of three blacks for every two whites until 25 percent of these jobs were held by blacks. Moreover, the court set a long-term goal of 30 percent for the fraction which blacks should comprise in the company's total work force.[12]

Besides the 55 percent of the company's work force which is employed in the city of Detroit, another 20 percent are employed in the remainder of Wayne County, and yet another 10 percent outside of Wayne County but still in the Detroit metropolitan area. As 15 percent of the company's workers were employed outside the Detroit SMSA at the time the case was being adjudicated and three counties—Lapeer, Livingston, and St. Claire—have since been included within the geographical boundaries of the Detroit SMSA, we assume that these additional workers resided in the three counties named.[13] Basic labor force data for the Detroit area are contained in Table 1.

In order to estimate the fraction of blacks in the company's labor market area using the model suggested here, one needs the values of q_i, the fraction of the firm's labor pool residing in each subarea. As applicant data were not available to us, the q_i's were first approximated by the fraction of the firm's jobs in each subarea, .55, .20, and .25 (outside Wayne County). Equation (1) then yields the following estimate of the percent of blacks in the firm's labor market:

$$(.55)(41.3) + (.20)(4.7) + (.25)(2.0)$$
$$= 24.2 \text{ percent}$$

Using the figures on where the firm's workers are employed does not take commuting patterns into account. From the 1970 Census of Population it is possible to obtain data on commuter flows from place of residence to place of work.[14] The basic premise in using these data is that commuting patterns of employed workers reflect desires as to where individuals wish to work. Thus, if x percent of the workers living in area A commute to area B, we assume that x percent of the labor force in area A would be working or looking for work in area B. In Table 2 we summarize the revelant data on commuting patterns in the Detroit SMSA. It is apparent from the table that the probabilities of commuting between areas by workers of both races are similar.[15] Since the commuting data were reported only for the SMSA, as defined prior to 1975, the calculations that follow restrict the labor force data to the SMSA as of that period.

Given the data in Tables 1 and 2, we can calculate the number of blacks working or looking for work in the city of Detroit as follows:

$$(.677)(249,647) + (.234)(33,978)$$
$$= 176,962$$

Similarly, the number of whites working or looking for work in the city of Detroit is:

$$(.656)(355,028) + (.240)(1,026,875)$$
$$= 479,348$$

Blacks form 27 percent of the city's available labor force of 656,310. Outside of the city, blacks number 106,663 of those working or looking for work, whites 902,555; so blacks form 10.6 percent of the available noncity work force of 1,009,218. Since 55 percent of the employees of Detroit Edison work in the city, the estimate from this approach is

$$(.55)(27.0) + (.45)(10.6) = 19.6 \text{ percent}$$

as the share of blacks among the total work force available to work for Detroit Edison or any other firm similarly situated.

Even though the probability of commuting between city and suburbs is the same

Table 1
Civilian Labor Force in the Detroit Area, by Race and Residence, 1970

Area	Total labor force	Black labor force	White, other labor force	Black as a percent of the total labor force
Detroit City.	604,675	249,647	355,028	41.3
Wayne County (excluding Detroit City).	457,310	21,518	435,792	4.7
Wayne County	1,061,985	271,165	790,820	25.5
Detroit SMSA (excluding Wayne County)	603,543	12,460	591,083	2.1
Detroit SMSA—pre-1975.	1,665,528	283,625	1,381,903	17.0
Added counties (1975)	84,662	1,014	83,648	1.2
Detroit SMSA—present	1,750,190	284,639	1,465,551	16.3
Detroit SMSA (excluding Wayne and added counties)	688,205	13,474	674,731	2.0

Sources: U.S. Bureau of the Census, *General Social and Economic Characteristics, Census of Population: 1970,* Final Report PC(1)–C24, Michigan, tables 85, 92, 121, and 126.

Table 2
Commuting Patterns of Workers

Item	Blacks		Whites	
	Living inside Detroit City	Living outside Detroit (in SMSA)	Living inside Detroit City	Living outside Detroit (in SMSA)
Work in city	122,623	5,672	194,742	210,167
Work outside city (in SMSA)	58,473	18,535	102,111	666,650
Total	181,096	24,207	296,853	876,817
Probability person works in city	.677	.234	.656	.240
Probability person works outside city	.323	.766	.344	.760

Source: U.S. Bureau of the Census, *Detailed Characteristics, Census of Population: 1970*, Final Report PC(1)–D24, Michigan, table 190.

for blacks and whites, there are a greater number of white suburbanites commuting into the city than black city residents commuting out of the city. Thus, the labor force available to the city is larger and "whiter" than its resident force. Nevertheless, the city labor force is "blacker" than the metropolitan labor force and the concentration of Detroit Edison's employment in the city yields a higher theoretical percentage of black workers, 19.6, than in the metropolitan area as a whole, 17.0.

An additional point is worth noting. The estimated proportion of blacks in the Detroit Edison labor pool is based on the commuting pattern of all workers. As most of the occupations in the departments cited as having few black employees were blue-collar occupations, the commuting pattern which is most relevant is that of blue-collar workers.[16] Of the blue-collar work force available in the city, 30.6 percent were black. The analogous proportion for the available work force outside the city was 13.8 percent. Repeating the previous calculation yields an estimate

$$(.55)(30.6) + (.45)(13.8) = 23.0 \text{ percent}$$

instead of 19.6 percent. The former figure reflects the fact that blue-collar workers are less likely to work at a distance from their place of residence than, say, professional workers, and since most of the firm's employment is inside the city, this increases the share of blacks in the labor pool.

FURTHER REFINEMENTS

The approach developed here is one approach to setting long-term fair employment goals for the work force of a plant or firm and to determining whether discrimination has occurred. In estimating the fraction of a firm's labor pool which is composed of minorities, this model takes account of the commuting patterns of an area's work force and the location of the firm's jobs within the area. It should be stressed that the approach presented here is applicable to the determination of *long-term* employment standards. For the purpose of setting short-term targets one might consider the unemployed as well as the expected flow of entrants into and withdrawals from the labor force. In any specific application, special circumstances, for example, the presence of a large military base or university, may need to be taken into account.

Discussion of the model has suggested that the setting of goals for a specific job requires careful definition of the potential labor force qualified for the job in question and consideration of the willingness of people in that occupation to travel long distances, or actually to move, to a new job. In some cases it may be necessary to use the educational level of current employees and to restrict the labor pool to those with the same educational level. For example, this was done in the *Rios* case previously cited. For high-paying professional jobs, a national market may be needed. In the case discussed, *Stamps* v. *Detroit Edison*, the court ruled that hiring discrimination was being practiced. The results of the model here support the court's finding though suggesting that the fair employment goal set in the decision may be somewhat high.

NOTES

Acknowledgment: It is a pleasure to acknowledge very helpful discussions of the use of statistics in the legal setting with Stephen N. Shulman, Robert T. Lasky, Patricia M. Vaughan, and Joseph A. Artabane, who are lawyers in Washington, D.C.

[1] Thus, hiring discrimination can have indirect external labor market effects that are similar to the direct effects of wage discrimination in internal labor markets. See, for example, Barbara R. Bergmann, "The Effect on White Incomes of Discrimination in Employment," *Journal of Political Economy* 79 (March–April 1971), pp. 294–313; and F. Y. Edgeworth, "Equal Pay to Men and Women," *Economic Journal* 32 (December 1922), pp. 431–57.

[2] The Supreme Court in the landmark *Griggs* v. *Duke Power* case (401 U.S. 424 (1971)) affirmed a lower court ruling that used data saying blacks throughout North Carolina could apply to the firm. The Fifth Circuit used data for the entire South, as well as Atlanta, in *United States* v. *Georgia Power Co.* (474 F.2d 906 (C.A. 5, 1973)) and statewide data in *Johnson* v. *Goodyear* (491 F.2d 1364 (C.A. 5, 1974)). The Sixth Circuit in *Afro-American Patrolman League* v. *Duck* (503 F.2d 294 (C.A. 6, 1974)) used the population of the city of Toledo, while the Eighth Circuit in *Parkam* v. *Southwestern Bell* (433 F.2d 421 (C.A. 8, 1970)) considered State (Arkansas)

data. Recently a District Court used the counties in which a New York union had jurisdiction in *Rios* v. *Enterprise Steamfitters Local 638* (9 CCH EPD pp. 10, 143 (D.C.–S.D.N.Y., 1975)).

[3] Indeed, the Second Circuit used the labor force in the *Rios* case cited above when it altered the original "goals" set by the District Court.

[4] See "New SMSA Criteria" in *Statistical Reporter*, December 1971, pp. 97–99.

[5] Carl Rosenfeld, "Jobseeking Methods Used by American Workers," *Monthly Labor Review*, August 1975, p. 42.

[6] Albert Rees and George P. Shultz, *Workers and Wages in an Urban Labor Market* (Chicago: University of Chicago Press, 1970), pp. 49–50. Long distances between home and work may result in reduced worker productivity and, hence, can be disadvantageous to the firm. In a third of the establishments studied by Rees and Shultz in the Chicago-Northwestern Illinois area, distance between home and work, travel time, and type of transportation available to the potential employee were used as criteria for hiring. The excluded occupation was accountant.

[7] In Rees and Shultz's study, 18 percent of the accountants traveled 15 miles or more to work, while 7 and 12 percent of the punch press and forklift truck operators, respectively, traveled this far. Among janitors, 9 percent traveled 15 miles or more to work, whereas only 5 percent of the janitresses, traveled as far. See Rees and Shultz, *Workers and Wages,* p. 66.

[8] This is precisely what a court attempted to do in a case involving the Detroit Edison Co.

[9] Time may also be used as an index of proximity, but generally distance and time are positively related.

[10] From a sample (or complete count) of applicants one can determine the proportion residing in each subarea of the total labor market area.

[11] The discussion of this case is limited to hiring issues; for further details, the reader is referred to "Significant Decisions in Labor Cases," *Monthly Labor Review*, January 1974, pp. 70–72.

[12] In setting the goal of 30 percent, the court also noted that 47 percent of the skilled unemployed in Detroit were black.

[13] Since only the fraction of blacks in an area enters into the calculations, and as all the suburban counties are predominantly white, a different choice of counties would not alter the conclusions.

[14] One reason why applicant flow data are preferred is that one can construct more detailed estimates of where applicants come from (for example, by area of the city or by county) than the overall census data allow. Moreover,

the applicant flow data will reflect the availability of transportation to the plant.

[15] This is consistent with the results of the Department of Labor's job search survey cited in footnote 5.

[16] For data underlying the calculations for blue-collar workers, see *General Social and Economic Characteristics,* Final Report PC(1)–C24, Michigan, Table 120 and *Detailed Characteristics,* Final Report PC(1)–D24, Table 86.

COMMENTARY

Labor market characteristics are of considerable importance to designing and implementing selection systems. This can be illustrated by focusing briefly on the phenomenon of the baby-boom generation. Generally, this group is defined as including persons born between 1946 and 1964. By the end of 1946, 3.4 million babies had been born in the United States, 20 percent more than in 1945 (Jones, 1980). The fertility rate (the number of children born to the average woman in her lifetime) increased to 3.8 during the mid-1950s and the number of births per year exceeded 4 million (*Business Week*, 1978). This compares to a fertility rate of 2.1 during the 1930s and a rate which had fallen to 1.76 by 1976. This group of relatively well-educated individuals will face increasing competition for middle-level managerial jobs just as they reach the prime age for such employment. Gottschalk (1981) reported that "demographers see a decade of frustrated employees with thwarted goals" (p. 1). He describes Bureau of Labor Statistics projections showing the number of jobs for managers and administrators to increase from 8.8 million to 10.5 million in the decade of the 1980s, an increase of 19 percent. This is contrasted with an increase in the number of persons aged 35–44 (prime middle-management years) from 25.4 million in 1980 to 36.1 million in 1990, a 42 percent increase. This is shown graphically in Figure 6–1.

Thus, by the early 1990s there is good reason to expect a general oversupply of relatively well-qualified individuals seeking middle-level managerial and professional-technical positions. However, as Young (1981) noted in the first reading, this same group will have moved through the educational system by the mid-1980s, thus changing the degree of competitiveness associated with securing entry-level employment. Young then described the potential for a relative shortage of new high school and college graduates and the resulting increased availability of entry-level jobs. This, of course, relates to how selective a firm will be able to be in making hiring decisions for this class of positions.

The article by Rumberger (1981) argued that the opportunity for skilled workers (as measured by the skill requirements of jobs) has increased in recent years, but not at a sufficient rate to keep pace with the supply of skilled labor. This imbalance has important implications for organizational specialists and selection specialists in particular. However, before pointing out some of these implications, it is important to note that for some occupational groups, this general prediction will not likely hold. For example, by 1990 the demand for computer programmers is expected to double while the nation's universities are not likely to produce sufficient numbers of qualified graduates in this field (Anders, 1981). In addition, as discussed by Young (1981), the baby-boom generation will have moved through the educational system by the mid-1980s, thus creating a smaller pool of persons from which to train computer specialists.

Taken together, the articles by Young (1981) and Rumberger (1981) should

Figure 6–1

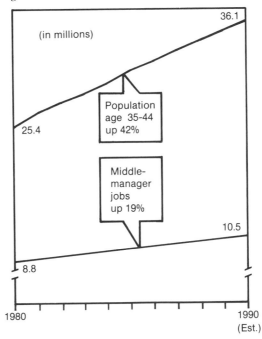

emphasize that the supply of and demand for labor changes as a function of many societal factors (e.g., the fertility rate, the level of educational attainment, and the emergence of new technological demand). These articles should illustrate the dynamic nature of this process. In fact, only a few years ago writers were worrying about a shortage of managerial talent. In 1970, Campbell, Dunnette, Lawler, and Weick stated that "more and more managerial jobs are going unfilled because fewer and fewer persons are available to take them. The number of people in the prime managerial age range of 35 to 45 is on the decline because of lowered birthrates during the depression of the 1930s and losses of young men during World War II and the Korean War" (p. 1). In addition, they point out that another societal factor (values toward managerial careers) had apparently shifted, thus creating a greater shortage as a lower proportion of college graduates entered business careers.

We now turn to some implications associated with labor market shifts. One simple way of considering the impact of the selection ratio and base rate on the usefulness of a given selection device is to recall the concept of a success ratio from the decision-making chapter. In 1939, Taylor and Russell published a series of tables characterizing the interaction of the selection ratio, the base rate, and the validity coefficient on the success ratio. The success ratio in this case is considered to be the index of usefulness. Recall that a success ratio is the proportion of selected applicants who are subsequently judged successful. Following the Taylor-Russell (1939) approach, the effect of the selection ratio and base rate on the usefulness of a given selection procedure is illustrated in Figures 6–2 and 6–3. When a selection procedure with a validity of .50 is utilized under conditions of varying selection ratios and base rates, different success ratios are produced. Since the success ratio is equal to $\dfrac{A}{(A + B)}$, it becomes more favorable from the firm's perspective as it

Figure 6–2.
Effect of Varying the Selection Ratio on the Success Ratio

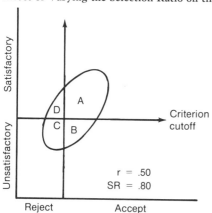

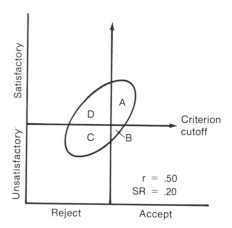

Figure 6–3
Effect of Varying the Base Rate on the Success Ratio

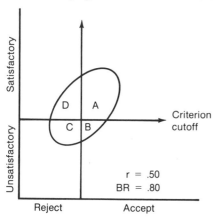

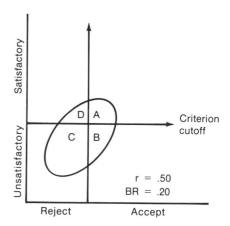

increases. Note that as the selection ratio shifts from .80 to .20, holding the base rate and validity coefficient constant, the success ratio becomes more favorable.

Likewise, a base rate shift from .20 to .80, holding the validity and selection ratio constant, will result in an increased success ratio. This is illustrated in Figure 6–3.

Thus, the size and quality of the applicant pool, in relation to the number of openings, or demand for labor, can influence the usefulness of a given selection device.

Recall, however, that there are a variety of problems associated with the Taylor-Russell definition of usefulness. A more sophisticated procedure for studying the utility of a selection procedure was advanced by Brogden (1949) and further refined by Cronbach and Gleser (1965). Brogden, it will be recalled, approached the problem in terms of the mean gain in utility per selectee. Following the example of Schmidt, Hunter, McKenzie, and Muldrow (1979), who build upon the earlier utility models, the following will illustrate how the supply of labor can affect resource allocation decisions. The prime concern will be to focus on the notion of a selection ratio.

Recall that Schmidt, Hunter, McKenzie and Muldrow (1979) offer the following equation as a means for estimating the productivity increase associated with the introduction of a new selection procedure:

$$\Delta U = tN_s(r_1 - r_2)SD_y\phi/p - N_s(C_1 - C_2)/p \qquad (6-1)$$

where ΔU = the gain in productivity in dollars from using the new selection procedure for one year; t = the length of time the average selectee will remain with the firm; N_s = the number of applicants actually hired during the given year; r_1 = the validity of the new procedure; r_2 = the validity of the procedure currently in use; C_1 = the per-applicant cost of the new procedure; C_2 = the per-applicant cost of the current procedure; SD_y = the standard deviation of job performance in dollars; ϕ = the ordinate in $N(0,1)$ at the point of cut corresponding to P (this, of course, is based on the assumption that test scores are normally distributed); and P = the selection ratio. This equation will give the estimated gain obtained from substituting the current procedure with a new procedure for one year, with the overall gains realized across the tenure of the new employees. That is, the gain is not realized during the first year, but accumulates as the new employees complete their length of service with the firm.

Assume that a medium-sized manufacturing firm expects to hire 10 clerical employees during the next year. These positions are of the typing, filing, public contact, and clerical service variety. Experience indicates that the average tenure of persons in these occupations equals two years while the yearly value to the firm of the typical performer has been estimated to be $10,000. The employee who performs better than 85 percent of his or her co-workers is estimated to contribute $11,000 of yearly value to the firm while persons performing at the 15th percentile generate a yearly outcome worth $9,000. Thus, one standard deviation in dollar terms equals approximately $1,000. In addition, the company currently uses a paper and pencil personnel test to hire clerical employees and makes selections on a top-down basis by hiring those persons with the highest scores. The cost per applicant of using the test is $5 and the test has an estimated validity of .20.

The question before the company's budget committee is whether or not to implement a new hiring procedure in the clerical area. The personnel director has reviewed a variety of alternative selection procedures and estimates that a currently available trainability test (a situational test that attempts to measure the potential to learn new clerical tasks) would result in better predictions of subsequent job performance. The estimated true validity for the new test is .50.

The relative productivity gain associated with the new predictor can be estimated by using equation (6-1). Other needed information in addition to that just provided includes knowledge of the selection ratio and the associated value of ϕ and the cost of the new selection procedure. The estimated productivity increases associated with the use of the new procedure for one year are shown in Table 6-1. Estimates are computed under three cost conditions ($25, $50, and $100 per applicant) and for three selection ratios (.05, .40, and .80). That is, assume that the cost of the new test could range from $25 to $100 and that the availability of labor could result in varying selection ratios for the firm.

As indicated in Table 6-1, if the new predictor costs $25 per applicant, the estimated productivity increase associated with the use of the new predictor for one year increases as the selection ratio becomes more favorable. To hire 10 new employees, testing 200 applicants and then hiring the top scoring individuals would result in a productivity gain of $8,000. If only 25 applicants are available for testing, the 10 selected from this group will likely provide only a $5,350 productivity increase, while a selection ratio of .80 would result in only a $1,925 gain. This

Table 6–1
Estimated Productivity Gains Associated with Using the Trainability
Test for One Year to Select Clerical Employees

Cost of net test	SR	Number tested	Total gain	Increased cost of testing	Net productivity gain
	.05	200	$12,000	$ 4,000	$8,000
$ 25	.40	25	5,850	500	5,350
	.80	approx. 12	2,175	250	1,925
	.05	200	$12,000	$ 9,000	$3,000
$ 50	.40	25	5,850	1,125	4,725
	.80	approx. 12	2,175	562	1,613
	.05	200	$12,000	$19,000	−$7,000
$100	.40	25	5,850	2,375	3,475
	.80	approx. 12	2,175	1,187	988

assumes that recruiting costs are constant and that the size of the applicant pool is a function of the number of persons available. That is, a constant recruiting cost will provide different numbers of applicants depending upon the aggregate supply of labor. When the new selection procedure costs $25, being highly selective and testing a large number of applicants results in the greatest productivity increase. Thus, the test will have the greatest impact under conditions supporting low selection ratios. Note that the cost of testing increases as more and more applicants are processed and that the productivity gain is not realized until each of the new employees completes two years of service.

What if the cost of testing reached $50 per applicant? Table 6–1 now indicates that while there is a clear productivity gain irrespective of the selection ratio, a selection ratio of .40 provides the greatest gain. This demonstrates that as testing costs increase in relation to the value of job performance, an extremely low selection ratio can work to the disadvantage of the firm. This is clearly illustrated when the cost of testing increases to $100 per applicant. Here, as shown in Table 6–1, the use of the new selection procedure would result in a loss of $7,000 if 200 applicants were tested (a selection ratio of .05). Thus, when the employer is free to determine the number of applicants to test (i.e., the size of the applicant pool is not severely constrained by labor market pressures), there is a need to determine the appropriate number in order to maximize productivity gains. A formula for solving this problem is provided by Cronbach and Gleser (1965, p. 309). This problem must be solved by iteration where only one value of the selection ratio will satisfy the Cronbach and Gleser equation.

In summary, the supply of labor can constrain the size of the applicant pool resulting in a situation in which the employer will not be able to maximize productivity gains by using the optimal selection ratio. Thus, productivity gains from selection are, in part, a function of employer control over selection ratios. The value of a test or any selection procedure varies as a function of the situation in which it is used. The favorableness of the situation is in large part determined by labor market characteristics.

The relative shortage of new high school graduates suggested by Young (1982) may constrain the supply of persons seeking clerical positions. Thus, the productivity gains associated with the introduction of more valid selection procedure will not

likely be as great in the mid- to late 1980s as the relative supply of clerical employees associated with the baby-boom generation passes through the system. Likewise,
the productivity gains associated with the use of more valid selection procedures are
likely to increase in the context of making hiring and promotional decisions for
middle management positions. The relative oversupply of qualified persons seeking
these positions will create a more favorable selection ratio from the firm's perspective.

There is one other issue that pertains to the decision to spend resources on a
new, more valid, selection procedure that requires some discussion at this time.
Note from Table 6–1 that the productivity gains associated with a new selection
procedure vary as a function of the situation. While productivity gains are to be
expected in most situations, the decision to introduce a new and more costly selection system should not be made in the abstract. That is, it is important to compare
the gain associated with a selection system modification with potential productivity
gains associated with other expenditures. For example, the use of an expensive
selection procedure may result in a productivity gain, but spending the same
amount of money on some form of physical plant improvement may generate a
greater return on investment. The point is, there may be situations in which the
introduction of a new, more valid selection system is not cost effective when compared to other system modifications. This is more likely to happen when the firm is
not able to maximize productivity gains through selection by using the optimal
selection ratio. Being able to choose the optimal selection ratio is a function of
important labor market considerations. Using our current example, spending
$2,000 on a word-processing unit may result in a greater net gain in productivity
than spending the same $2,000 on a new, more valid, selection system.

Finally, the third reading in this chapter by Gastwirth and Haber (1976) helps
focus on a different and yet crucial issue for selection specialists. Defining the
relevant labor market is central in cases where a plaintiff is attempting to establish a
prima facie case of discrimination. Recall that one type of evidence of adverse
impact compares the internal labor force associated with a particular firm with the
external labor force. This comparison is of the following type:

$$\frac{\text{Number of minorities employed}}{\text{Total number of employees}} \quad \begin{array}{c} \text{Compared} \\ \text{to} \end{array} \quad \frac{\text{Number of minorities in the relevant geographical area}}{\text{Total number of people in the relevant geographical area}}$$

While discussing the complexity of this issue in detail is beyond the scope of this
text, Gastwirth and Haber (1976) introduce the concept of transit cost, or the
degree to which distance and time between job and home influences the decision to
choose a job. They argue that since people prefer to work near home, greater
importance should be given to nearby rather than distant areas. Their procedure
represents a refined technique for making estimates of the relevant labor market
and is particularly useful in the context of equal employment opportunity litigation.
Note that this is a developing concept and that a more complete understanding of
what constitutes an appropriate definition of an external labor market will depend
upon forthcoming court decisions and technique refinements.

However, the concern for determining a relevant labor market is likely to be
important in a more general sense. Following Gastwirth and Haber, the distance and
time between job and home may relate to a variety of human resource outcomes.
Job choice, absenteeism, and the decision to resign may be influenced by a class of

variables of this type. Different recruiting strategies (e.g., local, regional, and extended regional, or national) may provide very different applicant pool characteristics. Precise information concerning the influence of recruiting strategy on applicant pool characteristics is not yet available but certainly defining an appropriate labor market has implications that go beyond those most often discussed in the context of the legal environment.

In summary, the labor market within which the firm makes hiring decisions will have a clear impact on the quality of those decisions. The degree to which the firm operates in a favorable selection environment will be a function of variety of factors, including both the numbers of and skill characteristics of persons seeking employment and the skill requirements associated with jobs. An oversupply of qualified applicants will mean that the optimal selection ratio can be determined and used by the firm, thus maximizing the productivity gains associated with the introduction of a more valid selection procedure. A firm operating under unfavorable labor market conditions may choose to allocate resources away from the personnel selection area to more cost effective changes to other organizational systems.

REFERENCES

Americans change. *Business Week,* February 20, 1978.

Anders, G. Colleges faltering in effort to ease critical shortage of programmers. *The Wall Street Journal,* August 24, 1981, p. 15.

Brogden, H. E. When testing pays off. *Personnel Psychology,* 1949, *2,* 171–183.

Campbell, J. P., Dunnette, M. D., Lawler, E. E., & Weick, K. E. *Managerial behavior, performance, and effectiveness.* New York: McGraw-Hill, 1970.

Cronbach, L. J., & Gleser, G. C. *Psychological tests and personnel decisions.* Urbana: University of Illinois Press, 1965.

Gastwirth, J. L., & Haber, S. Defining the labor market for equal employment standards. *Monthly Labor Review,* 1976, 99(3), 32–36.

Gottschalk, E. C. Promotions grew few as baby boom group eyes managers' jobs. *The Wall Street Journal,* October 22, 1981, pp. 1, 3.

Jones, L. Y. *Great expectations.* New York: Ballantine Books, 1980.

Rumberger, R. W. The changing skill requirements of jobs in the U.S. economy. *Industrial and Labor Relations Review,* 1981, *34,* 578–589.

Schmidt, F. L., Hunter, J. E., McKenzie, R. C., & Muldrow, T. W. Impact of valid selection procedures on work-force productivity. *Journal of Applied Psychology,* 1979, *64,* 609–626.

Taylor, H. C., & Russell, J. T. The relationship of validity coefficients to the practical effectiveness of tests in selection: Discussion and tables. *Journal of Applied Psychology,* 1939, *23,* 565–578.

Young, A. M. Educational attainment of workers, March 1981. *Monthly Labor Review,* April 1982, pp. 52–55.

Part 3

Methods of Selection

Chapter 7

Work Samples

INTRODUCTION

The purpose of this chapter is threefold. First, the conceptual thinking that justifies the development and use of work-sample tests will be presented. Why should miniature replicas of on-the-job behavior serve as particularly good estimates of subsequent on-the-job behavior? The first reading by Wernimont and Campbell (1968) addresses this issue by introducing the notion of "behavioral consistency" and elaborating on the conventional wisdom that "the best indicator of future performance is past performance." Their approach focuses on the use of preemployment behavior samples obtained in real or simulated situations. They argue that a variety of measurement problems can be alleviated using this strategy. This paper is of considerable historical importance since it helped establish the needed conceptual base for the then emerging technology of work-sample testing. Their work seems to be a reaction to the early conclusion that the validity of general-ability tests is either job or situationally specific. They apparently were arguing that there is something inherently wrong with the type of test and criterion variable commonly used in validation research. Their orientation seems consistent with the thinking of Ghiselli (1974) who argued for the impermanence of facts. Their approach is concerned with the situational context within which work is performed. Likewise, Ghiselli maintained that "the nature of the circumstances in which people work, together with the nature of their work, often change significantly over quite short periods of time" (1974, p. 84). He implies that these changes can disrupt the relationships between general attributes of employees and job performance. This thinking is contrary to the recent view provided by Schmidt and Hunter (1980). Recall that they explain complex and often chaotic validity results in terms of a variety of statistical artifacts, such as sampling error, range restriction, and criterion unreliability.

The second purpose of this chapter is to illustrate the steps that need to be followed in developing work-sample testing procedures and to relate this to the earlier discussion of content validity. The reading by Robinson

(1981) provides a concise example of how to go about operationalizing the "behavioral consistency" approach. This article is noteworthy because of its clarity and use of content-oriented test construction as the sole justification for the selection system's validity. This strategy is acceptable when successful job applicants already possess the knowledge and skill required for the job and the selection system is based on appropriate sampling from the job-content domain. Pay particular attention to the job-analysis method used by Robinson, since it and the other procedures used in developing the various tests seem to comply reasonably well with the content validity standards set forth in the Uniform Guidelines on Employee Selection Procedures (Equal Employment Opportunity Commission, Civil Service Commission, Department of Labor, and Department of Justice, 1978).

Finally, the third purpose of this chapter is to review available validity evidence regarding work sample tests. The literature review by Asher and Sciarrino (1974) serves this purpose and provides useful descriptive information about the wide variety of work sample tests designed for use in industry. Their review also compares the validity evidence surrounding work sample tests with validity evidence pertaining to other predictor types. The appropriateness of such a comparison will be of concern in the commentary and will be further discussed in the chapter that focuses on psychological tests.

REFERENCES

Asher, J. J., & Sciarrino, J. A. Realistic work sample tests: A review. *Personnel Psychology*, 1974, *27*, 519–533.

Equal Employment Opportunity Commission, Civil Service, Department of Labor, & Department of Justice. Adoption by four agencies of Uniform guidelines on employment selection procedures. *Federal Register*, 1978, *43*, 38290–38315.

Ghiselli, E. E. Some perspectives for industrial psychology. *American Psychologist*, 1974, *29*, 80–87.

Robinson, D. D. Content-oriented personnel selection in a small business setting. *Personnel Psychology*, 1981, *34*, 77–87.

Schmidt, F. L., & Hunter, J. E. The future of criterion-related validity. *Personnel Psychology*, 1980, *33*, 41–60.

Wernimont, P. F., & Campbell, J. P. Signs, samples, and criteria. *Journal of Applied Psychology*, 1968, *52*, 373–376.

Signs, Samples, and Criteria*

PAUL F. WERNIMONT
JOHN P. CAMPBELL

Many writers (e.g., Dunnette, 1963; Ghiselli & Haire, 1960; Guion, 1965; Wallace, 1965) have expressed concern about the difficulties encountered in trying to predict job performance, and in establishing the validity of tests for this purpose. In general, their misgivings center around the low validities obtained and misapplications of the so-called "classic validity model." To help ameliorate these difficulties it is proposed here that the concept of validity be altered as it is now applied to predictive and concurrent situations and introduce the notion of "behavioral consistency." By consistency of behavior is meant little more than that familiar bit of conventional wisdom, "The best indicator of future performance is past performance." Surprisingly few data seem to exist to either support or refute this generalization. It deserves considerably more attention.

* P. F. Wernimont and J. P. Campbell, "Signs, Samples, and Criteria," *Journal of Applied Psychology* 52 (1968), 372–76. Copyright 1968 by the American Psychological Association. Reprinted/Adapted by permission of the publisher and author.

SOME HISTORY

It is perhaps not too difficult to trace the steps by which applied psychologists arrived at their present situation. During both World War I and World War II general intelligence and aptitude tests were effectively applied to military personnel problems. Largely as the result of these successes, the techniques developed in the armed services were transported to the industrial situation and applied to the personnel problems of the business organization. From a concentration on global measures of mental ability, validation efforts branched out to include measures of specific aptitudes, interests, and personality dimensions. The process is perhaps most clearly illustrated by the efforts of the United States Employment Service to validate the General Aptitude Test Battery across a wide range of jobs and occupations. In general, testing seemed to be a quick, economical, and easy way of obtaining useful information which removed the necessity for putting an individual on the job and observing his performance over a trial period.

It was in the context of the above efforts that an unfortunate marriage occurred, namely, the union of the classic validity model with the use of tests as signs, or indicators, of predispositions to behave in certain ways (Cronbach, 1960, p. 457), rather than as samples of the characteristic behavior of individuals. An all too frequent procedure was to feed as many signs as possible into the classic validity framework in hopes that the model itself would somehow uncover something useful. The argument here is that it will be much more fruitful to focus on meaningful samples of behavior, rather than signs of predispositions, as predictors of later performance.

THE CONSISTENCY MODEL

To further illustrate the point, consider a hypothetical prediction situation in which the following five measures are available:

1. Scores on a mental ability test;
2. School grade-point average (GPA);
3. Job-performance criterion at Time 1;
4. Job-performance criterion at Time 2;
5. Job-performance criterion at Time 3.

Obviously, a number of prediction opportunities are possible. Test scores could be correlated with GPA; school achievement could be correlated with first-year job success; or the test scores and GPA could be combined in some fashion and the composite used to predict first-, second-, or third-year job performance. All of these correlations would be labeled validity coefficients and all would conform to the classic validity model. It is less clear what label should be attached to the correlation between two different measures of job performance. Few would call it validity; many would probably refer to it as reliability. There seems to be a tendency among applied psychologists to withhold the term validity from correlations between measures of essentially the same behavior, even

if they were obtained at two different points in time. That is, the subtleties of the concept of reliability and the ingredients of the classic validity model seem to have ingrained the notion that validity is a correlation between a predictor and a criterion and the two should somehow be dissimilar.

However, each of the 10 correlations that one could compute from the above situation represents the degree of common variation between the two variables, given the appropriateness of the linear correlation model. After all, that is what correlation is all about. In this sense there is no logical reason for saying that some of the coefficients represent validity and others reliability, although there certainly may be in other contexts. An implicit or explicit insistence on the predictor being "different" seems self-defeating. Rather one should really be trying to obtain measures that are as similar to the criterion or criteria as possible. This notion appears to be at least implicit in much of the work on prediction with biographical data where many of the items represent an attempt to assess previous achievement on similar types of activities. Behavior sampling is also the basis on which simulation exercises are built for use in managerial assessment programs.

At this point it should be emphasized that for the consistency notion to be consistent, the measures to be predicted must also be measures of behavior. For example, it would be something less than consistent to use a behavior sample to predict such criteria as salary progression, organizational level achieved, or subunit production. The individual does not always have substantial control over such variables, and, even with the more obvious biasing influences accounted for, they place a ceiling on the maximum predictive efficiency to be expected. Furthermore, they are several steps removed from actual job behavior. In this respect, the authors are very much in accord with Dunnette (1966) who argues strongly for the measurement of observable job behavior in terms of its effect on meaningful dimensions of performance effectiveness. A recently developed method for accomplishing this aim is the behavior retranslation technique of Smith and Kendal (1964). The applied psychologist should reaffirm his mandate and return to the measurement of behavior. Only then will one learn by what means, and to what extent, an individual has influenced his rate of promotion, salary increases, or work group's production.

In general terms, what might the selection or prediction procedure look like if one tried to apply a consistency model? First, a comprehensive study of the job would be made. The results of this effort would be in the form of dimensions of job performance well defined by a broad range of specific behavior incidents which in turn have been scaled with respect to their "criticalness" for effective or ineffective performance.

Next, a thorough search of each applicant's previous work experience and educational history would be carried out to determine if any of the relevant behaviors or outcomes have been required of him or have been exhibited in the past. Items and rating methods would be developed to facilitate judging the frequency of such behaviors, the intensity with which they were manifested, the similarity of their context to the job situation, and the likelihood that they will show up again. These judgments can then be related to similar judgments concerning significant and consistent aspects of an individual's job behavior.

Such a procedure places considerable emphasis on background data and is similar in form to the "selection by objectives" concept of Odiorne and Miller (1966). However, the aim is to be considerably more systematic and to focus on job behavior and not summary "objectives."

After the analysis of background data it might be found that the required job behaviors have not been a part of the applicant's past repertoire and it would be necessary to look for the likelihood of that job behavior in a variety of work-sample tests or simulation exercises. A number of such behavior measures are already being used in various management assessment programs.

Finally, individual performance measures of psychological variables would be given wider use where appropriate. For example, the Wechsler Adult Intelligence Scale (Wechsler, 1955) might be used to assess certain cognitive functions. Notice that such a measure is a step closer to actual performance sampling than are the usual kinds of group intelligence tests.

How does the above procedure compare to conventional practice? The authors hope they are not beating at a straw man if the usual selection procedure is described as follows. First, a thorough job analysis is made to discover the types of skills and abilities necessary for effective performance. This is similar to the consistency approach except that the objective seems to be a jump very quickly to a generalized statement of skills and abilities rather than remaining on the behavioral level. The conventional approach next entails a search for possible predictors to try out against possible criteria. Based on knowledge of the personnel selection and individual differences literature, personal experience, and "best guesses," some decisions are made concerning what predictors to include in the initial battery. It is the authors' contention that the classic validity model has forced an undue amount of attention on test and inventory measures at this stage. Witness the large amount of space devoted to a discussion of "test validation" in most books dealing with the selection problem. Again, signs seem to take precedence over samples. Lastly, one or more criterion measures are chosen. Too often the choice seems to be made with little reference to the previous job analysis and is based on a consideration of "objectivity" and relevance to the "ultimate" criterion. Unfortunately, even a slight misuse of these considerations can lead to criteria which are poorly understood. In contrast, working within the framework of a consistency model requires consideration of dimensions of actual job behavior.

It might be added that the above characterization of the conventional approach is meant to be somewhat idealized. Certain departures from the ideal might reinforce the use of signs to an even greater extent. For example, there is always the clear and present danger that the skill requirements will be stated in terms of "traits" (e.g., loyalty, resourcefulness, initiative) and thus lead even more directly to criteria and predictors which are oriented toward underlying predispositions.

RELATIONSHIP TO OTHER ISSUES

The consistency notion has direct relevance for a number of research issues that appear frequently in the selection and prediction literature. One important implication is that selection research should focus on individuals to a much greater extent than it has. That is, there should be more emphasis on intraindividual consistency of behavior. In their insightful discussion of the criterion problem, Ghiselli and Haire (1960) point out that intraindividual criterion performance sometimes varies appreciably over time, that is, is "dynamic." They give two examples of this phenomenon. However, after an exhaustive review of the literature, Ronan and Prien (1966) concluded that a general answer to the question, "Is job performance reliable?" is not really possible with present data. They go on to say that previous research has not adequately considered the relevant dimensions that contribute to job performance

and very few studies have actually used the same criterion measure to assess performance at two or more points in time. In the absence of much knowledge concerning the stability of relevant job behaviors it seems a bit dangerous to apply the classic validation model and attempt to generalize from a one-time criterion measure to an appreciable time span of job behavior. Utilizing the consistency notion confronts the problem directly and forces a consideration of what job behaviors are recurring contributors to effective performance (and therefore predictable) and which are not.

In addition, the adoption of signs as predictors in the context of the classic model has undoubtedly been a major factor contributing to the lack of longitudinal research. It makes it far too easy to rely on concurrent studies, and an enormous amount of effort has been expended in that direction. Emphasis on behavior samples and behavior consistency requires that a good deal more attention be devoted to the former, along with very explicit consideration of the crucial parameters of a longitudinal study.

The moderator or subgrouping concept also seems an integral part of the consistency approach. The basic research aim is to find subgroups of people in a particular job family for whom behavior on a particular performance dimension is consistent. Subgrouping may be by individual or situational characteristics but the necessity is clear and inescapable. Only within such subgroups is longitudinal prediction possible.

Lastly, the process the authors are advocating demands a great deal in terms of being able to specify the contextual or situational factors that influence performance. It is extremely important to have some knowledge of the stimulus conditions under which the job behavior is emitted such that a more precise comparison to the predictor behavior sample can be made. Because of present difficulties in specifying the stimulus conditions in an organization (e.g., Sells, 1964), this may be the weakest link in the entire procedure. However, it is also a severe problem for any other prediction scheme, but is usually not made explicit.

It is important to note that the authors' notion of a consistency model does not rest on a simple deterministic philosophy and is not meant to preclude taking account of so-called "emergent" behaviors. Relative to "creativity," for example, the question becomes whether or not the individual has ever exhibited in similar contexts the particular kind of creative behavior under consideration. If a similar context never existed, the research must investigate creative performance and outputs obtained in a test situation which simulates the contextual limitations and requirements in the job situation.

An additional advantage of the consistency approach is that a number of old or persistent problems fortunately appear to dissipate, or at least become significantly diminished. Consider the following:

1. Faking and response sets—Since the emphasis would be on behavior samples and not on self-reports of attitudes, beliefs, and interests, these kinds of response bias would seem to be less of a problem.

2. Discrimination in testing—According to Doppelt and Bennett (1967) two general charges are often leveled at tests as being discriminatory devices:

(a) Lack of relevance—It is charged that test items are often not related to the work required on the job for which the applicant is being considered, and that even where relationships can be shown between test scores and job success there is no need to eliminate low-scoring disadvantaged people since they can be taught the necessary skills and knowledge in a training period after hiring.

(b) Unfairness of content—It is further maintained that most existing tests, especially verbal measures, emphasize middle-class concepts and information and are, therefore, unfair to those who have not been exposed to middle-class cultural and educational influences. Consequently, the low test scores which are earned are not indicative of the "true" abilities of the disadvantaged. Predictions of job success made from such scores are therefore held to be inaccurate.

The examination of past behaviors similar in nature to desired future behavior, along with their contextual ramifications, plus the added techniques of work samples and simulation devices encompassing desired future behavior, should markedly reduce both the real and imagined severity of problems of unfairness in prediction.

3. Invasion of privacy—The very nature of the consistency approach would seem to almost entirely eliminate this problem. The link between the preemployment or prepromotion behavior and job behavior is direct and obvious for all to see.

CONCLUDING COMMENTS

The preceding discussion is meant to be critical of the concepts of predictive and concurrent validity. Nothing that has been said here should be construed as an attack on construct validity, although Campbell (1960) has pointed out that reliability and validity are also frequently confused within this concept. Neither do the authors mean to give the impression that a full-scale application of the consistency model would be without difficulty. Using available criteria and signs of assumed underlying determinants within the framework of the classic model is certainly easier; however, for long-term gains and the eventual understanding of job performance, focusing on the measurement of *behavior* would almost certainly pay a higher return on investment.

Some time ago, Goodenough (1949) dichotomized this distinction by referring to signs versus samples as indicators of future behavior. Between Hull's (1928) early statement of test validities and Ghiselli's (1966) more recent review, almost all research and development efforts have been directed at signs. Relatively small benefits seem to have resulted. In contrast, some recent research efforts directed at samples seem to hold out more promise. The AT&T studies, which used ratings of behavior in simulated exercises (Bray & Grant, 1966), and the In-basket studies reported by Lopez (1965) are successful examples of employing behavior samples with management and administrative personnel. Frederiksen (1966) has reported considerable data contributing to the construct validity of the In-basket. In addition, Ghiselli (1966) has demonstrated that an interview rating based on discussion of specific aspects of an individual's previous work and educational history had reasonably high validity, even under very unfavorable circumstances. In a nonbusiness setting, Gordon (1967) found that a work sample yielded relatively high validities for predicting final selection into the Peace Corps and seemed to be largely independent of the tests that were also included as predictors.

Hopefully, these first few attempts are the beginning of a whole new technology of behavior sampling and measurement, in both real and simulated situations. If this technology can be realized and the consistencies of various relevant behavior dimensions mapped out, the selection literature can cease being apologetic and the prediction of performance will have begun to be understood.

REFERENCES

Bray, D. W., & Grant, D. L. The assessment center in the measurement of potential for business management. *Psychological Monographs,* 1966, *80*(17, Whole No. 625).

Campbell, D. T. Recommendations for APA test standards regarding construct, trait, and discriminant validity. *American Psychologist,* 1960, *15,* 546–553.

Cronbach, L. J. *Essentials of pyschological testing.* (2nd ed.) New York: Harper & Row, 1960.

Doppelt, J. P., & Bennett, G. K. Testing job applicants from disadvantaged groups. *Test Service Bulletin* (No. 57). New York: Psychological Corporation, 1967, pp. 1–5.

Dunnette, M. D. A modified model for test validation and research. *Journal of Applied Psychology,* 1963, *47,* 317–323.

Dunnette, M. D. *Personnel selection and placement.* Belmont, Calif.: Wadsworth, 1966.

Frederiksen, N. Validation of a simulation technique. *Organizational Behavior and Human Performance,* 1966, *1,* 87–109.

Ghiselli, E. E. *The validity of occupational aptitude tests.* New York: Wiley, 1966.

Ghiselli, E. E., & Haire, M. The validation of selection tests in the light of the dynamic character of criteria. *Personnel Psychology,* 1960, *13,* 225–231.

Goodenough, F. *Mental testing: Its history, principles, and applications.* New York: Holt, Rinehart & Winston, 1949.

Gordon, L. V. Clinical, psychometric, and work sample approaches in the prediction of success in Peace Corps training. *Journal of Applied Psychology,* 1967, *51,* 111–119.

Guion, R. M. Synthetic validity in a small company: A demonstration: *Personnel Psychology,* 1965, *18,* 49–65.

Hull, C. L. *Aptitude testing.* New York: Harcourt, Brace Janovich, 1928.

Lopez, F. M., Jr. *Evaluating executive decision making: The In-basket technique.* New York: American Management Association, 1965.

Odiorne, G. S., & Miller, E. L. Selection by objectives: A new approach to managerial selection. *Management of Personnel Quarterly,* 1966, *5*(3), 2–10.

Ronan, W. W., & Prien, E. P. *Toward a criterion theory: A review and analysis of research and opinion.* Greensboro, N.C.: Richardson Foundation, 1966.

Sells, S. B. Toward a taxonomy of organizations. In W. W. Cooper, H. J. Leavitt, & W. W. Shelly, II (Eds.), *New perspectives in organization research.* New York: Wiley, 1964.

Smith, P. C., & Kendall, L. M. Retranslation of expectations: An approach to the construction of unambiguous anchors for rating scales. *Journal of Applied Psychology,* 1963, *47,* 149–155.

Wallace, S. R. Criteria for what? *American Psychologist,* 1965, *20,* 411–417.

Wechsler, D. *Manual for the Wechsler Adult Intelligence Scale.* New York: Psychological Corporation, 1955.

Reading 15

Content-Oriented Personnel Selection in a Small Business Setting*

DAVID D. ROBINSON

A "new emphasis" in the prediction of job behavior was proposed by Wernimont and Campbell (1969). The essence of their idea was that the classic model of criterion-related validity ought to be replaced by a "behavioral consistency" approach to prediction. This approach would rely upon "establishment of consistencies between relevant dimensions of job-behavior and preemployment-behavior samples obtained from real or simulated situations." Guion (1974) pointed out that industrial psychologists paid little attention to content validity until the term was thrust upon them by federal regulations, and concluded that content-referenced measurement constituted a "new window" to be opened. Concepts of job-relatedness and due professional care, emphasized by the courts, e.g., in *Griggs* v. *Duke Power*[1] and *Albemarle* v. *Moody*[2] have stimulated interest in content-oriented methodologies.

However, according to Lawshe (1957), the newness of the field and the proprietary nature of the work done by professionals practicing in industry has resulted in a paucity of literature on content validity in employment testing except with regard to the public sector. Prien (1977) has complained that textbooks treat job analysis in such a manner as to "suggest that any fool can do it," and that by doing so relegate it "to the lowest level technician." He asserted the job analysis in test selection and criterion development must not be done by rummaging around in an organization, but through application of highly systematic and precise methods. This paper is offered in response to the apparent needs identified by Lawshe and Prien. Its purpose is to describe a systematic procedure for identifying job content and to illustrate its application to recruiting and selection in a small business setting.

* D. D. Robinson, "Content-Oriented Personnel Selection in a Small Business Setting," *Personnel Psychology* 34 (1981), pp. 77–87. Copyright 1981 by Personnel Psychology, Inc. Reprinted/Adapted by permission of the publisher and author.

[1] *Griggs* v. *Duke Power Co.,* 401 U.S. 424 (1971).
[2] *Albemarle Paper Co.* v. *Moody,* 422 U.S. 407 (1975).

PROCEDURE

The basic job analysis model was designed for the purpose of comprehensively describing behavior in military junior officer jobs in order to develop training program content (Ammerman, 1965). According to Ammerman, the purpose of a task may be so taken for granted that it may not be evident in a task statement. Task statements often may simply describe muscle activity without reference to a state to be achieved. This job analysis procedure focuses on job objectives and goals as a basis for generating task statements.

One of the problems of describing job content is to settle on a level of analysis which is neither vague, e.g., "Supervises cafeteria operations" or "Handles customer complaints," nor so detailed as to constitute an undue burden of description if carried out on all parts of the job, e.g., "Identifies proper key to unlock door," "Inserts key into lock," "Turns key to the left," etc. Using the Ammerman procedure, task statements are generated which avoid both extreme generality and specificity. Task statements generated thusly can be used to develop training program content, which was Ammerman's purpose, and for recruitment and selection, to which purposes the model has been extended in the present case.

When a job analysis procedure generates information about the job performance domain which takes the form of observable behaviors, sound judgments can normally be made by incumbents, supervisors or others who can be shown to "know the job" Lawshe, (1975). This requires the following steps:

1. Convene a panel of experts. In a small business environment, this panel usually consists of investors, company officers and/or supervisors and/or job incumbents, and sometimes other professionals, e.g., certified public accountants.

2. Ask the panel to identify all the broad objectives to be met by an *ideal* incumbent on the target job. If objectives can be so quantified that they can properly be called *standards*, so much the better. This first meeting may require about four hours.

3. List specific behaviors required to meet each objective. These behaviors usually fall into three categories which are specified below and are illustrated with reference to the following objective specified for the manager of a sporting goods store, "keep the store profitable."

   a. Control activities: (e.g., "Maintains inventory based upon suggested inventory model," "Organize a special order system by which customers can take fastest possible delivery on merchandise not in stock" and "Return defective merchandise to supplier and follow through to get proper credit issued to store's account").

   b. Determinations: (e.g., "Determine suppliers' requirement for return of merchandise" and "Determine which items in inventory are not turning over and should be put on sale or discontinued").

   Task identification is facilitated by asking the panel such questions as: "What does the person have to do in order to meet this objective?" and "What does the person have to find out in order to be able to do that?"

4. Identification of "critical" tasks. When the panel is satisfied that all the job objectives have been stated and all relevant tasks have been specified, the next step is to request the panel to identify tasks critical to effective job performance. Tasks can be rated 0, 1, or 2 on the basis of frequency, importance, cost of error, or by some other means such as a one-zero/critical-non-critical basis. The critical tasks can be used subsequently as a basis for constructing selection tests and job performance evaluation checklists. This step can be recognized as "content sampling." The content sample will be valid to the extent that the critical

tasks reflect actual job performance requirements (Tenopyr, 1977; Guion, 1978a; 1978b).

5. Determination of interjudge agreement as to the importance of major dimensions of the job. Job objectives are vague when initially stated, but the process of task listing and identification of critical tasks sharpens their definition. After tasks are specified and critical tasks identified, members of the job analysis panel rank the job objectives from most to least important. The rank of each objective is summed across all judges, and the resulting rank sums themselves are ranked to provide an overall composite ranking. Intercorrelations are calculated using Spearman's Rho as a way of summarizing the degree of agreement between members of the panel as to the relative importance of the job objectives.

AN APPLICATION TO RECRUITING AND SELECTION IN A SMALL BUSINESS SETTING

The small business in point is a general contracting firm which built about 60 single family homes, and six 40–60 unit multi-family projects in 1979. In that year it had 10 employees and sales of about $10 million. The company estimates building costs for a given architectural configuration on a particular parcel of land, and invites sub-contractor bids. It supervises construction, and sells the properties to others or keeps them for investment. Business growth indicated the need for an additional construction superintendent. The scope of this assignment was limited to recruitment and selection with respect to that position.

Job Analysis

The job analysis panel consisted of the president of the company, the production vice president, the financial vice president and the incumbent construction superintendent. The job analysis resulted in identification of 11 broad objectives and 71 tasks, of which 20 were deemed critical (see Appendix 1). The job objectives were ranked independently from most to least important by members of the job analysis panel, and a composite ranking was calculted by the method described above. Rank order correlations are presented in Table 1.

Table 1
Correlation (Spearman's Rho) between Job Analysis Panelists' Rankings of Job Objectives from Most to Least Important

	Raters				
	(1)	*(2)*	*(3)*	*(4)*	*Overall*
1	1.00	.94	.81	.75	.95
2		1.00	.81	.60	.92
3			1.00	.79	.92
4				1.00	.88

Note: "Overall" is calculated by summing the rank of each job objective across all judges, then ranking these sums.

Test Development

Based upon consideration of the critical tasks, a test battery was constructed using work sample procedures, which have been successful elsewhere (e.g., Asher and Sciarrino, 1974; Campion, 1972; Gael, Grant, and Ritchie, 1975a; 1975b; Mount, Muchinsky, and Manser, 1977; Schoenfeldt, Schoenfeldt, Acker, and Perlson, 1976). Guion's (1978b) rules for scoring content domain samples were observed.

A multiple-hurdle selection strategy was devised. Objectively scored tests were administered first in order to eliminate less qualified candidates, avoiding consumption of expensive interview time. The tests described below were administered in the order in which they are listed.

Blueprint reading test. An architect was retained to help the panel to identify common architectural errors, and to incorporate them in his own drawings of buildings which had actually been executed by the company. Applicants were asked to mark the location of the errors on copies of the drawings with a felt-tipped pen. The test was scored by counting the number of markings visible through a mylar overlay scoring key which was developed for that purpose. The test was scored by the company receptionist. This test and the "Scrambled Subcontractor" Test were to be administered to all applicants, so these two tests constituted the first selection hurdle.

"Scrambled subcontractor" test. In the construction business, interruption of the critical construction path can be extremely costly. In that case, interest charges on construction financing accumulate. Subcontractors who are in the highest demand have commitments elsewhere and move to their next job, so rescheduling them is either difficult or impossible, depending upon how much lead time is available. Given the availability of critical construction materials, the most important factor in staying on the critical path is that subcontractors appear in the right order to do their work. Knowledge of the proper order of subcontractor appearance is a prerequisite to staying on the critical path. Ignorance of the particularities of the order of subcontractor appearance in residential construction would be a definite cause of failure on this job, and could lead to financial ruin of the company. In order to test this knowledge, applicants were given a list of 30 subcontractors (e.g., roofing, framing, plumbing, fencing) and were asked to list them according to order of appearance on the job site. The order of subcontractor appearance given by an applicant was compared with the order of appearance agreed upon by the incumbent construction superintendent and the vice president for production, and the applicants were given opportunity to discuss their rationale for particular orders. Minor deviations from the "school solution" were accepted.

Construction error recognition test. The construction superintendent is responsible for seeing that a building actually gets constructed according to the construction documents. Among many other duties, the job requires detection of errors in product fabrication including physical placement of plumbing, wiring, sheet metal and wooden structural and trim items, as well as evaluation of work quality along a number of dimensions, including correctness of installation of component items, strength, weathertightness, adherence to building code requirements and aesthetic considerations. By interviewing the job analysis panel, as well as a number of subcontractors, a list of 25 common and expensive construction errors was generated, and an 8' by 12' shed was constructed, incorporating the errors. For example: a window was installed upside down so that the "weep joint" was at the top, which would prevent moisture that might collect inside the window frame from draining out; four corners of plywood subflooring were joined at one point, which creates a weak joint; and "sway braces" were not attached to join floor and ceiling plates. Applicants were given unlimited time to examine the building inside and out, and to list the errors on a pad of paper. Applicants were given one point for each error perceived.

Scheduling test. Scheduling Analysis Problem #1 (The Lee K. Fawcett Company), an assessment center exercise purchased from Development Dimensions, Inc. was administered to test applicants' capability to plan, organize, schedule, anticipate and analyze problems, and to test adequacy of judgment. This exercise depicts a situation in which job assignments must be matched to capabilities and limitations of individual workers. Part way through the exercise, the job assignments must be changed due to an unexpected development. The validity of assessment center exercises has been well documented (e.g., Bray, Campbell, and Grant, 1974; Huck, 1973; Huck and Bray, 1976; Jaffee, 1972), but reservations expressed by Klimoski and Strickland (1977) regarding the possibility that the technique may introduce criterion contamination were noted, especially since members of the assessment team were also those to evaluate job performance later. In small business, this is inevitable. It was hoped that applicants who cleared the first four hurdles would be best qualified, and should be given the opportunity for personal interaction and assessment of behavior in structured situations by the owners of the company.

Structured interview. A structured interview was prepared which covered various aspects of the relationship between the construction superintendent and building inspectors, precautions to be taken with respect to the physical security of building materials and tools at the construction site, and typical subcontractor requests involving actions deemed by the panel to be inappropriate on the basis of company philosophy and business ethics. Interviews were conducted by the president and the production vice president.

Recruitment

A newspaper advertisement describing the company and listing the job objectives was run for three days. Attempts were made to circulate news of the position opening informally by stimulating as many industry contacts as possible. This activity resulted in assembly of 49 resumes which were screened down to 17 on the basis of "goodness of fit" to the job objectives and tasks.

Selection

The 17 candidates were telephoned to establish provisional availability. The job objectives were read, and applicants were asked if they could achieve these objectives. The selection process was described, and applicants were invited to call the telephone receptionist at the company to make an appointment for testing. All 17 candidates telephoned, expressed their availability, and all 17 appeared for testing. Each was given a copy of the objectives and tasks and asked to review them at leisure. This would be the first time any of them had seen the tasks. Upon reading this information, one applicant disqualified himself.

"Blueprint Reading" test results assumed a neat bivariate distribution, with eight each in high- and low-performing groups. The "Scrambled Subcontractor" test disqualified one, leaving seven. The "Construction Error Recognition" test eliminated four and left three in the field. These three were given the "Scheduling Test" and the structured interview. One candidate stood out clearly as the best suited to the job. An offer was extended and accepted. More than a year later the fit is reported to be satisfactory.

DISCUSSION

It might be instructive to examine the job objective identified as most important by all members of the panel: "Maintain a high level of integrity and honesty." The practical importance of this particular job objective can be easily understood, but the difficulty of it is probably more apparent to psychologists than to job analysis panels. In situations like this, the behavioral emphasis of the job analysis method guides the panel. Repeated requests to the panel for objective behavioral data pertinent to this objective yielded only two tasks. In cases like this, it helps the panel to understand the criterion definition problem by asking: "What do you hear the person say or see the person do (or avoid saying or doing) that allows you to conclude anything about _____? Where, when, in what situation does the person do/avoid it?" It also helps to point out that integrity and honesty (in this case) are "labels" that labels mean different things to different people, and that objectively described work behavior leads to far better measurement than is available through the use of labels.

This job analysis procedure is attractive for its direct emphasis on required job performance. Perhaps for this reason, it is readily accepted by job analysis panels, even after initial skepticism. The job analysis process enables reconciliation of divergent viewpoints about the job, and may ease friction in both large organizations and small businesses (Blum & Naylor, 1968). The rank order correlations provide quantitative indices of agreement among members of the panel as to the relative importance of the job objectives (as defined by the critical and non-critical tasks). High intercorrelations give members of the panel confidence in the process and the outcome (task information) of job analysis, and low ones may indicate the need to spend more time in job analysis and may signify that recruitment or selection activities are premature until agreement is reached.

As mentioned above, the Ammerman technique was developed for comprehensively describing jobs, i.e., generating the *population* of job behaviors, in order to develop junior military officer training programs. Ammerman identified 816 tasks performed by Nike Hercules Fire Control Platoon Leaders. Extension of the procedure for purposes of recruitment and selection may not require generating the entire population of job behaviors, since, presumably, training program development requires more task information than either personnel selection or performance evaluation. In other words, personnel selection or performance evaluation applications of the model employ a sampling strategy, rather than developing the entire population of job behaviors. An unsolved problem is de-

termination of sampling adequacy by some quantitative method.

When sufficient numbers of personnel are available for job analysis panels, some sort of retranslation procedures (Smith and Kendall, 1963) may improve validity. Lawshe's (1975) comments with regard to the makeup of job analysis panels are also germane in the context of a discussion of personnel available for job analysis. In one situation, a job analysis panel was made up of pizza restaurant managers. A group of pizza restaurant owners reviewed the output of the panel and generated a number of new critical tasks. The owners accepted 34 out of 35 tasks designated critical by the managers. In other words, the owners identified a number of job behaviors as important which were not even considered by a group of managers, although they accepted all but one of those identified by the managers. It seems evident that the perspective of these owners is broader than that of the managers. Hindsight suggests making the panel half managers and half owners.

The method of job analysis described in this paper appears to be practical and useful in situations wherein there are few incumbents. In such cases, the richness of task information may suggest procedures for measuring skills, abilities or interests taken directly, or logically related to the job content.

Such an approach may provide an alternative to the use of the "component validity" methodology used with the Position Analysis Questionnaire (PAQ) (McCormick, Jeanneret, and Mecham, 1972; Mecham, McCormick, and Jenneret, 1979) which establishes requirements in terms of general aptitude levels, interest and experience directly from structured job analysis information based on known relationships between job and human characteristics. Additionally, where the number of job applicants is large, job requirements established by the PAQ may be used to reduce the number of candidates before a more intensive and specific selection procedure based on content-oriented job analysis is used. This might prove to be especially true when an applicant might be considered for several jobs, and in instances where career counseling and/or placement might be primary objectives.

Finally, task information developed through this type of job analysis procedure may increase leadership effectiveness (Fiedler, 1967; Fiedler, Chemers, and Mahar, 1976). The economic importance of effective human resource utilization, which has been so clearly demonstrated on large scale bases (Pecorella, Bowers, Davenport, and Lapointe, 1978; and Schmidt, Hunter, McKenzie, and Muldrow, 1979) probably is even more apparent in small business settings.

REFERENCES

Ammerman, H. L. *A model of junior officer jobs for use in developing task inventories* (HumRRO Tech. Rep. 65–10). Alexandria, Va.: Human Resources Research Organization, November, 1965.

Asher, J. J. and Sciarrino, J. A. Realistic work sample tests: A review. *Personnel Psychology,* 1974, *27,* 519–533.

Blum, M. L. and Naylor, J. C. *Industrial psychology: Its theoretical and social foundations* (Rev. ed.). New York: Harper & Row, 1968, 492–494.

Bray, D. W., Campbell, R. J., and Grant, D. L. *Formative years in business: A long-term AT&T study of managerial lives.* New York: John Wiley & Sons, 1974.

Campion, J. L. Work sampling for personnel selection. *Journal of Applied Psychology,* 1972, *56,* 40–44.

Fiedler, F. E. *A theory of leadership effectiveness.* New York: McGraw-Hill, 1967.

Fiedler, F. E., Chemers, M. M., and Mahar, L. *Improving leadership effectivness: The leader match concept.* New York: John Wiley & Sons, 1976.

Gael, S., Grant, D. L., and Ritchie, R. J. Employment test validation for minority and nonminority telephone operators. *Journal of Applied Psychology,* 1975, *60,* 411–419.

Gael, S. Grant, D. L., and Ritchie, R. J. Employment test validation for minority and nonminority clerks with work sample criteria. *Journal of Applied Psychology,* 1975, *60,* 420–426.

Guion, R. M. Open a new window: Validities and values in psychological measurement. *American Psychologist,* 1974, *29,* 287–296.

Guion, R. M. "Content validity" in moderation. *Personnel Psychology,* 1978, *31,* 205–213.

Guion, R. M. Scoring of content domain samples: The problem of fairness. *Journal of Applied Psychology,* 1978, *63,* 499–506.

Huck, J. R. Assessment centers: A review of the external and internal validities. *Personnel Psychology,* 1973, *26,* 191–212.

Huck, J. R. and Bray, D. W. Management assessment center evaluations and subsequent job performance of white and black females. *Personnel Psychology,* 1976, *29,* 13–30.

Jaffee, C. L. *Effective management selection: The analysis of behavior by simulation techniques.* Reading, Mass.: Addison-Wesley, 1971.

Klimoski, R. J. and Strickland, W. J. Assessment centers—valid or merely prescient. *Personnel Psychology,* 1977, *30,* 353–361.

Lawshe, C. H. A quantitative approach to content validity. *Personnel Psychology,* 1975, *28,* 565–575.

Mecham, R. C., McCormick, E. J., and Jeanneret, P. R. *User's manual for the Position Analysis Questionnaire (PAQ): System II.* PAQ Services, Inc., Logan, Utah, 1979.

McCormick, E. J., Jeanerette, P. R., and Mecham, R. C. A study of job characteristics and job dimensions as based on the Position Analysis Questionnaire (PAQ). *Journal of Applied Psychology Monograph,* 1972, *56,* 347–368.

Mount, M. K., Muchinsky, P. M., and Hanser, L. M. The predictive validity of a work sample: A laboratory study. *Personnel Psychology,* 1977, *30,* 637–645.

Pecorella, P. A., Bowers, D. G., Davenport, A. S., and Lapointe, J. B. *Forecasting performance in organizations: An application of current value human resources accounting.* Center for Research on Utilization of Scientific Knowledge, Institute for Social Research. Ann Arbor: University of Michigan, 1978.

Prien, E. P. The function of job analysis in content validation. *Personnel Psychology, 1977, 30,* 167–174.

Schmidt, F. L., Hunter, J. E., McKenzie, R. C., and Muldrow, T. W. Impact of valid selection procedures on work-force productivity. *Journal of Applied Psychology, 1979, 64,* 609–626.

Schoenfeldt, L. F., Schoenfeldt, B. B., Acker, S. R., and Perlson, M. R. Content validity revisited: The development of a content-oriented test of industrial reading. *Journal of Applied Psychology, 1976, 61,* 571–588.

Smith, P. C. and Kendall, L. M. Retranslation of expectations: An approach to the construction of unambiguous anchors for rating scales. *Journal of Applied Psychology, 1963, 47,* 149–155.

Tenopyr, M. L. Content-construct confusion. Personnel Psychology, 1977, 30, 47–54.

Wernimont, P. F. and Campbell, J. P. Signs, samples, and criteria. *Journal of Applied Psychology, 1968, 52,* 372–376.

APPENDIX 1

	BR[a]	SS	CER	ST	SI
Ensure prompt adherence to oral commitments made to inspectors.					X
Do a walk-through inspection with customer or production supervisor.			X		
Complete superintendent's quality control checklist at specified intervals or phase of construction.			X		
Differentiate between possible and impossible conditions on the various classifications of construction (Section 8, custom, commercial, etc).	X		X		
Schedule work and materials in accordance with critical path set by company.		X			
Inspect work progress daily and determine adherence to critical path.		X	X		
Adjust schedule in accordance with work progress/delays.				X	
Notify subcontractors and suppliers of accelerated or delayed progress to negotiate their time in.				X	
Read and interpret plans and specifications.	X				
Recognize when plans are wrong.	X				
Correct and document errors in plans.	X				
Recognize when on-site changes create problems in other areas of the building.	X				
Identify common errors made by lay-out person or architect.	X				

	BR[a]	SS	CER	ST	SI
Recognize deviations from the plans or code.	X		X		
Call for subcontractor when job is ready for that phase of operation.		X		X	
Ask subcontractor about work methods, production, availability of workmen.					X
Inspect a subcontractor's work.			X		
Identify opportunities for theft and vandalism, and specify or take counter-measures, depending upon costs/benefits.					X
Recognize violations of OSHA safety standards.					
Keep an inventory of company equipment and tools.					X

"X" Tests used to estimate task performance capability.

[a] BR = Blueprint Reading; SS = Scrambled Subcontractor; CER = Construction Error Recognition; ST = Scheduling Test; SI = Structured Interview.

Reading 16

Realistic Work Sample Tests: A Review*

JAMES J. ASHER and JAMES A. SCIARRINO

Information with the highest validity seems to have a point-to-point correspondence with the criterion. For instance, in a review article of the scorable application blank, Asher (1972) concluded that biographical information showed substantially higher predictive validity when job proficiency was the criterion, than other predictors including tests of intelligence, personality, interest, perception, motor skill, and mechanical ability.

The generalization seemed to be that factual and verifiable historical information about applicants was the best predictor of future performance in specific positions. This implication was based on comparisons with tests designed to measure "simple" dimensions. Simple in this context means a pure or single dimension of behavior.

If there is merit in a theory about predictive power in a point-to-point connection between the predictor and criterion space, then tests of single dimensions should be less powerful predictors than more complex tests such as work sample tests designed to be a miniature replica of the criterion task. The intention was not to include

* J. J. Asher and J. A. Sciarrino, "Realistic Work Sample Tests: A Review," *Personnel Psychology* 27, (1974), pp. 519–33. Copyright 1974 by Personnel Psychology, Inc. Reprinted/Adapted by permission of the publisher and author.

in this review ready-made standardized tests, but only work samples especially created for specific criterion tasks.

In a search of the literature, work sample tests were classified into the categories of either motor or verbal. A work sample was identified as "motor" if the task was a physical manipulation of things as, for example, tracing a complex electrical circuit, operating a sewing machine, making a tooth from plaster, or repairing a gear box. A work sample test was classified as "verbal" if there was a problem situation that was primarily language-oriented or people-oriented. For instance, the in-basket problem required the subject to deal with a set of materials which a company manager might expect to find in his in-basket. The items ranged from telephone messages to detailed reports. In addition, the examinee had other materials to work with such as the union contract, the organizational chart, and stationery. The subject had three hours to review the materials and take appropriate action on each item.

The work sample tests classified as *motor* involved the manipulation of things as may be seen in the following list of predictors:

A carving dexterity test for dental students (Anderson and Friedman, 1952; Layton, 1953; Moore and Peel, 1951; Webb, 1956; Weiss, 1952).

A blueprint reading and tool identification test (Anonymous, 1954).

Shorthand and stenographic tests (Bender and Loveless, 1958).

A lathe test, a drill press test, and a tool dexterity test for machine operators (Bennett and Fear, 1943; Long and Lawshe, 1947; Tiffin and Greenly, 1939).

A sewing machine test for sewing machine operators (Blum, 1943; Inskeep, 1971).

A meat weighing test for meat scalers and packers (Bridgman, Spaethe, and Dignan, 1958).

Test for mechanics such as installing belts and pulleys, disassembling and repair

of a gear box, installing and aligning a motor, pressing a bushing into a sprocket and reaming it to fit a shaft (Campion, 1972).

Vehicle repairman test (Carpenter et al., 1954).

A clothesmaking test (Croft, 1959).

Motions tests for bench assembly jobs (Drewes, 1961).

Two hand coordination test for miner operators (Durrett, 1961).

A screw board test for machine operators in a register manufacturing company (Ekberg, 1947).

A rudder control test for pilots (Fleishman, 1953; Melton, 1947).

A direction control test for pilots (Fleishman, 1954a).

A code test for radio operators (Fleishman, 1955).

A complex coordination test for pilots (Fleishman, 1956).

A realistic typing test for office personnel (Giese, 1949; Skula and Spillane, 1954; West and Bolanovich, 1963; Ash, 1960).

A stitching test for sewing machine operators (Glanz, 1949).

A test for tracing trouble in a complex circuit (Grant and Bray, 1970).

A mechanical assembly test for loom fixers and spinning frame fixers (Harrell, 1937).

A test for the inspection of electronic defects (Harris, 1964).

A programming test for computer operators (Hollenbeck, and McNamara, 1965; McNamara and Hughes, 1961).

A driver's test (Lauer, 1955).

A tool dexterity test involving fastening or unfastening bolt, washer, and nut with wrenches and/or screw drivers. Designed for machine tool operators and aircraft construction riveters (Lawshe, 1949).

A map reading test for traffic control officers (Naylor, 1954).

An electrical and radio information test for radio receivers and transmitter repairmen (Personnel Research Branch, 1958).

A punched card test for computer machine operators (Saunders, Seil, and Rosensteel, 1956).

An optical test for relay adjusters who work with small parts and tools (Speer, 1957).

An electronic's test for electronic's technician trainees (Thorndike and Hagen, 1955).

A packaging test for production machine operators (Uhlmann, 1962).

The work sample tests classified as *verbal* were usually language-oriented or people-oriented as is shown in the following list:

A technical magazine editor's test which involved writing skill, the choice of picture headlines, layout, story organization, and design (Abt, 1949).

A test of common facts in law for law students (Adams, 1943).

A leadership test for supervisors in which S chooses a problem area and reports his recommendations to the group (Arbous and Maree, 1951; Weislogel, 1954).

The leaderless group discussion for supervisors and military trainees (Bass, 1954; Bass and Coates, 1954; Gleason, 1957; Wollowick and McNamara, 1969).

An oral fact-finding test for communication consultants (Bray and Campbell, 1968).

A small business game involving a manufacturing problem for managers (Bray and Grant, 1966; Hinrichs, 1969; Wollowick and McNamara, 1969).

The in-basket test for managers (Bray and Grant, 1966; Hinrichs, 1969; Meyer, 1970; Wollowick and McNamara, 1969).

A law school admission's test involving cases, data interpretation, and reading comprehension (Breslow, 1957).

Group discussion test for supervisors (Castle and Garforth, 1951; Glaser, Schwarz, and Flanagan, 1958; Handyside and Duncan, 1954; Mandell, 1950d).

A police test involving general information and judgment related to police work (DuBois and Watson, 1950).

A judgment and decision-making test for administrators (Forehand and Guetzkow, 1961; Mandell, 1950a, 1956).

A role playing test that simulates telephone contacts with customers (Gael and Grant, 1972).

Information test of navel organization and practices (Glickman, 1956).

Work sample tests in Chinese, Japanese, Spanish, or Russian for Peace Corps volunteers, interpreters, and interrogators (Gordon, 1967; Personnel Research Branch, 1957a, 1957b; Williams and Leavitt, 1947).

An information test about farming (Grigg, 1948).

A speech interview for foreign students (Jones and Michael, 1961).

A test of baking information and judgment of managerial problems in the baking industry (Knauft, 1949; 1954).

Skill in writing business letters (Kriedt, 1952).

A test for engineers involving processing of mathematical data and evaluating hypotheses (Mandell, 1950b).

A test of basic information in chemistry (Mandell, 1950c).

A test of supervisory judgment concerning employee relations, training, safety, and evaluation of performance (Mandell, 1947; Shultz, 1955).

A test for physical scientists involving mathematical formulations, science judgment, and information about physics (Mandell and Adams, 1948).

A test for promotion to Navy petty officer (Merenda, 1959).

A test for actuarial clerks involving basic mathematics and interpolation of tables (Poruben, 1950).

A study habits inventory and a test of organization for university students (Rubenowitz, 1958).

A test for government inspectors involving accuracy in handling testimony and understanding principles of U.S. Government (Snyder, 1955).

A test of ability to follow oral directions (Stern and Gordon, 1961).

A test of graphic reading and interpolation by students in optometry school (Warren and Canfield, 1948).

Aviation information for pilots, navigators, and bombardiers (Davis, 1947).

Life insurance information (Baier and Dugan, 1956).

The criteria were classified into either measures of job proficiency or success in training. When a study reported results from multiple samples, the median validity coefficient was selected as the most representative. The sample size in almost all studies was large enough so that a validity coefficient of .30 was significant beyond the .05 level. Most of the validities reported for either the motor or verbal work samples were significant beyond the .01 level.

In almost all studies of the motor work sample test, the job proficiency criterion was a supervisor's rating, usually with a graphic scale. In only a few studies was the reliability of the criterion ratings reported. In the few studies in which ratings were not used, some objective index of production was the measure of job proficiency.

When the criterion was success in training, the measure was either the completion of training or grades achieved. Again, the reliability of the training criteria was rarely reported.

For the verbal work sample tests, job proficiency in most studies was measured with supervisory ratings, usually a graphic scale or ranking. In rare instances reliability was reported for the criterion ratings, but often the problem of reliability was resolved by combining the judgments of raters who made decisions independently. When objective measures were used as criteria, they were, for instance, promotions, salary level, job level, sales or leadership offices held. For success in training, the criteria were grades achieved of a rating, usually with a graphic scale.

RESULTS

A predictive power of realistic work sample tests may be evaluated with greater clarity when compared with other predictors. Fortunately, Ghiselli (1966) has published the proportion of validity coefficients which resulted when tests were tried for specific jobs. For example, in his book are validity coefficients for mechanical repairmen on mechanical principles tests, general clerks on intelligence tests, bench workers on finger dexterity tests, and machine tenders on spatial relations tests. The criterion was job proficiency in all cases except mechanical repairmen for whom the criterion was success in training.[1]

As may be seen in Figures 1 through 3, the motor type work sample in which subjects physically manipulated things was second only to the biographical item in predictive power. The verbal work sample was consistently below the motor work sample in its ability to predict job proficiency, but still it was in the top half of the list.

Figure 4 suggests that the motor work sample tended to be a somewhat better predictor of job proficiency than of success in training. The reverse seems to be the case for the verbal work sample. As may be seen in Figure 5, the verbal work sample was distinctly more powerful in predicting success in training than in forecasting job proficiency.

When success in training was the criterion, Figure 6 shows that the verbal work sample had substantially more significant validity coefficients than the motor, especially in the range of .40 to .49.

---

[1] The validity coefficients for the personality tests in Figures 1 through 3 were estimated from Figure 1 in an article by Ghiselli and Barthol (1953) who reviewed 113 studies in which the personality trait appeared to have relevance for each specific job in eight different occupational categories.

The validity coefficients in Figures 1 through 3 for intelligence, mechanical aptitude, finger dexterity, and spatial relations were estimated from Figure 2–4 on page 29 of Ghiselli's book (1966), *The Validity of Occupational Aptitude Tests.*

Figure 1
Proportion of Validity Coefficients .50 or Higher with Job Proficiency As the Criterion

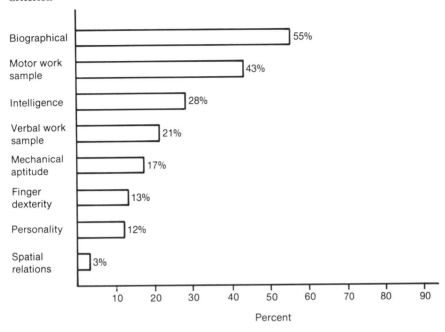

Figure 2
Proportion of Validity Coefficients .40 or Higher with Job Proficiency As the Criterion

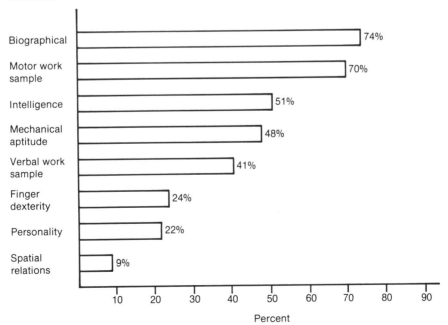

Figure 3
Proportion of Validity Coefficients .30 or Higher with Job Proficiency As the Criterion

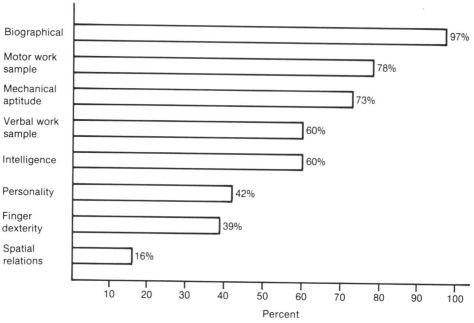

Figure 4
Motor Work Sample: Proportion of Validity Coefficients for Job Proficiency Versus a Training Criterion

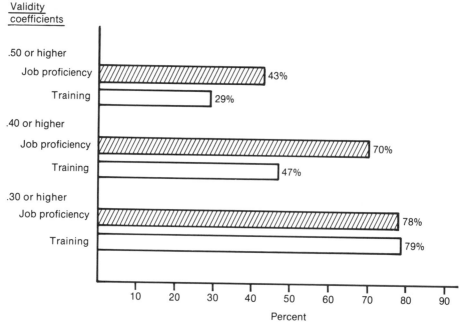

Figure 5
Verbal Work Sample: Proportion of Validity Coefficients for Job Proficiency Versus a Training Criterion

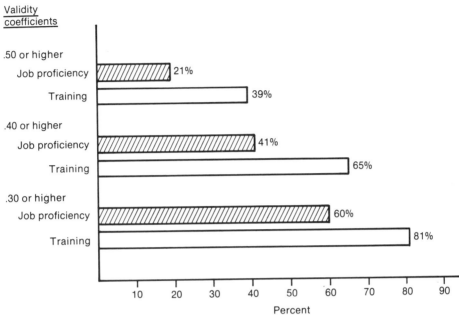

Figure 6
Proportion of Validity Coefficients for Motor Versus Verbal Work Samples When the Criterion Was Success in Training

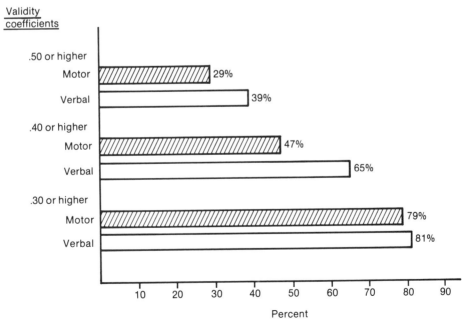

One explanation for the results is a point-to-point theory which states that the more points in common between the predictor and criterion space, the higher the validity coefficient. Of all the predictors, the realistic motor work samples had the most visible point-to-point connection with job proficiency criteria. Therefore, it should have had the highest proportion of large magnitude validity coefficients. It is puzzling that the realistic work sample was second to biographical information in predictive power.

For biographical data, the point-to-point connection between predictor and criterion space is less obvious. A dramatic example would be this single biographical item, "Did you ever build a model airplane that flew?", which was almost as good a predictor of success in flight training during World War II as the entire Air Force Battery (Henry, 1965, p. 913).

If a point-to-point theory has merit, then complex work sample tests that are miniature replicas of on-the-job behavior should have more predictive power than simple motor skills tests. The evidence, as presented in reviews by Fleishman (1953, 1954), supports this expectation. Fleishman concluded that simple motor skills tests, with occasional exceptions, have shown insignificant validities. However, in fairness it should be added that Fleishman's speculation was that sample motor tests had insignificant validity because they did not tap basic aptitudes needed in specific positions.

There is a strong attraction to a classic strategy of using factor analysis to analyze skills into single and basic dimensions called aptitudes, then patterning the single dimensions into a composite with a linear combination using a statistic as multiple regression. This is a mediator theory which assumes that criterion behavior is controlled or determined by generalized mediators as traits, aptitudes, or intelligence. The problem, then, is to measure the gen-

eral mediators. The more accurate the measurement, the higher the probability that the criterion behavior can be estimated with precision.

One difficulty with the mediator theory is interaction. It may be a complex stimulus-response task elicits an interaction effect which may not be additive, but configural calling for a yet undeveloped mathematic.

The interaction effect may be so powerful that it accounts for 50 percent of the variance in motor test performance alone. For instance, Fleishman and Hempel (1954) found that of 15 widely used printed and apparatus dexterity tests, only half of the variance was explained with the five factors isolated in the factor analysis. Since the reliabilities of the tests were high, error can only account for a rather limited portion of the unexplained variance.

Still another hypothesis to explain the predictive power of complex work sample tests in Seashore's (1939) concept of "work methods." It may be that a miniature work sample task is apt to elicit realistic work methods or work habits which individuals use to solve specific problems. These work methods may account for a greater proportion of individual differences than any linear additive combination of basic motor abilities.

Another possible explanation is experience. The miniature work sample may be sorting applicants into a continuum of individuals with progressively more criterion-related experience. Even if all the applicants do not have any prior experience in a specific position, the realistic work sample test may be measuring prior experience which has transfer to the criterion task.

SUMMARY

Realistic work sample tests that were miniature replicas of the criterion task were classified as motor or verbal. The motor work sample had subjects physically manipulate things as tracing a complex electrical circuit or operating a sewing machine, while verbal work samples required individuals to cope with people-oriented or language-oriented problems.

From the literature, the work sample tests selected were those especially designed to represent on-the-job criterion behavior in a specific situation rather than ready-made standardized tests unless the latter had an unmistakable surface relationship to the criterion.

The guiding hypothesis was a point-to-point theory which states that the more features in common between the predictor and criterion space, the higher the validity. In a previous review (Asher, 1972), it was found that historical information from the scorable application blank was data with a point-to-point relationship with the criterion and had the highest predictive power from a list of standard predictors including intelligence, personality, interest, perception, motor skill, and mechanical ability.

Complex work sample tests that were miniature replicas of specific criterion behavior should also have a point-to-point relationship with the criterion.

The results were as follows:

1. When job proficiency was the criterion, realistic motor work sample tests had the highest validity coefficients second only to biographical information. Verbal work sample tests were not as high as the motor, but they were in the top half of the predictors.

2. When the criterion was success in training, verbal work sample tests were more powerful in predicting success in training than in forecasting job proficiency. Verbal work sample tests had substantially more significant validity coefficients than the motor when there was a training criterion.

The point-to-point theory does not preclude other possible explanations such as the interaction hypothesis, the work-methods hypothesis, and the transfer-of-experience hypothesis.

REFERENCES

Abt, L. E. A test battery for selecting technical magazine editors. *Personnel Psychology,* 1949, *2,* 75–91.

Adams, W. M. Prediction of scholastic success in colleges of law: I. The experimental edition of the Iowa Legal Aptitude Test. *Educational and Psychological Measurement,* 1943, *3,* 291–305.

Anderson, A. V. and Friedman, S. Prediction of performance in a Navy Dental Prosthetic Technician Training Course (Abstract). *American Psychologist,* 1952, *7,* 288.

Anonymous. Validity information exchange No. 7-094. *Personnel Psychology,* 1954, *7,* 572.

Arbous, A. G. and Maree, J. Contribution of two group discussion techniques to a validated test battery. *Occupational Psychology,* 1951, *25,* 73–89.

Ash, P. Validity information exchange No. 13–07. *Personnel Psychology,* 1960, *13,* 456.

Asher, J. J. The biographical item: Can it be improved? *Personnel Psychology,* 1972, *25,* 251–269.

Baier, D. E. and Dugan, R. D. Tests and performance in a sales organization. *Personnel Psychology,* 1956, *9,* 17–26.

Bass, B. M. The leaderless group discussion as a leadership evaluation instrument. *Personnel Psychology,* 1954, *7,* 470–477.

Bass, B. M. and Coates, C. H. Validity information exchange No. 7-082. *Personnel Psychology,* 1954, *7,* 553–554.

Bender, W. R. G. and Loveless, H. E. Validation studies involving successive classes of trainee stenographer. *Personnel Psychology,* 1958, *11,* 491–508.

Bennett, G. K. and Fear, R. A. Mechanical comprehension and dexterity. *Personnel Journal,* 1943, *22,* 12–17.

Blum, M. L. Selection of sewing machine operators. *Journal of Applied Psychology,* 1943, *27,* 35–40.

Bray, D. W. and Campbell, R. J. Selection of salesmen by means of an assessment center. *Journal of Applied Psychology*, 1968, *52*, 36–41.

Bray, D.W. and Grant, D. L. The assessment center in the measurement of potential for business management. *Psychological Monographs*, 1966, *80* (17, Whole No. 625).

Breslow, E. The predictive efficiency of the Law School Admission Test at the New York University School of Law. *Psychology Newsletter*, 1957, *9*, 13–22.

Bridgman, C. S., Spaethe, M., and Dignan, F. Validity information exchange No. 11-21. *Personnel Psychology*, 1958, *11*, 264–265.

Campion, J. E. Work sampling for personnel selection. *Journal of Applied Psychology*, 1972, *56*, 40–44.

Carpenter, C. R., Greenhill, L. P., Hittinger, W. F., McCoy, E. P., McIntyre, C. J. Murnin, J. A., and Watkins, R. W. The development of a sound motion picture proficiency test. *Personnel Psychology*, 1954, *7*, 509–523.

Castle, P. F. C. and Garforth, F. I. de la P. Selection, training, and status of supervisors: I. Selection. *Occupational Psychology*, 1951, *25*, 109–123.

Croft, E. J. Prediction of clothing construction achievement of high school girls. *Educational and Psychological Measurement*, 1959, *19*, 653–655.

Davis, F. B. (Ed.) Army Air Forces Aviation Psychology Program Research Reports. *The AAF Qualifying Examination Report No. 6*, Chapter 6. Washington, D.C.: Government Printing Office, 1947.

Drewes, D. W. Development and validation of synthetic dexterity tests based on elemental motion analysis. *Journal of Applied Psychology*, 1961, *45*, 179–185.

DuBois, P. H. and Watson, R. I. The selection of patrolmen. *Journal of Applied Psychology*, 1950, *34*, 90–95.

Durrett, H. L. Validity information exchange No. 14–03. *Personnel Psychology*, 1961, *14*, 453–455.

Ekberg, D. L. A study in tool usage. *Educational and Psychological Measurement*, 1947, *7*, 421–427.

Fleishman, E. A. An evaluation of two psychomotor tests for the prediction of success in primary flying training. Lackland Air Force Base, Tex.: Human Resources Research Center, May 1953, *Research Bulletin* (53–9).

Fleishman, E. A. Evaluations of psychomotor tests for pilot selection: The direction control and compensatory balance tests. Lackland Air Force Base, Tex.: Air Force Personnel and Training Research Center, December 1954, *Technical Report* (AFPTRC-TR-54-131). (a)

Fleishman, E. A. Testing for psychomotor abilities by means of apparatus tests. *Psychological Bulletin*, 1954, *50*, 241–262.

Fleishman, E. A. Predicting code proficiency of radio telegraphers by means of aural tests. *Journal of Applied Psychology*, 1955, *39*, 150–155.

Fleishman, E. A. Psychomotor selection tests: Research and application in the U.S. Air Force. *Personnel Psychology*, 1956, *9*, 449–467.

Fleishman, E. A. and Hempel, W. E. A factor analysis of dexterity tests. *Personnel Psychology*, 1954, *7*, 15–32.

Forehand, G. A. and Guetzkow, H. The Administrative Judgement Test as related to descriptions of executive judgement behaviors. *Journal of Applied Psychology*, 1961, *45*, 257–261.

Gael, S. and Grant, D. L. Employment test validation for minority and nonminority telephone company service representatives. *Journal of Applied Psychology*, 1972, *56*, 135–139.

Ghiselli, E. E. *The validity of occupational aptitude tests.* New York: Wiley, 1966.

Ghiselli, E. E. and Barthol, R. R. The validity of personality inventories in the selection of employees. *Journal of Applied Psychology*, 1953, *37*, 18–20.

Giese, W. J. A tested method for the selection of office personnel. *Personnel Psychology*, 1949, *2*, 525–545.

Glanz, E. A grade test for power sewing machine operators. *Journal of Applied Psychology*, 1949, *33*, 436–441.

Glaser, R., Schwarz, P. A. and Flanagan, J. C. The contribution of interview and situational performance procedures to the selection of supervisory personnel. *Journal of Applied Psychology,* 1958, *42,* 69–73.

Gleason, W. J. Predicting Army leadership ability by modified leaderless group discussion. *Journal of Applied Psychology,* 1957, *41,* 231–235.

Glickman, A. S. The naval knowledge test. *Journal of Applied Psychology,* 1956, *40,* 389–392.

Gordon, L. V. Clinical, psychometric, and work sample approaches in the prediction of success in Peace Corps training. *Journal of Applied Psychology,* 1967, *51,* 111–119.

Grant, D. L. and Bray, D. W. Validation of employment tests for telephone company installation and repair occupations. *Journal of Applied Psychology,* 1970, *54,* 7–14.

Grigg, A. E. A farm knowledge test. *Journal of Applied Psychology,* 1948, *32,* 452–455.

Handyside, J. D. and Duncan, D. C. Four years later: A follow-up of an experiment in selecting supervisors. *Occupational Psychology,* 1954, *28,* 9–23.

Harrell, W. The validity of certain mechanical ability tests for selecting cotton mill machine fixers. *Journal of Social Psychology,* 1937, *8,* 279–282.

Harris, D. H. Development and validation of an aptitude test for inspectors of electronic equipment. *Journal of Industrial Psychology,* 1964, *2,* 29–35.

Henry, E. R. *Research conference on the use of autobiographical data as psychological predictors.* Greensboro, N.C.: The Richardson Foundation, 1965.

Hinrichs, J. R. Comparison of "real life" assessments of management potential with situational exercises, paper-and-pencil ability tests, and personality inventories. *Journal of Applied Psychology,* 1969, *53,* 425–432.

Hollenbeck, G. P. and McNamara, W. J. CUCPAT and programming aptitude. *Personnel Psychology,* 1965, *18,* 101–106.

Inskeep, G. C. The use of psychomotor tests to select sewing machine operators—some negative findings. *Personnel Psychology,* 1971, *24,* 707–714.

Jones, R. A. and Michael, W. B. The validity of a battery of tests in communication skills

for foreign students attending an American university. *Educational and Psychological Measurement,* 1961, *21,* 493–496.

Knauft, E. B. A selection battery for bake shop managers. *Journal of Applied Psychology,* 1949, *33,* 304–315.

Knauft, E. B. Validity information exchange No. 7-070. *Personnel Psychology,* 1954, *7,* 405–406.

Kriedt, P. H. Validation of a correspondence aptitude test. *Journal of Applied Psychology,* 1952, *36,* 5–7.

Lauer, A. R. Comparison of group paper-and-pencil tests with certain psychophysical tests for measuring driving aptitude of Army personnel. *Journal of Applied Psychology,* 1955, *39,* 318–321.

Lawshe, C. H. Hand-tool dexterity test. In O. K. Buros (Ed.), *The third mental measurements yearbook.* New Brunswick: Rutgers University Press, 1949.

Layton, W. L. Predicting success in dental school. *Journal of Applied Psychology,* 1953, *37,* 251–255.

Long, W. F. and Lawshe, C. H. The effective use of manipulative tests in industry. *Psychological Bulletin,* 1947, *44,* 130–148.

Mandell, M. M. The selection of foreman. *Educational and Psychological Measurement,* 1947, *7,* 385–397.

Mandell, M. M. The Administrative Judgment Test. *Journal of Applied Psychology,* 1950, *34,* 145–147. (a)

Mandell, M. M. Scientific selection of engineers. *Personnel,* 1950, *26,* 296–298. (b)

Mandell, M. M. Selecting chemists for the Federal Government. *Personnel Psychology,* 1950, *3,* 53–56. (c)

Mandell, M. M. Validation of group oral performance test. *Personnel Psychology,* 1950, *3,* 179–186. (d)

Mandell, M. M. Validity information exchange, No. 9-2. *Personnel Psychology,* 1956, *9,* 105.

Mandell, M. M. and Adams, S. Selection of physical scientists. *Educational and Psychological Measurement,* 1948, *8,* 575–581.

McNamara, W. J. and Hughes, J. L. A review of research on the selection of computer programmers. *Personnel Psychology,* 1961, *14,* 39–51.

Melton, A. W. (Ed.), Army Air Forces Aviation Psychology Program Research Reports. *Apparatus Tests,* Report No. 4., Chapter 8. Washington, D.C.: Government Printing Office, 1947.

Merenda, P. F. Navy petty officer promotion examinations as predictors of on-the-job performance. *Educational and Psychological Measurement,* 1959, *19,* 657–661.

Meyer, H. H. The validity of the in-basket test as a measure of managerial performance. *Personnel psychology,* 1970, *23,* 297–307.

Moore, B. G. R. and Peel, E. A. Predicting aptitude for dentistry. *Occupational Psychology,* 1951, *25,* 192–199.

Naylor, G. F. K. Aptitude tests for air traffic control officers. *Occupational Psychology,* 1954, *28,* 209–217.

Personnel Research Branch, The Adjutant General's Office, Department of the Army. Validity information exchange No. 10-41. *Personnel Psychology,* 1957, *10,* 485–486. (a)

Personnel Research Branch. The Adjutant General's Office, Department of the Army. Validity information exchange No. 10-42. *Personnel Psychology,* 1957, *10,* 487–489. (b)

Personnel Research Branch, The Adjutant General's Office, Department of the Army. Validity information exchange No. 11-18. *Personnel Psychology,* 1958, *11,* 257–259.

Poruben, A. A test battery for actuarial clerks. *Journal of Applied Psychology,* 1950, *34,* 159–162.

Rubenowitz, S. Predicting academic success: A follow-up study. *Occupational Psychology,* 1958, *32,* 162–170.

Saunders, W. J., Seil, W. R., and Rosensteel, R. K. Validity information exchange No. 9-34. *Personnel Psychology,* 1956, *9,* 379.

Seashore, R. H. Work methods: An often neglected factor underlying individual differences. *Psychological Review,* 1939, *46,* 123–141.

Shultz, M. Validity information exchange No.

8–09. *Personnel Psychology,* 1955, *8,* 118–119.

Skula, M. and Spillane, R. F. Validity information exchange No. 7-016. *Personnel Psychology,* 1954, *7,* 147–148.

Snyder, R. Validity information exchange No. 8-14. *Personnel Psychology,* 1955, *8,* 263.

Speer, G. S. Validity information exchange No. 10-5. *Personnel Psychology,* 1957, *10,* 80.

Stern, F. and Gordon, L. Ability to follow instructions as a predictor of success in recruit training. *Journal of Applied Psychology,* 1961, *45,* 22–24.

Thorndike, R. L. and Hagen, E. Validation of the Electronics Technician Selection test at selected class "A" schools. Bureau of Naval Personnel, *Technical Bulletin,* 55-3, April 15, 1955.

Tiffin, J. and Greenly, R. J. Experiments in the operation of a punch press. *Journal of Applied Psychology,* 1939, *23,* 450–460.

Uhlmann, F. W. A selection test for production machine operators. *Personnel Psychology,* 1962, *15,* 287–293.

Warren, N. D. and Canfield, A. A. An optometric aptitude test. *Educational and Psychological Measurement,* 1948, *8,* 183–191.

Webb, S. C. The prediction of achievement for first year dental students. *Educational and Psychological Measurement,* 1956, *16,* 543–548.

Weislogel, R. L. Development of situational tests for military personnel. *Personnel Psychology,* 1954, *7,* 492–497.

Weiss, I. Prediction of achievement success in dental school. *Journal of Applied Psychology,* 1952, *36,* 11–14.

West, L. and Bolanovich, D. J. Evaluation of typewriting proficiency: preliminary test development. *Journal of Applied Psychology,* 1963, *47,* 403–407.

Williams, S. B. and Leavitt, H. J. Prediction of success in learning Japanese. *Journal of Applied Psychology,* 1947, *31,* 164–168.

Wollowick, H. B. and McNamara, W. J. Relationship of the components of an assessment center to management success. *Journal of Applied Psychology,* 1969, *53,* 348–352.

COMMENTARY

In the first reading, Wernimont and Campbell (1968) provide a theoretical basis for the use of work-sample tests. They argue that predictors should be realistic samples of job behavior and therefore as similar to the criteria as possible. The goal is to create a point-to-point correspondence between predictor and criterion space. The more features in common between the predictor and criterion, the higher the likely validity coefficient. While the literature on work sampling has focused primarily on selecting people who are trained and therefore able to do the job immediately, the concept of a point-to-point correspondence can be used in the development of other predictor types. Perhaps the best illustration of this is the concept of a "trainability" test. Here, training content is sampled and the goal is to predict the ability of the applicant to learn the job. The interested reader should review the work of Robertson and Downs (1979) and Siegel (1978) for thorough discussions of this technique.

It is in the area of validating training samples that the necessity of conducting a criterion-related validity study is the greatest. The underlying construct measured (learning ability) is rather abstract and difficult to justify on the basis of content-oriented test construction alone. The use of content-oriented procedures to justify the use of a selection procedure is more appropriate with traditional work-sample tests. The second reading by Robinson (1981) provided a clear illustration of the development of work samples and the reliance on content-oriented validation techniques. Robinson's work is particularly noteworthy due to its concern for important principles outlined in the Uniform Guidelines (Equal Employment Opportunity Commission, Civil Service Commission, Department of Labor, and Department of Justice, 1978). A brief reflection on these principles in relation to Robinson's techniques should serve to clarify how to put sound conceptual thinking into practice.

First, the Uniform Guidelines stress that content validation (as sole justification for the use of a selection procedure) is appropriate only under limited conditions. Content validity is not an appropriate strategy when the selection procedure involves knowledge, skills, or abilities which an employee will be expected to learn on the job. The selection problem Robinson confronted involved hiring a construction superintendent for a general contracting firm. Clearly, this individual would have to be able to assume major job responsibility at the time of selection.

Next, a selection procedure based upon inferences about mental processes, such as intelligence, aptitude, personality, or leadership, cannot be defended solely on the basis of content validity. Robinson was very careful in attempting to measure task performance directly. For example, the tests were used to determine if applicants could do such things as adjust work schedules, recognize OSHA violations, and do walk-through inspections focusing on construction quality.

Third, the type of job analysis required when conducting a content-validity study is discussed at some length in the Guidelines. Essentially, the analysis should focus on work behaviors and associated tasks. The work behaviors selected for measurement should be critical and should constitute most of the job. The job analysis steps outlined by Robinson seem to meet these requirements and demonstrate that it is possible to conduct a high quality job analysis in the context of a small-business setting. Not only does Robinson's procedure focus on specific job behaviors but a systematic strategy for identifying critical tasks is central to the technique.

Finally, the content of the selection procedure should meet certain requirements. The Uniform Guidelines state that "as the content of the selection procedure less resembles a work behavior, or the setting and manner of the administration of the selection procedure less resembles the work situation, or the result less resembles a work product, the less likely the selection procedure is to be content valid, and the greater the need for other evidence of validity" (p. 38302). What better illustration of adherence to these principles than Robinson's "construction error recognition test"? The use of an 8 foot by 12 foot shed that incorporated common and expensive construction errors provided a highly realistic testing environment. Asking the applicant to identify these errors represents task behavior that is very similar to that expected on the actual job. In summary, Robinson produced tests that appropriately sampled from the relevant job content domain.

The last reading, by Asher and Sciarrino (1974), reviewed the validity results associated with work-sample tests especially created for specific criterion tasks. This article offers rich descriptions of the possible assortment of work-sample tests available. They then argue, however, that the predictive power of work-sample tests can be evaluated with greater clarity when compared to other predictors. While work-sample tests seem to correlate at relatively high levels with appropriate criteria, comparing these values with the coefficients associated with aptitude tests can be misleading. Since work-sample tests usually are designed to measure whether an applicant currently possesses required knowledge and skill, they are most useful when hiring experienced, trained individuals. Tests of this type would not be appropriate in selecting for low-skill or training positions. Thus, the technology of work-sample testing will not be correctly applied to entry-level hiring in many instances. Many of the comparisons Asher and Sciarrino provided must be interpreted taking this issue into consideration. While work-sample tests may provide relatively higher validity when applied to appropriate selection problems, there is no reason to expect similar results in different hiring contexts. Asher and Sciarrino compared work-sample results with estimates of aptitude-test validity provided by Ghiselli (1966). Many of Ghiselli's estimates involve selection problems for which work-sample tests would prove inappropriate. That is, traditional work-sample tests would not likely predict job performance when hiring for positions that did not require the immediate possession of certain job-related skills.

This issue can be characterized by focusing on the results provided in the often-cited study by Campion (1972). Advocates of the work-sample testing strategy may be pleased to note that Campion's work-sample test produced correlations ranging from .42 to .66 with three measures of job performance while a paper and pencil ability test (the Wonderlic Personnel Test) produced correlations ranging from $-.32$ to $-.19$. Campion was very careful to state that in this hiring context the work-sample tests were to be used to select from a pool of experienced maintenance mechanics. Success on the job depended upon the current possession of work skills. It is in this situation that the work sample is appropriate. He then discussed the situation where applicants would not be presumed to possess prerequisite work skills and would, if hired, be placed in training programs. Here, selection into training would normally be based on tests of general ability. In this context the Wonderlic Personnel Test may be perfectly acceptable. The point is, it makes little sense to compare the validity coefficients generated in this study. The various classes of tests were designed to measure very different constructs and were designed to be used in very different settings. Incidently, making a comparison by using the Campion data is not appropriate due to certain statistical artifacts that in all likelihood affected the tests differentially. For example, a test of mechanical comprehension was used to screen applicants while Campion conducted a current-employee study when investigating the validity of the work-sample tests. The Wonderlic correlated at a level of .56 with the test of mechanical comprehension, thus range restriction on both ability tests confounds the results.

Campion (1972) points out that when selecting for a training position an appropriate strategy would be to use a general-ability test to make initial hiring decisions, then use work-sample techniques to determine who should continue with the training experience. Candidates who could not acquire the skills required to do the job would then be eliminated or rerouted to other training programs. When general-aptitude tests are used to predict appropriate criteria in appropriate settings, much more respectable validity levels can be expected. For example, in a classic review article by Ghiselli (1973) (see Chapter 11) the average validity coefficient associated with tests of intellectual ability when predicting success in training was .41. Likewise, the average validity associated with tests of spatial and mechanical ability was .40. In both instances, these coefficients were specific to persons working in mechanical repair occupations and therefore it is meaningful to consider values of this magnitude in the context of Campion's sequential hiring strategy.

Finally, there are unique advantages associated with the use of work-sample tests that need brief comment. Obviously these need to be considered along with the considerable cost of testing associated with this approach. First, work-sample tests are likely to display a high degree of face validity. The meaning of face validity comes closest to what Mosier (1947) termed the *appearance of validity*. For Cascio (1978), face validity is "whether the measurement procedure looks like it is measuring the trait in question" (p. 68). This is of importance for at least two reasons. The most common argument is that applicants will be more motivated and more likely to react favorably to face valid selection procedures. In addition, Sackett and Dreher (1982) suggest that decisions regarding the use of selection systems may be influenced by user reaction to selection system components. They provide evidence that the perceived fairness and appropriateness of a test is partially a function of face validity.

Finally, work-sample tests may enable applicants to get a clearer understanding of the job. Their value in appraising the appropriateness of a job is explored in some detail by Downs, Farr, and Colbeck (1978). The broader issue of realistic job previews is discussed by Wanous (1980) in a book devoted to the organizational entry process.

REFERENCES

Asher, J. J., & Sciarrino, J. A. Realistic work sample tests: A review. *Personnel Psychology*, 1974, *27*, 519–533.

Campion, J. E. Work sampling for personnel selection. *Journal of Applied Psychology*, 1972, *56*, 40–44.

Cascio, W. F. *Applied psychology in personnel management*, Reston, Va.: Reston Publishing, 1978.

Downs, S., Farr, R. M., & Colbeck, L. Self-appraisal: A convergence of selection and guidance. *Journal of Occupational Psychology*, 1978, *51*, 271–278.

Equal Employment Opportunity Commission, Civil Service, Department of Labor, and Department of Justice. Adoption by four agencies of Uniform Guidelines on Employee Selection Procedures. *Federal Register*, 1978, *43*, 38290–38315.

Ghiselli, E. E. *The validity of occupational aptitude tests*. New York: John Wiley & Sons, 1966.

Ghiselli, E. E. The validity of aptitude tests in personnel selection. *Personnel Psychology*, 1973, *26*, 461–477.

Mosier, C. I. A critical examination of the concepts of face validity. *Educational and Psychological Measurement*, 1947, *7*, 191–205.

Robertson, I., & Downs, S. Learning and the prediction of performers: Development of trainability testing in the United Kingdom. *Journal of Applied Psychology,* 1979, *64,* 42–50.

Robinson, D. D. Content-oriented personnel selection in a small business setting. *Personnel Psychology,* 1981, *34,* 77–87.

Sackett, P. R., & Dreher, G. F. Face validity and empirical validity as determinants of selection decisions. Paper presented at the national meeting of the American Psychological Association, Washington, D.C., August, 1982.

Siegel, A. D. Miniature job training and evaluation as a selection/classification device. *Human Factors,* 1978, *20,* 189–200.

Wanous, J. P. *Organizational entry,* Reading, Mass.: Addison-Wesley, 1980.

Wernimont, P. F., & Campbell, J. P. Signs, samples, and criteria. *Journal of Applied Psychology,* 1968, *52,* 372–376.

Chapter 8

Assessment Centers

INTRODUCTION

The past decade has seen a rapid increase in the use of assessment centers both for internal promotion and external selection purposes. In an assessment center, job candidates participate in a variety of exercises designed to simulate the job for which they are being considered. Their performance in these exercises is observed and evaluated by a team of trained assessors, typically made up of higher-level managers. These evaluations are made on a number of dimensions determined to be important for success in the job in question. By using multiple exercises, multiple assessors, and multiple-performance dimensions a more complete portrait of the job candidate should be obtained than would be the case if the selection procedure relied on performance in a single situation, if performance were evaluated by a single assessor, or if performance on only one performance dimension were taken into account.

The first reading in this section is Byham's 1971 *Harvard Business Review* article describing what assessment centers are and how they compare with alternative selection procedures. Some may wonder why a more recent overview article was not included. We believe that the article serves a number of purposes. First, the article reached a wide audience and played a major role in stimulating the interest in assessment centers seen in the past 10 years. Thus, it is of historical interest. Second, the article includes a good description of a typical assessment center, giving the reader a feel for what assessment centers are like. Third it is worth noting that most assessment centers today are not noticeably different from those Byham described in 1971. While new developments have been made (see Moses & Byham, 1977), this early description is still remarkably representative of assessment centers. Fourth, inclusion of the article permits a comparison of what was known and believed about assessment centers at this relatively early stage with current concerns and issues.

As can be seen from Byham's article, a number of assessment center validation studies have been carried out. However, very few studies have been reported since the early 1970s. In fact, one factor contributing to the increasing popularity of assessment centers has been a belief that empirical validation is not necessary. Rather, it has been argued that since assessment centers constitute a simulation of on-the-job behavior, they can be justified on content-validity grounds. In fact, Jaffee and Sefcik (1980) have claimed that an assessment center developed on the basis of a job analysis is inherently content valid. In the second reading, Dreher and Sackett discuss problems with defending assessment centers on content-validity grounds. Reviewing the concept of content validity, the Uniform Guidelines, and relevant judicial decisions, they note that in many instances a content-validity strategy cannot be used. Of particular concern are situations where the applicant receives training before moving into a new position: it is not logical to use job-sampling justification when applicants will learn important job behaviors after the selection decision has been made. Dreher and Sackett argue that in many cases assessment centers are being used as measures of aptitude.

In the commentary, we attempt to sound a note of caution against the unquestioning acceptance of assessment centers and to point out that a number of important issues are still in need of clarification. We note potential shortcomings in all but a handful of validity studies, and question the contention that assessment centers have been shown to be more valid than other selection devices. We review validity evidence for women and minority group members and point out that the absence of differential validity does not preclude a finding of adverse impact, thus requiring a showing of job relatedness. Finally, we note that though there are a considerable number of ways in which assessment centers differ from one another, there is little research examining the impact of these variations on assessment decisions.

Assessment Centers for Spotting Future Managers*

WILLIAM C. BYHAM

FOREWORD

Under the controlled conditions that obtain in the assessment center, managers can observe promising young men in action and evaluate them objectively, both for specific job capabilities and for general management ability. From an assessment report, a company can get an excellent "gut" feel for whether a man will fit into its organization in the future, where he will do best, and how he ought to adapt and develop himself for the challenges he will meet as he moves up the management ladder. The assessment center technique has shown itself a better indicator of future success than any other tool management has yet devised; it also brings many valuable fringe benefits to the company that uses it. This article explains how the technique works, why it is superior to others, and the steps a company should go through in developing a center of its own.

Mr. Byham has developed three applications of the concept for J. C. Penney, where he is Manager of Selection, Appraisal and General Management Development. In 1969, he con-

ducted a survey of the design and effectiveness of all known industrial applications of the concept, which is the basis of a book he is now preparing on the subject. He has a background in industrial psychology and has worked in various personnel-related areas.

Deciding whom to promote to management from the rank and file is a classic difficulty. There is a great difference between the skills and talents required for rank and managerial positions, and a man's performance in the ranks provides scant basis for judging how well he would do if he were promoted to first-level management. Companies have learned from bitter experience that the best salesman or the finest mechanic does not necessarily make the best supervisor.

Usually, it is just about as hard to judge whether a man who is working well at one level of management will "take hold" at a higher level. The skills required may be more nearly alike in this case, but even experienced executives find it hard to assess the exact scope of a man's ability and the breadth of his shoulders. Previously developed yardsticks for measuring management potential have not really been worth their salt. Batteries of written tests, for example,

---

cannot assess the way a man works with people; supervisors' ratings can be highly biased; and so on.

To obtain a basis for making promotion decisions, a score or more of companies have resorted to the corporate assessment center approach. This assessment procedure simulates "live" the basic situations with which a man would be faced if he *were* moved up and develops information about how well he will cope at the higher level before the decision to promote him is actually made. AT&T, IBM, General Electric, J. C. Penney, Standard Oil (Ohio), and Sears, Roebuck, are a few of the companies that have established such centers.

In these centers, specially trained managers (and occasionally psychologists) act as "assessors" who evaluate candidates for promotion—either into management or within management—on their potential and their areas of weakness. Groups of men pass through series of standardized exercises such as management games, in-basket tests, and leaderless discussion sessions, while the assessors observe their behavior closely. Part A of the Appendix explains the schedule of a "typical" assessment center.

The assessors discuss each candidate's performance separately and then generate a comprehensive report on each candidate which management can combine with current performance information as it sees fit. As well as identifying the men most likely to succeed, the assessment reports spell out the individual deficiencies of each candidate and suggest guidelines for management to use in developing him.

These reports constitute powerful planning tools for management: it can use the reports to plan the orderly progression of management within the company; it can adjust its hiring patterns; if necessary, it can direct that jobs be designed which match and give growing space to particular men's abilities and potential; and, most impor-

tant, the company can plan a rational sensible route for the candidate to follow as he moves up the ladder.

Reports have proved to be remarkably valid. Longitudinal studies of thousands of employees assessed over the last few years indicate that this assessment method is much more accurate than traditional appraisal procedures, and these seem to be the reasons:

• The exercises used are designed to bring out the specific skills and aptitudes needed in the position(s) for which a group of candidates is being assessed.

• Since the exercises are standardized, assessors evaluate the candidates under relatively constant conditions and thus are able to make valid comparative judgments.

• The assessors usually do not know the candidates personally; so, being emotionally disengaged, they are unbiased.

• The assessors are shielded from the many interruptions of normal working conditions and can pay full attention to the candidates' behavior in the exercises.

• The procedures focus their attention on the primary kinds of behavior they ought to observe in evaluating a promotion candidate.

• They have been trained to observe and evaluate these kinds of behavior.

THE FIRST EXPERIMENTS

American Telephone & Telegraph first applied the assessment center idea 14 years ago as part of the data collection procedures for its Management Progress Study, a study of Bell System personnel the company undertook to gain insight into the management development process and to identify the variables related to success.[1]

Over four years, AT&T processed 422 men from six Bell Systems through a three-

[1] See Douglas W. Bray and Donald Grant, "The Assessment Center in the Measurement of Potential for Business Management," *Psychological Monographs,* 1966, 80 (17, Whole No. 625).

and-a-half day assessment center to obtain basic data on their experimental population. AT&T had got the idea for assessment centers from the pioneering work of the Office of Strategic Services, which used the method for selecting agents during the World War II. Descriptions of the ingenious exercises used by the OSS make both interesting and enjoyable reading.[2]

Some Bell executives who took part in the Management Progress Study assessment centers recognized the possibility that the technique could aid them with one of their critical problems—i.e., identifying potential among candidates for first-line management. They invited the AT&T researchers to set up an assessment center for them, and as a result the first nonresearch application of the method was made in 1958 by Michigan Bell. It achieved immediate and widespread acceptance throughout AT&T. Today, AT&T affiliates operate 50 centers all over the country, processing 10,000 candidates a year. The Bell centers are still primarily to evaluate the management potential of men being considered for first-level management positions.

TODAY'S APPLICATIONS

Other companies that have observed the success of the Bell System centers have also used the method primarily to identify candidates for first-level management. Today, however, there seems to be a trend toward using the method with higher levels of management. While still concentrating their primary use at the lower levels, companies such as Standard Oil (Ohio), IBM, General Electric, and AT&T have established middle-management centers for promotion and development purposes. Penney, for instance, is experimenting in how to assess middle-level managers in its retail stores to determine their aptitude for large- or medium-sized store management.

At these higher levels, centers usually focus on stimulating a man's self-development and career planning through increasing his self-knowledge. After the games and exercises, a participant is given time to critique his own performance and also that of his teammates. A "T-group" atmosphere is often created to increase self-learning. Conditions in such a center are sufficiently well controlled, however, that none of the negative effects which have occasionally characterized the T-group session have been noted here.

Middle-management assessment is already exerting profound impact on organizational planning. In meshing the company's projected manpower needs with its manpower resources as described in its assessment and development reports, Standard Oil (Ohio) goes so far as to consider, for each likely man, the kind of supervision under which he works at his best, the kinds of pressures he can tolerate, and so on, to find the best possible place for him to work and grow. The company also tries to tailor specific job responsibilities to the individual through changes in organization and areas of responsibility.

The concept has yet to be applied at the top level of management, and perhaps it never will be. Promotion and development decisions near the top are highly sensitive and highly personal, and a mechanical procedure for assessing candidates, however excellent, may not be suited to the situation.

So far as screening applicants for new employment at lower and middle levels is concerned, the assessment center method has little value for most companies, since there is seldom a large enough group of prospects at a given time to justify the expense of operating a program. Because of their great size, AT&T and Sears have been able to use the method in initial hiring.

[2] OSS Assessment Staff, *Assessment of Men* (New York, Rinehart, 1948), and "A Good Man Is Hard to Find," *Fortune,* March 1946, p. 92.

Sears operates a very short assessment program for college prospects in its eastern region, and college students who pass the campus interview are brought in large groups to Philadelphia for a day and a half of orientation and assessment. AT&T flies candidates for its "communications consultant" school to New York for assessment. Although this is expensive, research has shown that selection based on assessment pays off.

To my knowledge, 20 companies have been responsible for assessing more than 70,000 candidates in the last 10 years, but at least 100 more companies are developing centers or are in an advanced stage of center planning. Many others are "looking into the idea." As an indication of this interest, I might cite the fact that more than 200 company representatives attended conferences on the assessment center method during 1969.

Applications of the method have multiplied almost every year since the first industrial application of assessment centers by AT&T 14 years ago, and, within the limits I have outlined, these applications vary widely. The description of the typical center given in the Appendix is best described as a composite of many companies' centers. No center is exactly like the one described. Some centers process only 6 candidates at a time, while a few process more than 12. The ratio of assessors to candidates ranges from 3-to-1 to 1-to-1. While centers with a two-and-a-half consecutive day cycle are most common, some cycles are only two days long and these days are not necessarily consecutive. Others are five or six days long because assessment is integrated with training activities.

Obviously, there is no right or wrong way to structure a center—the specific application must be designed to meet specific company needs and operating requirements. This flexibility is reflected particularly in the variety and combinations of exercises used in centers. Each company

chooses exercises that bring out the behaviors they desire to assess. Parts B and C of the Appendix, however, demonstrate the kind of information the "typical" center might produce, and give some insight into the kind of assessment report a center can generate. I shall say more about the appropriate choice of exercises later.

Centers typically find that 30 percent to 40 percent of the candidates in a group fall into their acceptable outstanding category, 40 percent into their questionable category, and 20 percent to 30 percent into their unacceptable category.

Figures like these are often viewed askance by executives, and consequently I should like to discuss the question of validity next, before going into such topics as the "extra" benefits that centers bring and how centers are constructed and managed.

ARE THE ASSESSMENTS VALID?

In brief—yes, they *can* be. Unlike many other management development techniques that industry has widely accepted, the assessment center method has been well received partly because properly controlled research has shown it to be of value. This research has reassured both business executives and professional psychologists working in the personnel area that the assessment center method is almost certainly more valid than any other means of identifying and analyzing a candidate's management potential.

Four Kinds of Studies

Existing validity studies are of four kinds. Three of them focus on centers that are new or experimental, and the fourth focuses on the operational center that has existed for some period of time. To begin with, let me describe the three kinds of study that focus on the new centers.

First, where an assessment center is purely experimental and set up only for research purposes, a study usually compares assessment predictions with the candidates' later performance. Ordinarily, in these circumstances, the assessment reports are not released to management.

The work of Douglas W. Bray and Donald Grant on the original, experimental AT&T centers is of this kind, and it indicates that these centers' predictions were highly accurate. For instance, 64 percent of the candidates predicted to enter middle management had done so by the eighth year after assessment, while only 32 percent of those candidates predicted not to achieve middle-management positions had done so.

Second, a study may compare assessments made at a new, but "real life" center—that is, one that generates reports that are meant to be used—with candidates' later performance. An AT&T study of its new-salesman selection center reflects this pattern. The reports on the first 78 candidates who passed through this center were withheld from line management. All these men were subsequently hired as salesmen, and six months later their performance in the field was evaluated by trained observers who accompanied them on their calls. The results of both the original assessments and the performance review are shown in Exhibit 1. This exhibit shows, for example,

Exhibit 1
Validity Study of Assessment of Sales Representatives

Findings	Number of candidates		Validity of assessment
	Original assessment	Field review	
More than acceptable	9	9	100%
Acceptable	32	19	60
Less than acceptable	16	7	44
Unacceptable	21	2	10

Source: Douglas W. Bray and Richard J. Campbell, "Selection of Salesmen By Means of An Assessment Center," *Journal of Applied Psychology* 52, no. 1 (1968), p. 18.

that of the 32 salesmen assessed as "acceptable" at the center, 19 were still judged "acceptable" when their field performance was reviewed.

In this study, the correlation between assessment ratings and performance is .51. Interestingly, when these men's performance in the field was compared with the ratings of the men made by their supervisors, no significant correlation emerged. Similarly, no significant correlation was found between their field performance and the ratings given them by training personnel who worked with them in a sales training program.

(These two AT&T studies are somewhat unusual in that management was not notified of the assessment findings in either case. When management *is* notified of the findings and uses them in planning promotions and development activity, as in the next two kinds of study, bias is introduced and validity is harder to estimate.)

Third, a study may compare the success of a company's executive development program before and after a center has been set up. For example, one can contrast the "success" of the last 50 or 100 people promoted before the center's installation with the first 50 or 100 people promoted thereafter with the aid of assessment reports. Several studies of this kind report substantial improvement, and these are the ones executives find hardest hitting and most convincing.

From the executive's point of view, the basic question vis-à-vis validity is this: Is the assessment center a definite improvement over other means of identifying management potential—and, notably, is it a definite improvement over supervisory judgment? Once again, the answer is "Yes, it *can* be."

Of all studies, those of the third kind are the ones that can convince managers that the center approach really does work, because it allows them to contrast the effectiveness of relying on supervisory judgment alone (or even assisted by simple testing) with the superior effectiveness of using assessment reports to develop their people. Studies comparing the success of candidates promoted with assessment to those promoted without it consistently show a 10 percent to 30 percent improvement.

The *fourth* and most common kind of validity check is the follow-up study of candidates who have been assessed at an operating center and then promoted and developed by a management that is aware of the assessment findings.

Six such studies (some unpublished) report correlation between assessment findings and subsequent performance, the correlations ranging between .27 and .64. For instance, an IBM study of lower-level and middle-level managers reveals a correlation of .37. In general, assessments of potential for positions *above* the first level are more valid than assessments for positions *at* the first level.

Management Gains Better Judgments

While the weight of research is heavily on the side of the assessment center, this alone does not account for the method's phenomenal acceptance by management, which is less influenced by correlation coefficients than by evidence of the adequacy and fairness of a procedure. And a manager has only to act as an assessor or even sit through the assessor's deliberations to be convinced of the fairness, adequacy, and the accuracy of the method.

First timers observing an assessor discussion are always amazed by the extent and depth of information brought out. Like putting together a mosaic, assessors are able to integrate observations from various exercises to build a picture of how the candidate will perform in higher management. The candidate profiles in Parts B and C of the Appendix give only a pale idea of this dynamic synthesis.

Accurate judgments also convince management. In one instance, management insisted on "testing out" its center by putting through several candidates whom it considered "stars" and "bums." The assessors had no trouble spotting the bums, but in discussing a man that management considered a superstar, the assessors found their evaluations were all negative. After hours of discussion of possible extenuating circumstances, the assessors prepared a verdict of "low potential." The man was promoted anyway. He proved totally unable to handle the job and was replaced after two months. Management needed no more convincing.

In sum, it would appear that the validity of certain assessment centers can be established. But, of course, this does not mean that all assessment centers are valid, for, by their very nature, each company's center is and should be substantially different from any other company's. Still, the accumulation of research findings from a variety of types of centers lends considerable credibility to the general validity of the technique.

In a survey of the 20 companies that operated centers, I uncovered some 22 studies in all that showed assessment *more* effective than other approaches and only one that showed it exactly *as* effective as some other approaches. None showed it *less* effective. As I suggested before, these studies exhibit correlations between center predictions and achievement criteria such as advancement, salary grade, and performance ratings that range as high as .64. The companies appear satisfied that they are on the right track.

MANY INDIRECT BENEFITS

Over and above the explicit goals of assessment, companies have consistently found that a number of added dividends accrue from centers.

The first and most obvious of these dividends is candidate training. Even when candidate training is not a defined objective of a center, it does take place. Completing an in-basket, participating in group discussions, and playing management games are genuine training exercises, even if there is no immediate feedback of results. After all, such exercises were used as training exercises long before they were used in assessment centers.

Second, passing through an assessment center has a positive influence on morale and job expectations. Candidates see the center as a chance to show their ability in fair and realistic situations. They also obtain a realistic idea of the requirements of the positions for which they are being considered. After doing an in-basket, for example, some candidates from the ranks have withdrawn themselves from consideration because of their new understanding of the volume of paperwork involved in a manager's job.

Third, by designing the exercises carefully, it is possible to improve candidates' understanding and attitudes subtly while they are being assessed. For example, one company that routinely assessed service technicians for management potential designed a group discussion exercise that concentrated the candidates' attention on a service-facility staffing problem. This exercise was structured to lead the candidates logically to the conclusion that management sometimes has no alternative but to increase the overtime of the present staff. By participating in this exercise, the candidates who were incumbent technicians gained sympathetic insight into management's reasons for occasionally asking them to work overtime.

Fourth, by far the most valuable fringe benefit is assessor training. The actual training of an assessor prior to his assignment parallels a management training program. During training, assessors participate in management games, in-baskets, and

group discussions, followed by reviews of their performance in each of the activities.

An even more important training experience is actual participation as an assessor. In a normal work situation it is rare for managers to have the opportunity to spend uninterrupted time observing behavior and then comparing their observations with others. General Electric feels so strongly about the benefits of the assessment center to assessors that it has established a policy of a 1-to-1 assessor-candidate ratio to expose a substantial percentage of management to this experience.

Almost all of an assessor's training and experience is transferable to his job and should improve his ability to interview and appraise his subordinates. It is also possible for an assessor-manager to transfer some of the actual exercises from an assessment center to the everyday work situation. This has been done very successfully by managers in one company division, who use the in-basket and two exercises from the corporate assessment center as a screening device for hiring at the management level. These managers have found these procedures to be extremely useful in bringing out information not easily obtained through a personal interview with an applicant or a check on his background.

While these fringe benefits are important individually, they are even more important as an integral whole, since they indicate what may be the crucial advantage of the assessment center method over other, supplementary methods of identifying management potential. When a company uses psychological tests alone, or sends candidates to an outside psychologist for evaluation, it is in reality weakening itself because its executives are becoming dependent on others. Serving as assessor strengthens management skills. In addition, developing a center forces a company to focus on and resolve issues of job goals and define appropriate sources of manpower, things companies ought to do but frequently do not do.

BUILDING AND MANAGING CENTERS

The first and most important task in developing a center is establishing its goals and priorities. Management might ask itself these questions: Whom will we assess? Who will do the assessing? How will center reports be used—especially for manpower development? Who will see them? Will the reports be discussed with candidates? If so, how? The following discussion will develop some perspective on how these questions might be answered.

Identifying the Candidates

Candidates are commonly nominated for assessment by their supervisors. Usually supervisors are instructed to nominate employees who are performing adequately in their current jobs and who, in their estimation, have potential for advancement.

However, relying on supervisors' nominations represents a major philosophical inconsistency. One of the reasons for using the assessment center technique in the first place is to overcome some of the prejudices and biases inherent in supervisory judgment; yet the supervisor is ordinarily made the sole judge of whether a person should be assessed.

Companies can circumvent this potential bias by allowing candidates to nominate themselves or by establishing a rule that assessment will be automatic for all candidates who reach certain levels in the company. Both these alternatives mean that more candidates must be assessed, and this involves additional expense. Hence, they have been tried only on a limited basis.

Choosing the Assessors

Typically, assessors are line managers working two or three levels above the man being assessed. A group of junior foremen, for example, might be assessed by a team that includes division superintendents to whom the senior foremen report. These are the individuals who are responsible for promotion and who know most thoroughly the job requirements of the positions one level above the candidate's.

The job background of the assessor, of course, depends on the purpose of the specific assessment center. Where broader management aptitudes are being assessed, it is common for the assessors to be drawn from a number of areas in a company. This not only brings in a number of viewpoints, but exposes the candidate to representatives of a number of areas where he may find promotional opportunity. Having representatives of different areas also increases the acceptance of the findings throughout the company.

Assessors from management, like the candidates themselves, are usually nominated by their superiors (although in a few companies the center administrator makes an effort to recruit them). Naturally, the practice has its dangers. After a center has passed from the experimental to the operational phase, "purity" controls may be relaxed somewhat, and senior management may be tempted to send "cooperative" managers to centers to act as assessors. This temptation is particularly strong where the assessors serve for extended terms.

Center administrators have chosen to react to this problem in various ways. Some companies rely on their assessor training programs to screen out assessors who are unacceptable in the role, for one reason or another. The rationale here is that it is easy to spot an unqualified assessor during training and ease him out without bloodshed. As a fine point of strategy, for example, many center administrators suggest that it is wise to establish a pool of assessors, rather than train assessors for specific assignments. With the pooling arrangement, it is easy for the administrator to bypass unqualified assessors.

A major point of controversy among operators of assessment centers is the desirability of using professional psychologists rather than specially trained managers as assessors. Most arguments for using psychologists are based on their skills in observation; they are trained to recognize behavior not obvious to the untrained eye. While this argument is plausible, it has yet to be demonstrated in an operational center. Three studies have found no differences.

However, the superiority of psychologists over completely untrained managers is well established. Because of this superiority, companies often use psychologists as assessors in experimental or pilot programs, where training management assessors would be difficult. Psychologists are also used extensively for assessing higher levels of company management; at high levels, it is difficult to get and train managers who do not know the candidates personally, and the objective, independent psychologist is seen as the fairest evaluator.

By and large, companies now prefer to establish a pool of trained manager-assessors, each of whom serves more than once. Individual assessors are usually drawn from the pool to serve once or twice a year—a few companies ask assessors to serve only once. AT&T's practice is exceptional—it assigns assessors for six-month terms and center administrators for one year.

There are advantages and disadvantages to brief assignments. On the one hand, brief assignments usually mean that better men can be recruited, their enthusiasm and effort will be greater, more managers will benefit from the training involved in becoming an assessor, and more managers will be well prepared, after their tour of duty is over, to make judicious use of assessment reports. On the other hand, more managers must be trained and kept off their jobs; and those who serve briefly will not have as comprehensive an experience

as assessors as they would if they had served a longer period.

Where the appointment is for an extended period of six months or so, of course, more rigorous and lengthy assessor training is feasible—AT&T trains managers for a month—and longer experience in the role is very valuable to an assessor. One substantial disadvantage of the long assignment is that assessment becomes a routine matter, which it never should. Reports from fatigued assessors read like computer output, and it is hard to think of them as anything more. Currently, only AT&T appoints assessors for prolonged periods.

Training the Assessors

In the companies now operating assessment centers, there is a notable difference in the emphasis placed on training assessors. Some companies give new assessors as little as one hour of training, which really amounts to just an orientation to the whole procedure, while most others spend three or four days.

One can argue that the task of an assessor is similar to the requirements of most managers' jobs—a manager must interview individuals, observe groups, and evaluate presentations. Assessing requires skill in these same areas, and hence many feel that there is little justification for further training.

The principal rebuttal to these arguments is this: because a man has been doing something, he has not necessarily been doing it well. Companies report marked improvements in the reliability of supervisory ratings after the supervisors have been trained to work as assessors. Nonprofessionals need to be shown what to look for in observing group discussions and individual presentations, or they may focus on purely surface characteristics. While rigid scientific studies are lacking, it is obvious from comparing the reports presented by experienced and inexperienced assessors that training makes a very big difference in the quality of performance.

The most common method of training is by understudy. In the usual situation, an assessor-in-training sits through an entire assessment cycle as a nonvoting member. Another method of assessor training, particularly when assessment centers are being introduced, is to have the assessors go through the assessment experience first as candidates. Everything is the same except that there are no assessors present. In a typical training situation, the assessors go through an activity such as group discussion and then critique the discussion and identify possible areas of observation afforded by the situation. Several companies videotape activities to give assessors practice in making observations.

Selecting the Exercises

A center's success rests in large part on the thoughtful, accurate selection of assessment exercises, for they stimulate the behavior to be observed. Thus, the first step is to define the behavior one wants to observe. Key managers familiar with the positions for which the candidates are to be assessed should discuss this among themselves, and the center developer should ask them questions like these: "Can you describe the behavior of successful and unsuccessful people in the positions in question?" "How do you evaluate people for this position?" "What are the tasks to be performed?" "What characteristics will be needed in our managers 10 years from now?"

After a list has been compiled and agreed on, another meeting should be held to determine which of these characteristics can be assessed adequately on a man's current job. After eliminating these from the list, the characteristics that remain become the objectives of the assessment center program, and the assessment exercises should be selected to bring out these behaviors.

Because certain key forms of behavior, such as leadership, delegation, control, motivation, selling ideas, organization, and operation under time stress, are important to many companies, exercises that bring them out are common to many centers. Almost all centers have an in-basket, one or two leaderless group discussion exercises, and a management game. While these activities may be similar in type from center to center, the specific content may be quite different depending on the educational and organizational level of the candidates.

The whom-to-promote leaderless group discussion described earlier is more appropriate, for instance, for lower-level candidates because the decision to be made is relatively simple and straightforward. One higher-level variation puts the candidate in the role of a member of a school board. The board has just received a bequest of $100,000. Each candidate is told to advocate a different point of view, and he is given adequate time and information to develop his arguments. Unlike the promotion exercise, where only one decision can be reached, the board can allocate the money to one or any combination of the members' projects. The points of view specified for the candidates are rather weakly defined, and hence there is considerable opportunity for them to develop their arguments in a creative fashion.

Many jobs have a unique but highly important aspect, and if this can be simulated, the company ought to develop a special exercise. Here are two interesting examples of such special exercises:

Penney has developed an effective exercise called the Irate Customer Phone Call. During dinner on the first night of the program, the candidates are told that they are to play the role of a manager during the evening, and that they may receive a phone call between 8:00 and 10:00 that night.

This phone call is from an assessor playing an irate customer who makes several unreasonable demands on the candidate, after thoroughly convincing him of how upset he is about a service matter. The candidate's ability to handle this situation is evaluated along several dimensions, such as tact under stress.

The Peace Corps puts individual volunteers into a mock community development meeting with host nationals. The volunteer has been briefed in writing by the previous Peace Corps volunteer for the area, who has stated that the most important thing for the community is to bring in fresh, uncontaminated water from the nearby mountain. The purpose of this exercise is to determine the extent to which the new man will follow and push the ideas of the previous volunteer and the extent to which he will listen to the host nationals and form his own judgments.

At the meeting, the host nationals propose their own pet (and conflicting) projects. Depending on the characteristics of the people of the particular country being simulated, they ignore the volunteer's proposals, demonstrate impatience, pretend lack of understanding, exhibit hostility, and so on. They demand that the volunteer raise money or redesign plans, and a national might try to win over the volunteer to his own schemes through subtle persuasion or flattery.

Tests can also make a significant contribution to assessment if they are selected and used wisely. Intelligence, reading, arithmetic, and personality tests have all been found to increase the accuracy of certain assessment decisions. Tests should only be used under the direction of a psychologist, however, and great care should be taken in communicating test results lest they bias observations. Results are best reported to the assessors working at a center in broad terms such as "superior," "average," or "below average," since they can

easily misinterpret numbers or percentiles. It is good practice to hold back giving test findings until the very end of the assessment discussion of the candidate.

Management must also take extreme care in generalizing about the relative importance of various exercises. Depending on the objectives of the center and the content of the exercises (all games are not equally effective or appropriate), the relative importance of various assessment activities may vary greatly. One thing does seem clear: where it is included, the in-basket is usually the most important exercise in an assessment center.

Informing Candidates of Results

One of the most important, yet most hazardous, aspects of assessment center operation is feeding the reports back to the candidates. Companies handle this in widely different ways, depending on the purpose of their centers. Three companies offer candidates the option of receiving or not receiving feedback. Between 60 percent and 90 percent ask for it. These companies find that candidates who do very well and those who do very poorly usually know where they stand and do not request feedback, whereas those in the middle want to find out how they did and get hints for self-improvement. Some companies give feedback to all candidates automatically.

In almost all cases, and certainly in companies that are strongly concerned about management development, results are carefully couched in terms of the directions that a candidate's personal development should take in the future. The candidate's impact on his fellow candidates may be communicated to him to make him more objective about himself. His performance on individual tasks may be discussed with an eye to establishing a plan to overcome noted deficiencies.

When assessment and training are combined, it is possible to provide some feedback to candidates prior to their leaving the center. In some companies, a candidate must wait weeks for a feedback interview. Obviously, the sooner the feedback interview takes place, the more impact the training and development recommendations will have.

If a psychologist is available, he usually has the responsibility of discussing the center's result with the candidate. Otherwise, assessors or former assessors are given the responsibility.

The Place of Professionals

An industrial psychologist working in a large company was asked by a senior manager to aid in selecting supervisors for a newly created division. The psychologist suggested the assessment center method and submitted a report describing the technique and various exercises frequently used. The psychologist waited a month without receiving any reaction and finally telephoned the manager—who, to his surprise, reported that the assessment center was a big success and that he was very pleased with the outcome. Along with his subordinates, this manager had developed an assessment center for his own specific purpose, created his own exercises, and was running the center to his own satisfaction.

This vignette not only proves that managers can create assessment centers for their own specific purposes, but indicates also that a professional may not be needed. Yet psychologists do play an important role in center development. Psychologists are particularly valuable in these areas:

• Aiding managers to identify kinds of behavior that are critical to success.
• Developing or selecting assessment center exercises to bring out these kinds of behavior in the candidates.

• Training assessors.
• Administering pilot programs.
• Reviewing, critiquing, and improving the program.
• Researching the program's effectiveness.

Often psychologists' major contribution is to speed up the development of assessment centers. Some companies have spent as long as a year going through the various steps leading to the operation of their first center; with professional aid, other companies have accomplished the same thing in one month. As in so many areas, the difference seems to be in knowing what you are doing and benefiting from the experiences of others.

Just as there is no evidence that psychologists necessarily make better assessors than line managers, there is no evidence that psychologists make better assessment center administrators than line managers. Nevertheless, with the exception of AT&T, the majority of companies' centers are operated by industrial psychologists. This is partly the result of the newness of assessment centers in many companies. The appropriate role of the industrial psychologist seems to be that of developing and installing centers, rather than their continual operation. Psychologists should, however, retain responsibility for quality control and, in some cases, assessor training as well.

Negative Effects of Centers

When assessment centers are first explained to them, most managers immediately ask two questions: "What happens to the men who are not chosen for the center?" and, "What happens to the men who do not do well in the center?"

The effect of not being chosen. This depends primarily on how the center has been set up within a company. In some companies, centers have achieved the status of management development programs, and here, just as a young executive may feel he must go through T-group or grid training, he may feel he must be assessed. In these situations, anxiety develops among the ones not chosen, but to no greater extent than from failure to be chosen for any other development activity.

The effect of doing poorly. Candidates who do poorly in assessment centers are usually quite aware of their performance. A logical response from a candidate who has done poorly would be to start looking around for another job. Whether this actually happens is unclear: one study indicates a higher turnover among poorly rated candidates, but other studies find no differences.

Turnover among weak candidates may be viewed in different ways. Some companies see a moderate amount of turnover as beneficial, in that "dead wood" disappears and opportunities for advancement are increased. Of course, if the candidate represents a sizable investment in terms of company experience or technical know how, losing him may be a disaster. The key to preventing turnover is the method and content of the feedback of results to the candidate.

WHAT DO CENTERS COST?

It is obvious that assessment centers are not inexpensive. The costs vary, naturally, depending on the length of the program, its location, and whether the candidates' and assessors' time is counted. Considering only out-of-the-pocket expenses, Wolverine Tube estimates that the cost of assessing 12 men is equivalent to 12 lunches. AT&T, which has regional centers and usually must transport and house most of its candidates and assessors, figures total cost (including candidate and assessor salaries) as approximately $500 per candidate. A division of IBM which uses motels for its centers roughly figures $5,000 per 12 candidates exclusive of staff salary.

While these costs may appear high, they are probably quite small compared with the cost of executive failure. In general, the cost of operating an assessment center should be proportionate to the importance of the assessment decision to be made. Companies should be willing to spend much more money and time on assessing candidates for middle- or top-management positions than they are for assessing candidates for first-level positions.

Savings in Small Organizations

Many companies feel that they must have 10,000 or more employees to use assessment centers. This is not true. In the last two or three years, I have seen several effective applications in small organizations. There are many ways that costs and time requirements can be shaved:

A center can be run on company property, instead of taking men away to a motel or other expensive facility.

A center can be designed to fit into the normal workday, which cuts overtime costs. To avoid disrupting work, assessment can take place all in one day or in two or more separated days. Even Saturday and Sunday have been used.

To shorten time requirements, candidates may be required to do many exercises before coming to the center. For example, candidates may complete a personal information form, take tests, and go through an in-basket exercise before coming to the center. In one Penney center, the personal interview and in-basket interview are conducted at the common convenience of assessor and candidate; only group exercises are held on the one day allocated for assessment.

It is often possible to combine assessment activities with an existing training program without lengthening the training program. For instance, a two-day assessment center was integrated into a two-week training program for Junior Achievement professional staff by merely restructuring training activities already a part of the program.

The resulting training was more effective because of the increased self-awareness provided by the assessment and took no longer to accomplish. The one new activity added was an in-basket, which proved to be a needed addition to the training program. The only added costs were expenses for assessors, but there was a secondary payoff to this because the assessors' presence added greatly to the effectiveness of the training.

Using commercially available exercises instead of specifically modeled exercises is a significant source of savings, but sound judgment must be used in selecting them. The only company offering exercises specifically designed for assessment centers is Assessment and Development Designs of New York City.

The major problem reported by small organizations is that the assessors know the candidates and sometimes are their immediate superiors. While this kind of contamination is not ideal, most problems can be controlled by careful training of assessors coupled with judicious assignment of assessors to candidates.

CONCLUSION

The assessment center method may not be appropriate for many companies, even where the cost of operation is manageable. Particularly at higher level positions, most companies do not have enough candidates to warrant the operation of an assessment center. For these companies, a possibility may be the operation of multicompany centers where a number of companies send one or two individuals to a center operated by a consultant, a university, or another company.

Three such centers have been operated

on an experimental basis with seemingly good results. One center used psychologists and other professionals as assessors, while the other two relied on their managers. The latter seems preferable because it trains the managers, orients them to the proceedings, and helps them understand the use of the assessment center report.

While the effectiveness of an assessment center has not been proved beyond a shadow of a doubt, all the research, both published and unpublished, seems to indicate that the method has more validity than other existing methods. It is in this comparison that the strength of an assessment center lies. Granted that it is not perfect, it seems that using an assessment center for identifying management potential is a sounder and fairer method than those traditionally used by management.

APPENDIX

The material described in this Appendix is based largely on J.C. Penney's programs, but it reflects the practices of a number of other companies as well.

Part A: A Typical Assessment Cycle

I have arranged the following descriptions of assessment activities by periods, without attempting to manufacture a formal schedule. It is important to note that during any period, different groups can be engaged in different activities; in fact, schedules are commonly staggered and doubled up to economize on time and staff requirements.

Exact schedules vary greatly between companies, but they are always extremely tight. Any spare minutes are generally used for informal, coffee-break discussion between candidates and assessors, in the course of which both groups can gather and give a good deal of additional information. In Penney's centers, for example, we try to build in at least one half hour after each major group activity for open discussion among the candidates of how their performance might be improved. This technique, we find, strengthens the training effects of the program.

Sunday

Six management assessors meet at a conveniently located motel and organize materials for the week's activities. Late in the day, 12 candidates, all of them of comparable rank in the company, arrive and settle in.

Monday morning

Period 1: After orientation announcements the candidates are divided into teams of four, for participation in a management game. Each team is given a limited amount of capital to purchase raw materials, make a product, and sell it. The raw materials are usually tinker-toy parts which can be assembled into a variety of products of different complexity, each of which has a different, prespecified market value.

The players must first decide how to invest their capital to maximize profits and then organize the purchasing, manufacturing, and selling operations. Assessors observe the players for signs of leadership, organizational ability, financial acumen, quickness of thinking, and efficiency under stress.

Suddenly the players are notified that the prices of the raw materials and the products have been radically changed, requiring drastic redevelopment of capital and extensive operational reorganization. As soon as they have regrouped, these prices are abruptly changed again. The actions the players take allow the assessors to estimate their adaptability.

The game is then halted, and each candidate is asked to write a report evaluating his own performance and that of his fellow players.

Period 2: The candidates are divided into groups of six. While one group takes written psychological tests, the members of the other group are interviewed individually by the assessors. The assessors have been provided with detailed background information on each man, and they use this to probe for evidence of drive, motivation, and sense of self-development. This Assessment Interview, so called, is ordinarily the only exercise in the assessment process that focuses on the candidate's past behavior.

Monday afternoon

Period 1: The testing and interviewing groups are reversed.

Period 2: In two leaderless groups of six, the candidates join in discussion of a promotion decision. Here the candidates play the role of supervisors brought together on short notice by their boss to pick one man from a pool of six for advancement. Each candidate receives the file of one of the men in the pool, whom he is then to "champion" for the promotion. After each candidate has studied his protégé's folder, the group meets for an hour's discussion to choose the man it will recommend. Assessors observe the candidates' exchanges in the meeting for signs of aggressiveness, persuasiveness, expository skill, energy, flexibility, self-confidence, and the like.

Alternative exercise: In leaderless groups of six, candidates discuss the 20 most critical functions of a manager and list them in order of importance. (This forces them to think about the qualities on which they are being assessed.) Each group then chooses a spokesman who presents the list and the rationale behind it to the whole group of assessors and candidates.

Monday evening

Each candidate receives material on how best to conduct employment interviews and also the résumé of a job applicant. He studies these for use in one of the exercises on the following day. He may also receive special phone calls—for example, the Irate Customer Phone Call.

Tuesday morning

Tuesday morning is devoted to the In-Basket Exercise. This simulates the experience a candidate would have if he were suddenly and unexpectedly promoted a grade or two and arrived at work one morning to find his in-basket full of unfamiliar material typical of the sort he would then have to handle. He is instructed to go through this material and deal with the problems, answer the inquiries, request additional information where he needs it, delegate tasks to proper subordinates, and generally organize and plan just as he would if he had actually been promoted.

Tuesday afternoon

Period 1: The candidates conduct the employment interviews for which they prepared the night before, each interview taking place in the presence of an assessor. The applicants are college students who have been especially trained in the applicant's role. The interview itself lasts roughly half an hour, after which the applicant leaves and the assessor quizzes the candidate to determine what insights he has obtained about the applicant.

Period 2: The next exercise is the resolution of disciplinary cases. In groups of four, candidates decide how to allocate their time between three such cases and then decide the cases themselves, within one hour. This exercise provides the assessors with information on a candidate's appreciation of personnel problems and his sensitivity to subordinates' views of events and actions, as well as insight into his behavior within a group.

Alternative exercise: The candidates are assigned roles as city councilmen who meet to allocate a $1 million federal grant to the city departments. Each "councilman" interprets a briefing document provided by a city agency—the police department, sanitation department, water department, and so on—and tries to get as much of the grant allocated to this agency as possible. Again, effective discussion is limited to one hour.

Tuesday evening

Detailed data on a company are provided to all the candidates. Each is asked to examine its financial and marketing situation from the viewpoint of a consultant and to prepare a written recommendation for its board of directors on the future expansion of a particular part of its product line.

At the same time, also in preparation for the next day's activities, the assessors study the results of the candidates' In-Basket tests in detail.

Wednesday

Period 1: Four groups are formed, each consisting of three candidates and an assessor. Each candidate takes his turn presenting his oral analysis of the company data studied the night before and submitting written recommendations.

Period 2: These three candidates work together for an hour to reconcile and consolidate the recommendations.

Period 3: The In-Basket Interview follows, in which an assessor discusses with a candidate the various actions he took. This further defines each man's grasp of typical problems and opportunities.

Wednesday afternoon

In a final group session, the candidates rate each other and ask any questions they may have. They then leave for home.

Wednesday afternoon to Friday

The assessors discuss the candidates and prepare their ratings and reports.

Throughout all the exercises, the assessors have been rotated so that as many as possible have had a chance to observe each candidate closely. Thus, in these discussions, the assessor who conducted Jones's personal interview summarizes his background and his own impressions of his behavior in the interview; next the assessor who checked what Jones did in his In-Basket Exercise and interviewed him on it presents his impressions, and so on. Each assessor attempts to keep these descriptions nonevaluative and objective.

Only when all the assessors who have observed Jones have spoken does the group begin to judge his behavior from the viewpoint of his management potential and the directions in which he needs to develop. After they have reached a consensus, they prepare a final report.

Within two weeks a manager who has had experience as an assessor meets with Jones to communicate the results. In this meeting he lays stress on the areas in which Jones needs to develop himself and encourages him to set appropriate goals.

Part B: A Weak Candidate for General Management

John's overall performance must be considered a weak average. Individual opinions showed that four assessors considered his performance to be low to average, and two other assessors considered his performance to be much below average.

In appearance, he was poised, confident, and businesslike—well above average. In performance, however, he clearly displayed conflicting capabilities.

John is master of those situations that permit him to operate alone under well-planned and well-organized conditions. On the other hand, he loses confidence, retreats within himself, and fails to participate in unplanned and group operations. The latter was especially evident on those occasions where his leadership appeared to be challenged or tension of any type became noticeable.

For example, John turned in an above-average performance in the Applicant Interview, where he had complete control of the situation, and also in his oral presentation of the Financial Analysis Oral Presentation, where he had ample time to prepare his own analysis and presentation. (The content of his Financial Analysis was far below average.)

Yet, on the same day, assessors were unable to evaluate his performance in two group discussions at all, simply because he failed to participate and there was nothing to evaluate. His single remark during one entire exercise only succeeded in steering the group away from the logical conclusion.

In the In-Basket Exercise, John did exceptionally well in one sense, in that he handled all the items. But the depth and variety of his actions were below average. In the opinion of the assessor, he had little insight into the overall problems at the plant described and showed below-average judgment in his assignment on priorities and his resolutions of the more pressing problems. He assigned priorities chronologically, rather than by urgency.

His intent, as he stated in his In-Basket Interview, was to process the material by in-date as opposed to content of material. His overall diagnosis of the problems, his ability to delegate, and his judgment were below average. There was no indication that he noted the discrepancies in the financial areas or connected the interrelated incidents. The above-average points of the In-Basket Exercise were his self-confidence, his ability to communicate in writing, and his sensitivity toward the feelings of other people.

In the Commodities Market Game, John tended to avoid risks, and he checked and rechecked his calculations before reaching a decision. On occasion, he showed confusion and returned to his seat when he had prepared to make a transaction and then noted that the prices that he had used were no longer valid. In both games, he either ignored or failed to recognize the opportunity to establish his leadership and organize the team play, although the opportunity was clearly available.

In both the interview simulations, John demonstrated command of the situation. In fact, the assessor who conducted the Assessment Interview completely failed to throw him off balance, and throughout the whole exercise he demonstrated outstanding capabilities in salesmanship, leadership, interpersonal sensitivity, tactfulness, organizational ability, and patience. He communicated well and again showed his mastery over a situation that he had planned and in which he felt in control. His behavior in the Applicant Interview was similar, and he created a pleasant and relaxed atmosphere. He showed genuine concern for the applicant and was able to direct the applicant's thoughts and obtain vital information without conscious effort.

In all group discussions, including the discussions of the Financial Analysis in which his oral presentation had been above average, John again showed the tendency to disassociate himself from the group and the project. It was interesting to note that three different assessors expressed the feeling that, on those occasions when John felt he had something to contribute, his statements were directed toward the assessors and not toward the group participants.

It was also interesting to note that throughout the exercises, his peers rated him consistently higher than did the assessors. This may be partly the result of his bossy and confident attitude.

Throughout, the following characteristics were prominent:

Strengths
1. Plans and works well alone.
2. Exceptionally confident under conditions with which he is familiar and which he can control.
3. Displays strong appreciation of the ability in interpersonal relations.
4. Has average intellectual ability.

Weaknesses
1. Is not a "natural" leader.
2. Is not a team player.
3. Displays lack of ability to interpret unfamiliar situations and material.
4. Lacks ability to perform under tension.
5. Lacks management skills: i.e., organizational, planning, and decision making.
6. Displays little appreciation for or ability in delegation.

7. Analyzes situations superficially and makes hasty decisions.
8. Tends to retreat under opposition or unfavorable conditions.
9. Has high need for praise and security.

Suggestions for his development: The assessors are unanimously of the opinion that John has limited immediate capability to advance in line management. While his personal characteristics may have supported him adequately thus far in his career, it is doubtful that he can handle more complex and responsible jobs requiring more advanced management skills. Possible alternative career routes should be considered. His interviewing and interpersonal skills, for example, should make him an excellent personnel interviewer. But no matter what his next job assignment, his lack of administrative skills needs attention. His supervisor might use the In-Basket as an administrative training device.

Points to consider when presenting this assessment summary to the candidate: In the final peer ratings, John ranked himself as first in performance and as second in higher management potential. In informal talks with assessors he also indicated high expectations for the assessment results and a high opinion of his own performance. Feedback of these results should be planned carefully. It might be best to try to draw out his own views of his performance further, asking him to recall his action in the group discussions, while giving feedback slowly and carefully.

Part C: A Strong Candidate for Service-Center Management

Bob rated very high as compared with the other candidates. He is 40 years old, neat, and clean-cut in appearance.

In the Assessment Interview, Bob came across to the assessor as likable, relaxed, and tactful, and he communicated well. He stated realistic goals and displayed a strong interest in the company and in his work. His work and educational history showed considerable motivation and drive. For instance, after getting a technical-school education at night, he has continued to take at least one course of some kind each year. He is or has been an officer in almost

every organization to which he belongs, and the scope of his interests is quite broad.

During the interview, Bob mentioned two points about his present situation that make him unhappy: first, he feels badly about not being able to convince upper management of the value of some of his ideas and of his capabilities; and, second, he feels that he is spending too much time on clerical work as opposed to technical supervision.

In the one-to-one exercises, Bob's performance was mixed. He handled the Irate Customer Phone Call extremely well. Bob asked if the customer would hold the phone while he pulled the history, or if he could call back. He made it clear that he did not agree with the customer, but he also did not antagonize him and showed a great deal of tact. He finally agreed to come to the customer's home with a technician. The assessor who made the call rated him much above average.

He also handled the In-Basket Interview well. Bob may have talked a little too much, but he was calm, collected, and spoke with self-confidence. On the other hand, his Applicant Interview left much to be desired. Bob took extra time for preparation; yet he had formulated no plan or organization, and there was no rapport. He did not sell the company well, he did not spot the hole in the applicant's history, nor did he follow up on leads.

Bob was assessed in four different leaderless-group exercises and two management games, and in every case he was rated well above average in personal impact, in group relations, and in amount and quality of contribution. He was accepted by the groups, he offended no one, others listened when he spoke, and he was always sensitive to others. In one case (the Problem-Solving Task Force), another member of the group got himself into trouble; Bob recognized this and offered his help. Without fail, he was rated high in group situations, not only by the assessors but by his peers as well.

So far as leadership goes, Bob's performance was mixed. At the outset the Manufacturing Company Game, he was confused and unsure of himself. He caught on slowly, but became more aggressive as he realized what the game was about. He did not lead the group, but helped in decision making. In the Service Center Staffing

Discussion, he sat quietly and said practically nothing. During the group discussion of the discipline cases, Bob did not really push his ideas, and appeared to be afraid of offending someone. He had the leadership of the group for a small period of time, but did not hold it. In the Retail Store Game, he tried to lead, but the second member of his team was too frustrated by the game to understand and the third was operating strictly alone.

While no real leader emerged in the Supervisory Practices Group Discussion, Bob convinced two people to change their opinions. In the Financial Analysis Group Discussion, he sold the group on several ideas and was rated high by his peers.

Bob rated well above average on interpersonal sensitivity. At no time during the exercises, even with the Irate Customer, did he become offensive—he was always sensitive to others and considered their comments as he dealt with them.

Bob has a good understanding of financial matters, catches on to situations quickly, and tends to make accurate decisions. In the financial analysis of the lawnmower business, he diagnosed very well and came up with the proper answers. In the Retail Store Game, he caught on quickly and was not afraid to take a few risks. He handled the Irate Customer Phone Call well, without giving away any financial advantage. In the Manufacturing Company Game, he also diagnosed well and helped direct the group to the high-profit items. He came up with some very original and creative ideas that brought his team from a losing to a winning position.

Bob handled 17 items out of 30 in the In-Basket, and he handled these in depth. He recognized too late that he would not be able to complete all items. He caught on to the problems of the two troubled subordinates, noted the need for retraining other employees, and saw that the personnel area in general was not in satisfactory shape. He developed an organized approach to problems, set follow-up dates on material delegated, and recognized the need for planning. His treatment of the problems was often excellent.

Throughout, the following characteristics were prominent:

Strengths
1. Is motivated and wants to advance himself.
2. Shows strong interpersonal skills.
3. Is good in group relations.
4. Is tactful.
5. Withstands stress generally.
6. Has good management skills.
7. Has good financial comprehension.
8. Has average intellectual ability.

Weaknesses
1. Lacks good interviewing skills.
2. Has high need for approval.
3. Is rigid in his thinking once his mind is made up.

Suggestions for his development: Bob rates well above average as a candidate for service center manager. With counseling and guidance, he should be ready for promotion in less than one year. A careful development plan should be worked out to ensure his exposure to all aspects of center operation. Some exposure to regional operations is suggested to let him understand the rationale of the paperwork generated in a service center.

He needs experience in selection interviews and appraisals, and this should be provided under close guidance until he gets a feel for interviewing. His manager should contact the central training department for books or training programs on the subject.

Points to consider when presenting this assessment summary to the candidate: On several occasions, Bob indicated that he liked the assessment program and was glad to be involved. Also, he stated that he wants some experience in interviewing. It would be appropriate and helpful to discuss the training needs of this candidate openly and fully.

Some Problems with Applying Content Validity Evidence to Assessment Center Procedures*

GEORGE F. DREHER and PAUL R. SACKETT

. . . In a previous *Review* article, Norton suggested that "the assessment center [method] can properly be used (after content validation) to select among candidates for a position which is substantially managerial in content, even in the absence of an empirical validity study" (1977, p. 443). This view is shared by other authors who argue that one reason for the popularity of assessment centers is the degree to which the approach lends itself to validation based on content-oriented procedures (Byham, 1977, 1980a; Jaffee & Sefcik, 1980).

Since the publication of the Norton article, there has been considerable work devoted to the concept of content validity and legal clarification regarding the appropriateness of this type of validity evidence. Therefore, we believe that it is time to review this issue again, taking recent developments into account. We contend that those who argue for the content validation of the assessment center approach have not accurately characterized the complexity associated with this form of validation. In fact, certain key theoretical issues have been almost totally ignored. Also, the legal problems that organizations may encounter if they rely on content validation have not been clearly depicted in the literature on assessment centers.

To support these contentions, we will (1) review and integrate the current conceptual literature pertaining to content validity, (2) present an overview of the legal environment that relates to content validity, and (3) review current judicial decisions dealing with content validity. The Uniform Guidelines on Employee Selection Procedures (1978) and judicial decisions based on the Guidelines indicate that demonstrating the content validity of an assessment center simulation will be much more difficult than formerly believed, and that in some cases a content validity approach to demonstrating the job relatedness of such a simulation is inappropriate. We will also offer two potential solutions to the validation problem.

CONTENT VALIDITY

The concept of content validity, as used in the employment setting, has become increasingly complex. In his widely read book on personnel selection, Guion (1965) devoted one page to content validity, describing it as "the degree to which the total

* George F. Dreher and Paul R. Sackett, "Some Problems with Applying Content Validity Evidence to Assessment Center Procedures," *Academy of Management Review*, 6 (1981), pp. 551–60. Reprinted by permission of the Academy of Management.

variance of the sample (the actual test) is related to the variance in the total possible population of tasks or items" (p. 124). Since then, a variety of articles have appeared that attempt to distinguish between content validity and other approaches (e.g., criterion-related and construct validity) and outline the conditions that must be met before a personnel test or other selection procedure can be defended solely on the basis of content sampling (Guion, 1974, 1976, 1977, 1980; Lawshe, 1975; Messick, 1975; Tenopyr, 1977). Our purpose in this section is not to review these previous works, but to present an integrated view of content validity that accurately characterizes the difficulty, complexity, and limits associated with this type of validity evidence.

Content and construct approaches to validation focus on the test or selection device, while criterion-related approaches focus on the relationship between a hiring requirement and job behavior (Guion, 1976). In criterion-related work, the selection procedure, or what Grant (1980) calls the selector, is characterized as a *predictor* of future performance, not as a *measure* of performance. "No such assumption is made when content validity is invoked. Either experienced workers will be hired, or applicants will be expected to have already mastered certain prerequisite components of the job through prior training" (Guion, 1974, p. 291). Thus, as pointed out by Wernimont and Campbell (1968), it is appropriate to defend a selection procedure on the basis of content validity only when you want to sample a current level of performance. If a selection is used to predict future behavioral tendencies, the content approach is not appropriate.

Guion (1980) differentiates the concepts of *job content universe,* defined as all tasks, responsibilities, and required knowledge, skills, and abilities needed to perform the job, and *job content domain,* defined as the portion of the job content universe that the applicant is expected to

have already mastered. It is the job content domain that will be sampled when the work sample test is constructed, and the test is considered job related if it *adequately samples* the job content domain. What level of abstraction is permissible, however, before a selector no longer adequately samples this domain? Guion (1974) addressed this problem by placing methods for sampling job-relevant content on a continuum. He argued that the most direct sample is a probationary period. Those not able to meet minimum performance standards during probation are terminated. The level of abstraction becomes successively higher as one moves through the following list of selectors: (1) job training programs, (2) job simulations, (3) tests of specific knowledge and skills, (4) tests of general knowledge and skills, and (5) tests of general traits (e.g., verbal ability). Finally, the highest level of abstraction involves the use of tests that purport to measure basic traits or constructs (e.g., intelligence, aptitude, personality, or leadership).

The higher the level of abstraction, the less relevant content validity is in assessing the job relatedness of a selector. The most appropriate sampling methods can be characterized by reference to the following three dimensions:

1. There should be a *high degree of congruence between the test environment and the actual work environment.* For example, a selection procedure that presents applicants with hypothetical problems, using brief written case descriptions, or photographs of a typical situation, would be likely to produce a sterile, nonrepresentative test environment.

2. Respondents should be given a *high degree of response freedom.* That is, the measurement process should not impose severe limits on the possible actions taken by the persons being evaluated. For example, one might react in many different ways to a supervisory problem; asking a respondent to choose from three or four clearly stated al-

ternatives would represent a high degree of response restriction.

3. *Inferences drawn from a set of observations should be minimized.* For a leaderless group discussion, it may be appropriate to ask observers to rate the number and quality of verbal interactions initiated by the person(s) being evaluated. However, going on to rate the candidate(s) on personality and leadership traits would represent a long, and possibly invalid, inferential leap.

The first two dimensions, *congruence between test and work environment* and *response freedom,* are similar to those reviewed by Willems (1969) in a discussion of the generalizability of results generated by different research methods. He used *degree of manipulation of antecedent conditions* and *degree of imposition of units* as labels for a two-dimensional space for describing research activities. Willems's discussion of generalizability is useful because "people who talk about content validity are talking about how well a small sample of behavior observed in the measurement procedure represents the whole class of behavior that falls within the boundaries defining the content domain" (Guion, 1977, p. 3).

THE LEGAL FRAMEWORK

Before reviewing case law, it is important to outline the basic legal framework currently addressing content validation. The regulations put forward by the Equal Employment Opportunity Commission (EEOC) will serve as the focal point in the discussion. In 1966, the EEOC published the first of three sets of guidelines on employee selection. This was followed by the 1970 and 1978 regulations. These documents differed substantially regarding the role of content validity. Both Holt (1977) and Grant (1980) provide interesting analyses of the differences between the 1970 and 1978 documents. Essentially, the role of content validity has been enhanced as a

function of certain court decisions (e.g., *Washington* v. *Davis*) and the modified stance of the EEOC. The current Uniform Guidelines on Employee Selection Procedures (1978) include a more thorough discussion of content validity and define those situations in which this type of validation evidence is appropriate. In the remainder of this discussion of the legal framework, we will review the pertinent sections of the Uniform Guidelines.

The Uniform Guidelines

The current regulations now include an entire section on the technical standards for content validity studies (Sec. 14C). The areas most critical for our purposes will be reviewed in the order in which they appear in the document.

The appropriateness of content validity studies. A selection procedure can be supported by a content validity strategy if it is a representative sample of the relevant content of the job. Measures of knowledge, skills, and abilities can also be used if they are operationally defined and if the knowledge, skill, or ability is a necessary prerequisite to successful performance. Certain inferential extremes, however, are in violation of the Guidelines:

> A selection procedure based upon inferences about mental processes cannot be supported solely or primarily on the basis of content validity. Thus, a content strategy is not appropriate for demonstrating the validity of selection procedures which purport to measure traits or constructs, such as intelligence, aptitude, personality, common sense, judgment, leadership, and spatial ability. Content validity is also not an appropriate strategy when the selection procedure involves knowledges, skills, or abilities which an employee will be expected to learn on the job. (p. 38302)

This is a crucial statement because it not only refers to the degree to which inferences can be drawn from a set of observations, it also focuses on the inappropriateness of testing tasks or attributes that an applicant can be reasonably expected to learn after being hired or promoted. The appropriateness of content validity is also discussed earlier in the Guidelines when employers are cautioned against selection on the basis of knowledge, skills, or abilities that can be learned in a brief orientation (Sec. 5F, p. 38298).

Job analysis for content validity. The quality of any content validation effort depends on the thoroughness and appropriateness of the job analysis. The Guidelines set a stringent standard regarding job analytic procedures:

> There should be a job analysis which includes an analysis of the important work behavior(s) required for successful performance and their relative importance and, if the behavior results in work product(s), an analysis of the work product(s). Any job analysis should focus on the work behavior(s) and the tasks associated with them. . . . The work behavior(s) selected for measurement should be critical work behavior(s) and/or important work behavior(s) constituting most of the job. (p. 38302)

Thus, the work behaviors, the associated tasks, and work products need to be completely described. It also is clear that the link between a knowledge, skill, or ability and the appropriate work behavior must be established. The method used to determine this link must also be specified.

Standards for demonstrating content validity. Earlier, we argued that the most appropriate sampling method could be characterized as (1) displaying a high degree of congruence between the test environment and the work environment, and (2) allowing a high degree of response freedom. This viewpoint is reflected in the following Guideline statement: "As the content of the selection procedure less

resembles a work behavior, or the setting and manner of the administration of the selection procedure less resembles the work situation, or the result less resembles a work product, the less likely the selection procedure is to be content valid, and the greater the need for other evidence of validity" (p. 38302).

An interpretive guide to the Uniform Guidelines ("Questions and Answers on Uniform Guidelines . . . ," 1979) has been published. Certain key Questions and Answers will be cited in the following review of judicial decisions dealing with content validity.

JUDICIAL DECISIONS DEALING WITH CONTENT VALIDITY

A substantial number of judicial decisions involving content validity have been handed down. Kleiman and Faley (1978) reviewed court cases in which the content validity of paper and pencil tests was at issue; Byham (1979) reviewed court cases involving assessment centers and content validity. An exhaustive review here would be redundant; rather, illustrative cases will be cited.

Kleiman and Faley's review highlights the tremendous variability from case to case in the type of evidence required to demonstrate content validity. They report inconsistencies from case to case in terms of (1) whether or not a job analysis is viewed as a prerequisite for content validity, (2) if so, what will constitute an acceptable job analysis, (3) what evidence is necessary to group jobs for validation purposes, (4) whether the key determinant of content validity is the method by which a test is constructed or an item-by-item examination of content, (5) whether psychometric considerations (e.g., item difficulty, subtest weighting) play a part in the determination of content validity, and (6) whether or not the test must sample the entire job domain. Kleiman and Faley note substantial variation in judicial sophistication regarding personnel selection, and conclude that "due to the courts' inconsistency in applying existing standards, tests which are poorly constructed and/or improperly validated stand a chance of surviving a court test" (p. 711).

Developments since Kleiman and Faley's review make this conclusion somewhat questionable. It should be noted that the cases they reviewed were decided before the issuance of the 1978 Uniform Guidelines on Employee Selection Procedures. Subsequently, there have been several decisions involving content validity. These more recent decisions provide a more prudent basis for predicting the content validity standards that the courts will use than would decisions handed down under guidelines that differ substantially from those currently in effect.

In *U.S.* v. *Connelie,* a district court judge ruled that the selection procedure used by the New York State Police was not content valid. A two-part test, including a written "situations test" (which consisted of simulated police situations or activities) and a physical performance test (which consisted of subtests such as "mile run," "tire change," and "shotgun aiming"), was constructed based on a job-element method developed by Primoff (1973). The test was found to disqualify blacks, hispanics, and females at much higher rates than white males.

The judge thoroughly reviewed the federal guidelines on employee selection, as well as other professional standards, in determining that the test was not content valid. There were several areas in which the test or test-development procedures were found lacking: (1) the relationship of the test domain to a 20-week training program for new recruits was not examined; testing for knowledge, skills, or abilities acquired in training or on the job did not comply with professional standards or government

guidelines; (2) a task-oriented job analysis was not conducted, and the frequency and importance of job duties was not identified; (3) a number of the elements on which the examination was based "are at or near the abstract or unobservable end of the occupational continuum and are psychological processes. To the extent that the . . . examination attempted to measure such job constructs or psychological processes, this was not done in accordance with generally accepted professional standards or in compliance with federal guidelines" (p. 74); and (4) the fidelity with which the test situations matched the actual job situation was criticized. Similarly, for various aspects of the physical performance test: "There is nothing in the record concerning the likelihood that a State Trooper would very often be required to run a mile over flat terrain in pursuit of a suspect. Rather, the evidence would indicate that a foot chase would normally last for only a short distance" (p. 69).

Thus, in *Connelie,* the court relied heavily on the federal guidelines in determining the content validity of the selection procedure. The court, however, appeared to strike new ground in one of its conclusions regarding the determination of when content validity is an appropriate validation strategy:

> Jobs may be placed on a continuum. On one end of the continuum are jobs involving processes that are directly observable. At the other end of the continuum are jobs involving processes that are abstract or unobservable. . . . The more speculative the inference is from the observable, the greater is the "inferential leap." Therefore content validity alone is an appropriate strategy to follow only at or near the observation end of the continuum such as trade and craft jobs, where the inferential leap is small. (p. 69)

In *Firefighters Institute for Racial Equality* v. *City of St. Louis,* the 8th Circuit Court of Appeals considered the content validity of a promotional examination for the position of fire captain. The examination consisted of a multiple-choice portion and an assessment center portion.

The assessment center portion consisted of three exercises: (1) a fire scene simulation, involving viewing slides of a fire and responding to each in writing; (2) presenting a training lecture; and (3) a role-play simulation dealing with an interpersonal confrontation. The court objected to the fire scene simulation and cited Question and Answer No. 78: "Paper-and-pencil tests which are intended to replicate a work behavior are most likely to be appropriate where work behaviors are performed in paper-and-pencil form (e.g., editing and bookkeeping). Paper-and-pencil tests of effectiveness in interpersonal relations (e.g., sales or supervision), or of physical activities (e.g., automobile repair), or ability to function properly under danger (e.g., firefighters) generally are not close enough approximations of work behaviors to show content validity." The court noted that although the other two assessment exercises were somewhat flawed, in that candidates were observed for only a short period of time and assessors were insufficiently trained, these two exercises "more closely comply with the spirit of the guidelines" (p. 14079).

Thus, as in *Connelie,* the court in *Firefighters* relied on the Guidelines. Nevertheless, the two decisions differ substantially in their views on the appropriateness of content validity for various types of jobs. *Connelie* suggests that content validity may be appropriate only for trade or craft jobs, whereas *Firefighters* suggests that a content-valid selection procedure for a relatively complex position such as fire captain can be devised. Thus, while these cases suggest that courts will be making detailed use of the Guidelines, they also suggest that the inferences that will be drawn from the Guidelines regarding the appropriateness of content validity in various settings are likely to vary from case to case.

These two cases were selected for discussion because of their detailed treatment of content validity and because they present contrasting viewpoints as to the appropriateness of a content validity strategy. Other cases involving content validity between 1978 and the present uniformly rely on the Guidelines as a basis for ruling on the content validity of the selection procedure in question (*U.S.* v. *City of Montgomery, U.S.* v. *San Diego County, Vanguard Justice Society* v. *Hughes, U.S.* v. *Chicago, Detroit Police Officers Association* v. *Young, Allen* v. *City of Mobile, U.S.* v. *City of Buffalo, Guardians Association of the New York City Police Department* v. *Civil Service Commission*).

THE ASSESSMENT CENTER METHOD AND CONTENT VALIDITY

The research base on which the assessment center method rests consists primarily of criterion-related validity studies (Huck, 1977; Klimoski & Strickland, 1977). Nonetheless, one reason for its popularity, according to Byham (1977), is that it lends itself to content-based validation. Various authors differ as to how the content validity of an assessment center process can be demonstrated. According to Norton and Edinger (1978), "the content validity of an assessment center [selector] can be established by showing that the job in question is primarily managerial. If a job is primarily managerial, then a properly designed and implemented [selector] will be a valid predictor of success" (p. 22). A differing view is presented by Jaffee and Sefcik (1980), who state that content validity "is inherent in the assessment center process when the situational exercises are developed based on a thorough job analysis" (p. 42). Current sentiment is that the only practical method of establishing the job relatedness of assessment center exercises for most organizations is to rely on a content validity strategy (Byham, 1980b).

The *Firefighters* case discussed above represents the only court decision involving assessment center tests and content validity. The other cases reviewed by Byham (1980a) dealing with assessment center tests were cases in which the implementation of an assessment center approach was suggested or ordered in instances where validity evidence for paper-and-pencil tests was found lacking, or cases in which assessment center tests were challenged on grounds other than content validity (e.g., adequacy of assessor training, reliability). Thus, an examination of assessment center procedures in relation to content validity standards set forth in the Guidelines cannot be based on a history of judicial opinion.

One controversial issue regarding the job relatedness of an assessment center process is what is being measured. The Guidelines state that a content validity strategy is not appropriate for assessing selection procedures that purport to measure traits or constructs, giving as examples the commonly used assessment dimensions of judgment and leadership. At first glance, this opinion would seem to immediately rule out validating assessment center procedures using a content validity strategy. But Byham (1980b) maintains that a content-oriented strategy *is* appropriate, citing the answer to Question and Answer No. 75: "Some selection procedures, while labeled as construct measures, may actually be samples of observable work behaviors. Whatever the label, if the operational definitions are in fact based upon observable work behaviors a selection procedure measuring those behaviors may be appropriately supported by a content validity strategy." Byham defines a dimension as "a description under which behavior can be reliably classified" (p. 29), and maintains that, as such, dimensions are not constructs but merely convenient labels for observed

behavior. It is unclear whether this line of reasoning will withstand judicial scrutiny. Assessment procedures that attempt to score exercises objectively or use behavioral checklists or other means of making an explicit connection between a specific behavior and the rating given for a particular dimension, would seem to have a much greater likelihood of being consistent with the Guidelines than procedures that rely on global judgments by assessors following observation.

The use of job analysis in designing assessment center procedures is also an issue. The assessment center method has been plagued by a tendency to rely on established lists of dimensions and a few common exercises. All too frequently, the "job analysis" consists of having a handful of managers select from a list the dimensions that they feel are important for the position(s) in question. The selection of exercises is often equally haphazard. According to Crooks, "the decision to tailor-make exercises in the context of the company . . . may call for an investment in time, cost, and creative effort which may not be readily forthcoming, even with consultant help. If this is the case, selection then depends on buying or borrowing from others" (1977, p. 72). Crooks argues that tailor-made exercises are important for content validity.

Recent writing on assessment recognizes the need for thorough job analysis and for a well-documented relationship between the job analysis and the selection procedure (e.g., Byham, 1980b; Jaffee & Sefcik, 1980; Jeswald, 1977). Byham acknowledges the need for a sophisticated job analysis incorporating the requirements of the Guidelines.

One critical aspect of the Guidelines appears to have been completely ignored in previous writing on content validity applied to assessment center procedures. The Guidelines state that content validity evidence is not appropriate for tests of knowledge, skills, or abilities to be learned on the job. If an assessment center test is used to select individuals who will receive training to enable them to become fully functioning job incumbents, a content validity approach to demonstrating the job relatedness of the test is inappropriate. A test developed for a job may be content valid in some circumstances and not in others: assuming the test encompasses a representative sample of job behaviors, it may be content valid if applicants are expected to perform immediately at a high level of proficiency; the same test would not be content valid if applicants are to be given training after being selected for the job. The classic sign/sample distinction (Wernimont & Campbell, 1968) is useful here. A key component of the sign/sample distinction is time. When a measure is used as a sample, present behavior is of interest: Can the applicant *now* perform the task(s) that make(s) up the job? When a measure is used as a sign, future behavior is of interest: Will the applicant be able to perform the task(s) that make(s) up the job *after* training, job experience, or some other intervention? An assessment procedure used to select people who can immediately perform all aspects of the job is a sample; the same procedure used to select people who will receive training to perform the job is a sign. The assessment procedure is, in the latter case, being used as an aptitude test.

Examples of assessment center procedures being used as aptitude tests are commonly found among those used to select first-level supervisors. According to Byham (1977), this is the position for which assessment center simulations are most frequently used. Bender (1973) found that 49 percent of the simulations he surveyed were for first-level supervision; Cohen (1980) reported that 39 percent of those he sampled were for first-level supervision. It must be noted that, at this level, training programs are common. For example, Campbell, Dunnette, Lawler, and Weick

surveyed 33 large firms and found that "virtually all foremen had been through a supervisory training program designed to give basic skills necessary for management positions" (1970, p. 45). Therefore, we conclude that many simulations for first-level supervisor selection cannot be defended on grounds of content validity.

This leads us to conclude more generally that selection procedures for any position for which the job applicant will be given an opportunity to learn knowledge, skills, or abilities central to job performance cannot be defended on grounds of content validity. The recent court decision in *Guardians Association of the New York City Police Department* v. *Civil Service Commission* supports this conclusion. A selection test for police officers was based on a job analysis that identified 42 tasks making up the job. The judge found that "the applicant must secure training in substantially all of the designated tasks" (p. 15406), and therefore the test was not content valid under the Uniform Guidelines.

DISCUSSION

Assessment center selection procedures can be used in one of two ways: as a sample of job behavior or as a sign of future job performance. When a simulation is used as a sample—to determine whether a candidate is presently able to perform important job behaviors—a content validity strategy can be used to justify the simulation. Assessment center simulations as samples are often appropriate for selecting mid- to upper-level managers. However, the current reliance on common dimensions and common exercises is unlikely to withstand judicial scrutiny under the Uniform Guidelines. Detailed job analysis and careful exercise construction and scoring will be necessary to conform to the Guidelines.

When a procedure is used as a sign—to select individuals who will need training and experience before reaching adequate performance levels—then content validity does not apply. Because assessment center simulations for first-level supervisors are commonly used as signs, evidence of job relatedness will have to be based on a strategy other than content validity. Criterion-related validity studies may not be technically feasible in smaller organizations, but even if feasible from a sample-size viewpoint they are expensive and plagued by problems such as criterion contamination (e.g., Klimoski & Strickland, 1977). Establishing construct validity is acknowledged in the Guidelines as an extremely difficult procedure, incorporating both criterion-related and content validity studies. Thus, an organization attempting to use assessment center procedures to select supervisors is likely to find it difficult to demonstrate their job relatedness.

One response to this difficulty is to point out that, according to the Guidelines, a demonstration of job relatedness is not necessary if the selection procedure is shown not to have adverse impact on any of the classes protected by Title VII. Published research indicating that assessment center procedures are equally valid for majority and minority groups is a commonly cited advantage of assessment center screening of applicants (Byham, 1977; Huck, 1977). However, data such as those presented by Huck indicate that assessment center screening *can* have an adverse impact on members of protected classes; thus the occasional need to demonstrate the job relatedness of the selection procedures. Assessment center procedures may indeed be fair to all groups, but organizations that use them must be prepared to prove job relatedness if adverse impact is found.

One additional alternative considered in the Guidelines is the transfer of validity evidence from one setting to another. This possibility has not been examined in the assessment center context owing to the heavy reliance on content validity to justify

assessment center procedures. However, when the procedures are being used essentially as aptitude tests, validity evidence can be generalized in the same way as for more traditional selectors. Thus, if a technically sound validity study were done in one organization, the results could be generalized to a second organization if the jobs were highly similar, if the selector had been found to be fair to both sexes and to all racial and ethnic groups making up the second organization's workforce, and if there were no differences between the two settings that would be likely to affect validity results (Sec. 7B). Thus, a new strategy for assessment center users would be to engage in cooperative research including: (1) conducting technically sound validity studies, where feasible; (2) conducting cooperative job analyses to determine the similarity between target positions in various organizations; and (3) standardizing assessment center procedures between organizations. While obviously not a simple solution, validity generalization is certainly a potentially useful possibility for assessment center users.

Another possibility is to shift focus from job content to training content. If job sampling is inappropriate, the use of a sample of the training program as a selector may be defensible on content validity grounds. Siegel (1978) summarizes work done using a "miniature job training" approach to selection in which applicants receive training on a sample of job tasks and are evaluated on their ability to perform the tasks. Such a procedure not only samples job performance, but also includes a sample of the process by which the applicant is to acquire the necessary knowledge, skills, and abilities. The applicant demonstrates the ability to learn and perform, which mirrors the actual process involved when training follows selection. The application of the miniature training concept to first-line supervisory selection offers a potential solution to the content validity problem.

We hope our discussion has corrected misconceptions regarding content validity evidence for the job relatedness of assessment center procedures—misconceptions resulting from simplistic views of content validity presented in earlier writings. The Uniform Guidelines and judicial decisions based on the Guidelines indicate that demonstrating the content validity of an assessment center exercise will be a much more difficult process than formerly believed. Moreover, they indicate that in some cases the job relatedness of an assessment center procedure *cannot* be demonstrated using content validity evidence.

REFERENCES

Allen v. *City of Mobile,* 18 EPD 8845.

Asher, J. J.; & Sciarrino, J. A. Realistic work sample tests: A review. *Personnel Psychology,* 1974, *27,* 519–533.

Bender, J. M. What is "typical" of assessment centers? *Personnel,* 1973, *50,* 54–57.

Byham, W. C. Application of the assessment center method. In J. L. Moses & W. C. Byham (Eds.), 1977.

Byham, W. C. *Review of legal cases and opinion dealing with assessment centers and content validity.* Pittsburgh: Development Dimensions International, 1980. (a)

Byham, W. C. Starting an assessment center the correct way. *Personnel Administrator,* February 1980, pp. 27–32. (b)

Campbell, J. P.; Dunnette, M. D.; Lawler, E. E; & Weick, K. E. *Managerial behavior, performance, and effectiveness.* New York: McGraw-Hill, 1970.

Cohen, G. L. The bottom line on assessment center technology. *Personnel Administrator,* February 1980, pp. 50–56.

Civil Rights Act of 1964 as amended by the Equal Employment Opportunity Act of 1972 (Public Law 92-261). Washington, D.C.: U.S. Government Printing Office, 1972.

Crooks, L. A. The selection and development of assessment center techniques. In J. L. Moses & W. C. Byham (Eds.), 1977.

Detroit Police Officers Association v. *Young,* 16 EPD 8147.

Grant, D. L. Issues in personnel selection. *Professional Psychology,* 1980, *11,* 369–384.

Guardians Association of the New York City Police Department v. *Civil Service Commission,* 23 EPD 30,847.

Guidelines on employee selection procedures. *Federal Register,* 1970, *35,* 12333–12336.

Guion, R. M. *Personnel testing.* New York: McGraw-Hill, 1965.

Guion, R. M. Open a new window: Validities and values in psychological measurement. *American Psychologist,* 1974, *29,* 287–296.

Guion, R. M. Recruiting, selection, and job placement. In M. D. Dunnette (Ed.), *Handbook of industrial and organizational psychology.* Chicago: Rand McNally, 1976.

Guion, R. M. Content validity: The source of my discontent. *Applied Psychological Measurement,* 1977, *1,* 1–10.

Guion, R. M. On trinitarian doctrines of validity. *Professional Psychology,* 1980, *11,* 385–398.

Holt, T. Personnel selection and the supreme court. In W. C. Hamner & F. L. Schmidt (Eds.), *Contemporary problems in personnel.* Chicago: St. Clair Press, 1977.

Huck, J. R. The research base. In J. L. Moses & W. C. Byham (Eds.), 1977.

Jaffee, C. L.; & Sefcik, J. T. What is an assessment center? *Personnel Administrator,* February 1980, pp. 40–43.

Jeswald, T. A. Issues in establishing an assessment center. In J. L. Moses & W. C. Byham (Eds.), 1977.

Kleiman, L. S.; & Faley, R. H. Assessing content validity: Standards set by the court. *Personnel Psychology,* 1978, *31,* 701–713.

Klimoski, R. J.; & Strickland, W. J. Assessment centers: Valid or merely prescient? *Personnel Psychology,* 1977, *30,* 353–361.

Lawshe, C. H. A quantitative approach to content validity. *Personnel Psychology,* 1975, *28,* 563–575.

Messick, S. The standard problem: Meaning and values in measurement and evaluation. *American Psychologist,* 1975, *30,* 955–966.

Miner, M. G.; & Miner, J. B. *Employee selection*

within the law. Washington, D.C.: Bureau of National Affairs, 1978.

Moses, J. L.; & Byham, W. C. (Eds.). *Applying the assessment center method.* New York: Pergamon, 1977.

Norton, S. D. The empirical and content validity of assessment centers vs. traditional methods for predicting managerial success. *Academy of Management Review,* 1977, *2,* 442–453.

Primoff, E. S. *How to prepare and conduct job element examinations.* Washington, D.C.: U.S. Civil Service Commission, 1973.

Questions and answers on uniform guidelines on employee selection procedures. *Federal Register,* 1979, *44,* 11996–12009.

Siegel, A. D. Miniature job training and evaluation as a selection/classification device. *Human Factors,* 1978, *20,* 189–200.

Tenopyr, M. L. Content-construct confusion. *Personnel Psychology,* 1977, *30,* 47–54.

Uniform guidelines on employee selection procedures (1978). *Federal Register,* 1978, *43,* 38290–38309.

U.S. v. *Chicago,* 16 EPD 8141.

U.S. v. *City of Buffalo,* 18 EPD 8899.

U.S. v. *City of Montgomery,* 19 EPD 9238.

U.S. v. *Connelie et al. Government Employee Relations Report.* Washington, D.C.: Bureau of National Affairs, 1979, 829:47–829:88.

U.S. v. *San Diego County,* 20 EPD 30, 154.

Vanguard Justice Society, Inc. v. *Hughes,* 20 EPD 30,077.

Washington v. *Davis,* 12 FEP 1415.

Wernimont, P. F.; & Campbell, J. P. Signs, samples, and criteria. *Journal of Applied Psychology,* 1968, *52,* 372–376.

Willems, E. P. Planning a rationale for naturalistic research. In E. P. Willems & H. L. Raush (Eds.), *Naturalistic viewpoints in psychological research.* New York: Holt, Rinehart & Winston, 1969.

COMMENTARY: A CRITICAL LOOK AT SOME COMMON BELIEFS ABOUT ASSESSMENT CENTERS*

The assessment center has become a commonly used, well-regarded approach to managerial selection. Numerous descriptive and laudatory articles have appeared throughout the management literature; a much smaller number of data-based articles have been presented. The purpose of this commentary is to sound a cautionary note by attempting to differentiate what is commonly accepted as true regarding assessment centers from what has been empirically demonstrated regarding assessment centers.

The commentary is structured around what we will call six "tenets of conventional wisdom." These will be listed here and each will then be discussed in some detail:

1. The validity evidence for assessment centers is strong.
2. Assessment centers are more valid than conventional selection devices.
3. As job samples, assessment centers can be justified on content validity grounds.
4. Assessment centers do not illegally discriminate.
5. Research findings regarding assessment centers can be generalized from one organization to another.
6. Rating and reaching consensus regarding candidates is a straightforward, well-understood process.

The Validity Evidence

The cornerstone of the validity evidence for assessment centers remains the AT&T Management Progress Study (Bray & Grant, 1966). In this study, 422 candi-

* A slightly modified version of this commentary has also been published in *Public Personnel Management,* 11 (1982), pp. 140–47.

dates were assessed; the assessment results were then set aside to be used for research purposes only. Five to seven years after assessment, the assessment center predictions of which candidates would reach middle management were compared with the management level the candidates actually achieved. Dividing the sample into college and noncollege subsamples, the correlations between the assessment center prediction and level attained were .44 and .71 respectively.

A number of other validity studies have been reported. Cohen, Moses, and Byham (1974) summarize 18 and report an average correlation of .40 between assessment ratings and number of promotions received, and an average correlation of .63 with manager's ratings of a candidate's promotion potential. Byham (1970) reviewed 23 studies and reports that only one produced a negative validity coefficient.

It is important to realize that the Management Progress Study is one of only three instances in which complete secrecy as to assessment results was maintained. (An AT&T center for selecting salesmen (Bray & Campbell, 1968), and a center for selecting army recruiters (Borman, 1982) are the others.) Making the results available to the candidate's manager in an operational center makes the interpretation of validity results problematic due to the possibility of criterion contamination. Criterion contamination refers to the lack of independence between the assessment rating and the criterion: promotions received. For example, a candidate returns from assessment with a favorable evaluation; as a result, the candidate's manager forms a more favorable impression of the candidate; this impression becomes the basis for a recommendation that the candidate be promoted. In this case, an apparent relationship between assessment center performance and progress in the company would in fact be artifactual. A more subtle example: as a result of favorable assessment ratings, a candidate receives more challenging job assignments; due to these assignments, the candidate's skills develop and the candidate becomes promotable. Again we face the possibility that the promotions received are at least in part a result of being evaluated favorably in the assessment center. The result of such criterion contamination is an overestimate, of undeterminable magnitude, of what the actual validity would be if the assessment results were not used operationally.

Klimoski and Strickland (1977) point out another potential problem in interpreting validity results. They note that most studies have used advancement measures—salary change or promotions—as criteria. They suggest the possibility that assessment centers do not result in better selection decisions, but rather simply identify those individuals who are likely to be promoted using the organization's current standards. A correlation between assessment center evaluations and advancement may simply indicate that the assessment center can tell us what the organization would eventually do anyway. This is not necessarily bad: there may be value in the early identification of candidates with high promotion potential. But it is not evidence that assessment centers are valid predictors of performance. In addition, consider the possibility that an organization is adopting an assessment center due to dissatisfaction with existing promotion procedures. If this is the case, what interpretation should be placed on a positive correlation between assessment ratings and advancement? This could be interpreted as evidence that the assessment center is not useful. On the other hand, if one has enough confidence in the assessment center, one can view promotions as a predictor and assessment ratings as a criterion and view this correlation as a reaffirmation of the firm's promotion procedures.

In summary, only three validity studies are free from the criterion contamination problem, and the use of advancement measures rather than performance measures as criteria makes the results of validity studies difficult to interpret. The above discussion is not intended to suggest that assessment centers are not valid, but rather to point out that the evidence is not so overwhelming as to justifying closing the door on the issue of assessment center validity.

More Valid Than Other Predictors

"Perhaps the most dramatic and impressive feature of assessment centers is the greatly increased validity when compared to traditional selection and promotion techniques" (McNutt, 1979, p. 1). This statement represents the conventional wisdom with regard to assessment centers. Often cited as a basis for this conclusion is Byham's (1970) report of 22 studies in which assessment was found to be more effective than other approaches. Details of the studies, e.g., what the other approaches were, were not provided.

Hinrichs (1978) reports an interesting study in which assessment center participants were independently evaluated by management representatives based only on information in the participant's personnel files. Eight years later both the assessment center ratings and the evaluations based on personnel files were correlated with a measure of the managerial level attained. The evaluations based on personnel files correlated more highly with the criterion than did the assessment center evaluation.

Other studies also provide reason to question the superiority of assessment over other methods. Campbell, Dunnette, Lawler, and Weick (1970) review a number of studies examining the validity of different approaches to managerial selection. For example, in a large-scale validation study done by the Standard Oil Company of New Jersey, ability test, personality test, and biographical data blank information were used to develop and cross-validate a predictor of managerial effectiveness. The correlation between a prediction of success based on these various sources and managerial effectiveness, measured by a combination of advancement and performance appraisal data, was .70. Several other studies produce comparable findings. One important factor contributing to the success of these studies is that organization-specific keys were developed for the various tests. The rigor of this research is in sharp contrast to the "off-the-shelf" approach to the selection and use of tests.

These results compare favorably with the assessment center validities reported earlier and provide a basis for challenging assertions that assessment centers are more valid than other predictors. Several observations are in order at this point. First, the validity evidence for assessment centers is more consistent than the evidence for other predictors: while virtually all assessment center validity studies have produced positive results, there are numerous instances of testing programs failing to produce them. Second, it is recognized that validity is not the sole reason for choosing assessment over other approaches to managerial selection. Development value and user acceptability are among the other factors entering into such a decision. It does appear that claims for "greatly increased validity" may be overstated: other carefully developed predictors may be as or more effective at a substantially lower cost per candidate.

Use of a Content-Validity Strategy

As was seen in the reading by Dreher and Sackett (1981), it is a common belief that because assessment centers are job samples they can be justified on content-validity grounds, rather than requiring complex empirical validation. A key element of the content-validity idea is that the applicant is already expected to possess the skill or knowledge; content validity makes no sense if it is expected that the skill or knowledge will be acquired on the job or in training after hire. As Dreher and

Sackett (1981) point out, this requirement that job candidates possess the requisite knowledge and skill may not be met in many applications of the assessment center method. The most common use of assessment is the selection of first-level supervisors who commonly go through supervisory training programs after being selected. In this setting, reliance on content validity is clearly inappropriate. While the assessment center may be a useful selection device, it is being used as an aptitude test, rather than as a sample of necessary job skills. In a study by Moses and Ritchie (1976), one group of supervisors received interpersonal skills training, another did not. Both groups then went through a specially designed assessment center; the trained group performed significantly better. Thus, assessment center performance was higher after training. This study illustrates the problem in using a content-validity strategy: is it reasonable to assess whether or not a candidate has the level of interpersonal skills needed for a job, if the skills will be acquired or substantially improved in subsequent training?

Discrimination and Assessment Centers

One commonly hears such statements as "assessment centers don't discriminate," "assessment centers are court endorsed," or "assessment centers have EEOC approval." The legal status of assessment centers will be reviewed briefly to determine if such statements are warranted.

Considerable interest in assessment centers was generated by the 1973 consent degree between AT&T, the EEOC, and the Department of Labor. As part of the agreement, AT&T agreed to use an assessment center to evaluate college-graduate female employees as one mechanism for identifying promotable females. Over a 15-month period, 1,634 women were assessed, and 42 percent were evaluated as having management potential. Note that this center was part of an organization-specific program to increase minority representation and does not imply any sort of blanket endorsement of assessment centers.

Byham (1979) has reviewed a number of court cases involving assessment centers. *Berry* v. *City of Omaha* is the only case to date directly challenging the fairness and validity of an assessment center. The major issue raised dealt with the subjectivity of assessor judgments; the court ruled that the center was fair, since adequate assessor training produced reliable judgments. In a variety of other cases assessment centers were suggested or ordered by the court as an alternative to or supplement to paper and pencil tests. The courts are recognizing the potential value of assessment centers; nowhere is there anything to indicate that assessment centers will not be evaluated with any less scrutiny than is given to other selection devices.

Studies have been published which directly address the issue of discrimination in assessment centers on the basis of race and sex. Huck and Bray (1976) found a high degree of predictive validity for both a group of black female and white female candidates, and Moses and Boehm (1975) found assessment center evaluations to be fair and valid for both men and women. Thus no evidence of differential validity was found.

It is useful at this point to consider the "shifting burden of proof" model used in fair employment practice litigation: a selection device has adverse impact if it rejects significantly more members of a protected class than of a majority group; if adverse impact is found, the burden shifts to the employer to demonstrate the job relatedness (validity) of the selection device. If an assessment center was found to have adverse impact, the organization would have to demonstrate its validity for all groups. In a study by Huck (1974), 53 percent of white candidates and 29 percent of black candidates were evaluated as having high potential for advancement, indicating adverse impact against blacks. Moses and Boehm (1975) report no adverse impact on the basis of sex; however, one of the present authors has examined data from one center in which 16 percent of males and 10 percent of females were evaluated as having high potential. Note that adverse impact alone is not evidence of discrimination: if race or sex differences in assessment center evaluations correspond to comparable differences in on-the-job performance, the center does not discriminate. In many cases, it is likely that adverse impact may be found due to differences in the applicant population by race or sex. Consider an organization concerned with identifying promotable females; assume that a high proportion of the organization's work force is male. Assume all interested women are encouraged to go through assessment, while only a small proportion of men are selected for that. Due to the differences in candidate identification procedures, it is quite likely that a higher proportion of men than women will be evaluated favorably in assessment, despite the fact that the center may be highly valid.

Thus, while the evidence suggests that a well-designed assessment center does not discriminate, it is not unlikely that adverse impact will result, thus forcing the organization to defend the procedure. Organizations are cautioned against a belief that one does not have to be concerned about discrimination if an assessment center is used.

Generalizability of Research Findings

It is somewhat discomforting to note that despite the large number of organizations using assessment centers, the bulk of the reported research on assessment centers comes from only a handful of organizations. The main cause of concern is the lack of standardization among centers. Assessment is a complex process and variations exist from organization to organization on countless factors, including the number of exercises, the number of dimensions, the extent of assessor training, and the method of reaching consensus among assessors, to name but a few. A few comparative studies have been done. For example, Thompson (1969) found no difference between ratings made by psychologists and managers; Cohen and Sands (1978) found that the order of assessment center exercises had no impact on performance. However, the impact of most of the above factors on such outcomes as validity or fairness is unknown.

Recent research has also identified some interesting aspects of the judgment process in which differences between centers can be seen. Sackett and Dreher (1982) examined the correlations among the dimension ratings made at the conclusion of each exercise in three different organizations. In two of the organizations, the average correlation among ratings of different exercises (e.g., delegation in the in-basket compared with oral communication in a leaderless group discussion) was, as expected, near zero. In the third, however, the average of these correlations was .45. In essence, almost any rating, regardless of dimension or exercise, correlates relatively highly with almost any other rating. How these striking differences between organizations affect the validity of the process is an open question.

Whether some assessors have more influence than others in determining the final evaluation of a candidate is another issue of interest. Sackett and Wilson (1982) compared two centers and found negligible difference among assessors in the amount of influence exerted in one center, but fairly substantial differences in the second. Klimoski, Friedman, and Weldon (1980) noted that the role of the assessor team chairperson varies from center to center, and designed a laboratory study to examine the influences of the chairperson. They found that chairpersons with prior contact with the candidate and with formal voting rights exerted more influence on the group than chairpersons who had not observed the candidate's performance and who did not have a formal vote. The impact of differences in influence on the overall effectiveness of the assessment center is unknown.

In summary, it is not clear that research findings can be generalized from one center to another. Centers differ in a multitude of ways, some of which are obvious, e.g., the number of dimensions used. Others are not readily apparent, such as the findings discussed above regarding patterns of correlations among assessment center ratings and differences in influence. What is clear is that comparative research across organizations is needed to determine the impact of these differences from center to center.

The Rating Process

On paper, the rating process looks quite straightforward. Candidates are observed in a variety of exercises; they may or may not be evaluated at the end of each exercise. After all exercises have been concluded, the candidates are reviewed one at a time, with each assessor independently rating the candidate on each dimension. Differences are then reconciled by discussion; a similar process of independent judgment and reconciliation of differences is then followed for the overall rating.

An examination of ratings made by different assessors was made by Sackett and Hakel (1979). It was found that the overall rating in the center could be predicted with a very high degree of accuracy on the basis of only three dimensions—leadership, organizing and planning, and decision making. When asked to rate the importance of the dimensions, assessors consistently identified these three as the most important. Beyond these three dimensions, there was no agreement among assessors as to the importance of the remaining dimensions. These findings challenge the notion that the careful identification of multiple dimensions through job analysis makes a major contribution to the validity of assessment centers.

Moving from the individual ratings to the process of reaching consensus among assessors, Sackett and Wilson (1982) found that a simple mathematical rule could predict the outcome of the consensus discussion with 94.5 percent accuracy. It was observed that extreme ratings, e.g., 1s or 5s, had more impact on the group decision than mid-range ratings. These findings suggest that mid-range ratings may be used to indicate that an assessor has not had a chance to observe behavior relevant to the dimension or is not confident of his/her rating, rather than indicating that the assessor truly believes the candidate is average. Again, a departure from the intended process is indicated by this research.

Finally, Sackett and Dreher (1982) examined the dimensional ratings made upon the completion of each exercise. One disconcerting finding was that the average correlations among different ratings of the same dimension in different exercises (e.g., leadership rated in the in-basket, a role play, and a leaderless group discussion) were near zero in two different assessment centers. Central to the assessment center approach is the belief that stable behavior patterns exist, which can be categorized as representing the various dimensions. Multiple exercises are used in order to provide multiple opportunities for these behavior patterns to be manifested. These low correlations between exercises are a basis for concern as to what is actually being measured in an assessment center.

Thus, in looking at the rating process, one finds few dimensions contributing to the final evaluation, disagreement among assessors as to the importance of various dimensions, extreme ratings being given more weight in reaching consensus among assessors, and low agreement among the various post exercise ratings of the same dimension. An understanding of "what's going on" in the rating process is not complete; the dynamics of the assessor group and the processes of individual impression formation and decision making are in need of additional research.

Conclusions

This commentary has attempted to summarize empirical work and conceptual issues relevant to a select set of issues concerning the use of assessment centers. The predominant theme has been one of caution against overly rapid acceptance of some often-heard statements about the validity, legal status, and research base underlying the assessment center method. This should in no way be interpreted as an attempt to discredit assessment centers; the authors are advocates of work-sample/job-simulation approaches to selection. The intent of the commentary is to point out that far less is known about assessment than could or should be known, to encourage comparative research to determine the effects of various differences between centers, and to increase the knowledge base of individuals considering the use of assessment centers.

REFERENCES

Borman, W. C. Validity of behavioral assessment for predicting military recruiter performance. *Journal of Applied Psychology,* 1982, *67,* 3–9.

Bray, D. W., & Campbell, R. J. Selection of salesmen by means of an assessment center. *Journal of Applied Psychology,* 1968, *52,* 36–41.

Bray, D. W., & Grant, D. L. The assessment center in the measurement of potential for business management. *Psychological Monographs,* 1966, *80,* (17, Whole No. 625).

Byham, W. C. Assessment centers for spotting future managers. *Harvard Business Review,* 1970, *48,* 150–167.

—————. Review of legal cases and opinion dealing with assessment centers and content validity. Pittsburgh: Development Dimensions International, 1979.

Campbell, J. P., Dunnette, M. D., Lawler, E. E., & Weick, K. E. *Managerial behavior, performance, and effectiveness.* New York: McGraw-Hill, 1970.

Cohen, B. M., Moses, J. L., & Byham, W. C. *The validity of assessment centers: a literature review.* Monograph II. Pittsburgh: Development Dimension Press, 1974.

Cohen, S. L., & Sands, L. The effects of order of exercise presentation on assessment center performance: On standardization concern. *Personnel Psychology,* 1978, *31,* 35–46.

Dreher, G. F., & Sackett, P. R. Some problems with the applicability of content validity to assessment centers. *Academy of Management Review,* in press.

Hinrichs, J. R. An eight-year follow-up of a management assessment center. *Journal of Applied Psychology,* 1978, *63,* 596–601.

Huck, J. R. Determinants of assessment center ratings for white and black females and the relationship of these dimensions to subsequent performance effectiveness. Unpublished doctoral dissertation, Wayne State University, 1974.

Huck, J. R., & Bray, D. W. Management assessment center evaluations and subsequent job performance of white and black females. *Personnel Psychology,* 1976, *2,* 13–30.

Klimoski, R., Friedman, B., and Weldon, E. Leader influence in the assessment of performance. *Personnel Psychology,* 1980. *33,* 389–401.

Klimoski, R. J., & Strickland, W. J. Assessment centers—valid or merely prescient? *Personnel Psychology,* 1977, *30,* 353–361.

McNutt, K. Behavioral consistency and assessment centers: A reconciliation of the literature. *Journal of Assessment Center Technology,* 1979, *2,* 1–6.

Moses, J. L., & Boehm, V. R. Relationship of assessment center performance to management progress of women. *Journal of Applied Psychology,* 1975, *60,* 527–529.

Moses, J. L., & Ritchie, R. J. Supervisory relationships training: A Behavioral evaluation of a behavior modeling program. *Personnel Psychology,* 1976, *29,* 337–344.

Sackett, P. R., & Dreher, G. F. Constructs and assessment center dimensions: Some troubling empirical findings. *Journal of Applied Psychology,* 1982, *67,* 401–410.

Sackett, P. R., & Hakel, M. D. Temporal stability and individual differences in using assessment information to form overall ratings. *Organizational Behavior and Human Performance,* 1979, *23,* 120–137.

Sackett, P. R., & Wilson, M. A. Factors affecting the consensus judgment process in managerial assessment centers. *Journal of Applied Psychology,* 1982, *67,* 10–17.

Thomson, H. A. Internal and external validation of an industrial assessment program. Unpublished doctoral dissertation, Case Western Reserve University, 1969.

Uniform guidelines on employee selection procedures. *Federal Register,* 1978, *43,* 38290–38309.

Chapter 9

Biographical Data

INTRODUCTION

Past behavior predicts future behavior. This axiom forms the basis for the use of biographical, or life history, data as a predictor of job success. While information about various aspects of a person's past are commonly used unsystematically as part of the selection process (e.g., reference checks, subjective interpretations of application blank responses), our interest is in systematically scored biographical data. Two basic approaches to biodata are the weighted application blank (WAB) and the biographical information blank (BIB).

The WAB involves the development of a coding scheme to quantify applicants' responses to a standard application blank and the empirical determination of which items differentiate between successful and unsuccessful performers. The face validity of the coded items varies tremendously—previous experience and education, reasons for leaving past jobs, whether or not the applicant gives a middle initial, and whether the application is completed in pen or pencil may all be included in the coding scheme.

The BIB involves the use of an instrument other than the application blank, and is typically cast in a multiple-choice format. BIBs are usually much more detailed than application blanks, often including several hundred items. The nature of the items is also quite different: while application blanks primarily deal with factual, verifiable information, BIBs often include unverifiable items, such as conjecture about how one would act in a given situation or reaction to childhood experiences. Like the WAB, the BIB is typically scored by empirically determining which items are indicative of job success, although some attempts at scale development based on factor analysis have been made.

The first reading in the section is Asher's (1972) examination of the validity evidence for biographical data. Asher begins by reviewing the various types of information which may be viewed as biodata and argues for the use of historical, verifiable items. He then reviews the findings of studies using these types of items, and compares the results with validity evidence for a variety of other predictors. After documenting the effectiveness of biodata's success, Asher offers some speculations as to how to improve items even further.

The second reading is Thayer's (1977) account of the 50-year history of using biodata for selecting life insurance sales agents. Thayer points out numerous problems in maintaining the validity of a selection system over time, including the effects of economic changes, job changes, managerial sabotage by feeding responses to favored applicants, and organizational climate.

The commentary ties up a number of lose ends. Issues discussed include updating validity findings, fair employment practice implications of biodata use, and attempts to move beyond raw empiricism by identifying factors underlying responses to biodata items.

The Biographical Item: Can It Be Improved?*

JAMES J. ASHER

Biographical items may be found in measures that have names such as Application Blank, Biographical Information Blank, Individual Background Survey, and Life History Blank. Exactly what items should be classified as biographical is quite controversial (Henry, 1965). For example, a biographical item may vary on any of these dimensions: verifiable-unverifiable; historical-futuristic; actual behavior-hypothetical behavior; memory-conjecture; factual-interpretive; specific-general; response-response tendency; and external event-internal event. For specific examples of biographical items representing each dimension, see Table 1.

Some have advocated that only an individual's historical experiences, events or situations that are verifiable should be classified as biographical items (B-items). Using this system, most items on the usual application blank would be classified as B-items. For example, what was your rank in your high school graduating class? List each prior job with inclusive dates.

If only historical items that are verifiable are included as B-items, then questions such as this would *not* be asked. "Did you ever build a model airplane that flew?" Cureton (see Henry, 1965 p. 913) commented that this single item, although it cannot be easily verified for an individual, was almost as good a predictor of success in flight training during World War II as the entire Air Force Battery.

Other researchers feel that any person-type item which describes the individual may be classified as a B-item. This would include such items as personality, motivation, aspiration, attitudes, and values. From this enlarged classification, any item is included that answers one of these questions:

What have I done?
Where have I been?
What do I believe?
What do I want to be?
How do I feel?
What am I apt to do?
What interests me?
What relationships have I had with others?

While the enlarged classification of B-items obviously expands the amount of personal information collected, a more constrained classification may reduce a tendency towards fictionalization. B-items that are historical and verifiable may result in a narrow, yet representative set of data about

* J. J. Asher, "The Biographical Item: Can It Be Improved?" *Personnel Psychology* 25 (1972), pp. 251–69. Copyright 1972 by Personnel Psychology, Inc. Reprinted/adapted by permission of the publisher and the authors.

Table 1
A Taxonomy of B-Items

Verifiable How many full-time jobs have you had in the past five years?	*Unverifiable* What aspect of your last full-time job did you find most interesting?
Historical List your three best subjects in high school	*Futuristic* Do you intend to further your education?
Actual behavior Did you ever build a model airplane that flew?	*Hypothetical behavior* If you had the training, do you think you would enjoy building innovative model airplanes for a toy manufacturer?
Memory Before you were 12 years old, did you ever try to perform chemistry experiments at home?	*Conjecture* If your father had been a chemist, do you think you would have performed chemistry experiments at home before you were 12 years old?
Factual Do you repair mechanical things around your home such as appliances?	*Interpretive* If you had the training, how would you estimate your performance as an appliance repair man?
Specific As a child did you collect stamps?	*General* As a child were you an avid collector of things?
Response Which of the following types of cameras do you own?	*Response tendency* In buying a new camera, would you most likely purchase one with automatic features?
External event Did you ever have private tutoring lessons in any school subject?	*Internal event* How important did you view homework when you were in high school?

the individual, while the enlarged classification may be quite unrepresentative. For example, even when *S*s have a set to respond honestly, items calling for conjecture, interpretation, and supposition may have enough ambiguity to enable an individual to respond with a sort of leniency rating error about himself. Illustrations of such items would be:

Have you:

a. Often been double-crossed by people
b. Sometimes been double-crossed by people
c. Been double-crossed once or twice by people
d. Never been double-crossed by people

Were your parents:

a. Always very strict with you
b. Usually very strict with you
c. Seldom very strict with you
d. Never very strict with you

Using the constrained classification that B-items should be historical and verifiable, the reliability and validity of these items will be reviewed for 1960 through 1970. Then, what has been done to improve the B-item, and what innovations could be attempted in future research.

RESULTS

The scorable application blank was used to predict work behavior that ranged from unskilled to skilled, as may be seen in the following list:

* Adolescent girls (art and writing)
* Architects
College students
* Credit applicants
Door to door salesmen
Engineers
* Executives
* Female police personnel
Food company salesmen

Foreign service clerical workers
Foreign service junior officers
High school students
Hospital aids
Insurance salesmen
Life insurance salesmen
Peace corps workers
Petroleum research scientists
* Pharmaceutical research scientists
* Research scientists
* Unskilled workers
* Vocational rehabilitation trainees

From the list, studies were selected which had these characteristics: (*a*) there was cross-validation data expressed in a correlation statistic; (*b*) biographical items were used in a combination as a predictor rather than as single items; and (*c*) the definition of B-items was judged to be historical and verifiable. There were 11 studies with the attributes described and these were found in the categories marked with an asterisk. No study was selected in which B-items were used to predict grade points average for students, since this issue has been thoroughly reviewed by Freeberg (1967).

Using only cross-validated data from the 11 studies, there were 31 validity coefficients. The cross-validated correlations were distributed as follows: 35 percent were .60 or higher; 55 percent were .50 or higher; 74 percent were .40 or higher and 97 percent were .30 or higher.

In a recent review by Schuh (1967), it was found that in 19 of 21 studies, one or more biographical items had a predictive relationship with job turnover. Schuh concluded. ". . . some items in an applicant's personal history can be found to relate to tenure in most jobs" (p. 145).

COMPARED TO OTHER PREDICTORS

The predictive power of biographical items may be evaluated with greater clarity when compared with other predictors. Fortunately, Ghiselli (1966) has published the proportion of validity coefficients which resulted when tests were tried for specific jobs. For example, in his book are validity coefficients for: mechanical repairmen on mechanical principles tests; general clerks on intelligence tests, bench workers on finger dexterity tests, and machine tenders on spatial relations tests. The criterion was job proficiency in all cases except mechanical repairmen for whom the criterion was success in training.

In Figure 1, when the minimal cutoff for validity was .50, biographical items excelled the intelligence test by 2 to 1 and spatial relations by 18 to one.

In Figure 2, when the cutoff was arbitrarily taken as .40, B-items outperformed the intelligence test by 23 percent and the spatial relations test by eight to one.

In Figure 3, when .30 was the cutoff, B-items were still substantially ahead of all other predictors.

In Figures 1 through 3, B-items may be compared with another type of personal item which has a "cousin" relationship, the personality inventory. These data were taken from a paper by Ghiselli and Barthol (1953) who reviewed 113 studies from 1919 to 1953 in which the personality inventory was a predictor of work behavior. The results showed that B-items had 43 percent more validity coefficients of .50 or higher, 52 percent more validities at .40 or higher, and 55 percent more at .30 or higher.

*   *   *   *   *

For a complex range of work behavior, biographical items seem to yield higher validity coefficients than other predictors. By contrast, the usual selection interview has produced such low reliability and validity in study after study that many researchers have recommended its discontinuance (Dunnette, 1962; England and Paterson, 1960).

Figure 1
Proportion of Validity Coefficients .50 or Higher with Job Proficiency as the Criterion

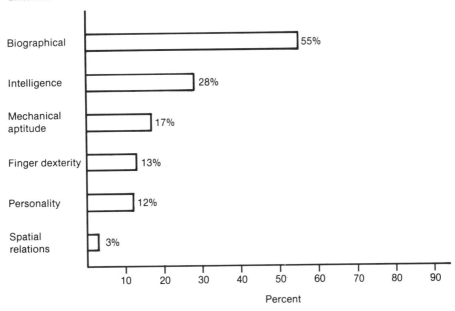

Percent

Figure 2
Proportion of Validity Coefficients .40 or Higher with Job Proficiency as the Criterion

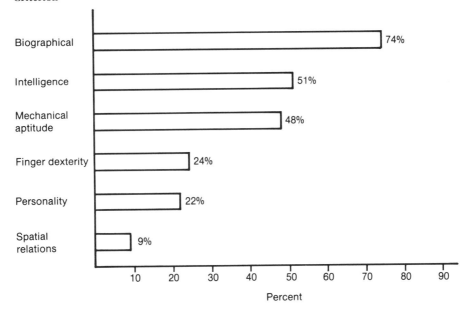

Percent

Figure 3
Proportion of Validity Coefficients .30 or Higher with Job Proficiency as the
Criterion

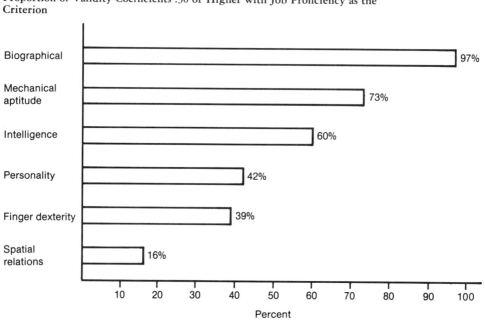

THREE THEORETICAL EXPLANATIONS

The Nonfiction Theory

Why is it that B-items seem to have accuracy in predicting specific work behavior? One explanation is that the scorable application blank is representative of an individual's history while other predictors, especially the unstructured selection interview, may be a caricature. For instance, in the interview, the individual can present a fictionalized concept of himself, while the scorable application blank is more apt to be a systematic, comprehensive collection of factual information about the individual. B-items may be to the selection interview what nonfiction is to fiction.

The Relevant Item Theory

Lykken and Rose (1963) have made the point that the validity of any test may be dampened because it is a set of "relevant"

and "irrelevant" items. For example, all parts of the predictor space are not likely to be equally valid. The predictor space for a test is heteroscedastic since all of the test items will not be relevant for predicting a specific criterion behavior.

The scorable application blank, by contrast, has a predictor space that is homoscedastic since only "relevant" items are selected in the set used to predict the specific criterion behavior in the cross-validation.

The Point-to-Point Theory

The scorable application blank may "work" because it escapes the fallacy of attempting to make predictions by measuring general mediators. For instance, a classic strategy in testing is to assume that criterion behavior is controlled or determined by generalized mediators as traits, aptitudes, or intelligence. The problem, then, is to measure the general mediators. The more accurate the measurement, the higher the probability that criterion behavior can be estimated with precision.

The data seem to suggest, however, that accurate prediction is a function of a point-to-point correspondence between predictor space and the criterion space. The more points they have in common, the greater the validity coefficient. As an illustration, the evidence gathered in the past 50 years rather consistently shows that the best single predictor of college grade point average is high school grade point average (Fishman and Pasanella, 1960; Freeberg, 1967), and the next best predictor is a measure of high school achievement.

Information with the highest validity seems to have a point-to-point correspondence with the criterion. This generalization was supported by a study of National Merit finalists (Holland and Nichols, 1964). The attempt, using samples of 500 boys and 500 girls, was not only to predict college freshman grades, but creative accomplishments in specific areas as leadership, science, drama, literature, music, and art. As might be expected, student achievement in high school was the best indicator of college achievement. The results further showed a point-to-point relationship between what the student did in high school and his behavior in college. For instance, high school grades predicted college grades, scientific activity in high school predicted similar achievement in college, and this specific, one-to-one relationship held for leadership, drama, writing, music, and art.

High school grade point average is predictive of college GPA, but if the one-to-one principle holds, then adult achievement probably *cannot* be predicted from information as college grade point average. Hoyt's review (1965) concluded that achievement in business, engineering, medicine, science, and law cannot be predicted, even with modest accuracy, from college GPA.

* * * * *

SUMMARY

In comparison with other predictors, such as intelligence, aptitude, interest, and personality, biographical items had vastly superior validity. This conclusion may be limited to "hard" rather than "soft" biographical items. Hard B-items would be those classified as historical and verifiable. For instance, here is a "hard" B-item: "What was your rank in your high school graduating class?" A "soft" B-item, for contrast, could be: "What subject in high school did you enjoy most?"

It may be that "hard" B-items, especially if the respondent is asked to grant his permission for item verification with former employers and schools, is a factual representation of the individual's past behavior. Beginning with these accurate data, the information is sorted to achieve a point-to-point correspondence with criterion behavior. This sorting of items to find only criterion-relevant items is rarely the analytic strategy with standardized measures. Usually a standardized predictor is applied as a ready-made collection of items many of which may or may not be criterion-relevant.

Future research with biographical items should attempt to discover how item dimensionality is related to predictive validity. For instance, how important are item dimensions as verifiable-unverifiable, historical-futuristic, actual behavior-hypothetical behavior, etc? There is some evidence (Walther, 1961; 1962) that certain "soft" B-items can have unusually high validity. A theoretical explanation is needed. It may be that item transparency and item fakability are more powerful variables than any classification of B-items as, for instance, hard or soft.

REFERENCES

Dunnette, M. D. Personnel management. *Annual Review of Psychology,* 1962, *13,* 285–314.

England, G. W., & Paterson, D. G. Selection and placement—the past ten years. In H. G. Heneman, Jr., L. C. Brown, M. K. Chandler, R. Kahn, H. S. Parnes, and G. P. Schultz (Eds.), *Employment Relations Research.* New York: Harper, 1960, pp. 43–72.

Fishman, J. A., & Pasanella, A. K. College admission-selection studies. *Review of Educational Research,* 1960, *33,* 298–310.

Freeberg, N. E. The biographical information blank as a predictor of student achievement: A review. *Psychological Reports,* 1967, *20,* 911–925.

Ghiselli, E. E., & Barthol, R. P. The validity of personality inventories in the selection of employees. *The Journal of Applied Psychology,* 1953, *37,* 18–20.

Ghiselli, E. E. *The validity of occupational aptitude tests.* New York: John Wiley & Sons, 1966.

Henry, E. R. *Research conference on the use of auto-biographical data as psychological predictors.* Greensboro, N.C.: The Richardson Foundation, 1965.

Hoyt, D. P. The relationship between college grades and adult achievement. A review of the literature. *American College Testing Program Research Reports,* 1965, No. 7.

Lykken, D. T., & Rose, R. Psychological prediction from actuarial tables. *Journal of Clinical Psychology,* 1963, *19,* 139–151.

Schuh, A. J. The predictability of employee tenure: A review of the literature. *Personnel Psychology,* 1967, *20,* 133–152.

Walther, R. H. Self-description as a predictor of success or failure in Foreign Service clerical jobs. *Journal of Applied Psychology,* 1961, *45,* 16–21.

Walther, R. H. Self-description as a predictor of rate of promotion of junior Foreign Service officers. *Journal of Applied Psychology,* 1962, *46,* 314–316.

Reading 20

"Somethings Old, Somethings New"*

PAUL W. THAYER

This paper is concerned with "somethings old, somethings new," and their interactions. The old things deal primarily with the study of individual differences in an applied setting. The new things deal primarily with organizational variables. You will see, however, that there are some old points to make concerning organizational variables and some new ones concerning individual differences.

The interaction of the old and the new are presented within the framework of the history of the development and validation of a selection instrument for life insurance agents, the *Aptitude Index.* That development and validation has been in progress since 1922, is still in process in 1977, and will continue, I suspect, as long as any of us is around.

Within this historical context, I will touch upon, at one time or another, the impact of: (*a*) societal changes upon validity and upon criteria; (*b*) organizational practices upon validity and upon criteria; (*c*) industry practices upon validity and upon criteria; (*d*) managerial behaviors upon validity and upon criteria. I will also touch on: (*e*) the statistical problems that one encounters in doing research in an industrial setting and (f) the fact that age is a powerful moderator variable.

Let me start with some history, LIMRA, or the Life Insurance Marketing and Research Association, is a nonprofit trade association. It is unusual in that it does not engage in lobbying or public relations. Its functions are to provide research, education, and consultation primarily to 350 member companies in the U.S. and Canada, and also to an additional 200 associates throughout the rest of the world. Although the research covers a wide spectrum—training, job attitudes, consumer opinion, costs, compensation, markets, etc.—LIMRA is probably best known for its selection research. Indeed, some of the earliest work done on biographical items was done back when LIMRA was the Life Insurance Sales Research Bureau.

Actually that research on bio data was begun not at the Bureau, but at Phoenix Mutual Life Insurance Company in 1922 by Gertrude V. Cope, manager of its Sales Research Division (Holcombe, 1922, Bureau of Public Personnel Administration, 1925). She analyzed bio data collected at the time of employment from over 400 men hired as agents in 1919, 1920 and 1921 and found several that were significantly related to success and failure:

1. Age
2. Number of dependents
3. Marital status
4. Education
5. Years since leaving school
6. Selling experience
7. Membership in social organizations
8. Offices held in social organizations
9. Home ownership
10. Number of investments
11. Life insurance ownership

Other companies such as the Guardian Life tried this same technique with positive results and in 1932 Albert K. Kurtz, then with the Sales Research Bureau, began research for the industry in general. He worked on biographical terms, while Arthur W. Kornhauser of the University of Chicago worked on a variety of personality tests.

Among the latter, Kornhauser tried such things as: an incomplete sentence form; a set of 12 men's photographs designed to measure the salesman's ability to "size up" people; and an interest test that required the salesman to guess how doctors, then lawyers, then clerks, and finally engineers would answer the items. The sets of guesses were then compared with how actual doctors, lawyers, clerks, and engineers answered the questions. None of these tests showed validity.

A fourth test contained 30 statements about economic, political, and social issues requiring the applicant to state his agreement or disagreement to varying degrees. The test was designed to measure confidence and also conservatism. Of interest here is that these items worked well in a concurrent study comparing more and less successful established agents, but failed to show validity in a follow-up predictive study.

Finally, there were over 100 conventional personality items designed to measure self-confidence, assertiveness, enthusiasm, extroversion, desire for power, etc. Of these, all worked but those designed to measure extroversion (Kornhauser, 1938).

Characteristics of Kurtz's and Kornhauser's separate research efforts was their clear understanding of the need for cross-validation of any empirically derived scoring method and the desirability of checking any tests that showed concurrent validity with a predictive study. In his report to Kurtz, Kornhauser points out that for his personality tests, ". . . the tests show definitely less agreement with success among new men in our recent studies than was previously shown among established agents. This may be due to the effects of success and failure on the established agents' test performance . . ." (ibid., p. 22). The fact that some of us have not yet learned the first lesson, cross-validation, is demonstrated by the need for Blumenfeld's (1972) note of a few years ago. The second lesson, the effects of job experience on test performance, is less widely recognized especially for personality, interest, and other "fakable" instruments.

To return to the story, Kurtz did a series of studies of bio items and published a number of reports during the 1930's. In 1937, he wrote a report based on a study of 10,111 agents contracted by 11 companies in which he first injected the use of age as a sort of moderator variable. Here is a brief, illustrative quote: "A little consideration will show that most items present in personal history rating charts are the type of items on which a man will receive progressively higher scores as he gets older—even though there may be no corresponding change in the man's ability. For example, most men of 45 have more dependents and higher living expenses than equally able men of 25; and they also belong to more organizations. Consequently, if a scoring system is to give the best results, it must make adequate allowance for these progressive changes" (Life Insurance Sales Research Bureau, 1937, p. 3). Kurtz handled the problem by a set of normative tables for several age groups so that the final predictor score would be the same for men with equal chances of success, regardless of age. This is a marked improvement over Cope's method in which age was a scored item. I hope that those using bio items are aware of the problem that Kurtz described and have taken appropriate steps. If not, they could be discriminating against certain age groups. Usually, the younger age groups will be penalized, but not always. Education is an item where the reverse might be true, assuming education is a valid item. Here is an example of changing societal standards having an impact on item scoring.

Table 1
Illustrative Validity Data

Aptitude index grades	*Success (combined survival and productive)*
A	233
B	116
C	69
D&E	41
	Base 100
(N = 372)	

The work of Kurtz and Kornhauser finally came together in 1938 with the introduction of the *Aptitude Index,* a combination of the bio and personality items (Kurtz, 1938). Kurtz did a number of things that we now commonly regard as good practice, but that were quite new then: He controlled on age for bio items, used multiple regression techniques for adding items to the scoring system, cross-validated his key, tested validity across a variety of companies in both the U.S. and Canada, differentially weighted the personality and bio items based on age because of differing validities (Kurtz, 1941), used a predictive validity model, and did continuing validity studies to be sure that the test continued to work.

Here are some data with the test in use with a sample of 372 indicating the kinds of validities Kurtz and Kornhauser obtained. (Life Insurance Sales Research Bureau, 1941). The validity model is predictive and the entries are ratios with a base of 100. One can see that companies involved had little faith in the test at the time as a strong validity relationship is obtained despite the test's use (Peterson and Wallace, 1966).

These data were originally reported at an APA symposium on September 2, 1940. A little more than 15 months later, the United States became a belligerent in World War II. Not much *Aptitude Index* research was done during the next four years. In addition, Kurtz left the Bureau to teach at Penn State.

Following World War II, a number of

things happened. First, Donald A. Peterson and S. Rains Wallace appeared on the scene to work with the *Aptitude Index*. Peterson was the primary architect of the test and he discovered several things. Not only had the world changed in a general sense as a consequence of the war, but the world of life insurance and agent selection had changed, too.

Consider:

1. The U.S. had gone from a deep depression with a manpower surplus to an inflationary period marked by sharp competition for manpower,
2. Economic and educational scales had skyrocketed, compared to pre-World War II,
3. Many changes in values had occurred.

And those are only a few changes.

What impact did this have on the *Aptitude Index* and agent selection?

1. Primarily because of economic changes, the *Aptitude Index* score distribution was now markedly negatively skewed. A very high percentage of applicants were getting scores of A and B. As a result, the *Aptitude Index* had lost most of its validity.
2. The nature of survival had changed, markedly affecting the criterion employed. Before the war, almost everyone was under a straight commission system. If agents sold some life insurance, they were paid; if not, they weren't. After the war, manpower competition was great. It was necessary to offer subsidies to the new agents to help them get established. If agents who were subsidized didn't sell any insurance, they had to be paid, anyway. Involuntary termination rose rapidly. And, because of company differences in subsidy level and differences in enforcement of subsidy-related production requirements, company criterion adjustments were now necessary before data were pooled.

3. New products were developed and a changing sales technology was evolving based upon need-identification, as opposed to selling a particular product to all comers. In other words, the job was changing.

Peterson and Wallace were able to restore the validity of the bio items by the simple device of rescaling. They restored the original distribution of scores and, as a result, restored the validity of the bio items.

The personality items could not be revived despite all the techniques those two skilled gentlemen could employ. In fact, the demise of the personality items developed by Kornhauser was the beginning of a long search involving almost every known personality, interest and temperament device. In a period of 20 years, over 25 such devices were tried out in a series of studies.

It wasn't until 1964 that one test was discovered consisting of some standard personality items that were scored with an empirical key. This test was developed by someone outside the organization. It was added to the *Aptitude Index* and had a life span of under five years. Again, LIMRA staff did not understand why such items survive such a short period of time. Testing firms that have done follow-up studies of personality measures report similar experiences.

To continue with the history, Peterson began to innovate, while utilizing the strong foundation prepared by Kurtz. First of all, he employed the growth curve concept of Binet, using curve fitting and standardized scaling to take age into account for individual items. The procedure is straightforward. Individual items are compared for various age groups from about 18 to 60 years. Where the relationships change across this broad range of ages, standard scores are developed by plotting age-growth curves. Standard scores are then run against the combined success criterion of survival with high production. Approximately 60 percent of the bio items yield improved prediction through the use of growth curves.

Age is also used in another way—as a moderator variable. The relationship of an item to the success criterion is examined across various age groups. Approximately 50 percent of the bio items exhibit changes in the slopes of the linear regression lines across age. Indeed, a substantial number change from an estimated slope of 0.00 to 0.25. None go from a negative to a positive relationship or vice versa as allowed by Saunders (1956), but there are a few in the latest test edition that might. The changes in slope, it should be noted, are orderly and gradual.

Thus age is employed in two ways: to develop growth curves and as a moderator variable. The search is on for other moderators.

Obviously, not all items are affected by age. Some are scored differently because of the country of the applicant (U.S. or Canada) or language (English or French).

The use of geographical and lingual distinctions and age as a moderator variable results in a number of keys instead of one. In fact, today, the *Aptitude Index* employs 27 keys and soon will employ over 50.

One final comment on age as a moderator variable. Kurtz discovered in 1938 and Edward J. Sweeney of the LIMRA staff rediscovered in 1964 that age also moderated the validity relationship of personality items to the criterion. Kurtz used age as a main effect variable, dividing the sample into two groups of 25 and younger, and 26 and older. The personality test was given one and one-half times the weight of bio items for the young group and vice versa for the older (Kurtz, 1941). Sweeney originally found a positive relationship for very young men between the 1964 personality test and success, which gradually reduced to zero for mid-30's or older ages. Thus age

can also moderate standard personality item validities, at least for a few years.

Returning to history now, Peterson also rediscovered a phenomenon which existed in the data developed by Cope in 1922, but which had been ignored during the ensuing quarter of a century. That phenomenon is heteroscedasticity. Very simply, variance increases on the criterion as test scores increase. Thus, as shown in Figure 1, the *Aptitude Index* predicts failure very accurately. It does not predict success well because of the high proportion of high scoring failures, or "false positives," which are responsible for the bulge in the lower right-hand quadrant. Obviously, in such a setting, one reports correlation coefficients at his or her own peril. In unrestricted samples, LIMRA staff still find that the success rate of these who pass the test is approximately four times greater than that of those who fail. They urge, however, that once an individual has passed the test, that that score not be given undue weight because the test's greatest strength is in identifying potential failures (Guion, 1965).

Peterson also paid considerable attention to the research done at the Prudential by Hughes, Dunn, and Baxter (1956) that demonstrated conclusively how rapidly a group of managers under strong recruiting pressure could destroy the validity of a test. That *Personnel Psychology* article showed that it took the managers little more than a year to destroy the test's validity. For this reason Peterson finally pushed LIMRA into a centralized scoring system that eliminates erroneous scoring—intended or otherwise—and permits monitoring of recruiting and selection practices of managers, etc. It also permits the manipulation of the scoring key as research reveals that experimental items do or do not work, and the consistent adding or subtracting of items from the keys so that their unrestricted validities can be estimated.

Just to bring the reader completely up to date and to dispel some misimpressions as

Figure 1
Schematic Representation of *Aptitude Index*
Validity Relationship

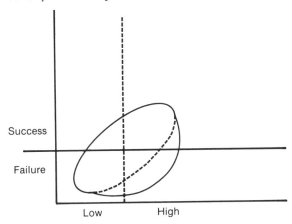

to bio item vulnerability to minority differences, the keys developed primarily upon white males demonstrated clear validity for male blacks and Spanish-surnamed Americans, as well as for females. The score distribution is slightly lower for black and Spanish-surnamed American males and lower still for females. Scaling adjustments eliminate male differences and reduce those for females to less than the federal definition of adverse impact with little or no effect on validity. Female distributions are rising as companies recruit more aggressively. Preliminary evidence suggests that using recruiting methods for minorities and females comparable to those used to find white males will result in a marked reduction or elimination of distribution differences.

The latest edition of the *Aptitude Index* does not use "sexist terminology," and also includes a number of items that have potential for improving the validity of the test for females and perhaps the pass rate. This latest edition also explicitly asks for information from applicants as to their age, sex, race, national origin, etc., in order to permit research that will prevent discrimination against any protected group. Such information is kept from those making the

hiring decision. The important point is that failure to ask such questions could result in discrimination. That point should be clear from the illustration using age as a moderator.

While mentioning that new edition, I should emphasize that the 1976 edition is the ninth printed version since 1938, or nine versions in 38 years. Some of those were published to permit the addition of new experimental items, but most resulted from the need to modify the range of alternatives, to drop items losing validity, etc. Since centralized scoring was installed in 1960, adjustments in scoring keys have been made on three or four occasions. Thus, there have been about a dozen revisions in 38 years. These revisions clearly demonstrate the need for maintaining tests. Even with the samples of thousands available to LIMRA for such maintenance research, there are still the problems of research on tests in use as demonstrated by Peterson and Wallace (1966).

The emphasis in this talk thus far has been on the old: individual differences. It is time to turn to the new: the interaction of organizational variables with individual measures. Recall that managers can destroy test validities by improper scoring or, in fact, by taking the test for the candidate. That is an extreme example.

Think back to a study done by Wallace and Twichell reported in *Personnel Psychology* in 1949. In that article, they suggested that the careful selection researcher ". . . will recognize that if he is to fulfill his major aims, he must investigate the other factors which may affect performance level or turnover and determine their relationships to the selection procedures and the groups from which the selection is made. In short, he will recognize that he probably never is concerned with a test's validity but with a number of validities which may vary for differing sub-groups of the population and under various administrative procedures" (Wallace and Twichell, 1949, p. 279). In the study referred to, Wallace and Twichell found a number of validities for the *Aptitude Index,* depending on whether the agents were receiving a subsidy or not and on whether their monthly financial needs were high or low.

During the 1960's, Peterson found very high validity for the *Aptitude Index* in selecting agents within a sample of managers rated as superior by home office officials and only modest validity for managers who were rated as poor (Life Insurance Agency Management Association, 1966). In a later, unreported study, Peterson and I did some similar research and found that validities varied substantially, depending on the characteristics of the managers involved. Unfortunately, in both studies, it was impossible to replicate the findings for the year following the initial study. Even though similar classifications of managers were used in both years, many managers changed their positions from good to poor and vice versa. We have continued studies from time to time in an attempt to stabilize the managerial classifications so that such findings would be replicable. Thus far, we have had no success.

Despite those mixed findings, research will continue. It makes good sense that one

should have maximum validities under good management. Following Dunnette's reasoning (Dunnette, 1973), a good manager should be able to help an individual with high potential to achieve high levels of performance. Little can be done to assist the individual with low potential. Thus, a predictor should exhibit high validity with such a manager. A poor manager probably does a poor job, regardless of the potential of the individual involved. Thus, zero or low validities are expected when the poor manager uses a normally valid predictor. The final bit of evidence with regard to local organizational impacts comes from the research done by Schneider (1975, p. 457) as part of his Cattell Award-winning work with Bartlett. He found substantial validities for the *Aptitude Index* in agencies where the climate was supportive of new employees.

Clearly, organizational variables do affect individuals and individual performance. Clearly, also, such variables alter validities. Unfortunately too little research has been done to clearly identify those variables that have consistent effects on validity relationships and to determine whether these are interactive or main effects. It is important to determine whether the variable under study has a main or interactive effect. If the variable is interactive, one does not get the full benefit if it is used as a main effect variable.

Thus far, I have given the history of a test that depends heavily upon bio items for its validity. I have also tried to point out how a number of environmental variables affect the test itself, the job, the criterion, and validities. As previously indicated, changes in the society, in the economy, and in company practices have marked impacts upon the nature of the criterion of survival and success or failure. Company practices in terms of enforcing a subsidy plan, of putting pressure on managers to recruit, of maintaining high quality managers, etc., also affect validity relationships. Societal emphases on education, or the joining of organizations, have age-related impacts on bio items. The quality of management and the climate within an organization alter validity relationships. Adding to that last point, LIMRA staff have observed that its very best member companies—the ones referred to as the "quality companies"—always show higher validity relationships with the *Aptitude Index* than is the case for other member companies.

Now for one final example of the effect of organizational variables upon validity relationships. In this case, the subject is not company practices, but industry practices. Some years ago, I persuaded LIMRA's Board of Directors to provide a substantial subsidy to the Conference Board to study factors related to turnover of salesmen in industries outside the life insurance business. Despite the fact that there are hundreds of life insurance companies in the U.S. and Canada (in fact, over 2,000), it was possible that practices were similar enough that important turnover relationships might be concealed by institutional restrictions of range.

The Conference Board strove diligently to gather data from hundreds of companies. It looked for correlates of turnover involving variables such as type or length of training, compensation practices, selection standards, territorial assignments, enforcement of productivity standards, etc. Unfortunately, only 9 percent of its membership could provide appropriate data. Despite the severe limitations imposed by this restriction, I am intrigued by the results.

Here are what I regard as extremely important findings from the Conference Board study of salesmen in all kinds of industries (National Industrial Conference Board, 1972). There is a significant relationship across companies with regard to level of starting pay and turnover. Companies starting their salesmen with low pay have significantly higher turnover rates than those with high starting pay. High

turnover is also associated with salesmen who sell direct to the public as opposed to salesmen who sell to organizational entities, such as corporations, universities, governments, hospitals, etc. Salesmen who are under some form of incentive compensation are more prone to turnover. The relationship is quite consistent in that salesmen on straight commission have higher turnover rates than those on salary plus bonus, whose turnover rates are higher than those on straight salary. Finally, salesmen who are required to meet some standard of performance early in their careers have higher turnover rates than those who need not achieve such standards until later in their careers. In summary, low starting pay, sales direct to the public, incentive compensation, and the imposition of early performance standards are all related to high turnover.

I am sure that the reader anticipates my next statement. I have just described the institutional practices of the life insurance business. It seems to me that selection research can't contribute much more to improving turnover rates until there are changes in the institutional practices of the business. That does not mean that it is desirable to change those practices. It may very well be that the particular way in which these variables are employed in the business results in the best utilization of our resources. Higher survival rates with lower productivity could well result in substantially higher costs to the public. Thus, the comment is not on the desirability of these practices. The important point is that institutional or industry practices undoubtedly put a ceiling on validity relationships.

In this paper, I may not have described anything new. The reader knows that society can have effects upon validity and criteria, that organizational practices have similar effects, that industry practices also have effects, that managerial behaviors have effects, that age is a powerful moderator, and that one can encounter some statistical problems working in industry not encountered in the laboratory. Perhaps the only thing accomplished is to give some new examples of things already known, "somethings old and somethings new." That, in and of itself, might be sufficient.

On the other hand, I hope for more than that. I hope I have reminded those who emphasize organizational variables at the expense of individual ones and those who emphasize individual variables at the expense of organizational ones that neither can make much progress. All of us should pay much more attention to both organizational and individual variables. I am encouraged by the increasing number of signs appearing in the literature, from the work of Forehand (1968), and Owens (1969) to more recent efforts of Dunnette and his colleagues (1973), and most recently Schneider's book, *Staffing Organizations* (1976). We can make very rapid strides and increase our contribution to society at large if we move toward an industrial/organizational psychology, as opposed to an industrial *or* an organizational psychology.

REFERENCES

Blumenfeld, W. I am never startled by a fish. *The Industrial/Organizational Psychologist,* May 1972.

Bureau of Public Personnel Administration. A method of rating the history and achievements of applicants for positions. Public Personnel Studies, 1925, pp. 202–209.

Dunnette, M. D. Performance equals ability and what? Unpublished manuscript. University of Minnesota, Department of Psychology. *Technical Report #4009,* 1973.

Forehand, G. A. On the interaction of persons and organizations. In R. Tagiuri and G. Litwin (Eds.), *Organizational climate: Explorations of a concept.* Boston: Division of Research, Harvard Business School, 1968.

Guion, R. M. *Personnel testing.* New York: McGraw-Hill, 1965.

Holcombe, J. M., Jr. A case of sales research: Report on first steps in a study of selection of life insurance salesmen. *Bulletin of The Taylor Society,* 1922, 7, 112–121.

Hughes, J. F., Dunn, J. F., Baxter, B. The validity of selection instruments under operating conditions. *Personnel Psychology,* 1956, 9, 321–324.

Kornhauser, A. W. Report on the Bureau's selection tests for life insurance salesmen 1932 to 1938. Personal communication to A. K. Kurtz. July 6, 1938.

Kurtz, A. K. Selection—The Aptitude Index. Life Insurance Sales Research Bureau, *Annual Meeting Proceedings,* 1938, pp. 170–180.

Life Insurance Sales Research Bureau. *How well does the Aptitude Index work?,* 1941.

Kurtz, A. K. Recent research in the selection of life insurance salesmen. *Journal of Applied Psychology,* 1941, 25, 11–17.

Life Insurance Agency Management Association, *LIAMA research in perspective: Recruiting selection, training and supervision in life insurance.* Hartford, 1966, pp. 55–56.

Life Insurance Sales Research Bureau. *Rating Prospective Agents,* 1937.

National Industrial Conference Board. *Salesmen's turnover in early employment,* 1972.

Owens, W. A. Cognitive, noncognitive and environmental correlates of mechanical ingenuity. *Journal of Applied Psychology,* 1969, 53, 199–208.

Peterson, D. A. and Wallace, S. R. Validation and revision of a test in use. *Journal of Applied Psychology,* 1966, 50, 13–17.

Saunders, D. R. Moderator variables in prediction. *Educational and psychological measurement,* 1956, 16, 209–222.

Schneider, B. Organizational climates: An essay. *Personnel Psychology,* 1975, 28, 447–479.

Schneider, B. *Staffing organizations.* Pacific Palisades, California: Goodyear Publishing, 1976.

Wallace, S. R. and Twichell, C. M. Managerial procedures and test validities. *Personnel Psychology,* 1949, 2, 277–292.

COMMENTARY

The two readings can be summarized succinctly: biodata works (Asher), but it requires constant care and attention to keep it working in an operational setting (Thayer). The two readings complement each other well: Asher's enthusiastic endorsement is tempered by Thayer's description of potential pitfalls in biodata use. The need for a dozen revisions of the *Aptitude Index* over a 38-year period and the fact that age moderates the validity of about 50 percent of the items in the *Aptitude Index* are but two of many arguments against a belief that biodata represents a quick and easy solution to the problem of developing valid methods of selection.

Validity Studies

Recall that Asher's review of the validity evidence focused solely on studies using objective, verifiable biodata items. A recent review by Reilly and Chao (1982) serves as both an update and expansion of Asher's work. Like Asher, Reilly and Chao included only cross-validated findings; unlike Asher, they included both verifiable and unverifiable data in their review. Across 44 studies, the mean validity coefficient was .35. Their results indicate success in predicting a number of criteria, including tenure (mean $r = .32$), performance in training (mean $r = .39$), performance ratings (mean $r = .36$), productivity (mean $r = .46$), and salary progress (mean $r = .34$). Their results also indicated that biodata has been found to be a valid predictor for a variety of occupational groups, including engineering (mean $r = .41$), clerical (mean $r = .52$), management (mean $r = .38$), sales (mean $r = .50$), and military occupations (mean $r = .30$). Reilly and Chao's review serves to strengthen Asher's conclusions that biodata is a promising alternative to more traditional selection techniques. While mean validities may be favorable, there are certainly instances where attempts to use biodata have been unsuccessful. For example, Schmidt, Hunter, and Caplan (1981) report a mean observed validity of $-.03$ across eight studies using a background survey to predict the performance of maintenance workers. Note that whenever different items and different weighting schemes are used across jobs and across organizations, the generalization of validity findings is unfeasible. Only when common items and weighting schemes are used will statements about generalized validity be possible. The use of the *Aptitude Index* in many insurance companies is the best example to date of using a common instrument across organizations.

Unfair Discrimination

The relatively scant literature dealing with possible discrimination in biodata use has been reviewed by Reilly and Chao (1982). Of eight studies examining mean score differences by race, four found whites scoring higher than blacks or Hispanics while four found no difference. Four studies found sex differences, some in favor of males, some in favor of females. In some studies rescaling was done to eliminate group differences. Thus, adverse impact appears to be relatively likely. However, validity differences between subgroups were not common; 10 to 12 studies found validity for all groups, but different scoring keys for different groups were sometimes needed.

Rationality versus Empiricism

Pace and Schoenfeldt (1977) argue that evidence of criterion-related validity may not be sufficient to justify biodata usage, and that some rational justification of the relationship between items and the nature of the job is necessary. They note that while some may equate showing job relatedness with demonstrating criterion-related validity, moving beyond raw empiricism and including only rationally defensible items may be prudent. They cite Rosenbaum (1976) as an example of problems with an empirical approach. Rosenbaum used a weighted application blank to predict employee theft in two Detroit area firms. In one firm his cross-validated scoring key included the item "has a Detroit address"; in the other the key included the item "is black." No attempt was made to examine validity for racial subgroups. Despite empirical validity evidence, using race, or a surrogate for race, as part of a scoring key would be difficult, if not impossible, to defend. Other items in Rosenbaum's scoring key include "weight over 150 pounds" and "does not wear eyeglasses." While not as inflammatory as the items above, there does not appear to be any logical basis for their relation to the criterion. The need to consider rationality as well as empirical validity is illustrated by a series of events which we recently encountered. An industry consortium commissioned the development and validation of a selection battery for a particular job. Upon completion, the validated battery was offered to member organizations. A number of organizations declined to use the system because of aspects of item content and scoring that did not "make sense" to decision makers in the organization. In a laboratory study, we found that the face validity of a selection device affects decisions about the fairness and appropriateness of using the device (Sackett & Dreher, 1982). Thus, we concur with Pace and Schoenfeldt's (1977) advice to inject the "hand of reason" into the development of biodata instruments.

A promising approach to moving toward rationality in biodata use is the identification of factors underlying responses to biodata items. For example, Baehr and Williams (1967) factored responses to a 150-item biodata questionnaire. Among the factors identified and named were school achievements, drive to achieve, leadership and group participation, financial responsibility, and early family responsibility. Logical hypotheses about relationships between dimensions and job content can be developed and tested. If stable biodata dimensions can be identified, cross-organizational comparisons becomes feasible, leading to the possibility of validity generalization.

Perhaps the most sophisticated use of biodata is the work of Owens and his colleagues (e.g., Brush & Owens, 1979; Schoenfeldt, 1974; Owens & Schoenfeldt, 1979) who have developed and done extensive research on an assessment-classification model. The model uses scores on biodata factors to form life-history subgroups, with the subgroups representing different patterns of life experiences. Membership in life history subgroups can then be related to membership in, performance in, and satisfaction with various job families. This model can be used for both selection and classification. For selection purposes, one focuses on a given job, determines which life-history subgroups are related to success on that job, and then seeks members of those subgroups to fill job openings. For classification purposes, one focuses on a given individual, determines the life-history subgroups to which the individual belongs, identifies job families where members of those subgroups are likely to succeed, and then places the individual in a job in one of those job families. Clearly, this represents a complex approach which is feasible only for large organizations. It illustrates, however, that the potential of biodata goes well beyond the straightforward empirical keying of application blank responses.

The validity evidence for biodata is strong. A weakness of many applications of biodata, however, is the raw empiricism of the development of the scoring scheme, often resulting in low face validity. A move toward rational item selection and the development of meaningful biodata dimensions through factor analysis may help make biodata more appealing to decision makers in organizations and enhance legal defensibility as well.

REFERENCES

Baehr, M., & Williams, G. B. Underlying dimensions of personal background data and their relationship to occupational classification. *Journal of Applied Psychology*, 1967, *51*, 481–490.

Brush, D. H., & Owens, W. A. Implementation and evaluation for an assessment classification model for manpower utilization. *Personnel Psychology*, 1979, *32*, 369–383.

Owens, W. A., & Schoenfeldt, L. F. Toward a classification of persons. *Journal of Applied Psychology*, 1979, *64*, 569–607.

Pace, L. A., & Schoenfeldt, L. F. Legal concerns in the use of weighted applications. *Personnel Psychology*, 1977, *30*, 159–166.

Reilly, R. R., & Chao, G. T. Validity and fairness of some alternative employee selection procedures. *Personnel Psychology*, 1982, *35*, 1–62.

Rosenbaum, R. W. Predictability of employee theft using weighted application blanks. *Journal of Applied Psychology*, 1976, *61*, 94–98.

Sackett, P. R., & Dreher, G. F. Face validity and empirical validity as determinants of selection decisions. Paper presented at the American Psychological Association Convention, 1982.

Schmidt, F. L., Hunter, J. E., & Caplan, J. R. Validity generalization results for two job groups in the petroleum industry. *Journal of Applied Psychology*, 1981, *66*, 261–273.

Schoenfeldt, L. F. Utilization of manpower: Development and evaluation of an assessment-classification model for matching individuals with jobs. *Journal of Applied Psychology*, 1974, *59*, 583–594.

Chapter 10

The Employment Interview

INTRODUCTION

The employment interview is one of the most intriguing paradoxes in the field of personnel psychology. Despite the fact that a large number of studies have shown that the interview is rarely a valid predictor of job success, the interview remains the most commonly used selection technique (Heneman, Schwab, Fossum, & Dyer, 1980). Thus a major task facing researchers in the personnel field is gaining an understanding of the factors contributing to the inability of the interview to successfully predict job performance.

In the early 1960s, researchers realized that there was little to be gained by further documenting the dismal validity of the employment interview. Two important reviews of the literature (Mayfield, 1964; Ulrich & Trumbo, 1965) concluded that a shift to studies of the decision-making process in the interview was necessary. Both of these reviewers advocated the use of a "microanalytic" strategy, which involved highly controlled experimental studies of the effects on interviewer decisions of a single variable (such as applicant appearance, applicant sex, or whether negative information about an applicant is weighted more heavily if it is obtained early or late in the interview). Through the systematic study of the large number of factors potentially affecting interviewer decisions, it was hoped that an understanding of the determinants of the observed low validity of interviews would emerge. The work of Webster and his students (Webster, 1964) has been viewed as providing the impetus for the microanalytic strategy of interview research, followed by the work of Mayfield and Carlson (e.g., Mayfield & Carlson, 1966; Carlson, Thayer, Mayfield, & Peterson, 1971), and Hakel and Dunnette and their colleagues (e.g., Hakel & Dunnette, 1970).

The use of the microanalytic strategy implied a major change in the research methodology used to study the interview. If one wanted to study the effects of having one negative piece of information about the applicant emerge either early or late in the interview, one needed to *control* when certain information was given. This control was difficult in actual real-life interviews. Thus, the notion of the simulated interview became popular.

Research subjects could be presented with a transcript of an alleged employment interview, asked to read it, and make employment decisions about the applicant. The transcript could easily be doctored by the researcher to present the negative information at the beginning or at the end of the "interview." Thus, the interview was studied without using "real" interviews. Variations on this simulation method included the use of audio or video tapes of interviews carefully scripted by the researcher, and the use of college students playing the part of "interviewer" in simulation studies. At its most extreme, the simulation became quite far removed from actual interviewing practice, e.g., simply presenting a research subject with a written list of characteristics of hypothetical applicant (white, male, 3.5 GPA, earned 30 percent of college expenses) and asking the subject to evaluate the suitability of the applicant for a given job. Due to the prevalence of this last type of research, interview simulation studies are often referred to as "paper people" studies.

The first reading in this section is Arvey and Campion's review of recent microanalytic research. They begin by summarizing the conclusions of six earlier review articles, thus providing a brief overview of the entire history of research dealing with the employment interview. They then discuss recent validity and reliability studies, decision-making studies, studies dealing with the effects of interviewer training, applicant race, sex, and handicap, applicant nonverbal behavior, applicant perceptions of the interviewer, and providing interview training to applicants. They conclude with some interesting speculations as to why the interview is still so extensively used despite all the problems noted in the literature.

The second reading in this section is a review, also by Arvey, of legal aspects of the interview. Arvey reviews how challenges to the interview have fared in court. He notes that there have been relatively few cases to date, but speculates that an increase in the number of suits challenging interview procedures is likely.

The commentary is devoted to two issues. Its first section presents a model of the interview process and argues that interview research has overlooked important aspects of the interview process. For example, many studies examine the effects of an applicant's sex on interview decisions, bypassing the issue of how or why sex affects decisions. Do interviewers ask different questions of men than of women? Or do they ask the same questions but evaluate the responses differently? We argue for the need to examine such questions as these.

The second section of the commentary deals with the issue of giving practical advice on how to conduct interviews. We note that many people are willing to give such advice, but that empirical support for the advice given is often lacking. We argue that any advice given should be research based and make a few cautious suggestions.

REFERENCES

Carlson, R. E., Thayer, P. W., Mayfield, E. C., & Peterson, D. A. Research on the selection interview. *Personnel Journal*, 1971, *50*, 268–275.

Hakel, M. D., & Dunnette, M. D. *Checklists for describing job applicants.* Minneapolis: University of Minnesota, 1970.

Heneman, H. G. III, Schwab, D. P., Fossum, J. A., & Dyer, L. D. *Personnel/Human Resource Management.* Homewood, Ill.: Richard D. Irwin, 1980.

Mayfield, E. C. The selection interview: A re-evaluation of published research. *Personnel Psychology,* 1964, *17,* 239–260.

Mayfield, E. C., & Carlson, R. E. Selection interview decisions: First results from a long term research project. *Personnel Psychology,* 1966, *19,* 41–55.

Ulrich, L., & Trumbo, D. The selection interview since 1949. *Psychological Bulletin,* 1965, *63,* 100–116.

Webster, E. C. *Decision making in the employment interview.* Montreal: Eagle Publishing Co., 1964.

The Employment Interview:
A Summary and Review of Recent Research*

RICHARD D. ARVEY and JAMES E. CAMPION

Industrial and organizational psychologists have been studying the employment interview for more than 60 years in an effort to determine the reliability and validity of judgments based on the assessment device and also to discover the various psychological variables which influence these judgments.

Hundreds of research articles have been published and a number of articles have appeared which summarize the current "state of the art" in this particular research domain. The present article falls within this tradition. Not since Schmitt's 1976 review article in this journal has there been a review of the literature in this area. And indeed, there has been much research dealing with this topic since that time.

The objective of the present article is

threefold: (1) to summarize the findings of relevant recent research dealing with the employment interview, (2) to provide some interpretation of these findings and offer some noticeable trends in this area, and (3) to spell out our thoughts about how and why the employment interview continues to be used despite its unimpressive research record.

Our plan is to first present a model or "schema" of the variables and processes inherent in the employment interview. Second, we will summarize the research findings as reported by earlier reviewers. Third, we will bring these reviews up-to-date by reviewing research published in the past few years. Finally, we will offer some suggestions about possible research avenues and potential methodologies which could be profitably utilized in future exploration of this topic area.

THE EMPLOYMENT INTERVIEW:
A MODEL

Perhaps one way of viewing the variables and processes involved in the em-

* R. D. Arvey and J. E. Campion, "The Employment Interview: A Summary and Review of Recent Research," *Personnel Psychology* 35 (1982), pp. 281–322. Copyright 1982 by Personnel Psychology, Inc. Reprinted/Adapted by permission of the publisher and author. This article is an expanded and revised version of a chapter prepared for *Interpersonal Perceptions* by Cook (in press).

Figure 1

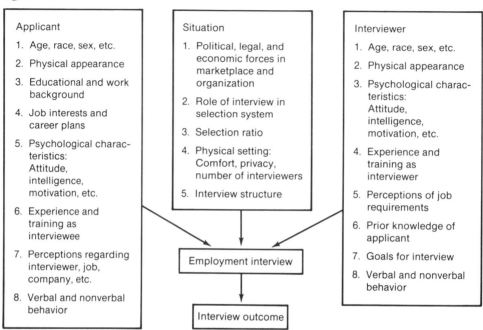

ployment interview is shown in Figure 1. For elaboration of a similar model, the reader is referred to Schmitt (1976). As may be seen in this figure, there are a number of applicant characteristics which may influence the perception of the interviewer and influence the resulting decision. In addition, there are a number of interviewer and situational factors which may also influence the perceptual and judgmental processes. Most of these classes of variables have been the object of research efforts bearing on decision making in the interview. It is expected that some of these variables will interact to influence subsequent decisions. For example, knowing the race and sex of an applicant may differentially shape the expectations, stereotypes, and behaviors of an interviewer which in turn may affect the interview outcome. We have intentionally omitted any hypotheses concerning causality among these variables. We simply do not have sufficient knowl-

edge, even after 60 years or so of research, to accurately pinpoint causal relationships between these variables at the present time.

PRIOR RESEARCH REVIEWS

Wagner (1949)

The first comprehensive review of the research associated with the employment interview was published by Wagner in 1949.

Wagner began his review by noting that one of the earliest investigations of the interview was published in 1911. In that article, Binet reported low reliability for interview-based assessments of intelligence collected from three teachers who had evaluated the same five children. However, the earliest industrial application was in 1915 when Scott reported low reliability for evaluations given by 6 personnel managers who had interviewed the same 36 sales applicants. These disappointing results have become persistent themes for research on the selection interview.

Wagner located 106 articles dealing with the employment interview. However, only 25 reported any empirical work and the remaining articles were nonempirical and represented a "hodgepodge of conflicting opinions." This early review was organized around several issues. One issue concerned the reliability and validity of interview judgments. Reliability was typically assessed by correlating evaluations of different interviewers who had assessed the same job candidates. Validity was typically assessed by correlating interview judgments with some measure of on-the-job performance. When the measure of performance was collected simultaneously with the interview judgments (e.g., interviews conducted with present employee groups), the design was called a concurrent study. In contrast, predictive designs involved following up at a later date those individuals who had been hired and put on the job. In his review, Wagner noted that reliabilities ranged from .23 to .97 with a median r of .57 for the 174 sets of ratings which were reported. Of the 22 validity coefficients summarized by Wagner, the range was from .09 to .94 with a median r of .27. This value was noted as not being particularly high.

Another issue addressed by Wagner was the capacity of interviewers to integrate information. He suggested that while interviewers may be useful in eliciting from candidates information which may not be obtained through other data gathering mechanisms, the combination of this information may best be done in a statistical rather than clinical fashion.

Wagner was favorably impressed with research results regarding the use of a standardized or patterned interview and recommended its use. He also suggested

interviewers consider using several "new" techniques. For example, he suggested that the interviewer might sit on the sidelines and evaluate the candidates as they perform job tasks such as giving a speech or participating in a group discussion—a procedure which today comprises an important component in the assessment center approach. He also recommended using the interviewer to rate the applicant while he (the applicant) carries out some practical job-related task, such as building a simple object. Again, this technique has found wide acceptance today in the work-sample approach to assessing applicant qualifications.

In conclusion, Wagner recommended that the interview may be useful in three situations: (1) where rough screening is needed, (2) where the number of applicants is too small to warrant more expensive procedures, and (3) where certain traits may be most accurately assessed by the interviewer. He also recommended the use of a standardized approach with an emphasis on assessing traits which have been demonstrated to be job related.

Mayfield (1964)

Fifteen years later, Mayfield (1964) summarized the interview research literature since the Wagner (1949) review. He noted that the literature still indicated relatively low reliabilities and validities for the employment interview. However, he went on to recommend that research in this area should shift to studying the decision-making processes inherent in the interview and to determine what factors were producing or influencing the interview judgments. Moreover, he suggested that research should focus on dividing the interview into smaller chunks and studying one or two variables at a time in a more controlled fashion. Thus, he suggested a re-orientation toward more micro-analytical research. After reviewing the literature, Mayfield felt that the research findings tended to support several general statements. Some of the most important of these statements are as follows:

1. General suitability ratings based on unstructured interviews have low reliability.
2. Material is not covered consistently in unstructured interviews.
3. Interviewers are likely to weight the same information differently.
4. Structured interviews result in higher inter-rater reliability.
5. Interview validity is low.
6. If the interviewer has valid test information available, his predictions based on the interview plus test information are usually no better and frequently less valid that the predictions based on the test alone.
7. Interviewers can reliably and validly assess intelligence but have not been shown to be effective in evaluating other traits.
8. The form of the question affects the answers given.
9. The attitude of the interviewer affects the interpretation of interviewees' responses.
10. In unstructured interviews, interviewers tend to talk most.
11. Interviewers are influenced more by unfavorable than favorable information.
12. Interviewers make their decisions quite early in unstructured interviews.

Ulrich and Trumbo (1965)

Published only six months after Mayfield's (1964) review, Ulrich and Trumbo (1965) reached many of the same conclusions. After agreeing that the interview again seemed deficient in terms of its reliability and validity, Ulrich and Trumbo

called attention to the utility of the interview. That is, they suggested that researchers should examine the information gained from the interview separately from information gained from other sources such as employment tests.

These authors also supported Wagner's recommendation for a structured approach to the interview. Further, their interpretation of the evidence suggested that the interview should be used as a selection device with more limited evaluation goals. Specifically, their review indicated that the interview could be useful in assessing interpersonal relations and career motivations. Finally, they reviewed more recent micro-analytic and decision-process research and characterized these studies as interesting and promising for providing insights into interviewing as well as for the field of interpersonal communication in general.

Wright (1969) and Schmitt (1976)

Wright (1969) and later Schmitt (1976) summarized many of the research studies generated in investigating the decision making processes of the employment interview. Both Wright (1969) and Schmitt (1976) relied heavily on the significant research conducted by Webster (1964) and his colleagues at McGill University. The studies summarized by Schmitt and Wright were, indeed, micro-analytical. In fact, Wright (1969) suggested that researchers might profit by returning to the earlier orientation of dealing with the interview more as a totality because the small micro-analytic approach would lead to fragmentation and meaningless results. In a similar vein, Schmitt (1976) indicated that with few exceptions, the studies reviewed suffered from a lack of integration and limited generalizability.

It is worthwhile here to summarize in more depth some of the specific variables and findings reviewed by Schmitt. He organized his review around specific variables and their impact on decision making in the interview.

1. *Information favorability.* A recurring research theme revolved around the relationship between an interviewer's final decision and the kind of information presented in the interview. Schmitt's review of the available data suggested that interviewers reach a final decision quite early in the interview—typically within the first four minutes (Springbett, 1958). Also, data revealed that interviewers weigh negative information more heavily than positive information (Springbett, 1958; Hollman, 1972). Webster (1964) suggests that this phenomenon may be due to the tendency for interviewers to receive feedback only about "bad" employees and, consequently, they may become more sensitive to negative or "knock-out" factors.

2. *Temporal placement of information.* Schmitt reviewed several studies dealing with when during an interview specific positive or negative information is presented. Some of these studies (Farr, 1973) indicated that order has a significant impact and that early impressions are more important than factual information in determining interviewer's judgments. An interpretation was offered by Farr (1973), who suggested that interviewers make up their minds early and then lose attention. Anderson (1960) found that after interviewers form a favorable decision, they spend more time talking than does the interviewee, perhaps to "sell" the candidates on the company. Schmitt suggests that the reason structured interviews are more reliable is because this format may force interviewers to be more attentive, which subsequently enhances their agreement with other raters.

3. *Interview stereotypes.* A considerable number of studies reviewed by Schmitt dealt with the stereotypes interviewers have of idealized job candidates. Research by Sydiaha (1961), Bolster and Springbett (1961), and Hakel, Hollman, and Dunnette (1970) tended to confirm the notion

that interviewers possess stereotypes of idealized successful applicants against which real applicants are judged. However, London and Hakel (1974) presented data suggesting that these stereotypes diminish or are altered as the evaluation of an applicant progresses.

4. *Job information.* Several studies reviewed by Schmitt indicated that as interviewers receive more information about the job to be filled, inter-rater reliability increases (Langdale & Weitz, 1973), and there is a reduction in the impact of irrelevant attributes on decisions (Weiner & Schneiderman, 1974).

5. *Individual differences in the decision process.* Schmitt reviewed several studies investigating whether interviewers use and weight information differently from one another. Hakel, Dobmeyer, and Dunnette, (1970) found evidence indicating that actual interviewers gave different weights to academic standing and job experience factors in evaluating applicants than did undergraduate students serving as raters. Valenzi and Andrews (1973) found wide individual differences in cue utilization resulting in considerable inter-rater differences in evaluating applicants.

6. *Visual cues.* Schmitt's review suggested that nonverbal sources of information were more important than verbal cues and that a combination of both kinds of cues were maximally responsible for obtained differences in ratings of job candidates (Washburn & Hakel, 1973).

7. *Attitudinal, sexual, and racial similarity.* In 1976, Schmitt reviewed a handful of studies which investigated the importance of attitudinal and racial similarities between the interviewer and interviewee. Generally, the findings suggested that attitudinal and racial similarity affected evaluations of candidates (Rand & Wexley, 1975; Wexley & Nemeroff, 1974). In addition, several studies (Dipboye, Fromkin, & Wibach, 1975; Cohen & Bunker, 1975) demonstrated that interviewers tended to give

lower evaluations to female applicants. However, both males and females were more likely to be recommended for traditionally role-congruent jobs.

8. *Contrast effects.* A number of studies reviewed by Schmitt had to do with the investigation of the quality of the preceding interviewees on interview ratings. There appears to be mixed findings in this area. Some studies found a significant, strong, and practical effect (Wexley, Yukl, Kovacs, & Sanders, 1972), while other studies suggest that the effect is either nonsignificant or trivial (Landy & Bates, 1973; Hakel, Dobmeyer, & Dunnette, 1970), especially when professional interviewers are used.

9. *Structured interview guides.* Again, Schmitt found evidence that the use of a structured interview guide increases inter-interviewer agreement.

10. *Miscellaneous.* Carlson, Thayer, Mayfield, and Peterson (1971) conducted a study showing that experienced interviewers were no more reliable than inexperienced interviewers, but that stress for quotas influenced the decisions of experienced interviewers more than the decisions of less experienced interviewers. Also, Carlson (1967) investigated the relative importance of appearance and personal history information.

The review by Schmitt was comprehensive and is illustrative of the kinds of variables and processes investigated in exploring the employment interview during the past 10 years or so.

Arvey (1979)

In 1979, Arvey summarized the research literature concerning evidence of bias in the employment interview with regard to blacks, females, the handicapped, and the elderly. Because of the increased probability that the interview will be subjected to legal scrutiny, Arvey reviewed the legal aspects of the interview. Eight legal cases concerning the employment inter-

view were summarized. It appears litigation has revolved around two basic themes:

1. Do particular kinds of questions convey an impression of an underlying discriminatory attitude or intent? That is, references to "girls" and inquiries to females into non-job related areas such as marital status, parenthood, child care, etc. when these same questions are not presented to male candidates may be sufficient to convince a court that discriminatory "animus" or intent was operating.

2. Does the inquiry operate in such a way as to demonstrate a differential impact or adverse impact on protected groups? If so, is the particular information valid or job related? Organizations should avoid interview questions which operate in such a way as to differentially affect minority groups, unless such questions are job related.

In his review, Arvey specified the processes inherent in the interview which potentially contribute to differential evaluations according to sex, race, etc.: (1) stereotyping and (2) differential behavior emitted during the interview.

Arvey reviewed a number of studies (17) investigating the effects of applicant's sex in interview evaluations. The studies showed in a reasonably consistent fashion that females were generally given lower evaluations than males when these candidates had similar or identical qualifications.

In addition to reviewing studies dealing with sex as a main effect, Arvey reported that research had also focused on several variables predicted to interact with sex to influence the evaluations given. The variable given the greatest attention was the type of job for which the candidates were being considered. Evidence supported the notion that females are given lower ratings for jobs typically "masculine" in nature, whereas males are also given lower ratings when being considered for typically "feminine" jobs (Shaw, 1972; Cohen & Bunker, 1975; Cash, Gillen & Burns, 1977).

A second variable commonly investigated in combination with sex was applicant competence or qualifications. Arvey reported that when qualifications were included, sex tended to account for a relatively small percentage of rating variance. A hypothesized interaction between sex and qualifications where competent females would receive lower evaluations than competent males was given only mixed support. Finally, attractiveness was investigated in combination with sex. Arvey's review indicates that attractive candidates are typically preferred regardless of sex.

Somewhat surprisingly, Arvey could locate only three studies dealing with the race of the applicant in interview evaluations. Even more surprising was that little evidence was found indicating that unfavorable evaluations were given to black candidates compared to whites (Wexley & Nemeroff, 1974; Haefner, 1977; Rand & Wexley, 1975).

In addition, Arvey reviewed two studies investigating the effects of candidates' age on interviewer evaluations and found a relatively strong pervasive effect due to applicant age (Haefner, 1977; Rosen & Jerdee, 1976).

Finally, Arvey reviewed four studies investigating the effects of applicants' handicap status on interview evaluations. Evidence supported the notion that handicapped applicants received lower evaluations in terms of hiring, but higher evaluations on motivational variables. Arvey suggests that interviewers might attribute higher motivation, effort levels, etc. to handicapped individuals filing applications for jobs because of the interviewer's attribution of greater efforts to overcome disabilities on the part of these applicants.

In his conclusion, Arvey identified a number of areas which need research attention.

1. *Methodological problems.* Arvey called attention to the overreliance on resume and paper-and-pencil methodologies in this area. He suggested that greater efforts should be made to study "real" interview situations and to utilize more full stimulus

fields. More use of videotape and face-to-face interview situations are needed. Arvey suggested that researchers need to tap subject pools other than undergraduate and graduate students and that subjects be given the opportunity to view more than *one* particular female, or handicapped individual in studies of this sort. Otherwise, any significant effect observed could be unique to the specific stimulus individuals presented due to other uncontrolled characteristics (hair color, height, etc.).

2. *More research on race, age, and the handicapped.* Arvey specified where more research is needed with each of these minority groups.

3. *Process research.* Arvey indicated that little is known about *why* differential evaluations are made and what goes on in the interview to influence the evaluations. In essence, he called for more research concerning the perceptual processes which might account for the phenomenon observed.

REVIEW OF RECENT RESEARCH

This section of the paper will consist of our summary of the recent literature concerning the employment interview. Basically, process research which has been published since the Schmitt (1976) article will be reviewed. Similarly, research dealing with bias and discrimination in the interview since the Arvey (1979) article will also be reviewed.

This review will be organized by focusing first on the general issues of interviewer reliability, validity, and some methodological concerns. Subsequently, we will review the research on a topic-by-topic basis dealing with many of the topics and variables discussed earlier by Schmitt.

Reliability and Validity

Recent research has not been as pessimistic about the validity and reliability as that of prior years. Interviews conducted by a board or panel appear to be promising as a vehicle for enhancing reliability and validity.

For example, reasonably favorable results were reported by Landy (1976) for the validity of board interviews for police officer selection. Data was gathered in a one-year period during which 399 white male applicants were interviewed and 150 applicants hired. The ratings made by the interviewing board at the end of each interview comprised the predictor variables. A principal components analysis of the averaged interview trait ratings indicated that there were three major components. A principal component analysis of supervisory ratings of performance identified four oblique performance factors. A validity analysis demonstrated rated performance could be predicted from averaged interview factor scores but not from the averaged overall recommendations of the interviewers. When the validity coefficients were corrected for restriction of range on the predictors, 4 of the 12 coefficients were significant (.26, .29, .33, and .34). However, given the number of validity coefficients computed and the statistical manipulations involved, these results are not overwhelming.

A more positive outcome was reported by Anstey (1977) in a 30-year follow-up on the British Civil Service Selection Board procedure. Using Civil Service ranks obtained 30 years later as a criterion measure, he found the validity coefficient for the interview was .35 for a sample of 301 employees. When the coefficient was corrected for restriction of range on the predictor it rose to .66. As in the previous study, the procedure employed here utilized a board interview.

Potential advantages of using group techniques for the interview were also reported by Rothstein and Jackson (1980). They had judges listen to a recording of a simulated interview and make judgments about (1) the possibility that an applicant

would manifest certain related behaviors, and (2) the suitability of the applicant for two occupations, accountant and engineer. They found that the group consensus judgments attributed a patterned of linked behaviors to the applicants that correlated with the known characteristics of those applicants.

However, less encouraging data were reported by Walden (1974) who used 9 psychologists to interview and predict the overall success of 118 candidates in the Royal Australian Navy. The interview did not yield any incremental validity to the predictions made separately from four tests and a life history form.

In another board interview study, Reynolds (1979) investigated the reliabilities for the oral interview used by the Louisiana Department of State Civil Service. Using the evaluations of three rater panels who interviewed 67 job applicants, he found that individual reliabilities varied from .54 to .66 across the seven rating dimensions and when averaged across the three raters the reliability varied from .78 to .85. Finally, the reliability coefficient for the composite final score across the 67 applicants was .90.

Several studies also investigated the general validity of the interview. Heneman, Schwab, Huett, and Ford (1975) found low validities for predicting the job success of social workers. These authors investigated the effects of interview structure, biographical information, and interviewee order on interviewer validity. Fifty-four undergraduates in personnel management and 36 social worker supervisors serving as judges rated 6 currently employed social workers assuming the role of job applicants in videotaped interviews. Non-significant validities were calculated using criterion scores where the criterion measure had been based on a job analysis of the social worker position. Analysis of variance results revealed that only interviewee order had an appreciable effect on interviewer validity. A factor to consider in this study, however, is that the results obtained may have been unique to only these six presently employed social workers who served as interviewees in the study.

Another study published during this time was reported by Latham, Saari, Purcell, and Campion (1980). These investigators utilized the critical incident technique to develop what they refer to as a "situational" interview. Critical incidents are reports by employees or supervisors very familiar with a job of unusually effective or ineffective job behavior. These critical incidents were converted into interview questions in which job applicants were asked to indicate how they would behave in a specific situation. Each answer was rated independently by two or more interviewers on a five-point Likert-type scale with benchmarks developed by job experts to facilitate objective scoring. They found interobserver reliability coefficients of .76 and .79 for hourly workers and foremen respectively. Similarly, the internal consistencies of the interview for the hourly workers and foremen were .71 and .67, respectively. The respective concurrent validity coefficients were .46 and .30. In another study, predictive validity coefficients of .39 and .33 were obtained for women and blacks, respectively. This research suggests that careful linking of job analysis and interview content can have beneficial effects on interviewer reliability and validity.

The themes suggested by research investigating the overall reliability and validity of the interview seem to be twofold:

1. The use of board or panel interviews appears promising as a means of improving the validity and reliability of the interview. Perhaps sharing different perceptions with the different interviewers forces interviewers to become more aware of irrelevant inferences made on non-job-related variables.

2. Use of directly related job analysis and other job information as a basis for interview questions is a useful method of improving the accuracy of the interview. This theme has been suggested previously by Schmitt (1976) and others (e.g., Langdale & Weitz, 1973).

Not much attention has been given to questions of the appropriateness of employment interview. When should an interview be used and when shouldn't it? Guion and Imada (1981) details a situation in which an organization had dropped the use of tests because of possible future litigation and relied on interviewer judgments to hire individuals into jobs requiring high levels of finger dexterity. A male applicant filed a law suit alleging discrimination; the interviewer had claimed to be able to assess dexterity by observing the applicant's hands. While the case was settled out of court, Guion indicates that this is an obvious misuse of the interview when applicants could have been more accurately assessed for dexterity using a test.

Methodological Issues

Two methodological issues have received research attention in recent years: The use of college students as interviewers and the use of paper-and-pencil stimulus "interviews."

Related to the first issue, recent research suggests that the threat to generalizability by using students as interviewers seems minimal. Bernstein, Hakel, and Harlan (1975) found no difference between professional interviewers and college students with respect to variances, inter-rater agreement, and main effects. These authors reviewed six studies and found that the only difference between college students and "real" interviewers was that college students were more lenient in their ratings.

Similar findings were reported by Dipboye, Fromkin, and Wiback (1975), who found no differences between professional interviewers and college students in their investigation of sex bias in the interview. Finally, McGovern, Jones, and Morris (1979) found that college students were equally as sensitive as professional personnel representatives to such interview behavior as eye contact, voice tone, body movements in making interview evaluations. Thus, the issue appears not to be as critical as previously believed.

Because many previous studies of the employment interview have not been based on actual interviews but instead on pencil-and-paper stimulus materials such as transcripts of interviews, application and resume data, and photographs, a serious paradigmatic quesion may be raised about the external validity or generalizability of results using these methods compared to actual interview contexts. Several recent studies suggest that the two kinds of settings and methods yield different results.

Gorman, Clover, and Doherty (1978) raised the question regarding external validity: "Can we learn anything about interviewing real people from interviews of paper people?" They had graduate students and experienced interviewers make judgments based on interviews and on test data alone. Based on the results, the authors concluded that the paper-and-pencil paradigm gives different results than the judgments based on actual interviews.

In a related study, Okanes and Tschirgi (1978) had 67 employment recruiters make pre-interview judgments based on a review of grades, job experiences, campus activity, and faculty references. Following 470 actual interviews of the same candidates, the data indicated significant shifts from an "unable to determine" rating category. Further, half the responses from the "probably recommend" category shifted, with the majority going to "probably not recommend." Huge increases occurred in the "probably not recommend" category. Thus, interviewers tended to be more neg-

ative in their evaluations following face-to-face interviews. This finding suggests two possibilities: (1) that references, resumes, etc. tend to be homogeneously positive and raters cannot make accurate discriminations and (2) interviewers may use face-to-face interviews again as a major source for "knock-out" or negative factors. A study which yielded somewhat contradictory results on this issue was conducted by Ferris and Gilmore (1977). In this study, 120 psychology students evaluated either a male or female applicant's resume, heard the applicant being interviewed, or saw a videotape of the interview, and then assigned a favorability rating to the applicant. Results indicated that mode of presentation had no effect.

Pre-interview information is not to be considered as irrelevant. In a provocative article, Dipboye (1980) argues that post-interview decisions are determined to a large extent by the impressions of applicants formed by interviewers before the interview. He suggests that pre-interview evaluations influence the way the interviewer conducts the interview and, in turn, the way the interview is conducted tends to evoke interviewee behaviors that confirm the interviewer's pre-interview evaluations. Also, Dipboye (1980) argues that interviewers tend to notice, recall, and interpret interviewee behavior in a manner which is consistent with their previous impressions.

An additional methodological note was discussed by Schuh (1978). He suggested that taking notes and avoiding interruptions are important in increasing interviewer listening accuracy. One hundred-twenty-eight were either required or forbidden to take notes and were either interrupted or not. On a 25-item listening accuracy test, the highest rate of accuracy (79 percent) was in the note-taking, no-interruption condition.

Finally, a study conducted by Newman and Kryzstofiak (1979) investigated the differences in research results obtained in resume research when the study was conducted unobtrusively versus the same study conducted when employees were aware that their responses were for a research study. Initially, resumes of a black and a white job applicant were sent to 240 employment managers who believed that these were actual job candidates. One year later, these same companies were contacted and employment managers (perhaps different subjects) asked to participate in a study where again resumes for black and white applicants were presented. These managers were asked to report their expected responses. When managers were aware of the study and asked to provide self-reports of expected responses, these responses were prone to treat the black and white candidates equally and somewhat more favorably. In contrast, employment managers who were unaware of their role in the study tended to make employment decisions based more on the race of the applicant.

In sum, the methodological nature of studies investigating the interview and interview processes seem to reflect a growing sophistication. There is an increasing recognition for the need to capture more realistic stimulus situations and interviewer responses. There is a growing concern about the potential contamination of research results due to method variance.

Decision-Making Studies

There were several studies reporting evidence for various rating errors in the interview. Kopelman (1975) found evidence of contrast bias in evaluations of videotaped interviews of candidates applying for medical school. Contrast effect counted for 11 percent of the decision variance and was most influential in the assessment of candidates of intermediate quality. Additional evidence for the contrast effect was provided by Schuh (1978) who had 120 employment interviewers and 180 managers

view videotaped interviews of four applicants for a management trainee position.

Farr and York (1975) investigated the influence of amount of information on primacy-recency effects in recruitment decisions. Seventy-two college recruiters evaluated hypothetical candidates described in a written booklet. The analysis indicated that recency effects occurred when interviewers were asked to make repeated judgments during the interview, whereas primacy effects were obtained when only a single judgment was required of each interviewer. The amount of information presented about each applicant had no effect upon judgments.

First-impression error was investigated by Tucker and Rowe (1979). They asked 72 students to read and evaluate interview transcripts after examining a letter of reference. Results suggested that interviewers who first read an unfavorable letter were more likely to give the applicant less credit for past successes and to hold the applicant more personally responsible for past failures. Results also indicated that the decision to hire is closely related to interviewers' causal interpretations of past outcomes.

Keenan (1977) reported evidence suggesting that interviewers' personal feelings about candidates influenced their general evaluations of them. In a study of 551 graduate recruitment interviews conducted by 103 interviewers, Keenan found fairly strong relationships between interviewers liking of the candidate and overall evaluations. The relationship between ratings of candidates' intelligence and general evaluation was only slightly reduced when the effect of liking was held constant. This was interpreted as suggesting that there are both affective and cognitive components in interviewers' evaluations of candidates.

London and Poplawski (1976) found sex differences in rating when they presented 120 male and 120 female undergraduates with information about two groups of hypothetical company employees. Their hypothesis that the distinctiveness in amount and favorability of information would result in differential stereotypes about the two groups was not confirmed. However, they did find that female subjects gave consistently higher ratings.

Finally, Leonard (1976) studied the relationship between cognitive complexity and similarity error in an interview context. Sixty-four undergraduates conducted interviews with confederates who played roles as job applicants. Similarity was manipulated by the confederate roles and by information given to the subjects. Subjects high on cognitive complexity were more likely to evaluate similar applicants more positively, suggesting that cognitive complexity may moderate the impact of similarity error.

A recent study by Osburn, Timmrick, and Bigby (1981) reported that interviewers made accurate discriminations among job candidates on the basis of a videotaped interview when they evaluated the candidates on specific and relevant job dimensions. However, interviewers making evaluations on more generalized job dimensions were not as accurate.

In sum, the recent studies tend to confirm earlier research demonstrating that indeed, interviewers tend to produce ratings or evaluations which are influenced by contrast, primacy-recency, first impressions, personal feelings, and other factors. On the positive side, some research again indicates that when evaluations are in the form of specific predictions of job behavior, less distortion is found.

There have been three studies published which investigated interviewer decision time. Huegli and Tschirgi (1975) examined a sample of 183 recruiting interviews conducted by 16 interviewers at Ohio University. Interviews were recorded and time monitored. The interviewers also completed a questionnaire describing their decision making during the interview. Find-

ings indicated that 77 percent of the interviewers reported making decisions during the interview itself but only 33 percent during the first half of the interview. This finding is at variance with those of previously reported studies which indicated that decisions were made very early in the interview. Huegli and Tschirgi also found that hire decisions were made sooner than no-hire decisions; however, interview length was unrelated to the hiring decision. Finally, decisions were unrelated to time of day.

A second study in this area was by Tucker and Rowe (1977), who conducted an experiment to determine whether consulting the application blank prior to the interview would delay the initial decision. Twenty-eight experienced recruiters interviewed a role-playing job candidate. Half the interviewers were provided with an application blank prior to the interview and half were not. Results indicated that not providing the application blank did not slow down the initial decision nor did it reduce the interviewer's confidence in the decision.

In a third study, Tullar, Mullins, and Caldwell (1979) investigated the effects of interview length (15 minutes versus 30 minutes) and applicant quality (high versus low) on interviewer decision time. Sixty experienced employment counselors observed a videotaped interview and made a decision as soon as they felt they had sufficient information. The interviewers took significantly more time to make the decision for the high quality candidates and for the longer interview.

Interviewer training. Several recent studies have been conducted investigating the effects of training on interviewer evaluations. For example, recent work by Vance, Kuhnert, and Farr (1978) investigated the use of behavioral rating scales in reducing interviewer error. Behavioral rating scales reflect the relevant dimensions of expected job behavior and have anchor points which illustrate in specific behavioral terms the behavior expected to be demonstrated by a candidate in order to be rated at each of the various points on the scales. Audiorecordings of interviews were rated by 112 undergraduates assigned to one of four conditions in a 2 × 2 factorial design. One independent variable was whether interviewers utilized the behavioral rating scales or a typical graphic rating scale to make their predictions. Use of the behavioral rating forms tended to reduce rater error and to increase rater accuracy. The second independent variable was whether the interviewers were trained or not trained to reduce rater error tendencies. However, no significant effects for training were found.

Heneman (1975) also investigated interviewer training in an effort to improve interview reliability and validity. Thirty-six students, half of whom were trained, viewed six videotapes of either structured or unstructured interviews. While the results showed no significant differences in interviewer validity, however, there was one significant finding involving inter-rater reliability. When untrained subjects observed an unstructured interview, reliabilities were lower. The training program consisted of a 90-minute lecture on use of job descriptions, rating scales, and how to avoid rating errors.

It should be noted that findings of no effects due to interviewer training is not consistent with earlier findings (Wexley, Sanders, & Yukl, 1973; and Latham, Wexley, & Purcell, 1975). This early work suggested that intensive workshops that included practice with feedback and group discussions helps to eliminate rating errors of contrast, halo, similarity, and first impression.

A recent field study shedding some indirect light on the impact of training interviewers was reported by Mayfield, Brown, and Hamstra (1980). After training life insurance managers to interview candidates using a particular kind of structured interview format and questions, their responses to a standard taped interview were analyzed in one study, and the actual ratings on specific interview items for 163 real job candidates were analyzed in a second study. Results demonstrated that it was possible for managers to reach agreement on a number of their evaluation ratings, that there was a stable factorial structure for the ratings which made good intuitive sense, and that many of these ratings were related to the final selection decision.

It is apparent that much, if not all, of the research dealing with interviewer training has focused largely on the psychometric aspects of interviewer ratings and evaluations as indicants of the success or failure of the training program. Alternative dependent variables should also be considered. For example, interviewer behavior during the interview should be examined. Do interviewers ask fewer "leading" questions during interviews as result of training? Are they less nervous? Do they elicit more information from interviewees? Do they follow a logical sequence during the interview? Are interviewees more comfortable with interviewers who have completed training? Note that these kinds of questions have relatively little to do with the psychometric aspects of their ratings (e.g., halo) but are more *behavioral* in nature. It may be profitable to focus on these kinds of questions when examining interviewer training.

One good example of this orientation is the work of Howard and Dailey (1979) and Howard, Dailey, and Gulanick (1979). These two studies examine the effectiveness of the University of Houston's Interviewing Institute using behavioral evaluation methodology. This training institute is conducted over five days and involves presentations, demonstrations, and exercises as well as three videotaped practice interviews occurring on the first, third, and fourth days. The subjects were 41 institute participants, heterogeneous with respect to employer and geographic location. All were engaged in jobs that involved interviewing and the median interviewing experience prior to the seminar was six months.

The researchers developed behavioral measures to evaluate interviewer improvement in six areas: questioning techniques, interview structure, interviewing supportiveness, techniques of rapport, active listening skills and attention to relevant material. Two types of evaluations were made. Behavioral data were collected for each interview, and these data were combined into six rationally developed scales for the six interviewing dimensions. The scaling of each behavior was accomplished by tallying and/or timing these target behaviors by the raters as they viewed the videotapes. Raters scored the tapes independently, and their mean scores were used as the unit of analysis. At the conclusion of each viewing, each rater also provided a subjective rating of the interviewer's skill level for each dimension on a nine-point scale. These evaluations were made on the first and last practice interviews. Undergraduate students, none of whom had any involvement in the Interviewing Institute, were used as judges. They participated in an 18-hour training program in which the scaled dimensions were explained and discussed. Archival Interviewing Institute tapes were viewed, rated, and discussed until all raters were confident that they understood the dimensions to be assessed. Finally, the trained judges were asked to evaluate first and last practice interview videotapes that had been coded and randomized.

Following this rather elaborate procedure, the researchers found significant and large differences in all six areas for both the count of behavioral incidence as well as the skill ratings. Another finding which might be of interest to future work was the close correspondence found between the behavioral change measure and the participant's self-report of change when based on a comparison between a retrospective pre-measure rather than a traditional pre-measure.

Minority characteristics. Since the review by Arvey (1979), several studies have investigated the effect of interviewee handicap on interviewer judgment. Stone and Sawatzki (1980) conducted a study where 90 MBA students observed one of six taped interviews which portrayed three conditions of disability (psychiatric, physical, and no disability) and two levels of work history (good or bad). Results indicated that applicants who were described as having two hospitalizations for nervous breakdowns had a lower probability of being hired. More obvious was the finding that applicants with good work histories were given significantly higher evaluations.

A study by Hastorf, Wildfogel, and Cassman (1979) reviewed acknowledgement of handicap as a tactic in social interaction. Subjects observed two videotapes of handicapped individuals being interviewed and then chose the one with whom they would prefer to work on a cooperative task. The results suggested that subjects prefer to work with interviewees who acknowledged their handicap.

In another study, Snyder, Kleck, Strenta, and Mentzer (1979) found that subjects avoided a person wearing a metal leg brace and chose to view movies with normal subjects, when avoiding the handicapped person could masquerade as a movie preference.

An excellent review of the literature involving employment decisions regarding the handicapped was provided by Rose (1980). In his review, Rose indicates that there are four classes of variables potentially related to discrimination against the handicapped. These are: (1) the nature of the handicap, (2) other personal attributes of the applicant or worker, (3) the nature of the job or occupation being considered, and (4) characteristics of the potential employing organizations, particularly the characteristics of the hiring and assessment procedures used by the organization. In addition, Rose delineates the methodological limitations of the research published in this area.

Applicant sex was examined as a potential factor influencing interview decisions by Simas and McCarrey (1979). Eighty-four male and female personnel officers who were classified into either high, moderate, or low authoritarian groups, evaluated male and female applicants in simulated videotaped recruitment interviews. The "high authoritarian" personnel officers of both sexes rated the male applicants more favorably than female applicants and indicated that they would make more job offers to the male applicants. Thus, this study is in line with research reported earlier.

Rosen and Mericle (1979) investigated the effects of applicant sex in selection decisions under conditions of strong or weak fair employment policy statements. Seventy-eight municipal administrators evaluated a resume of either male or female applicants in a condition when an organizational statement indicated strong emphasis on fair employment practices or a condition when only lip service was paid to fair practices. Results indicated that preference for male or female applicants was not influenced by strength of the policy statements. However, interviewers recommended lower starting salaries for females under the strong fair employment condition. The authors interpreted this finding as perhaps due to greater resistance on the part of managers or a reaction against hiring constraints imposed by strong affirmative action policies which represent a subtle attempt to undermine the career prospects for recently hired females.

The study by Ferris and Gilmore (1977) reviewed earlier revealed a marginally significant effect for male applicants to be given slightly higher favorability ratings than female applicants.

The impact of male and female applicant attractiveness was investigated by Heilman and Saruwatari (1979). These authors hypothesized that because attractive women are regarded as more feminine than unattractive women and attractive men are regarded as more masculine than unattractive men, attractive women would be at a disadvantage when being considered for stereotypically "male" jobs or jobs believed to require predominantly masculine talents for successful job performance. In this study, 45 male and female college students evaluated application forms and photos of male and female candidates who had been judged to be attractive or unattractive. The candidates were evaluated for either a clerical or management position on a number of dependent variables such as qualifications, hiring recommendation, starting salary, etc. Analyses revealed that attractive females were given higher evaluations when being considered for the clerical job compared to unattractive females, but attractive females were rated lower when considered for the management job. In contrast, for male candidates attractiveness always led to higher evaluations regardless of the job.

Cann, Siegfried, and Pearce (1981) conducted a study investigating whether sex and physical attractiveness would be less potent variables in influencing interviewers' decisions if the interviewers postponed an overall judgment and rated specific qualifications first. Results indicated that sex and physical attractiveness variables were still significant even after specific qualifications had been evaluated.

The recent studies dealing with applicant sex as it influences interviewers' decisions reflect a growing awareness that contextual and other personal variables need to be considered in combination with the sex variables. The phenomenon may be more complex than previously realized. An example of this thinking is reflected in a study by Heilman (1980) where she suggests "that situational factors can preclude, or at least reduce, the likelihood of discriminatory personnel decisions although they leave the decisionmaker's stereotypic belief system intact" (p. 387). As support for this proposition, Heilman (1980) reported the results of an investigation in which interviewers evaluated a female candidate's application form along with interviewing seven additional candidates. The sex of the applicant pool was manipulated so that the pool included either 12.5, 25, 37.5, 50, or 100 percent females. Results indicated that when women represented 25 percent or less of the total pool, the female applicant was evaluated more unfavorably than if the pool reflected a larger percentage of female applicants.

In a study involving a design where fictitious but realistic resumes were mailed to actual employers, McIntyre, Moberg, and Posner (1980) examined the pattern of responses made by organizations. Resumes of minority (black or female) and non-minority job candidates were sent to 458 companies. The data indicated that males were given preferential treatment compared to females. In addition, results indicated that the black applicants were given more favorable treatment than white applicants. This is one of the few studies examining the impact of race on interviewers' decisions. The results are in line with those noted by Arvey in his earlier review.

An earlier study conducted by Newman (1978) discussed the results of sending bogus resumes for black and white applicants to 240 companies. (This was the unobtrusive condition discussed in the Newman and Krzystofiak (1979) study above.) These data indicated a definite trend for larger companies to discriminate in favor of blacks. As noted previously, Newman and Krzystofiak (1979) found that this tendency did not generalize to situations where employment managers were aware of their role in the study. It should be noted, however, that these last examples are studies of recruitment rather than of employment interviews.

An unpublished doctoral study by Mullins (1978) used videotaped stimulus materials to examine interviewer ratings of high and low quality candidates role-played by black and white males. The study used a between-subjects design where 176 white business administration students viewed videotaped interviews. Results indicated that the most important variable influencing interview ratings was applicant quality, but that the black applicant was significantly favored over the white applicant. The study is difficult to interpret, however, because the differences obtained may be due to the specific individuals used in the stimulus condition.

One additional study focused on linguistic patterns as they related to interview judgments. Kalin and Rayko (1978) had 203 students evaluate audiotapes of job applicants for four jobs varying in social status. Five applicants spoke with an English-Canadian accent and five applicants spoke with a definite foreign accent (Italian, Greek, Portuguese, West African, and Slovac). Applicants with foreign accents were given lower ratings for the higher status jobs, but higher ratings for the lower status jobs.

No studies were found which investigated the effects of applicants' age in the interview.

In addition, no studies have fully examined the stereotyping process as it affects the interview. For example, McCauley, Stitt, and Segal (1980) reviewed the different definitions and conceptualizations of stereotyping, and proposed a Baysian model. This model might be a useful framework to examine bias in interview situations. As yet, little has been done to examine stereotyping or any other processes which might contribute to differential evaluations.

Nonverbal behavior. An area of considerable recent research interest has been in the study of interviewees' nonverbal behavior. For example, Amalfitano and Kalt (1977) examined eye contact effects on job interviewers' evaluations. Photographs were taken of a male and a female in two eye positions: looking straight into the camera and looking downward. Forty-four job interviewers in an employment agency were randomly assigned to one of the four photographs. Each subject was told to assume that he or she was interviewing the person for a job as a management trainee. Not surprisingly, the results showed interviewees were more likely to be hired if they looked straight ahead rather than down. In addition, straight-ahead lookers were rated as being more alert, assertive, dependable, confident, responsible, and as having more initiative.

In another study, Imada and Hakel (1977) examined the influence of nonverbal communication and of different methods of observing a job applicant. Seventy-two female subjects saw either an immediate or non-immediate applicant while serving as an interviewer, observer, or television observer. Immediacy was manipulated through several nonverbal modes of communication: eye contact, smiling, posture, interpersonal distance, and body orientation. Results again indicated that nonverbal communication had a significant effect on interviewer impressions and subsequent decisions.

In another study, Young and Beier (1977) examined the effects of nonverbal behavior of job applicants on subsequent hiring evaluations. Thirty-two interviewees were instructed to use one of four styles of nonverbal behavior during the videorecording of a short job interview with standard content. Videotaped interviews were watched by 22 raters who assessed nonverbal cue usage and by 50 judges who evaluated the applicants as prospective employees. Applicants who demonstrated greater amounts of eye contact, head moving, smiling, and other nonverbal behaviors were rated higher. In fact, these nonverbal behaviors accounted for more than 80 percent of the rating variance.

Tessler and Sushelsky (1978) investigated the effects of eye contact and social status on the evaluation of applicants in the employment interview. The dependent variable was interviewers' perception of how well the applicant was suited for a job requiring self-confidence. Using 60 undergraduates acting as interviewers, the results indicated statistically significant effects for eye contact and social status.

In another study, McGovern and Tinsley (1978) had 52 personnel representatives review videotaped job interviews in which verbal content was identical, but the interviewees' nonverbal behavior differed. An interviewee in the "low" condition exhibited minimal eye contact, low energy level, lack of affect, low voice modulation, and a lack of speech fluency. The "high" interviewee demonstrated opposite behavior. Nonverbal behavior was found to have a significant affect on almost every rating made by the subjects. Of the 26 subjects who saw the high nonverbal candidate, 23 would have invited him or her for a second interview. All 26 of the subjects who saw the low nonverbal candidate would not have recommended a second interview. This study was later replicated by McGovern et al. (1979) using college students as subjects; the obtained results closely paralleled results obtained with the professional interviewers.

In another study, Sigelman, Elias and Danker-Brown (1980) examined the effects of verbal and nonverbal interview behaviors of 88 mentally retarded adults on employability ratings given them by a panel of six students in a personnel management course. Verbal and nonverbal behaviors were relatively independent, with the former accounting for most of the predicted variance in the criterion variables. Persons whose speech was intelligible, who spoke at length, and who responded appropriately to questions were most likely to make a favorable impression.

A similar research finding was reported

by Sterrett (1978) who showed videotapes of a male job applicant displaying various intensities of body language to 160 managers in the insurance industry. The hypothesis that different body language intensities would result in differential perceptions of eight traits typically considered in the employment interview (ambition, motivational drive, self-confidence, self-organization, responsibility, verbal ability, intelligence, and sincerity) was *not* supported. Thus, these results are somewhat contradictory to other findings.

Hollandsworth, Kazelskis, Stevens, and Dressel (1979) performed a discriminant analysis to determine the relative importance of verbal and nonverbal dimensions of communication during 338 on-campus interviews conducted by 73 different college recruiters. The criterion variable was a four-point rating on "Would you hire?" The result showed the following order of importance among the independent variables: appropriateness of verbal content, fluency of speech, composure, body posture, eye contact, voice level, and personal appearance.

In sum, it appears that interviewees' nonverbal behavior influences interviewers' evaluations. However, the magnitude of influence appears to be generally less than what is communicated verbally by the candidate. One problem inherent in many of these studies is the possibility that interviewers use nonverbal information to provide them cues about the verbal skills of the interviewees. Thus, while researchers may manipulate the verbal-nonverbal variables in an orthogonal manner, interviewers may not view these factors as independent.

It is also possible that these factors do not operate in a linear fashion to influence interviewers. For example, it may be that interviewers first screen on verbal dimensions, and subsequently shift the perceptual-judgmental process into more nonverbal domains.

Interviewee variables. There were two studies which examined the impact of interviewees' self-perceptions on interview outcome. King and Manaster (1977) had 98 female undergraduates complete a body-image satisfaction scale, self-cathexis scale, Janis-Field-Eagly self-esteem scale, and a job-interview-performance-expectation scale prior to participating in a 15-minute simulated job interview. After the job interview, subjects rated their own performance. Independently, two judges rated each subjects' videotaped performance. Interviewees' expectations for job interview success were significantly related to both body satisfaction and self-esteem. High self-esteem interviewees tended to overestimate how well they had performed in the interview. However, actual interview performance was not related to either self-esteem or body attitudes.

In another study, Keenan (1978) asked job candidates in 551 employment interviews to give estimates of the level of their motivation to succeed immediately before and after each interview. Their level of state anxiety was also measured by a state-trait anxiety inventory before each interview. At the end of the interview, interviewees indicated how much they liked the interviewer personally. They estimated both the likelihood of their being successful in the interview and the likelihood that they would accept the job with the company. Interviewers were asked to evaluate each candidate and to estimate his or her chances of being offered a job. Not surprisingly, when candidates liked interviewers personally, they were more optimistic about their chances of success and were more willing to accept potential job offers. Candidates were also more confident of success at the end of the interview when their pre-interview motivation had been high. However, interviewer evaluations of candidates were most favorable when the level of the interviewee pre-interview motivation had been intermediate. The job candidates' state anxiety was unrelated to favorability of interviewers' evaluations.

These last two studies suggest that interviewees' pre-existing motives and expectations influence their own perceptions of performance during the interview. Interviewees who have high motivation to do well, have high self-esteem, etc. may tend to aggrandize their actual performance, and in some cases, this may operate to detract from their interview performance.

Relatively few studies have investigated the variables, motivational states, and perceptions of the interviewee as they impact the interview process. Yet it makes intuitive sense that conditional factors associated with interviewees will influence interview judgments.

Perceptions of interviewer. It is becoming increasingly apparent that interviewers must become more aware of their own impact on job applicants. In a recent article, Rynes, Henemen and Schwab (1980) reviewed research that examined the influence of organization recruitment practices on applicant attitudes and job choice behaviors. It was found that recruiting representatives, administrative practices, and evaluation procedures all are potentially important influences on job-seeker attitudes and behaviors.

The influence of the interviewer on interviewee attitudes and behavior was recently demonstrated by several investigators. Keenan and Wedderburn (1975) demonstrated the effects of the interviewer's nonverbal behavior on interviewees' impressions. They found that the interviewer's use of nonverbal approval in role-played interviews with 24 undergraduates resulted in a more favorable interviewee impression when compared to nonverbal disapproval. Contrary to expectations, interviewees' talking rate was not affected.

In a follow-up study, Keenan (1976) found that nonverbal approval by interviewers in mock interviews also resulted in the interview being evaluated as more re-

laxed and the interviewee as having made a better impression when judged by undergraduate observers.

In a related study, Schmitt and Coyle (1976) asked 237 college students who had been interviewed for jobs at a college placement center to describe their reactions to the interviewer and their subsequent decisions. Results indicated that perceived interviewer personality, manner of delivery, and adequacy of information influenced the interviewees' evaluations of the interviewer, the company, and the likelihood of job acceptance. Finally, Fisher, Ilgen, and Hoyer (1979) surveyed 90 undergraduate seniors and explored the effect of information favorability and source on applicant perceptions of source credibility and job offer acceptance. Results indicate that interviewers were the least credible source and that giving negative job information enhanced source credibility but decreased probability of job offer acceptance.

It is obvious that research investigating the characteristics of the interviewer and the subsequent impact on interviewee behavior and perceptions is sorely lacking. Equally lacking is research which investigates the role of tight or open labor markets on subsequent interviewer behavior and impact on interviewees. For example, in recent years the Houston labor market for professional engineers in the oil industry has been incredibly competitive. Since individuals with these skills are relatively rare, the role of interviewers and recruiters is considerably changed and reflect a "sell the company" perspective. The nature of job interviews is thus quite different.

Interviewee training. There have been numerous studies exploring how interviewees might be taught to present themselves more effectively in the employment interview. An early example of this was reported by Stevens and Tornatzky (1976), who assigned 26 clients from a drug abuse treatment program to a treatment group and a control group. The treatment was a workshop stressing behavioral interview skills, such as preparing for an interview, application completion, grooming, nonverbal communications, and phrasing of answers to interview questions. A six-month follow-up showed no significant attitudinal differences between the two groups but those who participated in the interview workshop obtained higher paying jobs.

Hollandsworth, Dressel, and Stevens (1977) developed a job interviewee skills workshop based on behavioral procedures such as modeling, role playing, and directive feedback, and compared it with a traditional lecture-discussion group approach, as well as with a no-treatment control group. Forty-five college seniors were randomly assigned to one of three groups. Subjects participated in a videotaped, simulated job interview prior to and following each workshop. Analyses of self-report and behavioral measures indicated that the group learning the behavioral procedures made significant gains in percentage of time eye contact was maintained during the interview. The discussion group was found to be superior to the behavioral and control groups in ratings of their ability to explain individual skills, and expression of feelings and personal opinions relevant to the interview. Also, interviewees in the discussion group demonstrated a significant increase in length of speaking time. Thus, both procedures seem to increase interviewee's effectiveness in the interview.

In a follow-up study, Hollandsworth and Sandifer (1979) developed a workshop combining the most effective components of behavioral and discussion group methods, and trained 46 masters level counselors in the use of the workshop. Subsequently, the counselors conducted over 320 workshops for approximately 4,100 secondary and post-secondary students. Data generated by these counselors indicate that the workshop was easily employed as a training procedure. Also, stu-

dent participants reported high levels of satisfaction with the procedure.

Keith, Engelkes, and Winborn (1977) also investigated training with 66 rehabilitation clients and found experimental support for training effects in improving knowledge of job openings and the number of job leads obtained. Further, 8 of the 19 trainees obtained jobs; whereas, only 6 of 47 control group members were able to find employment. Finally, Speas (1979) assigned 56 prison inmates to 1 of 4 treatment conditions or to a waiting list control group. The four instructional techniques were model exposure, role-playing, model exposure plus role-playing, and model exposure and role-playing with videotaped feedback. Judges' ratings of videotaped simulated pre- and post-treatment interviews, and personnel interviewers' ratings of follow-up interviews served as criterion measures. Post-test results indicated that both the model-plus-role-playing and the model-exposure-plus-role-playing-plus-videotaped-feedback treatments were significantly more effective than the control procedure on all dependent variables.

Lastly, two research efforts focused on issues related to what the interviewees can do to impress the interviewers. Harlan, Kerr, and Kerr (1977) administered questionnaires to 274 managers, supervisory personnel, clerical workers, and high school students, and asked them to indicate whether or not they would discuss various types of work-related factors if they were interviewed as applicants for employment. A systematic tendency was found for respondents to prefer to discuss motivator rather than hygiene factors. Responding to a modified version of the questionnaire, 20 professional employment interviewers indicated that it is, in fact, wise to emphasize motivator and de-emphasize hygiene factors if the applicant's intent is to maximize the likelihood of being offered a job.

In a second study, Campion (1978) investigated college recruiter evaluations of

170 job applicants. His findings suggested that undergraduate GPA, membership in fraternity or sorority, and membership in a professional society were significantly related to interviewers' overall general impression, personal liking, and the chances for further consideration in the interview.

This domain of investigation might profit by researchers becoming more acquainted with literature available on impression management. The recent text by Schlenker (1980) provides a review of the theory and research in impression management which may facilitate further research efforts in this area.

SUMMARY AND CONCLUSIONS

It is clear that research dealing with the employment interview is progressing. A number of themes seem to emerge when reviewing what has been happening in this area over the past five years or so.

1. *There has been an increase in research investigating bias in the interview.* One theme which has been fairly consistent is the increased interest in the employment interview as a vehicle for discrimination against women and minority group job candidates. While attention has focused predominantly on group membership variables and how they influence interview decisions, more recent research has investigated the effects of other variables in interaction with protected group status on interviewers decision making. However, as we noted earlier, much more research needs to be conducted in this area. With the potential for increased legal challenges to this selection devise, there is a pressing need for more research in this area before court decisions are made on the basis of preliminary and perhaps methodologically flawed studies.

2. *More variables associated with the interview have been under investigation.* Our review has revealed a number of studies dealing with variables which previously received little research attention. For example, researchers have begun to probe such topics as nonverbal behavior, interviewees' perceptions of interviewers, interviewees' self-perceptions, and interviewee training. For the most part, these factors are associated with the interviewee rather than with the interviewer. It is somewhat surprising that so little research has been conducted in the past dealing with applicant perceptions. Perhaps researchers felt that it would be somewhat intrusive to ascertain the perceptions, reactions, and so forth of actual candidates.

An important "hole" in the interview research area is the lack of investigations dealing with situational factors as they impact interviewers. For example, what effect does accountability have on interviewer decisions? Are the decisions of interviewers whose evaluations are more "public" more accurate and valid than interviewers who make their decisions with little visibility? Rozelle and Baxter (in press) conducted a study which shows that interviewers who were under conditions of higher accountability and responsibility were more discriminating in their judgments and showed more agreement with other interviewers.

3. *Researchers are becoming more sophisticated in their research methodologies and strategies.* As mentioned earlier, interview research in the past utilized resume designs for the most part. However, recent research efforts are incorporating more realistic stimulus sets into the designs. The use of videotape to capture the employment interview as it progresses is more frequent, due possibly to the lower costs and greater flexibility of these technologies.

Moreover, researchers are realizing the limitations of resume and other pencil-and-paper methodologies and conducting research to demonstrate the differences in results using these methodologies compared to more realistic stimulus and response settings. Some of the ethical issues associated with conducting research unobstrusively without informed consent are being discussed (e.g., Newman & Kryzsto-fiak, 1979). Yet, it is possible that results may have little relevance to employment interviews and associated evaluation processes unless interviewers and interviewees remain unaware of the purpose of the interview.

There has, however, been little attention to more sophisticated decision-making models and their incorporation into research on the interview. For example, the Brunswick lens model, policy-capturing methods, and Baysian techniques have seldom been employed. In one interesting, but complex study, Bigby (1977) used a Baysian model to determine the revisions of probabilities made by interviewers evaluating job candidates. His use of a Baysian framework seems particularly fruitful for future research.

Similarly, it appears as if some of the validity generalization models may be applicable. Distribution of validity coefficients based on the interview might be made available and applied to the same kinds of analyses indicated by Schmidt and Hunter (1977) and Callender and Osburn (1980).

4. *Research continues to be micro-analytic in nature.* The research reviewed here has most certainly been micro-analytic. Researchers have continued to examine a narrow range of variables when conducting their research on the employment interview. In our view, this approach still continues to have some usefulness despite Schmitt's (1976) admonition about conducting research which is too narrow. In our opinion, research efforts should focus on capturing more real or actual behavior and evaluation processes, but continue to focus on relatively small components of the interview and interview process.

5. *Researchers investigating the employment interview have neglected related research in the person-perception literature.* In review-ing recent research, one is struck by the almost complete lack of attention which has been paid to the person-perception literature by researchers in this area. It is almost as if industrial and organizational psychologists have studied the employment interview in isolation from the rest of psychology, perhaps even ignoring the fact that the phenomenon under investigation is essentially a perceptual process. Thus, one of the recommendations we can offer to researchers in this area is to pay far greater attention to what is going on in other domains regarding person-perception processes. Specifically, researchers could profit from examining the interview from various theoretical models and frameworks which stem from other areas. These include the following:

a. Attribution models. The employment interview and the evaluation judgments made by interviewers are surely a function of the attributions they make about interviewees. Hastorf, Schneider, and Polefka (1970) summarized the literature in this area some time ago, which suggests that interviewers form judgments about the success or failure of interviewees and frequently base their judgments on their attributions of cause of the success or failure experience was due to internal factors associated with interviewees or to external factors beyond the control of the interviewee. Moreover, attribution models differentiate between factors which are assumed to be stable (e.g., ability, difficulty of task) or relatively unstable (e.g., effort, luck). The implications which stem from attribution models are clear: Interviewers will form judgments about interviewees according to the attributions they make for the cause of past achievements on the part of job candidates. Yet, attribution theory has been virtually ignored in the investigation of the employment interview process.

b. Impression formation and management. A large body of literature has accumulated concerning how individuals form impressions and how impressions may be managed. For example, Schlenker (1980) summarizes a large number of studies dealing with the impact of nonverbal behavior on perceiver impressions and judgments. These studies have been conducted largely by social psychologists. Similarly, Hastorf, Schneider, and Polefka (1970) indicate that an area under investigation is how perceivers combine evaluation data. The same kind of question appears in the employment interview—How do interviewers combine informational cues? Yet, some of the scaling and weighting models developed by psychologists in person-perception research have received little or no attention from industrial psychologists.

   c. *Implicit personality theory.* The notion that individuals have their own idiosyncratic models of personality, which differ from those of other judges, is seldom recognized by researchers dealing with the employment interview as a broader phenomenon. With the exception of Hakel (1969), few researchers in industrial psychology pay much attention to this perceptual model.

   In short, the mainstream of research dealing with the employment interview typically has been without the benefit of the more broadly applicable person-perception models. The price has been somewhat shortsighted and situationally bound research, without the guidance of broader based theories.

Why the Interview Is Still Used

   Perhaps the glaring "black hole" in all previous reviews and in the current literature concerns the issue of why use of the interview persists in view of evidence of its relatively low validity, reliability, and its susceptibility to bias and distortion. We know of only one organization that hires a candidate sight unseen, based on resume

information only.[1] One only has to ask researchers in this area the question, "Would you hire somebody without an interview?" to learn that they most likely would also rely on the interview. Why is this so?

   The reasons for this persistence seems to fall into four major categories: (1) the interview is "really" valid, (2) the interview is not valid but certain practical considerations make it the popular choice, (3) the interview may not be valid but certain psychological processes act to maintain great faith in the selection tool, and (4) the interview is not valid but it does other things well. Let us examine each of these categories in more detail.

   1. *The interview is "really" valid.* Under this category fall two quite different explanations. First, some individuals will argue that while the evidence is quite pessimistic overall, the interview still yields valid judgments on several observable interpersonal dimensions of behavior which are manifested in the interview—such as sociability and verbal fluency. In essence, the interview is viewed as a "work sample" of these behaviors and is more likely to allow accurate assessment of these variables than of less observable dimensions. In fact, the evidence tends to support this contention. Validity coefficients are typically higher and more likely to be significant for dimensions of behavior which are more easily observed in the interview. Note, however, that this argument pertains to the accurate and valid assessment of these specific traits or behavioral dimensions and not necessarily to the job behavior.

   Similarly, there are some important areas than cannot be assessed well or easily with available psychometric technology. One obvious example is the prediction of work motivation. Attempts to develop motivation measures for predicting work be-

---

[1] Apparently, the Princeton University Philosophy Department hires on the basis of credentials only. (Personal communication, Dianne Horgan.)

havior generally have not been successful outside of a counseling context. Consequently, decision makers have relied on the interview and discussions of job interest, career plans, likes and dislikes, etc. to make assessments in this important area.

A second argument extended under this category is that while the interview is valid, typical psychometric models are not sufficiently capable of detecting interview validity. The reasoning here is that restriction of range, small samples, homogeneous applicant populations, and so forth, act to attenuate the correlations observed. We may simply expect too much in the way of psychometric evidence. A similar argument is that the linear model is not appropriate for tapping the relationships between interview judgments and on-the-job performance. Possibly more representative would be a multiple-hurdle approach, where candidates need to exhibit a certain "minimum" level of a variable, and subsequent differences beyond this minimum do not translate into differences in job performance.

A related issue concerns whether researchers have been validating the wrong theory. It may be that certain specific interviewers are more valid than others and that researchers perhaps should focus on differences among interviewers rather than the validity of the interview, collapsed across interviewers. In essence, the argument is "some interviewers are more valid than others."

2. *The interview may not be valid but certain practical considerations make it the popular choice.* For example, Wagner (1949) recommended the use of the interview when the number of applicants is too small to warrant more elaborate procedures. Historically, and especially since 1964, the use of other "more sophisticated" selection devices (such as tests) have been limited primarily to those jobs with a large number of incumbents where empirical validation was feasible and clearly cost effective. The vast majority of jobs have too few incumbents to permit traditional validation studies. This may be changing, however. It appears organizations have become increasingly interested in conducting cooperative and industry-wide validation studies. This taken together with recent successes in validity generalization research (Perlman, Schmidt, & Hunter, 1980; Schmidt, Gast-Rosenberg & Hunter, 1980) suggest that test usage may become more viable as an alternative or supplement to interviews for selection purposes.

Related to this are arguments regarding the practicality of using job tryouts as a means of assessing applicants' job skills and work experience claims. A practical alternative has been to have the applicant describe and discuss work history in the employment interview, a variation of the oral trade test. Here again, we anticipate change. This is due to the increased interest many organizations have shown for developing content-valid test and work samples as evaluation aids in assessing specific work skills and experience. Finally, some organizations use practicality arguments for removing tests and other scored selection devices in the aftermath of the 1964 Civil Rights Act. It was erroneously thought that total reliance on the unscored selection interview would lessen EEO problems. Of course, the courts have ruled otherwise (Arvey, 1979).

Finally, the interview may be used to forecast to applicants the nature of the job and the responsibilities. Wanous (1980) has called to our attention the importance of exposing job candidates to accurate information about the job which help create realistic job expectations for job candidates. Obviously, the interview can facilitate the communications of accurate job information.

3. *The interview is not valid, but interviewers maintain great faith and confidence in their judgments.* This argument stems predominantly from the work emerging from

the decision-making research. While evidence in clinical settings has clearly documented the superiority of statistical prediction over clinical, people are quite prone to place confidence in highly fallible interview judgments (Kahneman & Tversky, 1973).

Kahneman and Tversky (1973) and Einhorn and Hogarth (1978) discuss this phenomenon under the term, *the illusion of validity*. Essentially, interviewers ignore base rate information, do not pay attention to disconfirming evidence, and over-depend on case-specific information in making their judgments. Einhorn and Hogarth (1978) argue that the persistence of judgmental confidence is a function of the frequency and importance of both positive and negative feedback and the effects of experience. In actual employment settings, interviewers tend to receive very little feedback concerning their judgments, and some people have argued (e.g., Webster, 1964) that what evidence they do receive is about their errors, Thus, the feedback loops to interviewers seem tenous and distorted, which might well act to maintain confidence in the judgments made.

4. *The interview is not valid, but it does other things well.* In this category rest, for the most part, untested assumptions regarding the value of the interview for accomplishing objectives unrelated to the selection decision. One example is selling the candidate on the job. College recruiters often report that much of their time is devoted to this, especially in high demand areas in engineering and business. Interviewers also answer questions from the candidates. Many candidates, but especially those with experience, come prepared with specific questions important for their personal decisionmaking. Finally, many view the interview as an important public relations tool. Interviewers are potential consumers and recruiters, as well as voting citizens, and their perceptions of fair treatment could have important consequences. For these reasons, then, the elimination of the employment interview would probably be very unpopular among both interviewers and job applicants. Of course, whether these objectives are best met by the employment interview rather than by other means is an unanswered research question.

A Final Word

The employment interview continues to be widely used. While many industrial and organizational psychologists are well aware of the findings concerning the limited reliability and validity of this device, few would advocate eliminating the interview or not interviewing candidates to fill jobs in their own organizations (e.g., research assistants and secretaries). Thus, research on the interview continues and will continue as long as it is a widely used technique. One direction industrial psychologists should move toward is that of converting the findings and results stemming from research into applied guidelines for interviewers and interviewees. There is a dearth of guidelines and suggestions concerning the improvement of interview effectiveness based on research findings. Instead, many guidelines, suggestions, "how to interview" workshops, and techniques are founded on intuition, beliefs, and what seems more comfortable, rather than on research results. There need to be greater efforts made to merge research with application in this domain. There are some exceptions, however. Both Schmitt (1976) and Hakel (in press) have made efforts to translate research findings into practical guidelines. Perhaps these efforts should receive greater attention among practitioners.

REFERENCES

Amalfitano, J. G., & Kalt, N. C. Effects of eye contact on the evaluation of job applicants. *Journal of Employment Counseling,* 1977, *14,* 46–48.

Anderson, C. W. The relation between speaking times and decision in the employment interview. *Journal of Applied Psychology,* 1960, *44,* 267–268.

Anstey, E. A 30-year follow-up of the CSSB procedure, with lessons for the future. *Journal of Occupational Psychology,* 1977, *50,* 149–159.

Arvey, R. D. *Fairness in selecting employees.* Reading Mass.: Addison-Wesley Publishing, 1979.

Arvey, R. D. Unfair discrimination in the employment interview: Legal and psychological aspects. *Psychological Bulletin,* 1979, *86,* 736–765.

Bernstein, V., Hakel, M. D., & Harlan, A. The college student as interviewer: A threat to generalizability. *Journal of Applied Psychology,* 1975, *60,* 266–268.

Bigby, D. G. A Bayesian analysis of employment interviewers' errors in processing position and negative information. Unpublished masters thesis, University of Houston, 1977.

Binet, A. Nouvelles recherches sur la mesure du niveau intellectual, etc. *L'Annu Psychol,* 1911, *17,* 182.

Bolster, B. I., & Springbett, B. M. The reactions of interviewers to favorable and unfavorable information. *Journal of Applied Psychology,* 1961, *45,* 97–103.

Callender, J. C., & Osburn, H. G. Development of a test of a new model for validity generalizations. *Journal of Applied Psychology,* 1980, *65,* 543–558.

Campion, M. A. Identification of variables most influential in determining interviewers' evaluations of applicants in a college placement center. *Psychological Reports,* 1978, *42,* 947–952.

Cann, E., Siegfried, W. D., & Pearce, L. Forced attention to specific applicant qualification: Impact of physical attractiveness and sex of applicant biases. *Personnel Psychology,* 1981, *34,* 65–76.

Carlson, R. E. The relative influence of appearance and factual written information on an interviewer's final rating. *Journal of Applied Psychology,* 1967, *51,* 461–468. (b)

Carlson, R. E., Thayer, P. W., Mayfield, E. C., &

Peterson, D. A. Research on the selection interview. *Personnel Journal,* 1971, *50,* 268–275.

Cash, T. F., Gillen, B., & Burns, D. S. Sexism and "beautyism" in personnel consultant decision making. *Journal of Applied Psychology,* 1977, *62,* 301–307.

Cohen, S. L., & Bunker, K. A. Subtle effects of sex role stereotypes on recruiters' hiring decisions. *Journal of Applied Psychology,* 1975, *60,* 566–572.

Cook, M. *Interpersonal perceptions.* Metheuens, in press.

Dipboye, R. L. Self-fulfilling prophecies in the selection recruitment interview. Unpublished manuscript, 1980.

Dipboye, R. L., Fromkin, H. L., & Wiback, K. Relative importance of applicant sex, attractiveness, and scholastic standing in evaluation of job applicant resumes. *Journal of Applied Psychology,* 1975, *60,* 39–43.

Einhorn, H. J., & Hogarth, R. M. Confidence in judgment: Resistance of the illusion of validity. *Psychological Review,* 1978, *85,* 395–416.

Farr, J. L. Response requirements and primacy-recency effects in a simulated selection interview. *Journal of Applied Psychology,* 1973, *57,* 228–233.

Farr, J. L., & York, C. M. Amount of information and primacy-recency effects in recruitment decisions. *Personnel Psychology,* 1975, *28,* 233–238.

Ferris, G. R., & Gilmore, D. O. Effects of mode of presentation, sex of applicant, and sex of interviewer on simulated interview decisions. *Psychological Reports,* 1977, *40,* 566.

Fisher, C. D., Ilgen, D. R., & Hoyer, W. D. Source credibility, information favorability, and job offer acceptance. *Academy of Management Journal,* 1979, *22,* 94–103.

Gorman, C. D., Clover, W. H., & Doherty, M. E. Can we learn anything about interviewing real people from "interviews" of paper people? Two studies of the external validity of a paradigm. *Organizational Behavior and Human Performance,* 1978, *22,* 165–192.

Haefner, J. E. Race, age, sex, and competence as factors in employer selection of the disadvantaged. *Journal of Applied Psychology,* 1977, *62,* 199–202.

Hakel, M. D. Significance of implicit personality theories for personality research and theory. *Proceedings of the American Psychological Association,* 1969.

Hakel, M. D., Dobmeyer, T. W., & Dunnette, M. D. Relative importance of three content dimensions in overall suitability ratings of job applicants' resumes. *Journal of Applied Psychology,* 1970, *54,* 65–71.

Hakel, M. D., Hollman, T. D., & Dunnette, M. D. Accuracy of interviewers, certified public accountants, and students in identifying the interests of accountants. *Journal of Applied Psychology,* 1970, *54,* 115–119.

Hakel, M. D. Employment Interview. In K. M. Rowland & G. R. Ferris, (Eds.), *Personnel management: New perspectives.* Newton, Mass.: Allyn & Bacon, in press.

Harlan, A., Kerr, J., & Kerr, S. Preference for motivator and hygiene factors in a hypothetical interview situation: Further findings and some implications for the employment interview. *Personnel Psychology,* 1977, *30,* 557–566.

Hastorf, A. H., Schneider, D. J., & Polefka, J. *Person perception.* Reading, Mass.: Addison-Wesley Publishing, 1970.

Hastorf, A. H., Wildfogel, J., & Cassman, T. Acknowledgement of handicap as a tactic in social interaction. *Journal of Personality and Social Psychology,* 1979, *37,* 1790–1797.

Heilman, M. E. The impact of situational factors on personnel decisions concerning women: Varying the sex composition of the applicant pool. *Organizational Behavior and Human Performance,* 1980, *26,* 386–396.

Heilman, M. E., & Saruwatari, L. R. When beauty is beastly: The effects of appearance and sex on evaluations of job applicants for managerial and nonmanagerial jobs. *Organizational Behavior and Human Performance,* 1979, *23,* 360–372.

Heneman, H. G. III. The impact of interviewer training and interview structure on the reliability and validity of the selection interview. *Proceedings of Academy of Management,* 1975, 231–233.

Heneman, H. G. III, Schwab, D. P., Huett,

D. L., & Ford, J. L. Interviewer validity as a function of interview structure, biographical data, and interview order. *Journal of Applied Psychology,* 1979, *60,* 748–753.

Herzberg, F., Meusner, B., & Snyderman, B. B. The motivation to work (2nd ed.). New York: John Wiley & Sons, 1959.

Hollandsworth, J. G., Dressel, M. E., & Stevens, J. Use of behavioral versus traditional procedures for increasing job interview skills. *Journal of Counseling Psychology,* 1977, *24,* 503–509.

Hollandsworth, J. G., Jr., Kazelskis, A., Stevens, J., & Dressel, M. E. Relative contributions of verbal, articulative, and nonverbal communication to employment decisions in the job interview setting. *Personnel Psychology,* 1979, *32,* 359–367.

Hollandsworth, J. G., & Sandifer, B. A. Behavioral training for increasing effective job-interview skills: Follow-up and evaluation. *Journal of Counseling Psychology,* 1979, *26,* 448–450.

Howard, G. S., & Dailey, P. R. Response-shift bias: A source of contamination of self-report measures. *Journal of Applied Psychology,* 1979, *64,* 144–150.

Howard, G. S., Dailey, P. R., & Gulanick, N. A. The feasibility of informed pretests in attenuating response-shift bias. *Applied Psychological Measurement,* 1979, *3,* 481–494.

Huegli, J. M., & Tschirgi, H. An investigation of the relationship of time to recruitment interview decision making. *Proceedings of Academy of Management,* 1975, 234–236.

Imada, A., S., & Hakel, M. D. Influence of nonverbal communication and rater proximity on impressions and decisions in simulated employment interviews. *Journal of Applied Psychology,* 1977, *62,* 295–300.

Kahneman, D., & Tversky, A. On the psychology of prediction. *Psychological Review,* 1973, *80,* 251–273.

Kalin, R., & Rayko, D. S. Discrimination in evaluative judgments against foreign-accented job candidates. *Psychological Reports,* 1978, *43,* 1203–1209.

Keenan, A. Effects of the nonverbal behavior of interviewers on candidates' performance.

Journal of Occupational Psychology, 1976, *49*, 171–176.

Keenan, A. Some relationships between interviewers' personal feelings about candidates and their general evaluation of them. *Journal of Occupational Psychology*, 1977, *50*, 275–283.

Keenan, A. The selection interview: Candidates' reactions and interviewers' judgments. *British Journal of Social and Clinical Psychology*, 1978, *17*, 201–209.

Keith, R. D., Engelkes, J. R., & Winborn, B. B. Employment-seeking preparation and activity: An experimental job-placement training model for rehabilitation clients. *Rehabilitation Counseling Bulletin*, 1977, *21*, 259–265.

King, M. R., & Manaster, G. J. Bossy image, self-esteem, expectations, self-assessments, and actual success in a simulated job interview. *Journal of Applied Psychology*, 1977, *62*, 589–594.

Kopelman, M. D. The contrast effect in the selection interview. *British Journal of Educational Psychology*, 1975, *45*, 333–336.

Kryger, B. R., & Shikiar, R. Sexual discrimination in the use of letters of recommendation: A case of reverse discrimination. *Journal of Applied Psychology*, 1978, *63*, 309–314.

Landy, F. J., & Bates, F. Another look at contrast effects in the employment interview. *Journal of Applied Psychology*, 1973, *58*, 141–144.

Langdale, J. A. & Weitz, J. Estimating the influence of job information on interviewer agreement. *Journal of Applied Psychology*, 1973, *57*, 23–27.

Latham, G. P., Saari, L. M., Purcell, E. D., & Campion, M. A. The situational interview. *Journal of Applied Psychology*, 1980, *65*, 422–427.

Latham, G. P., Wexley, K. M., & Purcell, E. D. Training managers to minimize rating errors in the observation of behavior. *Journal of Applied Psychology*, 1975, *60*, 550–555.

Leonard, R. L. Cognitive complexity and the similarity-attraction paradigm. *Journal of Research in Personality*, 1976, *10*, 83–88.

London, M., & Hakel, M. D. Effects of appli-

cant stereotypes, order, and information on interview impressions. *Journal of Applied Psychology*, 1974, *59*, 157–162.

London, M., & Poplawski, J. R. Effects of information on stereotype development in performance appraisal and interview contexts. *Journal of Applied Psychology*, 1976, *17*, 239–260.

Mayfield, E. C. The selection interview: A reevaluation of published research. *Personnel Psychology*, 1964, *17*, 239–260.

Mayfield, E. C., Brown, S. H., & Hamstra, B. W. Selective interviewing in the life insurance industry: An update of research and practice. *Personnel Psychology*, 1980, *33*, 725–739.

McCauley, C., Stitt, C. I., & Segal, M. Stereotyping: From prejudice to prediction. *Psychological Bulletin*, 1980, *87*, 195–208.

McGovern, T. V., Jones, B. W., & Morris, S. E. Comparison of professional versus student ratings of job interviewee behavior. *Journal of Counseling Psychology*, 1979, *26*, 176–179.

McGovern, T. V., & Tinsley, H. E. Interviewer evaluations of interviewee nonverbal behavior. *Journal of Vocational Behavior*, 1978, *13*, 163–171.

McIntyre, S., Moberg, D. J., & Posner, B. Z. Preferential treatment in preselection decisions according to sex and race. *Academy of Management Journal*, 1980, *23*, 738–749.

Mullins, T. W. Racial attitudes and the selection interview: A factorial experiment. Unpublished doctoral dissertation, University of Houston, 1978.

Newman, J. M. Discrimination in recruitment: An empirical analysis. *Industrial and Labor Relations Review*, 1978, *32*, 15–23.

Newman, J. M., & Kryzstofiak, F. Self-reports versus unobstrusive measures: Balancing method variable and ethical concerns in employment discrimination research. *Journal of Applied Psychology*, 1979, *64*, 82–85.

Okanes, M. M., & Tschirgi, H. Impact of the face-to-face interview on prior judgments of a candidate. *Perceptual and Motor Skills*, 1978, *46*, 322.

Osburn, H. G., Timmrick, C., & Bigby, D. Effect of dimensional relevance and accuracy of simulated hiring decisions by employment interviewers. *Journal of Applied Psychology,* 1981, *66,* 159–165.

Pearlman, K., Schmidt, F. L., & Hunter, J. E. Validity generalization results for tests used to predict a job proficiency and training success in clerical occupations. *Journal of Applied Psychology,* 1980, *65,* 373–406.

Rand, T. M., & Wexley, K. N. Demonstration of the effect, "similar to me," in simulated employment interviews. *Psychological Reports,* 1975, *36,* 535–544.

Reynolds, A. H. The reliability of a scored oral interview for police officers. *Public Personnel Management,* 1979, *8,* 324–328.

Rose, G. L. Employment decisions regarding the handicapped: Experimental evidence. Presentation at American Psychological Association, Montreal, September 1, 1980.

Rosen, B., & Jerdee, T. H. The influence of age stereotypes on managerial decisions. *Journal of Applied Psychology,* 1976, *61,* 428–432.

Rosen, B., & Mericle, M. F. Influence of strong versus weak fair employment policies and applicants' sex on selection decisions and salary recommendations in management simulation. *Journal of Applied Psychology,* 1979, *64,* 435–439.

Rothstein, M., & Jackson, D. N. Decision making in the employment interview: An experimental approach. *Journal of Applied Psychology,* 1980, *65,* 271–283.

Rozelle, R. M., & Baxter, J. C. The influence of role pressure on the perceiver: Judgments of videotaped interviewers varying judge accountability and responsibility. *Journal of Applied Psychology,* in press.

Rynes, S. L., Heneman, H. G. III, & Schwab, D. P. Individual reactions to organizational recruiting: A review. *Personnel Psychology,* 1980, *33,* 529–542.

Schlenker, B. R. *Impression management.* Monterey, Calif.: Brooks/Cole Publishing, 1980.

Schmidt, F. L., & Hunter, J. E. Development of a general solution to the problem of validity generalizations. *Journal of Applied Psychology,* 1977, *62,* 529–540.

Schmitt, N. Social and situational determinants of interview decisions: Implications for the employment interview. *Personnel Psychology,* 1976, *29,* 79–101.

Schmitt, N., & Coyle, B. W. Applicant decisions in the employment interview. *Journal of Applied Psychology,* 1976, *61,* 184–192.

Schuh, A. J. Contrast effect in the interview. *Bulletin of the Psychonomic Society,* 1978, *11,* 195–196.

Shaw, E. A. Differential impact of negative stereotyping in employee selection. *Personnel Selection,* 1972, *25,* 333–338.

Sigelman, C. K., Elias, S. F., & Danker-Brown, P. Interview behaviors of mentally retarded adults as predictors of employability. *Journal of Applied Psychology,* 1980, *65,* 67–73.

Simas, K., & McCarrey, M. Impact of recruiter authoritarianism and applicant sex on evaluation and selection decisions in a recruitment interview analogue study. *Journal of Applied Psychology,* 1979, *64,* 483–491.

Snyder, M., Kleck, R., Strenta, A., & Mentzer, S. Avoidance of the handicapped: An attributional ambiguity analysis. *Journal of Personality and Social Psychology,* 1979, *37,* 2297–2306.

Speas, C. M. Job-seeking interview skills training: A comparison of four instructional techniques. *Journal of Counseling Psychology,* 1979, *26,* 405–412.

Springbett, B. M. Factors affecting the final decision in the employment interview. *Canadian Journal of Psychology,* 1958, *12,* 13–22.

Sterrett, J. H. The job interview: Body language and perceptions of potential effectiveness. *Journal of Applied Psychology,* 1978, *63,* 388–390.

Stevens, W., & Tornatzky, L. The effects of a job-interview skills workshop on drug-abuse clients. *Journal of Employment Counseling,* 1976, *13,* 156–163.

Stone, C. I., & Sawatzki, B. Hiring bias and the disabled interview: Effects of manipulating work history and disability information of the disabled job applicant. *Journal of Vocational Behavior,* 1980, *16,* 96–104.

Sydiaha, D. Bales' interaction process analysis of personnel selection interviews. *Journal of Applied Psychology,* 1961, *45,* 393–401.

Tessler, R., & Sushelsky, L. Effects of eye contact and social status on the perception of a job applicant in an employment interviewing situation. *Journal of Vocational Behavior,* 1978, *13,* 338–347.

Tucker, D. H., & Rowe, P. M. Consulting the application form prior to the interview: An essential step in the selection process. *Journal of Applied Psychology,* 1977, *62,* 283–287.

Tucker, D. H., & Rowe, P. M. Relationship between expectancy, causal attributions, and final hiring decisions in the employment interview. *Journal of Applied Psychology,* 1979, *64,* 27–34.

Tullar, W. L., Mullins, T. W., & Caldwell, S. A. Effects of interview length and applicant quality on interview decision time. *Journal of Applied Psychology,* 1979, *64,* 669–674.

Ulrich, L., & Trumbo, D. The selection interview since 1949. *Psychological Bulletin,* 1965, *63,* 100–116.

Valenzi, E., & Andrews, I. R. Individual differences in the decision process of employment interviewers. *Journal of Applied Psychology,* 1973, *58,* 49–53.

Vance, R. J., Kuhnert, K. W., & Farr, J. L. Interview judgments: Using external criteria to compare behavioral and graphic scale ratings. *Organizational Behavior and Human Performance,* 1978, *22,* 279–294.

Wagner, R. The employment interview: A critical summary. *Personnel Psychology,* 1949, *2,* 17–46.

Waldron, L. A. The validity of an employment interview independent of psychometric variables. *Australian Psychologist,* 1974, *9,* 68–77.

Wanous, J. P. *Organizational entry: Recruitment, selection, and socialization of newcomers.* Reading, Mass.: Addison-Wesley Publishing, 1980.

Webster, E. D., (Ed). *Decisionmaking in the employment interview.* Montreal, 1964.

Wexley, K. N., & Nemeroff, W. F. The effects of racial prejudice, race of applicant, and biographical similarity on interviewer evaluations of job applicants. *Journal of Social and Behavior Sciences,* 1974, *20,* 66–78

Wexley, K. N., Sanders, R. E., & Yukl, G. A. Training interviewers to eliminate contrast effects in employment interviews. *Journal of Applied Psychology,* 1973, *57,* 233–236.

Wexley, K. N., Yukl, G. A., Kovacs, S. Z., & Sanders, R. E. Importance of contrast effects in employment interviews. *Journal of Applied Psychology,* 1972, *56,* 45–48.

Wright, O. R., Jr. Summary of research on the selection interviews since 1964. *Personnel Psychology,* 1969, *22,* 341–413.

Young, D. M., & Beier, E. G. The role of applicant nonverbal communication in the employment interview. *Journal of Employment Counseling,* 1977, *14,* 154–165.

Reading 22

Unfair Discrimination in the Employment Interview*

R. D. ARVEY

LEGAL ASPECTS OF THE INTERVIEW

How has the employment interview fared when challenged in court by individuals claiming that they were discriminated against unfairly as a result of an interview? In almost all cases, the shifting-burden-of-

proof standard is used. Cases in which the use of the interview in employment deci-

* Excerpted from R. D. Arvey, "Unfair Discrimination in the Employment Interview: Legal and Psychological Aspects," *Psychological Bulletin* 86 (1979), pp. 736–65. Copyright 1979 by the American Psychological Association, Reprinted/Adapted by permission of the publisher and author.

Table 1
Litigation Concerning Interviews

Case	Alleged discrimination against	Adverse impact shown	Validity of interview shown	Comment
Rowe v. General Motors (1972)	Blacks	Yes	No	Subjective standards said to be ready mechanism for discrimination
Equal Employment Opportunity Commission Decision No. 72-0703 (1971)	Blacks	Yes	No	Hiring system must permit review
Hester v. Southern Railway Company (1974)	Blacks and females	No		Interview noted to be subjective
United States v. Hazelwood School District (1976)[a]	Females	Yes	No	
Weiner v. County of Oakland (1976)	Females	Yes	No	
Harless v. Duck (1977)	Females	Yes	Yes	Interview successfully defended on the basis of content validity
King v. New Hampshire Department of Resources and Economic Development (1977)	Females	Yes	No	Questions in interview were indicative of discriminatory intent
Bannerman v. Department of Youth (1977)	Females	No		Adverse impact not shown

[a] Later appealed to the Supreme Court, but issues associated with the interview were not a part of this later decision.

sions has been challenged are shown in Table 1.

Perhaps the first and most often cited case in this area is *Rowe* v. *General Motors*, decided by the Fifth Circuit Court of Appeals. The decision actually had to do with the performance appraisal used by the company in determining promotions, but because the case is used frequently as a controlling case, it is important to review it here. The decision dealt with the subjective nature of employment decisions, an obvious component of the interview. In this situation, foremen's subjective evaluations of hourly employees' ability, merit, and capacity were used in making promotion decisions. After determining that adverse impact had occurred regarding blacks, the court felt that the performance appraisal system violated Title VII in several ways: First, foremen were given no written instructions pertaining to the qualifications necessary for promotion; second, the standards that were determined to be in

control were vague and subjective. In summarizing the decision, the court added that

> all we do today is recognize that promotion/transfer decisions which depend almost entirely upon the subjective evaluation and favorable recommendation of the immediate foreman are a ready mechanism for the discrimination against blacks, much of which can be covertly concealed. (*Rowe* v. *General Motors*, p. 450)

Thus, this decision casts some doubt on the employer's use of a subjective decision-making process if such a process resulted in adverse impact.

In a 1971 decision, the EEOC ruled that an employer's decision not to hire a black woman because of her "poor attitude" during the interview was in violation of Title VII. In this case, the EEOC cited a number of court decisions to establish that if discriminatory impact of a hiring system is shown, "it is essential that the system be objective in nature and be such as to permit review" (EEOC Decision No. 72-0703, p. 437).

The employment interview was also given court scrutiny in *Hester* v. *Southern Railway Company*. A black female applicant was denied a clerical job partly as a result of the interview process. Although the district court ruled that an adverse impact had been demonstrated and that the interviewing procedure was faulty because of its subjective nature and because it was based on "no formal guidelines, standards and instructions," the court of appeals overturned the decision because there was no clear proof that these selection procedures (tests, interviews, etc.) had resulted in adverse impact.

A more recent case involved a court decision that struck down the use of the interview used in hiring teachers. In *United States* v. *Hazelwood School District,* the court noted that the subjective interview process used in making selection decisions was similar to the vague and subjective criteria used in *Rowe* v. *General Motors*. It is instructive to read what the court said in this instance:

> Principals are free to give whatever weight they desire to subjective factors in making their hiring decisions. Indeed, one principal testified that interviewing an applicant was "like dating a girl, some of them impress you, some of them don't." . . . No evidence was presented which would indicate that any two principals apply the same criteria—objective and subjective—to evaluate applicants. (*United States* v. *Hazelwood School District,* p. 7576)

An interesting 1976 case (*Weiner* v. *County of Oakland*) dealt specifically with the kinds of questions asked in the interview and their possible bias. Mrs. Weiner applied for the position of intermediate planner and was given an oral interview

that apparently was scored in some systematic way. Although Mrs. Weiner was ranked third on the list of eligible applicants, four men were hired to fill the available positions. As grounds for not hiring Mrs. Weiner, the county was only able to suggest some doubt about the flexibility of her approach to planning.

The court ruled that Mrs. Weiner had demonstrated an adverse impact. At this point, the burden of proof shifted to the county, which had to prove that it had valid business requirements justifying its conduct. The county attempted to defend the use of the interview by asserting that the decision reached was based on subjective evaluations made during the interview that were in no way the product of sex discrimination.

The court, however, reviewed the kinds of questions that were asked of Mrs. Weiner and found that they were suggestive of bias against women. Questions such as whether her husband approved of her working, whether her family would suffer if she were not home to prepare dinner, and whether she was able to work compatibly with young, aggressive men were asked. The court ruled that these kinds of questions during the interview, along with other facts, were sufficient to substantiate the charge of discrimination and awarded back pay and attorney's fees.

A recent case provided sufficient evidence to the court regarding the interview to survive challenge. *Harless* v. *Duck* involved a situation in which a woman brought a class action suit against a midwestern police department charged with discrimination in hiring because of sex. The department used, along with several other tests, a structured oral interview that consisted of approximately 30 questions posed to each candidate by a team of interviewers. The questions were designed to determine an "applicant's communication skills, decision-making and problem-solving skills, and reactions to stress situations." It was determined that 43 percent of the females failed the oral interview, compared with 15 percent of the males. After some discussion of proper sample sizes for detecting significant differences, the court determined that the discrepancy in pass rates was significant and that the interview did indeed have a discriminatory or adverse effect. In defending the validity of the interview, the organization relied on two sources of evidence:

1. The oral interview had construct and content validity. The expert witness for the organization testified that the structured oral interview portions of the exam, which consisted of hypothetical questions simulating situations likely to be encountered by patrolmen, measured several dimensions identified through job analysis that differentiate among persons who would be better patrol officers if put in a position to perform patrol functions.

2. A significant relationship between performance in the interview and performance at the police academy was shown. A previous Supreme Court decision (*Washington* v. *Davis;* . . . had affirmed the use of measures of training success as legitimate criteria against which to validate a selection instrument. The court found this evidence sufficient to demonstrate the validity of the interview.

Another recent case is *King* v. *New Hampshire Department of Resources and Economic Development,* in which a court of appeals found that the questions asked of a female who applied for the job of a state meter patrol officer helped to establish that discriminatory intent had occurred. In this instance, a female applicant was asked "whether she could wield a sledge hammer, whether she had any construction industry experience, and whether she could 'run somebody in' " (p. 670), none of which were related to the job in question. The court indicated that the employer's dis-

criminatory intent was proved largely by its own words and actions.

Finally, in *Bannerman* v. *Department of Youth Authority* the use of a panel interview was challenged. Candidates applying for a parole agent job were interviewed by a panel of three interviewers who were asked to judge each candidate in relation to stated "critical class requirements" (e.g., demonstrated ability to relate to youths and to gain their respect and confidence). However, the plaintiffs were not able to demonstrate to the satisfaction of the court any discriminatory bias against women; that is, there was no statistically significant difference between the pass rates of the males and females interviewed by the panel.

It is somewhat surprising that more cases dealing with interviews have not been litigated. It seems apparent that one direction in which the courts are moving is toward the exploration of the nature of and kinds of questions asked and the information elicited in the interview in more depth; that is, the content of the interview is being more fully examined. For example, inquiries during the interview that might convey to the applicant the impression that persons in a protected class will be discriminated against will now be viewed as discriminatory. In one case (cited in Babcock, Freedman, Norton, & Ross, 1975), the EEOC and the New York Human Rights Commission concluded that a New York law firm had violated Title VII when interviewers emphasized to female applicants that the firm had only one female lawyer and that she was assigned to an area of work traditionally performed by women. The conclusion was that "the interviews are conducted in such a manner as to express a preference for men and to discourage women from pursuing employment with respondent firm" (Babcock et al., 1975, p. 380).

Among these same lines, the specific kinds of information elicited on application forms and during interviews are being liti-gated. Managers are currently confused about what they may or may not ask dur-ing an interview. Although I do not pro-vide a review of these more specific in-terview inquiries, it should be noted that litigation revolves around two basic themes:

1. Do particular kinds of questions con-vey an impression of an underlying dis-criminatory attitude or intent? That is, ref-erences to "girls" and inquiries into non-job-related areas such as marital status, parenthood, child care, and so on, when these same questions are not presented to male candidates, may be sufficient to con-vince a court that discriminatory animus or intent is operating.

2. Does the inquiry operate in a way that demonstrates a differential impact or adverse effect on protected groups? If so, is the particular information valid or job re-lated? Thus, organizations should avoid in-terview questions that operate in such a way as to differentially affect minority groups, unless such questions are job re-lated.

Guidelines concerning preemployment inquiries have been set forth by a variety of state human rights commissions as well as by a set of guidelines issued by the EEOC. For example, the Washington State Human Rights Commission (1979, pp. 2923–2926) stated the following to be unfair and illegal preemployment inquiries when they cannot be shown to be job related: (a) all inquiries related to arrests; (b) any inquiry concerning citizenship; (c) specific inquiries concerning spouse, spouse's employment or salary, children, child care arrange-ments, or dependents; (d) overgeneral in-quiries (e.g., "Do you have any handi-caps?"—which would tend to divulge handicaps or health conditions that do not relate to fitness to perform the job); (e) whether the applicant is married; single, di-vorced, engaged, widowed, or any other in-quiry as to marital status; (f) type or condi-tion of military discharge; (g) any questions related to pregnancy; and (h) whether ap-plicant owns or rents a home.

To summarize, although there have not been an overwhelming number of lawsuits involving the discriminatory nature of the employment interview, the litigation that has evolved clearly indicates that the inter-view is vulnerable to such suits. Interviews will indeed be treated like tests and re-viewed by these same standards. I predict a greater number of suits in this area during future years. Organizations may find them-selves even more ill equipped to defend the interview because of the little attention paid to quantifying interview judgments or conducting research to determine the relia-bility, validity, or adverse effects of the in-terview process.

* * * * *

REFERENCES

Babcock, B., Freedman, A., Norton, E., & Ross, A. *Sex discrimination and the law: Causes and remedies.* Boston: Little, Brown, 1975.

Bannerman v. *Department of Youth Authority,* 17 FEP 820 (1977).

Equal Employment Opportunity Commission Decision No. 72-0703, 4 FEP 435 (1971).

Harless v. *Duck,* 14 FEB 1616 (1977).

Hester v. *Southern Railway Company,* 8 FEB 646 (1974).

King v. *New Hampshire Department of Resources and Economic Development,* 15 FEB 669 (1977).

Rowe v. *General Motors,* 4 FEB 445 (1972).

United States v. *Hazelwood School District,* 11 EPD 10854 (1976).

Washington v. *Davis,* 12 FEB 1415 (1976).

Washington State Human Rights Commission. State & local laws: Text of laws. *Fair Em-ployment Practices,* 1979, Sec. 457. 2723–2926.

Weiner v. *County of Oakland,* 14 FEB 380 (1976).

COMMENTARY

I. A Closer Look at the Interview Process

It is important to note that much of the interview research of the past 15 years has focused on interview outcomes, i.e., decisions. One result of this concentration has been a tendency for many studies to treat the interviewer as a passive recipient of information, which is then processed and a decision reached. The interviewer in his/her role as information seeker has tended to be ignored. While the effects of information received about the applicant prior to and in the course of the interview on interviewer judgments has been studied, the effects of these variables on the interviewer's behavior in the course of the interview, and particularly his/her information-seeking strategy, remain unexamined. For example, a number of "paper people" studies examined the effects of applicant sex on interview decisions, e.g., Dipboye, Fromkin, and Wiback, 1975, Dipboye, Arvey and Terpstra, 1977. What these studies do *not* tell us is the *process* by which applicant sex has an effect on interview decisions. Do interviewers ask different questions of males and females? Do interviewer nonverbal cues (e.g., body language) differ when interviewing males and females? Do interviewers evaluate the same information differently if it is received from a male or female candidate? Any one of these or any combination of these could explain why different decisions are made about males and females; the simulation methodology does not let us determine which process or processes are actually operating.

Arvey and Campion presented a model of the processes involved in the employment interview, but did not make any hypotheses about causality among the variables in the model, stating that sufficient knowledge to pinpoint causal relationships was not available. We believe that a major impediment to a thorough understanding of interview processes has been the failure to design research aimed at examining causal relationships. Thus, we are offering our own model of interview processes and will examine the extent of existing support for each linkage. Figure 10–1 presents a hypothesized model of the interview process which focuses on interviewer information seeking, receipt, and processing. The linkages in the proposed model are not viewed as the sole determinants of interview process and outcome, and examples of other determinants of the various aspects of the model are indicated by the dotted lines. The numbered linkages are those of primary importance for the model. The model makes explicit the processes by which applicant characteristics and applicant behavior may affect interview decisions, and recognizes the active role of the interviewer. A description of the model, with examples of research relevant to each linkage, follows. Classifying research in terms of the model linkages leads to a better understanding of what aspects of the interview process are in need of further investigation.

Linkage 1.   The first linkage is the relationship between applicant characteristics available to the interviewer prior to the interview and interviewer beliefs regarding individuals with those characteristics. Applicant characteristics would include information from resumes, conversations with previous supervisors, or other sources, and can include a variety of information ranging from demographic information, such as race and sex, to information regarding previous job performance, to test scores.

This linkage posits that characteristics of the applicant will affect the attitudes, beliefs, or expectations about the applicant held by the interviewer prior to the beginning of the interview, and subsequently (linkage 3) affect the interviewer's behavior in the interview. Only two studies directly relevant to this linkage were found.

Figure 10–1
Hypothesized Model of Interviewer Information Seeking, Receipt, and Processing

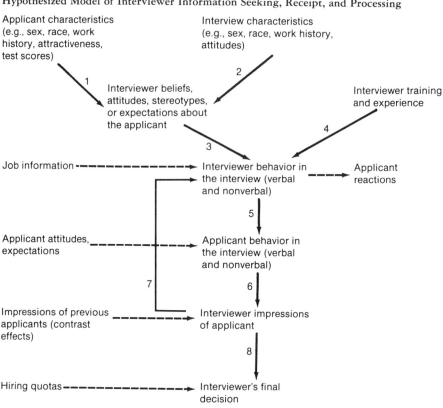

Tucker and Rowe (1979) presented college subjects with favorable, unfavorable, or neutral letters of reference prior to reading an interview transcript focusing on five previous successful work or educational experiences and five unsuccessful experiences. Significant differences in how applicants were expected to perform in the interview were found as a result of the letters of reference. In addition, subjects made more internal attributions of success and external attributions of failure in the interview when the favorable letter was received, and more external attributions of success and internal attributions of failure when the unfavorable letter was received.

London and Poplawski (1976) attempted to create stereotypes by presenting varying amounts of favorable and unfavorable information allegedly descriptive of employees of a hypothetical company. After receiving this information, subjects recorded their impression of company employees using a series of semantic differential scales. Subjects then read a description of one specific employee and rated that employee on the same scales. Strong differences between ratings of company employees and ratings of the specific employee were found, suggesting that individuals are evaluated on their own merits rather than on the basis of group sterotypes. However, low ratings of confidence in group evaluations suggests that a strong sterotype was not created by the experimental manipulation. Generalizability to situations where group stereotypes are stronger is in need of investigation.

There is a very large literature focusing on applicant characteristics; however, this literature examines the relationship between applicant characteristics and hiring decisions. In terms of the model, linkages 3 and 5 through 8 are bypassed. It is unclear whether the face-to-face interview would magnify or diminish the effects of, say, applicant sex compared to effects detected in a resume evaluation study. Does applicant sex have a substantial effect on interview questioning strategy, topic coverage, or nonverbal behavior, subsequently affecting applicant performance and resulting in a stronger sex effect than found in resume studies? Or do aspects of an applicant often not examined in resume studies (e.g., nonverbal behavior, communication skills) play a larger role in selection decisions, resulting in a weaker sex effect than found in resume studies? Sequential examination of the linkages in the model will be necessary for a thorough understanding of the role of applicant characteristics in the selection interview process.

Much of the literature on the effects of applicant characteristics has been discussed in the article by Arvey and Campion. All we wish to do here is note how much research has focused on the applicant characteristics—interviewer decisions linkage, bypassing interviewing process variables. Singe 1976, 20 studies have examined the effects of applicant sex, 10 the effects of applicant race, 7 the effect of physical attractiveness, 13 the effects of applicant qualifications, and smaller numbers of studies dealing with other characteristics, such as age, marital status, and handicap. Thus, despite a large amount of research dealing with applicant characteristics, little is known about the process by which these characteristics influence information formation and information seeking in the selection interview.

Linkage 2. The second linkage specified by the model is between interviewer characteristics, such as race, sex, attitude, and work history, and interviewer beliefs and expectations about the job applicant prior to the interview. As was the case with linkage 1, there is research dealing with the affects of interview characteristics on interviewer decisions; this research bypasses intervening linkages. For example, Mullins (1978) measured the racial attitudes of students who evaluated videotaped interviews with black or white applicants. A race x attitude interaction was found, but not in the predicted direction: highly prejudiced subjects rated blacks higher than whites. That subjects were giving socially desirable responses in an experimental situation appears to be a plausible explanation for these findings. Simas and McCarrey (1979) found that highly authoritarian personnel officers rated males higher than females while no differences were found for moderate or nonauthoritarian subjects. Muchinsky and Harris (1977) found that attitudes toward women as managers correlated with ratings of applicant suitability only for male raters. Finally, Keenan (1976) compared self-reports on the importance of various applicant characteristics made by personnel and nonpersonnel managers involved in campus recruiting. Personnel managers rated need for achievement and knowledge of the job and organization more important than did nonpersonnel managers, who emphasized an applicant's academic record. Thus, personality characteristics, attitudes, and organizational experiences have been found to influence decisions; how these factors affect interviewer expectations, interviewer behavior, and subsequent applicant behavior has not been examined.

Linkage 3. The third linkage specified by the model is between interviewer beliefs about the individual based on information obtained prior to the interview and the interviewer's behavior in the interview. Two studies were found which examine this linkage. Snyder and Swann (1978) examined the relationship between a hypothesis, or preconception, about another person and the hypothesis-testing strategy chosen when interacting with the person. The studies were variations of a question selection paradigm in which subjects were given hypotheses than an individual was an introvert or an extrovert and asked to select questions from a list, made up of introversion-oriented, extroversion-oriented, and neutral questions, to test the hypothesis. Snyder and Swann consistently found that introversion-oriented questions were asked more frequently in introvert-hypothesis conditions and extroversion-oriented questions were asked more frequently in extrovert hypothesis conditions. Snyder and Swann interpret this as evidence that people adopt confirmatory strategies in testing hypotheses about other people, and list the selection interview as one context in which the hypothesis-confirmatory strategy linkage would be expected to operate.

Sackett (1982) adapted the question selection paradigm to the selection interview context. Scenarios were designed to suggest that an applicant would or would not be acceptable for a job. Questions to ask the applicant were chosen by interviewers and college student subjects from a list of questions previously scaled as positive, negative, or neutral in intent. The type of hypothesis was found to be unrelated to the type of questions chosen. The study failed to support Syder and Swann's prediction that subjects would adopt hypothesis-confirming questioning strategies. Thus there is a very limited amount of research dealing with determinants of interviewer behavior. This research focuses on only one aspect of interviewer behavior—questioning strategy—and produces contradictory results.

Linkage 4. The fourth linkage specified by the model is between interviewer training and experience and interviewer behavior. Arvey and Campion reviewed the literature dealing with interviewer training and noted that it dealt almost exclusively with training to eliminate rating errors, such as halo. Arvey and Campion call for research focusing on the linkage we are specifying here, namely, the effects of training on interviewer behavior.

Of particular interest is the relative influence of applicant characteristics (e.g., race, sex) and interviewer training on interviewer behavior, and subsequently on interview decisions. We have previously noted the large number of studies examining the effects of applicant characteristics on interview decisions. Is training an effective mechanism for lessening the effects of sterotypes formed on the basis of applicant characteristics? Do interviewers apply what was learned in training to actual interviews? These and a variety of questions remain unanswered.

Linkage 5. The fifth linkage specified by the model is between interviewer behavior and applicant behavior. Interviewer behavior can be separated into the two components of content and style. With regard to content, specifying this linkage may at first glance seem trivial. The applicant's role in the interview is to respond to the interviewer's questions, and depending on the questions asked, a different behavior sample will be elicited from the applicant. However, a question of interest is, To what extent does an interviewer's selection of topics and questions result in a biased sample of applicant behavior? For example, in a continuation of the introvert-extrovert hypothesis testing research discussed above (Snyder and Swann, 1978), when the interviews were actually carried out using the questions which the interviewer had selected, interviewees in the different conditions were rated by observers as more introverted or extroverted depending upon the condition to which they were randomly assigned. Synder and Swann's work indicated that an interviewer's hypothesis regarding an interviewee produces a confirmatory information-seeking strategy, and this strategy elicits a biased behavior sample from the interviewee, resulting in a high probability that the hypothesis will be confirmed in the mind of the interviewer. While the use of a structured interview will reduce the possibility of such biases, many interviewers do not use a set structure, and in many cases structuring is limited to topics to be covered, rather than to specific questions. Odiorne and Hahn (1961) report that 71 percent of their sample of 94 college recruiters did not use a set pattern of questions.

With regard to style, a number of aspects of interviewer behavior have been found to affect interviewee behavior. For example, Matarazzo, Wiens, and Saslow (1965) found that interviewer speech duration, headnodding, and use of "mm-hmm" each significantly increased interviewee speech duration. Washburn and Hakel (1973) studied the effects of interviewer enthusiasm, defined as the use of eye contact, gestures, and smiling, on observer ratings of the applicant, and found that the applicant was evaluated more favorable when interviewer enthusiasm was high. Keenan and Wedderburn (1975) videotaped interviews with college students in which interviewers were trained to exhibit approving or disapproving nonverbal behavior (e.g., smile versus frown). The hypothesis that interviewees would talk more under the approval condition was not supported.

A second study by Keenan and Wedderburn (1980) also examines interviewer behavior, but does not examine the linkage with applicant behavior. They note that little is known about how interviewers obtain information in interviews: in fact, they report being unable to find a single empirical study of what questions are asked in interviewers. They asked college students to complete a questionnaire immediately after completion of campus recruiting interviews. For each of 26 items, students indicated the extent to which the item was covered. Results indicated wide variety in topics covered, many being treated superficially in a short time period, and low intrainterviewer consistency in topic coverage. In other words, two students interviewed by the same interviewer were likely to report substantial differences in topics covered. These descriptive findings are quite provocative: it would be extremely useful to examine the determinants of these differences in interviewer behavior as well as the effects of the differences in behavior on applicant behavior and subsequent interviewer decision making.

Linkage 6.   The sixth linkage is between the applicant's behavior in the interview and interviewer's impressions of the applicant. This linkage has been well documented in the interview literature. The relative effects of positive and negative information on interviewer impressions have been studied by a number of researchers (e.g., Springbett, 1958; Hollmann, 1972); the effects of the temporal placement of positive and negative information on interviewer impressions have been examined repeatedly (e.g., Blakeney & McNaughton, 1971; Farr, 1973); and the expression of attitudes similar to those of the interviewer has been found to result in more favorable impressions (e.g., Baskett, 1973; Peters and Terborg, 1975). In addition, the article by Arvey and Campion has reviewed the extensive literature on applicant nonverbal behavior, which generally indicates that nonverbal behavior does affect the evaluation received by the applicant.

Linkage 7.   The seventh linkage is the feedback loop between the impression of the applicant held at any point in the interview and the interviewer's subsequent behavior in the interview. Anderson (1960) found that interviewers spend more time talking with applicants they will accept than with those they will reject. Anderson speculates that interviewers form an impression of the applicant early in the interview and then talk more in an attempt to put a favorable-looking applicant at ease. Anderson's research does not, however, address the important issue of the effects of interviewer impressions on the content areas covered and the types of questions asked in the remainder of the interview. Sackett (1982) examined the effects of applicant responses on subsequent interviewer questioning strategy, but did not measure the intervening variable: interviewer impressions of the applicant. He found that applicant responses contradictory to initial impressions did not alter interviewer questioning strategy.

Linkage 8.   The eighth linkage specified in the model is between interviewer impressions of the applicant formed as a result of the interview and the interviewer's final decision about the applicant. While many studies examine the relationship between applicant characteristics or behavioral and final decisions directly, some studies obtain intermediate ratings of various dimensions of applicant performance. Thus, some insight into how dimensional information is used in making a final decision can be obtained. Rowe (1963) found that even when interviewers agree on the favorability of the information received about the applicant, there may be substantial differences in the percent of applicants accepted and rejected. Hollandsworth, Kazelskis, Stevens, and Dressel (1979) examined the relative contribution of evaluations of appropriateness of content, verbal fluency, and nonverbal behavior to final decisions, and found that while all three contributed to the final decision, appropriateness of content was most important and nonverbal behavior was least important. Stone and Sawatzki (1980) found that while a physical or psychiatric disability did not affect evaluation of performance in a audiotaped interview, psychiatric disability did result in a lowered likelihood of job offer. This is very useful for gaining an understanding of mechanisms by which handicap could ultimately affect employment decisions. In this study, disability did not appear to distort the perception or evaluation of applicant behavior; rather, interview performance is apparently discounted for individuals with psychiatric disability.

Summary

By reviewing recent literature in terms of the linkages of the model, limitations of current research strategies become apparent. Given the goal of understanding the processes by which interviewer characteristics, expectations and behavior affect interview decisions and ultimately the validity of these decisions, current research is often deficient. The process model notes the complex set of mechanisms intervening between an interviewer receiving initial information about an applicant and extending or failing to extend a job offer. Looking at current research in terms of the model highlights how little is known about the nature and malleability of impressions of an applicant based on information available prior to the interview, about the effects of these impressions on interviewer behavior, about the impact of interviewer behavior on applicant behavior, about how impressions of an applicant change in the course of the interview, and about how interviewer behavior changes in the course of the interview as a result of these changing impressions. Rather, the dominant themes in recent interview research have been the study of the effects of applicant characteristics and nonverbal aspects of applicant behavior on interviewer decisions, completely bypassing the intervening mechanisms specified in the model. The intent of this review is to sensitize future researchers to the need to explicitly consider the model linkages in designing research, and to point out the substantial gaps in our knowledge of interview processes.

II. Recommendations for Conducting Interviews

There certainly is no shortage of advice on to how to be a better interviewer. While this chapter may have left the impression that a lot of empirical work has been published dealing with the interview, the quantity of this work pales in comparison with the quantity of anecdotal writing in which, in the absence of any evidence, some expert reveals the key questions to ask or formula to follow in order to be an effective interviewer. The *Business Publications Index* lists more than 250 nonempirical articles between 1976 and 1981 alone.

We are displeased with amateur psychologizing and the contradictory recommendations found in these articles. One brief example. One author tells us that silence can be an effective interviewing tool. Waiting expectingly will be seen by the applicant as a cue that additional information is desired, and thus the applicant will elaborate on earlier responses and provide more complete information about him/

herself. A second author also advocates silence as an effective interviewing tool. The unsatisfactory applicant will begin talking again after a few seconds of silence; the good applicant will sit patiently and wait for the next question.

We feel strongly that speculative advice of this sort is inappropriate without empirical backing, and we are comfortable with some cautious recommendations based on the recent validity studies review by Arvey and Campion. We advise a thorough analysis of the target job, the careful development of a structured set of questions based on the job analysis, and the development of a behaviorally specific rating instrument for evaluating applicants. Carefully constructed interview procedures of this sort have achieved some degree of success. Note that the validities obtained in these studies do not exceed those commonly found with other predictors, leading one to question whether comparable success could be attained at lower cost with other predictors. Nonetheless, if an organization is committed to the use of interviews, the above procedures may be useful.

In addition to the limited research on factors affecting interview validity is research on factors affecting applicant reactions to the interview. Since one purpose of the interview is to interest the applicant in the organization, the results of this research can lead to useful suggestions for interviewers, and thus will briefly be reviewed here.

Schmitt and Coyle (1976) mailed a 74-item questionnaire to students, asking them to describe the interviewer who conducted their most recent interview, to respond to questions about the likelihood of being offered and of accepting a job, and to give overall perceptions of interviewer competence and likability. The questionnaire was factored and factor scores were used to predict the dependent variables. A warm personality/good citizen factor was the best predictor of all dependent variables. An interviewer mannerisms factor, a job knowledge factor and a factor dealing with providing job information were all related to willingness to accept an offer and to overall impression of the interviewer. Similar findings are reported by Karol (1977): interviewer interpersonal skills and the provision of job information were the best predictors of satisfaction with the interview. In addition, interviewer-applicant similarity in age, race, and vocational orientation were related to satisfaction with the interview.

Concerned about the retrospective nature of the Schmitt and Coyle study, Keenan (1978) obtained applicant ratings of the importance of the interview and likelihood of accepting an offer immediately before and after an interview, as well postinterview ratings of likelihood or receiving a job offer and liking for the interviewer. In addition, interviewers rated the applicant's overall qualifications and the likelihood of a job offer immediately after the interview. Applicants felt a job offer was more likely and were more willing to accept a job offer if they liked the interviewer. These findings hold up when interviewer evaluation of the candidate is partialed out, suggesting that liking an interviewer and confidence in a job offer are not due to the applicant accurately perceiving how he/she is being evaluated. In addition, applicants indicating a moderate level of preinterview motivation were most likely to be evaluated favorably.

Herriot and Rothwell (1981) also obtained ratings of the likelihood of accepting a job offer before and after an interview, and found that intention to accept declines after an interview. Unmet expectations are presented as explanation: applicants report that the interview was less formal, that there was less opportunity for discussion or questions, fewer questions about themselves, and less information presented about the organization than expected.

Rowe (1976) collected postinterview ratings from college students interviewing for jobs as part of a work-school cooperative program. Students rank-ordered their preferences for jobs after a series of interviews; interviews for the most preferred job were longer, interviewers provided more information, gave the applicant more time to sell him/herself, and did a better job of putting the applicant at ease.

Two experimental studies dealt with applicant reactions to interview/interviewer characteristics. Rogers and Sincoff (1978) varied interviewer age, title (director of recruiting versus no title) and verbal fluency in playing an audiotaped interview to college students. The major factor influencing impressions of the interviewer was title, with age also an important factor. A 30-year-old interviewer was preferred to one either 20 or 50 years old. Verbal fluency had minimal effect.

Keenan and Wedderburn (1975) trained interviewers to exhibit approving or disapproving nonverbal cues. College student subjects reported than an approving interviewer was more likable and friendly, and made them more at ease and less nervous.

This body of research uniformly indicates that interviewer behavior is a determinant of applicant impressions of a company. While some conclusions are less than startling (e.g., be warm and open), others seem quite useful (e.g., provide job information, be knowledgeable about the firm, allow ample opportunity for applicants to talk about themselves and to ask questions). The most pressing research need at present is to move away from campus recruiting interviews. Due to the availability of such data to university-based researchers, all studies of applicant reactions to interviewer behavior were done in this context, which represents a small fraction of all interviews conducted.

In conclusion, the interview remains a troubling area—an almost universally used device whose validity appears to be no greater than less expensive predictors even under the best of conditions; an area where unsubstantiated, contradictory how-to-do-it advice abounds; and an area in need of research more carefully conceived than has been the case in the past.

REFERENCES

Anderson, C. W. The relation between speaking times and decision in the employment interview. *Journal of Applied Psychology*, 1960, *44*, 267–268.

Baskett, C. D. Interview decisions as determined by competency and attitude similarity. *Journal of Applied Psychology*, 1973, *58*, 343–345.

Blakeney, R. N., & MacNaughton, J. F. Effects of temporal placement of unfavorable information on decision making during the selection interview. *Journal of Applied Psychology*, 1971, *55*, 138–142.

Dipboye, R. L., Arvey, R. D., & Terpstra, D. E. Sex and physical attractiveness of raters and applicants as determinants of resume evaluations. *Journal of Applied Psychology*, 1977, *62*, 288–294.

Dipboye, R. L., Fromkin, H. L., & Wiback, K. Relative importance of applicant sex, attractiveness, and scholastic standing in evaluation of job applicant resumes. *Journal of Applied Psychology*, 1975, *60*, 39–43.

Farr, J. L. Response requirements and primacy-recency effects in a simulated selection interview. *Journal of Applied Psychology*, 1973, *58*, 228–233.

Herriot, P., & Rothwell, C. Organizational choice and decision theory: Effects of employers' literature and selection interview. *Journal of Occupational Psychology*, 1981, *54*, 17–31.

Hollandsworth, J. B., Kazelskis, R., Stevens, J., and Dressel, M. T. Relative contributions of verbal, articulative, and nonverbal communication to employment decisions in the job interview setting. *Personnel Psychology*, 1979, *32*, 359–367.

Hollmann, T. D. Employment interviewer's errors in processing positive and negative information. *Journal of Applied Psychology,* 1972, *56,* 130–134.

Karol, B. L. Relationship of recruiter behavior, perceived similarity, and prior information to applicants' assessments of the campus recruitment interview. Unpublished doctoral dissertation, Ohio State University, 1977.

Keenan, A. Interviewers' evaluation of applicant characteristics: differences between personnel and non-personnel managers. *Journal of Occupational Psychology,* 1976, *49,* 223–230.

Keenan, A. The selection interview: Candidates' reactions and interviewers' judgments. *British Journal of Social and Clinical Psychology,* 1978, *17,* 201–209.

Keenan, A., & Wedderburn, A. A. I. Effects of the non-verbal behavior of interviewers on candidates' impressions. *Journal of Occupational Psychology,* 1975, *48,* 129–132.

Keenan, A., & Wedderburn, A. A. I. Putting the boot on the other foot: Candidates' descriptions of interviewers. *Journal of Occupational Psychology,* 1980, *53,* 81–89.

London, M., & Poplawski, J. R. Effects of information on stereotype development in performance appraisal and interview contexts. *Journal of Applied Psychology,* 1976, *61,* 199–205.

Matarazzo, J. D., Weins, A. N., and Saslow, G. Studies of interview speech behavior. In L. Krasner and L. P. Ullman (Eds.), *Research in behavior modification.* New York: Holt, Rinehart, & Winston, 1965.

Muchinsky, P. M., & Harris, S. L. The effect of applicant sex and scholastic standing on the evaluation of job applicant resumes in sex-typed occupations. *Journal of Vocational Behavior,* 1977, *11,* 95–108.

Mullins, T. W. Racial attitudes and the interview—A factorial experiment. Unpublished doctoral dissertation, University of Houston, 1978.

Odiorne, G. S., & Hahn, A. S. *Effective college recruiting.* Ann Arbor: Mich.: Bureau of Industrial Relations, University of Michigan, 1961.

Peters, L. H., & Terborg, J. R. The effects of temporal placement of unfavorable information and of attitude similarity on personnel selection decisions. *Organizational Behavior and Human Performance,* 1975, *13,* 279–293.

Rogers, D. H., & Sincoff, M. Z. Favorable impression characteristics of the recruitment interviewer. *Personnel Psychology,* 1978, *31,* 495–504.

Rowe, P. M. Individual differences in selection decisions. *Journal of Applied Psychology,* 1963, *47,* 305–307.

Rowe, P. M. Effects of expected job characteristics and interview factors on organizational choice. *Psychology Reports,* 1976, *38,* 1011–1018.

Sackett, P. R. The interviewer as hypothesis tester: The effects of impressions of an applicant on interviewer questioning strategy. *Personnel Psychology,* 1982, *35,* 789–804.

Schmitt, N., & Coyle, B. W. Applicant decisions in the employment interview. *Journal of Applied Psychology,* 1976, *61,* 184–192.

Simas, K., & McCarrey, M. Impact of recruiter authoritarianism and applicant sex on evaluation and selection decisions in a recruitment interview analogue study. *Journal of Applied Psychology,* 1979, *64,* 483–491.

Snyder, M., & Swann, W. Hypothesis-testing processes in social interactions. *Journal of Personality and Social Psychology,* 1978, *36,* 1202–1212.

Springbett, B. M. Factors affecting the final decision in employment interview. *Canadian Journal of Psychology,* 1958, *12,* 13–22.

Stone, C. I., & Sawatzki, B. Hiring bias and the disabled interviewee: Effects of manipulating work history and disability information of the disabled job applicant. *Journal of Vocational Behavior,* 1980, *16,* 96–104.

Tucker, D. H., & Rowe, P. M. Relationships between expectancy causal attributions, and final hiring decisions in the employment interview. *Journal of Applied Psychology,* 1979, *64,* 27–34.

Washburn, P. V., & Hakel, M. D. Visual cues and verbal content as influences on impressions after simulated employment interviews. *Journal of Applied Psychology,* 1973, *58,* 137–140.

Chapter 11

Psychological Tests

INTRODUCTION

The use of tests for personnel selection has a long and controversial history. Studies investigating the validity of occupational tests began appearing in the early 1900s. As discussed in Chapter 1, Burtt (1917) summarized data originally collected by Munsterberg and conducted the equivalent of a criterion-related validity study. Recall that while the study was flawed according to current standards, a variety of what Munsterberg (1913) called mental tests distinguished between high- and low-ability employees in different firms. The mental tests of the early 1900s were very much like current aptitude tests. Aptitude tests, unlike achievement tests, are used to measure person-centered traits and focus on predispositions to act. Achievement tests attempt to measure current knowledge and skill levels. The work-sample and knowledge tests described by Asher and Sciarrino (1974) are best characterized as achievement tests. The primary focus of this chapter will be on aptitude tests. In particular, the approach used by Ghiselli (1966) in selecting tests for review in his classic book entitled *The Validity of Occupational Aptitude Tests* will be used to help define this common test type. Ghiselli's five major aptitude test categories included tests of intellectual abilities, spatial and mechanical abilities, perceptual accuracy, motor abilities, and personality. Personality tests commonly include both personality inventories and interest inventories. The goal of this chapter will be to present information pertaining to the validity and usefulness of aptitude tests. The commentary will then reflect on the validity, fairness, and feasibility of standardized aptitude tests versus alternative selection procedures.

The first reading by Ghiselli (1973) represents an abbreviated and updated version of his 1966 book. His goal was to summarize the substantial amount of information pertaining to the validity of various tests that had been accumulating since the early 1900s. An enormous amount of information is summarized in this article. Validity studies published during the period 1920 through 1971 were reviewed along with unpublished material obtained from a variety of sources. Keep in mind that the validity generalization models developed by Schmidt and his colleagues and Callender and

Osburn (1980) were not available to Ghiselli. He did not correct for a variety of statistical artifacts when estimating the validity of tests. Thus, the validity averages reported in the article will almost always be underestimates. Ghiselli notes that these attenuated findings are likely to be the result of three general problems. First, the criterion used in most early studies was a global measure of performance (covering all or most aspects of the job). It is unlikely that a test designed to measure a restricted range of traits will be highly correlated with a multidimensional criterion variable. Second, a restriction of range in both the test and criterion scores will lead to attenuated validity estimates. Finally, the unreliability of common indices of job performance will serve to limit the validity of tests used to predict them. Even given these problems, Ghiselli concludes that the validity of many aptitude tests is quite respectable and that a rather high degree of generality has been achieved.

Ghiselli's review focused on the validity of individual tests. The predictive power of single tests is not likely to be as high as some optimal combination of tests. A single test, as noted earlier, will generally not be highly correlated with a multidimensional measure of job performance since the test is designed to measure only some of the abilities or traits necessary for success on a given job. The likelihood of measuring other required abilities and traits should increase as the number of different tests used also increases. Thus, combinations of two or more tests of differing type should have higher validity than tests taken alone. To illustrate the usefulness of carefully developed test batteries, Sparks (in the second reading) describes one of the best-known testing programs in industry. Originally developed by what was then the Standard Oil Company of New Jersey (SONJ), this operational system relies on what is termed a *purely statistical* or *actuarial approach* to collecting and combining predictor information. Standardized test scores were generated across multiple tests. Often, empirical scoring keys were developed and cross-validated to maximize the predictive accuracy of each individual predictor. The strategy was then to use the various predictor scores in a multiple regression equation to predict managerial job performance. The original scoring and combination rules developed by SONJ have continued to generate good predictive validities. Note that the original testing program included measures of verbal ability, inductive reasoning, management judgment (the ability to choose an effective action when confronted with hypothetical human relations problems), personality, and biographical data covering such things as home and family background, educational and vocational planning, finances, health history, and social relations. Thus, one component of the program (the biographical inventory) does not correspond with the general focus of this chapter (i.e., standardized aptitude tests). Nevertheless, the overall success of this approach leads to important conclusions regarding the usefulness of standardized aptitude tests and illustrates what can be done with a carefully designed program of validation research.

In Chapter 3, Schmidt and Hunter (1980) provided the essentials of a procedure developed to examine the question of whether validity coefficients actually are situationally specific. In order to estimate the variation in true validities, it is necessary to take the statistical artifacts of range restriction and criterion unreliability into account. Recall that the best estimate of a test's validity is the mean of the corrected validity distribution. If a large percentage of the values lie above the minimum useful level of validity, one can conclude that the estimate of true validity in a new situation (i.e., similar test and job type) will be at or above this minimum useful level. In the third reading, Schmidt and Hunter (1981) provide evidence that professionally developed cognitive-ability tests are valid predictors of performance on the job and in training for all jobs in all settings. They further present evidence that cognitive tests are equally valid for and fair to minority and majority applicants and that the use of such tests can result in very large labor cost savings. When reviewing this article, it will be important to note two issues. First, these authors discuss only the results generated by applying the validity generalization model to cognitive tests. Cognitive tests in this case refer to professionally developed objective tests of verbal ability, quantitative ability, mechanical comprehension, spatial ability, and inductive and deductive reasoning. Also, they conclude that of the tests studied the validities are neither specific to situations or jobs. This is a particularly strong statement that requires a critical examination. This will be provided in the commentary.

Finally, Tenopyr (1981), in the fourth reading, concludes that at present there are few alternatives to tests when validity, adverse impact, and feasibility are taken into account. Given the high degree of usefulness that can be attributed to tests, she then provides evidence that the use of tests is on the decline. This curious state of affairs is discussed in terms of the current legal and regulatory environment. Tenopyr also makes insightful comments regarding the impact the recent work on validity generalization will have on the work of the selection specialist. Her conclusion is that this work will have little impact in the real world for some time. This, along with the article by Schmidt and Hunter (1981), should help focus our attention on the serious problems associated with translating research knowledge into professional and regulatory practice. Also, Tenopyr raises some relevant questions regarding the use of supervisory ratings of performance in the studies used in the application of the validity generalization models and expresses concern over the relationship between validity generalization and ability theory.

REFERENCES

Asher, J. J., and Sciarrino, J. A. Realistic work sample tests: A review. *Personnel Psychology,* 1974, *27,* 519–533.

Burtt, H. E. Professor Munsterberg's vocational tests. *Journal of Applied Psychology,* 1917, *1,* 210–213.

Callender, J. C., & Osburn, H. G. Development and test of a new model for validity generalization. *Journal of Applied Psychology,* 1980, *65,* 543–558.

Ghiselli, E. E. *The validity of occupational aptitude tests.* New York: John Wiley & Sons, 1966.

Ghiselli, E. E. The validity of aptitude tests in personnel selection. *Personnel Psychology,* 1973, *26,* 461–477.

Munsterberg, H. *Psychology and industrial efficiency.* Boston: Houghton Mifflin, 1913.

Schmidt, F. L. & Hunter, J. E. The future of criterion-related validity. *Personnel Psychology,* 1980, *33,* 41–60.

Schmidt, F. L., & Hunter, J. E. Employment testing: Old theories and new research findings. *American Psychologist,* 1981, *36,* 1128–1137.

Tenopyr, M. L. The realities of employment testing. *American Psychologist,* 1981, *36,* 1120–1127.

The Validity of Aptitude Tests in Personnel Selection*

EDWIN E. GHISELLI

Traditionally Munsterberg's experiment with motormen is taken to be the beginning of research in the use of tests for personnel selection. Nevertheless, anecdotal evidence strongly suggests that even before 1910 other psychologists conducted similar studies with tests, studies which were small in scope and which went unpublished and unpublicized. Furthermore, under the impetus of the scientific management movement some of the so-called efficiency experts at about that time were using a few simple tests for evaluating applicants for jobs, and even reported fragmentary evidence of validity in the attempt to justify and to publicize their activities. During World War I the large scale testing both of soldiers and industrial workers provided stimulation, methodology, and respectability to the examination of the utility of tests in the assessment of occupational aptitude. This all led to a great post-war surge of systematic research in personnel testing. So beginning about 1920 substantial amounts of data pertaining to the validity of various sorts of tests for the evaluation of workers in many different jobs began to become available.

For something over half a century, then, there has been an accumulation of experience with the use of tests as devices for assessing men and women for positions in business and industrial establishments, and an enormous amount of information has been collected. The purpose here is to summarize this information in as simple and compact form as is possible. Such a summary will at least permit an examination of general trends in the validity of tests for personnel selection.

METHOD

The description of the utility of a particular test for the selection of personnel for a given job is commonly given as the Pearsonian coefficient of correlation between test and criterion scores, the familiar validity coefficient. The findings of the different researches which have to do with the occupational validity of tests, then, have the unique ability of being expressed in the form of the same numerical index. As a consequence, they can be quite conveniently summarized by means of averages, the averages of the validity coefficients that have been reported for each type of test for each type of job. On an earlier occasion the author (1966) has summarized the literature pertaining to the occupational validity of tests in this way. The present report brings up to date the most recent of these summaries.

The classification of tests which was used is as follows:

Tests of Intellectual Abilities

Intelligence. This category includes all tests which are termed intelligence or mental alertness tests, as for example, the Otis and Wesman tests.

Immediate memory. These tests present material, e.g., 5- to 10-place numbers, which the individual studies and after a very short period of time tries to recall.

Substitution. With these tests the individual learns and applies a code.

Arithmetic. These devices involve the computation of arithmetic problems of various kinds, which are presented in simple form or as practical problems such as making change.

Tests of Spatial and Mechanical Abilities

Spatial relations. Spatial judgments about the size and form of figures are required by these tests. The Minnesota Paper Form Board is a good illustration.

Location. With these tests the individual must identify the location of a series of points, and make judgments about the distances between them. Examples are furnished by the copying and location subtests of the MacQuarrie Mechanical Ability Tests.

Mechanical principles. Tests of this sort, such as the Bennett Mechanical Comprehension Test, present in pictorial form problems which require knowledge of various mechanical principles to solve.

Tests of Perceptual Accuracy

Number comparison. The stimulus material in these tests consist of a series of pairs of numbers, both members of each pair consisting of the same number of digits. The digits in some of the pairs are exactly the same, and in others one digit is different. As in the number comparison part of the Minnesota Clerical Test the individual is required to indicate which pairs are the same and which are different.

Name comparison. These tests are similar to the number comparison tests except that they consist of pairs of names instead of pairs of numbers. The Minnesota Clerical Test includes items of this sort.

Cancellations. A continuous series of numbers or letters in random order is presented by these tests, and the individual crosses out all numbers of letters of a specified sort.

Pursuit. This type of test presents a tangle of lines, and by eye alone the individual is required to follow each line from its beginning to its end. The pursuit subtest of the MacQuarrie Mechanical Ability Test is an example.

Perceptual accuracy. The speed and accuracy with which similarities and differences between simple figures can be perceived is measured by these tests.

Tests of Motor Abilities

Tracing. With measuring devices of this sort the individual is required to follow a path with a pencil, both speed and accuracy being important in the performance. The tracing subtest of the MacQuarrie Mechanical Ability Test is an illustration.

Tapping. These tests present a series of circles or squares into each of which the individual places two, or perhaps three, dots with a pencil. The tapping part of the MacQuarrie Mechanical Ability Test is representative.

Dotting. These tests are similar to the tapping tests except that by using smaller circles or squares precision of movement is stressed. For instance, in the dotting subtest the MacQuarrie Mechanical Ability Test the individual places a single pencil dot in each of a series of quite small circles.

Finger dexterity. This category includes all pegboard tests, together with tests which involve mating simple assemblies such as placing washers on rivets which are then inserted into holes. The O'Connor Finger Dexterity Test and the Purdue Pegboard Test are examples.

Hand dexterity. While to some extent these tests do involve finger dexterity, their purpose is to measure grosser manual motions involving the wrist. In The Minnesota Turning Test, for example, blocks are picked up, turned over, and replaced in their original positions.

Arm dexterity. As in the Minnesota Placing Test, these tests involve the very gross movements of picking up blocks and placing them in another position.

Personality Traits

Personality. Included here are all of the sundry inventories that ask questions which presumably are indicative of one or another of the many personality characteristics. A number of different trait names are used to distinguish the various aspects of personality. In some cases different names are used to denote the same, or very nearly the same, quality, and in others the same name is used to denote quite different qualities. As a consequence it is impossible to classify the measured traits into specific categories. Furthermore, in some instances inventories are developed for a given job and are not identified by a specific trait name. Therefore, only those results were included in the present summary where the trait seemed pertinent to the job in question, or where the inventory

was developed specifically for the job through item analysis, and cross-validation data were reported. An example of this category of tests is the Guilford-Zimmerman Temperament Survey.

Interest. Inventories of this sort ask questions about interests in, and preferences for, such matters as avocations, occupations, and school subjects. Interest inventories were included in this summary on the basis as were personality inventories.

The following classification of occupations was used:

Managerial occupations
    Executives and administrators (e.g., plant managers, department heads)
    Foremen (e.g., first-line industrial supervisors)
Clerical occupations
    General clerks (e.g., coding clerks)
    Recording clerks (e.g., typist, stenographers)
    Computing clerks (e.g., bookkeepers, calculating machine operators)
Sales occupations
    Salesclerks (e.g., retail sales persons)
    Salesmen (e.g., insurance salesmen, industrial salesmen)
Protective occupations (e.g., policemen, firemen)
Service occupations (e.g., waiters, hospital attendants)
Vehicle operators (e.g., taxicab drivers, bus drivers)
Trades and crafts
    Mechanical repairmen (e.g., automobile mechanics, typewriter repairmen)
    Electrical workers (e.g., electricians, radio repairmen)
    Structural workers (e.g., carpenters)
    Processing workers (e.g., petroleum refinery workers, electric substation operators)
    Complex machine operators (e.g., printers, weaving machine operators)

Machine workers (e.g., machinists, turret lathe operators)

Industrial occupations

Machine tenders (e.g., punch press operators, bottle-capping machine operators)

Bench workers (e.g., assemblers)

Inspectors (e.g., pottery inspectors, gaugers)

Packers and wrappers (e.g., package wrappers)

Gross manual workers (e.g., unskilled laborers)

The literature summarized here includes reports which pertain to the occupational validity tests that were published during the period form 1920 through 1971. To these published findings was added a great amount of unpublished material which was obtained from private sources in a number of business, industrial, and governmental organizations. In all instances validity was expressed as the coefficient of correlation between test and criterion scores. The criteria, of course, were different for different jobs. In all but a very few instances the criteria were intended to be a measure of overall success, and were generally in the form of ratings, although occasionally they consisted of objective measures or combinations of different kinds of measures. The validity coefficients were differentiated in terms of whether they referred to the prediction of success in training, or to the level of proficiency attained on the actual job itself. Only those cases were included in the prediction of training where the training was preparation given the individual before he was actually placed on the job, and was not refresher training.

For each of the 20 types of tests, 21 types of jobs, and 2 types of criteria, the mean of the validity coefficients was calculated. Because of the nature of the Pearsonian coefficient, the means were obtained through Fisher's z transformation, the coefficients entering into a mean being weighted in terms of the number of persons on which each of those coefficients were determined.

The circumstances in which studies of validity of occupational aptitude tests are conducted are of such a nature that in almost all instances, if not all, their findings were attenuated. As a consequence the validity coefficients that are reported for the tests almost invariably are underestimates of their true predictive power.

To begin with, the criteria ordinarily used are global, covering all aspects of job performance and consequently a broad spectrum of traits. A single test, measuring as it does a restricted range of traits, cannot possibly be highly related to such a variable. Second, there is almost certain to be a restricted range both in test and criterion scores. If scores on the test being examined are not themselves used to select and reject candidates for the job, it is quite possible that they will have some relationship to whatever assessments are used for this purpose. Furthermore, poor workers on a job tend to be eliminated and superior ones to be promoted out of it. Since criterion scores must be obtained on workers who stay on the job for extended periods, those available for a validation study will have a smaller range of criterion scores than will those who are working on it at any given time. Restriction in the range of scores of variables being related, of course, results in a reduction in the magnitude of the coefficient of correlation between them. Measures of human performance invariably have some degree of unreliability. The reliability coefficients of indices of job performance rarely reach as high as .90, while not infrequently they are lower than .50. Values of the order of .60 to .80 can be taken to be characteristic of the reliability with which job performance is measured. It is, therefore, apparent that the magnitude of the reliability of the criteria which are used substantially limits the validity of tests which are used to predict them.

In view of the foregoing it is apparent that the average validity coefficients presented here must be considered to be understatements of the predictive power of occupational aptitude tests. Furthermore, the very process utilized here of classifying both tests and jobs into broad categories further diminishes the magnitude of those average coefficients. The sheer size of Buros' *Mental Measurements Yearbook* and the *Dictionary of Occupational Titles* is ample testimony to the fact that the types of tests and jobs can be numbered into the hundreds if not thousands. Yet in the summary here, a mere 20 classes of tests and 21 classes of jobs were used. Had more refined rubrics been employed the average validity coefficients would, of course, have been smaller in some instances, but in others they would have been much larger. Furthermore, the heterogeneity resulting from bundling together studies conducted at different times in different organizations, and utilizing widely different samples of individuals varying markedly in education, age, and social and ethnic backgrounds, while giving the findings a good deal of generality also certainly attenuates them.

It is to be recalled that in the studies summarized here validity is described solely by means of the Pearsonian coefficient of correlations. Thus a linear model, with at least the implication of homoscedasticity, is forced upon all relationships between test and criterion scores. Certainly in some instances nonlinear heteroscedastic models would give a much more favorable picture of the validity of occupational aptitude tests.

As will be seen in the following discussion and in the tables, while there is a wealth of information it is not equally distributed among the various types of tests, jobs, and criteria. For some jobs there are no data at all in important areas of aptitude, and for others it is quite limited. Nevertheless, it is possible to ascertain at least general trends for most jobs, and for many of them the data are quite complete.

RESULTS

Managerial Occupations

The average validity coefficients for the managerial occupations are given in Table 1. It should be noted that the studies of the prediction of trainability which were included here were only those wherein the attempt was made to provide total training for the job and not just training in some specific area such as leadership.

In Table 1 it will be observed that in general the prediction of training criteria is better for foremen than it is for executives and administrators, whereas the reverse is true for job proficiency criteria. For both types of criteria, tests of intellectual abilities, spatial and mechanical abilities, and perceptual accuracy tend to be the best, and are of moderate validity for both types of managerial occupations. Tests of motor abilities have lesser, though apparently some, validity for proficiency criteria. Measures of personality and interest also are of moderate value in predicting the level of proficiency executives and administrators attain on their jobs, but they are much less useful for foremen.

Clerical Occupations

As may be seen in Table 2, while there are some differences in terms of the validity of the various sorts of tests for the three types of jobs which constitute the clerical occupations, there is, nevertheless, a considerable degree of consistency among them. Success in training for the clerical occupations is exceptionally well predicted by tests of intellectual abilities, and nearly as well by those indicative of perceptual accuracy. Oddly enough, tests of spatial and mechanical abilities also give rather good prediction of training success. More limited validity for training criteria is exhibited

Table 1
Validity Coefficients for Managerial Occupations

	Executives and Administrators		Foremen		All Managers	
	Training	Proficiency	Training	Proficiency	Training	Proficiency
Intellectual abilities	.27[b]	.30[e]	.33[b]	.26[e]	.30[c]	.27[f]
Intelligence	.28[b]	.30[e]	.31[b]	.28[e]	.29[b]	.29[f]
Arithmetic	.25[b]	.29[c]	.36[b]	.20[d]	.33[b]	.23[d]
Spatial and mechanical abilities	.25[b]	.23[e]	.36[a]	.22[e]	.28[b]	.22[e]
Spatial relations	.25[b]	.22[e]	.36[a]	.21[d]	.28[b]	.21[d]
Mechanical principles		.42[a]		.23[e]		.23[e]
Perceptual accuracy	.18[b]	.24[c]	.26[b]	.27[b]	.23[b]	.25[e]
Number comparison		.14[a]		.37[b]		.31[b]
Name comparison	.18[b]	.23[b]	.26[a]	.14[b]	.21[b]	.21[c]
Cancellation		.32[b]				.22[b]
Pursuit			.25[a]		.25[a]	
Motor abilities	.02[b]	.13[d]	.38[a]	.15[b]	.02[b]	.14[d]
Tapping	.09[b]	.17[b]	.04[a]	.20[a]	.07[b]	.18[c]
Finger dexterity	−.02[b]	.13[b]		.23[a]	−.02[b]	.14[c]
Hand dexterity	−.02[b]	.10[b]		.02[a]	−.02[b]	.09[c]
Personality traits	.53[a]	.29[e]		.16[e]	.53[a]	.22[f]
Personality		.28[e]		.15[e]		.21[f]
Interest	.53[a]	.30[d]		.17[e]	.53[a]	.28[d]

[a] Less than 100 cases.
[b] 100 to 499 cases.
[c] 500 to 999 cases.
[d] 1,000 to 4,999 cases.
[e] 5,000 to 9,999 cases.
[f] 10,000 or more cases.

by measures of motor abilities. The personality and interest inventories which have been tried for this purpose have not proven to be of any great value.

Forecasts of success attained on the actual job is equally well given by tests of intellectual ability and perceptual accuracy, both of which have moderately high validity coefficients. Tests which measure spatial and mechanical abilities, and motor abilities, and inventories which are designed to measure various personality traits have much more restricted utility.

Sales Occupations

No investigations of the validity of tests for training in the sales occupations were found that met the standards adopted in this study. The average validity coefficients for job proficiency criteria are listed in Table 3. An examination of the data present in this table will show that there is a sharp distinction between the lower sales occupations, the sales clerks, and the higher ones, the salesmen, in the utility of the various kinds of tests. For all practical purposes tests of intellectual abilities, perceptual accuracy, and motor abilities are of no value for the selection of sales clerks, whereas tests of intellectual abilities are rather good for the assessment of applicants for the job of salesman, and tests of perceptual accuracy and of motor abilities are of modest, but some, value. Measures of spatial and mechanical abilities have moderate validity for the job of salesman, and are of somewhat lesser value for the job of sales clerk. For both types of sales occupations measures of personality are rather good, perhaps being better for sales clerks than for salesmen.

Table 2
Validity Coefficients for Clerical Occupations

	General clerks		Recording clerks		Computing clerks		All clerks	
	Training	Proficiency	Training	Proficiency	Training	Proficiency	Training	Proficiency
Intellectual abilities	.47[f]	.28[f]	.46[f]	.26[f]	.52[e]	.25[e]	.47[f]	.28[f]
Intelligence	.46[f]	.32[f]	.43[f]	.26[e]	.54[d]	.23[d]	.46[f]	.30[f]
Immediate memory	.21[b]	.29[d]	.32[d]	.36[b]	.46[a]	.26[c]	.32[d]	.31[d]
Substitution		.24[d]	.24[c]	.23[c]	.34[b]	.24[c]	.25[d]	.24[e]
Arithmetic	.49[f]	.25[f]	.50[f]	.27[d]	.51[d]	.29[d]	.50[f]	.26[f]
Spatial and mechanical abilities	.35[f]	.12[e]	.30[f]	.17[d]	.52[d]	.26[d]	.34[f]	.17[f]
Spatial relations	.39[e]	.11[d]	.32[e]	.15[d]	.55[c]	.25[d]	.35[f]	.16[e]
Location		.05[b]	.24[c]	.12[c]	.49[a]	.30[b]	.27[c]	.16[d]
Mechanical principles	.32[e]	.20[c]	.29[f]	.23[d]	.50[c]	.26[e]	.32[f]	.23[d]
Perceptual accuracy	.36[b]	.27[e]	.41[f]	.27[d]	.31[b]	.31[d]	.40[e]	.29[f]
Number of comparison	.42[b]	.28[e]	.28[b]	.29[d]	.35[b]	.32[d]	.34[c]	.30[e]
Name comparison	.34[b]	.25[d]	.35[b]	.35[d]	.19[b]	.33[d]	.33[c]	.30[e]
Cancellation		.22[c]	.58[b]	.19[d]	.11[a]	.24[e]	.49[b]	.22[d]
Pursuit		−.17[a]	.21[b]	.12[b]		.35[b]	.15[b]	.12[b]
Perceptual speed		.40[b]	.42[e]			.46[b]	.42[e]	.45[c]
Motor abilities	.07[b]	.16[e]	.14[d]	.18[d]	.14[b]	.14[d]	.14[d]	.16[f]
Tracing		−.09[a]	.17[b]	.11[b]	.08[a]	.42[b]	.16[b]	.16[b]
Tapping	.00[b]	.20[d]	.23[b]	.25[c]	.16[b]	.15[c]	.21[c]	.20[d]
Dotting	.32[b]	.14[c]	.15[b]	.17[c]	.16[a]	.03[c]	.18[b]	.12[d]
Finger dexterity	.01[b]	.16[d]	.09[c]	.18[c]		.18[c]	.08[d]	.17[d]
Hand dexterity	.06[b]	.14[d]	.30[a]	.17[e]		.12[c]	.14[b]	.14[d]
Arm dexterity		.13[b]	.09[a]	−.09[a]		.34[a]	.09[a]	.14[b]
Personality traits	.17[d]	.30[c]		.15[c]		.19[b]	.17[d]	.22[d]
Personality		.30[c]		.18[c]		.17[b]		.24[d]
Interest	.17[d]			−.01[b]		.23[b]	.17[d]	.12[b]

[a] Less than 100 cases.
[b] 100 to 499 cases.
[c] 500 to 999 cases.
[d] 1,000 to 4,999 cases.
[e] 5,000 to 9,999 cases.
[f] 10,000 or more cases.

Table 3
Validity Coefficients for Sales Occupations

	Sales clerks	Salesmen	All sales occupations
	Proficiency	Proficiency	Proficiency
Intellectual abilities	−.03[d]	.33[d]	.19[e]
Intelligence	−.06[d]	.34[d]	.19[e]
Immediate memory	−.06[b]		−.06[b]
Substitution	−.16[a]		−.16[a]
Arithmetic	.10[b]	.29[d]	.25[d]
Spatial and mechanical abilities	.14[b]	.20[b]	.18[e]
Spatial relations	.14[b]	.20[b]	.18[e]
Mechanical principles		.16[a]	.16[a]
Perceptual accuracy	−.02[d]	.23[b]	.04[d]
Number comparison	−.14[b]	.27[b]	.05[b]
Name comparison	.00[b]	.19[b]	.05[e]
Cancellation	.02[c]		.02[c]
Motor abilities	.09[c]	.16[b]	.12[d]
Tapping	.21[b]	.17[b]	.19[b]
Finger dexterity	−.05[b]	.18[b]	.06[b]
Hand dexterity	.11[b]	.13[b]	.12[b]
Personality traits	.35[d]	.30[e]	.32[e]
Personality	.36[d]	.29[d]	.31[d]
Interest	.34[e]	.31[d]	.32[d]

[a] Less than 100 cases.
[b] 100 to 499 cases.
[c] 500 to 999 cases.
[d] 1,000 to 4,999 cases.
[e] 5,000 to 9,999 cases.
[f] 10,000 or more cases.

Protective Occupations

The available information pertaining to the validity of various tests for the protective occupations is summarized in Table 4. It will be observed that good to very good predictions of trainability are provided by tests of intellectual abilities, spatial and mechanical abilities, and perceptual accuracy. Measures of personality apparently are of no use at all for this purpose. None of the various individual types of tests have more than modest predictive power for proficiency criteria in the protective occupations. Yet all apparently do have some, though perhaps small, value.

Service Occupations

The average validity coefficients for the sundry jobs that are grouped together in the service occupations are shown in Table 5. The best predictions in these occupations, whether for trainability or job proficiency, are given by tests of intellectual abilities. In the case of trainability the validity is substantial, and it is considerably less for job proficiency. Tests of spatial and mechanical abilities, perceptual accuracy, and motor abilities in that order have reasonably good to moderate utility as measures of aptitude for training in the service occupations. These same three tests together with measures of personality traits all have low validity for job proficiency.

Vehicle Operators

The findings for the relatively homogenous occupation of vehicle operator are given in Table 6. Tests of spatial relations

Table 4
Validity Coefficients for Protective Occupations

	Training	Proficiency
Intellectual abilities	.42[d]	.22[d]
Intelligence	.65[b]	.23[d]
Immediate memory	.28[a]	.26[b]
Arithmetic	.30[c]	.18[c]
Spatial and mechanical	.35[c]	.18[d]
Spatial relations	.31[b]	.17[d]
Mechanical principles	.38[b]	.23[b]
Perceptual accuracy	.30[b]	.21[e]
Number comparison		.16[b]
Name comparison		.23[c]
Perceptual speed	.30[b]	
Motor abilities		.14[d]
Tapping		.16[b]
Finger dexterity		.15[c]
Hand dexterity		.08[b]
Personality traits	−.11[b]	.21[c]
Personality	−.11[b]	.24[c]
Interest		−.01[b]

[a] Less than 100 cases.
[b] 100 to 499 cases.
[c] 500 to 999 cases.
[d] 1,000 to 4,999 cases.
[e] 5,000 to 9,999 cases.
[f] 10,000 to more cases.

Table 5
Validity Coefficients for Service Occupations

	Training	Proficiency
Intellectual abilities	.42[d]	.27[d]
Intelligence	.42[d]	.26[d]
Arithmetic	.42[d]	.28[d]
Spatial and mechanical abilities	.31[d]	.13[d]
Spatial relations	.31[d]	.13[d]
Perceptual accuracy	.25[c]	.10[d]
Number comparison		.14[b]
Name comparison	.25[c]	.15[c]
Cancellation		−.27[b]
Motor abilities	.21[d]	.15[d]
Tapping	.18[c]	.22[c]
Finger dexterity	.21[c]	.13[c]
Hand dexterity	.23[c]	.13[c]
Arm dexterity		−.01[b]
Personality traits		.16[b]
Personality		.16[b]

[a] Less than 100 cases.
[b] 100 to 499 cases.
[c] 500 to 999 cases.
[d] 1,000 to 4,999 cases.
[e] 5,000 to 9,999 cases.
[f] 10,000 or more cases.

Table 6
Validity Coefficients for Vehicle Operators

	Training	Proficiency
Intellectual abilities	.18[d]	.16[d]
Intelligence	.21[d]	.15[d]
Immediate memory	.10[b]	
Arithmetic	.17[d]	.25[e]
Spatial and mechanical abilities	.31[d]	.20[d]
Spatial relations	.23[d]	.16[e]
Location		.18[b]
Mechanical principles	.38[d]	.22[d]
Perceptual accuracy	.09[c]	.17[b]
Number comparison		.37[a]
Name comparison	.11[a]	.15[b]
Perceptual speed	.08[c]	
Motor abilities	.31[b]	.25[d]
Tapping	.27[a]	.28[e]
Dotting		.28[b]
Finger dexterity	.44[a]	.22[b]
Hand dexterity	.21[a]	.16[b]
Personality traits		.26[b]
Interest		.26[b]

[a] Less than 100 cases.
[b] 100 to 499 cases.
[c] 500 to 999 cases.
[d] 1,000 to 4,999 cases.
[e] 5,000 to 9,999 cases.
[f] 10,000 or more cases.

and mechanical ability, and of motor abilities have average validity coefficients of moderate magnitude for training criteria. Tests of intellectual abilities have much lower validity, and tests of perceptual accuracy have little or no validity. In the prediction of job proficiency tests of motor abilities and of personality traits are the best, though having only modest validity. Measures of intellectual ability and of perceptual accuracy while not completely without value, have relatively low validity.

Trades and Crafts

While the jobs included in the category of the trades and crafts are rather different from each other in their specific nature they all do involve the exercise of a high degree of skill, and require an extensive

Table 7
Validity Coefficients for Trades and Crafts

	Mechanical repairmen		Electrical workers		Structural workers		Processing workers		Complex machine operators		Machine workers		All trades and crafts	
	Training	Proficiency	Training	Proficiency	Training	Proficiency	Training	Proficiency	Training	Proficiency	Training	Proficiency	Training	Proficiency
Intellectual abilities	.41[f]	.23[e]	.49[f]	.29[e]	.31[f]	.25[d]	.46[e]	.24[d]	.26[e]	.26[e]	.35[e]	.19[d]	.41[f]	.25[f]
Intelligence	.40[f]	.23[d]	.47[f]	.31[d]	.33[e]	.25[d]	.36[d]	.24[d]	.34[d]	.25[d]	.34[d]	.18[d]	.41[f]	.25[f]
Immediate memory	.30[d]		.31[c]	.21[a]	.13[c]	.13[b]	.31[b]	.15[b]		.30[b]	.12[b]	-.02[b]	.28[e]	.17[c]
Substitution	.34[a]		.34[a]	-.17[a]	.31[c]	.31[a]		.34[a]		.26[b]	.27[b]	-.21[b]	.31[e]	.21[b]
Arithmetic	.42[f]	.24[d]	.53[f]	.28[d]	.30[e]	.25[d]	.50[e]	.22[c]	.28[b]	.27[d]	.39[d]	.22[c]	.43[f]	.25[f]
Spatial and mechanical abilities														
Spatial relations	.40[f]	.20[d]	.47[f]	.21[d]	.33[e]	.22[d]	.33[d]	.24[d]	.35[d]	.25[d]	.40[e]	.27[d]	.41[f]	.23[f]
Location	.42[f]	.18[d]	.46[e]	.19[d]	.33[e]	.23[d]	.35[d]	.25[d]	.35[d]	.25[d]	.44[d]	.28[d]	.41[f]	.23[f]
Mechanical Principles	.24[b]	.28[a]	.24[a]	.23[b]	.23[b]	.23[b]	.24[b]	.21[b]	.28[a]	.25[b]	.24[b]	.04[b]	.25[d]	.20[d]
Perceptual accuracy	.40[f]	.25[d]	.49[f]	.25[d]	.34[d]	.10[b]	.13[c]	.28[b]		.40[a]	.38[d]	.44[b]	.41[f]	.26[d]
Number	.40[f]	.20[d]	.27[f]	.24[d]	.28[d]	.25[d]	.29[c]	.25[c]	.26[c]	.26[d]	.27[d]	.13[c]	.35[f]	.24[e]
Comparison	.22[a]	.23[a]	.25[c]	.17[a]	-.04[b]	.08[b]	.24[b]	.21[a]	.42[a]	.14[b]	.10[b]	.12[a]	.20[d]	.14[c]
Name comparison	.34[b]	.20[d]	.25[b]	.21[c]	.31[d]	.25[b]	.14[b]	.31[b]	.30[b]	.26[d]	.21[b]	.23[b]	.28[d]	.25[e]
Cancellation		.04[a]		.21[a]		.21[a]			.20[b]	.23[a]	.28[b]	.01[b]	.24[e]	.16[b]
Pursuit	.17[c]	.36[b]	.16[c]	.29[b]	.18[a]	.24[a]	-.13[a]	.17[d]	.41[a]	.33[b]	.20[b]	-.12[a]	.16[d]	.25[d]
Perceptual speed	.40[f]	.03[a]	.43[c]	.36[a]	.29[d]	.35[b]	.34[c]	.19[b]		.28[a]	.35[c]	.12[d]	.40[f]	.25[c]
Motor abilities	.15[d]	.16[d]	.15[d]	.16[a]	.26[d]	.21[c]	.17[b]	.27[d]	.26[d]	.19[e]	.17[d]	.06[b]	.20[f]	.19[f]
Tracing	.21[b]	.27[a]	.24[b]	.15[a]	.24[a]	.30[b]	.17[b]	.24[b]	.22[a]	.19[b]	.21[b]	.14[c]	.22[d]	.20[c]
Tapping	.05[c]	.16[d]	.20[c]	.17[c]	.14[d]	.18[d]	-.01[b]	.31[b]	.24[b]	.20[d]	.10[b]	.06[d]	.17[d]	.19[c]
Dotting	.20[b]	.11[a]	-.14[a]	.01[a]	.13[b]	.20[b]	.02[b]		.26[a]	.11[b]	.10[b]	.10[d]	.13[c]	.11[c]
Finger dexterity	.21[c]	.18[d]	.15[d]	.17[d]	.26[d]	.20[d]	.22[c]	.28[d]	.27[c]	.18[d]	.22[d]	.21[b]	.21[e]	.19[f]
Hand dexterity	.11[b]	.13[d]	.03[b]	.12[c]	.33[c]	.22[d]		.25[c]	.27[c]	.18[d]	.20[b]	.11[b]	.23[d]	.18[e]
Arm dexterity	.08[a]	.07[a]	-.10[a]			.24[a]		.22[a]	.34[a]	.33[a]	-.03[b]	-.13[b]	.06[b]	.15[c]
Personality traits									.31[a]	.24[b]				.24[c]
Personality								.30[b]		.24[b]				.29[b]
Interest	.16[e]		.16[e]			.28[b]		.22[b]				-.13[b]	.16[f]	.17[b]

[a] Less than 100 cases.

[b] 100 to 499 cases.

[c] 500 to 999 cases.

[d] 1,000 to 4,999 cases.

[e] 5,000 to 9,999 cases.

[f] 10,000 or more cases.

Table 8
Validity Coefficients for Industrial Occupations

	Machine tenders		Bench workers		Inspectors		Packers and wrappers		Gross manual workers		All industrial workers	
	Training	Proficiency	Training	Proficiency	Training	Proficiency	Training	Proficiency	Training	Proficiency	Training	Proficiency
Intellectual abilities	-.31ᵃ	.21ᶠ	.27ᵈ	.18ᶠ	.24ᶜ	.21ᵈ	.49ᶠ	.18ᵈ	.25ᵇ	.22ᵉ	.38ᵉ	.20ᶠ
Intelligence	-.31ᵃ	.21ᵉ	.20ᵈ	.18ᶠ	.22ᶜ	.23ᵈ	.50ᵈ	.17ᵈ	.23ᵇ	.21ᵈ	.38ᶜ	.20ᶠ
Immediate memory		.17ᵈ		.06ᵈ		.14ᵇ		.24ᵇ				.15ᵈ
Substitution		.19ᶜ		.12ᵈ		-.01ᵇ		.16ᵇ				.14ᵈ
Arithmetic		.21ᵉ	.37ᶜ	.20ᵉ	.26ᵇ	.24ᵈ	.43ᶜ	.16ᵈ	.37ᵃ	.24ᵈ	.38ᶜ	.21ᶠ
Spatial and mechanical abilities		.20ᶠ	.35ᵈ	.22ᶠ	.25ᵈ	.22ᵈ	.46ᵉ	.15ᵈ	.30ᵇ	.19ᵈ	.40ᵉ	.20ᶠ
Spatial relations		.22ᶠ	.32ᵈ	.21ᶠ	.28ᵈ	.24ᵈ	.43ᵈ	.15ᵈ	.30ᵇ	.19ᵈ	.40ᶜ	.21ᶠ
Location		.11ᵈ		.19ᵉ	.19ᶜ	.18ᶜ		.16ᶜ			.19ᶜ	.15ᶜ
Mechanical principles			.63ᵇ	.41ᵇ		.42ᵇ	.50ᵈ	.14ᵇ	.24ᵃ	.21ᵈ	.50ᵈ	.24ᵈ
Perceptual accuracy		.20ᶠ	.22ᶜ	.21ᶠ	.18ᵈ	.19ᵈ		.19ᵈ			.20ᵈ	.20ᶠ
Number comparison		.20ᵈ	.38ᵃ	.15ᵈ		.04ᵈ		.13ᵈ			.38ᵃ	.13ᵈ
Name comparison		.21ᶜ	.05ᵇ	.21ᵉ	.13ᵇ	.24ᶜ		.22ᵈ	.24ᵃ	.21ᵈ	.11ᵇ	.21ᶠ
Cancellation		.25ᵈ		.36ᶜ		-.11ᵃ		.24ᵇ				.31ᵈ
Pursuit		.15ᵈ	.29ᵇ	.15ᵈ	.09ᵇ	.09ᵇ		.16ᵈ			.15ᵇ	.15ᵈ
Perceptual speed	.21ᵃ	.24ᵇ	.26ᵇ	.27ᵈ	.22ᶜ	.58ᵃ					.24ᵈ	.29ᵈ
Motor abilities		.20ᶠ	.36ᵈ	.25ᶠ	.07ᵈ	.14ᵉ		.17ᵉ	.24ᵇ	.27ᵉ	.28ᵈ	.22ᵈ
Tracing		.16ᵈ	.16ᵈ	.18ᵇ	.09ᵃ	.20ᵇ		.12ᵇ			.14ᵇ	.16ᵉ
Tapping		.22ᵉ	.13ᵇ	.22ᵉ	.11ᵇ	.14ᶜ		.22ᵈ	.16ᵇ	.23ᵈ	.13ᶜ	.22ᶠ
Dotting		.15ᵈ	.22ᵇ	.16ᵈ	.08ᵃ	.06ᵇ		.13ᵇ			.18ᵇ	.15ᵈ
Finger dexterity	.21ᵃ	.18ᶠ	.41ᵈ	.26ᶠ	.02ᵇ	.16ᵈ		.10ᵈ	.29ᵇ	.26ᵈ	.34ᵈ	.22ᶠ
Hand dexterity		.27ᵈ	.41ᶜ	.27ᵉ	.03ᵇ	.25ᶜ		.20ᵈ	.25ᵇ	.30ᵈ	.33ᵉ	.26ᶠ
Arm dexterity		.15ᶜ	.54ᵇ	.24ᶜ		.00ᵈ		.24ᵈ		.43ᵇ	.69ᵇ	.18ᵈ
Personality traits		.26ᵃ		.26ᵃ								.26ᵃ
Personality				.50ᵃ								.50ᵃ
Interest		.26ᵃ		.02ᵃ								.14ᵃ

ᵃ Less than 100 cases.
ᵇ 100 to 499 cases.
ᶜ 500 to 999 cases.
ᵈ 1,000 to 4,999 cases.
ᵉ 5,000 to 9,999 cases.
ᶠ 10,000 or more cases.

preparation through training. The average validity coefficients for these various jobs are to be found in Table 7.

As would be expected from the characteristics of the jobs which constitute the trades and crafts, tests of intellectual abilities and of spatial and mechanical abilities have fairly substantial validity for the prediction of trainability. Tests of perceptual accuracy are almost as good, and those measuring motor abilities and personality traits have only limited validity. When it comes to measuring aptitude for performing the actual job itself, tests of intellectual abilities, spatial and mechanical abilities, perceptual accuracy, and personality traits are all found to be equally effective, having moderate validity. The validity of tests of motor abilities is more restricted.

Industrial Occupations

The many semiskilled and unskilled jobs which are to be found in industrial organizations are grouped together here to form the industrial occupations. The effectiveness of the various sorts of tests for these occupations are to be found in Table 8.

Measures of intellectual abilities, and of spatial and mechanical abilities are quite good measures of aptitude for training in the industrial occupations, being nearly as good for this purpose as they are in the case of the trades and crafts. The utility of tests of motor abilities is somewhat less, but still satisfactory. While the validity of tests of perceptual accuracy is still lower, they, too, are not without some value. Tests of intellectual abilities, spatial and mechanical abilities, perceptual accuracy, and motor abilities all have just about the same level of validity for proficiency criteria. Though this falls short of what is ordinarily desired, nonetheless it is apparent that these tests do give predictions of job proficiency which clearly are better than chance.

THE PREDICTIVE POWER OF OCCUPATIONAL APTITUDE TESTS

Considering the considerable differences in the times when the investigations summarized here were performed, together with the large differences in the nature of the organizations in which they were conducted, and the marked variations among the samples in such factors as age, sex, education, and background, the average validity coefficients presented here can be said to have a good deal of generality. Furthermore, since most of them are based upon a number of separate and distinct determinations they have a substantial measure of dependability and meaningfulness.

The general run of the validity coefficients is quite respectable for training criteria, and it is somewhat less so for proficiency criteria. The grand average of the validity coefficients for all tests for all jobs taken together is .39 for training criteria and .22 for proficiency criteria. However, for every job there is at least one type of test which has at least moderate validity. If for each job the highest average validity coefficient is observed, it will be found that for the 21 jobs these values range from .28 to .65 for training criteria, and from .24 to .46 for proficiency criteria. The averages of these maximal validity coefficients are .45 for training criteria and .35 for proficiency criteria. In view of the attenuating effects upon validity coefficients which were discussed earlier the foregoing values clearly are conservative as descriptions of the predictive power of occupational aptitude tests. It will be recalled that single tests are being considered here, and that judiciously selected combinations of tests would have been higher validity.

REFERENCE

Ghiselli, E. E. *The validity of occupational aptitude tests.* New York: John Wiley & Sons, 1966.

Paper-and-Pencil Measures of Potential*

C. PAUL SPARKS

This paper is written retrospectively. The author has been continuously associated with the research and operation of the program since it was begun by Standard Oil Company (New Jersey) in 1955 as The Early Identification of Management Potential or, colloquially, as EIMP. The availability of data on the program through published literature is quite limited. However, general familiarity has been gained by many persons through oral presentations at seminars, conventions, and workshops and through numerous doctoral dissertations prepared with the aid of material collected in the course of administering the tests and questionnaires. A large number of proprietary in-house research reports has been written and many of these have been made available to scholars interested in the subject.

The use of demographic information as an aid to personnel planning is a very recent development, particularly the use of sophisticated models that permit testing of the later effects of various scenarios based on the input of age, education, attrition, and other variables. Yet, in the early 1950s some organizations were making work force projections in which the low birth rate of the depression years was seen as having dire implications. This problem of the 30s was also shown as compounded by the effects of World War II, both a decimation of talent and an upset to the traditional educational system. In Jersey Standard this information was translated into a projected personnel shortage, particularly a shortage of able, qualified middle managers. The traditional identification process—trial, evaluation, and promotion of those deemed most fit—was considered as unlikely to continue to meet the demand. Management approached the Social Science Research Division of the Employee Relations Department and asked for a proposal. Perhaps the industrial psychologists employed there did not realize the enormity of the task they were being asked to perform, and they may not have heeded an observation made by George Washington:

> One of the difficulties is bringing about change in an organization is that you must do so through the persons who have been most successful in that organization, no matter how faulty the system or organization is. To such persons, you see, it is the best of all possible organizations, because look who was selected by it and look who succeeded most within it. Yet these are the very people through whom we must bring about improvements.

---

* This is an original article written specifically for this book.

The industrial psychologists employed by the Social Science Research Division were all empiricists. That is, their approach to a selection problem was typically the gathering of objective information about a candidate and the correlating of this information with some pertinent criterion of success. Hinrichs (1966) defines this procedure in this way:

> *The statistical approach.* The psychologist who is oriented to the statistical approach says that selection should be viewed as a process of evaluating the extent to which a candidate will resemble currently successful employees in terms of characteristics which research has shown to be related to success in the organization. The hiring decision usually is based on a statement that, as a result of the selection factors evaluated, the probability is x that the candidate will be a successful employee. (p. 87)

He contrasts this with:

> *The clinical approach.* The psychologist who is clinically oriented views each selection decision as an individual case. He attempts to learn as much as possible about each candidate and each specific job and to evaluate these independently without considering in any way the total pool of candidates available or the statistical probabilities of group differences. He uses his knowledge of people and his experience to arrive at an essentially subjective judgment about the appropriateness of hiring each individual candidate. Although he may evaluate the same data that are used in the statistical approach, he interprets them intuitively rather than comparing the candidate against statistical norms. (p. 88)

As the Jersey Standard industrial psychologists were drafting their research proposal they were keenly aware of a highly successful empirical program inaugurated by Sears in 1942 with the assistance of the late Dr. L. L. Thurstone. As described by Bentz (1968):

> The battery of tests . . . selected by Thurstone at the beginning of our effort reflects the nature of our company. The company is relatively nontechnical in nature, and executive development takes place largely through job rotation. The original intent was not the prediction of success in specific or specialized kinds of assignments. Rather, a test battery was desired which would tap *general* executive competence: the ability to move effectively and flexibly through a range of different tasks and assignments. (p. 59)

The Sears Executive Battery of Psychological Tests was as follows (Benz, 1968, p. 60):

> American Council on Education Psychological Test.
>
> Guilford-Martin Personality Inventories.
>
> Allport-Vernon Study of Values.
>
> Kuder Preference Record.

During this time, another development was emerging, one that would have a profound effect on identification of managers for many years. The formal title of the research was the Management Progress Study of AT&T, a study which is still ongoing after 25 years and is contributing much-needed longitudinal knowledge on the growth and development (or decline and decay) of persons in a business/industrial environment. However, the point of interest here is that the initial measurement of the persons to be included in the study as potential managers would be through what is known as an assessment center. Details of the operation of an assessment center are beyond the scope of this paper, as are the evaluations to be made at the conclusion of the assessment. Suffice it to be noted here that most of the basic data are derived from interactions among candidates on a number of different exercises which are observed by trained assessors. Bray, Campbell & Grant (1974) list the attributes to be rated and describe the exercises to be performed. They also discuss findings of the study in some detail.

The reader should note that throughout this period the persons mentioned here were professional colleagues and many were personal friends. Thus, many things which were not written down until much later were discussed at length, sometimes quite heatedly. All of the above information, and much more not discussed here, was available to the Jersey Standard industrial psychologists as they designed their study.

Laurent (1968, p. 4) characterized the beliefs underlying the EIMP study as:

There are significant individual differences between the most successful and least successful members of a group of managers.

Some of these differences can be measured.

A candidate for a management position will have a better chance of being successful if his individual characteristics and background are more like those of the most successful than the less successful managers.

These characteristics can be measured early in an employee's career.

The research was conceived as a concurrent validity study rather than a predictive study because of time constraints. Data that would be derived from a longitudinal study would not be available at the time of projected need. Accordingly, a sample of subjects was sought which would include some of the most successful and some of those with less success (failures were not included) who, at least on the surface, had the same opportunity as the most successful. A total of 600 individuals in SONJ and affiliates with organizational units in the metropolitan New York area met the specification imposed. These ranged from the chairman of the board and the president of

the parent company to about the second level of supervision in the parent company or one of the affiliates. Staff specialists, e.g., medical, law, and accounting, at levels equivalent to those of the managers were included. All participants were told that they were taking part in a research project and that individual results would not be used for administrative purposes.

Data collection was to be accomplished in a variety of ways—tests, questionnaires, interviews, and extractions from company records. Listed below are the various pieces of information:

Miller Analogies Test, a standardized measure of verbal reasoning.

Non-Verbal Reasoning Test, a standardized measure of abstract reasoning.

Guilford-Zimmerman Temperament Survey, a standardized measure of 10 personality or temperament measures according to its authors. The 300 items were also considered "experimental" for item-analysis purposes.

Individual Background Survey, a multiple-choice inventory of life experiences constructed specifically for the project.

Management Judgment Test, verbally described written situations which called for a decision or a choice of action from among several alternatives. This was constructed specifically for the project though some of the situations had been used earlier with manufacturing first-line foremen.

Self-Performance Report, a forced-choice type rating form which the job incumbent completed. The form was an amalgam of materials used earlier by superiors rating their subordinates.

Survey of Management Attitudes, questions on a variety of occupational, social, and educational items developed specifically for the project.

Picture Technique, a set of eight TAT-type pictures flashed on a screen for 10 seconds and then removed. Examinee wrote a brief narrative describing what was going on in each picture.

Personal History Record, a cumulative record of numbers and kinds of assignments throughout his career. The record was reviewed with the incumbent and the assignments were classified as line/staff, overseas/domestic, functional/general, etc.

Interview. One-on-one interview between incumbent and researcher centering on career planning before entering the company, critical period for advancement, most important achievement, and person who contributed most to his advancement. Interview data were recorded on two checklists, one on the information developed and the other on human relations skills exercised during the interview.

The complete file on each individual contained more than 1,000 experimental items with about 5,400 alternative responses.

The criteria used to select potential participants in the study were quite broad—location somewhere in the organizational hierarchy as shown by job title and location on an organization chart of one of the six participating companies. Obviously, this was insufficient as a criterion against which to perform incisive statistical analyses. Also, the criterion had to make sense to management. Significant correlations against an index which seriously violated the opinions of top management would be of no value in gaining acceptance of any tools or techniques developed by the project.

Though the study was being performed in what was ostensibly one organization, there was no uniformity in the collection and recording of information that could be used as a criterion of success. The parent company and the five affiliates had independent job classification systems and no method for equating them. There were no uniform performance appraisal data. Even the promotional data were clouded. At one point in the criterion construction one of the researchers mused that Mrs. Doe must have real trouble conveying to the Tuesday

bridge group that Mr. Doe had been promoted from vice president of company X to deputy coordinator of marketing in company Y. On the other hand, Mrs. Doe had no trouble convincing herself as she compared the paychecks for the two jobs.

Criterion variables finally used in the study were three: *position level attained, managerial effectiveness,* and *salary.* These are simple to state, but it took four years to develop them. In the process a complete dossier was built for each participant in the study. An example of the problem of position level was illustrated earlier in the discussion of Mrs. Doe and her bridge club. Each job move of each participant was checked against his salary history and other variables to determine whether the move was a promotion or a lateral move. These other variables included such things as the in-company classifications of other managers at his level, the size of the company, previous or following job incumbents, and subsequent assignments. The reader must also be aware that these participants could have moved into or out of any one of hundreds of Jersey Standard organizations anywhere in the world. In the long run each participant was assigned to 1 of 16 position levels based on the job held in 1955 where the tests were given and the other information was collected.

The managerial effectiveness criterion was derived by means of the alternation ranking technique. Lists of managers at approximately the same level in the hierarchy and in the same activity were prepared. The number on each list ranged from 6 to 30. Names of persons not in the study were frequently included in order to develop the base for comparison. An effort was made to find at least three superiors who would know the work of a large proportion of the men on each list. More than 100 managers were involved in the ranking task. Rankings were to be made on the "effectiveness of this man as a manager." Each set of rankings was converted to a set of normalized scores based on the number of persons ranked. The score for each participant was the average of all of his standard scores. The reader will note here that the effects of status, assignment, company size, etc., were minimized by this procedure. Thus, the highest-ranked individual in a group of second-level supervisors could have the same effectiveness score as the highest-ranked individual in a group of vice presidents.

Most merit salary administrations are based on the premise that the amount of salary received by an employee should reflect the value of the job being held and how well the incumbent is performing it. Jersey Standard had a merit salary policy. However, use of 1955 salary figures had some built-in hazards. For example, one individual might have just received a substantial salary increase while a counterpart might be just one month away from a similar increase. Also, the effects of previous salaries are inevitably built into the system. A 10 percent raise is not the same amount for two individuals if one has a base of $20,000 and the other has a base of $30,000. In addition, tenure, both company and job, affects salaries. Given the same job and the same level of performance, the individual with 20 years of service is likely to have a higher salary than will the individual with 10. The effects were minimized by creating standard scores for each participant for each year of a five-year period, 1954–58, and averaging these scores. An adjustment for age was then applied to minimize the effect of tenure. Age, rather than service, was used because some participants had relevant experience outside Jersey Standard. A third salary criterion was constructed by comparing age-adjusted indexes for each individual from a beginning date of 1950 to an ending date of 1958. Changes between the two indexes gave one more measure of "success."

The research design called for the development of scoring keys based on item analysis against a success criterion. By 1959 the number of pieces of predictor and criterion information had grown to such an extent that even programming to handle 5,400 bits of data for each participant was well nigh impossible, not to mention the difficulties of interpretation imposed on the researchers. Also, the reader must remember that the computers of the 50s were hardly comparable to those of the 80s.

The researchers chose to attack the criterion problem through the technique of factor analysis. All of the criterion variables just discussed, plus several additional descriptive variables thought likely to have an effect, were entered into the factor-analysis program. Several factors emerged but the strongest clearly reflected the three criteria posited by the researchers early in the study: *position level, managerial effectiveness* (ranking), and *salary*. However, age and service were also related to this factor despite the efforts of the researchers to minimize their impact. A weighting system was designed to remove the effects of age and service and a "success index" was computed for each participant.

By now the original research sample had shrunk to 443. Eliminations were due solely to large gaps in the predictor or criterion data files. For example, 20 individuals were eliminated because no ranking information could be obtained, they had not been in their current position long enough. Some individuals had been transferred to foreign assignments before their interviews were secured. Others simply failed to show up for testing sessions, including make-up sessions. A very few specifically declined to participate in the research.

The total sample was divided into two subsamples of 222 and 221 for a double cross-validation of the items. A general purpose item-analysis computer program was written to take care of the mass of data and the response alternatives were analyzed against the overall success index (SI).

The alternation ranking criterion (AR) was used separately for another item analysis, the rationale being that it was largely unaffected by position level. Age was also included as a criterion for still another item analysis, the rationale being that certain biographical data items might reflect age.

Scoring keys based on right and wrong answers existed for the two ability tests, verbal reasoning and nonverbal reasoning. Commercially available keys were available for scoring the Guilford-Zimmerman Temperament Survey on 10 scales. (For further information about these scales see Guilford & Zimmerman, 1949, and Guilford, Zimmerman, & Guilford, 1976.) However, as mentioned previously, the 300 items of the GZTS were also to be treated as experimental and were thus to be subjected to item analysis. The self-performance report had a graphic rating scale format with values to be recorded directly. It also had a theoretical forced-choice key built around the relationships among six constructs. All other instruments simply provided undifferentiated item data.

The double cross-validation technique provides that keys constructed on one subsample be compared with the criterion on the other subsample. Thus, keys constructed on subsample A would be used to score materials of subsample B for validation and vice versa. The general purpose item-analysis computer program used provided the researchers with two pieces of information. The first was the Pearsonian correlation between the response to a given item and the criterion of interest. The second was the mean criterion score for all participants marking a particular response to that item. Said differently, if being an only child tended to be more often a characteristic of high-criterion participants, a positive correlation of appropriate magnitude would be shown on the computer printout. At the same time, the mean criterion score for those who were only children would be shown. The latter statistic

was extremely important for multiple-choice items where only one alternative could be chosen. Such an item might well have more than one keyed response.

These statistics were generated for each item in the data base, not once but three times—once for the overall success index, once for the ranking score, and once for age. The amount of computer output was voluminous, to put it mildly. Space to inspect the output was at a premium. The author can still remember working with two other researchers on the floor of a nearby apartment living room because that was the only space large enough to spread out the computer paper. Several decision rules had been established but the computer programming available at that time was insufficient to eliminate the necessity of human judgment.

The basic decision rules were these:

1. The validity coefficient should attain the .10 level of significance. For samples of this size this typically meant a correlation of at least .07 for the item.
2. The alternative should have been marked as applicable by at least 10 percent of the respondents.
3. The alternative should not have a significant (.05) correlation with age.

This last decision rule warrants some explanation. Among the biographical data items were a number that were time bound. For example, by 1955 few young people built crystal radio sets. While many of these participants were growing up, building a crystal radio set was an achievement. Since the ages of the participants had a range of more than 30 years, the correlation with age was a very important datum.

Keys were finally built, a set based on the item analyses for subsample A and another set for subsample B. The original forms were even broken down into logical subparts based on hypotheses or hunches of the researchers.

A generalized computer scoring key was

written, one which would add algebraically +1, 0, and −1, the only item weights assigned. Differential item weighting was discussed, weighting based either on the size of the item validity coefficient or the significance level of mean differences. No-differential weighting was a conscious, not a default, decision. A constant was added to all scores to eliminate the possibility of a negative total score on any instrument or a subpart thereof.

As the keying proceeded it appeared to the researchers that each of several pieces of data contributed to an understanding of the relationship of an item to the criterion being employed. Many of these related to the shape of the distribution of responses among the item alternatives while others related to the criterion distribution of the participants checking a particular response. For example, a given response might distinguish high-criterion respondents from both middle- and low-criterion respondents but fail to distinguish middle from low. For some instruments this led to use of a new set of item-analysis data, the percentage of high, middle, and low criterion respondents marking the response.

Earlier it was noted that the managerial success criterion developed through the alternation ranking procedure would be used as one criterion for item analysis and keying, even though it was also a part of the success index criterion. This meant that four studies were going on simultaneously:

1. Item analysis and keying based on the success index (SI) with subsample A and validation on subsample B.
2. Item analysis and keying based on the success index (SI) with subsample B and validation on subsample A.
3. Item analysis and keying based on the alternation ranking (AR) with subsample A and validation on subsample B.
4. Item analysis and keying based on the alternation ranking (AR) with subsample B and validation on subsample A.

Basic validation data for 45 sets of scores are shown in Table 1 for each of the 4 studies. Details of the data behind each set of scores are beyond the scope of this paper. The reader should be able to fathom much of the thought processes of the researchers through the notes that follow each key identification. Also, the reader should remember that the correlations reported for each of the item analysis based keys are cross-validations.

Many of the correlations are statistically significant (.01 level) across all four studies, even when SI keys are validated against AR criterion scores and vice versa. In addition, the researchers had available distributions of scores, means, standard deviations, and a complete matrix of intercorrelations. The task was now to put together some trial batteries based on these data. At this point a new consideration obtruded. The test battery would be administered to persons with no track record if it were to be used for early identification of management potential. A simple regression of the variables would not be a satisfactory solution. For example, the aspects of the interview which reflected prior experience were unsuited to short-service employees, though they had contributed to an understanding of managerial success. Skipping over the experimental trials, the researchers retained the two reasoning ability tests, the Individual Background Survey, the new scores on the Temperament Survey, the Management Judgment Test, and the Self-Performance Report. The two studies against each criterion (SI and AR) were combined and a new set of keys was constructed for each of the two criteria (SI and AR). These keys were built by comparing the item-analysis keys for subsamples A and B, as well as inspecting the item analysis of the composite. Certain decision rules were established to ensure that a keyed item had a significance level of at least .05, and was not characterized by an extremely noticeable imbalance in either of the subsamples. Some judg-

Table 1
Validities of Different Keys against the Two Final Criteria

Score	SI-A	SI-B	AR-A	AR-B
Verbal reasoning, raw score	.18†	.17*	.18†	.20†
Verbal reasoning, age adjusted	.18†	.19†	.16*	.16*
Nonverbal reasoning, raw score	.20†	.08	.29†	.26†
Nonverbal reasoning, age adjusted	.21†	.09	.25†	.20†
GZTS—general activity	.05	.08	.07	−.02
GZTS—restraint	.03	.05	.04	.08
GZTS—aggressiveness	−.08	−.07	.06	−.01
GZTS—sociability	−.07	−.01	.02	−.08
GZTS—emotional stability	.14*	.13*	.14*	.04
GZTS—objectivity	.08	.17*	.17*	.07
GZTS—friendliness	.04	.11	.10	−.01
GZTS—thoughtfulness	−.01	−.10	−.01	−.06
GZTS—personal relations	.05	.20†	.14*	.11
GZTS—masculinity	.06	.04	.23†	.16*
GZTS—SI *r*'s and frequencies	.31†	.32†	.30†	.17*
GZTS—SI *r*'s and M's	.27†	.31†	.29†	.15*
GZTS—AR *r*'s	.18†	.29†	.29†	.22†
GZTS—AR *r*'s and M's	.11	.30†	.24†	.22†
Self-performance report—graphic	.13*	−.05	.05	−.05
Self-performance report—forced-choice theory	.21†	.09	−.03	.01
Self-performance report—SI M's	.24†	.23†	.09	.17*
Self-performance report—AR M's	.00	−.04	.07	.04
Interview (003) check list—SI *r*'s	.21†	.19†	.11	.06
Interview (003) check list—AR *r*'s	.23†	.05	.21†	.06
Interview (310) a priori—theoretical	.17*	−.03	.13*	.15*
Interview (310) SI *r*'s	.20†	.29†	.20†	.18†
Interview (310) SI *r*'s & M's	.19†	.19†	.19†	.15*
Interview (310) AR *r*'s	.13*	.11	.32†	.20†
Interview (310) AR *r*'s & M's	.11	.14*	.32†	.19†
Background—basic items—SI % differentiation	.40†	.32†	.30†	.18†
Background—entire form—AR % differentiation	.35†	.32†	.37†	.28†
Background—experience only—SI *r*'s & M's	.64†	.60†	.32†	.20†
Background—college items—SI *r*'s & M's	.32†	.24†	.26†	.09
Background—entire form—AR % & M's	.32†	.33†	.35†	.28†
Background—marriage items—SI *r*'s & M's	.35†	.31†	.14*	.06
Background—entire form—SI *r*'s & M's	.63†	.50†	.38†	.19†
Background—entire form—AR *r*'s & M's	.37†	.36†	.44†	.33†
Management attitudes—SI *r*'s & M's	.25†	.14*	.09	.10
Management attitudes—AR *r*'s & M's	.12	.04	.08	.09
Management judgment—SI %, 1st choice	.32†	.22†	.23†	.06
Management judgment—SI %, 1st & 2d choice	.51†	.47†	.22†	.25†
Management judgment—SI *r*'s & M's, 1st choice	.32†	.31†	.23†	.12
Management judgment—AR *r*'s & M's, 1st choice	.11	.30†	.16*	.17*
Management judgment—AR % distribution, 1st	.13*	.27†	.11	.20†
Picture technique—a priori scale A	.03	.09	−.01	.15*

* p < .05.
† p < .01.

ment did enter into the final decision. For example, certain items had a linear relationship with the criterion and a linear relationship with age, e.g., years of schooling. The researchers assayed the probable relationship with a younger population and keyed accordingly.

The data bank of items for the entire 443 participants was accessed and the instruments of interest were rescored, once with the keys built for the SI criterion and once for the keys built for the AR criterion. Scores obtained were then correlated with the appropriate criterion. No cross-comparisons were made, i.e., SI scores versus AR criterion and vice versa. The purist will note here a touch of "fold-back validation" in that keys were constructed, in part, on the criterion and resulting scores were then used to predict that criterion. In defense, I would point out here that the original decision rules provided for an item significance level of .10 or better in a subsample. This meant that a keyed item in the total would have a significance level of .001 or better (.10 × .10).

A multiple correlation coefficient was then computed between the instrument scores and the two principal criteria. This was done for the entire group, for each of the six participating companies, for different functional groups, e.g., marketing, accounting and research, and for persons whose careers had been general management versus professional specialization. The researchers were looking for deviant data, information that would indicate a problem. They found none of any practical significance.

Using all the data at hand, the researchers established a set of weights that could be used operationally, one which personnel specialists without sophisticated statistical training could use and interpret. The weights recommended were then used in preparation of a report to Jersey Standard management.

An example of the report to management is shown in Table 2. Scores of the 443 participants on the EIMP battery were used to rank the participants. Scores on the appropriate criterion were used independently to develop another rank order. The multiple correlation of .70 was reported as a technical aside. What was reported was an empirical expectancy table comparing the two. This table reported how the members of each test score decile compared with the criterion in terms of placement in a high third, middle third, or low third. An example of this presentation is shown here for the SI scoring versus the SI criterion.

Table 2
Relations of Test Scores to SI Criterion

Rank on test	Criterion group			N
	Low $^1/_3$	Middle $^1/_3$	High $^1/_3$	
1–44	0%	5%	95%	44
45–88	2	23	75	44
89–132	5	38	57	44
133–176	10	45	45	44
177–220	25	55	20	44
221–265	40	47	13	45
266–310	53	38	9	45
311–355	56	33	11	45
356–399	64	29	7	44
400–443	79	21	0	43
N	148	148	147	443

Jersey Standard management accepted the report with congratulations for a job well done. In discussion after the presentation, a somewhat curious question arose. Paraphrased, it was this, "Should we not keep this information proprietary since it represents the possibility of a competitive edge?" This, of course, is contrary to the canons of our profession and is currently the source of many of our problems with federal regulatory agencies, advocate groups, and the "academically" oriented members of the profession. The answer solved the immediate, if not the later, problem. Paraphrased, it was, "Anyone who tries to follow us will always be behind us. Hopefully, by the time they are where we are today, we will be ahead of that point."

The presentation to management was concentrated on showing the validity of the tests and inventories researched. However, it was also necessary to develop a recommendation on how the battery could be used operationally. The researchers first set about packaging the materials for field administration. The reasoning tests were no problem. They could be used as delivered from their commercial publishers. Permission was obtained from Sheridan Supply to reprint the Guilford-Zimmerman with a different format but without any modification of items or response alternatives. The biggest problem was with the background survey. The researchers felt strongly that they had learned much from working with the item-analysis data, though they would probably have had difficulty in quantifying or otherwise detailing what they had learned. For example, both data and rational judgment indicated that some biodata items would have little applicability until the respondent had a full-time job and an opportunity for making choices of what to do with money, time, energy, etc. Others were clearly applicable to the development and education years. Still others appeared to have no time or experience boundaries. The biodata items were sorted into three years: early, later, and immaterial. Also, some items were noted as obsolete if used with new hires; note the example given earlier of building a crystal radio set. In contrast, new hires of the 60s would have had opportunities not available to those of the research participants. Some of these were added to the form. For example, astronaut as a potential occupational aspiration was added to the form, even though it could not be scored. The rationale was that later research would demonstrate whether it was valid. Also, even then, the researchers were envisaging development of techniques that would permit statistical identification of underlying dimensions so that forms could be revised without criterion-based item analysis. Ultimately, two background survey forms were produced, one of which could be given at the time of hire and one that could be given after the individual had from five to seven years of full-time work experience, not necessarily in a Jersey Standard company.

Jersey Standard's management gave a recommendation which might surprise some researchers and practitioners. It said, in effect, that the researchers should take their program and see if they could sell it to the operating companies. They first approached Humble Oil & Refining Com-

pany, the largest domestic affiliate. Presentations were made to that top management. The program was neither endorsed nor criticized. Instead, the researchers were told to see if they could sell it to functional management. Finally, one vice president agreed on a trial. He invited 21 of his managers to take the Personnel Development Series (PDS), as it had been renamed. Nineteen accepted the invitation. The tests and questionnaires were scored and interpreted on the basis of tentative norms developed by the researchers on the basis of results obtained by the original 443 participants. The result, consternation! All 19 scored above average and many were in the top decile according to the norms. The vice president smiled wryly and said that he would hope so, that these were all individuals whom he had nominated as having potential for top jobs in the company. Parenthetically, he was right. One of the 19 later became a senior vice president of Exxon Corporation. Another became manager of a major function in Humble. Most of the others had or are having successful careers. Satisfied with his own little validation study, this vice president asked that PDS be offered to all of the professional/technical employees in units under his supervision.

This experience was repeated several times during the next few years until virtually all functions and units within Humble had experience with PDS. There was much variation in the approach taken by different managers. Some restricted the testing to short service personnel, typically those with less than two years of service. Others asked that their entire professional/technical work force be included. This meant that opportunities existed for a large number of concurrent validity studies and also for the development of a base from which follow-up predictive studies could be run later. An example of the kind of concurrent studies performed is shown in Table 3. This series investigated validity across professional/

Table 3
Concurrent Validity Coefficients by Function/Specialization

Function/specialization	N	Predictor		Criterion		r
		M	σ	M	σ	
Series I only						
Marketing—retail	603	20.3	3.4	41.0	3.1	.52†
Marketing—industrial	106	20.8	3.2	41.8	2.8	.47†
Marketing—operations	73	17.6	3.8	37.8	4.2	.52†
Marketing—administrative	42	19.0	3.9	37.2	4.6	.54†
Production—engineers	179	21.5	3.1	42.8	3.4	.49†
Production—geologists	90	20.9	3.1	41.9	1.8	.28†
Exploration—geologists	107	21.5	3.3	42.6	2.1	.21*
Exploration—geophysicists	49	20.3	2.9	42.5	1.5	.22
Exploration—landmen	58	21.5	3.2	40.9	2.0	.31*
Refining—engineers	185	22.3	3.1	45.2	2.9	.40†
Controllers—accounting	141	19.5	3.1	38.8	3.8	.45†
Employee relations	32	23.2	3.0	42.4	2.8	.35*
Planning—engineers	38	21.2	3.2	41.7	3.3	.45†
Series I & II						
Marketing—retail	145	21.1	3.4	41.4	3.3	.56†
Refining—engineers	51	22.5	3.7	45.9	4.2	.55†
Production—engineers	106	21.4	3.0	43.2	4.1	.64†
Production—geologists	51	19.7	3.0	42.3	2.5	.30*
Exploration—geologists	65	21.4	2.9	32.6	2.2	.41†
Controllers—accounting	67	19.5	3.0	38.9	3.9	.57†

* p < .05.
† p < .01.

technical specialties in several functions of the company. The criterion employed was a slightly different version of the original success index (SI), i.e., job level attained, job performance as measured by a performance report, and salary, all with the effects of age and service partialed out. It should probably be noted here that the ingredients of this success index were taken from company records and were not subject to the careful attention given to the construction of the original success index. In all probability this new success index had lower reliability, a condition which would automatically bring about lower correlations, even if the "true" validity was constant. Also, two sets of data are reported here, one with only PDS-I and one with PDS-I & II (Series I augmented by the experience based form of the Background Survey). In Humble the Management Judgment Test had been included in Series

I based on research which showed a nonsignificant relationship to age and service.

The perceptive reader will deduce several things from the data shown in Table 3. I call particular attention to the criterion standard deviation for the geologists and the geophysicists. The validity coefficient is obviously affected by a severe restriction of range on the criterion. During the time that these data were being collected, exploration activity was at a low ebb; there was virtually no hiring of geologists and many employees with geological specialties were being transferred to other functions, particularly if they appeared to have talent for general management. For example, the manager of the General Services Department had been trained as a geologist.

In the meantime the program was being introduced into other affiliates of Jersey Standard, both domestic and foreign. This author does not have access to the details of most of these introductions but was made aware of them through correspondence and visits of the psychologists of these affiliates. The Canadian affiliate introduced the program in its marketing function, including a translation into Quebec French. The Central and South American affiliates introduced the program with administration in both English and Spanish. The materials were translated into Japanese and a small pilot program executed. By far the most ambitious was the program of the European affiliates. One of the principal researchers had been transferred from Jersey Standard to Esso Europe. Laurent (1969) published some of his research, that covering translation, installation, and validation in Norway, Denmark, and the Netherlands. Even a digest of his work is beyond the scope of this paper. Suffice it to say here that validities were comparable to those obtained in the original EIMP research. Laurent extended this research to other European countries, including Finland and West Germany.

The Jersey Standard companies have a long history of supporting graduate research. This had been done through the provision of internships, assistance in the collection of data, direct financial support, and actual provision of data that were available in-house from operational or research programs. It was only natural that the EIMP data would be made available to students with appropriate research designs. The first of these (Hobert, 1965, Hobert & Dunnette, 1967) investigated the possible use of moderator variables to explain off-diagonal cases. Baker (1967) factored the biographical data items to develop a better prediction of salary levels. Cassens (1966) used the Central and South American data to examine similarity of cultural dimensions through analyses of biographical data. Taylor (1968) used the early Humble Oil data bank to compare three quite different occupational specialties and determine the

accuracy with which one could predict membership through scoring of biodata.

These kinds of research continued in Humble Oil (now Exxon Company, U.S.A.) and are still continuing. Herring (1969) performed the first predictive study. Jernigan (1970) used 4,186 sets of responses to investigate the factor structure of the GZTS and compare these findings with the 10 commercial keys (Guilford & Zimmerman, 1949; Guilford, Zimmerman, & Guilford, 1976). Woodward (1971) used the same data for a multiple discriminant analysis of five different occupational groups. Manese (1971) compared a group of employees who had spent their entire careers to date with the company with a group who had spent a significant amount of time in other companies before joining Humble/Exxon. Schrader (1975a, 1975b) investigated fakability of biodata scores and also studied ways of forming biodata dimensions. Frank (1976) compared an actuarial with a linear model for forming biodata dimensions. Brousseau (1976) used original GZTS responses and gathered later ones in order to investigate the effects of experience on personality profiles. Vicino (1978) added situational variables to PDS scores in an attempt to improve prediction of managerial success. Vandaveer (1981) investigated sex differences on the various PDS scores as well as the relative validity of sex.

This last study merits particular comment. The reader will probably have noted that all participants up to now have been referred to as "men." This was not an editorial usage; they *were* men. Beginning about 1970, the number of women professionals hired began to reach sizable proportions. Other women were moved from administrative jobs into more demanding professional jobs and, occasionally, into supervisory jobs. Where appropriate, these women were given the PDS. They complained that the forms were biased, particularly the Background Survey and the Management Judgment Test. A revision of these two instruments was undertaken. Revising the Management Judgment Test was accomplished by desexing the language, by rewriting so that a neutral pronoun was used or rewriting slightly so that the offending language was not necessary. The Background Survey presented more problems. Cosmetic changes were easily effected, "actor" as an early vocational aspiration was simply changed to "actor/actress." Other items were more difficult to modify. Consider this cluster of early vocational aspirations. It might be considered sexist today to have added such items as nurse, cosmetologist, and librarian, but much research evidence pointed to the fact that many women did (and still do) consider these as suitable vocations. Of course, items such as these could not be scored on any a priori basis and the small number of women with test results and with relatively short service precluded criterion-based item analysis. Inclusion was still recommended on the grounds that they would form a data base for future key construction. In the meantime both the revised form and the original form were given to females at the same testing sessions and they were asked to compare the two for coverage and appropriateness.

In 1970 the U.S. Equal Employment Opportunity Commission issued a new set of guidelines for use of employment tests. In 1971 the U.S. Department of Labor through its Office of Federal Contract Compliance issued an order on testing. In 1971 the U.S. Supreme Court handed down a decision in *Griggs* v. *Duke Power Company,* which interpreted the proper use of tests. Exxon U.S.A. decided to bring together as much information as possible and validate the PDS with the guidance given by these regulations and court decisions. Between 1973 and 1976, 12 major studies were completed, each designed to give evidence on one or more aspects of test use or validation that had been challenged by the EEOC, the OFCC, or in a federal court. The most important of these are discussed below.

Study A was aimed at determining the predictive value of the overall PDS results 10 years after testing, with the tests given during the first 2 years of employment. The criterion of success was the level achieved in the company hierarchy as measured by the classification level of the job held the 10th year after testing. The results were based on 339 individuals hired during the period 1962–1965 and tested between 1964–1966. These 339 were the active survivors of approximately 700 such employees hired and tested during that period. At the time of testing, virtually all of these employees were located in one of the four major operating functions—marketing, production, exploration, and refining. By their 10th year about 20 percent were in functions other than these. A few of the original examinees were lost because of transfer to the parent company or to other affiliates of Exxon U.S.A., both foreign and domestic. Table 4 presents the accumulated data. To help put this in perspective a few comments on the job grade structure are offered. Grades 21–23 are generally lower-level professional/technical jobs; 24–26 are intermediate professional/technical jobs or lower-level supervisory jobs; 27–29 are senior professional/technical jobs or middle-level supervisory jobs; 30 begins the executive payroll and also includes a few exceptionally high professional/technical jobs, and 34 is just a shade away from senior management. The correlation representing the relationship shown was .47, both statistically and practically significant. The reader will note that this is substantially below the .70 reported in the original EIMP study. It must also be noted that only one of the criterion aspects (job level attained) was used and that only the

Table 4
Predictive Validity of Personnel Development Series I, Job Grade 10 Years after Testing

Job grade	PDS scale scores							
	<13	13–15	16–18	19–21	22–24	25–27	>27	N
34	—	—	—	—	—	1	1	2
33	—	—	—	—	2	1	—	3
32	—	1	—	—	4	2	1	8
31	—	—	—	1	—	3	—	4
30	—	2	2	2	4	2	1	13
29	—	—	3	6	4	4	3	20
28	—	3	4	9	4	7	5	32
27	2	2	7	12	11	5	3	42
26	3	13	25	17	18	4	—	80
25	4	8	10	9	18	1	—	50
24	11	12	15	16	7	2	—	63
23	—	3	2	1	—	—	—	6
22	2	4	3	2	1	—	—	12
21	3	—	—	1	—	—	—	4
N	25	48	71	76	73	32	14	339

early portion of the PDS was used (later background omitted). There is the possibility that PDS affected the promotional history. Unit managers did have access to the results, but they do not have promotional authority except at the lowest levels and PDS results were not available to the committee on executive development.

Perhaps a mention of one of the favorite uses of PDS by unit managers will give additional perspective. Each year, an estimate of career potential is made for each employee in each unit. The managers would compare this with PDS, looking for discrepancies. Where such were found, the employee would be placed in a work situation with a respected superior and thus maximally exposed for verification of either the PDS score or management's estimate of potential. The unit manager truly did not care. He/she would be judged on the future performance of those nominated as having potential for advancement, not on the PDS score.

Laying aside for the moment the extent of predictor-criterion contamination, let us proceed to study B. There is one point in time at which such contamination is not

possible—the year in which the PDS was taken. The PDS data files were searched for individuals who had three or more years of service at the time of PDS completion and for whom complete data on job grade attained, potential estimate, and performance appraisal were available. A total of 685 individuals met the prescribed specifications. An index of relative achievement was constructed. Technically, this index was computed as the first factorial component derived from appropriate weighting of job grade, potential, appraisal, service, and age. Achievement index scores were categorized by scale scores to match the seven PDS categories as closely as possible. The cross-tabulated scores are shown in Table 5. The correlation represented by this tabulation was .53, quite comparable to the 10-year follow-up previously discussed though the individuals shown here ranged from 3 to 25 years of service.

As the data were being recorded for study A the records of several individuals suggested that validity appeared to increase with additional service. If this were true, it would run counter to the belief expressed in many personnel selection texts, the

Table 5
Concurrent Validity of Personnel Development Series I

Achievement index	PDS scale scores							
	<13	13–15	16–18	19–21	22–24	25–27	>27	N
27	1	2	1	8	8	13	10	43
25–27	1	3	6	23	23	23	19	98
22–24	1	6	21	35	30	28	7	128
19–21	11	12	27	42	28	18	7	145
16–18	18	9	38	32	27	9	1	134
13–15	20	18	18	19	9	1	2	87
13	23	12	6	5	2	2	—	50
N	75	62	117	164	127	94	46	685

Table 6
Personnel Development Series I versus Job Grade Attained

Years of service	Reasoning	Background	Judgment	Temperament	Total
3	.29†	.27†	.22†	.16†	.31†
4	.30†	.21†	.24†	.21†	.34†
5	.30†	.28†	.22†	.20†	.35†
6	.29†	.30†	.27†	.18†	.38†
7	.28†	.30†	.30†	.14*	.40†
8	.27†	.34†	.29†	.20†	.41†
9	.28†	.34†	.32†	.20†	.44†
10	.30†	.35†	.35†	.24†	.47†
11	.30†	.35†	.32†	.24†	.45†
12	.32†	.34†	.35†	.24†	.46†

* $p < .05$.
† $p < .01$.

American Psychological Association *Standards for Educational & Psychological Tests* (1974), and the Uniform Guidelines (1978) of EEOC and OFCC that validity deteriorates with time. The facts for the PDS were investigated statistically, not only for the total PDS score but for each subpart. The subjects were 304 of the 339 shown in Table 4. A few were lost because of gaps in their records due to service in some other affiliate though they were in Exxon U.S.A. during their 10th year. A few others were lost because they had not yet completed their 12th year of service and the researchers wished to extend the study as far as possible.

The observations of those posting the data had been correct. There was a consis-tent increase in the validity coefficients, not only for the total PDS but for each part. The predictor data were, of course, constant. What did change was the range of job grades, the criterion in this instance, as reflected in greater standard deviations as years of service increased.

Despite the change reflected in the standard deviations, some might say that the increase was due to use of the PDS in making (or denying) promotions. This suggested a look at the participants of study B. These 685 individuals varied widely in terms of length of service at the time of testing and no criterion contamination was possible. The results are shown in Table 7.

The correlations are generally higher for comparable years of service. The criterion

Table 7
Validity of PDS-I Total and Subparts by Length of Service Correlations
with Achievement Index

Years of service	N	Reasoning	Background	Judgment	Temperament	Total
3	173	.33†	.10	.27†	.21†	.31†
4	106	.30†	.33†	.35†	.28†	.44†
5	95	.41†	.28†	.38†	.07	.39†
6	57	.31*	.41†	.24	.22	.38†
7	38	.60†	.64†	.56†	.43†	.73†
8	32	.35*	.54†	.33	.20	.50†
9–11	38	.41†	.53†	.36*	.30	.63†
12–14	34	.28	.58†	.47†	.35*	.60†
15–17	55	.52†	.68†	.53†	.48†	.74†
18–25	57	.64†	.52†	.47†	.22	.60†
Total	685	.38†	.44†	.41†	.29†	.53†

* p < .05.
† p < .01.

is better. This is the achievement index of study B as contrasted with only the job-grade part, which was the criterion for study A and in Table 6. In general, the correlations increase with service. The results are less precise as sample sizes were small for some years. In fact, some combinations were necessary to obtain even a minimally acceptable sample.

Other studies included a replication of the concurrent validity study by function/specialization discussed earlier and reported in Table 3. Particularly noteworthy here was the fact that the validity for 172 research scientists and engineers was .54 against the achievement index and the PDS subparts also behaved in the same way that they did for the other functions.

Another study involved 395 individuals who had PDS-I close to the time of hire and who had PDS-II several years later. Validity against the achievement index at the time of taking PDS-II was .59 for Series I only and .64 for Series I & II combined. The addition of Series II resulted in an increase of 18 percent in the amount of variance accounted for.

Still another study involved validation for EEO "protected groups." Against the achievement index the validity for 67 black

males was .38 (p < .01; for 49 Hispanic males was .52 (p < .01), and for 66 white females was .31 (p < .05). The white females included several who had been recently promoted from nonexempt positions and thus had lower job grades while having a considerable amount of service.

The most ambitious of the studies, by far, was an attempt to define the content of the background, judgment, and temperament subparts of PDS-I in terms that would be meaningful to operational management. This activity was also expected to result in definitions that would be meaningful to EEO enforcement personnel. Furthermore, legislation was being proposed that would require reporting of data such as these to employees after they had taken PDS. The files yielded complete personnel data on 1,745 employees tested at various times prior to 1973 and still active in 1973. Item data from all three subparts of PDS-I were also available on computer tape. A modified co-variance program was written to cluster the items of each subpart. Each form was rescored to give a subscore reflecting these clusters. No changes were made in the item weights. The total score from each instrument was unchanged.

Three major clusters of items emerged

from analysis of the background items. These were:

Developmental influences. Relationships with family, peers, friends, and others that contributed experiences, attitudes, aspirations, etc.

Achievements: academic years. Direct academic or academic-related experiences but also including socialization experiences of high school and college.

Present self-concept. Evaluations of own abilities, achievements, probable future successes, personal characteristics, etc.

Four major clusters of items emerged from analysis of the Judgment items. These were:

Staff communication and participation. How an organization should be run in terms of superior/subordinate relations, planning, decision-making, idea generation, etc.

Employee selection and development. Characteristics of good/poor employees. The way to develop employees and attain achievement of the objectives of the organization.

Employee motivation and labor relations. Development of reward and recognition strategies; problem resolution and complaint handling.

Management style and decision-making. Reactions to company policies and practices; preferred methods of operation as a subordinate and as a superior.

Four major clusters of items emerged from analysis of the Temperament items. These were:

Behavioral consistency. The extent to which day-to-day activities were influenced by patterns of mood or behavior.

Energy level and time use. Approaches to situations with varying pressure demands, physical and/or mental-emotional.

Confidence and conviction. Willingness to take a stand as opposed to compromising for the sake of maintaining smooth relations.

Behavior understanding and tolerance. Understanding the underlying reasons for the behavior of others and acceptance of differing points of view.

Each of these 11 subscales was normed to fit the same interpretive scale as that used for the three instruments involved and the total PDS score. It was recognized that the subscales would probably not be as valid as the total instrument score. Each subscale was shorter and was thus probably less reliable. However, it was hoped that each would have at least a modicum of validity. A criterion of job grade and present performance, adjusted for age and service, was constructed for each of the 1,745 individuals. Instrument and subscale scores were correlated with this criterion. Results are presented in Table 8.

Table 8
Validity of Subscales and Total Scores of Three Major Instruments

Predictor	Correlation	
Background record total	.44*	
Development influences		.35*
Achievement: academic years		.38*
Present self-concept		.36*
Judgment record total	.27*	
Staff communication		.19*
Employee selection		.16*
Employee motivation		.13*
Management style		.18*
Temperament record total	.20*	
Behavioral consistency		.08*
Energy level—time use		.10*
Confidence—conviction		.21*
Behavior understanding		.09*
Total (without reasoning tests)	.46*	

* $p < .01$.

The subscales performed essentially as the researchers had predicted. All were statistically significant ($p < .01$) though the practical significance of some of the Temperament subscales was questionable. Again, the criterion used here was only a portion of what had been the best criterion based on a variety of researches.

The reader will have noted that a variety of criteria have been used in these studies. The reason is a very pragmatic one. Personnel Research did not always have access to data which would have allowed development of a complete file on each individual except by special permission from top management. Job grade, age, and service were always available. Estimates of potential and performance appraisal were available up to a specified job grade. Data on individuals transferred from Humble/Exxon U.S.A. were not available. Where missing data would have influenced the results of a study by eliminating significant parts of the desired sample, that study was not done or other criteria were substituted. With the exception of inability to compare certain correlation coefficients across studies, this did not cause trouble. Weaknesses could be expected to affect equally comparison of functions, instruments, sex or race/ethnic groups, length of service groups, etc.

A new study is under way. Job grades attained by several thousand examinees will be the criterion, with appropriate adjustments for age and service. The majority of these are still employed in Exxon U.S.A. and special permission was obtained to secure the job grades of those still active in the Exxon Corporation, wherever they are. The company now has a uniform classification system so that jobs in foreign affiliates are classified on the same variables as those in the domestic affiliates. It is quite important that these jobs outside Exxon U.S.A. be included since Exxon's employees with the very highest potential are generally expected to have a tour of foreign service during their careers. Also, inclusion of individuals outside Exxon U.S.A. will greatly extend the grade level representation and thus the criterion.

Standard E11 of the APA *Standards for Educational and Psychological Tests* (1974) reads:

To the extent feasible, a test user who intends to continue employing a test over a long period of time should develop procedures for gathering data for continued research. (p. 45)

Much data have been gathered, maintained, and used in research. It is perhaps difficult to divine a plan of research from the material contained in this article. What actually happened, and is still happening, was that the data base was accessed as questions were raised or, in the case of graduate-student research, as hypotheses were developed.

A survey of members of the Division of Industrial Psychology of the American Psychological Association and from the industrial representatives of the Foundation for Research in Human Behavior was conducted in the late 60s (Campbell, Dunnette, Lawler, & Weick, 1970). These individuals were asked to nominate firms "doing research in areas related to the identification or enhancement of managerial talent" (p. 19). Standard Oil of New Jersey had more nominations than any other organization. This paper should show that this research interest has not abated. The few studies reported here are only a small portion of those in the file, selected to illustrate points and not to deify PDS. Not reported at all are studies on issues generated by the PDS research but performed on data collected with other instruments. An example of this was the doctoral dissertation of Matteson (1969) on a methodology for constructing homogeneous keys for a biographical inventory. (See also Matteson, Osburn, & Sparks, 1969, 1970.) This was performed with a wage-earner biodata form. Others could be given. The research continues. Almost completed is an extensive job analysis of what Exxon U.S.A. executive-managerial-professional-technical employees (from entry level through upper management) do on the job, what individual abilities contribute to good performance, and what environmental and contextual variables surround the job.

REFERENCES

American Psychological Association. *Standards for educational and psychological tests.* Washington, DC: Author, 1974.

Baker, B. L. *The use of biographic factors to moderate prediction and predict salary level.* Unpublished doctoral dissertation, Purdue University, 1967.

Bentz, V. J. The Sears experience in the investigation, description, and prediction of executive behavior. In J. A. Myers (Ed.), *Predicting managerial success.* Ann Arbor, Mich.: Foundation for Research on Human Behavior, 1968, 59–152.

Bray, D. W., Campbell, R. J., & Grant, D. L. *Formative years in business: A long-term AT&T study on managerial lives.* New York: John Wiley & Sons, 1974.

Brousseau, K. R. Effects of job experience on personality: A theoretical and empirical investigation. Unpublished doctoral dissertation, Yale University, 1976.

Campbell, J. P., Dunnette, M. D., Lawler, E. E. III, & Weick, K. E., Jr. *Managerial performance and effectiveness.* New York: Mc-Graw-Hill, 1970.

Cassens, F. P. Cross cultural dimensions of executive life history antecedents (biographical information). Unpublished doctoral dissertation, Louisiana State University, 1966.

Frank, B. A. A comparison of an actuarial and a linear model for predicting managerial behavior. Unpublished doctoral dissertation, University of Houston, 1976.

Griggs v. *Duke Power Company.* 401 U.S. 424 (1971).

Guilford, J. P., & Zimmerman, W. S. *The Guilford-Zimmerman temperament survey: Manual of instructions and interpretations.* Beverly Hills, Calif.: Sheridan Supply Co., 1949.

Guilford, J. S., Zimmerman, W. S., & Guilford, J. P. *The Guilford-Zimmerman survey handbook.* San Diego: Edits, 1976.

Herring, J. W. Predictive value of a management aptitude test battery. Unpublished doctoral dissertation, University of Houston, 1969.

Hinrichs, J. R. *High talent personnel: Managing a critical resource.* New York: American Management Association, 1966.

Hobert, R. D. *Moderating effects in the prediction of managerial success from psychological test scores and biographical factors.* Unpublished doctoral dissertation, University of Minnesota, 1965.

Hobert, R. D., & Dunnette, M. D. Development of moderator variables to enhance the prediction of managerial effectiveness. *Journal of Applied Psychology,* 1967, *51,* 50–64.

Jernigan, L. R. A principal components analysis of the Guilford-Zimmerman temperament survey. Unpublished doctoral dissertation, Texas Christian University, 1970.

Laurent, H. Research on the identification of management potential. In J. A. Myers (Ed.), *Predicting managerial success.* Ann Arbor, Mich.: Foundation for Research on Human Behavior, 1968, 1–34.

Laurent, H. Cross-cultural cross-validation of empirically validated tests. *APA Experimental Publication System,* 1969, *2,* 042C.

Manese, W. R. Correlates of organizational tenure. Unpublished doctoral dissertation, University of Houston, 1971.

Matteson, M. T. An exploratory investigation of a methodology for constructing homogeneous keys for a biographical inventory. Unpublished doctoral dissertation, University of Houston, 1969.

Matteson, M. T., Osburn, H. G., & Sparks, C. P. *A computer-based methodology for constructing homogeneous keys with applications to biographical data* (Personnel Psychology Services Center Report 1). Houston, Tex.: University of Houston, December 1969.

Matteson, M. T., Osburn, H. G., & Sparks, C. P. The use of non-empirically keyed biographical data for predicting job success of refinery operating personnel. *APA Experimental Publications System,* 1970, *5,* 158C.

Schrader, A. D. An investigation of the fakability of an empirically scored biographical inventory with variations in the subtleness of specificity of subject response set. Unpublished master's thesis, University of Houston, 1975. (a)

Schrader, A. D. A comparison of the relative utility of several rational and empirical strategies for forming biodata dimensions. Unpublished doctoral dissertation, University of Houston, 1975. (b)

Taylor, L. R. A quasi-actuarial approach to assessment. Unpublished doctoral dissertation, Purdue University, 1968.

U.S. Department of Labor, Office of Federal Contract Compliance. Employee testing and other selection procedures. *Federal Register,* 1971, *36,* 19307–19310.

U.S. Equal Employment Opportunity Commission. Guidelines on employee selection procedures. *Federal Register,* 1970, *35,* 12333–12335.

U.S. Equal Employment Opportunity Commis-

sion, U.S. Civil Service Commission, U.S. Department of Labor, & U.S. Department of Justice. Adoption by four agencies of Uniform guidelines on employee selection procedures. *Federal Register,* 1978, *43,* 38290–38315.

Vandaveer, V. V. Investigation of sex differences in managerial profiles. Unpublished master's thesis, University of Houston, 1981.

Vicino, F. L. Situational correlates of organizational success. Unpublished doctoral dissertation, University of Rochester, 1978.

Woodward, J. A. A multiple discriminant analysis of five occupational groups based on thirteen personality measures. Unpublished masters thesis, Texas Christian University, 1971.

Reading 25

Employment Testing

*Old Theories and New Research Findings**

FRANK L. SCHMIDT
JOHN E. HUNTER

This article contains two messages: a substantive message and a methodological message. The substantive message is this: *(a)* Professionally developed cognitive ability tests are valid predictors of performance on the job and in training for all jobs (Hunter, 1980; Schmidt, Hunter, & Pearlman, 1981) in all settings (Lilienthal & Pearlman, in press; Pearlman, Schmidt, & Hunter, 1980; Schmidt, Gast-Rosenberg,

& Hunter, 1980; Schmidt, Hunter, & Caplan, 1981; Schmidt, Hunter, Pearlman, & Shane, 1979; Sharf, Note 1; Timmreck, Note 2; Schmidt, Hunter, Pearlman, & Caplan, Note 3); *(b)* cognitive ability tests are equally valid for minority and majority applicants and are fair to minority applicants in that they do not underestimate the expected job performance of minority groups; and *(c)* the use of cognitive ability tests for selection in hiring can produce large labor cost savings, ranging from $18 million per year for small employers such as the Philadelphia police department (5,000 employees; Hunter, Note 4) to $16 billion per year for large employers such as

* Excerpted from F. L. Schmidt and J. E. Hunter, "Employment Testing: Old Theories and New Research Findings," *American Psychologist* 36 (1981), pp. 1128–37. Copyright 1981 by the American Psychological Association. Reprinted/Adapted by permission of the publisher and author.

the federal government (4,000,000 employees; Hunter, Note 5).

The methodological message is this: In the last 10 years the field of personnel selection has undergone a transformation in viewpoint resulting from the introduction of improved methods of cumulating findings across studies. Use of these methods has shown that most of the "conflicting results" across studies were the result of sampling error that was not perceived by reviewers relying on statistical significance tests to evaluate single studies. Reviews in our field were also subject to systematic distortion because reviewers failed to take into account the systematic effects of error of measurement and restriction in range in the samples studied. The real meaning of 70 years of cumulative research on employment testing was not apparent until state-of-the-art meta-analytic procedures were applied. These methods not only cumulate results across studies but correct variance across studies for the effect of sampling error and correct both mean and variance for the distorting effects of systematic artifacts such as unreliability and restriction of range.

Tests have been used in making employment decisions in the United States for over 50 years. Although occasional use has been made of personality tests, and content-validated job knowledge and job sample tests have been used with some frequency, the most commonly used employment tests have been measures of cognitive skills—that is, aptitude or ability tests. Examples include tests of verbal and quantitative ability, perceptual speed, inductive and deductive reasoning, and spatial and mechanical ability. A great deal of new knowledge has accumulated over the last 10 years on the role of cognitive abilities in job performance and in the employment-selection process. In the middle and late 1960s certain theories about aptitude and ability tests formed the basis for most discussion of employee selection issues

and, in part, the basis for practice in personnel psychology. At that time, none of these theories had been tested against empirical data. However, they were plausible at face value, and some were accepted by personnel psychologists as true or probably true. Two important events occurred during the 1970s: *(a)* new methods were developed for quantitatively integrating research findings across studies to provide strong tests of theories, and *(b)* these methods were used to cumulate the empirical research evidence needed to determine whether these theories were true or false. We now have this evidence, and it shows that the earlier theories were false.

THE THEORIES AND THE RESEARCH EVIDENCE

The Theory of Low Utility

The first theory holds that employee selection methods have little impact on the performance and productivity of the resultant workforce. From this theory, it follows that selection procedures can safely be manipulated to achieve other objectives, such as a racially representative workforce. The basic equation for determining the impact of selection on workforce productivity had been available for years (Brogden, 1949; Cronbach & Gleser, 1957), but it had not been employed because there were no feasible methods for estimating one critical equation parameter: the standard deviation of employee job performance in dollars *(SDy)*. *SDy* indexes the magnitude of individual differences in employee yearly output of goods and services. The greater *SDy* is, the greater is the payoff in improved productivity from selecting high-performing employees.

During the 1970s, a method was devised for estimating *SDy* based on careful estimates by supervisors of employee output (Hunter & Schmidt, in press; Schmidt, Hunter, McKenzie, & Muldrow, 1979).

Applications of this method showed that *SDy* was larger than expected. For example, for entry-level budget analysts and computer programmers, *SDy* was $11,327 and $10,413, respectively. This means that a computer programmer at the 85th percentile in performance is worth $20,800 more per year to the employing organization than a computer programmer at the 15th percentile. Use of valid selection tests substantially increases the average performance level of the resultant workforce and therefore substantially improved productivity. For example, use of the Programmer Aptitude Test in place of an invalid selection method to hire 618 entry-level computer programmers leads to an estimated productivity improvement of $54.7 million ($68 million in 1981 dollars) over a 10-year period if the top 30 percent of applicants are hired (Schmidt, Hunter, McKenzie, & Muldrow, 1979). Estimates have also been made of the impact of selection on national productivity. Based on extremely conservative assumptions, Hunter and Schmidt (in press) calculate that the gross national product would be increased by $80 to $100 billion per year if improved selection procedures were introduced throughout the economy.

These findings mean that selecting high performers is more important for organizational productivity than had been previously thought. Research has established that mental skills and abilities are important determinants of performance on the job. If tests measuring these abilities are dropped and replaced by the interview and other less valid procedures, the proportion of low-performing people hired increases, and the result is a serious decline in productivity in the individual firm and in the economy as a whole. The rate of growth in productivity in the United States has slowed markedly in recent years—from about 3.5 percent to zero or even negative rates. One possible reason for this decline is the decline in the accuracy with which

employers sort people into jobs. In response to pressures from the federal government, American employers have substantially reduced the use of valid tests of job aptitudes in making hiring and placement decisions. Many companies have abandoned the use of such tests entirely. Over a period of 8–10 years, this change would manifest itself in lower productivity gains. Consider two examples. Seven or eight years ago, the General Electric Company (GE) responded to government pressure by dropping all tests of job aptitude and "getting their numbers right" in the hiring process. Like many firms, GE has a policy of promoting from within. About two years ago, several plants realized that a large percentage of the people hired under the new selection standards were not promotable. GE had merely transferred the adverse impact from the hiring stage to the promotion stage. These plants have now resumed testing (Hawk, Note 6). Some years ago, U.S. Steel selected applicants into their skilled trades apprentice programs *from the top down* based on total score on a valid battery of cognitive aptitude tests. They then lowered their testing standards dramatically, requiring only minimum scores on the tests equal to about the seventh-grade level and relying heavily on seniority. Because their apprentice training center kept excellent records, they were able to show that (*a*) scores on mastery tests given during training declined markedly, (*b*) the flunk-out and drop-out rates increased dramatically, (*c*) average training time and training cost for those who *did* make it through the program increased substantially, and (*d*) average ratings of later performance on the job declined (Braithwaite, Note 7).

The theory that selection procedures are not important is sometimes presented in a more subtle form. In this form, the theory holds that all that is important is that the people hired be "qualified." This theory results in pressure on employers to set low minimum qualification levels and then to hire on the basis of other factors from among those who meet these minimum levels. This is the system U.S. Steel adopted. In our experience, minimum levels on cognitive ability tests are typically set near the 15th percentile for applicants. Such "minimum competency" selection systems result in productivity losses 80 percent to 90 percent as great as complete abandonment of valid selection procedures (Mack, Schmidt, & Hunter, in press). For example, if an organization the size of the federal government (4 million employees) were to move from ranking on valid tests to such a minimum competency selection system with the cutoff at the 20th percentile, yearly productivity gains from selection would be reduced from $15.6 billion to $2.5 billion (Hunter, Note 5), an increase in labor costs of $13.1 billion per year required to maintain the same level of output. In a smaller organization such as the Philadelphia police department, the loss would be $12 million per year, a drop from $18 million to $6 million (Hunter, Note 4).

The problem is that there is no real dividing line between the qualified and the unqualified. Employee productivity is on a *continuum* from very high to very low, and the relation between ability test scores and employee job performance and output is almost invariably linear (APA, 1980; Hunter & Schmidt, in press; Schmidt, Hunter, McKenzie, & Muldrow, 1979). Thus a reduction in minimum acceptable test scores at any point in the test-score range results in a reduction in the productivity of employees selected. A decline from superior to average performance may not be as visible as a decline from average to poor performance, but it can be just as costly in terms of lost productivity. The finding that test-score/job-performance relationships are linear means that ranking applicants on test scores and selecting from the top down maximizes the productivity

of employees selected. This finding also means that any minimum test score requirement (test cutoff score) is arbitrary: No matter where it is set, a higher cutoff score will yield more productive employees, and a lower score will yield less productive employees. On the other hand, it means that if the test is valid, all cutoff scores are "valid" by definition. The concept of "validating" a cutoff score on a valid test is therefore not meaningful.

Most of the productivity loss in minimum competency selection systems comes from majority, not minority, group members. Minimum competency systems usually reduce standards for all applicants. Since most people hired are majority group members, the cumulative productivity loss from hiring less productive members of the majority group is much greater than the loss due to less productive minority workers.

The usual purpose of minimum competency systems is to eliminate discrepancies in minority and majority employment rates. However, despite the productivity losses, such systems typically merely reduce this discrepancy; they do not eliminate it. On the other hand, selection systems based on top-down hiring within each group completely eliminate "adverse impact" at a much smaller price in lowered productivity. Such systems typically yield 85 percent to 95 percent of the productivity gains attainable with optimal nonpreferential use of selection tests (Cronbach, Yalow, & Shaeffer, 1980; Hunter, Schmidt, & Rauschenberger, 1977; Mack et al., in press). However, such selection systems raise a host of legal, social, and moral questions (Lerner, 1977, 1979).

The Theory of Subgroup Validity Differences

This theory holds that because of cultural differences, cognitive tests have lower validity (test-criterion correlations) for minority than for majority groups. This theory takes two forms. The theory of single-group validity holds that tests may be valid for the majority but "invalid" (that is, have zero validity) for minorities. Although it was erroneous (Humphreys, 1973), the procedure adopted by psychologists to test for single-group validity involved testing black and white validity coefficients for significance separately by race. Since minority sample sizes were usually smaller than those for the majority, small-sample single-group validity studies produced a high frequency of white–significant, black–nonsignificant outcomes. Four different cumulative studies have now demonstrated that evidence for single-group validity by race does not occur any more frequently in samples than would be expected solely on the basis of chance (Boehm, 1977; Katzell & Dyer, 1977; O'Connor, Wexley, & Alexander, 1975; Schmidt, Berner, & Hunter, 1973).

The theory of differential validity holds that population validities are different for different groups, but are not necessarily zero for any group. This theory was tested by applying a statistical test of the difference between observed sample validities. Individual studies obtained varying results. More recent studies have cumulated findings across studies. The first such review was done by Ruch (Note 8), who found that differential validity occurred in samples at only chance levels of frequency. Two more recent reviews claim to have found somewhat higher frequencies: Boehm (1977) found a frequency of 8 percent and Katzell and Dyer (1977) reported frequencies in the 20 percent–30 percent range. But it has been shown (Hunter & Schmidt, 1978) that the data preselection technique used in these studies results in a Type I bias—rejecting the hypothesis of no difference when it is true—which creates the false appearance of a higher incidence of differential validity. Two more recent

studies that avoid this Type I bias have found differential validity to be at chance levels (Bartlett, Bobko, Mosier, & Hannan, 1978; Hunter, Schmidt, & Hunter, 1979). Bartlett et al. (1978) analyzed 1,190 pairs of validity coefficients for blacks and whites and found significant black–white differences in 6.8 percent of the pairs, using an alpha level of .05. Hunter et al. (1979) found the frequency of differential validity among the 712 pairs with a positive average validity to be 6 percent. Similar results have been obtained for Hispanic Americans (Schmidt, Pearlman, & Hunter, 1980). Thus the evidence taken as a whole indicates that employment tests are equally valid for all groups (Linn, 1978). The earlier belief in differential validity apparently resulted from excessive faith in individual small-sample studies in which significant difference occurred by chance.

The Theory of Test Unfairness

This theory holds that even if validity coefficients are equal for minority and majority groups, a test is likely to be unfair if the average test score is lower for minorities. There are numerous statistical models of test fairness, and these differ significantly in their properties (Cole, this issue; Jensen, 1980, Chap. 10; Hunter & Schmidt, 1976; Hunter et al., 1977). However, the most commonly accepted model of test fairness is the regression model (Cleary & Hilton, 1968). This model defines a test as unfair to a minority group if it predicts lower levels of job performance than the group in fact achieves. This is the concept of test fairness embedded in the Uniform Guidelines on Employee Selection Procedures (Equal Employment Opportunity Commission, Civil Service Commission, Department of Labor, & Department of Justice, 1978; Ledvinka, 1979). The theory of test unfairness is based on the assumption that the factors causing lower test scores do not also cause lower job performance. The accumulated evidence on this theory is clear: Lower test scores among minorities are accompanied by lower job performance, exactly as in the case of the majority (Bartlett et al., 1978; Campbell, Crooks, Mahoney, & Rock, 1973; Gael & Grant, 1972; Gael, Grant, & Ritchie, 1975a, 1975b; Grant & Bray, 1970; Jensen, 1980, Chap. 10; Schmidt, Pearlman, & Hunter, 1980; Ruch, Note 8; Tenopyr, Note 9). This finding holds true whether ratings of job performance or objective job sample measures of performance are used. Tests predict job performance of a minority and the majority in the same way. The small departures from perfect fairness that exist actually favor minority groups.

These findings show that employment tests do not cause "adverse impact" against minorities. The cumulative research on test fairness shows that the average ability and cognitive skill differences between groups are directly reflected in job performance and thus are *real*. They are *not* created by the tests. We do not know what all the causes of these differences are, how long they will persist, or how best to eliminate them. For many other groups in the past, such differences have declined or disappeared over time. But at the present time, the differences exist and are reflected in job performance.

The Theory of Test Invalidity

This theory holds that cognitive employment tests are frequently invalid for all (majority and minority alike). This theory takes two forms. The first subtheory holds that test validity is situationally specific—a test valid for a job in one organization or setting may be invalid *for the same job* in another organization or setting. The conclusion is that a separate validity study is necessary in each setting. The second form of this theory holds that test validity is job specific—a cognitive test valid for one job may be invalid for another job. The conclusion is that a separate validity study is necessary for every job.

Subtheory 1: Is validity situationally specific? The empirical basis for the subtheory of situational specificity was the considerable variability in observed validity coefficients from study to study even when jobs and tests appeared to be similar or identical (Ghiselli, 1966). The older explanation for this variation was that the factor structure of job performance is different from job to job and that the human observer or job analyst is too poor an information receiver and processor to detect these subtle but important differences. If so, empirical validation would be required in each situation, and validity generalization would be impossible (Albright, Glennon, & Smith, 1963; Ghiselli, 1966; Guion, 1965).

A new hypothesis was investigated during the 1970s. This hypothesis is that the variance in the outcomes of validity studies within job-test combinations is due to statistical artifacts. Schmidt, Hunter, and Urry (1976) showed that under typical and realistic validation conditions, a valid test will show a statistically significant validity in only about 50 percent of studies. As an example, they showed that if true validity for a given test is constant at .45 in a series of jobs, if criterion reliability is .70, if the prior selection ratio on the test is .60, and if sample size is 68 (the median over 406 published validity studies—Lent, Aurbach, & Levin, 1971b), then the test will be reported to be valid 54 percent of the time and invalid 46 percent of the time (two-tailed test, $p = .05$). This is the kind of variability that was the basis for the theory of situation-specific validity (Ghiselli, 1966; Lent, Aurbach, & Levin, 1971a).

If the variance in validity coefficients across situations for job-test combinations is due to statistical artifacts, then the theory of situational specificity is false, and validities are generalizable. We have developed a method for testing this hypothesis (Pearlman et al., 1980; Schmidt, Gast-Rosenberg, & Hunter, 1980; Schmidt & Hunter, 1977; Schmidt, Hunter, Pearlman, & Shane, 1979). One starts with a fairly large number of validity coefficients for a given test-job combination and computes the variance of this distribution. From this variance, one then subtracts variance due to various sources of error. There are at least seven sources of error variance: (*a*) sampling error (i.e., variance due to $N <$ ∞); (*b*) differences between studies in criterion reliability; (*c*) differences between studies in test reliability; (*d*) differences between studies in range restriction; (*e*) differences between studies in amount and kind of criterion contamination and deficiency (Brogden & Taylor, 1950); (*f*) computational and typographical errors (Wolins, 1962); and (*g*) slight differences in factor structure between tests of a given type (e.g., arithmetic reasoning tests).

Using conventional statistical and measurement principles, Schmidt, Hunter, Pearlman, and Shane (1979) showed that the first four sources alone are capable of producing as much variation in validities as is typically observed from study to study. Results from application of the method to empirical data bear out this prediction. To date, distributions of validity coefficients have been examined for 152 test-job combinations (Lilienthal & Pearlman, in press; Pearlman et al., 1980; Schmidt, Gast-Rosenberg, & Hunter, 1980; Schmidt & Hunter, 1977; Schmidt, Hunter, & Caplan, 1981; Schmidt, Hunter, Pearlman, & Shane, 1979; Schmidt, Hunter, Pearlman, & Caplan, Note 3; Linn, Harnisch, & Dunbar, Note 10). The first four artifacts listed above accounted for an average of 72 percent of the observed variance of validity coefficients. About 85 percent of the variance in validities accounted for by artifacts

is accounted for by simple sampling error. Corrections for sampling error alone lead to the same conclusions about validity generalizability as corrections for the first four artifacts (Pearlman et al., 1980; Schmidt, Gast-Rosenberg, & Hunter, 1980). Had it been possible to partial out variance due to all seven rather than to only four artifacts, all observed variance would probably have been accounted for.

These findings are quite robust. Callender and Osburn (1980) have derived alternative equations for testing validity generalizability and have shown that these produce identical conclusions and virtually identical numerical results. These findings effectively show the theory of situational specificity to be false. If one looks at the estimated distributions of operational (or true) validities (that is, validities corrected for the effects of criterion unreliability and range restriction; cf. Schmidt, Gast-Rosenberg, & Hunter, 1980), one finds that in 84 percent of 152 test-job combinations, even the validity value of the 10th percentile is positive and substantial enough in magnitude to have practical value in improving workforce productivity. These findings show that cognitive test validities can typically be generalized with confidence across settings and organizations, and there is no factual basis for requiring a validity study in each situation.

Subtheory 2: Is test validity job specific? Job differences might moderate the validity of a given test in one of two ways. First, the test could be valid for all jobs but more valid for some jobs than for others. Second, the test could be valid for some jobs but invalid for others. The latter is the moderating effect postulated by the theory of job-specific validity. But sampling error and other artifacts can falsely cause a test to appear to be invalid. Just as sampling error can produce the appearance of inconsistency in the validity of a test for the same job in different settings, sampling error in validity coefficients can cause tests to appear to be valid for one job but invalid for another job.

The first large-sample tests of this hypothesis were recently completed. Based on an analysis of data from almost 370,000 clerical workers, Schmidt, Hunter, and Pearlman (1981) show that the validities of seven cognitive abilities were essentially constant across five different task-defined clerical job families. All seven abilities were highly valid in all five job families. They next examined the validity patterns of five cognitive tests determined on a sample of 23,000 people in 35 highly heterogeneous jobs (for example, welders, cooks, clerks, administrators). Validities for each test varied reliably from job to job. But the variation was small, and *all tests were valid at substantial levels for all jobs.*

This finding has now been replicated and extended to the least complex, lowest-skill jobs. The U.S. Employment Service has conducted over 500 criterion-related validity studies on jobs that constitute a representative sample of jobs in the *Dictionary of Occupational Titles* (U.S. Department of Labor, 1977). In a cumulative analysis of these studies, Hunter (1980) showed that cognitive abilities are valid for all jobs and job groupings studied. When jobs were grouped according to complexity of information-processing requirements, the validity of a composite of verbal and quantitative abilities for predicting on-the-job performance varied from .56 for the highest-level job grouping to .23 for the lowest. These studies disconfirm the hypothesis of success in job training. Thus, even for the lowest-skill jobs, validity is still substantial. These studies disconfirm the hypothesis of job-specific test validity. There is no empirical basis for requiring separate validity studies for each job; tests can be validated at the level of job families. These cumulative analyses of existing studies show that the most frequently used cognitive ability tests are valid for all jobs and job families.

In conclusion, our evidence shows that the validity of the cognitive tests studied is neither specific to situations nor specific to jobs.

* * * * *

REFERENCE NOTES

1. Sharf, J. C. Recent developments in the field of industrial and personnel psychology. Paper presented at the conference, *Recent directions in testing and fair employment practices.* Washington, D.C.: The Personnel Testing Council of Metropolitan Washington and BNA Systems, April 23, 1981.

2. Timmreck, C. W. *Moderating effect of tasks on the validity of selection tests.* Unpublished manuscript, University of Houston, 1981.

3. Schmidt, F. L., Hunter, J. E., Pearlman, K., & Caplan, J. R. *Validity generalization results for three occupations in the Sears, Roebuck Company.* Chicago: Sears, Roebuck Company, 1981.

4. Hunter, J. E. *An analysis of validity, differential validity, test fairness, and utility for the Philadelphia Police Officer Selection Examination prepared by Educational Testing Service.* Unpublished manuscript, Michigan State University, 1980.

5. Hunter, J. E. *The economic benefits of personnel selection using ability tests: A state of the art review including a detailed analysis of the dollar benefit of U.S. Employment Service placements and a critique of the low cutoff method of test use.* Report prepared for U.S. Employment Service, U.S. Department of Labor, Washington, D.C., January 15, 1981.

6. Hawk, J. Personal communication, November 20, 1978.

7. Braithwaite, D. Personal communication, January 15, 1976.

8. Ruch, W. W. *A re-analysis of published differential validity studies.* Paper presented at the meeting of the American Psychological Association, Honolulu, September 1972.

9. Tenopyr, M. L. *Race and socioeconomic status as moderators in predicting machine-shop*

training success. Paper presented at the meeting of the American Psychological Association, Washington, D.C., September 1967.

10. Linn, R. L., Harnisch, D. L., & Dunbar, S. B. *Validity generalization and situational specificity: An analysis of the prediction of first year grades in law school.* Unpublished manuscript, University of Illinois at Urbana-Champaign, 1980.

REFERENCES

Albright, L. E., Glennon, J. R., & Smith, W. J. *The uses of psychological tests in industry.* Cleveland, Oh.: Allen, 1963.

American Psychological Association, Division of Industrial and Organizational Psychology. *Principles for the validation and use of personnel selection procedures* (2nd ed.). Berkeley, Calif: Author, 1980. (Copies may be ordered from Lewis E. Albright, Kaiser Aluminum & Chemical Corporation, 300 Lakeside Drive—Room KB 2140, Oakland, Calif. 94643.)

Bartlett, C. J., Bobko, P., Mosier, S. B., & Hannan, R. Testing for fairness with a moderated multiple regression strategy: An alternative to differential analysis. *Personnel Psychology,* 1978, *31,* 233–241.

Berliner, D. C. Tempus Educare. In P. Peterson & H. Walberg (Eds.), *Research in teaching: Concepts, findings and implications.* Berkeley, Calif.: McCutchan, 1979.

Boehm, V. R. Differential prediction: A methodological artifact? *Journal of Applied Psychology,* 1977, *62,* 146–154.

Brogden, H. E. When testing pays off. *Personnel Psychology,* 1949, *2,* 171–183.

Brogden, H. E., & Taylor, E. K. A theory and classification of criterion bias. *Educational & Psychological Measurement,* 1950, *10,* 159–186.

Callender, J. C., & Osburn, H. G. Development and test of a new model of validity generalization. *Journal of Applied Psychology,* 1980, *65,* 543–558.

Campbell, J. T., Crooks, L. A., Mahoney, M. H., & Rock, D. A. *An investigation of sources of bias in the prediction of job perfor-*

mance: A six year study (Final Project Report No. PR-73-37). Princeton, N.J.: Educational Testing Service, 1973.

Cleary, T. A., & Hilton, T. I. Test bias: Prediction of grades of Negro and white students in integrated colleges. *Journal of Educational Measurement,* 1968, *5,* 115–124.

Cole, N. S. Bias in testing. *American Psychologist,* 1981, *36,* 1067–1077.

Cronbach, L. J., & Gleser, G. *Psychological tests and personnel decisions.* Urbana: University of Illinois Press, 1957.

Cronbach, L. J., Yalow, E., & Schaeffer, G. A mathematical structure for analyzing fairness in selection. *Personnel Psychology,* 1980, *33,* 693–704.

Equal Employment Opportunity Commission, Civil Service Commission, Department of Labor, & Department of Justice. Adoption by four agencies of Uniform guidelines on employee selection procedures. *Federal Register,* 1978, *43,* 38290–38315.

Gael, S., & Grant, D. L. Employment test validation for minority and nonminority telephone company service representatives. *Journal of Applied Psychology,* 1972, *56,* 135–139.

Gael, S., Grant, D. L., & Ritchie, R. J. Employment test validation for minority and nonminority clerks with work sample criteria. *Journal of Applied Psychology,* 1975, *60,* 420–426. (a)

Gael, S., Grant, D. L., & Ritchie, R. J. Employment test validation for minority and nonminority telephone operators. *Journal of Applied Psychology,* 1975, *60,* 411–419. (b)

Ghiselli, E. E. *The validity of occupational aptitude tests.* New York: Wiley, 1966.

Grant, D. L., & Bray, D. W. Validation of employment tests for telephone company installation and repair occupations. *Journal of Applied Psychology,* 1970, *54,* 7–14.

Guion, R. M. *Personal testing.* New York: McGraw-Hill, 1965.

Humphreys, L. G. Statistical definitions of test validity for minority groups. *Journal of Applied Psychology,* 1973, *58,* 1–4.

Hunter, J. E. *Validity generalization for 12,000 jobs: An application of synthetic validity and validity generalization to the General Apti-*

tude Test Battery (GATB). Washington D.C.: U.S. Employment Service, U.S. Department of Labor, 1980.

Hunter, J. E., & Schmidt, F. L. A critical analysis of the statistical and ethical implications of five definitions of test fairness. *Psychological Bulletin*, 1976, *83*, 1053–1071.

Hunter, J. E., & Schmidt, F. L. Differential and single group validity of employment tests by race: A critical analysis of three recent studies. *Journal of Applied Psychology*, 1978, *63*, 1–11.

Hunter, J. E., & Schmidt, F. L. Fitting people to jobs: Implications of personnel selection for national productivity. In E. A. Fleishman (Ed.), *Human performance and productivity*. Hillsdale, N.J.: Erlbaum, in press.

Hunter, J. E., Schmidt, F. L., & Hunter, R. Differential validity of employment tests by race: A comprehensive review and analysis. *Psychological Bulletin*, 1979, *86*, 721–735.

Hunter, J. E., Schmidt, F. L., & Rauschenberger, J. M. Fairness of psychological tests: Implications of four definitions for selection utility and minority hiring. *Journal of Applied Psychology*, 1977, *62*, 245–260.

Jensen, A. R. *Bias in mental testing*. New York: Free Press, 1980.

Katzell, R. A., & Dyer, F. J. Differential validity revived. *Journal of Applied Psychology*, 1977, *62*, 137–145.

Ledvinka, J. The statistical definition of fairness in the federal selection guidelines and its implications for minority employment. *Personnel Psychology*, 1979, *32*, 551–562.

Lent, R. H., Aurbach, H. A., & Levin, L. S. Predictors, criteria and significant results. *Personnel Psychology*, 1971, *24*, 519–533. (a)

Lent, R. H., Aurbach, H. A., & Levin, L. S. Research and design and validity assessment. *Personnel Psychology*, 1971, *24*, 247–274. (b)

Lerner, B. Washington v. Davis: Quantity, quality, and equality in employment testing. In P. Kurland (Ed.), *The 1976 Supreme Court Review*. Chicago: University of Chicago Press, 1977.

Lerner, B. Employment discrimination: Adverse impact, validity, and equality. In P. Kurland & G. Casper (Eds.), *The 1979 Supreme Court Review*. Chicago: University of Chicago Press, 1979.

Lilienthal, R. A., & Pearlman, K. *The validity of federal selection tests for aid/technicians in the health, science, and engineering fields*. Washington, D.C.: U.S. Office of Personnel Management, Personnel Research and Development Center, in press.

Linn, R. L. Single-group validity, differential validity, and differential predictions. *Journal of Applied Psychology*, 1978, *63*, 507–514.

Mack, M. J., Schmidt, F. L., & Hunter, J. E. Estimating the productivity costs in dollars of minimum selection test cutoff scores. Washington, D.C.: U.S. Office of Personnel Management, Personnel Research and Development Center, in press.

O'Connor, E. J., Wexley, K. N., & Alexander, R. A. Single group validity: Fact or fallacy? *Journal of Applied Psychology*, 1975, *60*, 352–355.

Pearlman, K., Schmidt, F. L., & Hunter, J. E. Validity generalization results for tests used to predict training success and job proficiency in clerical occupations. *Journal of Applied Psychology*, 1980, *65*, 373–406.

Schmidt, F. L., Berner, J. G., & Hunter, J. E. Racial differences in validity of employment tests: Reality or illusion? *Journal of Applied Psychology*, 1973, *53*, 5–9.

Schmidt, F. L., Gast-Rosenberg, I., & Hunter, J. E. Validity generalization results for computer programmers. *Journal of Applied Psychology*, 1980, *65*, 643–661.

Schmidt, F. L., & Hunter, J. E. Development of a general solution to the problem of validity generalization. *Journal of Applied Psychology*, 1977, *62*, 529–540.

Schmidt, F. L., & Hunter, J. E. Moderator research and the law of small numbers. *Personnel Psychology*, 1978, *31*, 215–231.

Schmidt, F. L., Hunter, J. E., & Caplan, J. R. Validity generalization results for two jobs in the petroleum industry. *Journal of Applied Psychology*, 1981, *66*, 261–273.

Schmidt, F. L., Hunter, J. E., McKenzie, R., & Muldrow, T. The impact of valid selection procedures on workforce productivity. *Journal of Applied Psychology,* 1979, *64,* 609–626.

Schmidt, F. L., Hunter, J. E., & Pearlman, K. Task differences and validity of aptitude tests in selection: A red herring. *Journal of Applied Psychology,* 1981, *66,* 166–185.

Schmidt, F. L., Hunter, J. E., Pearlman, K., & Shane, G. S. Further tests of the Schmidt-Hunter Bayesian validity generalization procedure. *Personnel Psychology,* 1979, *32,* 257–281.

Schmidt, F. L., Hunter, J. E., & Urry, V. M. Statistical power in criterion-related validity studies. *Journal of Applied Psychology,* 1976, *61,* 473–485.

Schmidt, F. L., Pearlman, K., & Hunter, J. E.

The validity and fairness of employment and educational tests for Hispanic Americans: A review and analysis. *Personnel Psychology,* 1980, *33,* 705–724.

Sewell, W. H., Hauser, R. M., & Featherman, D. L. (Eds.). *Schooling and achievement in American society.* New York: Academic Press, 1976.

U.S. Department of Labor. *Dictionary of occupational titles* (4th ed.). Washington, D.C.: U.S. Government Printing Office, 1977.

Wiley, D. E. Another hour, another day: Quality of schooling, a potent path for policy. *Studies of Educational Processes,* No. 3, University of Chicago, July 1973.

Wolins, L. Responsibility for raw data. *American Psychologist,* 1962, *17,* 657–658.

Reading 26

The Realities of Employment Testing*

MARY L. TENOPYR

Since the early 1960s, employment testing has been in a storm of controversy. It is probably one of the most emotion-laden sources of dissension associated with the civil rights movement. The perplexing thing about the debates is that the importance of testing as a vehicle for employee selection is probably overrated, and the furor about testing appears disproportionate in relation to the current extent of test use. If employment testing were outlawed tomorrow, the effect on the employment of minorities and women in business and industry would scarcely be noticeable. However, in those areas of the public sector in

which merit systems are in effect, there could be some discernible effects associated with the elimination of tests.

Unfortunately, any statements about the current amount of test use have to be to some extent speculative. There have not been any recent, thorough surveys of the extent of test use in private employment in this country. The most recent data available appear to be those of Prentice-Hall and the American Society for Personnel Administration (1975). Their survey involved sending a questionnaire to 2,000 ASPA member companies, of whom 67 percent responded. Results indicate that there is considerable range in the amount of test usage. Approximately 60 percent of employers with more than 25,000 employees did at least some testing, whereas only about 39 percent of employers with fewer than 100 employees used tests. Fewer than

* M. L. Tenopyr, "The Realities of Employment Testing," *American Psychologist* 36 (1981) pp. 1120–27. Copyright 1981 by the American Psychological Association. Reprinted/Adapted by permission of the publisher and author.

one out of five employers said that they disqualified applicants on the basis of tests alone. The survey also gave some indication of the type of testing done: More than 25 percent of the respondents said that they test only to fill clerical job openings. About three fourths reported that their employment testing programs had been cut back in the preceding five years, and about 14 percent were planning to eliminate most testing at some time in the future. Thus, it appears that testing by private employers is far from universal. Where it is used, it is generally not the sole factor in determining employment decisions; it is often selectively used, so not all prospective employees are tested in a given company; and test use is on the wane. Further evidence on the last point is provided by Mitchell, Reynolds, and Elliot (1980), who report that there has been a 10 percent decline in submissions of new vocational tests to the Buros Institute since the publication of the *Eight Mental Measurements Yearbook* (Buros, 1978).

In the public sector, 36 states have statewide merit systems; the other 14 have merit systems for agencies that receive federal funds. It is difficult to estimate the extent of merit system coverage, but one source (Savas & Ginsburg, 1978) suggests that the merit system "covers more than 95 percent of all permanent federal (civilian) employees, all state and county employees paid by federal funds, most state employees, many county employees (particularly in the northeastern states), most employees in more than three fourths of America's cities, and almost all full-time policemen and firemen" (pp. 257–258). Data on the proportion of merit systems that use tests are generally unavailable, but a survey of 526 agencies (Quaintance, Note 1) suggests that about three fourths of the merit systems use tests of some sort. Thus it appears that employment testing is far more influential in the public sector than in the private sector. The most common type of test

is the job-knowledge test. However, even in the public sector, testing is not universal.

In view of the publicity given to the Uniform Guidelines on Employee Selection Procedures (Equal Employment Opportunity Commission et al., 1978), it is likely that most employers know of the legal difficulties they may encounter if they use tests. The legal requirements for testing are probably the primary cause of the decline in test use. Nothing in the literature indicates that tests are less valuable selection tools than they were, but many articles (e.g., Grant, 1980; Manning, 1978; Robertson, 1978) inform employers of the regulations and governmental advisories on test use. The general reaction appears to be to flee from objective selection procedures rather than to attempt to comply with the guidelines.

The extent to which those employers who still use tests are conducting the extensive research required to justify testing is also open to question. Certainly they recognize that they may have legal difficulties if they do not conduct validation studies, but Boehm (Note 2) reports a marked decline in the number of validation studies appearing in the scientific literature. There can be a number of reasons for this decline, but it may well be that researchers fear public criticism of their work, prior to its use, in legal proceedings and are keeping their studies away from the critical eyes of their peers. If such is the case, it is unfortunate not only for the science of psychology but also for the smaller employers who look to the better funded, larger corporations for guidance and standards in personnel research. Lack of published research regarding test validity will probably only result in less use of testing for employment purposes.

THE REAL WORLD

Tests do not discriminate against various groups; people do. This fact seems to have become lost in the debates about matters such as fairness models and possible differential validity. The term *test bias* has been commonly used in scientific circles for years (e.g., Cleary, 1968; Flaugher, 1978), but bias is a function of the way a test is used, not a property of the test itself (see Cole, this issue; Reschly, this issue). The unfortunate emphasis on the test itself has led most writers in psychology to ignore the fact that employment tests are usually only part of a complex decision-making process, the dynamics of which are often not known. The same test may be used in a biased way in one situation and in an unbiased way in another situation. The focus should be on analyzing the whole employment decision-making process with the aim of making it as valid and fair as is feasible, not on the testing portion of the process alone. However, possibly because it is easier to study tests than total decision-making processes, there is a dearth of literature on such processes.

There is, of course, a substantial literature on many aspects of testing in relation to group differences, and a number of notions, differential validity being a prime example, have been reduced to a point at which they have become mainly sociopolitical issues rather than scientific ones. Consequently, many of the studies in the psychological literature, no matter how statistically elegant and logically unassailable they may be, have little immediate meaning for the real world of employee selection. For example, the conclusion (Hunter, Schmidt, & Hunter, 1979; Linn, 1978; Schmidt & Hunter, this issue) that marked differences in test validity for blacks and whites are rare is not particularly meaningful in the real world. In the local situation, the typical employer simply does not have the large N (Trattner & O'Leary, 1980) required to appropriately test the hypothesis that validities differ for the races. The rare employer who can do such studies for some high-population jobs

will probably continue to do so until the U.S. Supreme Court deems such studies unnecessary. Unless the findings of the psychological researchers are clearly articulated to the major policymakers and result in appropriate changes in policy, all of the research in the world will not change the way employers function. Official government pronouncements, which are essentially policy documents, will prevail (Novick, this issue).

The developments regarding selection fairness models will also probably have little impact on the actual way employment selections are made. The controversies about fairness models have little meaning in the real world. The study of fairness will undoubtedly continue to be incorporated into validity studies whenever feasible, but its purpose will be defense against challenges; it will not be used with an eye toward using tests differently for different groups. Very simply, employers cannot afford to use different tests for subgroups, nor can they interpret tests differently for such groups. For example, having different critical scores for different groups is not a viable employment policy for either a public or a private employer. In the present social era, almost all employers espouse an official policy of equal employment opportunity. To the best of my knowledge, however, employers do not further equal employment efforts by having officially different employment standards for different groups unless compelled to do so by applicable court orders.

A number of authors have developed fairness models that require expression of utilities for the hiring of different groups (Cronbach, 1976; Darlington, 1976; Gross & Su, 1975; Novick & Ellis, 1977; Novick & Petersen, 1976; Petersen & Novick, 1976). For practical use, these models pose even more problems than the traditional models. Certainly, no employer is officially going to place different numerical values on the selection of persons of different races or sexes. The situation with differential validity notions and fairness models is basically the same. Even if differential validity were a viable phenomenon, it would not be a factor in developing employee selection procedures. If the controversies about the appropriateness of various fairness models were to end today, employers would not use tests differently for different groups. If it were agreed that a model requiring prior specification of the utilities were appropriate, employers simply would not utilize the model, because it would mean openly expressing preferences for some groups.

One of the more noteworthy recent contributions to the field of personnel psychology is the work suggesting that validities generalize to a far greater extent than had been believed previously (Callender & Osburn, 1980; Schmidt, Gast-Rosenberg, & Hunter, 1980; Schmidt & Hunter, 1977; Schmidt, Hunter, McKenzie, & Muldrow, 1979; Schmidt, Hunter, Pearlman, & Shane, 1979). This work is just making its impact on thinking in the discipline. The ultimate fate of the concept of broad generalization of ability tests will depend on many factors. One of these is the inevitable debate (which has yet to take place) that will arise over the relationship of validity generalization to ability theory. The results of the validity generalization studies done to date suggest that almost any test is valid for any job (Schmidt & Hunter, this issue). This implies a general factor like that commonly called *intelligence*. A reasonable alternative is a theory akin to Spearman's (1927), which allows for a general factor and specific factors. Those who espouse theories based on group factors, for example, Guilford (1959), may have difficulty accepting the implications of validity generalization studies. A relevant question that has been raised (Tenopyr & Oeltjen, in press) concerns the nature of criteria employed in the studies showing validity to generalize so widely. Although there is evi-

dence of validity generalization for other criteria, supervisor's ratings are apparently the main criteria used in many of these studies (Schmidt & Hunter, 1977). There are many problems with supervisor's ratings (Landy & Farr, 1980). It is clear that no matter how carefully the rating form and associated procedures are designed, halo effect and its related general factor are still problems with the kind of ratings typically used in validation studies. Factor analysis of personnel ratings typically yields only a small number of interpretable factors (Tenopyr & Michael, 1964), and this finding is associated with the problem of the general factor. Many job trainee evaluations, the results of which are often used as criteria, may also involve a general factor, or at the most, a small number of factors.

If the general factor or the other factors involved in personnel ratings reflect only broad abilities and these are essentially all that supervisors recognize in employee behavior, it should not be surprising that validities have been found to generalize so widely. However, the phenomenon of a general factor or a limited number of group factors might not be artifactual and may be a reality reflecting the organization of abilities. The only answer to the dilemma thus posed is carefully designed research involving performance measurement instrumentation that will allow general, group, or specific factors to manifest. Different methods of measuring performance should be systematically applied so that method variance can be assessed. Some such studies have been done in laboratory settings (Fleishman, 1978; Forbes & Barrett, 1978), but research in real organizational settings is needed.

The concept of broad validity generalization, however appealing it may be to the practitioner, probably will have little impact on events in the real world for some time. The idea of validity specificity, which has come under some question, has been entrenched in personnel psychology for some time (American Psychological Association, Division of Industrial and Organizational Psychology, 1980), and old established ideas are hard to dislodge. A more important problem is that the Uniform Guidelines on Employee Selection procedures (Equal Employment Opportunity Commission et al., 1978) and numerous legal decisions (Novick, this issue) reflect the notion of validity specificity. Also, many of today's practitioners still remember the days when it was a common practice in business and industry to administer a short, unvalidated, general intelligence test to every applicant. Despite the fact that this procedure may have had some merit, conscientious practitioners do not want to see a return to the days of highly indiscriminate test use. It can probably be expected that these psychologists will recommend to their employers some middle ground that acknowledges validity generalization but still calls for validation studies on major groups of jobs.

These examples of the relationship between psychological research and reality are not exhaustive, but they should indicate that the psychological literature can have only minimal impact on the real world of employing organizations. Whether the political forces will completely overwhelm the scientific forces remains to be seen, but the political forces are strong and to ignore them in any discussion of employment testing would be folly. What happens regarding the real world will, until legislative bodies and the courts face the issues squarely, continue to be a function more of politics than of science.

ALTERNATIVES TO EMPLOYMENT TESTS

"Tests should not be the sole device for making selection decisions." "Test results should always be used along with other information." These are platitudes often heard about the use of tests. Employers and educational institutions utter words like

these sanctimoniously and claim that they never make decisions on the basis of tests alone. But what are the other selection devices? What is the other information? How should it be combined with tests? The Uniform Guidelines on Employee Selection Procedures (Equal Employment Opportunity Commission et al., 1978) call for a search for alternatives to tests, but what are the valid alternatives?

Tests, because of their high visibility and political unacceptability in some quarters, have been singled out as requiring validation (Ledvinka & Schoenfeldt, 1978). Yet where are the validation studies on the commonly used additions to or alternatives for tests? The interview is probably the most widely used selection procedure in the country, but in a recent review of the literature (Tenopyr & Oeltjen, in press), only one published validation study on the interview was found for the three years from 1978 to 1980. During the same period, however, there were approximately 50 published studies indicating how vulnerable interviews and typical resume reviews are to biases or irrelevancies of various sorts. The history of validity for the interview is, to say the least, dismal (Ulrich & Trumbo, 1965). The interview, despite various innovations over the years, has never been consistently shown to improve selection. At best it introduces randomness to the selection process; at worst, it colors selection decisions with conscious or unconscious biases. As such, the interview represents a poor alternative to testing, although it may be viewed favorably by groups who stand to profit from its potential biases.

Experience and educational variables are probably as widely used in selection as the interview. Who has seen an employment application blank that does not require supplying at least some education and work history? Yet, there is little validation evidence to support the widespread use of these variables. Caplan and Schmidt (Note

3) report little evidence of validity for experience, and O'Leary (Note 4) reports a low-to-modest average relationship between school grades and occupational success. There appear to have been few recent attempts to determine the validity of education and experience as usable criteria (Tenopyr & Oeltjen, in press). It is clear to the most naive observer that for certain jobs, certain types of experience and education could be useful, but there is a dearth of information about the validity of this type of variable. The available data suggest that the validity of experience and education is not likely to be impressive and may vary depending on how relevant education and experience are determined (Johnson, Guffey, & Perry, Note 5). On a logical basis, these variables have little to recommend them as alternatives to tests. Not only do they appear to have low validity, but they may also serve to exclude members of groups who have been denied job opportunities and educational advantages.

Another possible alternative to tests is the scored biodata blank. Well-developed biodata instruments have had fairly good track records insofar as validity is concerned (Brown, 1978; Life Insurance Marketing & Research Association, Note 6). There are also some indications that items can be developed and selected so as to reduce adverse effect on various groups (Life Insurance Marketing & Research Association, Note 6). There are, however, a number of problems in developing a biodata blank that must be overcome to obtain an instrument of high enough quality to be a suitable alternative to a test. Many items that would contribute to validity may be either illegal under some state or local laws or be of such a nature as to give rise to questions of fairness. For example, a question like, "How old were you when you opened your first bank account?" might be criticized by certain groups.

Another serious problem is that large samples, preferably involving thousands of cases, are required to establish stable item weights and thus ensure continuing validity. This difficulty is not insurmountable if employers join in consortia to conduct the necessary research; even fairly large employers would have difficulty in obtaining enough subjects to establish a comprehensive selection program involving biodata unless they had cooperation from other companies. Another difficulty is that biodata can suffer from face validity problems that make them especially open to charges from unions or other groups. Under such circumstances, the security of the key may be in jeopardy.

All in all, formally scored biodata may be a satisfactory alternative to tests, but only if their development is careful and based on sufficient subjects to provide stable results.

Assessment centers, which involve simulation as well as pencil-and-paper exercises, are becoming more difficult to evaluate as their popularity increases. In the beginning they were only applied to managerial selection (Bray & Grant, 1966), but now they are being used for many purposes (Fitzgerald, Note 7), and extreme variations of them have come to be called "assessment centers" themselves. Many of these variations bear little resemblance to the typical assessment center on which most of the research in the literature is based. Although studies using combinations of techniques in assessment have generally resulted in moderate validity coefficients for the criterion of success at management (Bray, Campbell, & Grant, 1974; Moses & Byham, 1977), little criterion-related evidence is available for validity of assessment-center-like procedures used for selecting such diverse groups as police officers, firefighters, and sanitation workers.

No definitive statement can be made about any adverse effect that assessment-center-like activities have on various groups. Not only is there little published information in this area, but it is unlikely that any findings relative to adverse effect of assessment-center-like methods would generalize to all of the selection procedures that are now being called assessment centers.

One factor preventing the use of assessment centers in situations in which there are a large number of job candidates is cost. Although Cascio and Silbey (1979) have shown that under some assumptions, assessment centers can be cost effective when used for some jobs, an assessment center's average cost, which may be several hundred dollars per candidate, would prohibit its use for any except high-level jobs.

Thus, the assessment center cannot be recommended unequivocally as a general alternative to tests. Its cost, coupled with the lack of information about its effect on the selection of various groups, suggests that practitioners should approach the use of assessment approaches with some deliberation.

If it is impossible to screen at the initial hiring stage, the most obvious recourse an employer has is to make a reversible selection decision at the hiring point. The screening then moves further along in the employment process. For example, either training or the probationary period can be used as a selection device. Goldstein (1980) has reviewed studies relative to validity of training and reported generally positive results, but nothing definitive can be said about the adverse effect of training. There is a lack of studies on either the validity or the impact of probationary periods. One problem in deferring the final selection decision until after the employee has been placed on the payroll is the cost of using posthiring activities as a screen. These costs would undoubtedly vary as a result of differences in jobs and training practices, but they could nevertheless be substantial.

In a major review of the literature on alternatives to testing, Reilly and Chao (Note 8) cover various alternatives in de-

tail, including some of those just discussed. It appears that there are no alternatives better than tests when validity, degree of adverse effect on various groups, and feasibility of use are all taken into account. With few exceptions, most alternatives are less useful than tests. Thus it seems that a practitioner undertaking a search for alternatives will primarily just be going through an exercise to satisfy government requirements. Those who would still advocate a search for alternatives in light of the accumulated evidence indicating that such alternatives are not useful should be reminded that the whole history of the development of mental testing has been based on the fact that the alternatives used before tests were ever developed were not useful. The government-mandated search for alternatives is in a sense a turning back of the clock to pre-Binet times.

Two further technical points need to be made about alternatives. First, as Ironson and Guion (Note 9) point out, in any discussion of alternatives, one must separate the methodology and the constructs that are the basis for measurement. Thus, one cannot compare an interview and a test without considering whether they are measuring the same constructs. How much of the difference in the results of the application of various techniques is due to methodology and how much is a function of what is being measured is unknown.

A second technical point relates to the combination of test variables and other variables in the employment decision-making process. All psychologists, are surely aware of the inferiority of clinical decision making as opposed to the actuarial use of decision tools (Meehl, 1956; Sawyer, 1966). Yet why is less than optimal use of tests advocated so widely? For example, the addition of invalid interview results to valid test results has to reduce validity. Even if some of the information used with test results is valid, the chances are that it will not be combined with the tests in an optimal manner (Meehl, 1956; Sawyer,

1966). Thus, it appears that the clinical use of other information, whatever it may be, in conjunction with valid test results, no matter how intuitively appealing the notion may be, has little scientific merit.

Despite the compelling evidence that valid and otherwise suitable alternatives to tests will not be found and that the clinical combination of other data with test results weakens overall validity, employers will probably still continue to seek alternatives. The legal and regulatory pressure to do so can be expected to continue despite the scientific facts involved.

SUMMARY

At least in the private sector, employment testing is not the bar to minority and female employment that many of its critics might claim it to be. In the public sector, where testing is used more heavily, the type of test most widely used is the job-knowledge test, not the much-maligned aptitude test. Thus, one really wonders what the uproar about employment tests is all about. This is not to say that the critical examination of employment testing has been without merit. However, at present, heavy public and professional emphasis on the use of tests in employment may be akin to beating a dead horse.

It is unfortunate that government regulations and legal precedents have developed more in line with sociopolitical aims than with scientific knowledge. Many of the resources that could be devoted to solving the educational and social problems that underlie the testing issue are being squandered on needless research and legal activities. If the amount of money spent on legal activities alone were used constructively to fund educational research and programs for the disadvantaged, a great deal could be done both for those who have been excluded from the benefits of our society and for the country as a whole. Just throwing money after problems is not enough; scientists and professionals of many disciplines must clearly define the problems before programs can be developed. Possibly the greatest impediment in this area is that previously programs were developed before problems were defined. Problem definition is probably the most important thing that psychologists can contribute to the employment prospects for minority groups and women. However, they cannot make this contribution while they are preoccupied with the instruments that indicate symptoms; they must attend to the disease itself.

It is clear that a complete abandonment of employment testing and the substitution of alternatives, which are in many cases no more useful than a lottery for jobs, will not work to anyone's advantage in the long run. Growth in productivity in the American economy has declined for the past several years. Clearly, valid tests can contribute to making the work force more productive (Schmidt, Hunter, McKenzie, & Muldrow, 1979). On the surface, it might appear that the strategies for improving productivity and those for fostering social progress are at odds, but they probably need not be. The inflation and other adverse factors associated with generally low productivity probably affect disadvantaged groups more than other groups. Certainly, the appropriate social policies are those that will afford equal employment opportunity and at the same time provide for increased productivity. Selection testing has an important role in these policies. In the long run, the constructive use of employment tests can benefit everyone.

REFERENCE NOTES

1. Quaintance, M. K. Personal communication, 1981.

2. Boehm, V. R. *Are we validating more but publishing less?* Unpublished manuscript, Cleveland, Standard Oil of Ohio, 1981.

3. Caplan, J. R., & Schmidt, F. L. *The validity of education and experience ratings.* Paper presented at the meeting of the Interna-

tional Personnel Management Association, Assessment Council, Kansas City, Mo., 1977.

4. O'Leary, B. S. *College grade point average as an indicator of occupational success: An update* (Personnel Research and Development Center Report PRR-80-23). Washington, D.C.: U.S. Office of Personnel Management, 1980.

5. Johnson, J. C., Guffey, W. L., & Perry, W. R. *When is a T & E rating valid?* Paper presented at the meeting of the International Personnel Management Association Assessment Council, Boston, 1980.

6. Life Insurance Marketing and Research Association. *Profits and the AIB in United States ordinary companies* (Research Report No. 1978-6). Hartford, Conn: Life Insurance Marketing and Research Association, 1978.

7. Fitzgerald, L. F. *The incidence and utilization of assessment centers in state and local governments* (Research Report). Washington, D.C.: International Personnel Management Association, 1980.

8. Reilly, R. R., & Chao, G. T. *Validity and fairness of alternative employee selection procedures.* Unpublished manuscript. Morristown, N.J.: American Telephone & Telegraph Company, 1981.

9. Ironson, G. H., & Guion, R. M. *Adverse impact from a psychometric perspective: A case study in evaluating group differences.* Unpublished manuscript, Bowling Green State University, 1981.

REFERENCES

American Psychological Association, Division of Industrial and Organizational Psychology. *Principles for the validation and use of personnel selection procedures* (2nd ed.). Berkeley, Calif.: Authors, 1980. (Copies may be ordered from Lewis E. Albright, Kaiser Aluminum & Chemical Corporation, 300 Lakeside Drive, Room KB 2140, Oakland, California 94643.)

Bray, D. W., Campbell, R. J., & Grant, D. L. *Formative years in business: A long-term AT&T study of managerial lives.* New York: Wiley, 1974.

Bray, D. W., & Grant, D. L. The assessment center in the measurement of potential for business management. *Psychological Monographs,* 1966, *80*(17, Whole No. 625).

Brown, S. H. Long-term validity of a personal history item scoring procedure. *Journal of Applied Psychology,* 1978, *63, 673–676.*

Buros, O. K. (Ed.). *Eight mental measurements yearbook.* Highland Park, N.J.: Gryphon, 1978.

Callender, J. D., & Osburn, H. G. Development and test of a new model for validity generalization. *Journal of Applied Psychology,* 1980, *65, 543–558.*

Cascio, W. F., & Silbey, V. Utility of the assessment center as a selection device. *Journal of Applied Psychology,* 1979, *64, 107–118.*

Cleary, T. A. Test bias: Predicting grades of Negro and white students in integrated colleges. *Journal of Educational Measurement,* 1968, *5, 115–124.*

Cole, N. S. Bias in testing. *American Psychologist,* 1981, *36, 1067–1077.*

Cronbach, L. J. Equity in selection—Where psychometrics and political philosophy meet. *Journal of Educational Measurement,* 1976, *13, 31–42.*

Darlington, R. B. Defense of "rational" personnel selection and two new methods. *Journal of Educational Measurement,* 1976, *13, 43–52.*

Equal Employment Opportunity Commission, Civil Service Commission, Department of Labor, & Department of Justice. Adoption by four agencies of Uniform guidelines on employee selection procedures. *Federal Register,* 1978, *43, 38290–38315.*

Flaugher, R. L. The many definitions of test bias. *American Psychologist,* 1978, *33, 671–679.*

Fleishman, E. A. Relating individual differences to the dimensions of human tasks. *Ergonomics,* 1978, *21, 1007–1019.*

Forbes, J. B., & Barrett, G. V. Individual differences and task demands in relation to performance and satisfaction on two repetitive monitoring tasks. *Journal of Applied Psychology,* 1978, *63, 188–196.*

Goldstein, I. L. Training in work organizations. In M. R. Rosenzweig & L. W. Porter (Eds.),

Annual review of psychology. Palo Alto, Calif.: Annual Reviews, 1980.

Grant, D. L. Issues in personnel selection. *Professional Psychology,* 1980, *11,* 369–384.

Gross, A. L., & Su, W. Defining a "fair" or "unbiased" selection model: A question of utilities. *Journal of Applied Psychology,* 1975, *60,* 345–351.

Guilford, J. P. *Personality.* New York: McGraw-Hill, 1959.

Hunter, J. E., Schmidt, F. L., & Hunter, R. Differential validity of employment tests by race: A comprehensive review and analysis. *Psychological Bulletin,* 1979, *86,* 721–735.

Landy, F. J., & Farr, J. L. Performance rating. *Psychological Bulletin,* 1980, 87, 72–107.

Ledvinka, J., & Schoenfeldt, L. F. Legal developments in employment testing: Albermarle and beyond. *Personnel Psychology,* 1978, *31,* 1–13.

Linn, R. L. Single-group validity, differential validity, and differential prediction. *Journal of Applied Psychology,* 1978, *63,* 507–512.

Manning, W. H. Test validation and EEOC requirements: Where we stand. *Personnel,* 1978, *55,* 70–77.

Meehl, P. E. Clinical versus actuarial prediction. In *Proceedings, Invitational Conference on Testing Problems, 1955.* Princeton, N.J.: Educational Testing Service, 1956.

Mitchell, J. V., Reynolds, C. R., & Elliott, S. N. Test news from the Buros Institute. *Measurement News,* 1980, *23,* 6, 16.

Moses, J. L., & Byham, W. C. (Eds.). *Applying the assessment center method.* New York: Pergamon, 1977.

Novick, M. R. Federal guidelines and professional standards. *American Psychologist,* 1981, *36,* 1035–1046.

Novick, M. R., & Ellis, D. D. Equal opportunity in education and employment. *American Psychologist,* 1977, *32,* 306–320.

Novick, M. R., & Peterson, N. S. Towards equalizing educational and employment opportunity. *Journal of Educational Measurement,* 1976, *13,* 77–88.

Petersen, N. S., & Novick, M. R. An evaluation of some models for culture-fair selection. *Journal of Educational Measurement,* 1976, *13,* 3–29.

Prentice-Hall & American Society for Personnel Administration. PS/ASPA survey probes employee testing and selection procedures. In *Personnel management policies and practices report.* Englewood Cliffs, N.J.: Prentice-Hall, 1975.

Reschly, D. J. Psychological testing in educational classification and placement. *American Psychologist,* 1981, *36,* 1094–1102.

Robertson, D. E. New directions in EEO guidelines. *Personnel Journal,* 1978, *57,* 360–363, 394.

Savas, E. S., & Ginsburg, S. C. The civil service. A meritless system? In F. S. Lane (Ed.), *Current issues in public administration.* New York: St. Martins Press, 1978.

Sawyer, J. Measurement *and* prediction, clinical *and* statistical. *Psychological Bulletin,* 1966, *66,* 178–200.

Schmidt, F. L., Gast-Rosenberg, I., & Hunter, J. E., Validity generalization results for computer programmers. *Journal of Applied Psychology,* 1980, *65,* 643–661.

Schmidt, F. L., & Hunter, J. E. Development of a general solution to the problem of validity generalization. *Journal of Applied Psychology,* 1977, *62,* 529–540.

Schmidt, F. L., & Hunter, J. E. Employment testing: Old theories and new research findings. *American Psychologist,* 1981, *36,* 1128–1137.

Schmidt, F. L., Hunter, J. E., McKenzie, R. C., & Muldrow, T. W. Impact of valid selection procedures on work-force productivity. *Journal of Applied Psychology,* 1979, *64,* 609–626.

Schmidt, F. L., Hunter, J. E., Pearlman, K., & Shane, G. S. Further tests of the Schmidt-Hunter Bayesian validity generalization procedure. *Personnel Psychology,* 1979, *32,* 257–281.

Spearman, C. *The abilities of man.* New York: Macmillan, 1927.

Tenopyr, M. L., & Michael, W. B. The development of a modification in the normal varimax method for use with correlation matrices containing a general factor. *Educational and Psychological Measurement,* 1964, *24,* 677–699.

Tenopyr, M. L., & Oeltjen, P. D. Personnel selection and classification. In M. R. Rosenzweig & L. W. Porter (Eds.), *Annual review of psychology.* Palo Alto, Calif.: Annual Reviews, in press.

Trattner, M. H., & O'Leary, B. S. Sample sizes for specified statistical power in testing for differential validity: *Journal of Applied Psychology,* 1980, *65,* 127–134.

Ulrich, L., & Trumbo, D. The selection interview since 1949. *Psychological Bulletin,* 1965, *63,* 100–116.

COMMENTARY

Taken as a whole, this section's readings suggest that useful levels of validity are associated with standardized ability tests. Personality and interest inventories, on the other hand, seem much less appropriate in employment settings even though they did make a significant contribution to the Exxon testing program and apparently have produced favorable results in other studies involving managerial and sales occupations (for a further discussion of the validity of personality inventories in personnel selection see Guion & Gottier, 1965; Korman, 1968; and Gough, 1976). Since few studies have demonstrated a significant relationship between measures of personality and job success, the remaining comments regarding ability tests should not be taken to include traditional personality and interest inventories. Note however, that there is continuing controversy regarding the appropriateness of the research designs used to evaluate the usefulness of personality testing in industry. See Busch and Hogan (1982) for a discussion of these issues. Also, there seems to be little support for using projective measures of personality in the employment context (e.g., Rorschach Test, Thermatic Apperception Test). Reilly and Chao (1982) in a major review article, which subsequently will be discussed in greater depth, state that "for purposes of predicting occupational success, projectives appear to lack the basic requirements of sufficient reliability and validity" (p. 52).

Perhaps it would be useful to reconsider Tenopyr's comments regarding alternatives to employment tests. She concludes that "with a few exceptions, most alternatives are less useful than tests" (1981, p. 1124). When attempting to make judgments about occupational tests it is not possible to do so in the abstract. The notion of usefulness is a relative concept. Thus, even though tests have generated positive results they must be judged in comparison to potential alternatives. In their major review article Reilly and Chao (1982) cover seven classes of alternatives to testing. These include biographical data, peer evaluations, self-assessments, reference checks, academic performance, expert judgments, and projective tests. Taking validity, adverse impact, and feasibility into account, they conclude that only biographical data and peer evaluations should in some situations be considered as alternatives. However, a variety of administrative problems serve to limit the usefulness of even these two approaches. Apparently, peer evaluation systems may be troubled by the participants' low degree of acceptance of the process. For instance, Cederblom and Lounsbury (1980) note that a relatively low degree of user acceptance of the practice was observed among 174 faculty of a university where peer evaluations had been used for six years. This, along with the problem of generating a sufficiently large peer group possessing adequate exposure to the candidate, renders this technique useless in many situations. For example, it is unlikely that peer evaluations would serve the needs of an entry-level selection system. Also, Exxon's experience and Tenopyr's comments regarding the complexities of a biographical data research program leads to the conclusion that only a small number of employers have sufficient resources to develop a selection system dependent upon this type of predictor.

Of the remaining alternatives reviewed by Reilly and Chao (1982), none compared to tests when considering the basic requirement of validity. To illustrate, the average validity coefficients associated with interviews, self-assessments, reference checks, academic performance, expert judgments, and projective techniques were .19, .15, .14, .20, .17, and .28 respectively. The .28 associated with projective tests included one clear outlier of .69 and becomes .18 when this coefficient is not included in the average. While it is difficult to make direct validity comparisons between procedures designed for use in different selection contexts, these low values suggest that these alternatives are not well suited for most selection situations.

The Reilly and Chao (1982) review did not include work-sample tests or assessment center techniques. However, it is clear that work-sample tests have been quite successful in predicting job proficiency. Recall that motor work-sample tests (i.e., tests that involve the manipulation of things, such as a drill press test for machine operators) have produced particularly high-validity coefficients when job proficiency is used as the criterion. For example, 43 percent of the validity coefficients summarized by Asher and Sciarrino (1974) were at .50 or higher while 70 percent of the coefficients were .40 or better.

Even though work samples and assessment center techniques have produced favorable validity results (note that the previous discussion of assessment centers in Chapter 8 cautioned against an overreliance on previous assessment center research) a major conceptual issue regarding their use almost has been totally ignored by users. This issue has already been discussed in the context of assessment centers and work-sample tests in previous chapters, but a brief review seems appropriate here. The work-sample tests summarized by Asher and Sciarrino (1974) often required the applicant to possess considerable technical job knowledge or skill. For example, they described a life insurance information test (Baier & Dugan, 1956), an accuracy in handling testimony and understanding principles of the U.S. government test (Snyder, 1955), a test for tracing trouble in a complex circuit (Grant & Bray, 1970), and tests for mechanics, such as disassembling and repairing a gear box (Campion, 1972). Tests of this type are appropriate only when hiring fully functioning, experienced workers. They are of little use when making entry-level or low-skill-level selection decisions. When a test is being used to measure technical knowledge and to select from a group of experienced applicants it can be misleading to compare validity results in this situation with validity results generated when using an aptitude test to preduct entry-level job performance. As pointed out by Ironson and Guion (1981) it is difficult to compare aptitude tests with alternatives when the two predictor types are designed to measure different underlying constructs. It is not possible in this situation to separate methodology (e.g., aptitude tests versus work-sample tests) from the intended measurement constructs. Only when the various predictor types are designed to measure the same underlying construct and are to be used in similar selection contexts does a one-to-one comparison become meaningful. Thus, since work-sample tests and assessment center exercises are often designed to measure current levels of job-related knowledge and skill while aptitude tests are often designed to measure constructs like mechanical comprehension or learning ability, it is difficult to make direct validity comparisons. These two predictor types are likely to prove useful in very different selection situations.

Finally, some cautionary remarks regarding the application of the Schmidt and Hunter validity generalization model to the area of cognitive tests are in order given the impact this work is having on the field of personnel selection. Tenopyr (1981) already discussed potential problems associated with relying on studies where the main criteria used are supervisory ratings. Two other issues will be reviewed. First, the nature of the prior distribution of validity coefficients used in the model needs further clarification. Then, the meaning of Schmidt and Hunter's (1981) assertion that "professionally developed cognitive ability tests are valid predictors of performance on the job and in training for all jobs in all settings" (p. 1128) will be discussed. This is a rather strong statement that needs further clarification.

Recall that the approach to validity generalization provided by Schmidt and Hunter (1977) is based on estimating the variance of the true unrestricted, unattenuated validities generated in many past studies. If the variance of these validities is low, this implies that the true validities are not situation specific. This distribution is thought of as a Bayesian "prior" distribution with the mean representing the most likely true validity to be found in future studies. Of course, it is possible for a researcher to conduct an original validity study, enter the resulting coefficient into the prior distribution, and use all available data to make an estimate about the validity of a particular test in the situation of interest. As the number of validity coefficients entering this Bayesian prior increase, a more and more stable estimate is generated.

The use of a prior distribution creates a potentially serious problem that is essentially the "file drawer" problem described by Rosenthal (1979). The data used in validity generalization studies comes from past investigations. Normally, published research is reviewed and organizations are asked to provide unpublished reports of validity estimates. The extreme view of this problem is that behavioral-science journals are "filled with the five percent of the studies that show Type I errors, while the file drawers back at the lab are filled with the 95 percent of the studies that show nonsignificant (e.g., $p > .05$) results" (Rosenthal, 1979, p. 638). The possibility here is that the prior distribution used in validity generalization studies are biased in favor of positive validity findings. The current legal environment may result in a reluctance on the part of investigators to publish or make public in any form negative validity findings. While there are multiple explanations, there has been a marked decrease in the number of articles that report validity results during the years 1960–79 in the *Journal of Applied Psychology* and *Personnel Psychology* (Boehm, 1982). Also, there is no indication that these two journals have declined in terms of their key role in disseminating selection research (Boehm, 1982). While past validity generalization studies have assured companies of complete anonymity, the possibility exists that a form of nonresponse bias could be operating.

One way to deal with this potential problem is to consider a suggestion by Rosenthal (1979). He describes a procedure for computing the tolerance for filed null results. Essentially, this provides an estimate of the number of filed null reports required to bring the overall p value from a combination of reported validity coefficients to the "just significant" .05 level. Callender and Osburn (1981) used this procedure and generated file drawer figures that were quite large in a petroleum industry validity generalization study. However, the number of unreported null studies required to bring the overall p value down to the "just significant" level says little about the magnitude of the estimated true validities. In the Callender and Osburn (1981) study the estimated true validities for four ability tests (when using a job-performance criterion) ranged from .20 for a test of arithmetic reasoning to .32 for a test of learning ability. Unreported negative results could lower the estimated true validities to the point at which they are no longer useful, applying general utility concepts.

Finally, recall that in the third reading for this chapter Schmidt and Hunter (1981) concluded that of the cognitive tests studied, validities were neither specific to situations nor to jobs. However, they cite a study by Hunter (1980) that showed a composite ability score to correlate with on-the-job performance in the range of .23 to .56. Apparently, validity values systematically varied with the information-processing requirements of the job. Validities were highest in jobs requiring complex information-processing demands. Hunter's study represents a cumulative analysis of more than 500 validity studies covering a representative sample of jobs in the *Dictionary of Occupational Titles*. Thus, while there is evidence that many ability tests are valid across situations and jobs, the magnitude of the validity estimates is likely to systematically vary with certain job characteristics.

In summary, cognitive-ability tests seem well suited for certain hiring situations, particularly when used to select persons who will enter training programs. Also, as predictors of job performance, validity values are high enough to be of practical utility in most selection settings. When compared to existing alternatives, cognitive tests do very well when simultaneously taking validity, feasibility, and adverse impact into account. While validity values may not seem particularly high, the question of what to use as an alternative to testing takes on major importance. Only when hiring fully functioning, skilled employees do such alternatives as work-sample tests offer some potential advantage.

REFERENCES

Asher, J. J. & Sciarrino, J. A. Realistic work sample tests: A review. *Personnel Psychology*, 1979, 27, 519–533.

Baier, D. E., & Dugan, R. D. Tests and performance in a sales organization. *Personnel Psychology*, 1956, 9, 17–26.

Boehm, V. R. Are we validating more but publishing less? (The impact of governmental regulation on published validation research—An exploratory investigation). *Personnel Psychology*, 1982, 35, 175–187.

Busch, C. M., & Hogan, R. T. Validity reconsidered: The usefulness of personality measures in personnel selection. Paper presented at the 90th annual American Psychological Association Convention, Washington, D.C., August, 1982.

Callender, J. C., & Osburn, H. G. Testing the constancy of validity with computer-generated sampling distributions of the multiplicative model variance estimate: Results for petroleum industry validation research. *Journal of Applied Psychology*, 1981, 66, 274–281.

Campion, J. E. Work sampling for personnel selection. *Journal of Applied Psychology*, 1972, 56, 40–44.

Cederblom, D., and Lounsbury, J. W. An investigation of user acceptance of peer evaluation. *Personnel Psychology*, 1980, 33, 567–579.

Dreher, G. F., & Sackett, P. R. Some problems with applying content validity evidence to assessment center procedures. *Academy of Management Review*, 1981, 6, 551–560.

Grant, D. L., & Bray, D. W. Validation of employment tests for telephone company installation and repair occupations. *Journal of Applied Psychology*, 1970, 54, 7–14.

Gough, G. Personality and personality assessment. In M. D. Dunnette (Ed.), *Handbook of industrial and organizational psychology*. Chicago: Rand McNally, 1976.

Guion, R. M., & Gottier, R. F. Validity of personality measures in personnel selection. *Personnel Psychology,* 1965, *18,* 135–164.

Hunter, J. E. *Validity generalization for 12,000 jobs: An Application of synthetic validity and validity generalization to the General Aptitude Test Battery (GATB).* Washington, D.C.: U.S. Employment Service, U.S. Department of Labor, 1980.

Ironson, G. H., & Guion, R. M. *Adverse impact from a psychometric perspective: A case study evaluating group differences.* Unpublished manuscript, Bowling Green State University, 1981.

Korman, A. K. The prediction of managerial performance: A Review. *Personnel Psychology,* 1968, *21,* 295–322.

Reilly, R. R., & Chao, G. T. Validity and fairness of some alternative employee selection procedures. *Personnel Psychology,* 1982, *35,* 1–62.

Rosenthal, R. The "file drawer problem" and tolerance for null results. *Psychological Bulletin,* 1979, *86,* 638–641.

Schmidt, F. L., and Hunter, J. E. Development of a general solution to the problem of validity generalization. *Journal of Applied Psychology,* 1977, *62,* 529–540.

Schmidt, F. L., & Hunter, J. E. Employment testing: Old theories and new research findings. *American Psychologist,* 1981, *36,* 1128–1137.

Snyder, R. Validity information exchange No. 8–14. *Personnel Psychology,* 1955, *8,* 263.

Tenopyr, M. L. The realities of employment testing. *American Psychologist,* 1981, *36,* 1120–1127.